Praise for
The Rescue Turn and the Politics of Holocaust Memory

"The assistance, both individual and collective, provided to Jews by their neighbors during the Holocaust is one of the few heartening features of this tragic period. In recent years, with the widespread rise of populism, this has often been instrumentalized to provide a more positive image of the national past during the Nazi occupations and to obscure the fact that assistance of this type was never widespread and often went side-by-side with cooperation with the Nazis in carrying out the anti-Jewish genocide. This comprehensive and well-researched volume provides a balanced evaluation of these hotly disputed issues in ten European countries. It is essential reading for all those interested in the complex and difficult questions of assistance, indifference, and collaboration under Nazi occupation."

—Antony Polonsky, emeritus professor of Holocaust studies, Brandeis University

"This volume is a significant multidisciplinary contribution to scholarship on the public valorization of narratives of rescue. Bringing together established and emerging scholars, this anthology draws attention to the different scales of the representation of rescue at transnational, national, local, and individual levels and explores their relationships in public discourse across different national contexts."

—Hannah Holtschneider, professor of contemporary Jewish cultural history, University of Edinburgh

"In this timely volume, scholars from diverse disciplines scrutinize Holocaust narratives of rescue efforts in ten European countries. Illuminating the intricacies of memory deployment, they offer insightful analysis on the cosmopolitanization of memories and the contestations that ensue. A must-read for anyone interested in the politics of historical memories."

—Daniel Levy, professor of sociology, Stony Brook University

"Since the Holocaust became a European foundational past, and the question of the reactions of 'bystanders' one of its most controversial themes, its better understanding is of more than academic importance. This comprehensive volume offers advanced analysis of relevant politics in key European countries and insightful case studies, pointing to some highly disturbing tendencies."

—Dariusz Stola, professor, Polish Academy of Sciences

"This collection offers an enlightening European tour of Holocaust commemorations. The case studies analyze the rescue turn: a growing emphasis on assistance given to Jews in memory politics, observable at international, national, and individual levels. Written by an interdisciplinary team of proficient researchers, this volume gives fresh insights on how the image of the rescuer both relates to globalization of Holocaust memory and to scant national sensibilities, eager to promote a guilt-free and politically usable narrative, often tending to blur their responsibilities."

—Audrey Kichelewski, associate professor in contemporary history, University of Strasbourg

THE RESCUE TURN *and the* POLITICS *of* HOLOCAUST MEMORY

THE RESCUE TURN *and the* POLITICS *of* HOLOCAUST MEMORY

EDITED BY
NATALIA ALEKSIUN, RAPHAEL UTZ,
AND ZOFIA WÓYCICKA

WAYNE STATE UNIVERSITY PRESS
DETROIT

ISBN 9780814350836 (paperback)
ISBN 9780814349502 (hardcover)
ISBN 9780814349519 (e-book)

Library of Congress Control Number: 2023932576

On cover: Photos of mural project commemorating Zegota secret council in Warsaw (*images at right and top left*). Mural designed by Adam Quest; painted by Good Looking Studio, 2017. Used by permission of Adam Quest Studio. Cover design by Shoshana Schultz.

Publication of this book was made possible through the generosity of the Bertha M. and Hyman Herman Endowed Memorial Fund.

The research and editorial work for this volume was possible thanks to the financial and logistical support of the Centre for Historical Research Berlin of the Polish Academy of Sciences; the Imre Kertész Kolleg Jena; the German Historical Institute Warsaw; and the Bud Shorstein Center for Jewish Studies, University of Florida.

PAN CENTRUM BADAŃ HISTORYCZNYCH Polskiej Akademii Nauk w Berlinie

IMRE KERTÉSZ KOLLEG JENA
Europas Osten im 20. Jahrhundert. Historische Erfahrungen im Vergleich

Deutsches Historisches Institut Warschau
Niemiecki Instytut Historyczny w Warszawie

UF BUD SHORSTEIN CENTER FOR JEWISH STUDIES
Liberal Arts *and* Sciences

Wayne State University Press rests on Waawiyaataanong, also referred to as Detroit, the ancestral and contemporary homeland of the Three Fires Confederacy. These sovereign lands were granted by the Ojibwe, Odawa, Potawatomi, and Wyandot Nations, in 1807, through the Treaty of Detroit. Wayne State University Press affirms Indigenous sovereignty and honors all tribes with a connection to Detroit. With our Native neighbors, the press works to advance educational equity and promote a better future for the earth and all people.

Wayne State University Press
Leonard N. Simons Building
4809 Woodward Avenue
Detroit, Michigan 48201-1309

Visit us online at wsupress.wayne.edu.

Contents

The Rescue Turn

An Introduction

NATALIA ALEKSIUN, RAPHAEL UTZ, AND ZOFIA WÓYCICKA

In June 1989, Yad Vashem informed Polish citizen Marianna Chęć-Wieczorkiewicz that it had decided to bestow the title "Righteous Among the Nations" on her and her parents for rescuing a young Jewish child in eastern Poland during the Holocaust. Part of the institution's mission since its inception, the designation serves to recognize non-Jews who "had risked their lives in order to save Jews."[1] While reflecting on the role of non-Jewish rescuers and seeking to honor and assist them dated back to the immediate postwar period, the category took formal shape only after Yad Vashem established its program for the Righteous Among the Nations in 1962.[2] Within a year it developed procedures for handling candidates' files such as that of the Chęćs, who put their lives in danger not only during the war but also in its aftermath.[3]

In March 1943, two months before the destruction of the ghetto in Bełżyce, near Lublin, a Jewish tailor, Szmul Leib Sznajderman, asked Stanisław and Karolina Chęć, from the neighboring village of Jaroszewice, to hide his newborn son, Moszek (Moshe). Feeling sorry for the baby, they agreed.[4] The Chęćs struggled to provide for the sick baby, whose parents perished shortly after they had handed over their young child. In his letter to the Central Committee of Jews in Poland, Stanisław recalled that "even when there was no [money] for a piece of bread for me, we had it for milk for the child."[5] The whole family cherished the boy, whom they called Mundek, and tried to protect him. Even after the area was liberated in July 1944, Moshe remained with the Chęćs. One day, however,

Moshe's maternal uncle, Szol Fersztman, arrived to claim the child, and he took Moshe back with him to Lublin. Marianna, the Chęćs's daughter, who had looked after the boy and was especially close to him, accompanied Moshe to facilitate his adjustment to the new environment.[6] The family's attachment and continued devotion to the Jewish child met with communal censure.

The Chęćs struggled during the war, but after the war they faced continued threats and violence in retribution for what they had done. In 1947 Marianna's father, Stanisław Chęć, sent a desperate letter to the Central Committee of Jews in Warsaw asking for assistance in his "critical situation" in the wake of a raid by a "band of native fascists."[7] The attackers had smashed his apartment, kicked and battered Stanisław, and cut the hair of his wife, Karolina, and daughter, Marianna. With their home destroyed, the family was forced to live in a stable. They were targeted for violence and humiliation as punishment for having rescued a Jewish child.[8]

Official recognition of the Chęćs's courage during the German occupation was neither immediate nor a given. From the social censure and isolation of the Chęćs, who could only hope for the assistance provided by the organization created by the remnants of Polish Jewry, until the state authorities' involvement in preparing their file and submitting it to Yad Vashem, much seems to have changed in the country's treatment of Poles who helped Jews during the Holocaust. On the eve of the fall of communism in Eastern Europe, the authorities recognized the political potential of the award and more broadly of the discourse centering around ethnic Poles rescuing Jews under the German occupation. As a result of the application for the medal and of its approval, the family was presented with their certificate at a ceremony in Warsaw in 1991. By then Poland had already undergone a peaceful political transformation from communist dictatorship to democracy. Seen over time, the Chęćs's story reflects shifting agencies and a growing public interest and investment in the recognition of the wartime sacrifices of non-Jewish Polish citizens who gave aid to Holocaust victims. With some variation, this dynamic web of changing social attitudes, institutions and their memory politics, and survivors' efforts and agency applies not only to Poland but to most European countries.

In particular, over the last two decades in Europe and beyond, the subject of assistance given to Jews during the Holocaust has attracted tremendous attention among both scholars and the general public. This interest translated into numerous publications, conferences, commemorative initiatives, monuments, films, plays, museums, and exhibitions. Those partaking in academic, popular, and political discussions often invoked the category of the Righteous Among the Nations as established by Yad Vashem. However, in recent years the interest in this historical phenomenon has exceeded referencing the well-established honoring ceremony organized by Yad Vashem. One could even say that Yad Vashem has fallen victim to its own success, for it has produced a brand so appealing that it has been appropriated by a variety of actors with diverse agendas and has begun to live an independent life of its own.[9]

The "fashion" has been engendered by the mass media and most prominently by Steven Spielberg's 1993 film *Schindler's List*.[10] Furthermore, transnational and intergovernmental organizations, such as the Council of Europe, the European Parliament, and the International Holocaust Remembrance Alliance (IHRA), as well as by transnational NGOs, such as Gariwo (Gardens of the Righteous Worldwide) have propagated the topic of the Righteous. In fact, the joint declaration signed in 2000 by the delegates to the Stockholm International Forum on the Holocaust already highlighted the importance of preserving the memory of those "who defied the Nazis, and sometimes gave their own lives to protect or rescue the Holocaust's victims."[11] In 2007 member states of the Council of Europe signed a "Solemn Tribute to the 'Righteous' of Europe." In 2012 the European Parliament established the European Day of the Righteous. These international developments were triggered by and resonated with the politics of remembrance led by various governmental and civil society actors. In recent years, as discussed in this volume, a number of European states have established state holidays and organized official ceremonies predominantly honoring their own "national" Righteous. Indeed, streets have been named after the rescuers, and museums and monuments dedicated to them have been erected all over Europe.[12]

In some European countries the efforts to salvage and underscore the memory of people who rescued Jews during World War II were a direct response to scholarly and public debates about collaboration in the persecution and murder of Jews.[13] Focusing on rescuers has seemingly helped to neutralize difficult and painful conversations about the past. It has offered a strategy for inscribing oneself into the global trend of commemorating the Holocaust without challenging or diminishing a sense of national pride. Moreover, the development of the human rights discourse and the growing tendency to universalize history increasingly have led people to understand the Holocaust as a reservoir of role models to emulate. This shift also helps to explain the "fashion" for the Righteous, who offer very persuasive examples of activism and courage in the face of undeniable evil.

In their important book, *The Holocaust and Memory in the Global Age*, sociologists Daniel Levy and Natan Sznaider suggested the emergence of a new, globalized, "cosmopolitan" memory of the Holocaust. They argued that the process of the cosmopolitanization of memory, visible already in the 1980s, greatly accelerated in the early 1990s. After the end of the Cold War, as the binary world order collapsed and anticommunism as the common ideology of the West lost its power, public attention refocused on crimes committed by the Nazis. As a result of political transformation, in a short period of time archives in Russia, Poland, and other former Eastern Bloc states opened up to researchers, and the sites where many of the crimes of the Holocaust actually took place, including Auschwitz-Birkenau, Babi Yar, Maly Trostinec, and the Operation Reinhardt extermination camps, became accessible to foreign visitors, making Holocaust history more tangible for them. These changes were also triggered by the Rwandan genocide in 1994 and to an even greater extent by the practice of ethnic cleansing during the Bosnian War (1992–95) and the Kosovo War (1998–99). These tragic events made Europeans realize that war, ethnic hatred, and mass murder were still acute and present in their midst. As a result, these phenomena led to the strengthening of the human rights discourse for which the Holocaust served as a significant point of reference.[14]

The 1990s were also the period in which the Holocaust became an evermore important element of the culture of remembrance in the United States, as exemplified by the opening of the United States Holocaust Memorial Museum in Washington, DC, and the release of *Schindler's List*, both in 1993.[15] They represented a process that created a pervasive presence of representations of the Holocaust in American popular culture. However, the "Americanization" of the Holocaust meant not only that the topic was turned into a consumable media product, but also that it was taken out of its original geographical and historical contexts and redesigned into a universal story of the struggle between good and evil.[16] Thus it became more appealing to people who had no discernable biographical or familial connection to these events. Consequently, the Jews became "archetypical victims" so that others could identify with their suffering, and the Holocaust became a "globally understandable code for all forms of human rights violations."[17] This mode of thinking about the Holocaust was also partly emulated in Europe and other parts of the globe. As a result, Holocaust memory was transformed into something more "future-oriented" and began to serve as a moral yardstick for contemporaries.[18]

The cosmopolitan memory, as defined by Levy and Sznaider, is characterized by its focus on victims of war and genocide. Such a focus has strengthened what historians Jan Eckel and Claudia Moisel called a "culture of victimization," in which social groups increasingly define themselves not by their glamorous past and heroic deeds but by the suffering they endured.[19] This new mode of remembering is highly personalized: Victims are no longer commemorated as a national or ethnic group but as individuals with whom everybody can empathize. At times "the distinction between memories of victims and perpetrators" gets blurred, and one makes individual choices about with whom to identify.[20]

Finally, according to Levy and Sznaider, cosmopolitan memory is reflexive. It abandons the old heroic narratives in favor of a more self-critical vision of one's own community, in which attitudes toward persecuted minority groups become the ultimate measure of good and evil: "While traditional and exemplary narratives deploy historical events to promote foundational myth, the critical narrative emphasizes events that focus on past injustices of one's own nation. Cosmopolitan memory thus implies some recognition of the history (and the memories) of the 'Other.'"[21]

Levy and Sznaider did not claim that this new form of memory eliminated traditional national master narratives altogether. They underlined that "speaking about the cosmopolitanization of Holocaust memory does not imply some progressive universalism subject to a unified interpretation. The Holocaust does not become one totalizing signifier containing the same meanings for everyone. Rather its meanings evolve from the encounter of global interpretations and local sensibilities. The cosmopolitanization of Holocaust memories thus involves the formation of nation-specific and nation-transcending commonalities."[22] Levy and Sznaider also recognized that there would always be tension between local, national, and global and cosmopolitan memories. Later focus group research conducted by Daniel Levy, Michael Heinlein, and Lars Breuer in Poland, Austria, and Germany confirmed that one can hardly speak about the existence of a unified European memory in regard to World War II and the Holocaust. Nevertheless, these scholars maintained that the new mode of remembering questions and weakens national frameworks and leads to "shared cosmopolitan memory practices" that manifest themselves "in the following repertoires of memory work—affirmative but ambivalent perceptions of Europeanness, skeptical narratives about the nation emphasizing injustice and perpetratorship, and an increased recognition of the Other."[23]

In their work, Levy and Sznaider did not make a clear distinction between global and European memory. Rather, it seems as if they saw both as moving in a similar direction. While their analysis focused predominantly on Israel, the United States, and Germany, they argued that, due to developments in Europe, the Holocaust has been firmly established as the negative founding myth of the European Union. Consequently, the recognition of its significance and singularity became, as formulated by historian Tony Judt, an "entry ticket" to Europe.[24]

Over the last two decades, scholars have largely confirmed Levy and Sznaider's insights while also honing their theory. The critique went in two directions.

Some authors noted that "cosmopolitan memory" was not solely an analytical concept but also a normative claim.[25] In fact, Levy and Sznaider seemed to be fervent advocates of this mode of remembering, while other researchers hinted at its limitations, such as the sole focus on the victims and their individualized suffering, which neglects the biographies and motivations of the perpetrators and the mechanisms of escalating violence. This perspective—the critics argued—weakened the force of Holocaust education as a tool in preventing racism and genocide. As formulated by sociologist Geffrey Olick, coming to terms with the past requires learning from the experiences and perspectives of both victims and perpetrators: "For only through developing realistic images of both sides [. . .] can we avoid turning ordinary victims into martyrs and ordinary perpetrators into psychopaths, as so many commemorative images and claims do."[26]

Other commentators pointed out that the spread of a reflexive, unheroic memory leads to a blurring of responsibilities. The growing awareness that wide strata of nearly all European societies were in some way implicated in the genocide of the Jews—by showing indifference to its victims or by profiteering, or by directly participating in the mass murder—turned the Holocaust from a German into a European phenomenon.[27] However, this notion of wide-ranging implication in the Holocaust sometimes obscures the difference in the degree of responsibility and the form of complicity in the genocide among the Third Reich, its allies, and the governments and societies of the occupied and neutral countries. As critically noted by Eckel and Moisel, in the European politics of remembrance, "the German responsibility for the Holocaust and other crimes committed during World War II [. . .] move into the background."[28]

Furthermore, memory scholar Aleida Assmann pointed out that cosmopolitan memory could be, not without reason, perceived as a Western European project that was being imposed on others.[29] Taking this one step further, historian and political scientist Anna Cento Bull and memory scholar Hans Lauge Hansen argued that the cosmopolitan mode of remembering, "far from having superseded the antagonistic mode associated with 'first modernity' in the European context, has proved unable to prevent the rise of, and is being increasingly challenged by, new antagonistic collective memories constructed by populist neo-nationalist movements."[30]

Moreover, while Levy and Sznaider were among the first to highlight the impact of globalization processes on collective remembering, other researchers have nevertheless expressed doubts concerning the direction of these developments. Although we do not yet fully understand the nature and results of the interplay between the global and the local, scholars tend to agree that, contrary to initial optimistic assertions about cosmopolitanization of memory, recent changes have not led to a general alignment of local war narratives.[31] Indeed, anthropologist and museologist Sharon Macdonald notes: "What has emerged here, then, is a dynamic of potentially cosmopolitan developments that are sometimes appropriated to other ends or bump up against limits and other agendas in practice."[32] In some cases the confrontation with transnational discourses even reinforces nationalistic master narratives.[33] Therefore, Macdonald proposed to speak not about globalization but rather about a "glocalization" of memory understood as the "local reworking of global patterns."[34]

As this volume demonstrates, the transnational context plays an important role in generating and shaping local rescue narratives. However, the essays included here also suggest that, despite the common subject, narratives vary from place to place, and in some cases the topic is presented very differently from the self-reflexive, inclusive, cosmopolitan mode of remembering. In fact, many of the case studies assembled in this volume demonstrate exactly the opposite: a process of claiming the Righteous for national narratives. By appropriating Yad Vashem's moral standards of honoring outstanding individual behavior, they are, in fact, applied to entire populations and transformed into statements about societies and, indeed, national character.

Rather than universal values reflected in cosmopolitan memory, in many cases nationalism appears to be particularly relevant. In his influential study, Benedict Anderson identified the imagining of a particular community as the central element of any nationalism.[35] At the heart of this process is always a search for a politically meaningful way to link the past with the present and, indeed, the future—in other words, the creation of a usable past.[36] Furthermore, Liah Greenfeld has argued that the specificity of nationalism is one of perspective: It is not to look at a specific object but to look at an object in a specific way.[37] All this is at play in the present reframing of the Righteous as standard bearers of moral goodness, as examples of wider societal behavior and attitudes, as pars pro toto for entire nations.

How this process unfolds is illustrated well by the following episode from Poland. In 2017 the deputy minister of culture and national heritage, Jarosław Sellin, announced a plan to build a Museum of the Righteous of the Auschwitz Region (Muzeum Sprawiedliwych spod Auschwitz). The new museum was to be dedicated to those Polish inhabitants of Oświęcim and the surrounding villages who had aided prisoners of the Auschwitz camp during World War II. The overwhelming majority of these beneficiaries were political prisoners of Polish and other nationalities; only a few of them were Jews. The local authorities implementing the project pointed to the European Day of the Righteous, established by the European Parliament in 2012: "Although it is a relatively recent holiday [. . .]—as explained on the Oświęcim district website—the varied forms by which it is commemorated in many countries show how important it is for Europeans to preserve the memory of good, selfless, decent and heroic people."[38] However, the International Auschwitz Council rejected the working name of the museum to avoid any confusion with the Righteous Among the Nations designation bestowed by Yad Vashem.[39] Consequently the institution was opened under the name "Memorial Museum to the Inhabitants of the Oświęcim Region" (Muzeum Pamięci Mieszkańców Ziemi Oświęcimskiej) in spring 2022.[40]

What is remarkable here is not the eventual failure to make use of the concept and name of the Righteous but the explicit attempt to create a usable past repositioning and effectively marginalizing the history of the Holocaust by changing the contexts even while consciously preserving the original brand name. Even where such departures from the standard established by Yad Vashem do not occur, the case studies in this volume show how the narrative pattern of the Righteous has been implemented in different European countries. The pattern remains the same, but it is employed in diverging ways, and it is more often than not used as a tool to integrate the history and memory of the Holocaust into histories that remain predominantly national.

Composition of the Volume

The idea for this edited collection draws on the workshop "Rescue of Jews during the Holocaust in European Memory," which was held in Berlin in June 2018, at the Centre for Historical Research of the Polish Academy of Sciences.[41] Co-organized by the Imre Kertész Kolleg Jena and the German Resistance Memorial Center in Berlin, it brought together a diverse group of scholars from Europe, Israel, and the United States. Following productive and challenging discussions at the workshop, we asked some of the participants to build on their presentations and expand them into chapters. Additionally, we have invited Anna Bikont, Liliana Hentosh, Hana Kubátová, Mark Roseman, and Anika Walke to write about themes and countries not represented during the workshop. Thus this edited volume consists of ten chapters, each dealing with a different country—Belarus, Denmark, France, Germany, Greece, the Netherlands, North Macedonia, Poland, Slovakia, and Ukraine—and focusing on different aspects and manifestations of the memory of the rescue and rescuers of Jews. While the focus of most of the essays is on recent developments, these chapters also offer insights into how the treatment of the topic evolved after World War II.

Read together the chapters, authored by historians and social scientists, delve into a number of individual national case studies from diverse perspectives. They also look at the different "scales" on which memory operates and at how these different scales interact with each other.[42] The volume proceeds from dealing with the interrelations between the transnational and the national and then moves down to the local and individual—though these distinctions may not always be clear cut. The first section, "(Trans)National Memory?" underscores the influence of global developments on national memory cultures and policies and the role of rescue stories in cultural diplomacy. It opens with a text by Ido de Haan, who examines the intertwined roots of recognizing the failure of Dutch society during the Holocaust and the nation's pride in the rescue efforts undertaken by only a small number of citizens. Both narratives, that of shame and that of pride, coexisted with and competed against each other from the early postwar years. As argued by de Haan, the dynamic of this relationship and the evolution of the image of the rescuers in the Netherlands can be understood only by looking at the interplay between national and international memory agents. As one of the examples, the author cites the extraordinarily high numbers of Dutch Righteous Among the Nations honored by Yad Vashem and often referred to in public discourse. He claims that, far from being a reflection of historical realities, this phenomenon must be seen in the light of postwar developments, including the role played by networks of Dutch immigrants to Israel.

The chapter by Sofie Lene Bak also draws attention to how international developments influence domestic memory politics and national discourses. The author discusses the clash between the public memory of the famous Danish rescue operation from October 1943, on the one hand, and the latest historical findings on the subject on the other. During the rescue operation, nearly eight thousand Danish Jews, or 95 percent of the entire Jewish population, were transferred by sea to neutral Sweden, thereby evading the deportation to Nazi death and concentration camps. However, recent research shows that the rescue action would not have been possible if not for the specific character of the Nazi occupation of Denmark and the far-reaching collaboration of the Danish civil administration with the Germans in some areas. This modus vivendi allowed the Danes to first protect and then rescue the vast majority of Danish Jews from deportation and death with the tacit approval of the occupation authorities. Historians point also to the questionable practice of some of the fishermen, who demanded exorbitant prices for the boat transfer to Sweden. However, as discussed by Bak, this nuanced narrative, with its different shades of gray, is hardly received in Danish politics and by Danish society, even by those generally critical of their own national history. The main reason for this is that the nuanced narrative is not easily accommodated with the predominant cosmopolitan, universalized, and deterritorialized memory of the Holocaust and the Righteous, which often overlooks the local, specific circumstances and favors individual heroism and clear distinctions between good and evil.

Naum Trajanovski takes the discussion of the political tension a step further by examining how the topic of survival is played out in diplomatic relations. The author discusses the narratives of Jewish rescue in the Macedonian culture of remembrance and memory politics, and highlights the role these stories play in the relations between North Macedonia and Bulgaria. Fewer than two hundred of the more than seven thousand Macedonian Jews survived the Holocaust, most of them in Albania. Trajanovski shows how the topic was first appropriated by Macedonian and Yugoslav communists to highlight their antifascist stance and internationalism. After the establishment of the Republic of Macedonia in 1991, the stories of aid provided to the persecuted Jews were designed to reveal Macedonian heroism and suffering against the backdrop of the crimes committed by the Bulgarian occupiers. Needless to say, Bulgaria has strongly opposed this narrative, as it questions its own politics of remembrance, which celebrates the rescue of the Bulgarian Jews and places all the blame for the deportation of Jews from Bulgaria-annexed Thrace and Vardar Banate on the Germans. Trajanovski looks specifically at the Holocaust Memorial Center for the Jews of Macedonia in Skopje, opened in 2011, as a site of political and diplomatic dissent.

The second section, "National Memory—Local Memory," explores what is happening at the level of national policy and in the interactions among the state and local administrations and civil society. However, as observed already by Aleida Assmann and Sebastian Conrad, today "trajectories of memory" on the local and national levels cannot be understood "without a global frame of reference."[43] Sarah Gensburger's chapter delves specifically into this triangle of local, national, and transnational memory politics and activism. She demonstrates how, after the meteoric rise of the Justes de France (Righteous of France), which peaked with their introduction to the Pantheon in 2007, French commemoration of the Righteous became in the last decade both much more widespread and more diverse and polyphonic. This diffusion of the category of the Righteous was triggered by a feedback loop among foreign institutions, such as Yad Vashem, top-down governmental politics of remembrance, and bottom-up commemorative and educational initiatives coming from both local administration and civil society. However, as Gensburger argues, in France the influence of public policy in the field of memory is restrained. Thus the state promotes certain topics but does not directly interfere in the content and form of such commemorations. This, she claims, is characteristic of a state that exercises its influence through infrastructural power rather than through "despotic power" and content-related memory politics.

Hana Kubátová writes about the challenges to official memory politics in a civil society influenced by right-wing agents. She examines Slovak memory politics and the public discourse about Jewish rescue, and the ways in which they are closely connected with the memory of Slovak resistance and, in particular, the Slovak National Uprising of August–October 1944. Kubátová also notes the influence of transnational developments on local policymakers. She describes how, on the eve of Slovakia's accession to the European Union, the country's political representatives expressed regret for the role played by the Slovak State in persecuting the Jews and confirmed their commitment to commemorating and educating about the Holocaust. At the same time, the story of the uprising and the help delivered to Jews by its supporters and participants served to mitigate the negative image evoked by such public apologies. It also served to boost Slovak national self-esteem and helped to unite society around an example of courage and resistance against fascism. However, this narrative was undermined by national conservative parties and organizations striving to rehabilitate the Slovak State and to present Jozef Tiso as a "savior of Jews." The comparison of this case with the French example seems to suggest that in Slovakia—as in Poland and some other, mostly Eastern and Central European countries—official memory politics has a much more centralized and content-related character than in France and most other Western European countries, which makes divergent interpretations less visible.

The chapter by Liliana Hentosh traces the often ambiguous process of transforming helpers into national heroes. The author analyzes recent discussions in Ukraine surrounding the religious and national leadership of the former Greek Catholic archbishop of Lviv, Andrei Sheptytsky, and the role he played in rescuing Jews and at the same time supporting Ukrainian cooperation with the Third Reich during the German occupation. While in Soviet times Sheptytsky was portrayed as a Nazi collaborator, after 1991 he was made into a national hero and praiseworthy supporter of the Ukrainian national cause. However, it is only in recent years that his aid for Jews gained broader recognition in Ukraine. This shift must be seen against the backdrop of Ukrainian aspirations to join the European Union and NATO. Several actors, among them Ukrainian politicians, Jewish survivors who believed they owed their lives to Sheptytsky, and representatives of the Jewish community in Ukraine, have advocated for his recognition as Righteous Among the Nations. However, until now Yad Vashem has rejected their recommendation.

The Belarussian case, examined by Anika Walke, stands in stark contrast to the other national case studies. While most chapters in this volume describe different ways rescuers and rescue stories were appropriated by national policymakers, in Belarus the opposite seems to be the case—the few civil society actors seeking to commemorate this aspect of wartime history have met with total disinterest on the part of the state. Such policy stands in a long Soviet tradition of not recognizing the specificity of the Nazi genocidal policy toward the Jews and their fate during the occupation. In addition, Soviet state-sponsored antisemitism after World War II, life behind the Iron Curtain, and the rupture of diplomatic relations between the USSR and Israel in 1967 hindered the official recognition of Belorussian Righteous Among the Nations. Only in the 1990s did the remaining survivors—in cooperation with historians and memory activists—begin to document the rescue stories in Belarus. They were driven not only by the urge to inscribe Belarus in the global discourse about the Holocaust but also by a desire to honor their benefactors. These efforts, supported by Yad Vashem and other international organizations, ran against official memory policies. Belorussian state authorities, generally not interested in commemorating the Holocaust, were also afraid that dealing with the history of Jewish rescue could reveal other, less favorable aspects of the stance of Belorussian society under German occupation and so undermine the central narrative of the Great Patriotic War as a unified antifascist front of all Soviet nations.

The last section in this volume, "Individual Memory—Public Remembrance," focuses on the interconnectedness between public remembering and personal testimonies, and foremost on how the former influences and alters the latter. Anna Maria Droumpouki examines changing oral history testimonies of Greek Holocaust survivors against the backdrop of official Greek politics of memory. As described by the author, in recent years Greek policymakers have discovered the stories of Jewish rescue as a tool of cultural diplomacy and an argument to refute allegations of Greek society's indifference, profiteering, and participation in the genocide. Comparing oral history accounts given at different times by Greek Holocaust survivors living in Greece and North America, Droumpouki shows how individual accounts are altered and adjusted to the official interpretation of the past. She argues that such embellished narratives serve to uphold the image of good relations between the two communities, and also between Greece and Israel, and to confirm the sense of rootedness of the Greek Jews in the majority society.

While Droumpouki's article analyzes the changing testimonies of Holocaust survivors, Anna Bikont and Mark Roseman underscore that accounts given by rescuers were also subject to constant reworking. Anna Bikont studies the story of Irena Sendler, a social worker from Warsaw. During the war, together with her mostly female colleagues from the Warsaw city council's welfare department, and in collaboration with the Polish Council to Aid Jews (Żegota), Sendler rescued numerous Jewish children from the Warsaw Ghetto. After 1945 her wartime activity, like that of others who helped persecuted Jews, was not a matter of public interest. However, after the publication of Jan Tomasz Gross's *Neighbors* in Poland in 2000, Sendler was rediscovered and turned into a heroine, "the mother of the Children of the Holocaust."[44] This shift was part of a backlash to the scholarly and public debate over Polish implication in the Holocaust, triggered by publication of *Neighbors*. Sendler's deeds were to serve as a synecdoche for the stance of the entire nation. Bikont meticulously reconstructs Sendler's biography, uncovering how it was turned into a myth and how Sendler herself largely contributed to this mythmaking process. The author describes how Sendler altered and enriched her personal accounts to better fit public expectations.

Mark Roseman problematizes the memory of the Righteous in Germany by examining postwar private and group narratives of the helpers in the Bund—Gemeinschaft für sozialistisches Leben (The league—Community for socialist life). During the Nazi era and World War II, members of the Bund, a leftist self-study circle formed in the Ruhr area in the 1920s, aided Jews and other people persecuted by the regime by helping them to leave Germany, providing them with shelter and false papers and later also by sending parcels to transit and concentration camps. Roseman discusses how the group narrated, and on various occasions rewrote, its experience after the war. While the basic facts remained intact, what changed was the overall interpretation of the group's actions and the motivations they ascribed to their deeds. Confronting these postwar versions with earlier testimonials, the author argues that the shifts in the narrative were mainly due to the changing political situation in West Germany and the changing attitude of West German society toward the recent past. He also draws attention to the role of Yad Vashem in creating an image of the Righteous as selfless, lone individuals, acting out of an inner moral drive, which often overlooks many important aspects of the rescue stories, including the role of social networks and personal acquaintances. This image also impacts how the war experience has been retrospectively narrated by the helpers and the aid-receivers.

While the essays collected in this volume vary in the lens adopted by the authors, they all raise questions about the interplay of the local, national and transnational, social and governmental, Jewish and non-Jewish agents and initiatives, and their roles in creating (useful) national rescue narratives. They also show how individual testimonies of Holocaust survivors and their helpers can shape public discourse and vice versa. When read together, all the case studies assembled here provide new insights into what has emerged as one of the most important and most visible trends in recent Holocaust memory. As shown in the following chapters, in many countries this has become a "rescue turn" in its nautical sense indeed: a maneuver to change direction of a ship. Here, the meaning is a change of narrative direction by bringing (back) the tropes of rescuing the Jews and individual or collective righteousness into the center of Holocaust commemoration. The many ways this recalibration is underway across Europe highlights the importance of looking closely at those changes and their contexts.

We would like to thank the Centre for Historical Research of the Polish Academy of Sciences in Berlin, the Imre Kertész Kolleg Jena, and the German Resistance Memorial Center for hosting and co-organizing the workshop, "Rescue of Jews during the Holocaust in European Memory." Zofia Wóycicka cowrote this introduction and completed her work on this volume thanks to the grant of the National Science Centre (Narodowe Centrum Nauki, NCN) OPUS22, "Help Delivered to Jews during World War II and Transnational Memory in the Making" (grant no. 2021/43/B/HS2/01596). The Centre for Historical Research of the Polish Academy of Sciences in Berlin, the Imre Kertész Kolleg Jena, the German Historical Institute Warsaw, and the Center for Jewish Studies at the University of Florida financed the editorial work on this volume, including the copyediting of the manuscripts and the translation of two chapters. We also owe gratitude to the copyeditor, Nicolas Hodge, and the two translators, Jasper Tilbury (translating from Polish) and Asia Fruman (translating from Ukrainian), for their tremendous job. Last but not least, our thanks to the two anonymous reviewers, whose feedback was very important in improving the texts.

Notes

1 See "The Yad Vashem—Holocaust Martyrs' and Heroes' Remembrance Authority Law 5713/1953," Yad Vashem, https://www.yadvashem.org/about/yad-vashem-law.html, accessed January 30, 2022.

2 Boaz Cohen, "Holocaust Survivors and Early Israeli Holocaust Research and Commemoration: A Reappraisal," in *How the Holocaust Looks Now: International Perspectives*, ed. Martin L. Davies and Claus-Christian W. Szejnman (Palgrave Macmillan, 2006), 139–48; Kobi Kabalek, "The Commemoration before the Commemoration: Yad Vashem and the Righteous Among the Nations, 1945–1963," *Yad Vashem Studies* 39, no. 2 (2011): 169–211.

3 "The Righteous Among the Nations—About the Program," Yad Vashem, https://www.yadvashem.org/righteous/about-the-program.html, accessed January 30, 2022.

4 See testimony for the Jewish tailor Shmul Leib Sznajderman submitted by Regina Sznajderman Tauber, in the Central Database of Shoah Victims' Names, Yad Vashem, https://yvng.yadvashem.org/index.html?language=en&s_id=&s_lastName=Sznajderman&s_firstName=&s_place=Belzyce&s_dateOfBirth=&cluster=true, accessed January 30, 2022. He was married to Leah Sznajderman, née Fersztaman.

5 Archiwum Żydowskiego Instytutu Historycznego (Archive of the Jewish Historical Institute, hereafter AŻIH), CKŻP, Wydział Opieki Społecznej, 303/VIII, 223.

6 Yad Vashem Archives (hereafter YVA), M.31.2/4231.

7 AŻIH, 303/VIII, 223.

8 AŻIH, 303/VIII, 223. For the broader context see Alicja Podbielska, "'That's for Hiding Jews!' Post-Liberation Violence against Holocaust Rescuers in Poland, 1944–1948." *SIMON. Shoah: Interventions, Methods, Documentation* 6, no. 2 (2019): 110–121.

9 One of the first scholars to describe this phenomenon was Sarah Gensburger. See Sarah Gensburger, "La diffusion transnationale de la catégorie de 'Juste Parmi les Nations.' (Re)penser l'articulation entre diffusion des droits de l'homme et globalisation de la mémoire," *Revue internationale de politique comparée* 22, no. 4 (2015); Sarah Gensburger, *National Policy, Global Memory: The Commemoration of the "Righteous" from Jerusalem to Paris, 1942–2007* (New York: Berghahn, 2016), 105–36. See also Alicja Podbielska, "Toruńskie Yad Vashem," *Zagłada Żydów. Studia i Materiały* 16 (2020), 874–883; Zofia Wóycicka, "A Global Label and Its Local Appropriations: Representations of the Righteous Among the Nations in Contemporary European Museums," *Memory Studies* 15, no. 1 (2022).

10 On how the movie triggered the commemoration of the assistance given to Jews during World War II, among others, in Great Britain and Germany, see Erin Bell, "'Britain's Secret Schindler': The Impact of Schindler's List on British Media Perceptions of Civilian Heroes," in *A Companion to Steven Spielberg*, ed. Nigel Morris (Chichester, West Sussex: Wiley Blackwell, 2017); Kobi Kabalek, "The Rescue of Jews and the Memory of Nazism in Germany, from the Third Reich to the Present" (PhD diss., University of Virginia, 2013), 309–13.

11 International Holocaust Remembrance Alliance (IHRA), "Stockholm Declaration: The Declaration of the Stockholm International Forum on the Holocaust, January 27–29, 2000," https://www.holocaustremembrance.com/about-us/stockholm-declaration, accessed January 2, 2022.

12 On this, see also Gensburger, "La diffusion transnationale"; Gensburger, *National Policy, Global Memory*; Wóycicka, "A Global Label and Its Local Appropriations."

13 Gensburger, "La diffusion transnationale," 542–43; Gensburger, *National Policy, Global Memory*, 106–8; Dariusz Libionka, "Polskie piśmiennictwo na temat zorganizowanej i indywidualnej pomocy Żydom (1945–2008)," *Zagłada Żydów. Studia i Materiały* 17, no. 4 (2008): 65–76.

14 Daniel Levy and Natan Sznaider, "Sovereignty Transformed: A Sociology of Human Rights," *British Journal of Sociology* 57, no. 4 (2006): 669–70.

15 Hilene Flanzbaum, "Introduction: The Americanization of the Holocaust," in *The Americanization of the Holocaust*, ed. Hilene Flanzbaum (Baltimore: Johns Hopkins University Press, 1999), 5–15.

16 Flanzbaum, "Introduction," 7–8, Peter Novick, *The Holocaust in American Life* (Boston: Houghton Mifflin, 1999), 239–63.

17 Jan Eckel and Claudia Moisel, "Einleitung," in *Universalisierung des Holocaust? Erinnerungskultur und Geschichtspolitik in internationaler Perspektive. Beiträge zur Geschichte des Nationalsozialismus* 24, ed. Jan Eckel and Claudia Moisel (Göttingen: Wallenstein Verlag, 2008), 18. (All translations by the authors.)

18 Daniel Levy and Natan Sznaider, "Memory Unbound: The Holocaust and the Formation of Cosmopolitan Memory," *European Journal of Social Theory* 5, no. 1 (2000): 101.

19 Eckel and Moisel, "Einleitung," 18.

20 Levy and Sznaider, "Memory Unbound," 103.

21 Levy and Sznaider, "Memory Unbound," 103.

22 Levy and Sznaider, "Memory Unbound," 92.

23 Daniel Levy, Michael Heinlein, and Lars Breuer, "Reflexive Particularism and Cosmopolitanization: The Reconfiguration of the National," *Global Networks* 11, no. 2 (2011): 141.

24 Tony Judt, *Postwar: A History of Europe since 1945* (New York: Penguin Books, 2005), 803.

25 Sharon Macdonald, *Memorylands: Heritage and Identity in Europe Today* (New York: Routledge, 2013), 190.

26 Jeffrey K. Olick, *The Politics of Regret: On Collective Memory and Historical Responsibility* (New York: Routledge, 2003), 148.

27 Jacob S. Eder, "Holocaust Memory in a Globalizing World: Introduction," in *Holocaust Memory in a Globalizing World*, ed. Jacob S. Eder, Philipp Gassert, and Alan E. Steinweis (Göttingen: Wallstein Verlag, 2017); Harald Schmidt, "Europäisierung des Auschwitzgedenkens. Zum Aufstieg

des 27. Januar 1945 als 'Holocaustgedenktag' in Europa," in *Universalisierung des Holocaust?* 174–202.

28 Eckel and Moisel, "Einleitung," 25.

29 Aleida Assmann, "The Holocaust—A Global Memory? Extensions and Limits of a New Memory Community," in *Memory in a Global Age: Discourses, Practices and Trajectories*, ed. Aleide Assmann and Sebastian Conrad (New York: Palgrave Macmillan, 2010), 113.

30 Anna Cento Bull and Hans Lauge Hansen, "On Agonistic Memory," *Memory Studies* 9, no. 4 (2016): 390–91.

31 Eder, "Holocaust Memory in a Globalizing World: Introduction"; Schmidt, "Europäisierung des Auschwitzgedenkens."

32 Macdonald, *Memorylands*, 215.

33 Chiara De Cesari and Ann Rigney, "Introduction," in *Transnational Memory: Circulation, Articulation, Scales*, ed. Chiara De Cesari and Ann Rigney (Berlin: De Gruyter, 2014), 6.

34 Sharon Macdonald, *Difficult Heritage: Negotiating the Nazi Past in Nuremberg and Beyond* (New York: Routledge, 2009), 123.

35 Benedict Anderson, *Imagined Communities: Reflections on the Origin and Spread of Nationalism* (London: Verso, 1991), 6–7.

36 See David Roskies, *The Jewish Search for a Usable Past* (Bloomington: Indiana University Press, 1999); Raphael Utz, *Rußlands unbrauchbare Vergangenheit. Nationalismus und Außenpolitik im Zarenreich* (Wiesbaden: Harrassowitz Verlag, 2008), 23–28.

37 Liah Greenfeld, *Nationalism: Five Roads to Modernity* (Cambridge, MA: Harvard University Press, 1992), 3.

38 "Sprawiedliwi spod Auschwitz," Starostwo Powiatowe w Oświęcimiu, published online June 9, 2017, http://www.powiat.oswiecim.pl/aktualnosci/sprawiedliwi-spod-auschwitz, accessed November 27, 2021 (now unavailable).

39 Memorial and Museum Auschwitz-Birkenau, "Report from the XXXII IAC Meeting, July 2–3, 2017," http://auschwitz.org/en/museum/auschwitz-council/iac-meetings/meeting-xxxii-2-3-july-2017,28.html, accessed November 17, 2021.

40 For the broader political context, see Jan Grabowski and Marc Grimm, "The Holocaust and Poland's 'History Policy,'" *Israel Journal of Foreign Affairs* 10, no. 3 (2016): 481–86.

41 https://cbh.pan.pl/de/workshop-rescue-jews-during-holocaust-european-memory, accessed August 30, 2022.

42 De Cesari and Rigney, "Introduction."

43 Aleida Assmann and Sebastian Conrad, "Introduction," in *Memory in a Global Age*, ed. Assmann and Conrad, 2.

44 Anna Mieszkowska, *Irena Sendler: Mother of the Children of the Holocaust*, trans. Witold Zbirohowski-Koscia (Santa Barbara, CA: Praeger, 2011).

Bibliography

Anderson, Benedict. *Imagined Communities: Reflections on the Origin and Spread of Nationalism*. London: Verso, 1991.

Assmann, Aleida. "The Holocaust—A Global Memory? Extensions and Limits of a New Memory Community." In *Memory in a Global Age: Discourses, Practices and Trajectories*, ed. Aleida Assmann and Sebastian Conrad, 97–117. New York: Palgrave Macmillan, 2010.

Assmann, Aleida, and Sebastian Conrad. "Introduction." In *Memory in a Global Age: Discourses, Practices and Trajectories*, ed. Aleida Assmann and Sebastian Conrad, 1–6. New York: Palgrave Macmillan, 2010.

Bell, Erin. "'Britain's Secret Schindler': The Impact of Schindler's List on British Media Perceptions of Civilian Heroes." In *A Companion to Steven Spielberg*, ed. Nigel Morris, 320–35. Chichester, West Sussex: Wiley Blackwell, 2017.

Cento Bull, Anna, and Hans L. Hansen. "On Agonistic Memory." *Memory Studies* 9, no 4 (2016): 390–404.

Cohen, Boaz. "Holocaust Survivors and Early Israeli Holocaust Research and Commemoration: A Reappraisal." In *How the Holocaust Looks Now: International Perspectives*, ed. Martin L. Davies and Claus-Christian W. Szejnman, 139–48. Basingstoke: Palgrave Macmillan, 2006.

De Cesari, Chiara, and Ann Rigney. "Introduction." In *Transnational Memory: Circulation, Articulation, Scales*, ed. Chiara De Cesari and Ann Rigney, 1–25. Berlin: De Gruyter, 2014.

Eckel, Jan, and Claudia Moisel. "Einleitung." (Introduction.) In *Universalisierung des Holocaust? Erinnerungskultur und Geschichtspolitik in internationaler Perspektive*. (Universalization of the Holocaust? Culture and Politics of Memory in International Perspective.) *Beiträge zur Geschichte des Nationalsozialismus* 24, ed. Jan Eckel and Claudia Moisel, 9–25. Göttingen: Wallenstein Verlag, 2008.

Eder, Jacob S. "Holocaust Memory in a Globalizing World: Introduction." In *Holocaust Memory in a Globalizing World*, ed. Jacob S. Eder, Philipp Gassert, and Alan E. Steinweis, 7–30. Göttingen: Wallstein Verlag, 2017.

Flanzbaum, Hilene. "Introduction: The Americanization of the Holocaust." In *The Americanization of the Holocaust*, ed. Hilene Flanzbaum, 5–15. Baltimore: Johns Hopkins University Press, 1999.

Gensburger, Sarah. "La diffusion transnationale de la catégorie de 'Juste Parmi les Nations.' (Re)penser l'articulation entre diffusion des droits de l'homme et globalisation de la mémoire." (The transnational diffusion of the category of "Righteous Among the Nations": (Re)thinking the relationship between the diffusion of human rights and the globalization of memory.) *Revue internationale de politique comparée* 22, no. 4 (2015): 537–55.

———. *National Policy, Global Memory: The Commemoration of the "Righteous" from Jerusalem to Paris, 1942–2007*. New York: Berghahn, 2016.

Grabowski, Jan, and Marc Grimm. "The Holocaust and Poland's 'History Policy.'" *Israel Journal of Foreign Affairs* 10, no. 3 (2016): 481–86.

Greenfeld, Liah. *Nationalism: Five Roads to Modernity*. Cambridge, MA: Harvard University Press, 1992.

International Holocaust Remembrance Alliance. "Stockholm Declaration: The Declaration of the Stockholm International Forum on the Holocaust, 27–29 January 2000," https://www.holocaustremembrance.com/about-us/stockholm-declaration, accessed January 2, 2022.

Judt, Tony. *Postwar: A History of Europe since 1945*. New York: Penguin Books, 2005.

Kabalek, Kobi. "The Commemoration before the Commemoration: Yad Vashem and the Righteous Among the Nations, 1945–1963." *Yad Vashem Studies* 39, no. 1 (2011): 169–211.

———. "The Rescue of Jews and the Memory of Nazism in Germany, from the Third Reich to the Present." PhD diss., University of Virginia, 2013.

Levy, Daniel, Michael Heinlein, and Lars Breuer. "Reflexive Particularism and Cosmopolitanization: The Reconfiguration of the National." *Global Networks* 11, no. 2 (2011): 139–59.

Levy, Daniel, and Natan Sznaider. *The Holocaust and Memory in the Global Age*. Philadelphia: Temple University Press, 2006.

———. "Memory Unbound: The Holocaust and the Formation of Cosmopolitan Memory." *European Journal of Social Theory* 5, no. 1 (2002): 81–106.

———. "Sovereignty Transformed: A Sociology of Human Rights." *British Journal of Sociology* 57, no. 4 (2006): 657–76.

Libionka, Dariusz. "Polskie piśmiennictwo na temat zorganizowanej i indywidualnej pomocy Żydom (1945–2008)." (Polish writing on organized and individual aid to Jews [1945–2008].) *Zagłada Żydów. Studia i Materiały* 17, no. 4 (2008): 17–79.

Macdonald, Sharon. *Difficult Heritage: Negotiating the Nazi Past in Nuremberg and Beyond*. New York: Routledge, 2009.

———. *Memorylands: Heritage and Identity in Europe Today*. New York: Routledge, 2013.

Memorial and Museum Auschwitz-Birkenau. "Report from the XXXII IAC Meeting, July 2–3, 2017," http://auschwitz.org/en/museum/auschwitz-council/iac-meetings/meeting-xxxii-2-3-july-2017,28.html, accessed November 17, 2021.

Mieszkowska Anna. *Irena Sendler: Mother of the Children of the Holocaust.* Trans. Witold Zbirohowski-Koscia. Santa Barbara, CA: Praeger, 2011.

Novick, Peter. *The Holocaust in American Life.* Boston: Houghton Mifflin. 1999.

Podbielska, Alicja. "'That's for Hiding Jews!' Post-Liberation Violence against Holocaust Rescuers in Poland, 1944–1948." *SIMON. Shoah: Interventions, Methods, Documentation*, 6, no. 2 (2019): 110–121.

Podbielska, Alicja. "Toruńskie Yad Vashem." *Zagłada Żydów. Studia i Materiały*, 16 (2020): 874–883.

Roskies, David. *The Jewish Search for a Usable Past.* Bloomington: Indiana University Press, 1999.

Olick, Jeffrey K. *The Politics of Regret: On Collective Memory and Historical Responsibility.* New York: Routledge, 2007.

Schmidt, Harald. "Europäisierung des Auschwitzgedenkens. Zum Aufstieg des 27. Januar 1945 als 'Holocaustgedenktag' in Europa." (Europeanization of Auschwitz Remembrance. On the Rise of January 27, 1945 as "Holocaust Memorial Day" in Europe.) In *Universalisierung des Holocaust? Erinnerungskultur und Geschichtspolitik in internationaler Perspektive. Beiträge zur Geschichte des Nationalsozialismus*, 24, ed. Jan Eckel and Claudia Moisel. Göttingen: Wallenstein Verlag, 2008, 174–202.

Starostwo Powiatowe w Oświęcimiu. "Sprawiedliwi spod Auschwitz." (Righteous from the vicinity of Auschwitz.) Published online June 9, 2017. http://www.powiat.oswiecim.pl/aktualnosci/sprawiedliwi-spod-auschwitz, accessed November 27, 2021 (now unavailable).

Utz, Raphael. *Rußlands unbrauchbare Vergangenheit. Nationalismus und Außenpolitik im Zarenreich.* (Russia's unusable past: Nationalism and foreign policy in the Tsarist empire.) Wiesbaden: Harrassowitz Verlag, 2008.

Wóycicka, Zofia. "A Global Label and Its Local Appropriations: Representations of the Righteous Among the Nations in Contemporary European Museums." *Memory Studies* 15, no. 1 (2022): 20–36.

PART I

(Trans)National Memory?

1

Shame and Pride

The Memory of the Rescue of Jews in the Netherlands, 1945 to the Present

IDO DE HAAN

On February 1, 1956, a local Dutch newspaper in The Hague, *Het Haagsch Dagblad*, ran the headline, "Mr. F.M.A. Schokking Ordered the Arrest of a Jewish Family in 1942. Father, Mother, and Child Dead." The article revealed that during the German occupation, the mayor of The Hague, Frans Schokking, had been instrumental in the arrest of a Jewish family. In the small town of Hazerswoude, where Schokking had been serving as mayor in 1942, he had called the *Sicherheitsdienst* to inform them that a Jewish family named Pino had been hidden in his community. Only after Schokking called for a second time was the family arrested.

After the war Schokking survived the purge of government personnel without a scratch, and in 1952 he even experienced a boost in his career when he became mayor of The Hague. When his role in the arrest of the Jewish family in 1942 came to light, Schokking's defense was that he had acted in the best interests of many others, Jews and non-Jews, who had been in hiding in Hazerswoude. He claimed that the Pino family had acted irresponsibly by going outside all the time. He even suggested they might have been secret agents in German service, deployed to reveal resistance against the German authorities. Initially, Schokking's line of defense was backed by an official committee established to investigate the case by the minister of the interior, Louis Beel, and led by the president of the Supreme Court, Jan Donner, which published a report exonerating Schokking of all accusations. It emphasized that, at the time of the incident, the mayor had long pondered what to do before he called the

Sicherheitsdienst for the second time to ask for the *verwijdering* ("removal") of the Pino family.[1] "And thus it happened," concluded the committee, without mentioning that Jakob Pino had committed suicide in prison after being separated from his wife and daughter, who were both deported to Auschwitz, where they were killed.[2]

The committee warned against judging Schokking with hindsight, but that did not stem the wave of publications that compared his behavior under German occupation to that of other Dutch gentiles, some testifying to heroic acts of rescue, but others to reluctance or even rejection of helping to Jews. Remarkably, Jewish survivors hardly participated in the debate, and were even actively discouraged from doing so, most forcefully by the party leader Carl Romme of the Catholic People's Party (KVP)—the largest party in parliament. When Jakob Pino's sister, who had survived, asked the prosecutor general to open a criminal case against Schokking, Romme qualified it as "dirty politics [. . .] to file a complaint after literally ten years."[3] The most vocal participants in the debate were members of the former resistance. *Het Haagsch Dagblad*, the daily that had first revealed the case, belonged to a newspaper syndicate that had emerged from the social-democratic resistance newspaper *Het Parool*, which was clandestinely published from February 1941 and continued to appear after the liberation—until the present day. The communist newspaper *De Waarheid*, published from November 23, 1940, onward (until 1990), also paid ample attention to the affair. When Schokking's case was finally discussed in parliament, the Labour MP and resistance hero Johan Scheps recalled his own experience rescuing Jews, and noted, "We always urged Jews who did not look too Jewish to go out and act like born Christians."[4] On the other hand, the conservative-liberal MP Govert Ritmeester argued that, as a mayor of Den Helder, he had known many Jews, some brave, some cowards, but many also "unruly," like the Pino family: "They had to be disciplined, very forcefully."[5] Anton Roosjen, MP for the orthodox Protestant Antirevolutionary Party, started his contribution to the debate with his recollection of his imprisonment in Buchenwald, where he had seen 250 Dutch Jews arriving in March 1941:

> Six weeks after their arrival, 52 of them had already died of dismal mistreatment, and when the others were deported to Mauthausen, we all understood that their fate was sealed. And we felt tortured by the knowledge that we were unable to offer any help. We can be grateful that the willingness to lend aid to the hunted Jews in the Netherlands could often be turned into action and that in very many cases this was done. As a result, thousands of our Jewish compatriots have

> certainly escaped a horrible death, and for that we must be grateful, above all to those who have risked their own lives by providing this assistance. But because of that we are all the more tormented by the question regarding the incident in Hazerswoude: Could these three lives not also have been spared? At the moment everyone will give an affirmative answer to this question. An error was committed there in Hazerswoude, a serious error; that is calling the S.D. That should never have happened—irrespective of whether this was a trap. That is why I repeat: That was wrong.[6]

The term Roosjen used here for "wrong" was *fout*, which in the context of the war meant collaboration, and if that had resulted in the loss of life—which was generally the case when Jews were denounced—the death penalty was imposed in some of the postwar trials. Of the 154 people who received the death sentence for collaboration, thirty-nine were executed, while all but four were released within fifteen years after their death sentences were reversed.[7] Not so in the case of Schokking. After a series of debates, he resigned as mayor of The Hague, but he lived a long and happy life, fulfilling less illustrious public functions until his death in 1990.

The Memory of Rescue in a Dutch Context

The revelations about Schokking and the debates about his role in the demise of the Pino family reflect the contradictory images in the public commemoration of the rescue of the Jews in the Netherlands. On the one hand, this is a history of failure. Around 74 percent of the total number of Dutch Jews perished during the Holocaust. More Jews were deported from the Netherlands than from any other part of Western Europe. As a result, some 104,000 Jews from the Netherlands were killed. Contrary to the popular notion that all Dutch, like so many others in Europe, flatly denied responsibility for the destruction of European Jewry, it is argued here that, from the immediate postwar period onward, the failure to rescue Dutch Jews and the inaction of the majority of the Dutch population in the face of genocide have been central issues in many of the public debates in the Netherlands.[8] To apply Michael Rothberg's concept, there has been an extensive debate in the Netherlands about the moral responsibility emerging from the fact that Dutch society and its institutions were implicated in the Holocaust, because of the sole fact that the mass murder happened "in our midst."[9]

Yet on the other hand, alongside this discourse of shame, there has been a persistent tendency to boast about rescue efforts, most significantly about the general strike of February 1941 in protest against the deportation of Jews. Another remarkable symptom of excessive pride about rescue activity is that the second largest group of Righteous Among the Nations recognized by Yad Vashem comes from the Netherlands. Up until 2019, 5,778 Dutch gentiles had been awarded this title for helping Jews. While the highest number of Righteous comes from Poland, the Dutch contingent is by far the largest of any national group of Righteous gentiles in relation to the size of the Dutch population, to the number of victims of the Holocaust in the Netherlands, or to the number of survivors.

Addressing the questions as to why there are so many Dutch Righteous Among the Nations in a country that failed significantly more than other nations to rescue its Jewish fellow citizens, and more generally, how to account for the contradictory tendencies of the memory of rescue in the Netherlands, has an intrinsic relevance. Even if the Holocaust was transnational in nature, its impact was first of all experienced and has been remembered locally. These two aspects, of the impact and resonance of the experience of rescue, matter equally to the memory of rescue, and both history and memory are conditioned by local political, social, and cultural circumstances, and by the boundaries of the nation-state. The Dutch case is of crucial importance to a better understanding of the international developments in the field of Holocaust memory. The high number of Dutch Righteous is not the only intriguing issue. The legacy of Anne Frank and the failure to rescue her have also given global Holocaust memory a distinctive Dutch twist, which is generally invisible in the debate over whether Anne Frank is a Jewish or a universal icon.[10] But the amount of scholarly studies on the memory of the Holocaust in the Netherlands accessible to a non-Dutch speaking audience is very limited.

However, the intrinsic relevance of the Dutch case has clear limits. The aim to fill in lacunae in scholarship runs the risk of contributing to the predicament of memory studies already identified in 2011 by Astrid Erll, namely that it turns "into an additive project: we add yet another site of memory, we address yet another historical injustice."[11] Equally troubling is the tendency toward methodological nationalism, in which the national context is treated as an impermeable and immutable framework for studying developments of Holocaust memory. Even if one acknowledges the relevance of the national context, it should not entail a reified and static notion of a national culture of remembrance.

This chapter strives to circumvent methodological nationalism by emphasizing the contradictory and layered nature of the memory of Jewish rescue and the interplay between national and international developments. As Michael Rothberg argued, we need to conceptualize "multidirectional memory" as an articulation of the past in the context of networks of communication, institutions of the state, and social groupings within society, the impact of which is characterized by "displacements and contingencies" and highly ambivalent affective impacts.[12] Schokking's case serves as an example of how a historical reconstruction of a rescue story in the Netherlands needs to take into account the voices of the members of the former resistance, Jewish survivors, and politicians, as well as of people claiming a professional capacity to interpret the past, such as journalists, historians, and judges, but also novelists, documentary filmmakers, and playwrights.[13] Therefore, the first two sections of this chapter focus on the memory of rescue as a source of shame and pride, emerging from the interaction among Dutch professionals, politicians, as well as other Jewish and non-Jewish memory activists, as reflected in key publications and debates in postwar Netherlands.[14]

Yet another way to overcome methodological nationalism is to locate the memory of the rescue of Dutch Jews in a transnational context. In contrast to studies on the globalization of Holocaust memory, emphasizing its deterritorialization and universalization, the following account of the memory of rescue in the Netherlands underlines the relevance of reterritorialization.[15] The final section of the chapter demonstrates that Dutch Jewish immigrants in Israel played a crucial role in the high number of Dutch citizens recognized as Righteous Among the Nations.

The Failure of Rescue

The first issue to address is how Dutch society dealt with the high percentage of Jewish victims from the Netherlands. In 1940, around 140,000 Jews were living in the Netherlands. Some 107,000 were deported, of whom only about 5,200 survived. All in all, fewer than 30 percent of Dutch Jewry survived the Holocaust, and this stands in sharp contrast to the 75 percent of the French Jews who survived, or the 60 percent of Belgian Jewish survivors. Indeed, in the Netherlands the death rate in the Holocaust approaches the number of victims in Eastern Europe—the heartland of the destruction.[16]

Although comparative research aiming to explain the widely divergent percentage of Jewish victims in Western European countries began only in the 1980s, the failure to come to the rescue of the Dutch Jews had already become an issue of public awareness in the immediate postwar years. At the time, many members of the former resistance and of the postwar political elite were concerned about the high level of antisemitism among large sections of the Dutch population. Some commentators even argued that antisemitism was more widespread in the country after the German occupation than before.[17] In an attempt to explain this, Hilda Verwey-Jonker, one of the most influential social democratic intellectuals of the immediate postwar years, suggested that there was a link between the guilt over failing to help the Jews and the rise of antisemitism. She wrote in November 1945: "The great majority of the Dutch people are very well aware that their behavior towards their Jewish fellow citizens was utterly miserable. They try to justify this in hindsight and find such justification in a critique of the Jews. At this point, antisemitism thus fulfils the same role as the exuberant national joy that fills our streets: a compensation for a lack of national pride demonstrated during the occupation."[18]

Such failure was documented, for example, in a well-known collection of war diaries published in 1954 by the Dutch National Institute of War Documentation (NIOD), for a long time the most influential guardian of the memory of World War II in the Netherlands. In one of the accounts, a man described his response to a police raid that occurred on June 20, 1943, while he was looking forward to a family outing: "There goes a fine day," he writes. "I can already imagine the long faces of my wife and kid." When he reached the train station, he reflected on the Jews he saw: "Herded together, carried off like cattle. . . . They might not be a pleasant people. But they are still human beings. How can our good Lord tolerate this?"[19]

In the 1950s several literary accounts addressed the failure to provide help, as well as the mixed feelings this failure engendered. An important example is Adriaan van der Veen's *Het wilde feest* (The wild party [1952]), which opens with an epigraph: "the thought of it filled him with that sort of impersonal but unbearable shame with which we are filled, for instance, by the notion of physical torture, of something that humiliates humanity." While the book demonstrated a deeply felt concern for the fate of the Jews, the story about the attempts of the main character, a non-Jewish man, to win the heart of a Jewish woman "by fully identifying with the fate of the Jewish people" also illustrated how such empathy was mixed with the author's exoticizing fascination with Jews.[20] The motivations behind identifying with the fate of the Jews were also questioned by Willem van Maanen in *Al lang geleden* (Long ago [1956]): "You only love me because I am Jewish, not because I am Mirjam."[21] Other authors testify about the feeling of powerlessness with regard to the fate of the Jews. In a popular novel intended "for the older girl," *Een baantje bij de krant* (A job at the newspaper [1963]), Martje witnessed the arrest of Jews and noted: "And there we stood powerless before the window, safe in our own house; we were [safe], but they were not."[22] The same sentiment was expressed in the popular novel by Willy Corsari, *Die van ons* (One of us [1945]), which sold seventy thousand copies (thereby saving the former resistance publishing house De Bezige Bij from bankruptcy).[23] A more highbrow example is the first publication of one of the most successful Dutch authors of the twentieth century, Gerard Reve. In *De ondergang van de familie Boslowits* (The demise of the Boslowits family [1946]), he documented in a seemingly detached but ultimately chilling way the fate of the titular family from the perspective of a young, passive neighbor.[24]

Recollections of Dutch indifference and failure to rescue Jews also played a role in the first systematic historical study of the persecution of the Jews in the Netherlands, written by the Dutch Jewish lawyer Abel Herzberg, *Kroniek van de Jodenvervolging 1940–1945* (Chronicle of the persecution of the Jews, 1940–1945 [1950]). In his account of one of the largest police raids in Amsterdam, which took place on June 20, 1943, and led to the arrest of 5,700 people, he remarks: "One of the assembly places during the police raid was the Olympiaplein. The weather was beautiful that day, and the usual games were played on the sports field. The Jews waiting there were witnessing this loud and clear. These were no NSB [National Socialist movement] members playing there. These were not men from the resistance. It was the majority of the Dutch people. One had grown accustomed to so much."[25]

An important impetus in the growing public awareness of the failure to rescue Dutch Jews was the disappointment of former resistance members over the swift return of collaborators to prominent positions in society, as a result of which many former resistance members were left feeling their efforts to fight Nazism had been futile. An influential example was the work of criminologist Willem Nagel. In 1953, under his resistance alias, J. B. Charles, he published the book *Volg het spoor terug* (Follow the trace), in which he criticized Dutch society for its cowardly attitude in the face of the Nazi regime, lambasted the tendency to forgive and forget, and warned against a reemergence of fascism and its most heinous aspect—the racist persecutions. His book was an immediate success, partly because it provoked fierce criticism, which became even stronger after *Volg het spoor terug* was awarded the literary prize of the Jan Campert Foundation—named after another resistance icon. In the end, ironically, Nagel received the prize from the hands of the mayor of The Hague, Frans Schokking, who was about to play a prominent role in the political scandal sketched earlier in this chapter.[26]

The downfall of Schokking underlined the continued influence of former resistance members on the memory of rescue in postwar Dutch society. Their impact was reinforced by a series of newspapers that had initially been established as underground publications but continued to appear after 1945, attracting a large readership: the daily *Het Parool* with a social-democratic leaning (and a series of affiliated local newspapers, including *Het Haagsch Dagblad*); *Trouw* (neo-Calvinist); *De Waarheid* (communist); and the weekly progressive journal *Vrij Nederland*, founded and edited by Henk van Randwijk. In 1960 Van Randwijk began writing a series of reflections on life in the Netherlands during the German occupation, "In the Shadow of Yesterday," which was published under his resistance alias, Sjoerd van Vliet. In 1970 his articles appeared again in one volume, which was distributed in hundreds of thousands of copies among the Dutch youth by the national committee to commemorate the twenty-fifth anniversary of the liberation (Nationaal Comité, 25 jaar bevrijding—5 mei 1970).[27] It created a platform for a deeply pessimistic account of the unwillingness of the Dutch to rescue the Jews: "You who read this, did you belong to those who, by so many pretexts, refused to hide Jews? I advise the youth who read this to ask their parents, their teachers, their minister or priest about this. Not to set them up against the authorities or to let them take all these pretexts at face value [. . .] but to temper their expectations with regard to human nature and human solidarity in German-occupied territory."[28]

The failure of rescue became an even more prominent theme after the publication of Jacques Presser's history of the Holocaust in the Netherlands, *Ondergang: De vervolging en verdelging van het Nederlandse jodendom (1940–1945)* (Downfall: The persecution and destruction of Dutch Jewry [1940–1945]; 1965). On the one hand, Presser described the persecution of the Jews as a cat-and-mouse game between Germans and Jews in which Dutch non-Jews played no role. In other parts of his account, however, he emphasized that the latter fell short of the solidarity that ideally would have been required of anyone aware of the injustice done to Jews. In reality many were less determined to assist, although their attitude was more varied than could be expressed by the simple terms of right and wrong, "goed en fout": "almost unwieldly simplifications," according to Presser.[29] Some were too eagerly misled by German evasions, but many more felt excused for their failure to help Jews due to the similar failure of Dutch officials. In this way, Presser drew attention to the attitudes of the Dutch government in exile, the secretaries-general (the Dutch civil servants in charge of the ministries after the government had gone into exile), police officials, and people from many other sectors of Dutch society, who had all tried to accommodate the German demands. Some argued that collaboration was justified because it prevented a far worse outcome; but in other cases their accommodation was carried out to profit from the opportunities the German occupation offered. This attitude also characterized the leadership of the Jewish Council, which according to Presser demonstrated the same misguided utilitarianism as the non-Jewish establishment.[30]

Just like Van Randwijk's critique, Presser's condemnation of the political establishment set the tone for a public debate over whether the failure to save the Jews was a symptom of a fundamental flaw in Dutch society. In this context, the comparatively high number of casualties among Dutch Jews played a pivotal role. From the middle of the 1980s, the scholarly discussion of this issue was framed in terms of the "Dutch paradox," and interpreted as the mirror image of the Belgian and French paradoxes.[31] While Jews in Belgium were more isolated, and prewar antisemitism was stronger in France than in most other parts of Europe, more Jews were deported from the Netherlands than from any other part of Western Europe, both in absolute and relative numbers. As Hans Blom, the historian and, later, director of the NIOD, argued in 1987, this happened despite the fact that no successful antisemitic political mobilization had occurred in prewar Dutch society, even if anti-Jewish stereotypes were widespread. Until the German invasion of May 1940, Dutch Jews generally seemed to have lived peacefully among other Netherlanders. Geographical explanations were deemed equally unconvincing: The argument that the Netherlands was such a flat country that Jews were unable to find a place to hide was belied by the fact that 300,000 non-Jewish Dutch men had successfully avoided German attempts to deploy them as forced laborers in Germany.[32]

Echoing Presser's arguments, the journalist and historian Nanda van der Zee ascribed the failure of rescue primarily to the Dutch political elite, especially Queen Wilhelmina. In a widely read yet critically received study, Van der Zee argued in 1997 that the flight of Wilhelmina and the government to London in the first days after the German invasion had demoralized the Dutch people and created an opportunity for the Germans to install a civil authority with a much wider reach than the military occupying regimes established in France and Belgium. In addition, Van der Zee held the Dutch civil service responsible for the implementation of German policies: They had developed a formalistic and subservient attitude, legitimized by a prewar administrative ruling that, in the event of a foreign occupation, all civil servants should remain at their posts to mitigate and distribute the burden of occupation evenly. The willingness to accommodate increasingly harsh measures against Jews was thus legitimized as an attempt to prevent the worst outcome. The failure to understand that this meant Dutch Jews were sacrificed was exacerbated by the lack of interest in their fate.[33] In a more structural argument, Hans Blom suggested that the willingness to accommodate the German demands resulted from a deeply ingrained deference to authority and general predilection to mitigate between conflicting positions, stemming from an age-old Dutch political culture of mutual tolerance and organizational entrenchment (*verzuiling*) of confessional differences—an attitude that, due to the high level of assimilation, also characterized the Jewish population.[34]

These critical accounts of the role of the Dutch were concisely summarized in the title of Max Arian's article, published in 1992: "Nederland Deportatieland" (The Netherlands: Land of deportation).[35] It expressed a widespread national consensus that is still to a large extent in place, about the lack of help offered to the Jews during the occupation of the Netherlands. Telling examples of this consensus are two speeches given by Queen Beatrix in 1995. Fifty years after the end of World War II, she addressed the Israeli Knesset and the Dutch Parliament, and stated that the memory of the "most gruesome genocide in history" was a cause for "a deep feeling of shame" about the fact that the "courageous resistance" of a few "could not prevent the destruction of their Jewish fellow citizens," because many other Dutchmen had remained "passive" or had even given "active support to the occupier."[36] Recently, this consensus was reinforced by formal apologies by the Dutch prime minister Mark Rutte for the failure of the Dutch government: "Certainly, there were individual cases of resistance within the government, but too many Dutch officials carried out what the occupiers demanded of them. Others endured the great evil in hope of being able to do something good—which sometimes worked, but much more often it did not. And the bitter consequences of registration and deportation were not recognized in time and were not recognized sufficiently."[37]

Despite the widespread agreement that the Dutch failed to rescue their Jewish compatriots, the explanation of that failure has remained a topic of continuous debate in recent years. Much of the disagreement concerns the question of knowledge about the fate of the Jews. For instance, the writer Ies Vuijsje has argued that many members of the elite had actually been aware of the plight of the Dutch Jews but had failed to pay proper attention to it. The main culprit in his story is Loe de Jong, whose career as reporter for Radio Oranje, the radio station of the Dutch government in exile in London, continued when he established the Rijksbureau voor Oorlogsdocumentatie on May 5, 1945 (later renamed Rijksinstituut voor Oorlogsdocumentatie, and after 1999, Nederlands Instituut voor Oorlogsdocumentatie [NIOD]), and served as its director. He was also the author of the canonical work, *Het Koninkrijk der Nederlanden in de Tweede Wereldoorlog* (The kingdom of the Netherlands in the Second World War), published between 1969 and 1988.[38] According to Vuijsje, during and after the war, De Jong deliberately ignored information about the annihilation of the Jews. Vuijsje ascribed this attitude less to antisemitism than to a psychological tendency to repress the horrifying news about the fate of the Jews.[39] While Vuijsje emphasized the repression of knowledge as the motive for inaction, the historian Bart van der Boom explained the failure to assist Jews, but also the limited attempts of Jews to find refuge, as resulting from an incomplete understanding of the murderous nature of Nazi anti-Jewish policies. Although most people were convinced that the deportations spelled disaster, only a few believed all Jews would actually be killed. Most, including the majority of Jews, therefore made a seemingly rational calculation that resistance to the arrests and deportation of Jews would be more harmful than accommodating the German demands.[40] Both publications led to further and extensive public as well as scholarly debate, in which Vuijsje's accusatory perspective was rejected by some as too one-sided, while Van der Boom's exculpatory approach was seen as an attempt to whitewash the reputation of Dutch society for its failure to rescue its Jewish population.[41]

The Pride of Rescuers

In contrast to the apparent consensus on the notion that Dutch society was practically and morally responsible for the failure to assist its Jewish citizens during the German occupation, there has always been an alternative recollection of the Holocaust, which emphasized that the Dutch demonstrated remarkable courage in their attempts to rescue the Jews.[42] This image consisted of two parts: nationalization of the rescue and the focus on individual acts of heroism. On the one hand, solidarity with the Jews was seen as an expression of a collective or even national spirit of resistance. The main expression of this nationalization and incorporation of the memory of rescue into the memory of resistance was the commemoration of the strike of February 1941. After the German authorities arrested 427 Jewish men in Amsterdam on February 22 and 23, 1941, communist resistance groups called for a general strike to express solidarity with the Jews. After just two days, this strike was violently suppressed, on February 26, 1941. The commemoration of the strike as a collective rescue effort was contested during the early years of the Cold War, but it became consolidated in the 1960s. On the other hand, it was emphasized that the rescue of Jews resulted from individual courageous acts of gentiles, mainly by providing shelter to Jews. A crucial source for this aspect of heroic memory of rescue was the diary of Anne Frank and the history of the Franks' secret annex. Equally telling was the very high number of individual rescuers from the Netherlands who were recognized as Righteous Among the Nations by Yad Vashem.

The commemoration of the strike of February 1941 has long occupied a central place in the memory of rescue. During the first national commemoration of the strike, on February 25, 1946, fifty thousand people attended a ceremony where Queen Wilhelmina—herself seen as the "mother of the resistance"—bestowed an honor on the city of Amsterdam by adding the motto "Valiant,

Steadfast, Compassionate" to the city's coat of arms. Since then, the yearly commemoration has served as a constant affirmation. In 1948 the sculptor Mari Andriessen was commissioned to design a statue in tribute to the strike. He sculpted an Amsterdam dockworker, to express his admiration for the fact that "for the first time in history Christians had tried to protect Jews."[43] The monument itself became an icon of the Dutch "spirit of resistance," displayed in countless schoolbooks and commemorative volumes and on posters devoted to the period of the Nazi occupation. International recognition came in 1960, when the mayor of Amsterdam, Gijs van Hall, planted a tree on the Mount of Remembrance at Yad Vashem to commemorate the strike—one of five trees planted at Yad Vashem to honor collective rescue efforts.[44]

Despite its aim to express solidarity with the Jews, the commemoration of the strike of February 1941 turned out to be very divisive. In the context of the Cold War, the working-class nature of the strike and the prominent role of its communist organizers made the memory of the strike a heavily contested event. Between 1951 and 1966, two competing ceremonies were held each year on the same day: In the morning a "national" commemoration took place, followed by another, generally much larger event organized by the communists, with up to thirty thousand people attending the ceremony. The unveiling of the statue of the *Dokwerker* happened on a "neutral" date in December 1952. The fierce contestation of the memory of the strike of February 1941 undermined the unitary, national nature of this aspect of collective memory. At the same time, however, it made the status of the strike of February an even more prominent symbol of collective pride.[45]

In 1966 the national and communist commemorations of the strike were reconciled again in a joint commemoration, indicating that the 1960s, frequently characterized as an era of increased contestation, represented a time when the national imagery of Dutch efforts to rescue the Jews became consolidated. A crucial role in the emergence of this national perspective was played by Loe de Jong, who had made the NIOD into a national repository of knowledge regarding World War II and had himself become the conscience of the nation with regard to the period of war, occupation, and persecution. Between 1960 and 1965, De Jong presented a series of television documentaries, *De Bezetting* (The occupation), in which the heroic attempts to rescue the Jews were emphasized in the final scenes of each of the twenty-one episodes. Each final scene showed the *Dokwerker*, accompanied by a soundtrack of "Merck toch hoe sterck" (See how strong), a seventeenth-century popular song celebrating Dutch resistance to Spanish rule in the Low Countries.[46]

The outline of the TV series was also the framework for De Jong's history of the Netherlands under German occupation. Published between 1969 and 1988 in twenty-seven hefty volumes, De Jong's work painted an image of a quickly growing popular resistance against Nazi rule: "From month to month, feelings of irritation and indignation were growing among the public at large."[47] This public resistance also included protests against anti-Jewish measures: first of all, of course, the strike of February 1941, but also the distribution of leaflets (entitled "Jew and Non-Jew Are One") from the roof of the Amsterdam department store De Bijenkorf, in protest of the May 1, 1942, order that Jews must wear a yellow star.[48] According to De Jong, the Nazi terror sometimes made it too dangerous to voice this kind of protest in public. Still, De Jong argued: "What could not be voiced publicly in occupied territory was stated with clarity by Queen Wilhelmina" in her speeches for Radio Oranje, thus making her majesty's voice the mouthpiece of the general mood of the Dutch public.[49]

In the context of the nationalization of the memory of rescue, the perspective and contributions of Jews were marginalized. In 1946 the Amsterdam city council turned down a request from the Nederlands-Israëlietische Hoofdsynagoge Amsterdam (the Netherlands' Israelite Main Synagogue Amsterdam, the governing body of the Amsterdam Ashkenazi Jewish community) to build a memorial to the Jewish victims in the city center. The council argued that the commemoration of victims needed to take place in a national context, which did not allow for a separate treatment of different minorities. Moreover, the location at the Jonas Daniël Meyerplein, between the main synagogues, was deemed unfit for the purpose—although it was assigned two years later as the location for the erection of *De Dokwerker*.[50] And in 1950, a couple of hundred meters down the road, the *Monument van Joodse Erkentelijkheid* (Monument of Jewish gratitude) was unveiled. The initiator of the monument was a member of the Amsterdam city council, Maurits de Hartogh, who had survived the war due to the special protection of the Dutch secretaries-general Karel Johannes Frederiks and Jan van Dam. Having being interned in the Netherlands from 1942 until September 1944 among other "prominent" Jews, De Hartogh was then deported to Theresienstadt, where he survived the Holocaust. Addressing the Amsterdam city council, De Hartogh explained that "certainly, our people were not able to prevent the majority of Dutch Jews from being taken abroad, from where regrettably only a small portion returned." Yet the aim of the monument was to express "the deep gratitude which fills the hearts of the Jews in the Netherlands for the fact that in these five frightful years, they were considered to be Netherlanders, with whom solidarity was declared."[51] According to the sculptor of the monument, Jobs Wertheim—also a survivor of Theresienstadt—it conveyed among other things:

> Resignation: The characteristic attitude of the specifically persecuted group of Jews, who saw no way out. [. . .] Protection: The love of the non-Jew for his fellow man, the particularly hard-hit Jew, expressing himself in hiding, assistance with escaping, care of hidden ones etc. Resistance: The moral support given to the Jew by the non-Jew, his resistance and combative spirit in the active struggle against the occupier. Mourning: The mourning by the non-Jew and Jew for the dead and the suffering in the jointly borne ordeal of the Fatherland in the war years.[52]

In contrast to this rather one-sided division of roles between resigned and passive Jews and actively resisting non-Jews, Amsterdam mayor Arnold d'Ailly voiced a more nuanced view. At the unveiling on February 23, 1950, he expressed not only pride in the honor bestowed on the Dutch people but also shame, "because even though there was much resistance, very many failed."[53] The latter sentiment apparently prevailed among a substantial part of the Jewish community and its religious leaders, most of whom declined to attend the ceremony. As Jo Melkman, the chief editor of the Jewish journal *Nieuw Israelietisch Weekblad*, declared ironically in his editorial about the ceremony, the Dutch Jews "serve only to glorify the Dutch national consciousness. They are nothing more than an opportunity to present a noble deed, worthy to be written down in the annals of a great liberation struggle."[54]

An additional source of frustration was that the contribution of Jews to their own rescue was largely ignored. In fact, Jacques Presser, in the aforementioned book *Ondergang*, was the first to emphasize that, in relative terms, more Jews participated in the resistance movement than non-Jews.[55] He also contrasted the collaboration of the Dutch and Jewish leadership with the example of the Jewish economist and mystic Friedrich Weinreb, who had led Jews in Southern Holland to believe he could rescue them through his connections with the German authorities; in the end he was forced by these same authorities to hand over his Jewish contacts. Weinreb was convicted in 1946 by the Dutch Special Court of Justice for the betrayal of Jews to the Germans—and in 1948 in cassation to an even higher sentence of six years. However, according to Presser and the accused's defenders, Weinreb had deployed creative yet ultimately highly risky methods to save Jews, which demonstrated his persistent ingenuity in resisting and deluding the German authorities. Weinreb thus was seen by some as a quixotic but nevertheless positive example of *Zivilcourage*, inspiring resistance against injustice in postwar society as well. The novelist Harry Mulisch argued that Weinreb was the "Che Guevara of bureaucracy" who fought an "administrative guerrilla action" against a system that remained in place.[56] Presser was less concerned about the revolution than with the abandonment of the Jews when he described Weinreb's postwar conviction for betrayal as turning "the Jew Weinreb into a scapegoat, who paid for the failure of so many non-Jews. He must have failed, also failed, because they had failed."[57] In the end, the debate between Weinreb's supporters, who claimed he had rescued several hundred Jews, and those who argued that Weinreb had deluded these Jews and contributed to their demise to save his own skin, was decided in favor of the latter.[58] Yet Presser's plea for the recognition of Jewish resistance led to a modest but steady stream of research.[59] But the image of perceived Jewish passivity persisted. Only in 1988 was the first monument dedicated to Jewish resistance unveiled, on the occasion of which the mayor of Amsterdam, Ed van Thijn, deplored the prejudicial notion that "Jews went like sheep to the slaughter."[60]

The memorialization of individual rescuers focused primarily on people who had provided opportunities for *onderduiken* (diving under), as hiding from the German authorities was referred to in Dutch. This focus was by no means self-evident. As Bob Moore has demonstrated in his detailed study, *Survivors: Jewish Self-Help and Rescue in Nazi-Occupied Western Europe*, rescue attempts involved public and private protests, assistance in escaping abroad, the forging of identity cards and food stamps, the manipulation of the process by which people were identified as Jews, and outright acts of sabotage, such as the torching of the Amsterdam civil registry office on March 28, 1943.[61] One possible explanation for the fact that, despite this diversity of rescue efforts, *de onderduik* became the central component of the memory of rescue is the impact of the diary of Anne Frank. The secret annex where the Frank and Van der Pels families were hidden has become an iconic place for the commemoration of the Holocaust, currently attracting around 1.3 million visitors a year, while Anne Frank's diary and its many adaptions—as plays, graphic novels, movies, and even a musical—have reached one of the widest audiences any book has ever achieved.[62] Some of the people who helped those hiding in the secret annex, notably Miep Gies, who found and saved the diary, were important spokespersons for the memory of Anne Frank and the attempt to rescue the Frank family. As Gies declared in the opening lines of her memoir, *Anne Frank Remembered*: "I am not a hero. I stand at the end of a long, long line of good Dutch people who did what I did or more—much more—during those dark and terrible times many years ago."[63]

Yet another reason why *de onderduik* played such a central role is that it was seen as a distinctively Dutch type of rescue. In the chapter "Het onderduiken" in the commemorative book series *Onderdrukking en verzet* (Repression and resistance; published in four volumes between 1949 and 1954 by an editorial board of prominent figures from all political and cultural sections of Dutch society), Hendrik van Riessen, one of the leading figures in the National Organization for Help to People in Hiding (Landelijke Organisatie voor hulp aan onderduikers, or LO), set the tone by arguing that in the Netherlands more than anywhere else, "providing shelter had developed into a mighty movement for the protection of Dutch citizens against German measures." The reasons for this exceptional strength of "shelter work" (*onderduikerswerk*) were "the mental disposition of our people, on which Christianity has not yet lost its hold," as well as "a sense of order and awareness of responsibility, which generally characterized the Dutch."[64] But the chapter paid only limited attention to the hiding of Jews and focused mainly on non-Jewish men evading the German actions to round up men for forced labor. As Presser noted in 1965, in the introduction to his lengthy chapter about "De onderduik," there was a growing awareness in the Netherlands that "the Jews who most needed the support of organizations for shelter [*onderduikorganisaties*] and the hospitality of families who gave shelter [*onderduik-verlenende gezinnen*] [. . .] received it by far the least."[65] He discussed estimates of some 20,000 to 30,000 Jews who had been hidden, out of whom some 8,000 to 10,000 were captured, only to conclude that precise information was lacking. More recently Bert Jan Flim, a researcher for Yad Vashem, has estimated that there were only 15,900 Jews in hiding; 700 of these had only one Jewish parent, while 700 were in mixed marriages. According to Flim, the limited numbers are explained by the fact that the National Organization for Help to People in Hiding started operating only in 1942, when the first deportations began, at a moment when it was already very difficult for Jews to travel. However from 1943 onward, the successful attempts to hide some 300,000 men who were attempting to evade forced labor, as well as tens of thousands of strikers after the railway strike of September 1944, indicate that the potential to hide Jews was never fully realized.[66]

Remembering rescue offered an opportunity not only to sing the praises of the Dutch spirit of resistance but also to comment on the behavior of Jews in hiding. In *Het Grote Gebod* (The great command, 1951), the commemorative volume of the National Organization for Help to People in Hiding, the author and journalist Klaas Norel presented a number of examples of "remarkable resignation by which Jews subjected themselves to the German measures," suggesting that "to accept their fate seemed to most Jews preferable to an attempt to avoid the control of the Nazis, as that would entail the risk of very cruel punishment if they were to be found."[67] He likewise made the following observation:

> Hiding was no fun, neither for Jews, nor for those who offered shelter. There were reproaches from both sides. "We are plundered and abused," was sometimes a legitimate complaint from the Jews, since there were actually "helpers" who pinched from their guests. Unruly, disobedient and always creating problems, many hosts would argue [about their guests], who then wanted to get rid of them. Of course, some Jews will have been difficult, but bear in mind under what circumstances and with which psychological burden they had to live for years.[68]

Norel's remarks were echoed in later accounts, and they were not dissimilar from the comments made about the Pino family in the Schokking affair, five years after the publication of Norel's article. The reason Schokking's opponents reacted with such vehemence to his line of defense might have stemmed from the suspicion that such comments were inspired by anti-Jewish sentiment. Neither was Norel beyond reproach in this respect. In another article published in 1947, he had argued that the passivity of Jews ended only when their property was at stake: "And then, with a vengeance, with great cunning, they hid millions from the enemy. But this could not be accomplished by cunning alone. They needed help. And help was generously offered, by the Dutch."[69] The remarks led to a legal complaint filed by the Jewish lawyer Hans Warendorf, who argued that Jews had actually actively resisted the persecution. Nevertheless, Norel was acquitted by a judge who claimed that Norel had demonstrated a "lack of tact" but had not intended any "deliberate insult."[70]

Positive accounts of the rescue of Dutch Jews created a connection between the national spirit of resistance and the fate of the Jews. However, this was often to the detriment of the memory of the Jews and their fate during the Holocaust, not only because of the instrumentalization of their suffering for buttressing a sense of Dutch national pride, but also because of the sometimes forceful marginalization of their experiences and concerns. In the first decades after the war, when the rescue of Jews was a source of national pride, it was very hard to address the aggression Jews were subjected to as a result of their victimization and the trauma they experienced, not just by the Nazis, but also as a result of their dependency on rescuers who took advantage—in terms of money, labor, service, or sex—of the Jews in their care.[71] This changed only in the late 1970s, when the traumatic effects of persecution, and also the impact of the Shoah on children and later generations, became topics of concern.[72] The psychological discourse offered a new vocabulary for discussing the experience of persecution and rescue, yet at the risk of turning it into an individual trauma that had to compete with many other kinds of hurtful experiences, likewise engendering a competition between victim groups.[73]

A Nation of Righteous Gentiles

As Bob Moore remarked, the centrality of acts of rescue by non-Jewish helpers providing shelter for Jewish *onderduikers* might also be an artifact of the requirements for the recognition of people as Righteous Among the Nations, which require survivor testimony about individual acts of rescue.[74] The recognition of saviors as Righteous Among the Nations plays a significant and also puzzling role in the memory of rescue in the Netherlands. In 1962, the Israeli Memorial Authority of Yad Vashem established the Commission for the Designation of the Righteous. The commission drafted the criteria for recognition and from 1963 awarded the first certificates to non-Jews who provided help to Jews at the risk of their own lives, without reward, for primarily humanitarian motives, and without otherwise having harmed Jews.[75] From the beginning of this program until 2019, 27,362 persons have been recognized as Righteous Among the Nations. As the Israeli historian and director of research at Yad Vashem Dan Michman once stated, the title of the Righteous "has become a kind of Nobel Prize for Humanitarianism."[76]

The designation of the Righteous Among the Nations has become an important asset in both international and domestic Dutch politics. The relevance for foreign policy became evident, for instance, in the speech the Dutch prime minister Mark Rutte gave during his official visit to Israel in 2013. He celebrated "the natural—and at the same time emotional—bond between the Netherlands and Israel. I really felt that bond this morning when I visited Yad Vashem. This impressive memorial also commemorates the many Dutch Jews who were murdered in the Holocaust. What's more, Yad Vashem honors 5,269 Dutch nationals as 'Righteous Among the Nations,' for their efforts to help the Jews in their hour of need."[77] Yet also domestically, the conferral of the Righteous Among the Nations honorific has become an important aspect of national commemorative practices. The ceremony where rescuers or their families receive the certificate takes place in the local synagogue or town hall, at the ministry of foreign affairs, or at the Israeli embassy in The Hague, generally in the presence of the Israeli ambassador, the Dutch mayor, the secretary of state, or some other official.[78]

It is not just the high symbolic value, but even more the sheer number of Righteous Among the Nations from the Netherlands that is remarkable. In early 2019, there were 5,778 Dutch citizens who were acknowledged as Righteous Among the Nations. For a considerable time in the 1970s and 1980s, the Dutch Righteous were the largest group in absolute numbers. The Dutch are still in second place after Poland, which has 6,992 Righteous officially acknowledged. In relative terms, the Dutch number is exceptionally high, both in comparison to the size of the country and its population, as well as in comparison to the number of Jewish victims and the number of survivors. In the 1940s the Dutch population was around 9 million; some 36,000 Jews survived. Given that one in every 1,500 Dutch citizens was designated as Righteous, there was one Righteous for every six Jewish survivors. In France, which had an overall 1940 population of roughly 40 million people, and a Jewish population of 320,000 people, some 77,000 Jews perished. France has 4,099 citizens designated Righteous, thus one in every 10,000 French was designated Righteous, or one Righteous for every 20 survivors. Hungary, with 550,000 Jewish victims and around 255,000 Jewish survivors, has 867 Righteous. In Bulgaria, where most of its 50,000 Jewish citizens were saved, there are only 20 Righteous.[79]

It is not easy to explain why there are so many Dutch Righteous Among the Nations, and why this number does not correlate with either the size of the population or the number of Jewish victims and survivors. There seem to be two main lines of argument to explain the discrepancy: one referencing the conditions of rescue under the Nazi occupation and the other pointing to varying conditions in the postwar remembrance of rescue. The first line of argument presupposes that the context of the persecution, and therefore the opportunities for rescue, differed in the various countries. According to the Dutch-Jewish historian Joseph Michman (previously known as Josef Melkman—the chief editor of the *Nieuw Israelietisch Weekblad* mentioned earlier—until his *aliyah* in 1957), the long-time director of research at Yad Vashem and member of the Commission for the Designation of the Righteous, the high number of Dutch Righteous can be explained by two key factors:

> the extremely cruel nature of the wartime persecution of Jews in the Netherlands, and the protracted reign of its occupying regime. The character of the German regime and its tremendous efficiency made it more dangerous to rescue Jews in Holland than in Belgium or France. Anyone caught helping Jews in the latter countries would suffer a relatively mild punishment, but in Holland he or she was likely to be executed or sent to a concentration camp, where the chances of survival were very slim.[80]

The argument would then be that Dutch rescuers ran a higher risk than rescuers in other countries—for which they were acknowledged by their recognition as Righteous. However, there is little evidence to support this claim. Actually, it seems hard to deny that the Nazi regime was much more lethal in the "bloodlands" in Eastern and southeastern Europe than in the West, not only for Jews, but also for non-Jews.[81] Moreover, the violence of German repression does not explain the case of France, for instance. During World War II, some 250,000 Dutch citizens died from violent causes—2.7 percent of the total population—of which approximately 40 percent were victims of the Holocaust. Around 2,000 of those died in retaliation for acts of resistance, which included providing shelter for Jews, although their exact number is unknown.[82] That is also the case in France, yet there around 54,000 people died in retaliation for acts of resistance, in the repression of armed partisans, and as deportees to German concentration camps (apart from Jewish deportees).[83] If the level of violence and risk had been decisive, there would have to be more French Righteous than there actually are.

Another argument to explain the variation in Righteous gentiles related to the specific conditions of rescue can be derived from Bob Moore's study, *Survivors*. He argues that in France and Belgium the rescue of Jews was, to a much larger degree than in the Netherlands, embedded in strong social and economic networks, both of Jews and non-Jews. As a result, rescue was often a byproduct of social and economic interdependencies, stemming less from altruistic motives. A consequence might be that fewer rescue efforts qualified for recognition by the Commission for the Designation of the Righteous, which requires purely humanitarian motives and individual agency. There are, in principle, no collective forms of recognition, with three important exceptions: (1) The Danish resistance presented its remarkable evacuation of 7,220 of Denmark's 7,800 Jews as a collective act, and it was recognized as such; (2) the Dutch community of Nieuwelande received collective recognition in 1983, along with 202 of its inhabitants who were also individually acknowledged; (3) following the precedent set by Nieuwelande, the French community of Chambon-sur-Lignon in France received collective recognition in 1990 (along with 40 individual recognitions).[84] The Dutch rescuers much better fit the criterion that help should have been motivated by humanitarian motives: Not only were many more rescuers operating individually, but the networks were also more often linked to churches or other denominational or ideological organizations, which inspired the "altruistic personality" the commission deemed essential for the recognition of the Righteous Among the Nations. However, Moore is the first to warn against "glib categorizations of religious or humanitarian motivations or the stereotyping of national reactions towards the persecution of Jews [which] have dominated popular literature on the subject for too long." In the end, the opportunity and actuality of rescue are determined by more complex factors, as they are "conditioned by both national and local circumstances and social structures."[85]

A third argument involving the conditions of rescue to explain the high number of Righteous focuses on the intensity and duration of the relations between rescuers and the Jews they hid. As Joseph Michman argued, "The fear and hope that accompanied the Jews in hiding created many cases of strong bonds between rescuers and survivors."[86] There are reasons to believe this is at least a partial explanation. Most Dutch Jews who went into hiding did so in the summer of 1942, and remained hidden until May 1945. In some parts of Europe, the period in which Jews were in hiding did not last that long, because the Jews were persecuted more brutally and were captured before they had been able to find a place to hide (which might be the case in the Baltic states). Another possibility is that they were threatened with deportation at a later period in the war, as was the case for Hungarian and Greek Jews. Or the German occupation ended earlier, as in France and Belgium. Combined with a more individualized form of rescue, the Dutch circumstances might have contributed to closer relations between rescuers and survivors, and to the remarkable tokens of gratitude Dutch Jews displayed both collectively and individually after the liberation, including the monument of Jewish gratitude discussed earlier. Similar motives might have played an important role in Dutch Jewish survivors' requests to Yad Vashem to recognize their helpers as Righteous Among the Nations. Yet the argument centered on the duration of assistance also has weaknesses: In many parts of Poland, Ukraine, and Belarus, the persecution took place over an extended period—in this respect, not fundamentally different from the period of persecution in the Netherlands. Also, this argument assumes that Jews were hidden by the same people over an extended period. But Dutch Jews in hiding often stayed at several addresses—ranging from two or three up to twenty-five and more—limiting the possibilities for forging a lasting connection with their rescuers.[87]

Another line of explanation for the high number of Dutch Righteous Among the Nations suggests it is an artifact of the circumstances conditioning its recognition by Yad Vashem, rather than a reflection of the circumstances of rescue. This perspective was first emphasized by the Commission for the Designation of the Righteous itself, which rightly argued that "the numbers of Righteous recognized do not reflect the full extent of help given by non-Jews to Jews during the Holocaust; they are rather based on the material and documentation that was made available to Yad Vashem."[88] The commission argued that the recognition depends on "requests made by the rescued Jews," who might refrain from doing so because of "the difficulty of grappling with the painful past," or because they were unaware of the program, or unable to do so. This was especially the case for "people who lived behind the Iron Curtain during the years of the Communist regime in Eastern Europe."[89] The latter argument might explain some of the variance between Western and Eastern European countries, but it definitely fails to account for the difference between, say, Poland and Hungary. More important, the factors addressed by the commission fail to explain the differences between, for instance, France and the Netherlands: Jews from every country had difficulties in facing the past.

A more promising line of argument related to the conditions of recognition is to determine whether the creation of the program recognizing and recording the deeds of the Righteous Among the Nations and the procedures that were established for the recognition of rescuers of Jews might have led to a Dutch overrepresentation. As Irena Steinfeldt, director of the Department of the Righteous at Yad Vashem, demonstrated, the initiative for the program was taken in 1955 by Rachela (Rachel) Auerbach, who worked on survivor testimonies and had represented Yad Vashem in a meeting to commemorate Joop Westerweel. As happened frequently on all kinds of celebratory and commemorative occasions in Israel, a tree was planted, in this instance in memory of Westerweel's efforts to rescue members of the Chalutz movement in the Netherlands and his death at the hands of the Nazis in 1944.[90] Auerbach suggested that the commemoration of Westerweel should serve as a template for the Righteous Among the Nations program, and several individuals in the group around Westerweel were among the first to be acknowledged as Righteous Among the Nations. In the first year of the program, Joop and Wilhelmina Westerweel were recognized as Righteous, and the year after most of the twenty-three newly awarded Netherlanders belonged to the group posthumously named the Westerweel Group. It was a mixed group of Jews and non-Jews; many of the Jewish members were Zionists who migrated to Israel after the war. Their collective efforts to have Westerweel and his non-Jewish collaborators acknowledged as Righteous Among the Nations paid off, and moreover created an example for other Dutch Jewish immigrants to Israel.[91]

This tendency might have been reinforced by the strong ties among Dutch immigrants (or their difficulty in becoming integrated in Israeli society), who stayed in touch through the Irgun Olei Holland (Organization of Immigrants from the Netherlands). This was established in 1943 to serve the interests of Dutch Jews in Palestine and later Israel, and today it still counts among its members almost 20 percent of all Jews of Dutch descent in Israel.[92] As Joseph Michman declared: "Many of the Jews who survived in the Netherlands immigrated to Israel and recognized Yad Vashem and its work at a time when the institution was still unfamiliar in Europe."[93] A confirmation of this analysis can be found in the reverse situation in France. It was one of the main French initiators for the recognition of French Righteous, Jacques Pulver, who deplored the lack of awareness of the honor these rescuers could have, and should have, received through an application to Yad Vashem. In 1990 he "noted the shameful slowness of France compared to Holland, and even Poland. We shall not catch up, since in Holland 2200 people were recognized at the end of [19]89, in France 680. But we do our best."[94]

An additional factor might also be that Joseph Michman was for a long time a member of the Commission for the Designation of the Righteous. As his son Dan Michman declared, "The prominent position of my father may have played a role. [. . .] Dutch Jews were well aware of Yad Vashem and told each other there was an award for the Righteous."[95] The activism of Michman and the group of Dutch Jews in Israel might very well explain the remarkable rise, and especially the boom, of Dutch applications and recognitions from the end of the 1970s until the late 1980s, when Michman was active in the commission. The impact of the Dutch migrant community in Israel on the Dutch memory of rescue poses an ironic reversal of the argument that Holocaust memory has become diasporic in nature, creating an "elective affinity between Jewish memory and newly emerging forms (and practices) of memory in Second Modernity."[96] In this case, it is not the Jewish diaspora but the Dutch diaspora in Israel that plays a pivotal role in Holocaust memory.

Shame and Pride and the Drive for Recognition

Although such situational explanations go a long way toward clarifying the remarkably high number of Dutch Righteous Among the Nations, a more fundamental reason why the Dutch applications snowballed in this way, might—in the end—also have much to do with two other factors that lead us back to the remarkable tension between the sense of collective shame and pride in the Dutch memory of rescue. In a way, the applications Dutch Jews filed for the acknowledgment of the courage of their rescuers might be motivated by the same anger with which Presser defended Friedrich Weinreb in the 1960s. Weinreb was considered one of the few who had actually dared to resist the Nazis and to come to the rescue of the Jews. In the same manner, Jews applying for the recognition of their rescuers might send the message that their humanitarian help was so much appreciated because so many others failed to offer it.

In a similar way, many of the rescuers might have been keen on gaining recognition as a Righteous gentile. Not only was their courage a scarce commodity during the war, but they shared the feelings of disappointment of many other former members of the resistance about the unsuccessful purge of collaborators and their return to high places in postwar Dutch society. Moreover, the national ideology of a widespread "spirit of resistance" among the Dutch public, contrasting so starkly with the reverse image of blatant failure, might have contributed to the need for a more individual form of recognition, which the Jews they had saved were very willing to provide. Finally, the abundant recognition of these scattered, individual rescue efforts might be important for the Dutch population at large, which has permanently vacillated between deep-felt shame and wavering pride. It is through this tension of shame and pride that the Righteous Among the Nations could become such a crucial category in the Dutch memory of the rescue of the Jews.

Notes

1 "Nota naar aanleiding van de publikaties in verschillende bladen betreffende de burgemeester der gemeente 's-Gravenhage." *Verslag der Handelingen van de Tweede Kamer der Staten-Generaal Zitting 1955–1956*, no. 4271.1 (The Hague: Staatsdrukkerij, 1956). In Dutch, the highly unusual expression *difficulteerde* was used—meaning "considering something strenuously and at length." The verb *difficulteerde* is used very infrequently and only in a political context; see https://www.neerlandistiek.nl/2018/06/taalkundige-fact-check-wie-gebruikt-het-werkwoord-difficulteren/, accessed July 1, 2019.

2 For a detailed analysis of the Schokking affair, see Ido de Haan, *Na de ondergang. De herinnering aan de Jodenvervolging in Nederland 1945–1995* (The Hague: SDU, 1997), 106–16.

3 "Het zij genoeg geweest," *De Volkskrant*, March 10, 1956.

4 *Verslag der Handelingen van de Tweede Kamer der Staten-Generaal Zitting 1955–1956*, July 5, 1956, p. 2009.

5 *Verslag der Handelingen van de Tweede Kamer der Staten-Generaal Zitting 1955–1956*, July 5, 1956, p. 2021.

6 *Verslag der Handelingen van de Tweede Kamer der Staten-Generaal Zitting 1955–1956*, July 5, 1956, p. 2015.

7 Ido de Haan, "Failures and Mistakes: Images of Collaboration in Postwar Dutch Society," in *Collaboration with the Nazis: Public Discourse after the Holocaust*, ed. Roni Stauber (London: Routledge 2010), 71–90.

8 The assumption that the failure to rescue the Jews of Europe has been ignored and repressed is central to books like Judith Miller, *One by One,*

by One: Facing the Holocaust (London: Weidenfeld & Nicolson, 1990), and Géraldine Schwarz, *Les Amnésiaques* (Paris: Flammarion, 2017).

9 Michael Rothberg, *The Implicated Subject: Beyond Victims and Perpetrators* (Stanford, CA: Stanford University Press, 2019); see also Omer Bartov, *Murder in Our Midst: The Holocaust, Industrial Killing, and Representation* (Oxford: Oxford University Press, 1996).

10 See Daniel Levy and Natan Sznaider, *The Holocaust and Memory in the Global Age*, trans. Assenka Oksiloff (Philadelphia: Temple University Press, 2006), 59–63, 188–90.

11 Astrid Erll, "Travelling Memory," *Parallax* 17, no. 4 (2011): 4–18, at 4.

12 Michael Rothberg, *Multidirectional Memory: Remembering the Holocaust in the Age of Decolonization* (Stanford, CA: Stanford University Press, 2009).

13 Astrid Erll has conceptualized this as memory "travelling" between genres; see Erll, "Travelling Memory," 12–15.

14 For the wider context of this analysis, see De Haan, *Na de ondergang*. Some of the complexity of studying the memory of rescue becomes apparent in the discussion of the French case by Renée Poznanski, "Rescue of the Jews and the Resistance in France: From History to Historiography," in "The Rescue of Jews in France and Its Empires during World War II: History and Memory," special issue, *French Politics, Culture & Society*, 30, no. 2 (2012): 8–32.

15 Aleida Assmann, "The Holocaust—A Global Memory? Extensions and Limits of a New Memory Community," in *Memory in a Global Age: Discourses, Practices and Trajectories*, ed. Aleida Assmann and Sebastian Conrad (Basingstoke: Palgrave MacMillan, 2010), 97–117; Levy and Sznaider, *The Holocaust and Memory in the Global Age*.

16 See United States Holocaust Memorial Museum. "Jewish Losses during the Holocaust: By Country," in *Holocaust Encyclopedia*, https://encyclopedia.ushmm.org/content/en/article/jewish-losses-during-the-holocaust-by-country, accessed July 1, 2019.

17 Dienke Hondius, *Return: Holocaust Survivors and Dutch Antisemitism* (Westport, CT: Praeger, 2003).

18 Hilda Verwey-Jonker, "Kijk NIET naar zijn neus," *Vrij Nederland*, November 24, 1945, as quoted in Martin Bossenbroek, *De meelstreep. Terugkeer en opvang na de Tweede Wereldoorlog* (Amsterdam: Bert Bakker, 2001), 266.

19 T. M. Sjenitzer-van Leening, ed., *Dagboekfragmenten 1940–1945* (Utrecht: Veen, 1985 [1954]), 305.

20 Adriaan van der Veen, *Het wilde feest* (Amsterdam: Amber, 1952), 51. The epigraph is from G. K. Chesterton, *Dickens* (1906). See Hans Anten, "Adriaan van der Veen. Het wilde feest," in *Lexicon van literaire werken 38*, ed. Ton Anbeek, Jaap Goedegebuure, and Bart Vervaeck (Groningen/Antwerp: Wolters-Noordhoff/Garant-Uitgevers, 1998), 1–11; Van Veen's story dealt with Dutch Jews, yet was set in the United States and heavily influenced by similar stories, including Arthur Miller, *Focus* (1945); L. Z. Hobson, *Gentleman's Agreement* (1946), and Saul Bellow, *The Victim* (1947). Cf. Sidra Ezrahi, *By Words Alone: The Holocaust in Literature* (Chicago: University of Chicago Press, 1980), 192.

21 Quoted from Joseph Melkman, *Geliefde vijand. Het beeld van de Jood in de naoorlogse Nederlandse literatuur* (Amsterdam: De Arbeiderspers, 1964), 54.

22 Annie Winkler-Vonk, *Een baantje bij de krant* (Amsterdam: Ploegsma, 1963), 93.

23 Willy Corsari, *Die van ons* (Amsterdam: De Bezige Bij, 1945); see Xandra Schutte, "Willy Corsari," *De Groene Amsterdammer* 122, no. 21, May 20, 1998.

24 Simon [Gerard] van het Reve, "De ondergang van de familie Boslowits," *Criterium* 1, no. 15 (December 1946): 788–813. The young boy observing the demise of the family Boslowits is called Simon, which was also the alias used by the author, Gerard van het Reve, when he published the novella.

25 Abel Herzberg, *Kroniek van de Jodenvervolging 1940–1945* (Amsterdam: Querido, 1985), 154. Herzberg's chronicle was first published as part of a four-volume history on the Netherlands under German Occupation: J. Bolhuis, C. D. J. Brandt, H. M. van Randwijk, and B. C. Slotemaker, eds., *Onderdrukking en verzet. Nederland in oorlogstijd*, vol. 3 (Arnhem/Amsterdam: Van Loghum Slaterus/J.M. Meulenhoff [1949–54]), 7–256.

26 J. B. Charles, *Volg het spoor terug* (Amsterdam: De Bezige Bij, 1953); Kees Schuyt, *Het spoor terug. J.B. Charles/W.H. Nagel 1910–1983* (Amsterdam: Balans, 2010), 269.

27 Gerard Mulder and Paul Koedijk, *H.M. van Randwijk. Een biografie* (Amsterdam: Nijgh & van Ditmar, 1988), 712.

28 H. M. van Randwijk, *In de schaduw van gisteren. Kroniek van het verzet 1940–1945* (Amsterdam: Bert Bakker, 1967), 197.

29 Jacques Presser, *Ondergang: De vervolging en verdelging van het Nederlandse jodendom (1940–1945)*, vol. 2 (The Hague: Staatsuitgeverij, 1965), 126; an incomplete English translation was published under the

title *Ashes in the Wind: The Destruction of Dutch Jewry*, trans. Arnold J. Pomerans (London: Souvenir Press, 1968).

30 See Conny Kristel, *Geschiedschrijving als opdracht. Abel Herzberg, Jacques Presser en Loe de Jong over de jodenvervolging* (Amsterdam: Meulenhoff, 1998).

31 Wout Ultee and Henk Flap, "De Nederlandse paradox. Waarom overleefden zoveel Nederlandse joden de Tweede Wereldoorlog niet?" in *Verklarende sociologie. Opstellen voor Reinhard Wippler*, ed. Harry Ganzeboom and Siegwart Lindenberg (Amsterdam: Thesis, 1996), 185–97; Maxime Steinberg, "Le paradoxe xénophobe dans la solution finale en Belgique occupée," *Revue du Nord*, 2, vol. 2, Special Issue: *L'occupation en France et en Belgique, 1940–1944*, ed. Etienne Dejonghe (1988): 653–64. Maxime Steinberg, "Le paradoxe français dans la Solution Finale à l'Ouest," *Annales. Économies, société, civilisations*, 48 (1993): 583–94; Ido de Haan, "The Paradoxes of Dutch History: Historiography of the Holocaust in the Netherlands," in *Holocaust Historiography in Context: Emergence, Challenges, Polemics and Achievements*, ed. David Bankier and Dan Michman (Jerusalem/New York: Yad Vashem/Berghahn, 2008), 355–76.

32 Hans Blom, "The Persecution of the Jews in the Netherlands: A Comparative Western European Perspective," *European History Quarterly* 19, no. 3 (1989): 333–51.

33 Nanda van der Zee, *Om erger te voorkomen. De voorbereiding en uitvoering van de vernietiging van het Nederlandse jodendom tijdens de Tweede Wereldoorlog* (Amsterdam: Meulenhoff, 1997). The general attitude toward the book is expressed in the title of a review by the then director of the Dutch Institute of War Documentation (NIOD): Hans Blom, "Een droevig boek" (A sad book), *Historisch Nieuwsblad* 6, no. 2 (1997): 4–5, and even more vocally by Jan Kuyk, "Een indrukwekkend monument van incompetentie en dilettantisme" (An impressive monument of incompetence and dilettantism), *Trouw*, April 11, 1997. The violent response to the book is documented in René Zwaap, "Nanda van der Zee veegt de stoep goed schoon," *De Groene Amsterdammer* 121, no. 16, April 16, 1997, who explained the reaction as a defense of elite interests against Van der Zee's challenge to their reputation.

34 Blom, "The Persecution of the Jews in the Netherlands."

35 Max Arian, "Nederland deportatieland," *De Groene Amsterdammer* 116, no. 49, December 2, 1992. The article was written by Max Arian, who as a Jewish child had been hidden by the rescuers of the "NV-groep." The group was established in July 1942, immediately after the first larger

deportations started, to hide Jews from Amsterdam with families in the south and east of the Netherlands.

36 Queen Beatrix, "Toespraak tijdens de herdenkingsbijeenkomst in de Ridderzaal Den Haag, 5 mei 1995," in *Koningin Beatrix aan het woord. 25 jaar troonredes, officiële redevoeringen en kersttoespraken*, ed. Carla van Baalen et al. (The Hague: SDU, 2005), 382–88, at 384.

37 *Toespraak van minister-president Mark Rutte bij de Nationale Holocaust Herdenking, Amsterdam* (January 26, 2020), https://www.rijksoverheid.nl/documenten/toespraken/2020/01/26/toespraak-van-minister-president-mark-rutte-bij-de-nationale-auschwitzherdenking-amsterdam, accessed March 2, 2020.

38 For De Jong, see Boudewijn Smits, *Loe de Jong 1914–2005. Historicus met een missie* (Amsterdam: Boom, 2014); Conny Kristel, *Geschiedschrijving als opdracht*.

39 Ies Vuijsje, *Tegen beter weten in: Zelfbedrog en ontkenning in de Nederlandse geschiedschrijving over de Jodenvervolging* (Antwerp: Uitgeverij Augustus, 2006). Like the response to Nanda van der Zee, Vuijsje's work was also very critically received by professional historians, demonstrating a large divide between them and the wider pubic. See Hella Rottenberg, "Voor de gemoedsrust van de natie," *Trouw*, June 24, 2006; Nelleke Noordervliet, "Barmhartige leugen," *Historisch Nieuwsblad* 15 no. (2006).

40 Bart van der Boom, *Wij weten niets van hun lot. Gewone Nederlanders en de Holocaust* (Amsterdam: Boom, 2012).

41 For a critique see, for instance, Evelien Gans, "Disowning Responsibility: The Stereotype of the Passive Jew as a Legitimizing Factor in Dutch Remembrance of the Shoah," in *The Jew as Legitimation: Jewish-Gentile Relations beyond Antisemitism and Philosemitism*, ed. David Wertheim (London: Palgrave Macmillan, 2017), 173–95; Pinchas Bar-Efrat, *Denunciation and Rescue: Dutch Society and the Holocaust* (Jerusalem: Yad Vashem, 2017), 43–49. An analysis of the debate is presented by Krijn Thijs, "Ordinary, Ignorant, and Noninvolved? The Figure of the Bystander in Dutch Research and Controversy," in *Probing the Limits of Categorization: The Bystander in Holocaust History*, ed. Christina Morina and Krijn Thijs (New York: Berghahn Books, 2019), 247–65.

42 See Frank van Vree, *In de schaduw van Auschwitz: Herinneringen, beelden, geschiedenis* (Groningen: Historische Uitgeverij, 1995); Rob van Ginkel, *Rondom de stilte. Herdenkingscultuur in Nederland* (Amsterdam: Bert Bakker, 2011).

43 Quoted in Annet Mooij, *De strijd om de Februaristaking* (Amsterdam: Balans, 2006), 29.

44 https://www.amsterdam.nl/stadsarchief/stukken/beroemd/burgemeester-israel/, accessed July 1, 2019, and https://www.yadvashem.org/righteous/about-the-righteous/related-sites.html, accessed July 1, 2019.

45 For further details, see Mooij, *De strijd om de Februaristaking*.

46 For discussions of *De Bezetting*, see Van Vree, *In de schaduw van Auschwitz*; Chris Vos, *Televisie en bezetting. Een onderzoek naar de documentaire verbeelding van de Tweede Wereldoorlog in Nederland* (Hilversum: Verloren, 1995); Chris van der Heijden, *Dat nooit meer: De nasleep van de Tweede Wereldoorlog in Nederland* (Amsterdam: Contact, 2011). The national impact of *De Bezetting* was also considerable because until 1964 there was only one television channel in the Netherlands.

47 Loe de Jong, *Het Koninkrijk der Nederlanden in de Tweede Wereldoorlog. Deel 4 mei '40–maart '41. Tweede helft* (The Hague: Martinus Nijhoff, 1972), 844.

48 Loe de Jong, *Het Koninkrijk der Nederlanden in de Tweede Wereldoorlog. Deel 5 maart '41–juli '42. Tweede helft* (The Hague: Martinus Nijhoff, 1974), 1092.

49 Loe de Jong, *Het Koninkrijk der Nederlanden in de Tweede Wereldoorlog. Deel 5 maart '41–juli '42. Eerste helft* (The Hague: Martinus Nijhoff, 1974), 22.

50 Bianca Stigter, "Beelden om nooit te vergeten. Monumenten ter nagedachtenis aan de Tweede Wereldoorlog in Amsterdam 1945–1991," *Kunst en beleid in Nederland* 6 (1993): 13–62, at 41–42; David A. Duindam, "Signs of the Shoah: The Hollandsche Schouwburg as a Site of Memory," PhD diss., University of Amsterdam, 2016, 44–46.

51 *Gemeenteblad Amsterdam*, Tweede Afdeling, Verslag van de vergaderingen van den Gemeenteraad, 21 november 1945, p. 20, quoted in Roel Hijink and Gerrit Vermeer, "Het monument van Joodse erkentelijkheid, teken van trots en schaamte," *Amstelodamum* 105, no. 2 (2018): 51–67, at 51. See also Wim de Wagt, *Vijfhonderd meter namen. De Holocaust en de pijn van de herinnering* (Amsterdam: Boom, 2021).

52 Quoted in Hijink and Vermeer, "Het monument van Joodse erkentelijkheid," 60.

53 Quoted in Hijink and Vermeer, "Het monument van Joodse erkentelijkheid," 58.

54 Quoted in Mooij, *De strijd om de Februaristaking*, 50.

55 Presser, *Ondergang*, vol. 2, 3–7.

56 Harry Mulisch in *Vrij Nederland*, March 6, 1971, quoted by Regina Grüter, *Een fantast schrijft geschiedenis. De affaires rond Friedrich Weinreb* (Amsterdam: Balans, 1997), 277.

57 Presser, *Ondergang*, vol. 2, 109–10.

58 Grüter, *Een fantast schrijft geschiedenis.*

59 Jac. van de Kar, *Joods verzet: terugblik op de periode rond de Tweede Wereldoorlog*. Tweede herziene druk (Amsterdam: Stadsdrukkerij Van Amsterdam, 1984); Ben M. Braber, *Passage naar vrijheid: joods verzet in Nederland 1940–1945* (Amsterdam: Balans, 1987); Bill Minco, *Koude voeten: begenadigd tot levenslang. Het relaas van een joodse scholier uit het Geuzenverzet: Oranjehotel, Untermassfeld, Mauthausen, Auschwitz, Dachau*, Tweede druk (Nijmegen: SUN, 1997). Bob Moore, *Survivors: Jewish Self-Help and Rescue in Nazi-Occupied Western Europe* (Oxford: Oxford University Press, 2010); Bernard Wasserstein, *The Ambiguity of Virtue: Gertrude van Tijn and the Fate of the Dutch Jews* (Cambridge, MA: Harvard University Press, 2014), Richter Roegholt and Hans Wiedema, *Walter Süskind en de Hollandse Schouwburg: De geschiedenis van de redding van joodse kinderen 1942–1943* (Amsterdam: Walter Süskind Stichting, 1992); Mark Schellekens, *Walter Süskind: Hoe een zakenman honderden joodse kinderen uit handen van de nazi's redde* (Amsterdam: Atheneaeum–Polak & Van Gennep, 2012).

60 Quoted in Van Ginkel, *Rondom de stilte*, 421.

61 See Moore, *Survivors.*

62 For analyses of the "Anne Frank phenomenon," see Gerrold van der Stroom, ed., *De vele gezichten van Anne Frank. Visies op een fenomeen* (Amsterdam: De Prom, 2003); Barbara Kirshenblatt-Gimblett and Jeffrey Shandler, eds., *Anne Frank Unbound: Media, Imagination, Memory* (Bloomington: Indiana University Press, 2012); David Barnouw, *The Phenomenon of Anne Frank*, trans. Jeannette K. Ringold (Bloomington: Indiana University Press, 2018).

63 Miep Gies and Alison Leslie Gold, *Anne Frank Remembered: The Story of the Woman Who Helped to Hide the Frank Family* (New York: Simon and Schuster, 1987) 11. The documentary based on the book, *Anne Frank Remembered*, by Jon Blair (1995), received an Academy Award and an Emmy Award.

64 Hendrik van Riessen, "Het onderduiken," in *Onderdrukking en verzet*, vol. 3, ed. J. Bolhuis et al., 689–721, at 689.

65 Presser, *Ondergang*, vol. 2, 244.

66 Bert Jan Flim, "Opportunities for Dutch Jews to Hide from the Nazis, 1942–1945," in *Dutch Jews as Perceived by Themselves and by Others*, ed. Chaya Brasz and Yosef Kaplan (Leiden: Brill, 2001), 289–305; Bert Jan Flim, "Joodse onderduikers en de drievoudige tragiek van de onderduik-organisaties," in *Wat toeval leek te zijn maar het niet was. De organisatie van de jodenvervolging in Nederland*, ed. Henk Flap and Marnix Croes, eds. (Amsterdam: Het Spinhuis, 2001), 145–60; Bert Jan Flim, "De Holocaust in Nederland," in *Rechtvaardigen onder de Volkeren. Nederlanders met een Yad Vashem-onderscheiding voor hulp aan joden*, ed. Israel Gutman et al. (Amsterdam/Antwerp L.J. Veen/NIOD, 2004), 26–44.

67 Klaas Norel, "De onderduiker," in *Het Grote Gebod. Gedenkboek van het verzet in LO en LPK*, vol. 2, ed. Hendrik van Riessen et al. (Kampen/Bilthoven: J.H. Kok N.V/H. Nelissen, 1951), 3–48, at 7.

68 Norel, "De onderduiker," 9.

69 Klaas Norel and L. D. Terlaak Poot, *De tyrannie verdrijven* (Wageningen: Keuning, 1947), quoted by Evelien Gans, "The Meek Jew—and Beyond," in *The Holocaust, Israel and "the Jew": Histories of Antisemitism in Postwar Dutch Society*, ed. Remco Ensel and Evelien Gans (Amsterdam: Amsterdam University Press, 2017), 83–105, at 84.

70 Gans, "The Meek Jew—and Beyond," 87; see also Evelien Gans, "Disowning Responsibility."

71 Ziporah Valkhoff, *Leven in een niet-bestaan, beleving en betekenis van de joodse onderduik. Met een inleiding van Jolande Withuis* (Utrecht: Stichting ICODO, 1992).

72 For the increased interest in children and the second generation, see Hans Keilson, *Sequentielle Traumatisierung. Deskriptiv-klinische und quantifizierend-statistische follow-up Untersuchung zum Schicksal der jüdischen Kriegswaisen in den Niederlanden* (Stuttgart, Enke, 1978); Deborah Dwork, *Children with a Star: Jewish Youth in Europe* (New Haven, CT: Yale University Press, 1991); Bloeme Evers-Emden and Bert Jan Flim, *Ondergedoken geweest. Een afgesloten verleden? Joodse "kinderen" over hun onderduik, vijftig jaar later* (Kampen: Kok, 1995); Bloeme Evers-Emden, *Geschonden bestaan. Gesprekken met vervolgde Joden die hun kinderen moesten "wegdoen"* (Kampen: Kok, 1996); Bloeme Evers-Emden, *Je ouders delen. Een eerste onderzoek naar de gevoelens van eigen kinderen in pleeggezinnen in de oorlog en nu* (Kampen: Kok, 1999); Diane L. Wolf, *Beyond Anne Frank: Hidden Children and Postwar Families in Holland* (Berkeley: University of California Press, 2007).

73 For the psychological turn in Holocaust memory, see Ido de Haan, "Openbaar leedwezen. Over de betekenis van het vervolgingstrauma," *Psychologie en Maatschappij* 73 (1995): 329–50; Ido de Haan, "Paths of Normalization after the Persecution of the Jews: The Netherlands, France and West Germany in the 1950s," in *Life after Death: Approaches to a Cultural and Social History during the 1940s and 1950s*, ed. Richard Bessel and Dirk Schumann (Washington, DC: German Historical Institute, 2003), 65–92; Ido de Haan, "Persecution Remembered: The Construction of a National Trauma," *Netherlands' Journal of Social Sciences* 34, no. 2 (1998): 196–217; Pieter Lagrou, "The Nationalization of Victimhood: Selective Violence and National Grief in Western Europe, 1940–1960," in *Life after Death*, ed. Bessel and Schumann, 243–58; Jean-Michel Chaumont, *La concurrence des victimes. Génocide, identité, reconnaissance* (Paris: Éditions La Découverte, 1997).

74 Bob Moore, "The Rescue of Jews from Nazi Persecution: A Western European Perspective," *Journal of Genocide Research* 5 no. 2 (2003): 293–308.

75 See Mordecai Paldiel, "The Righteous Among the Nations at Yad Vashem," *Journal of Holocaust Education* 7, nos. 1–2 (1998): 45–66, at 47.

76 Herman Vuijsje, "Schuld en hulde; Nederland is recordhouder in Yad Vashem," *De Groene Amsterdammer* 138, no. 6, February 5, 2014.

77 Speech by the Dutch prime minister, Mark Rutte, at a working dinner in Israel, December 8, 2013, https://www.government.nl/ministries/ministry-of-general-affairs/documents/speeches/2013/12/08/speech-by-mark-rutte-at-a-working-dinner-in-israel, accessed July 1, 2019 (now unavailable).

78 E.g., "Uitreiking onderscheiding Yad Vashem in de synagoge van de Joodse gemeenschap," *BN/De Stem*, March 22, 1999; "Yad Vashem voor drie Limburgse families," *Trouw*, March 3, 2014; "Onderscheiding Yad Vashem voor Beekse burgers," *De Limburger*, December 3, 2018.

79 "Names of Righteous by Country," https://www.yadvashem.org/righteous/statistics.html, accessed July 1, 2019.

80 Joseph Michman, "Rescue and Righteous Among the Nations in Holland," https://www.yadvashem.org/righteous/resources/rescue-and-righteous-among-the-nations-in-holland.html, accessed July 1, 2019.

81 Timothy Snyder, *Bloodlands: Europe between Hitler and Stalin* (New York: Basic Books, 2010).

82 Loe de Jong, *Het Koninkrijk der Nederlanden in de Tweede Wereldoorlog. Deel 8 Gevangenen en gedeporteerden. Tweede helft* (The Hague: Martinus Nijhoff, 1978), 886.

83 Olivier Wieviorka, *Histoire de la Résistance 1940–1945* (Paris: Perrin, 2013), 455.
84 "Related Sites," https://www.yadvashem.org/righteous/about-the-righteous/related-sites.html, accessed July 1, 2019.
85 Moore, *Survivors*, 367.
86 Michman, "Rescue and Righteous Among the Nations in Holland."
87 Loe de Jong, *Het Koninkrijk der Nederlanden in de Tweede Wereldoorlog. Deel 7 mei '43–juni '44. Eerste helft* (The Hague: Martinus Nijhoff, 1976), 471–72.
88 "Names of Righteous by Country," https://www.yadvashem.org/righteous/statistics.html, accessed July 1, 2019.
89 "Names of Righteous by Country," https://www.yadvashem.org/righteous/statistics.html, accessed July 1, 2019.
90 Irena Steinfeldt, "Commemorating the Righteous Among the Nations at Yad Vashem: The History of a Unique Program," *Diasporas: Circulations, Migrations, Histoire* 21 (2013): 82–90.
91 Hans Schippers, *Westerweel Group: Non-Conformist Resistance against Nazi Germany—A Joint Rescue Effort of Dutch Idealists and Dutch-German Zionists* (Berlin: De Gruyter Oldenbourg, 2019).
92 Chaya Brasz, *Irgoen Olei Holland. De ontstaansgeschiedenis van de Nederlandse Immigrantenvereniging in Israel* (Jerusalem: Ahva, 1993); Chaya Brasz, "Dutch Jews as Zionists and Israeli Citizens," in *Dutch Jews*, ed. Brasz and Kaplan, 214–34.
93 Michman, "Rescue and Righteous Among the Nations in Holland."
94 Quoted in Sarah Gensburger, "The Righteous Among the Nations as Elements of Collective Memory," *International Social Science Journal* 62, nos. 203–4 (March–June 2011): 135–46, at 140; see also Sarah Gensburger, *Les Justes de France. Politiques publiques de la mémoire* (Paris: Les Presses de Sciences Po, 2010).
95 Quoted in Vuijsje, "Schuld en hulde."
96 Levy and Sznaider, *The Holocaust and Memory in the Global Age*, 51.

Bibliography

Anten, Hans. "Adriaan van der Veen. Het wilde feest." (Adriaan van der Veen. The wild party.) In *Lexicon van literaire werken* 38, ed. Ton Anbeek, Jaap Goedegebuure, and Bart Vervaeck, 1–11. Groningen: Wolters-Noordhoff/Garant-Uitgevers, 1998.

Arian, Max. "Nederland deportatieland." (The Netherlands, land of deportations.) *De Groene Amsterdammer*, December 2, 1992.

Assmann, Aleida. "The Holocaust—A Global Memory? Extensions and Limits of a New Memory Community." In *Memory in a Global Age: Discourses, Practices and Trajectories*, ed. Aleida Assmann and Sebastian Conrad, 97–117. Basingstoke: Palgrave MacMillan, 2010.

Bar-Efrat, Pinchas. *Denunciation and Rescue: Dutch Society and the Holocaust*. Jerusalem: Yad Vashem, 2017.

Barnouw, David. *The Phenomenon of Anne Frank*. Trans. Jeannette K. Ringold. Bloomington: Indiana University Press, 2018.

Bartov, Omer. *Murder in Our Midst: The Holocaust, Industrial Killing, and Representation*. Oxford: Oxford University Press, 1996.

Beatrix [Queen]. "Toespraak tijdens de herdenkingsbijeenkomst in de Ridderzaal Den Haag, 5 mei 1995." (Speech at the commemorative meeting in the Ridderzaal, The Hague, May 5, 1995.) In *Koningin Beatrix aan het woord. 25 jaar troonredes, officiële redevoeringen en kersttoespraken*, ed. Carla van Baalen, 382–88. Den Haag: SDU, 2005.

Blom, Hans. "Een droevig boek." (A sad book.) *Historisch Nieuwsblad* 6, no. 2 (1997): 4–5.

———. "The Persecution of the Jews in the Netherlands: A Comparative Western European Perspective." *European History Quarterly* 19, no. 3 (1989): 333–51.

Bolhuis, Jan, C. D. J. Brandt, H. M. van Randwijk, and B. C. Slotemaker, eds. *Onderdrukking en verzet. Nederland in oorlogstijd*. (Repression and resistance. The Netherlands during the war.) Arnhem/Amsterdam: Van Loghum Slaterus/J.M. Meulenhoff, 1949–54.

Boom, Bart van der. *Wij weten niets van hun lot. Gewone Nederlanders en de Holocaust*. (We know nothing about their fate. Ordinary Dutch people and the Holocaust.) Amsterdam: Boom, 2012.

Bossenbroek, Martin. *De meelstreep. Terugkeer en opvang na de Tweede Wereldoorlog*. (The line of flour. Return and reception after the Second World War.) Amsterdam: Bert Bakker, 2001.

Braber, Ben M. *Passage naar vrijheid: joods verzet in Nederland 1940–1945*. (Passage to freedom: Jewish resistance in the Netherlands 1940–1945.) Amsterdam: Balans, 1987.

Brasz, Chaya. "Dutch Jews as Zionists and Israeli Citizens." In *Dutch Jews as Perceived by Themselves and by Others*, ed. Chaya Brasz and Yosef Kaplan, 214–34. Leiden: Brill, 2001.

———. *Irgoen Olei Holland. De ontstaansgeschiedenis van de Nederlandse Immigrantenvereniging in Israel*. (Irgoen Olei Holland. The history of the

establishment of the society of Dutch immigrants in Israel.) Jerusalem: Ahva, 1993.
Charles, J. B. *Volg het spoor terug*. (Follow the trace back.) Amsterdam: De Bezige Bij, 1953.
Chaumont, Jean-Michel. *La concurrence des victimes. Génocide, identité, reconnaissance*. (The victim competition. Genocide, identity, recognition.) Paris: Éditions La Découverte, 1997.
Corsari, Willy. *Die van ons*. (Those of us.) Amsterdam: De Bezige Bij, 1945.
Duindam, David A. "Signs of the Shoah: The Hollandsche Schouwburg as a Site of Memory." PhD diss., University of Amsterdam, 2016.
Dwork, Deborah. *Children with a Star: Jewish Youth in Europe*. New Haven, CT: Yale University Press, 1991.
Erll, Astrid. "Travelling Memory." *Parallax* 17, no. 4 (2011): 4–18.
Evers-Emden, Bloeme. *Geschonden bestaan. Gesprekken met vervolgde Joden die hun kinderen moesten "wegdoen."* (Violated existence. Conversation with persecuted Jews who were forced to "give away" their children.) Kampen: Kok, 1996.
———. *Je ouders delen. Een eerste onderzoek naar de gevoelens van eigen kinderen in pleeggezinnen in de oorlog en nu*. (Sharing your parents. A first investigation of feelings of biological children in foster families during and after the war.) Kampen: Kok, 1999.
Evers-Emden, Bloeme, and Bert Jan Flim. *Ondergedoken geweest. Een afgesloten verleden? Joodse "kinderen" over hun onderduik, vijftig jaar later*. (Having been in hiding. A closed past? Jewish "children" about hiding, fifty years later.) Kampen: Kok, 1995.
Ezrahi, Sidra. *By Words Alone: The Holocaust in Literature*. Chicago: University of Chicago Press, 1980.
Flim, Bert Jan. "De Holocaust in Nederland." (The Holocaust in the Netherlands.) In *Rechtvaardigen onder de Volkeren. Nederlanders met een Yad Vashem-onderscheiding voor hulp aan joden*, ed. Israel Gutman, 26–44. Amsterdam/Antwerpen: L.J. Veen/NIOD, 2004.
———. "Joodse onderduikers en de drievoudige tragiek van de onderduikorganisaties." (Jewish people in hiding and the threefold tragedy of organizations for hiding Jews.) In *Wat toeval leek te zijn maar het niet was. De organisatie van de jodenvervolging in Nederland*, ed. Henk Flap and Marnix Croes, 145–60. Amsterdam: Het Spinhuis, 2001.
———. "Opportunities for Dutch Jews to Hide from the Nazis, 1942–1945." In *Dutch Jews as Perceived by Themselves and by Others*, ed. Chaya Brasz and Yosef Kaplan, 289–305. Leiden: Brill, 2001.

Gans, Evelien. "Disowning Responsibility: The Stereotype of the Passive Jew as a Legitimizing Factor in Dutch Remembrance of the Shoah." In *The Jew as Legitimation: Jewish-Gentile Relations beyond Antisemitism and Philosemitism*, ed. David Wertheim, 173–95. London: Palgrave Macmillan, 2017.

———. "The Meek Jew—and Beyond." In *The Holocaust, Israel and "the Jew": Histories of Antisemitism in Postwar Dutch Society*, ed. Remco Ensel and Evelien Gans, 83–105. Amsterdam: Amsterdam University Press, 2017.

Gensburger, Sarah. *Les Justes de France. Politiques publiques de la mémoire.* (The Righteous of France. Public politics of memory.) Paris: Les Presses de Sciences Po, 2010. English ed.: *National Policy, Global Memory: The Commemoration of the "Righteous" from Jerusalem to Paris, 1942–2007.* New York: Berghahn, 2016.

———. "The Righteous Among the Nations as Elements of Collective Memory." *International Social Science Journal* 62, nos. 203–4 (March–June 2011): 135–46.

Gies, Miep, and Alison Leslie Gold. *Anne Frank Remembered: The Story of the Woman Who Helped to Hide the Frank Family.* New York: Simon and Schuster, 1987.

Ginkel, Rob van. *Rondom de stilte. Herdenkingscultuur in Nederland.* (Around the silence. Memory culture in the Netherlands.) Amsterdam: Bert Bakker, 2011.

Grüter, Regina. *Een fantast schrijft geschiedenis. De affaires rond Friedrich Weinreb.* (A dreamer writes history. The affairs around Friedrich Weinreb.) Amsterdam: Balans, 1997.

Haan, Ido de. "Failures and Mistakes: Images of Collaboration in Postwar Dutch Society." In *Collaboration with the Nazis: Public Discourse after the Holocaust*, ed. Roni Stauber, 71–90. London: Routledge, 2010.

———. *Na de ondergang. De herinnering aan de Jodenvervolging in Nederland 1945–1995.* (After the destruction. The memory of the persecution of the Jews in the Netherlands 1945–1995.) Den Haag: SDU, 1997.

———. "Openbaar leedwezen. Over de betekenis van het vervolgingstrauma." (Public grief. On the meaning of the persecution trauma.) *Psychologie en Maatschappij* 73 (1995): 329–50.

———. "The Paradoxes of Dutch History: Historiography of the Holocaust in the Netherlands." In *Holocaust Historiography in Context: Emergence, Challenges, Polemics and Achievements*, ed. David Bankier and Dan Michman, 355–76. Jerusalem/New York: Yad Vashem/Berghahn, 2008.

———. "Paths of Normalization after the Persecution of the Jews: The Netherlands, France and West Germany in the 1950s." In *Life after Death: Approaches to a Cultural and Social History during the 1940s and 1950s*, ed. Richard Bessel and Dirk Schumann, 65–92. Washington, DC: German Historical Institute, 2003.

———. "Persecution Remembered: The Construction of a National Trauma." *Netherlands' Journal of Social Sciences* 34, no. 2 (1998): 196–217.

Heijden, Chris van der. *Dat nooit meer: De nasleep van de Tweede Wereldoorlog in Nederland.* (Never again. The aftermath of the Second World War in the Netherlands.) Amsterdam: Contact, 2011.

Herzberg, Abel. *Kroniek van de Jodenvervolging 1940–1945.* (Chronicle of the persecution of the Jews 1940–1945) Amsterdam: Querido, 1985.

Hijink, Roel, and Gerrit Vermeer. "Het monument van Joodse erkentelijkheid, teken van trots en schaamte." (The monument of Jewish gratitude, sign of pride and shame.) *Amstelodamum* 105, no. 2 (2018): 51–67.

Hondius, Dienke. *Return: Holocaust Survivors and Dutch Antisemitism.* Westport, CT: Praeger, 2003.

Jong, Loe de. *Het Koninkrijk der Nederlanden in de Tweede Wereldoorlog.* (The history of the Kingdom of the Netherlands during the Second World War.) 12 vols. The Hague: Martinus Nijhoff, 1969–94.

Kar, Jac. van de. *Joods verzet: terugblik op de periode rond de Tweede Wereldoorlog.* (Jewish resistance: A retrospective on the period around the Second World War.) Amsterdam: Stadsdrukkerij Van Amsterdam, 1984.

Keilson, Hans. *Sequentielle Traumatisierung. Deskriptiv-klinische und quantifizierend-statistische follow-up Untersuchung zum Schicksal der jüdischen Kriegswaisen in den Niederlanden.* (Sequential traumatization. Descriptive-clinical and quantitative-statistical follow-up research on the fate of Jewish war orphans in the Netherlands.) Stuttgart: Enke, 1978.

Kirshenblatt-Gimblett, Barbara, and Jeffrey Shandler, eds. *Anne Frank Unbound: Media, Imagination, Memory.* Bloomington: Indiana University Press, 2012.

Kristel, Conny. *Geschiedschrijving als opdracht. Abel Herzberg, Jacques Presser en Loe de Jong over de jodenvervolging.* (History as command. Abel Herzberg, Jacques Presser and Loe de Jong on the persecution of the Jews.) Amsterdam: Meulenhoff, 1998.

Kuyk, Jan. "Een indrukwekkend monument van incompetentie en dilettantisme." (An impressive monument of incompetence and dilettantism.) *Trouw*, April 11, 1997.

Lagrou, Pieter. "The Nationalization of Victimhood: Selective Violence and National Grief in Western Europe, 1940–1960." In *Life after Death: Approaches to a Cultural and Social History during the 1940s and 1950s*, ed. Richard Bessel and Dirk Schumann, 243–58. Washington, DC: German Historical Institute, 2003.

Levy, Daniel, and Natan Sznaider. *The Holocaust and Memory in the Global Age.* Trans. Assenka Oksiloff. Philadelphia: Temple University Press, 2006.

Melkman, Joseph. *Geliefde vijand. Het beeld van de Jood in de naoorlogse Nederlandse literatuur.* (Beloved enemy. The image of the Jew in post-war Dutch literature.) Amsterdam: De Arbeiderspers, 1964.

Michman, Joseph. "Rescue and Righteous Among the Nations in Holland," https://www.yadvashem.org/righteous/resources/rescue-and-righteous-among-the-nations-in-holland.html, accessed July 1, 2019.

Miller, Judith. *One by One, by One: Facing the Holocaust.* London: Weidenfeld & Nicolson, 1990.

Minco, Bill. *Koude voeten: begenadigd tot levenslang. Het relaas van een joodse scholier uit het Geuzenverzet: Oranjehotel, Untermassfeld, Mauthausen, Auschwitz, Dachau.* (Cold feet: Delivered to a life-long sentence. The story of a Jewish student from the Geuzen-resistance. Oranjehotel, Untermassfeld, Mauthausen, Auschwitz, Dachau.) Nijmegen: SUN, 1997.

Mooij, Annet. *De strijd om de Februaristaking.* (The struggle around the February strike.) Amsterdam: Balans, 2006.

Moore, Bob. "The Rescue of Jews from Nazi Persecution: A Western European Perspective." *Journal of Genocide Research* 5 no. 2 (2003): 293–308.

———. *Survivors: Jewish Self-Help and Rescue in Nazi-Occupied Western Europe.* Oxford: Oxford University Press, 2010.

Mulder, Gerard, and Paul Koedijk. *H.M. van Randwijk. Een biografie.* (H.M. van Randwijk. A biography.) Amsterdam: Nijgh & van Ditmar, 1988.

Noordervliet, Nelleke. "Barmhartige leugen." (Merciful lie.) *Historisch Nieuwsblad* 5 (2006).

Norel, Klaas. "De onderduiker." (The person in hiding.) *Het Grote Gebod. Gedenkboek van het verzet in LO en LPK.* vol. 2, ed. Hendrik van Riessen, 3–48. Kampen/Bilthoven: J.H. Kok N.V/H. Nelissen, 1951.

Norel, Klaas, and L. D. Terlaak Poot. *De tyrannie verdrijven.* (Expelling tyranny.) Wageningen: Keuning, 1947.

"Nota naar aanleiding van de publikaties in verschillende bladen betreffende de burgemeester der gemeente 's-Gravenhage." (Memorandum in response to the publications in various magazines concerning the mayor of the municipality of The Hague.) *Verslag der Handelingen van de Tweede Kamer der Staten-Generaal Zitting 1955–1956*, no. 4271.1. The Hague: Staatsdrukkerij, 1956.

Paldiel, Mordecai. "The Righteous Among the Nations at Yad Vashem." *Journal of Holocaust Education* 7, no. 1–2 (1998): 45–66.

Poznanski, Renée. "Rescue of the Jews and the Resistance in France: From History to Historiography." In "The Rescue of Jews in France and Its Empires during World War II: History and Memory." Special issue, *French Politics, Culture & Society* 30, no. 2 (2012): 8–32.

Presser, Jacques. *Ondergang: De vervolging en verdelging van het Nederlandse jodendom (1940–1945)*. The Hague: Staatsuitgeverij, 1965. English ed.: *Ashes in the Wind: The Destruction of Dutch Jewry*. Trans. Arnold J. Pomerans. London: Souvenir Press, 1968.

Randwijk, Henk M. van. *In de schaduw van gisteren. Kroniek van het verzet 1940–1945*. (In the shadow of yesterday. Chronicle of the resistance 1940–1945.) Amsterdam: Bert Bakker, 1967.

Reve, Simon van het. "De ondergang van de familie Boslowits." (The demise of the Boslowits family.) *Criterium* 1, no. 15 (December 1946): 788–813.

Riessen, Hendrik van. "Het onderduiken." (Hiding.) In *Onderdrukking en verzet. Nederland in oorlogstijd*, vol. 3, ed. Jan Bolhuis et al., 689–721. Arnhem/Amsterdam: Van Loghum Slaterus/J.M. Meulenhoff, 1952.

Roegholt, Richter, and Hans Wiedema. *Walter Süskind en de Hollandse Schouwburg: De geschiedenis van de redding van joodse kinderen 1942–1943*. (Walter Süskind and the Hollandse Schouwburg: The history of the rescue of Jewish children 1942–1943.) Amsterdam: Walter Süskind Stichting, 1992.

Rothberg, Michael. *The Implicated Subject: Beyond Victims and Perpetrators*. Stanford, CA: Stanford University Press, 2019.

———. *Multidirectional Memory: Remembering the Holocaust in the Age of Decolonization*. Stanford, CA: Stanford University Press, 2009.

Rottenberg, Hella. "Voor de gemoedsrust van de natie." (For the peace of mind of the nation.) *Trouw*, June 24, 2006.

Schellekens, Mark. *Walter Süskind: Hoe een zakenman honderden joodse kinderen uit handen van de nazi's redde*. (Walter Süskind: How a businessman saved hundreds of Jewish children from the hands of the Nazis.) Amsterdam: Atheneaeum–Polak & Van Gennep, 2012.

Schippers, Hans. *Westerweel Group: Non-Conformist Resistance against Nazi Germany—A Joint Rescue Effort of Dutch Idealists and Dutch-German Zionists*. Berlin: De Gruyter Oldenbourg, 2019.

Schutte, Xandra. "Willy Corsari." *De Groene Amsterdammer*, May 20, 1998.

Schuyt, Kees. *Het spoor terug. J.B. Charles/W.H. Nagel 1910–1983*. (The trace back. J.B. Charles/W.H. Nagel 1910–1983.) Amsterdam: Balans, 2010.

Schwarz, Géraldine. *Les Amnésiaques*. Paris: Flammarion, 2017. English ed.: *Those Who Forget: My Family's Story in Nazi Europe—A Memoir, a History, a Warning*. Trans. Laura Marris. Pushkin Press: London, 2020.

Sjenitzer-van Leening, Jitty T.M., ed. *Dagboekfragmenten 1940–1945*. (Diary fragments 1940–1945.) Utrecht: Veen, 1954.

Smits, Boudewijn. *Loe de Jong 1914–2005. Historicus met een missie*. (Loe de Jong 1914–2005. The historian on a mission.) Amsterdam: Boom, 2014.

Snyder, Timothy. *Bloodlands: Europe between Hitler and Stalin*. New York: Basic Books, 2010.

Steinberg, Maxime. "Le paradoxe français dans la Solution Finale à l'Ouest." (The French paradox in the Final Solution in the West.) *Annales. Économies, société, civilisations* 48 (1993): 583–94.

———. "Le paradoxe xénophobe dans la solution finale en Belgique occupée." (The xenophobe paradox in the Final Solution in occupied Belgium.) *Revue du Nord* 2, vol. 2, Special Issue: *L'occupation en France et en Belgique, 1940–1944* (1988): 653–64.

Steinfeldt, Irena. "Commemorating the Righteous Among the Nations at Yad Vashem: The History of a Unique Program." *Diasporas: Circulations, Migrations, Histoire* 21 (2013): 82–90.

Stigter, Bianca. "Beelden om nooit te vergeten. Monumenten ter nagedachtenis aan de Tweede Wereldoorlog in Amsterdam 1945–1991." (Images you'll never forget. Monuments commemorating the Second World War in Amsterdam 1945–1991.) *Kunst en beleid in Nederland* 6 (1993): 13–62.

Stroom, Gerrold van der, ed. *De vele gezichten van Anne Frank. Visies op een fenomeen*. (The many faces of Anne Frank. Views about the phenomenon.) Amsterdam: De Prom, 2003.

Thijs, Krijn. "Ordinary, Ignorant, and Noninvolved? The Figure of the Bystander in Dutch Research and Controversy." In *Probing the Limits of Categorization: The Bystander in Holocaust History*, ed. Christina Morina and Krijn Thijs, 247–65. New York: Berghahn Books, 2019.

Ultee, Wout, and Henk Flap. "De Nederlandse paradox. Waarom overleefden zoveel Nederlandse joden de Tweede Wereldoorlog niet?" (The Dutch paradox. Why did so many Jews not survive the Second World War?) In *Verklarende sociologie. Opstellen voor Reinhard Wippler*, ed. Harry Ganzeboom and Siegwart Lindenberg, 185–97. Amsterdam: Thesis, 1996.

United States Holocaust Memorial Museum. "Jewish Losses during the Holocaust: By Country." In *Holocaust Encyclopedia*, https://encyclopedia.ushmm.org/content/en/article/jewish-losses-during-the-holocaust-by-country, accessed 1 July 2019.

Valkhoff, Ziporah. *Leven in een niet-bestaan, beleving en betekenis van de joodse onderduik. Met een inleiding van Jolande Withuis*. (Living in nonexistence, experience and meaning of Jewish hiding.) Utrecht: Stichting ICODO, 1992.

Veen, Adriaan van der. *Het wilde feest*. (The wild party.) Amsterdam: Amber, 1952.

Vos, Chris. *Televisie en bezetting. Een onderzoek naar de documentaire verbeelding van de Tweede Wereldoorlog in Nederland*. (Television and occupation. A research into the documentary imagination of the Second World War in the Netherlands.) Hilversum: Verloren, 1995.

Vree, Frank van. *In de schaduw van Auschwitz: Herinneringen, beelden, geschiedenis.* (In the shadow of Auschwitz: Memories, images, history.) Groningen: Historische Uitgeverij, 1995.

Vuijsje, Herman. "Schuld en hulde; Nederland is recordhouder in Yad Vashem." (Guilt and homage: The Netherlands is a record holder in Yad Vashem.) *De Groene Amsterdammer*, February 5, 2014.

Vuijsje, Ies. *Tegen beter weten in: Zelfbedrog en ontkenning in de Nederlandse geschiedschrijving over de Jodenvervolging.* (Against all knowledge: Self-deception and denial in the Dutch historiography of the persecution of the Jews.) Antwerp: Uitgeverij Augustus, 2006.

Wagt, Wim de. *Vijfhonderd meter namen. De Holocaust en de pijn van de herinnering.* (Five hundred meters of names. The Holocaust and the pain of memory.) Amsterdam: Boom, 2021.

Wasserstein, Bernard. *The Ambiguity of Virtue: Gertrude van Tijn and the Fate of the Dutch Jews.* Cambridge, MA: Harvard University Press, 2014.

Wieviorka, Olivier. *Histoire de la Résistance 1940–1945.* (History of the resistance 1940–1945.) Paris: Perrin, 2013.

Winkler-Vonk, Annie. *Een baantje bij de krant.* (A job at the newspaper.) Amsterdam: Ploegsma, 1963.

Wolf, Diane L. *Beyond Anne Frank: Hidden Children and Postwar Families in Holland.* Berkeley: University of California Press, 2007.

Zee, Nanda van der. *Om erger te voorkomen. De voorbereiding en uitvoering van de vernietiging van het Nederlandse jodendom tijdens de Tweede Wereldoorlog.* (To prevent a worse outcome. The preparation and execution of the destruction of Dutch Jewry during the Second World War.) Amsterdam: Meulenhoff, 1997.

Zwaap, René. "Nanda van der Zee veegt de stoep goed schoon." (Nanda van der Zee sweeps the sidewalk well.) *De Groene Amsterdammer*, April 16, 1997.

2

Danish Heroism Revisited

The Rescue of the Danish Jews between National and Global Memory

SOFIE LENE BAK

At 9 PM on October 1, 1943, all telephone communication in Copenhagen was cut off. Columns of trucks manned by German police drove out into the streets of the capital. The objective was a surprise attack on Denmark's Jewish community, which consisted of approximately eight thousand people, mostly living in the capital area. Neutral Denmark had been occupied by Germany in April 1940, yet a swift capitulation meant that Denmark was never formally at war with Germany. This in turn allowed the Danish government to insist on the formal sovereignty of the kingdom, creating a unique and illusory construction in a Europe controlled by Nazi forces. "The peaceful occupation" of Denmark allowed for an active and voluntary policy of cooperation with the Germans, intended as a means of fending off German pressure for further political and economic integration into the German *Grossraum*. Throughout the occupation, the Danish government and administration sought to preserve democracy and protect the population. In principle, Denmark was still ruled by the king, parliament, and government, headed by a Social Democratic-Liberal coalition. The Danish courts, administration, and even the army and police maintained an independent status. The bilateral affairs of the two countries were directed through the German embassy and the Ministry of Foreign Affairs, the *Auswärtiges Amt*, in Berlin. Denmark never came under the control of the Nazi Party or the SS.[1]

However, during the summer of 1943, a wave of sabotage and strikes directed at the German *Wehrmacht* swept the country. This sedition, which began among industrial workers, spread, and was supported by a growing number of resistance groups dissatisfied with the compliance and national humiliation implied by Danish-German cooperation. By the summer of 1943, the Danes believed the collapse of the German regime was imminent and looked forward to the prospect of an Allied invasion. "Hitler's pet canary," as Denmark was nicknamed by Winston Churchill, now revolted against the Germans. As the Danish authorities lost control of the masses, Berlin issued an ultimatum to the Danish government, demanding martial law, curfew regulations, and the death penalty for sabotage operations against the *Wehrmacht*. Presented on August 28, it was promptly rejected by the government and a united front of political parties. In the early morning of August 29, the *Wehrmacht* assumed executive power and declared a state of martial law. The government and parliament resigned, the king was put under house arrest, and the officers and soldiers of the Danish army and navy were interned.[2]

Still, the rupture was not absolute. The Danish police and courts remained free of German influence. The permanent secretaries of the ministries stayed in their positions and now represented "official" Denmark—a modus vivendi that served both German and Danish interests in maintaining the status quo. Still, the political restraints that had guided German conduct were lifted, and terror campaigns against the enemies of the Third Reich began immediately, with preparations for the mass arrest and deportation of the Jews in Denmark.[3]

During the last days of September, more than 1,500 German policemen designated for the roundup of the Jews arrived in Denmark to assist the by then still limited Gestapo resources in the country. They were provided with detailed lists of addresses of Jewish families and were accompanied by Danes who knew the locality, among them Danish volunteers in the Waffen-SS, home in Denmark on furlough. On the night of the raid on October 1, within three hours, 198 men, women, and children had been arrested in Copenhagen. Despite the strong police force, by the morning of October 2, the total number of Jews arrested in the country during the roundup was only 281. Thousands of people were on the run. In the course of just a few weeks, 95 percent of Danish Jews reached safety in neighboring Sweden, in an operation affectionately referred to as "little Dunkirk," supported by the altruistic help and assistance of their fellow Danes.[4] The story of the rescue is rightfully world famous and plays a prominent part in global memory of the Holocaust. However, both at home and abroad, a range of myths and "silences" has clouded the memory of the events, and the chasm between collective memory and the historiography of the rescue is currently deepening.

This chapter presents the first in-depth analysis of national and global memory regarding the rescue of the Danish Jews. In doing so, this study reveals the preconception of the rescue as a widely admired act of courage as the chapter discusses the most recent historical scholarship on the subject. Danish historians have been battling quite fiercely over the interpretation of the rescue and producing insights that are barely acknowledged outside of Denmark. In the last section of the chapter, the national particularities of the rescue are weighed against the concept of a cosmopolitan memory culture, as national memory is dissolving into a decontextualized and heroizing global memory culture. In this process, vital insights may be lost, but if the pitfalls of idealized interpretations are avoided, global patterns might offer new approaches to historical research and to the viability of public memory. In general, by highlighting the implications of decontextualization and deterritorialization of memory, this chapter proposes an innovative contribution to the field of memory studies. However, challenging the myths about the rescue is not only an academic exercise. As the chapter proposes, a more realistic perception of the rescue has much to offer. Not only does it enhance the understanding of the preconditions of rescue and survival during the Holocaust, but it also acknowledges personal memories of the survivors that have long been disregarded and neglected in public memory culture.

Early Writing on and Collective Memory of the Rescue

In the first decades after the war, Danish public memory of the rescue had an exclusive focus on the showdown between the Danes and the Germans, with the Danes firmly cast as rescuers and the Germans as perpetrators. The clever and resolute Danes who tricked the Gestapo comprised the central theme in memoirs and monographs. The Germans were portrayed as stupid and simple-minded, thus explaining why so many Jews managed to escape and why so few rescuers were arrested.[5]

However, most literature on the subject refrained from individualization, and most rescuers remained anonymous. The rescue was vigorously promoted as a collective effort. In 1963, when Yad Vashem in Israel asked for names of Danes entitled to the honorary title "Righteous Among the Nations," veterans of the Danish resistance requested that no individual be honored in preference to others. Thus three trees with plaques were planted in honor of the Danish king, Christian X, the Danish resistance, and the Danish population.[6]

The postwar narrative of resilience and solidarity idealized the spontaneity of the rescuers, portraying their reactions to the persecution of Jews as something *natural*, just as the stories of the wit and skill of the rescuers tended to romanticize them. However, public memory neither heroized nor universalized the rescue. In early writings, the rescuers were portrayed as humble, common people not motivated by abstract altruistic principles but simply provoked by the assault on their friends, colleagues, and neighbors. The aspect of personal risk was rarely accentuated. According to the narrative, for the first time during the occupation, the people stood undivided by political and partisan interests. The event was cultivated as a source of national pride that reaffirmed the morale of and united the population after the humiliating defeat of occupation and collaboration.[7]

This master narrative of a unanimous and fearless people, united in their resistance against the German occupation, had an enormous influence on public memory and historiography alike. This narrative remained virtually unchallenged until the 1990s, when a new generation of historians embarked on a critical revision that acknowledged the transnational nature of the Holocaust. Only then was the event situated in the European context of the Holocaust and no longer exclusively in the national context of the German occupation. The comparative perspective illuminated not only striking similarities but also exceptional differences between Denmark and other countries occupied by Nazi Germany. A closer look at the events in the autumn of 1943 will illuminate the extraordinary conditions at play in the Danish case.

The Germans implemented the roundup of the Danish Jews on the evening of October 1, when most Jews were expected to be in their homes celebrating Rosh Hashanah, the Jewish New Year. The operation was well planned and executed carefully and efficiently. The orders stipulated that it had to be concluded in just three hours. Fortunately, most Jewish families had already left their homes, because they had been warned of the coming roundup. Several Germans had leaked the time and date of the roundup, and the warning spread like wildfire.[8] As a result, the element of surprise was almost completely absent. Although the Germans had the police forces needed to hunt down and capture the Jews of Copenhagen, they evidently had taken several steps to ensure that the roundup would not produce results.

There were no roundups of Jews after the central operation on October 1, 1943. The fifteen hundred German policemen available for the roundup were never used to search for Jews, or for patrolling the Danish coast. The pursuit of Jews after the roundup was now left to a small group of Gestapo officers, employees of the German security police's department IV-B-4, which dealt with the so-called Jewish question.[9] By no means did they have the resources to control a coastline of more than two hundred kilometers. This left the Gestapo completely dependent on Danish informers. The limited resources dedicated to the operation obviously affected the results. The total number of arrests *after* the roundup was 197. More than a quarter were arrested on one single occasion, when an informer betrayed Jews hiding in the fishing town of Gilleleje on October 6.[10] Furthermore, the Germans did not plan to catch Jews escaping across the sea. There was no German police surveillance over the strait between Denmark and Sweden in October 1943. German patrol boats only performed naval duties. All surveillance boats available were allocated to minesweeping. German police did not seize *any* of the six hundred to seven hundred illegal transports carrying Jewish refugees over the sea.[11] Jews were often caught by coincidence or imprudence, usually at harbors crowded with people. An illustrative example is found in Taarbaek, a small fishing hamlet north of Copenhagen. On October 9, two Gestapo agents who had been tipped off arrived at the port in Taarbaek just as a fishing boat with refugees was leaving the quay. Thirteen people were arrested that night; five were subsequently deported to the Theresienstadt Ghetto. However, witnesses at the war crimes trials in Denmark after the war reported that there were quite a lot of people at the harbor, among them several Danish police officers who assisted in the escape. Nevertheless, Danish law during the occupation prohibited leisure boating and unauthorized traffic in the harbors. A crowd of thirty or maybe forty people in the middle of the night, during curfew, can hardly be considered discreet. The situation was all too obvious—and triggered an informer, who alerted the Gestapo.[12]

When contextualized, the events of October 1943 show how reluctantly and restrainedly the Germans acted in Denmark. This implies several challenges to the master narrative: If the Germans deprioritized the persecution of Jews after the roundup on October 1, what does that mean for the risk implicit in helping Jews? How and why, then, was this master narrative of the rescuers constructed, and what forces of memory politics were at play? And how can the German conduct in Denmark be empirically explained?

Supply and Demand

A humorous prologue to the most sensitive aspect of the Danish rescue is provided by a cartoon printed in the popular cartoon yearbook *Svikmøllen* (an almost untranslatable term meaning "vicious circles") in late 1945, the first "free" issue after liberation. A distinguished-looking gentleman is approaching the ticket office of the ferry service between Copenhagen and the Swedish city

Figure 2.1. *Svikmøllen* cartoon, late 1945.

of Malmö, on the other side of the Oresund, the narrow strait between Denmark and Sweden. The dialogue reads:

> [CUSTOMER]: What is the price for a ticket to Sweden?
> [TICKET AGENT]: 5 kroner and 60 Øre.
> [CUSTOMER]: That is cheap! Last time I paid 3,000 kroner.

The cartoon suggests that it was commonly known in Denmark that the Jews had paid a considerable amount of money for their illegal transport to Sweden. The amount mentioned—three thousand kroner (Danish crowns [DKK])—is at the top end of the average price of a thousand crowns per person, as estimated by later research.[13] The historical amount is the equivalent of 150 dollars or 130 euros. However, this is at a time when the average hourly wage for an industrial worker was about two Danish crowns. To get an idea of the value in present-day money, multiply the amount by twenty.

The question of money has always been extremely sensitive. National debate on the issue either has been openly apologetic or has played down the consequences. Overall, the payment for passage has long been rationalized as life insurance for the fishermen who risked their lives, safety, and livelihoods in case of arrest, or the destruction or confiscation of their boats. Jewish testimonies after the war supported this narrative. In Jewish memoirs there was no taboo surrounding the payment, yet neither the rationale nor the fairness of the payment was questioned explicitly.[14] However, more than two decades have passed since meticulous Danish research in the 1990s established that the fishermen did not actually risk their lives to help Jews. Neither did they risk deportation to German concentration camps. Rescuers caught by the Gestapo were handed over to the Danish courts to be charged with assisting illegal migration. The maximum penalty was three months' imprisonment under relatively lenient conditions in a Danish prison. Most of the cases, however, never even came to court, or court officials let the rescuers slip away through the back door.[15] Thus the rescuers faced only very limited punishments.

The combination of the limited risk of helping and the fact that Jews paid large sums for the rescue leads to the conclusion that the Danish Jews were exploited and that the fishermen took advantage of the desperate predicament of the Jews. Yet is that just a cynical rationalization made years after the events—from a safe and cozy distance? Obviously, it is essential to consider the difference between assessments made today and the perceptions of the people involved at the time, who did not perceive—or only partly perceived—the real risk of their actions. However, even in testimonies given by the rescuers, their personal risk is often downplayed, neglected, or made light of in comparison to the perceived risk of other illegal activities, such as sabotage.[16]

It is a vital conclusion, therefore, that money was a precondition for the success of the rescue. Money ensured that there were enough fishermen willing to sail. The money supplied made it possible to transport almost eight thousand people out of Denmark in a few weeks—minimizing the risk of exposure and arrest in hiding. According to estimates, the rescue amounted to twenty million Danish crowns in total. The Jewish refugees contributed about half of the amount, while the rest was obtained through private and corporate donations, which covered the cost for less fortunate families.

While honoring the subjective fears of the rescuers and fishermen, one must still inevitably confront the fact that—regardless of the need for insurance for the material risk taken by the fishermen, or security for their families in case of arrest—prices were subjected to the mechanisms of supply and demand. As the demand declined in November 1943, when the transports of Jews came to an end, the average price for the crossing dropped to one hundred Danish crowns, 10 percent of the average October price. It should also be added that the rescuers operating on land—finding secure hiding places, housing, and assisting refugees on their way to the coast, guiding the refugees to the harbors and beaches, collecting money, clothes, and food supplies—were all accomplices in the crime of illegal migration and faced the same penalties as the fishermen. As far as we know, they did not receive payment.[17]

The historical findings documenting the limited risk entailed in helping Jews and the marginal German resources dedicated to hunting down rescuers and fishermen clash with the public perception of the motives of the rescuers.[18] For the fishermen, humanitarian motives intertwined with the desire to profit from the situation. It is a fact that several fishermen made a living—and a fortune—on the rescue. Not only had the fishermen claimed ample payment for their deeds; since the prices were subjected to the mechanisms of supply and demand, the fishermen were also equivalent to human smugglers. This complicates the symbolic value of the celebrated icon of the rescue, the fishing boat, featured at Holocaust museums all over the world—prominently at the United States Holocaust Memorial Museum in Washington, DC, and at Yad Vashem in Jerusalem. Furthermore, Danes also were among the perpetrators, since the Gestapo received assistance from Danish informers and collaborators.

However, since the late 1990s public memory has proven remarkably resilient to historical findings. Even if it has been generally accepted that the Jews had to pay for their rescue, the gravity of the moral dilemma depends on just how much the fishermen knew about the limited risk of arrest, an argument that is eagerly applied in their defense. Additionally, the scope and consequences of the payments are still ignored or minimized.[19] As historians question the motives of the Danish people, the public narrative has increasingly promoted the self-sacrifice and moral fiber of the rescuers. This represents a change compared to the first postwar decades, when Danish politicians and members of the resistance opposed a heroizing and individualizing narrative, and witnesses and historians kept a more levelheaded and more humble attitude toward the rescue effort.

In the new millennium, national memory is being subjected to a mythical narrative that has always been vivid in global memory, the key feature being the heroic national character of the Danes. In recent years, a series of the most resilient myths about Denmark has been eliminated from global Holocaust memory: for example, the legend that King Christian X had worn the yellow star in solidarity with his Jewish subjects,[20] or the myth that the Danes risked their lives to save their Jewish fellow citizens. However, other inaccurate assumptions about conditions in occupied Denmark still frequently appear in both international scholarship and public memory: for example, that Danes who helped Jews escape to Sweden were sent to concentration camps, even though no Dane was deported to concentration camps merely for aiding fleeing Jews.[21] Moreover, payment is rarely mentioned, as it is inconsistent with the heroic narrative. Payment is specifically also incompatible with the definition of the Righteous Among the Nations as formulated by Yad Vashem. According to Yad

Vashem and Israel's ministry of foreign affairs, recognition of the Righteous depends on the criteria that "the rescuer was aware that in extending such aid he was risking his life, safety and personal freedom." Additionally, the condition was and remains that "no material reward or substantial compensation was exacted by the rescuer from the rescued as a condition for extending aid."[22] Heroism requires risk, which explains why public memory is fiercely resisting the latest research findings, deepening the chasm between public memory and historiography.

The Perspective of the Victim

The fishing hamlet of Taarbaek mentioned earlier—the overcrowded harbor where thirteen Jews were arrested on a night in October 1943—was the site of one of the best-documented events during the rescue operation, because of a tragic accident. Just as the boat with the Jewish refugees was leaving the harbor, the Gestapo arrived and fired what they claimed were warning shots. However, a young man assisting the fleeing group was hit and died immediately.

Figure 2.2. This photograph was taken in Sweden in October 1943, just after the safe arrival of the four Jewish siblings pictured. The rowboat also carried their aunt and a fisherman. During the crossing, one of the oars broke—fortunately the boat was already close to the Swedish coast. The broken oar is on display at the Museum of Danish Resistance in Copenhagen. Courtesy of the Museum of Danish Resistance.

The young man, Claus Heilesen, who was killed by the Gestapo, was only eighteen years old and a promising student of engineering. He has been honored for his deed on several memorials in Denmark and is frequently mentioned in the literature on the rescue as an example of the bravery of the rescuers and the deadly risks they faced.[23] However, nobody paid attention to the fact that Claus Heilesen's mother was Jewish, hence according to the Nazis he was a "Mischling," and that he was fleeing to Sweden himself. He *did* arrange and organize the illegal transport—but he, too, was on his way into the boat bound for the Swedish safe haven. Claus Heilesen's death was exceptional but not his deeds. Personal memories and oral history accounts of Danish Jewish survivors challenge the notion of the Jews as passive victims. Rather than passive objects of persecution and rescue, they were active subjects who tried their best to secure their possessions and belongings. Likewise, with little time on their hands, they managed to obtain the cash needed for the flight, and many organized transport not only for their nearest family but for more distant relatives and friends as well.[24]

When the flight started in late September 1943, the earliest transports were often conducted in small rowboats. These crossings were extremely dangerous—not because of the risk of exposure but because the rowboats the Jews had purchased were in very poor condition. Many of the known accidents in which people drowned happened at the beginning, when small boats were used. At least twenty Jewish refugees drowned on their way to Sweden.[25] Transports by larger fishing vessels made it possible for more refugees to make the crossing in greater safety.

Another example of how a victim's perspective can reveal new aspects of the rescue involves the heartbreaking stories of Jewish children left behind in Denmark. At least 150 Jewish children—20 percent of the total number of children from newborn to five years of age who were affected by the Nazi persecution—never made it to Sweden. The dangers of the flight and the uncertainty of refuge prompted their parents to leave their children behind. Small children were considered a security risk, some rescue organizations refused to accept small children, and false rumors circulated that children who could not keep quiet were strangled. The children were placed with foster families or in children's homes. Most stayed with their foster families for another twenty-two months, until the liberation. They are the "hidden children" of Denmark.

The foster parents were not hardened partisans with finely honed skills in conducting clandestine activities. The cover stories and the children's hastily constructed identities speak volumes about their inexperience. However, families, neighbors, and communities supported the foster parents and closed ranks

Figures 2.3 and 2.4. These charming photos are of a little boy named Lennart, who was only four weeks old when his mother had to leave him in Denmark so she could flee Nazi persecution. The photo album containing these two pictures was the only thing Lennart had to remind him of his foster parents, who cared for him as if he was their own. His biological parents broke off all contact with the couple after the war, because of the emotional strain on both families. Courtesy of the Danish Jewish Museum.

around the children. Not a single child was handed over to the Gestapo. No systematic mission was carried out, yet the children participated in the daily lives of the families, including a diet heavily dependent on pork, Christian holidays, and church attendance. In general, the children were cared for and loved, and payment was rare. The stories display a compassion and altruism that validates the solidarity of the Danes toward the Jews. Still, it was their parents—motivated by fear—who had made the difficult decisions to part with their children and place them with foster families, as a conscious choice to save the children's lives. Both the children and their parents paid a high emotional price.

During my research, I accidentally stumbled on individual examples of children who were left behind in Denmark when their parents fled, and I called for more testimonies in a major Danish newspaper in 2009. The response was overwhelming. Finally, after sixty-five years, the hidden children of Denmark understood that they were far from alone in their experiences, and they gained a common identity as hidden children.[26] Although the vast majority of the children reunited with their parents after the war, the children could not escape the feeling of a double betrayal. First, their parents abandoned them, and then they had to leave the foster parents with whom they had formed strong emotional bonds. Several of the hidden children emphasize that they never reestablished an intimate relationship with their biological parents and were unable to embrace them. The rejection experienced by the parents was a heavy burden on the family, which together with feelings of shame and guilt prompted suppression and silence. The hidden children continued to live in hiding, concealing both who they were and what they could remember.[27]

Why have these experiences of the victims been downplayed for so long in historiography as well as in public memory? In the first postwar decades, the celebration of the resistance movement and the victims of political persecution often overshadowed the persecution of the Jews, both in Denmark and in many other European countries. The defeated and divided nations in Europe, in the East as well as in the West, needed patriotic martyrs who had sacrificed their lives in a national fight for freedom against fascism, not victims of a senseless racist ideology. In collective memory the Jewish victims either were included in a patriotic discourse that implied restitution and acknowledgment or excluded and discriminated against as supposedly passive victims who were segregated from the political prisoners of the camps.[28]

However, due to the rescue, the persecution of the Danish Jews has always been an integral part of the commemoration of the resistance. Though most of the rescuers returned to their daily lives when the rescue operation was over and never again participated in illegal activities,[29] in memory culture the rescue was a landmark of the Danish resistance, representing one of its greatest achievements and a popular breakthrough. October 1 was established as a day of remembrance, alongside the anniversary of the 1943 rebellion on August 29 and Liberation Day on May 5—all considered victory days for the antifascist resistance. The need for national cohesion meant that the victims were assimilated and included in the discourse of resistance. Jews who drowned on their way to Sweden or died in the camps were hence commemorated as "Fallen in the fight for the Freedom of Denmark."[30] Danish Jews were included in the patriotic memory due to this amalgamation, just as the rescue was integrated into a national narrative of resistance against the German occupation.[31]

However, patriotic memory did not leave much room for mourning the dead or acknowledging the racist and antisemitic motives behind the persecution. The national memorial to victims of the resistance (*Mindelunden*) was first unveiled in 1945, on the biennial of the August 29 rebellion, and officially inaugurated on May 5, 1950. Erected in a field on the outskirts of Copenhagen which had been used by the Germans as an execution and burial ground for members of the Danish resistance, the memorial functions as a cemetery for the resistance members executed at the site and as a memorial park for Danish victims of the concentration camps. However, only political prisoners are included in the commemoration. Despite being expanded with new monuments over the years—to Danish civilian mariners in Allied service in 2017 and recently, in 2019, to the Danish soldiers who lost their lives during the war—the memorial park does not include Jewish victims. They are commemorated separately, at the Jewish cemetery in Copenhagen, with a monument that was erected by the Jewish community in 1946.

In public memory the focus was on the rescuer rather than the victims, and with time a narrative with a fixed set of stereotypes of the "survivors," "perpetrators," and "rescuers" evolved. The interests in such a narrative in Danish society as well as in the Jewish community were convergent. While the deeds of ordinary Danes washed away the shame of defeat and collaboration, the Jewish community was overwhelmed by gratitude—and by fear of antisemitic reactions.

During exile in Sweden, the leadership of the Jewish community knew that their eventual return to Denmark was of the utmost importance. As the chairman of the community put it: "We have to return as persecuted refugees, as soldiers after a victorious war, not as the Jews who instantly want to reclaim their old status."[32] When the war finally ended, the fear expressed by the community leaders had not disappeared. Any claims Jewish families might raise for restitution for damages entailed the risk of provoking prejudice against supposedly demanding Jews, who could be seen as exploiting their victimization rather than conforming to the expectation of humility and gratitude. On returning home, the exiled Jews were frequently confronted with stories of the hardship suffered by Danes during the last years of the German occupation and implicit insinuations that during this time the Jewish refugees had lived in comfort and abundance in neutral Sweden. Among former members of the resistance, the Jews were accused of not having engaged in active resistance toward the Germans.[33] Danish Jews felt their status more challenged than ever. The Jewish community never made collective claims for restitution nor questioned the conduct of their fellow Danes. They embarked on a strategy of undivided gratitude toward Denmark. All attention was diverted toward the rescuers, while any hardship during exile or on returning was excluded from public memory.[34]

Yet memory culture did not remain static. The Holocaust emerged as a frame of reference in Danish public memory from the late 1980s, as publications and periodicals on Jewish life in Denmark—published for a wider audience—largely undertook the commemoration of the rescue.[35] The changing political landscape of Europe following the fall of the communist regimes and the reunification of Germany, paired with the shocking atrocities in former Yugoslavia, moved victims of National Socialism into the center of public attention. In 1989 the first Holocaust monument commemorating the genocide of European Jews was established in Denmark next to the Copenhagen synagogue. However, it was not until 2008 that a monument commemorating the deportation of *Danish* Jews was inaugurated in Copenhagen harbor. The monument is placed in a public space, and it confronts passersby with the stories of the victims, thus embodying a definitive shift from the segregated postwar memory culture, where the commemoration of Jewish victims of the concentration camps was an internal Jewish matter. For the first time the Jewish deportees and those who perished in the camps were commemorated in public both as Jews and as Holocaust victims.[36]

Thus national memory is moving from an exclusive focus on the rescue—and the rescuers—toward a gradual acknowledgment of the victims and the European context of the Holocaust. However, integration and interpretation of the rescue action itself in terms of the European experience of the Holocaust do not necessarily illuminate the Danish case. By the new millennium, as the last witnesses are passing away, the experience of rescue is increasingly instrumentalized and universalized. This was evident in the Danish commemorations on the seventieth and seventy-fifth anniversaries of the rescue in 2013 and 2018. On the occasion of the seventieth anniversary in 2013, the then Danish prime minister, Helle Thorning-Schmidt, was awarded the Raoul Wallenberg Centennial Medal—on behalf of the Danish people—from the International Raoul Wallenberg Foundation, as a tribute to "one of the most heroic performances in modern history."[37] The most popular book on the rescue, published on the seventieth anniversary, had an explicit message for present-day populism: "When it is so easy to arouse national chauvinism, it is not because we all in the end fear and despise those who are different. It is because we from time to time allow leading politicians to turn suspicion toward 'the others' into their political instrument."[38] On the seventy-fifth anniversary, the then Danish prime minister, Lars Løkke Rasmussen, stated: "We shall use the 75th anniversary to look each other in the eyes and remember the core values that constitute our shared civilization."[39] Public memory is increasingly submitting to a heroizing tone, far from the meek and level-headed accounts of the original narrative. Moreover, the decontextualization, deterritorialization, and universalization of the event do not add to the explanation of how the rescue was possible. Quite the contrary.

The Benefits of Collaboration

The escape and survival of 95 percent of the Danish Jewish community are often portrayed as a miracle beyond rational explanation. "Nor was it Nazi behavior that made the crucial difference, because it was murderous everywhere," it is commonly concluded.[40] Such popular sentiments leave us, at best, with very limited insight into the causes and conditions of altruistic behavior; at worst, we have to resort to clichés relating to national character. Since the late 1990s, various aspects of the persecution of the Jews in Denmark have been highlighted and revised in a wave of new, more critical approaches. Not only has the consensus among historians changed during the past two decades, but the focus and context have shifted from methodological nationalism to growing attention toward an international audience and incipient comparative and transnational research. Central to the historical debate is the question of the conditions of the mass escape. Did the Germans proceed with similar brutality and determination all over Europe, regardless of local political circumstances? Was the roundup actually a failure from a German viewpoint? Was the mass escape over the small strip of water separating Denmark from Sweden a result of German incompetence and deficiency?

As a case of historical irony, it was the utterly unheroic collaboration between the Danish government and the Germans that diverted German persecution of the Jews throughout most of the occupation, and helped them escape when the German police finally struck. Denmark capitulated after just a few hours of fighting in 1940 and tried hard to comply with German demands afterward. Yet this "policy of cooperation"[41] allowed for mutual concessions, as the Danish government refused to allow any special measures regarding the Jews.[42] On this point they were in consonance with the majority of the Danish population. The Germans realized that any further action against the Jews in Denmark would make further cooperation impossible and cause unrest among the Danish population. Hence actions against the Jewish community were postponed, and when the roundup orders finally came, the operation was actively sabotaged by the Germans from within. Yet from a German viewpoint, the roundup on October 1 was not necessarily a failure. It was a revival of an alternative policy of frightening and terrorizing the Jews into leaving the country. Within a few weeks, thousands of people were driven into exile. To the Third Reich's plenipotentiary (*Reichsbevollmächtigter*) in Denmark, Werner Best, a forced expulsion accommodated both his ideological convictions and his pragmatic view of the policy of cooperation in Denmark. *Kopfjagd* ("head-hunting") was never in question. Within weeks, the result was a *judenrein* ("cleansed of Jews") territory.[43]

Furthermore, even the fate of the Danish Jews who were deported illuminates the far-reaching capacity of the policy of cooperation. In total, 472 people were deported from Denmark because of their Jewish descent; 470 were sent to the Theresienstadt Ghetto in the protectorate of Bohemia and Moravia. Over the course of the nineteen months they spent in the ghetto, fifty-four died. Yet according to a deal made between the plenipotentiary, Werner Best, and Adolf Eichmann, who were in charge of the mass deportation, all Jews deported from Denmark were to stay in the Theresienstadt Ghetto and were not selected for transport to the extermination camps.[44] Only one Dane was deported from Theresienstadt to Auschwitz, presumably by mistake.[45] The camp inmates were allowed to receive letters and parcels with clothes, and from February 1944 they were granted permission to receive monthly food parcels from Denmark. Even more remarkable is the fact that these privileges were extended to German nationals deported from Danish soil. The remaining prisoners from Denmark were liberated from the ghetto in April 1945 and evacuated to Sweden in a joint operation by the Swedish Red Cross and Danish authorities. These extraordinary conditions were the result of tireless efforts by the Danish civil administration, left intact when the government resigned in August 1943, as they relentlessly asked for information on deportees, negotiated releases, and pleaded for a visit to Theresienstadt by the International Red Cross.[46]

In conclusion, neither the rescue operation in October 1943 nor the protection of Danish deportees would have been possible without German consent and approval. In fact, the protection of the Jewish community in Denmark is the most conspicuous achievement of the Danish-German cooperation policy. After the war, however, neither pragmatic diplomacy nor Jewish agency was useful for a nation defeated and liberated by foreign forces. In addition, Denmark desperately needed any positive publicity that could ameliorate Allied suspicions regarding the true motives of the Danes.

The first historian to systematically investigate the events, the Israeli researcher Leni Yahil, emphasized that a key factor in explaining why the Jews in Denmark were rescued from German persecution was the fact the Danes possessed a "special character . . . with its high ethical standard and its love of freedom and democracy."[47] Yahil's early interpretation established the Danish case as an example of the potential achievement of courageous active resistance to Nazi persecution, and it was adopted by most Danish and international scholars and became the core of the master narrative about the "Danish Rescue," acknowledged worldwide as a rare shining light in the darkness of the European Holocaust.

Yet as recent historical findings show, the cooperation policy was of paramount importance for Jewish survival in Denmark. This forces us to reinterpret the roles of perpetrators, bystanders, and rescuers, with the German perpetrators collaborating in the rescue, the bystander government acting as rescuers, and some ordinary Danes acting as perpetrators informing on and assisting in the arrest of fellow citizens. Furthermore, research points to the crucial importance of the military situation and to the exceptional character of the occupying regime in Denmark. Most comparative research has difficulties in placing Denmark in categories or types of occupying regimes, due to the extraordinary nature of the peaceful occupation and cooperation policy. Denmark was a *Sonderfall* ("special case").[48] However, the protection of human life came with the price of economic collaboration with Germany and support for the German war industry. It likewise entailed political collaboration on combating communism, including assistance in the arrest of Danish citizens, as the Danish government outlawed the Communist Party in the wake of the German attack on the Soviet Union in 1941 and eventually signed the Anti-Comintern Pact—committing Denmark to combat communism alongside the fascist allies Germany and Japan—later that same year.

In recent years the cooperation policy has been heavily criticized and politicized in Danish public debate, most notably by then Danish prime minister, Anders Fogh Rasmussen. In 2003, on the sixtieth anniversary of August 29, 1943, the Liberal-Conservative prime minister denounced the strategy as naïve, reprehensible, and cowardly, rejecting the motivation, urgency, and rationale of the cooperation policy. Fogh Rasmussen's assault on the cooperation policy marked a previously unseen attempt at instrumentalizing the past to legitimize the turn in Danish foreign policy toward active military engagement in Afghanistan in 2002 and in Iraq in 2003–7. It was an ironic fact, obviously not mentioned by the prime minister, that his party, Venstre, represented rural and agricultural interests that had profited extensively from cooperation with Nazi Germany during the war. The debate following the statement demonstrated how decontextualized the past had become and illuminated a growing distance between professional historians and the general public.[49]

The Price of Silence

On October 3, 1943—two days after the roundup of Danish Jews—the city of Copenhagen dispatched a group of civil servants to the Copenhagen synagogue. In the report from the scene, they stated:

> The Germans had used it as a collection point during the roundup of the Jews and it still exhibited the signs of this. Prayer shawls were thrown over the seats of the chairs and prayer books were spread over the floor. On the elevated area, the floor was strewn with cigarette butts, and the trustees' top hats, which were usually kept in a cupboard in the entrance, had been used as footballs and kicked across the floor and underneath the rows of benches. The Social Service [of Copenhagen municipality] removed what they assessed to be of value: some Torah scrolls, various silver objects and books. These effects were moved, along with some boxes of items from the Museum of the Jewish Community, to the crypt of one of Copenhagen's old churches with the help of the Museum of Copenhagen. And from there they were delivered back to a representative of the Jewish Community after the German capitulation.[50]

The account of the disrespectful treatment of the synagogue is reminiscent of the behavior of the German occupying forces all over Europe, where Jewish property was vandalized and destroyed. However, it also tells of the exceptional occupation conditions that were in effect in Denmark, as German authorities in Denmark tolerated neither destruction nor theft of Jewish property.

For the civil servants who inspected the synagogue, this was just the first of many similar tasks. Just hours after the German roundup was completed, the ministry of welfare requested that the municipality of Copenhagen safeguard the belongings of the Jews who had fled their homes and property. In the months to follow, the city dealt with 1,970 inquiries about empty homes and other suspicious circumstances around the capital. When the social workers received an inquiry, they visited the residence, checked the conditions, and made a complete inventory of the household effects. If it was possible to keep the flat for the original tenants, the city authorities paid the rent for the rest of the occupation. Had the flat already been rented out again, or circumstances indicated that it was sublet, all personal property and furniture were put in storage. Contracts with trustees for property and businesses were established with neighbors, relatives, and employees, preventing thefts and larceny. In all, the city paid rent and all other costs for ninety-seven flats, while storage was provided for the goods of 350 households, through municipal efforts. The ministry of welfare covered all expenses.[51]

The work of the municipality of Copenhagen reflects a unique set of circumstances: During the German occupation a Danish public agency managed to protect the abandoned property of the Jews. The rationale behind the undertakings was that the Jews should have homes to return to. No less remarkable is the fact that the arrangements were partly due to an agreement with the German authorities. Although the agreement with the German security police concerned only the safekeeping of the property and flats of *deported* Jews, the Danish authorities interpreted the agreement loosely as covering "anyone, who because of the circumstances, has deemed it necessary to take themselves out of harm's way, whether in this country or abroad."[52] The flats inspected by the municipality had only in a very few cases been vandalized by the German police. There were no cases of looting. Nevertheless, they encountered frequent cases of theft, apparently perpetrated by other Danes in the aftermath of the roundup.

On October 1, 1945, the Danish parliament passed the Law of Compensation to the Victims of the Occupation, in recognition of the considerable need for public assistance for people whose existence had been shattered by the events of the war. The law was primarily aimed at members of the resistance and political deportees, but included the category "Persons persecuted because of their descent." "Descent" as a concept had the linguistic advantage of disassociation from Nazi racist ideology—and with it the politically problematic concept of race—and it did not exclude anyone from compensation in advance. The law guaranteed compensation for death and disability due to events that took place during the war, including persecution, imprisonments, internments, and deportations carried out by the Germans. Tort compensation for imprisonment, internment, and deportation was paid out at a fixed rate for every week the imprisonment had lasted. In addition, the law contained the possibility for compensation for damage to property and support to begin or continue business activity or education as well as restoration of particularly severe losses. The provision for restitution of severe losses included compensation for the expenses Danish Jews had had in connection with the flight to Sweden. The law granted support for repayment of loans taken to pay for the flight and compensation for the use of private means—both ready money and the sale of personal effects and property. By way of compensation, the Danish state thus contributed to financing the flight of the Danish Jews to Sweden with an estimated sum of more than 700,000 Danish crowns. The compensation was a very important symbolic acknowledgment of the sufferings of the Jewish community and shut down any political and moral discussions about the legitimacy of the price of the rescue before it had even begun.[53]

According to the dominant narrative expressed in testimonies and memoirs, not only were the Danish Jews enthusiastically welcomed home by their fellow citizens, but their living conditions, housing, and material status had also remained untouched by flight and exile, thanks to the care given to their homes and possessions by fellow citizens.[54] Undoubtedly, numerous families returned and found their homes and property well cared for and intact, and some Danish private individuals had unselfishly and carefully kept an eye on the property of their Jewish neighbors and friends. However, it was the municipality of Copenhagen that took responsibility in large part for the safekeeping of Jewish homes and property. Thus public authorities played an important role in guaranteeing that many Danish Jews had homes to return to, and their efforts prevented large-scale theft and larceny by fellow Danes.

Yet the fact that a significant segment of the Danish Jews received compensation for the losses they suffered during the war was erased from individual memory, and it never became part of collective memory either. The explanation is political. To a great extent, these losses were caused by theft and misuse: Families came home and found that all their valuables and desirable objects had disappeared from their homes, or prior to their flight they had had to sell furniture, jewelry, silver, and businesses at prices that were way below market value. They were grateful for the price they could get, which was most advantageous for the buyer. Loans and repurchase agreements were made, which, at best, were on market terms and, at worst, were an exploitation of their wretched situation. The compensation cases involved painful conflicts, which, accompanied by a discussion of the reasonableness of the sums the Jews had been charged for the crossing to Sweden, could have driven a serious wedge into Danish society. The broad government coalition of politicians and members of the resistance that passed the law on compensation in 1945 wanted to avoid this at any price. The restitution process underlines the dedication of the Danish authorities to the reintegration of the Jewish community and their interest in silencing potential ethnic conflict. Their stand on the question of the payment charged to the Jewish families during the rescue was remarkably clear: "It is commonly known that a lot of people, particularly fishermen, assisted the illegal transports [to Sweden] for personal gain exclusively and have made huge profits out of these fantastic 'fares' (especially in the period around 1 October 43)," as the internal guidelines for handling restitution cases stated.[55]

The prompt and inclusive state assistance provided to Danish Jews on their return in 1945 is unique in the European context and confirms Denmark's status as the exception both during and in the immediate aftermath of the Holocaust. Not only did the law of compensation include Jews as a matter of course, it included the exiled Jews and the losses they had suffered in Denmark in their absence and the price they had paid for their illegal transport to Sweden. The compensation was an extension of the efforts by the municipality of Copenhagen to mitigate and ameliorate the consequences of Nazi persecution. At first,

Danish politicians and authorities had attempted to prevent persecution. When it did finally occur, from the very beginning all legal means were used to ward off its consequences. Without the compensation, a significant number of people would have been impoverished, facing severe difficulties in getting back on their feet. Yet the compensation was also a factor in the veil of silence that fell over the considerable economic costs of the flight.

A Cosmopolitan Memory Culture

The notion of a "cosmopolitan memory culture," as argued by Daniel Levy and Natan Sznaider, implies a memory that is decontextualized from historical time and space, fueling universalism and a generalization, which "diffuses the distinction between memories of victims and perpetrators."[56] As this essay has clearly demonstrated, national memory of the rescue in Denmark has increasingly assimilated into such global patterns.[57] In this process of cosmopolitanization, the complex and ambiguous aspects of the event are smoothed over, and the experience of the historical actors universalized. The universal tale derived from the experience of the victims, as well as from that of the perpetrators, can be utilized in a myriad of personal and political agendas. However, the pivotal conclusion is that local historical context is paramount for the understanding of the Danish rescue. The exceptional character of the occupying regime in Denmark and the nature of the cooperation policy during the war make comparison with other countries and rescue operations an intricate endeavor and the Danish case a very unsuitable universal measuring stick for either good or evil.

Moreover, it is a widely accepted argument that the cosmopolitan memory contributes to the creation of a common European culture of memory, as cosmopolitan memory transforms the Holocaust into a transcendent idea that might provide a basis for a European identity.[58] This constitutes a paradox, since most of the examples of mediated representations, especially film and television, are American (though in the case of *Schindler's List* with a deliberate attempt at Europeanization as to casting, location, and style). The common patterns of the cosmopolitan memory could just as well be considered an *Americanization* of memory, as argued by Alvin Rosenfeld. By this he means "a tendency to individualize, heroize, moralize, idealize, and universalize"[59] the Holocaust, favoring the affirmative figures of "the survivor," Jews who did not die, and the "rescuer," who saved them. These types are moved from the margins to the center of the narrative, despite the obvious disproportion and asymmetry as to the historical reality of the Holocaust. When rescue is the focus of the narrative—as in the Danish case—there is a risk of stereotyping the figures of the "victim," "perpetrator," and "rescuer" according to current cultural, political, and religious values and needs. Thus the nuances carefully exposed by historiography as to the crucial role of payment in the rescue, the aspects of Danish collaboration, and the conflated roles of the bystander and rescuer in the case of the Danish politicians and civil servants are frequently marginalized.

However, as argued by Levy and Sznaider, the core of the cosmopolitan memory is "a reflexive choice to incorporate the suffering of the 'Other,'"[60] which emphasizes the victims' suffering and draws inspiration from their struggle. This has also been true in the Danish case. As an outcome of the Stockholm International Forum on the Holocaust in 1999, Denmark has been committed to commemorating the International Holocaust Remembrance Day on January 27, since 2003, and to developing and providing adequate teaching materials for state schools. In 2000 the Danish government provided a sizable research grant for a comprehensive examination of the restrictive Danish refugee policy in the 1930s, when thousands of refugees, among them many Jews, sought asylum in Denmark, and most were turned down. The project yielded six volumes and an official apology. The apology was explicitly concerned with the expulsion of Jewish refugees during the German occupation, described as a "shameful act" and "a stain on Denmark's otherwise good reputation."[61] Public attention to the results and to stories of the individual tragedies caused by the expulsions has been immense.[62] A cosmopolitanization of national memory might potentially entail that the fate of the Jews of Denmark is acknowledged as a part of the European and Jewish ordeal of the Holocaust, which might facilitate a new and long overdue focus on the victims and survivors.

The Danish myth of the struggle against evil tells of the ultimate victory of the good, due to the belief in the superiority of Danish democratic culture. The comprehension that conscious and strategic German restraint rather than Danish heroism was of paramount importance for Jewish survival may appear less affirmative. Still, a more nuanced and contextualized memory of the rescue in 1943 has much to offer. Danish politicians, dismissing any German talk of "a Jewish problem" throughout the occupation, were in consonance with the vast majority of the Danish population. Solidarity with the Jewish minority was the norm rather than the exception in Denmark. It allows us to understand that, in October 1943, active engagement in political protest or rescue activities was a mass phenomenon. A moving and illustrative example is the reaction at the largest university in Denmark, University of Copenhagen. On the morning after the roundup, all teaching classes were canceled for one week, and the rectorate signed an official protest that was delivered to the German plenipotentiary, Werner Best. In addition, the most senior member of the student union personally handed an official protest on behalf of the students to the chief of the Gestapo in Denmark.[63] Meanwhile, groups of students searched the parks and woods of Copenhagen, looking for Jews who had fled their homes. As one of the leading members of a rescue network explains in his memoirs: "We didn't know any Jews. But my sisters searched all the backyards of the Adelgade and Borgergade neighborhood where the poor Eastern [European] Jews lived."[64] Imagine that: Students actively seeking out Jews to rescue! Exploring the reasons and preconditions for this consensual reaction across class, age, and gender remains an academic and human challenge and privilege. The master narrative may need corrections, but the events in October 1943 and the dedication of the Danish authorities to alleviate the effects of the German persecution of the Danish Jews still stand as one of the finest hours in Danish history.

Notes

1 The most thorough volume on the occupation of Denmark is Claus Bundgård Christensen et al., *Danmark besat. Krig og hverdag 1940–45*, 4th rev. ed. (Occupied Denmark: War and everyday life, 1940–45) (Copenhagen: Informations Forlag, 2015). In English, Nathaniel Hong, *Occupied Denmark's Adaptation and Resistance to German Occupation 1940–1945* (Copenhagen: Frihedsmuseets Venners Forlag, 2012), introduces the exceptional circumstances of the occupation and the cooperation policy.

2 The main and still uncontested work on the events of August 1943 is Hans Kirchhoff, *Augustoprøret 1943. Samarbejdspolitikkens Fald. Forudsætninger og Forløb. En studie i kollaboration og modstand I–III* (The August sedition 1943: The Fall of the cooperation policy—Conditions and process. A study of collaboration and resistance I–III) (Copenhagen: Gyldendal, 1979).

3 Henrik Lundtofte, *Gestapo! Tysk politi og terror i Danmark 1940–45* (The Gestapo! German police and terror in Denmark, 1940–45) (Copenhagen: Gad, 2003).

4 Sofie Lene Bak, *Nothing to Speak of: Wartime Experiences of the Danish Jews 1943–1945* (Copenhagen: Danish Jewish Museum, 2011).

5 For early examples of the narrative, see Torben Meyer, *Flugten over Øresund* (The flight over the Oresund) (Copenhagen: Jespersen & Pio, 1945), and Jørgen Gersfelt, *Saadan narrede vi Gestapo* (How we tricked the Gestapo) (Copenhagen: Gyldendal, 1945).

6 Bjarke Følner, "Memorials and Memorial Culture," in *Nothing to Speak of: Wartime Experiences of the Danish Jews 1943–1945*, by Sofie Lene Bak (Copenhagen: Danish Jewish Museum, 2011), 215–49. As a result, only 22 individual Danes are awarded the honor, most accorded since "the global turn" in public memory by the new millennium. https://www.yadvashem.org/righteous/statistics.html, accessed September 30, 2022.

7 Sofie Lene Bak, *Jødeaktionen oktober 1943. Forestillinger i offentlighed og forskning* (The persecution of the Jews, October 1943: Perceptions in research and public opinion) (Copenhagen: Museum Tusculanum Press, 2001).

8 The German shipping expert Georg Ferdinand Duckwitz played an important role in sabotaging the roundup. As soon as he heard about the planned action, he took steps to obstruct it and mitigate its effect. He is a central character in collective memory of the event, inside as well as outside Denmark. Duckwitz served as the Federal Republic of Germany's ambassador to Denmark after the war and was given the distinction of Righteous Among the Nations by Yad Vashem. He is generally perceived as "the savior of Danish Jews." However, recent research emphasizes that he operated with the consent and within the strategy of the plenipotentiary in Denmark, Werner Best. For a lengthy discussion of the warning given by Best and the relationship between Duckwitz and Best, see Bak, *Jødeaktionen*, and Hans Kirchhoff, *Holocaust i Danmark* (The Holocaust in Denmark) (Odense: University Press of Southern Denmark, 2013).

9 Lundtofte, *Gestapo!*

10 On the case of Gilleleje, see Christian Tortzen, *Gilleleje oktober 1943. Under jødernes flugt for nazismen* (Gilleleje, October 1943: When the Jews fled from Nazism) (Copenhagen: Fremad, 1970).

11 Rasmus Kreth and Michael Mogensen, *Flugten til Sverige. Aktionen mod de danske jøder oktober 1943* (The Escape to Sweden: The persecution of the Danish Jews, October 1943) (Copenhagen: Gyldendal, 1995).

12 Bak, *Nothing to Speak of.*

13 Kreth and Mogensen, *Flugten til Sverige.*

14 For a published collection of testimonies, see Bent Blüdnikow and Klaus Rothstein, eds., *Dage i oktober 43. Vidnesbyrd* (Days in October 1943: Testimonies) (Copenhagen: Centrum/Det Mosaiske Troessamfund, 1993). However, some testimonies by rescuers tell of Jewish refugees reluctant to pay the requested amount; see, e.g., Tortzen, *Gilleleje*; testimony in *Fem Aar. Indtryk og Oplevelser* (Five years: Impressions and

experiences), ed. Christian Refslund and Max Schmidt (Copenhagen: H. Hagerup, 1946), 117.

15 Kreth and Mogensen, *Flugten til Sverige.*

16 For a prominent example, see Aage Bertelsen, *October 1943* (London: Museum Press, 1955).

17 Kreth and Mogensen, *Flugten til Sverige.*

18 The book by Rasmus Kreth and Michael Mogensen, *Flugten til Sverige*, published in 1995, first triggered the newspaper debate; see, e.g., *Weekendavisen*, May 18, 1995, and *Politiken*, May 5, 1995. The debate resurfaced in 2010, when a journalist published a book dedicated to the topic; see Thomas Hjortsø: *Den dyre flugt—pengenes strøm under redningen af de danske jøder i 1943* (The expensive flight: The money supply during the rescue of the Danish Jews in 1943) (Copenhagen: People's Press, 2010).

19 See, e.g., Bo Lidegaard, *Countrymen: The Untold Story of How Denmark's Jews Escaped the Nazis, of the Courage of Their Fellow Danes—and of the Extraordinary Role of the SS* (New York: Knopf, 2013); Denmark in the USA/Ministry of Foreign Affairs of Denmark, "Commemoration of the 70th Year of the Rescue of Danish Jews during World War II," http://usa.um.dk/en/70thcommemoration/ accessed July 4, 2019 (now unavailable).

20 The myth prominently features in the novel *Exodus* by Leon Uris (1958) and appears in Hannah Arendt's *Eichmann in Jerusalem* (1963), as well as in Gerald Reitlinger's *The Final Solution* (1953, and in the 2d ed. from 1961). It is worth mentioning that the passage on the yellow star in *Exodus* was edited out in the 1959 Danish version. "The lovely story" is falsified in Leni Yahil, *The Rescue of Danish Jewry: Test of a Democracy* (Philadelphia: Jewish Publication Society of America, 1969). See also the Holocaust encyclopedia from the United States Holocaust Memorial Museum, https://encyclopedia.ushmm.org/content/en/article/king-christian-x-of-denmark, accessed September 30, 2022. Even the children's book *The Yellow Star*, by Carmen Agra Deedy (Atlanta: Peachtree Publishers Ltd., 2000), debunks the myth in the epilogue.

21 See examples in Bak, *Jødeaktionen.*

22 See Israel Ministry of Foreign Affairs, https://mfa.gov.il/MFA/MFA-Archive/2003/Pages/The%20Righteous%20Among%20the%20Nations.aspx, accessed October 23, 2019, and Yad Vashem https://www.yadvashem.org/righteous/faq.html, accessed September 30, 2022.

23 Memorial plaques to Claus Heilesen have been installed in Taarbaek harbor and at his engineering college in Copenhagen (*Polyteknisk Læreanstalt*, now Copenhagen University). On both plaques he is

commemorated as "Fallen fighting for the freedom of Denmark." The trend of portraying Heilesen as a rescuer began in Aage Bertelsen's memoir, *October 1943*. The narrative is repeated in Kreth and Mogensen, *Flugten til Sverige*, and Lidegaard, *Countrymen*.

24 Sofie Lene Bak, *Da krigen var forbi. De danske jøders hjemkomst efter besættelsen* (When the war was over: The return of the Danish Jews after the occupation) (Copenhagen: Gyldendal, 2012).

25 Bak, *Nothing to Speak of*.

26 Children of the Holocaust gained international recognition at the beginning of the 1990s; see André Stein, *Hidden Children: Forgotten Survivors of the Holocaust* (Toronto: Viking, 1993), and Jane Marks, *The Hidden Children: The Secret Survivors of the Holocaust* (New York: Ballantine Books, 1993).

27 The stories of the hidden children in Denmark are explored in Bak, *Nothing to Speak of*. Interviews with hidden children in Denmark are published in Kirsten Nilsson, *De gemte børn—Beretninger fra anden verdenskrig* (The hidden children: Testimonies from the Second World War) (Copenhagen: Gyldendal, 2012).

28 Pieter Lagrou, "Victims of Genocide and National Memory: Belgium, France and the Netherlands 1945–1965," *Past and Present* 154 (1997): 181–222; Zofia Wóycicka, *Arrested Mourning: Memory of the Nazi Camps in Poland, 1944–1950* (Frankfurt am Main: Peter Lang, 2014); and Joanna Wawryzniak, *Veterans, Victims, and Memory: The Politics of the Second World War in Communist Poland* (Frankfurt am Main: Peter Lang, 2015).

29 Henrik Dethlefsen, *De illegale Sverigesruter 1943–45. Studier i den maritime modstands historie* (The illegal routes to Sweden: Studies of the history of maritime resistance) (Odense: Odense University Press, 1993).

30 Følner, "Memorials." From the late 1950s, groups of veterans of the resistance published multiple periodicals that document the commemorative practice: e.g., *Gestapo-Fangen* (The Gestapo prisoner), *FV-bladet* (Veterans of the fight for freedom), and *Pigtråd* (Barbed wire).

31 Bak, *Jødeaktionen*.

32 Arthur Henriques and Erik Henriques Bing, *Møder i Sverige. Det Mosaiske Troessamfunds forhandlingsprotokol fra flygtningetiden i Sverige 1943–45* (Meetings in Sweden: Minutes of the Jewish community from the exile in Sweden, 1943–45) (Copenhagen: Tågaliden, 2011), 25.

33 See, e.g., the biography of a prominent resistance leader, Morten Møller, *Mogens Fog* (Copenhagen: Gyldendal, 2009).

34 Bak, *Krigen*.
35 Chiefly, the periodical *Dansk Jødisk Historie* (Danish Jewish history; published between 1980 and 1990), from 1992, with the title *Rambam. Tidsskrift for jødisk kultur og forskning* (Rambam: Periodical for Jewish culture and research), published by the Danish Jewish Historical Society (established in 1980); see Bak, *Jødeaktionen*. See also Karl Christian Lammers, "The Holocaust and Collective Memory in Scandinavia: The Danish Case," *Scandinavian Journal of History* 36, no. 5 (2011): 570–86.
36 Følner, "Memorials."
37 On the Raoul Wallenberg Centennial Medal, see https://www.stm.dk/presse/pressemeddelelser/hts-statsministeren-modtager-raoul-wallenberg-medalje/, accessed October 10, 2023.
38 The Danish version of Bo Lidegaard, *Landsmænd* (Countrymen) (Copenhagen: Politikens forlag, 2013), 449.
39 Official statement by the Danish prime minister on the seventy-fifth anniversary in 2018: http://www.stm.dk/_p_14736.html, accessed October 25, 2019 (now unavailable).
40 Irving Greenberg, "The Righteous Rescuers," in *The Courage to Care: Rescuers of Jews during the Holocaust*, ed. Carol Rittner and Sondra Myers (New York: NYU Press, 1986), 3.
41 The underground press coined the term during the war. The politicians themselves preferred the term "policy of negotiation." A third term, "policy of collaboration," was introduced into Danish historiography in 1979 by the historian Hans Kirchhoff but has never gained wide acceptance in either historiography or public debate. Sofie Lene Bak, "Between Tradition and New Departure—The Dilemmas of Collaboration in Denmark," in *Collaboration with the Nazis: Public Discourse after the Holocaust*, ed. Roni Stauber (London: Stephen Roth Institute for the Study of Contemporary Antisemitism and Racism, Tel Aviv University/Routledge, 2010), 110–24.
42 However, the logic of the policy of cooperation did lead the government to accept informal discrimination of Danish Jewish businesses and public employees, the first losing German import and export contracts, the second promotions to public offices; Jakob Halvas Bjerre, "Samarbejdets diskrimination" (Discrimination caused by cooperation), *Rambam. Tidsskrift for jødisk kultur og forskning* 26 (2017): 107–21.
43 Bak, *Jødeaktionen*.
44 Yahil, *The Rescue*, 1969.
45 Silvia Goldbaum Tarabini Fracapane, "Myter og misforståelser om deportationerne til Theresienstadt" (Myths and misconceptions about

the deportations to Theresienstadt), *Rambam. Tidsskrift for jødisk kultur og forskning* 17 (2008).

46 Although the consequences of the visit are disputed and controversial, to the Danish deportees—and to the Germans—the visit signified that the deportees were not forgotten. For a critical approach, see Ingrid Lomfors, *Blind fläck. Minne och glömska kring svenska röda korsets hjälpinsats i Nazityskland 1945* (Blind spot: Memory and oblivion on the relief effort of the Swedish Red Cross in Nazi Germany, 1945) (Stockholm: Bokförlaget Atlantis, 2005), and Silvia Goldbaum Tarabini Fracapane, *The Jews of Denmark in the Holocaust—Life and Death in Theresienstadt Ghetto* (London: Routledge, 2021).

47 Yahil, *The Rescue*, xviii. Although Yahil's idealized conclusions about the moral and democratic standing of the Danes and her assumption of the national spirit as a causal variable have faced much criticism in Denmark, her theory concerning Best's double-dealing remains unchallenged.

48 John T. Lauridsen, "'Særtilfældet'—Tysk besættelsespolitik i Danmark i europæisk perspektiv" ("The special case"—German occupation policy in Denmark in a European perspective), in *Tysk besættelsespolitik i Danmark 1940–1945* (German occupation policy in Denmark, 1940–1945) (Copenhagen: Royal Library/Museum Tusculanum Press, 2013), 151–65.

49 Claus Bundgård Christensen, "'The five evil years': National self-image, commemoration and historiography in Denmark, 1945–2010—Trends in historiography and commemoration," in *Hitler's Scandinavian Legacy: The Consequences of the German Invasion for the Scandinavian Countries, Then and Now*, ed. John Gilmour and Jill Stephenson (London: Bloomsbury Academic, 2013).

50 Report from June 25, 1946, Social Directorate Information Service: The Social Service, 1943–45, Copenhagen City Archive.

51 Bak, *Krigen*.

52 Letter of October 23, 1943, to the Chief Administrative Officers in the Regions in Denmark, from the permanent Under-secretary of the Ministry of Welfare, Archives of the Ministry of Welfare, National Archives.

53 Bak, *Krigen*. The total compensation paid out to Jewish victims under the Law of Compensation to the Victims of the Occupation was 2.2 million Danish crowns by 1958. The present-day value is approximately 30 million Danish crowns. See also Sofie Lene Bak, "Repatriation and Restitution of Holocaust Victims in Post-war Denmark," in *Jewish Studies in the Nordic Countries Today* (*Scripta Instituti Donneriani Aboensis* 27),

ed. Ruth Illman and Björn Dahla (Turku: Turku University Press 2016), 134–52. The law covered only Danish citizens. Stateless Jewish refugees were excluded from compensation whether or not they had a residence permit in Denmark and regardless of their loss.

54 See a prominent example in the memoirs of the chief rabbi Marcus Melchior, *A Rabbi Remembers* (New York: Lyle Stuart, 1968). See, in addition, Blüdnikow and Rothstein, eds., *Dage*, and Bak, *Jødeaktionen*, 109ff.

55 Guidelines for the Handling of Restitution Cases, Restitution Office, box 28, Central Office for Special Affairs, National Archives. For the numerous examples of how the authorities attended to special religious needs, acted as mediator, and supported the Jews' efforts to overcome the consequences of deportation and flight, see Bak, *Krigen*.

56 Daniel Levy and Natan Sznaider, "Memory Unbound: The Holocaust and the Formation of Cosmopolitan Memory," *European Journal of Social Theory* 5, no. 1 (2002): 103.

57 Although in commemorative practices, as Sharon Macdonald argues, cosmopolitan memory does not replace the nation as the framework of interpretation but rather "the nation presenting itself as cosmopolitan through harnessing more widely shared pasts as parts of its own." Sharon Macdonald, *Memorylands: Heritage and Identity in Europe Today* (London: Routledge, 2013), 215. This is illustrated by the Danish case, where the rescuers are ascribed universalized and universally held values as motivation.

58 Sharon Macdonald, *Difficult Heritage: Negotiating the Nazi Past in Nuremberg and Beyond* (London: Routledge Taylor & Francis Group, 2009), 132.

59 Alvin H. Rosenfeld, "The Americanization of the Holocaust," in *End of the Holocaust* (Bloomington: Indiana University Press 2011), 60.

60 Levy and Sznaider, "Memory Unbound," 103.

61 Then prime minister Anders Fogh Rasmussen on the sixtieth anniversary of the liberation in 2005, https://www.stm.dk/statsministeren/taler/statsminister-anders-fogh-rasmussens-tale-i-mindelunden-4-maj-2005/, accessed September 30, 2022.

62 During the war, twenty Jewish refugees were deported from Denmark and sent back to Nazi Germany, where they were sent to concentration or death camps. Eighteen were murdered. See Hans Kirchhoff and Lone Rünitz, *Udsendt til Tyskland. Dansk flygtningepolitik under besættelsen* (Expulsions to Germany: Danish refugee policy during the occupation)

(Odense: Syddansk Universitetsforlag, 2007). In 2000 the newly established Centre for Holocaust and Genocide Studies (DCHF) in Copenhagen was entrusted with the investigation and with organizing an annual Holocaust Remembrance Day and educational activities. However, in 2002 the DCHF was deprived of its independent status and integrated into the Danish Institute for International Studies (DIIS) with a drastically reduced budget; subsequently the research unit for Holocaust and genocide studies was dissolved. Finally, in 2017 DIIS lost the government contract for Holocaust educational activities to a private supplier of teaching materials.

63 Yahil, *The Rescue*, 210, 437.

64 Jørgen Kieler, *Hvorfor gjorde I det?* (Why did you do it?) (Copenhagen: Gyldendal, 2001).

Bibliography

Bak, Sofie Lene. "Between Tradition and New Departure—The Dilemmas of Collaboration in Denmark." In *Collaboration with the Nazis: Public Discourse after the Holocaust*, ed. Roni Stauber, 110–24. London: Stephen Roth Institute for the Study of Contemporary Antisemitism and Racism, Tel Aviv University/ Routledge, 2010.

———. *Da krigen var forbi. De danske jøders hjemkomst efter besættelsen.* (When the war was over: The return of the Danish Jews after the occupation.) Copenhagen: Gyldendal, 2012.

———. *Jødeaktionen oktober 1943. Forestillinger i offentlighed og forskning.* (The persecution of the Jews, October 1943: Perceptions in research and public opinion.) Copenhagen: Museum Tusculanum Press, 2001.

———. *Nothing to Speak of: Wartime Experiences of the Danish Jews 1943–1945.* Copenhagen: Danish Jewish Museum, 2011.

———. "Repatriation and Restitution of Holocaust Victims in Post-war Denmark." In *Jewish Studies in the Nordic Countries Today* (*Scripta Instituti Donneriani Aboensis*, vol. 27), ed. Ruth Illman and Björn Dahla, 134–52. Turku: Turku University Press, 2016.

Bertelsen, Aage. *October 1943*. London: Museum Press, 1955.

Bjerre, Jakob Halvas. "Samarbejdets diskrimination." (Discrimination caused by cooperation.) *Rambam. Tidsskrift for jødisk kultur og forskning* 26 (2017): 107–21.

Blüdnikow, Bent, and Klaus Rothstein, eds. *Dage i oktober 43. Vidnesbyrd.* (Days in October 1943: Testimonies.) Copenhagen: Centrum/Det Mosaiske Troessamfund, 1993.

Bundgård Christensen, Claus. "'The Five Evil Years': National Self-Image, Commemoration and Historiography in Denmark, 1945–2010—Trends in Historiography and Commemoration." In *Hitler's Scandinavian Legacy: The Consequences of the German Invasion for the Scandinavian Countries, Then and Now*, ed. John Gilmour and Jill Stephenson, 147–59. London: Bloomsbury Academic, 2013.

Bundgård Christensen, Claus, Joachim Lund, Niels Wium Olesen, and Jakob Sørensen. *Danmark besat. Krig og hverdag 1940–45*, 4th rev. ed. (Occupied Denmark: War and everyday life, 1940–45.) Copenhagen: Informations Forlag, 2015.

Dethlefsen, Henrik. *De illegale Sverigesruter 1943–45. Studier i den maritime modstands historie.* (The illegal routes to Sweden: Studies of the history of maritime resistance.) Odense: Odense University Press, 1993.

Fracapane, Silvia Goldbaum Tarabini. *The Jews of Denmark in the Holocaust—Life and Death in Theresienstadt Ghetto*. London: Routledge, 2021.

———. "Myter og misforståelser om deportationerne til Theresienstadt." (Myths and misconceptions about the deportations to Theresienstadt.) *Rambam. Tidsskrift for jødisk kultur og forskning* 17, no. 1 (2008): 56–65.

Følner, Bjarke. "Memorials and Memorial Culture." In *Nothing to Speak of: Wartime Experiences of the Danish Jews 1943–1945*, by Sofie Lene Bak, 215–49. Copenhagen: Danish Jewish Museum, 2011.

Gersfelt, Jørgen. *Saadan narrede vi Gestapo*. (How we tricked the Gestapo.) Copenhagen: Gyldendal, 1945.

Henriques, Arthur, and Erik Henriques Bing. *Møder i Sverige. Det Mosaiske Troessamfunds forhandlingsprotokol fra flygtningetiden i Sverige 1943–45.* (Meetings in Sweden: Minutes of the Jewish community from the exile in Sweden, 1943–45.) Copenhagen: Tågaliden, 2011.

Hjortsø, Thomas: *Den dyre flugt—pengenes strøm under redningen af de danske jøder i 1943*. (The expensive flight: The money supply during the rescue of the Danish Jews in 1943.) Copenhagen: People's Press, 2010.

Hong, Nathaniel. *Occupied Denmark's Adaptation and Resistance to German Occupation 1940–1945*. Copenhagen: Frihedsmuseets Venners Forlag, 2012.

Kieler, Jørgen. *Hvorfor gjorde I det?* (Why did you do it?) Copenhagen: Gyldendal 2001.

Kirchhoff, Hans. *Augustoprøret 1943. Samarbejdspolitikkens Fald. Forudsætninger og Forløb. En studie i kollaboration og modstand I–III*. (The August sedition 1943: The fall of the cooperation policy—Conditions and process. A study of collaboration and resistance I–III.) Copenhagen: Gyldendal, 1979.

———. *Holocaust i Danmark*. (Holocaust in Denmark.) Odense: University Press of Southern Denmark, 2013.

Kirchhoff, Hans, and Lone Rünitz. *Udsendt til Tyskland. Dansk flygtningepolitik under besættelsen.* (Expulsions to Germany: Danish refugee policy during the occupation.) Odense: Syddansk Universitetsforlag, 2007.

Kreth, Rasmus, and Michael Mogensen, *Flugten til Sverige. Aktionen mod de danske jøder oktober 1943.* (The escape to Sweden: The persecution of the Danish Jews, October 1943.) Copenhagen: Gyldendal, 1995.

Lagrou, Pieter. "Victims of Genocide and National Memory: Belgium, France and the Netherlands, 1945–1965." *Past and Present* 154 (1997): 181–222.

Lammers, Karl Christian. "The Holocaust and Collective Memory in Scandinavia: The Danish Case." *Scandinavian Journal of History* 36, no. 5 (2011): 570–86.

Lauridsen, John T. *Tysk besættelsespolitik i Danmark 1940–1945.* (German occupation policy in Denmark, 1940–45.) Copenhagen: Royal Library/Museum Tusculanum Press, 2013.

Levy, Daniel, and Natan Sznaider, "Memory Unbound: The Holocaust and the Formation of Cosmopolitan Memory." *European Journal of Social Theory* 5, no. 1 (2002): 87–106.

Lidegaard, Bo. *Countrymen: The Untold Story of How Denmark's Jews Escaped the Nazis, of the Courage of Their Fellow Danes—and of the Extraordinary Role of the SS.* New York: Knopf, 2013.

———. *Landsmænd.* (Countrymen.) Copenhagen: Politikens forlag, 2013.

Lomfors, Ingrid. *Blind fläck. Minne och glömska kring svenska röda korsets hjälpinsats i Nazityskland 1945.* (Blind spot: Memory and oblivion on the relief effort of the Swedish Red Cross in Nazi Germany, 1945.) Stockholm: Bokförlaget Atlantis, 2005.

Lundtofte, Henrik. *Gestapo! Tysk politi og terror i Danmark 1940–45.* (The Gestapo! German police and terror in Denmark, 1940–45.) Copenhagen: Gad, 2003.

Macdonald, Sharon. *Difficult Heritage: Negotiating the Nazi Past in Nuremberg and Beyond.* London: Routledge Taylor & Francis Group, 2009.

———. *Memorylands: Heritage and Identity in Europe Today.* London: Routledge, 2013.

Marks, Jane. *The Hidden Children: The Secret Survivors of the Holocaust.* New York: Ballantine Books, 1993.

Melchior, Marcus. *A Rabbi Remembers.* New York: Lyle Stuart, 1968.

Meyer, Torben. *Flugten over Øresund.* (The flight over the Oresund.) Copenhagen: Jespersen & Pio, 1945.

Møller, Morten. *Mogens Fog.* Copenhagen: Gyldendal, 2009.

Nilsson, Kirsten. *De gemte børn—Beretninger fra anden verdenskrig.* (The hidden children: Testimonies from the Second World War.) Copenhagen: Gyldendal, 2012.

Refslund, Christian, and Max Schmidt, eds. *Fem Aar. Indtryk og Oplevelser.* (Five years: Impressions and experiences.) Copenhagen: H. Hagerup, 1946.

Rittner, Carol, and Sondra Myers, eds. *The Courage to Care: Rescuers of Jews during the Holocaust.* New York: NYU Press, 1986.

Rosenfeld, Alvin H. *End of the Holocaust.* Bloomington: Indiana University Press 2011.

Stein, André. *Hidden Children: Forgotten Survivors of the Holocaust.* Toronto: Viking, 1993.

Tortzen, Christian. *Gilleleje oktober 1943. Under jødernes flugt for nazismen.* (Gilleleje, October 1943: When the Jews fled from Nazism.) Copenhagen: Fremad, 1970.

Wawryzniak, Joanna. *Veterans, Victims, and Memory: The Politics of the Second World War in Communist Poland.* Frankfurt am Main: Peter Lang, 2015.

Wóycicka, Zofia. *Arrested Mourning: Memory of the Nazi Camps in Poland, 1944–1950.* Frankfurt am Main: Peter Lang, 2014.

Yahil, Leni *The Rescue of Danish Jewry: Test of a Democracy.* Philadelphia: Jewish Publication Society of America, 1969.

3

The Rescue of the Macedonian Jews during World War II

Between Collective Agency and Individual Stories

NAUM TRAJANOVSKI

"The Holocaust in Macedonia shall never be forgotten. We are stressing loud and clear that we will never forget the Holocaust, we will never allow it to be denied and we will never let the historical facts be distorted," stated North Macedonia's speaker of the parliament, Talat Džaferi, in his commemorative speech on March 11, 2018, the annual day of mourning for the 7,144 Macedonian Jews deported to the Treblinka extermination camp in 1943.[1] The following day, the Macedonian parliament issued a declaration condemning the Holocaust and "all the other forms of genocide and human rights violations such as antisemitism, discrimination, hate speech, xenophobia, exclusion and racism."[2] The same day, the former prime minister Boyko Borisov became the first high-ranking Bulgarian official to attend a Holocaust remembrance event in Skopje—laying flowers at the memorial site of the tobacco warehouse (Maced., Monopol), the former temporary detention center for Macedonian Jewry, and participating in Skopje's "March of the Living."[3] The initiative, generally applauded by the public in both Bulgaria and North Macedonia, should be seen in the context of the signing of the Bulgarian-Macedonian Friendship Treaty in August 2017. Apart from economic partnership, the treaty envisioned a bilateral historical commission (a joint commission) and joint commemorations of shared historical figures and commemorative events.[4]

Borisov's act, however, did not mark a breakthrough in Bulgarian-Macedonian relations. In October 2019, all the parties in the Bulgarian parliament backed an "Explanatory Memorandum" that accused North Macedonia of "ethnic and linguistic engineering" after 1944, state-sponsoring "anti-Bulgarian ideology," and failing to acknowledge their understanding of "joint history."[5] The memorandum was circulated among European Union institutions, and it soon became the rationale behind Bulgaria's refusal to allow North Macedonia to begin EU accession talks in the following years. The Bulgarian veto was eventually lifted in June 2022, after negotiations between Bulgaria and North Macedonia orchestrated by the French presidency of the EU Council. The weaponization of history and memory in the public discourses in both countries, in turn, not only blocked the work of the joint commission but also hindered the bilateral dialogue. In Skopje, the political opposition mobilized to reject the so-called French proposal for resolving the stalemate. The protestors argued against alleged concessions relating to ethnic Macedonian identity, language, and constitution which the Republic of North Macedonia would have to make in the coming accession negotiations with the EU. In Bulgaria the governmental coalition cracked over the North Macedonia dispute, as the leader of the populist party, Slavi Trifonov, announced he would leave the government after Prime Minister Kiril Petkov revealed his plans to lift the veto.[6]

As one of the most contested issues, the deportation of 7,144 Macedonian Jews to Treblinka in March 1943 reemerged in this period. In brief, the Bulgarian side—via the Bulgarian members of the joint commission—reacted to the description of a "Bulgarian fascist occupation of Macedonia" during World War II in Macedonian textbooks and memorials, which claimed that the kingdom of Bulgaria was a "pro-Nazi" or a "pro-fascist" state.[7] This Bulgarian critique, in turn, provoked various critical reactions among the Macedonian public; some suggested that the asymmetric bilateral negotiations facilitated by the EU would result in whitewashing the role of the Bulgarian state in the Holocaust. A statement to that effect was jointly issued in December 2020 by the Jewish community in the Republic of North Macedonia (Maced., Evrejska zaednica vo Republika Severna Makedonija) and the Holocaust Fund of the Jews of Macedonia (Maced., Fond na holokaustot na Evreite od Makedonija), which urged the Bulgarian authorities to acknowledge international Holocaust scholarship and "apologize and claim responsibility" for the killing of the Macedonian Jews.[8] In September 2021, the Jewish community and the Holocaust Fund published another statement that disapproved of the deletion of the term "Bulgarian" before "fascist occupation" in Macedonian textbooks and memorial plaques. A more precise solution, according to the joint statement, would be to add "erstwhile" and "government" to every reference to wartime Bulgaria.[9] These tensions did not calm down with the lifting of the Bulgarian veto, however. The Bulgarian government continued to sponsor the newly opened Bulgarian cultural clubs in North Macedonia that were named after pro-Nazi political activists, including the "Vančo Mihajlov" club in Bitola. The Macedonian Jewish organizations' reactions were, again, among the most vocal, now urging the authorities in North Macedonia to check the legal justification and validity of the Bulgarian clubs.[10]

This essay aims to discuss the narratives pertaining to the rescue of Macedonian Jews, exploring how wartime experiences were handled in the Macedonian cultures of remembrance after World War II. The chapter will provide an outline of the evolution of the Macedonian rescue narratives by looking at how these stories have been presented, from the early historiographic writings in the 1950s until the most recent public debates. I will also analyze how the rescue stories are being told in the two permanent exhibitions opened at the Holocaust Memorial Center for the Jews of Macedonia in Skopje (HMC) in 2011 and 2019. The establishment of the HMC in 2011 will be highlighted as a critical juncture in the development of Holocaust memory in North Macedonia. I discuss the HMC focusing not only on museum exhibitions but also on the public reception of the HMC and the debates related to the museum.[11] I will also look at these materials against the background of the recent developments in relations between Bulgaria and North Macedonia, highlighting, as well, organizations and institutions that stepped up as leading "memory agents" of the Holocaust in North Macedonia.[12] The first of these is the Macedonian Jewish community, which has played a key role in organizing commemorations of the Shoah since 1946, publishing Jewish accounts of the rescue in the late 1980s and establishing the HMC. Likewise, several veterans' organizations have been and continue to be significant stakeholders in the memorialization of World War II across North Macedonia. I argue that the many and various references to rescue stories in North Macedonia illuminate not only the modes of remembering, commemorating, and memorializing the Holocaust of the Macedonian Jews, but also the negotiation of Holocaust memory by historians, curators, and decisionmakers in the spatial context of southeast Europe.

Historical Background

The Axis powers' attack on Yugoslavia was launched on April 6, 1941, and the unconditional surrender of the Royal Yugoslav Army was signed on April 17, 1941. The Bulgarian army invaded the Vardar Banate (Maced., Vardarska

Banovina) and a portion of eastern Serbia on April 19, 1941, while on May 14, 1941, it annexed western Thrace and eastern Aegean Macedonia (today's Northern Greece). The Yugoslav province of Vardar Banate, which roughly translates into the territory of today's North Macedonia, was divided and put under Bulgarian, German, and Italian administration: The western part of the region was administered by Italian forces in the first years of the war, while Bulgarian state administration was installed in the territory of the other major part of today's North Macedonia. German forces established army headquarters and "head offices for the exploitation of the mines and the railroads in Skopje."[13] As a result, the multiethnic and multiconfessional population of the most economically underdeveloped region of interwar Yugoslavia experienced a radically new political reality. In the major part of Vardar Macedonia, the locals, facilitated by the already initiated pro-Bulgarian action committees (Maced., Bugarski centralni akcioni komiteti), saluted the Bulgarian troops as liberators from Serbian rule. However, this political sentiment gradually changed due to the rigorous cultural and identity policies pursued by the Bulgarian authorities, which were aimed at integrating the local Slavic population into the Bulgarian *ethnie*. Local resistance would eventually culminate in the formation of the Communist Party of Macedonia (CPM) in 1943, as well as broad support for the cause promoted by Tito's partisans in the two final years of World War II.

The Macedonian Jews, alongside the Macedonian Roma and Turks, were in a considerably worse position than the ethnic Macedonians.[14] Even though "the decrees restricting the rights of the Jews" had been introduced by the First Yugoslav Cvetković-Maček government as early as 1940, the community of more than 7,700 Macedonian Jews duly became subjected to a new set of antisemitic and racist laws after falling under Bulgarian jurisdiction.[15] On February 22, 1943, Theodor Dannecker, the Reich Central Security Office's representative in Bulgaria, and Aleksandar Belev, the head of the Commissariat for Jewish Affairs, signed an agreement to deport twenty thousand Jews from the "new Bulgarian territories of Thrace and Macedonia," with "no reference" to the Jews from the "old" territories of Bulgaria proper.[16] The regional representatives of the Commissariat for Jewish Affairs monitored the arrests carried out by the Bulgarian police and army, "supported by members of the state-run Brannik Youth."[17] The Macedonian Jews from Bitola, Skopje, Štip, and the smaller Jewish settlements were rounded up on the night of March 10, and deported by rail to the Treblinka extermination camp between March 22 and 29, 1943. Given that these deportations were "implemented swiftly, with no advance warning," the Jewish victims had very limited opportunities to escape and find a safe haven, contrary to the Jews from Bulgaria proper, who managed to avoid deportation thanks to the protests by a group of politicians and the Orthodox Christian religious authorities.[18] In the aftermath of the war, an estimated 196 Jews returned to the former People's Republic of Macedonia. Among them, 116 returned from hiding in neighboring Albania and Italy, 65 from detention centers in Bulgaria, 15 as former prisoners of war in Germany, and 20 from the partisan units.[19]

The Rescue Narratives in Macedonian Historiography

The first scholarly publications on the Holocaust in Macedonia appeared in the late 1950s.[20] In 1957 a book titled *The Crimes of the Fascist Occupants and Their Collaborators against Jews in Yugoslavia*, edited by Zdenko Löwenthal and published by the Belgrade-based Federation of Jewish Communities of the Federal People's Republic of Yugoslavia (FJC; Serbo-Croat., Savez jevrejskih opština Jugoslavije), presented the results of a late 1940s state-sponsored documentation project on the wartime crimes against Yugoslav Jewry.[21] The three-hundred-page study only touched on Macedonian Jewry's history during World War II *en passant*, as a five-page account on the political background of the period "from the occupation to the detainment of all Macedonian Jews."[22] As observed by historian Holly Case, Löwenthal's failure to acknowledge the involvement of the Macedonian Jews in the Yugoslav People's Liberation War (Maced., Narodnoosloboduvačka borba) set the tone of early Macedonian historiography on the Holocaust.[23] Shortly afterward, in 1958, the Macedonian medievalist and former partisan fighter Aleksandar Matkovski published a lengthy article in *Glasnik*, the official periodical of the Institute of National History, titled "The Tragedy of the Jews from Macedonia."[24] In 1958 the Yugoslav Federation of Jewish Communities praised the article, and an English translation of the text appeared in Yad Vashem's yearbook in 1959.[25]

However, as noted by Stefan Troebst, "With Matkovski's publications, the subject of the Holocaust was opened and at the same time closed again in Macedonian historiography."[26] Only in the 1980s did the Holocaust reemerge as a subject of analysis in the works of Macedonian historians. Matkovski published *A History of the Jews in Macedonia* in 1982, and Jamila Kolonomos and Vera Veskoviḱ-Vangeli's two-volume collection of wartime documents pertaining to the deportation of the Macedonian Jews appeared just four years later.[27] There are various theories why the Holocaust was neglected by scholars prior to the 1980s. Nadège Ragaru ascribes this vacuum in historical research to the absence of Macedonian Jewish voices in the wake of the Holocaust;[28] Troebst points to the deterioration of Yugoslav-Israeli and Yugoslav-Bulgarian relations in the 1960s;[29] while Jovan Ḱulibrk stresses the link to the Yugoslav context of the production of historical knowledge.[30] Postwar Yugoslav historiography overlooked the interethnic wartime cleavages in order to preserve Yugoslavia's founding myth of "brotherhood and unity," a policy that sought to avoid jeopardizing the postwar multiethnic state-building project.[31] The impact of these limitations on historical research was even more severe in the Macedonian context, as there was only one institution entitled to carry out research on Macedonian history—the Institute of National History in Skopje, founded in 1948.[32]

The earliest narratives about Jewish rescue in Macedonian historiography ascribed agency to the Communist Party of Yugoslavia (CPY) and the Communist Party of Macedonia (CPM). The first rescue story was published by the Institute of National History in 1976. It was an eyewitness account of roundups and deportations from the town of Štip by Isak Sion, titled "Participation of the Jews from Štip in the Peoples' Liberation Movement from Štip" (Maced., Učestvoto na Evreite od Štip vo narodnoosloboditelnoto dviženje). Sion, a member of the Communist Party and after the war a member of the first Macedonian government, saw the Bulgarian police tanking up with suspiciously large quantities of petrol on March 9, 1943, and suspected "some sort of activity against the Jews [who were associated with] the illegal and discredited communists." Himself of Jewish origin, he strove to mobilize the local Jewish community and the local party branch to convince the locals to search for hiding places, a task which, according to Sion, was successful in the case of only one of his Jewish comrades.[33] Sion, however, did not question the role of the party drawing on this episode: He positioned it at the center of wartime resistance, claiming it was instrumental in mobilizing the multiethnic Macedonian population against the occupiers.

This function of the partisan movement was made official on August 4, 1944, shortly after the initial military success and the consolidation of the liberated territories in today's western North Macedonia, when the CPM's Central Committee issued its "Proclamation to the Peoples and Nationalities in Macedonia" (Maced., Proglasi). The part dedicated to "national minorities," or the Macedonian Albanians, Turks, Vlachs, and Jews, restates the "brotherhood and unity" ideal and announces that the minority groups should "contribute a lot" to the formation of the new fatherland—the Macedonian state within the democratic and federal Yugoslavia.[34] This view became a normative trope, in contrast to individual rescue stories and the failed attempts of the Communist Party to provide safe havens during the roundups. It crystallized as a focal point of the official historiographic narrative of the rescue of Macedonian Jews, and in the 1980s it became the key reference point in the wartime history of Macedonian Jews. Thus the Communist Party was depicted as the sole rescue facilitator for Macedonian Jews—a discourse based on the considerable support of the Macedonian Jewish community for the communist parties of Yugoslavia and of Macedonia, as well as the significant number of Jews who had joined the armed resistance.

The two cornerstones of Macedonian Holocaust studies, Matkovski's *A History of the Jews in Macedonia* and *The Jews in Macedonia during World War II (1941–1945)*, the latter authored by Kolonomos and Vesković-Vangeli, also helped to establish a narrative about the rescue of Macedonian Jews. Their focus was on the collective agency of the CPM in the rescue of Macedonian Jews, while individual stories of Jews who managed to escape the Holocaust were mentioned only briefly. Drawing on Bulgarian archival materials and the report of the Yugoslav State Commission, Matkovski listed a number of names of Macedonian rescuers, some of them already recognized as Righteous Among the Nations by Yad Vashem, others not.[35] Kolonomos and Vesković-Vangeli published a slightly longer account and a more comprehensive picture of those Macedonian Jews who escaped the Holocaust by fleeing to Greece and Albania, naming almost all of them, as well as discussing the local developments in the three Macedonian cities with significant prewar Jewish communities.[36] The two studies also touched on the cases of the Jewish physicians and pharmacists who were released from the Skopje detention camp due to the demand for qualified members of these professions. Following their release, these people were dispersed across the territory of wartime Bulgaria, along with their families.[37]

Moreover, from the early 1970s to the mid-1980s, three conferences took place in Skopje, leading to the publication of the three-volume study *Skopje in the People's Liberation War*.[38] Besides the general effort to position the postwar Macedonian capital city as the center of the antifascist struggle, the attendees of these conferences unequivocally confirmed the already established narrative of "brotherhood and unity" among the Skopjans, as well as the unifying role played by the Communist Party in the course of World War II and the support it gave to Skopje's Jews. At the same time, Skopje's Jews were accused of "passivity" and a reluctance to join the armed resistance movement. Mustafa Karahasan, a former member of the party in Skopje and a famed postwar novelist, explained this reluctance as due to a "fear of repercussions" against the Jewish community. According to Karahasan, the two meetings of the party members and the members of the Skopje's Jewish community in 1941 were unsuccessful in bringing about an agreement that would ensure the support of Skopje's Jews for the armed resistance.[39]

The three Skopje-based conferences can be viewed as the culmination of the narrative ascribing a collective effort to save the Macedonian Jews to the CPY and

CPM. This discourse, promoted by official state institutions, functioned as a legitimizing tool in the Yugoslav state-building process. Moreover, the state-founding "anti-fascist myth" of a struggle against Nazism and fascism neglected alternative historical interpretations and considered working through the past as a nonissue. Similar to the developments in the postwar German Democratic Republic noted by Jacqueline Nießer, Yugoslav Macedonia perceived the very establishment of the state as an act that overcame any historical issues "by its mere existence."[40] The various episodes of rescue of Jews in Yugoslavia during World War II were hence subordinated to the motives of a joint struggle against the wartime enemies. The rescue narratives were also formatted on the major partisan operation of rescuing two thousand Jews from an Italian camp for Jews in the autumn of 1943. However, as Emil Kerenji notes, the communist primary sources highlight the joint antifascist struggle and do not speak of rescuing or saving Jews.[41] The Yugoslav communist leadership, moreover, was not prone to antisemitism, "unlike in the Soviet Union, and certainly unlike in Poland and Hungary," and the Yugoslav communists "had no experience of anti-Semitic Communist Party purges."[42]

The first responses to the notions of Jewish "passivity" and the heroic stance of the CPM in the rescue of Macedonian Jews appeared in the 1980s with the publication of the first Jewish wartime biographies and autobiographies. These discourses came against the background of Jaša Romano's book on the Yugoslav Jews in the years 1941 to 1944, published in Belgrade in 1980, where he argued that the CPM underperformed in "working with the Jews," although the Macedonian Jews were mostly sympathetic to the communists and actively helping the resistance.[43] Ženi Lebl's chapter, dedicated to the rescue of Macedonian Jews, from her book *Tide and Wreck* (Maced., *Plima i Slom*), provides another clear counterpoint to the rescue narratives promoted by the Communist Party. An Israeli-based Serbian Jew who had experienced detention in Yugoslavia, Lebl actively engaged in "destroying the fame of the Bulgarians and Tsar Boris as saviors of Jews."[44] Lebl's book, originally published in Hebrew in 1986 and translated into Serbian in 1990, focuses on the stories of the Macedonian Righteous Among the Nations, mentioning, as well, affiliates of the Bulgarian authorities, Spanish and Italian diplomats, and Albanian rescuers—all of them active in the rescue of Macedonian Jewry. She also questions the notion of Jewish passivity by stressing that the Jewish community provided substantial support, safe havens, and financial aid to the Communist Party in its formative period, prior to the establishment of the CPM and during the intraparty purges in 1941 and 1942. Lebl writes that the argument that the "Jews were called to join the resistance, but they failed to appear" is "particularly hurtful"—since the "facts are completely opposite."[45]

The party's failure to mobilize the local Jews was highlighted by Jamila Kolonomos in her autobiography.[46] Even though she praised the partisan struggle and the People's Liberation War, Kolonomos shed light on the complexities in the cooperation between the Jewish community and the Macedonian wartime resistance.[47] A Francophone herself, Kolonomos joined the partisans in 1941 and "worked her way up from being a deputy company political officer, that of a battalion, then of a brigade, eventually becoming deputy political commissioner of the 42nd Division of the Yugoslav Army."[48] The prehistory of her work is particularly interesting, as she coauthored a paper on the linguistic features of the Judeo-Spanish in Bitola with her Sorbonne supervisor, Israel Revah, in 1963 and wrote the first ethnographic study on Macedonian Jews of Sephardic origin as early as 1978. She also coauthored one of the two major studies of the destruction of Macedonian Jewry during the Holocaust, before focusing her research on personal accounts of the Holocaust and individual rescue stories in the 1990s.[49]

Over the last three decades, the discursive struggle between the official narrative of rescue and the individual rescue stories in North Macedonia shifted from historiography to the fields of museology and public remembrance. To illustrate this, I will discuss five temporary exhibitions presented in the Museum of the City of Skopje (Maced., Muzej na grad Skopje) and the Museum of Macedonia (Maced., Muzej na Makedonija) in Skopje from the 1980s up until the early 2000s in the next section. There have been several recent attempts, however, to instigate a debate over the role of the party in the rescue of the Macedonian Jews. Once such attempt was a 2019 publication by Todor Čepreganov, one of the leading Macedonian historians of World War II, where he called for a general "reconsideration" of the role of the party in the rescue of Macedonian Jews. Čepreganov stressed that, due to "both objective and subjective reasons, political and military circumstances," the rescue of Macedonian Jews was "hindered" in wartime Macedonia. As for the Communist Party, he wrote, "It is quite clear [that] even in the cities with considerable Jewish populations, the partisan organization [PO] was clueless on how to save the Jews."[50] However, there was no followup to this text, and it failed to provoke a debate among the Macedonian historians.

Museum Representations of the Holocaust and Macedonian Jews

The reactions to the official rescue narrative promoted by former PO members in the late 1980s and early 1990s coincided with a period of major sociopolitical change in North Macedonia. Even though it was successful in avoiding getting entangled in the Yugoslav Wars (1991–95), the state failed to address the key transitional issues of the early 1990s, which alongside the Greek embargo (1994) and the Kosovo War (1995–99) "undermined the internal fragile inter-ethnic balance" in Macedonia.[51] The interethnic tensions culminated in an armed conflict between Macedonian forces and Albanian radicals in 2001.

The displays from the 1980s dedicated to the history of Macedonian Jews and the Holocaust exhibited the wartime Jewish fate in the context of the victory of the partisan units, thus appropriating the general historiographic trope of interpreting the Macedonian experience of World War II. One part of the exhibition "The Tragedy of Macedonian Jewry" (Maced., Tragedijata na makedonskite Evrei), shown at the Museum of the City of Skopje in 1980 and organized by Skopje's Union of Veteran Organizations (Maced., Sojuz na borečkite organizacii na Skopje), was entirely dedicated to the "victory of the anti-fascist forces" from a global perspective. The section on the antifascist victory was preceded by another section on the deportations of the Macedonian Jews which did not refer to the rescue stories at all.[52] In a similar manner, the 1981 exhibition titled "11 March 1943" (Maced., 11 mart 1943) and the 1988 exhibition "45 Years after the Deportation of the Macedonian Jews" (Maced., 45 godini od deportiranjeto na makedonskite Evrei), presented in the Museum of the City of Skopje, focused above all on the decimation of Macedonian Jewry. The exhibitions did not mention the Jews who managed to escape the Holocaust, or the people who aided them.[53]

Against this backdrop, the exhibition that opened at the Museum of the City of Skopje in 1994, "The Jews in Macedonia" (Maced., Evreite vo Makedonija), can be read as a narrative shift in the representation of the Holocaust in post-Yugoslav Macedonia. The exhibition had a more ethnographic character and depicted the Jewish presence in Macedonia and the everyday peaceful coexistence of the multiethnic and multiconfessional Macedonian population prior to World War II.[54] Thus this exhibition anticipated the new post-Yugoslav paradigm of presenting the history of the Macedonian Jews and the Holocaust, shifting from the narrative of the "common struggle" under communist leadership to a story of multicultural Macedonian heritage. While in Yugoslav Macedonia the Holocaust was instrumentalized to legitimize the PO, CPM, and the CPY, in the post-Yugoslav period it was adjusted to new domestic and international political circumstances. The two major museum events organized in 2003 on the sixtieth anniversary of the deportation of the Macedonian Jews illustrate the aforementioned dynamics. The first was the opening of the temporary exhibition "The Echo of the Macedonian Sephardim" (Maced., Ehoto na makedonskite Sefardi) at the Museum of Macedonia. The display highlighted the "continuity" of the Jewish presence on Macedonian soil.[55] As formulated by Bojan Ivanov, the former director of the museum, the exhibition was "dedicated to the future" and was intended to express the idea that the "two nations, the Macedonian and the Jewish [. . .], suffered together for thousands of years, but never lost their national consciousness, their spirit."[56] The second temporary exhibition opened in 2003, titled "The Phoenix Trail" (Maced., Po tragite na Feniksot), was organized by the Museum of the City of Skopje. The introduction to the exhibition catalog outlined its narrative strategy, opening with the statement: "On this day, we remember the pain and the horrors, horrors we are not guilty of, yet we must memorize them in our minds and not let them happen again."[57] This account contains all three components of the official Macedonian Holocaust narrative: The Holocaust is presented as the ultimate tragedy of a Macedonian ethnic and religious minority group; it is used to champion peace in postconflict North Macedonia; and finally, it serves to assign the sole responsibility for the crimes to others, namely Nazi Germany and especially neighboring Bulgaria.

The Holocaust Memorial Center for the Jews of Macedonia in Skopje

The founding of the Holocaust Memorial Center for the Jews of Macedonia in Skopje (Maced., Memorijalen centar na holokaustot na Evreite od Makedonija) constitutes a break from the Yugoslav Macedonian official Holocaust narrative, and a reaction to the Holocaust exhibitions from the 1990s and the early 2000s. The institution itself can be interpreted, in Barbara Kirshenblatt-Gimblett's term, as a European Jewish museum that is an "imperfect fit." Herein, if the "perfect-fit cases are essentially success stories—the success of the immigrant Jewish communities or the success of the State of Israel," the imperfect-fit museums aim at recovering the "stories of success that have been overshadowed by the failure represented by the Holocaust and the persisting stigma of antisemitic stereotypes."[58] The proposal to build a Holocaust Memorial Center in North Macedonia was advanced by a number of predominantly Macedonian Jewish actors. According to Kolonomos's personal account, the initial idea of establishing the HMC was formulated by Ivan Dejanov, the former president of the Macedonian-Israeli Friendship Society, and it was immediately endorsed by the Macedonian Jewish community.[59] Shortly afterward, the plans received a significant political response. In the late 1990s, the Macedonian parliament discussed the question of restitution of Jewish property. The debate was concluded in 2002 with the adoption of the Denationalization Law (Maced., Zakon za denacionalizacija), which also acted as a legal basis for the formation of the Holocaust Fund of the Jews from Macedonia (April 23, 2002). The fund was intended to be an institutional body for safeguarding the property rights of the deported Jews who had no living heirs, as well as a legal entity for developing the concept of and running the HMC—the first such museum in the region.[60] The HMC was finally inaugurated on March 10, 2011. The content of the first permanent exhibition was developed by a team of internationally renowned museum-design experts, under the leadership of Michael Berenbaum and Edward Jacobs. As stated in a brochure published by the HMC in 2014, the institution is dedicated to "cultivating Jewish culture and tradition" and "researching the life and work of the Jews in the region."[61] However, the program of the HMC, similar to the programs and agendas of Holocaust museums elsewhere, was far from being "shaped in a vacuum."[62] The main mission of the museum was "presenting, educating and researching multiethnic societies, freeing them from any kinds of danger coming from various forms of intolerance, chauvinism, antisemitism" and thus, "aiming to build a society in which ethnic and religious diversity will present a civilizational asset and a basis for further prosperity." Therefore, the HMC recognized the need for postconflict reconciliation in North Macedonia.

The museum is located at the center of the former Jewish quarter in Skopje (Maced., Evrejsko maalo), near the historical and present-day city center. Thus the academic debate over the HMC has, up until now, focused on the institution's links to its surroundings and the history of the Jewish quarter.[63] The exhibition narrative itself remained surprisingly under-researched, both in the wake of its inauguration in 2011 and after the opening of the new permanent exhibition in 2019. Both exhibitions were created by the same experts. In 2016 the Holocaust Fund of the Jews from Macedonia published Michael Berenbaum's booklet, *The Jews in Macedonia during World War II*, which can be read as a catalog of the first permanent exhibition at the HMC. In the introduction Berenbaum deconstructs the categories of perpetrators, victims, collaborators, bystanders, rescuers, and resistors, which are used to classify the behavior of individuals and collective agents during the Holocaust. He also questions the classification of Bulgaria as a "defiant" state. As stated by Berenbaum, Bulgaria's role in the Holocaust, "part murderer, part persecutor, part rescuer," and the story of the Macedonian Jews, who alongside the Jews of Thrace "faced each stage of the Holocaust," would all need to be redefined in the Macedonian museum.[64] The rescue stories thus lie at the core of the exhibition narrative at the HMC, enabling the "complexity of the stories of those who were rescued, as well as the rescuers," to be explored. This claim resonates with another article authored by Berenbaum, where he also calls for a contextualization of the rescue stories. In Berenbaum's words, "If there are 22,000 men and women honored by

Yad Vashem for their efforts to save Jews, there are at least 22,000 stories" that are essential to be told, as a crucial counterbalance to the "unrelenting story of evil and despair that is the core of the Holocaust."[65]

The Rescue Stories in the HMC's New Permanent Exhibition

In March 2010 the wartime Catholic bishop of Skopje, Dr. Smiljan Franjo Čekada, was recognized as Righteous Among the Nations, with the certificate and the medal presented to his brother, Vladimir, at the official inauguration of the HMC in March the following year. Čekada not only actively protested against the detention of Macedonian Jewry in March 1943, he also opened the premises of the Catholic church in Skopje to five Jewish children. This event illustrates the HMC's policy of promoting individual rescue stories as well as providing a platform for the stories of the Macedonian Righteous Among the Nations. The lives of the ten Macedonian Righteous Among the Nations recognized until now play a crucial role in the center's public and educational activities. For example, in 2017 the HMC took part in the coproduction, alongside the Macedonian public broadcaster, of a three-part documentary film on the history of Macedonian Jewry, with the final part dedicated exclusively to the Macedonian Righteous Among the Nations. In 2018 the HMC hosted a temporary exhibition titled "The Lost Sephardic World of the Western Balkans," a joint effort of HMC and Centropa. The exhibition documented the story of Bogoja Siljanovski, who hid five Jewish children during the roundup in Skopje in March 1943. The exhibition placed the rescue of the Macedonian Jews in a wider context by presenting similar stories from other parts of former Yugoslavia, including Belgrade, Zagreb, and Dubrovnik. The rescue stories were displayed alongside a presentation on the resistance by Yugoslav Jews, in the section "Resistance and Rescue." The narrative here was straightforward, stressing that, out of the very few Western Balkan Jews who survived World War II, "almost all of those who did were rescued by neighbors or strangers, joined the partisans, or fled to Italy. [. . .] Jews fleeing to Albania were often protected by local Muslims."[66] The theme of Albanian rescuers, novel to the Macedonian public, was further pursued by the HMC. For instance, in March 2019 the HMC organized a lecture by the Macedonian historian Besnik Emini titled "The Jewish Refugees in Albania during World War II."

The new 2019 multimedia exhibition brings a more nuanced discourse on the rescuing activities in Macedonia. The section "Hiding and Rescue" names three ways of escaping the Holocaust: "those who hid or were rescued by neighbors or strangers, those who fought with the partisans and survived, and those who were rescued because they were physicians and pharmacists or foreign nationals of Axis or neutral countries." This section follows a part of the exhibition dedicated to the partisan struggle, which describes the "unique history of the resistance in Yugoslavia, with the Jews as its integral part," while the next section is titled "Tragedy and Triumph" and deals with the experiences of Macedonian Jews in the immediate postwar years. The "Hiding and Rescue" section presents the stories of the ten Macedonian Righteous Among the Nations in the context of the "total moral collapse"—endorsing them as "ordinary people [who,] acting out of political, ideological or religious convictions [. . .], mustered extraordinary courage to uphold human values." Moreover, the exhibition displays a wall of bystanders—a set of blurred onlookers—on the left side of the corridor stairs linking the museum section dedicated to prewar history to the section depicting World War II and the Holocaust. The bystanders trope had been completely missing from Macedonian historiography, and prior to the publication of Lebl and Kolonomos's works was rarely publicly discussed. The exhibition also presents the persecuted Jews not as passive victims but as protagonists of the story in their own right. For example, it tells the stories of Jews who hid in the countryside, fled to Albania, or joined the resistance. At the same time the exhibition also increases the number of rescuers by bringing in stories of gentile aid-providers not yet recognized as Righteous Among the Nations.

The HMC and Bulgarian-Macedonian Relations (2010–19)

The reception of the HMC in Macedonia was conditioned by the immediate national and regional political contexts. Postconflict (North) Macedonia pursued European integration and NATO membership as its main political objectives, in the hope that both would also consolidate its multicultural society. However, after the 2008 Greek veto of North Macedonia's full NATO accession, the then ruling center-right coalition led by the Internal Macedonian Revolutionary Organization–Democratic Party for Macedonian National Unity (IMRO–DPMNU) (Maced., Vnatrešna makedonska revolucionerna organizacija–Demokratska partija za makedonsko nacionalno edinstvo) put the promotion of an ethnic Macedonian national identity at the top of its political agenda. This policy culminated in the "Skopje 2014" project, an umbrella term endorsing the 137 monuments and memorials erected in Skopje's city center in the early 2010s. The HMC, despite being on the margins of this memory policy, physically found itself in the midst of a new memorial landscape. The former Jewish quarter was surrounded by the new Museum of the Macedonian Struggle for Statehood and Independence (2011), the new building of the Archaeological Museum (2014), the State Archive and Constitutional Court (2014), and the refurbished city square "Macedonia" (Maced., Ploštad Makedonija). The significance of these spatial constructions for the new mnemonic canon promoted by the government was aptly observed by Irena Stefoska and Darko Stojanov, who called them the "national trinity" serving to disseminate the novel nationalistic narrative.[67] "Skopje 2014" has also been criticized as a project dividing the local population and provoking regional tensions.[68]

In addition, the inauguration of Skopje's HMC in 2011 also coincided with a debate by Bulgarian experts on the fate of Jews during World War II. While the Bulgarian debates of the 1990s and 2000s focused solely on the rescue of Bulgarian Jewry, critical voices in the early 2010s questioned the rescue paradigm by stressing the antisemitic legislation, the violent evictions, the deportations of Jews from the annexed territories, as well as the role of the Bulgarian interwar radical right in promoting antisemitism. They also challenged the "salvation myth" and its discursive development by highlighting the difference between the treatment of the Jews in Bulgaria proper and in the annexed territories.[69] However, these voices were opposed by many Bulgarian historians and politicians.

In this context, the HMC became the object of attacks by some Bulgarians, who regarded not only the museum but the whole "Skopje 2014" project as a political provocation. The HMC was depicted as a key repository of a Macedonian "anti-Bulgarian campaign" and an attack on the international image of contemporary Bulgaria. The rescue issue became a focal point of this discursive collision. Already prior to the opening of the HMC, at a conference organized in 2011 by the Bulgarian Academy of Sciences (BAS) on the sixty-eighth anniversary of the "salvation of Bulgarian Jewry," Georgi Markov, a Bulgarian scholar and member of the BAS, stated that the politics behind the Skopje's Holocaust museum are "too sad to remain uncommented upon."[70] Furthermore, he repeated the exculpatory argument that Nazi Germany had put pressure on Bulgaria to deport its Jewish population, and he reminded his audience of Bulgaria's ultimate refusal to hand over the Bulgarian Jews to the Nazis. The conference proceedings concluded that the Skopje museum would "tarnish the reputation and the international image of Bulgaria."[71] The HMC was also attacked in Bulgaria on other occasions. For instance, the Bulgarian-born and Israel-based journalist Sylvia Avdala described the HMC as a failed institution: a historical "falsification" embedded in the Macedonian nationalistic discourse that served as a tool in an anti-Bulgarian defamation campaign. In 2012 both a Bulgarian version and an English translation of the book *The Deportation of the*

Jews from Vardar Macedonia and Aegean Region: Facts and Myths, authored by Spas Tashev, an associate of the Institute for Population and Human Studies at the BAS, was published in Sofia. In his book Tashev criticized Skopje's politics of memory and the way the destruction of Macedonian Jewry is depicted at the HMC while whitewashing the Bulgarian role in the Holocaust.[72]

The Bulgarian criticism culminated in 2012 after the premiere of *The Third Half* (Maced., Treto poluvreme), a Macedonian historical film directed by Darko Mitrevski. The film, based on the personal account of Blagoja Mladenovski, is set in Skopje during World War II. Its plot focuses on a love story between a Sephardi Jewish girl and a Macedonian craftsman, with the history of the football club "Makedonija" in the background. It also shows the roundups of the Jews in Skopje in March 1943, the violent behavior of Bulgarian camp guards, and the deportations to Treblinka in trains bearing Bulgarian signage. This was the most expensive state-sponsored film production ever made in North Macedonia and the only Macedonian nomination for the 2013 Academy Awards. It was treated by the then prime minister, IMRO–DPMNU's Nikola Gruevski, as a "project of national interest." The fate of the Macedonian Jews thus becomes a pattern for interpreting the Bulgarian wartime treatment of the entire Macedonian population. In other words, the Holocaust was used as a vehicle for telling the story of the ethno-Macedonian struggle during the long twentieth century, epitomized by the wartime history of FC "Makedonija." The Serbian historian of the Holocaust Jovan Ḱulibrk describes this discursive strategy as a "metonymy" or an equation of the destruction of the Jewish community with the overall treatment of the locals of other ethnic groups and religious denominations.[73]

The film also illustrates the "nationalistic turn" in Macedonian artistic production.[74] This turn becomes evident if one compares *The Third Half* with the documentary series *The Skopje Dossier* (Maced., Dosie Skopje), made by the same director in 2000, which also dealt with FC "Makedonija" in one of its episodes. The documentary presents the locals' sympathy for the wartime football club as just another "form of resistance" against the occupiers, a trope used in postwar Yugoslav Macedonian historiography, while the feature film provides a different interpretative framework for the football club, its wartime activities, and the local, communist-driven resistance.[75] For instance, in the feature film the main character claims his motivation for joining the partisan units to be private and not ideological (he is not a communist, but just wants to save his family)—in line with the revision of the socialist history promoted by the IMRO–DPMNU government. At the same time, both the feature and the documentary film draw attention to the Bulgarian and pro-Bulgarian members of the managerial board of the club, but fail to mention that it was one of the first sports clubs to ask for confiscated Jewish property in the wake of the deportations.[76] The movie provoked harsh criticism from Bulgaria, resulting in an appeal to the European Parliament and the European Council to halt the accession talks with Macedonia in 2012, a political initiative that did not, however, result in a suspension of the negotiation process at that particular point.[77]

Newest Bilateral Developments

In 2016–17, the government in Macedonia changed. As of October 2017, the center-left Social Democratic Union of Macedonia (SDUM) (Maced., Socijaldemokratski Sojuz na Makedonija) has been the main political power. One of the key factors in bringing about this change was opposition to the IMRO–DPMNU's memory politics, with the SDUM taking a hard line against "Skopje 2014" and participating in the so-called Colorful Revolution—a series of protests against the IMRO–DPMNU–led government—targeting and color-bombing monuments erected as part of the "Skopje 2014" project. The initial period of the SDUM government was also marked by a set of proactive bilateral foreign policy measures, such as signing the Bulgarian-Macedonian Friendship Treaty (2017) and the Greek-Macedonian Name Agreement (2018). Both accords opt to enhance bilateral cooperation by a joint effort of revisiting national histories. In the case of the Greek-Macedonian agreement, the emphasis is on the revision of North Macedonia's public monuments and memorials, delineating the semiotic domains of "Macedonia" between the Greek region of Macedonia and the Republic of North Macedonia, as well as endorsing the ancient Macedonian past as global cultural heritage and not as an exclusively national feature. The Bulgarian-Macedonian Treaty, as hinted in the introductory section, envisions the creation of a binational expert commission for reviewing history textbooks and suggested joint commemorations of shared historical figures and events. An initial consensus was reached in regard to the ancient and the medieval past, yet the interpretation of late nineteenth-century history, or the roles played by the Macedonian Revolutionary Organization and the 1903 Ilinden Uprising, provoked heated public debates in both countries. Even though the joint commission has not yet approached the period of World War II, the Holocaust, and the fate of the Macedonian Jews, one can anticipate a similar bout of intense public and expert debates.[78]

The initial reconciliatory gestures in the aftermath of the Bulgarian-Macedonian Friendship Treaty came from both the Macedonian and Bulgarian Jewish communities. They established an institutional communication channel and worked to reduce the interpretational differences in relation to the history of the Holocaust in Bulgaria and North Macedonia. During a meeting held under the auspices of the Organization of the Jews in Bulgaria ("Shalom") in 2017, the representatives of the two communities discussed a revision of the official position of "Shalom" regarding the events leading up to the roundups and the deportation of Macedonian Jews.[79] The Bulgarian prime minister Borisov's participation in Skopje's "March of the Living" in 2018 reflects those attempts to come up with a transnational reading of the Holocaust. Nevertheless, the 2018 Skopje commemoration was criticized in the Macedonian public as too accommodating toward Bulgaria's reluctance to recognize its role in the deportations of Macedonian Jews. Several commentators highlighted Borisov's failure to deliver an apology to the Macedonian Jews and the Macedonian public.[80] This failure is paradigmatic of the current Bulgarian politics of memory, an "unassailable historiographic a priori" that stresses the rescue of Bulgarian Jews, silencing the shared responsibility for the deportations of the Jews from the annexed territories.[81]

As an illustration, one can look at the seventy-sixth anniversary of the "Salvation of Bulgarian Jews during World War II" (Salvation Day) in 2019. Under the banner "Together for Bulgaria, Together for Europe," the 2019 Salvation Day commemoration highlighted the contrast between wartime terror and present-day European integration. Against this background, the fate of the Macedonian Jews was depicted in line with the official Bulgarian narrative of state rescue of Bulgarian Jews. The statement of Kaloyan Pargov, a high-profile member of the major opposition Bulgarian Socialist Party, expresses this consensus very well: He portrayed the Jews from the annexed territories who perished during the war as those who were "not saved" by the Bulgarian state.[82] The denial of the Bulgarian state's agency in the deportations of Macedonian Jews has long been expected to come under discussion within the framework of the joint Bulgarian-Macedonian joint commission. Still, the gap between the memory regimes in North Macedonia and Bulgaria remains too big to deal with this issue.

At the same time, rescue narratives reappeared in both the Macedonian and Bulgarian public discourses as a step away from the conflicting "national aspirations of the conflicting parties."[83] One of the major events in this regard is the declaration signed by a number of Bulgarian intellectuals in March 2023 which calls on the Bulgarian government to acknowledge its responsibility for the deportations of the Jews from Macedonia, western Thrace, and Pirot.[84] Prior to this expert mobilization, the Bulgarian historian Dimitar Bechev—in an interview for the Macedonian weekly *Globus* from 2012—proposed joint Bulgarian-Macedonian commemorations of the Bulgarian and the Macedonian Righteous Among the Nations—including Vlado Kurtev, the Skopjans Todor

Hadži Mitkov and Trajko Ribarev, as well as Dimitar Čkatrov, the wartime president of FC "Makedonija." The key to unlocking the bilateral struggle over the Holocaust, according to Bechev, is a "direct dialogue" with witnesses of the Holocaust.[85] However, this initiative to integrate the local and individual rescue stories in the transnational mnemonic domain remained unnoticed by the Macedonian public and did not translate into a commemorative practice—mostly due to the affiliation of the aforementioned rescuers with the Bulgarian wartime authorities. The 2013 exhibition pavilion of the Holocaust History Museum at Yad Vashem's Department for the Righteous Gentiles presented another possible model for commemorating the contested rescuers. Herein, Dimitar Peshev, one of the most famous Bulgarian Righteous Among the Nations, was portrayed as a "man who first supported the anti-Jewish legislation, but who in 1943 acted in a frenzied manner to stop the deportation."[86] This narrative construction shows the reconciliatory potential of the shared Bulgarian-Macedonian rescuers for contemporary Bulgarian-Macedonian relations.

Finally, in North Macedonia, one can trace a certain shift of public attention toward the diplomatic history of World War II and its link to the rescue stories of Macedonian Jews. This topic was initially mapped in the works of Lebl and Kolonomos, but remained under-researched up until the mid-2000s. In 2019 an edited volume titled *Diplomacy and Deportations of Macedonian Jews in 1943* focused on the diplomatic history of rescue in North Macedonia and the region. The diplomatic history of rescue was also the subject of the exhibition "More Than a Duty" (Maced., Poveḱe od dolžnost), organized by the Skopje-based NGO "Cultural Information Center" and dedicated to all the diplomats around the world recognized as Righteous Among the Nations. The rescue of the Macedonian Jews in Albania is also highlighted in the most recent brochure published by the HMC, dedicated to the new permanent exhibition. The brief description of the exhibition chapter titled "Hiding and Rescue" stressed that "Albania was crucial for the few surviving Jews from Macedonia," as it provided safe heavens.[87]

Conclusion

This essay examines the development of the historical narratives pertaining to the rescue of the Macedonian Jews in North Macedonia since the 1950s. During the 1980s, the debate about the rescue of Macedonian Jews evolved into a discursive struggle between the official narrative, which credited the partisan organizations and the communist parties of Macedonia and of Yugoslavia with a collective effort to aid the persecuted Jews, and individual rescue stories, which shed light on the complicity of the process. In post-Yugoslav Macedonia, this discursive struggle shifted from historiographic debates to the field of public history. In the 1990s and 2000s, state-sponsored museums and historical exhibitions strove to integrate the Holocaust into the emerging Macedonian national-historical canon. Stripped away from some of the socialist historiographic tropes, the history of Macedonian Jews was presented as part of the multicultural and multiconfessional Macedonian heritage. However, the collective rescue agency of the partisan organizations in post-Yugoslav Macedonia was not questioned until the opening of the HMC in 2011, which proved to be a turning point. Hence, both exhibitions showcased at the HMC up to this point (2011 and 2019) contributed to a further contextualization of the rescue stories and presented them in line with the Jewish voices and some of the recent models of interpreting the Holocaust of European Jewry.

At the same time, the rescue stories of the Macedonian Jews were among the most disputed topics of the Bulgarian-Macedonian controversies over Macedonian history. Both communist and postcommunist historiographies and historical debates in North Macedonia and Bulgaria utilized the decimation of Macedonian Jewry, as well as the rescue of the Jews in wartime Bulgaria proper, to reinforce ethnonational historical canons. Although the political initiative culminating in the 2017 Bulgarian-Macedonian Friendship Treaty sought to open new opportunities for resolving the dispute over Holocaust history, it heretofore has not led to a shared understanding of the history of the Holocaust in Macedonia. On the contrary, the heated reactions to the work of the Bulgarian-Macedonian Joint Commission resulted in a weaponization of wartime history in both countries. In this very context, the HMC assumed the role of a gatekeeper of the history and memory of Macedonian Jewry, with regard to both its exhibitions and activities beyond the museum space. While critical of historical interpretations put forward by some Macedonian scholars and curators, it is also outspoken about the failure of the Bulgarian state to acknowledge its involvement in the extermination of Macedonian Jewry. The HMC continues to use its leverage to argue against the uncritical and politically motivated rendering of the history of World War II in the region.

Notes

I would like to thank the coordinators, staff, and colleagues at Charles University's VITRI research center, which allowed me to present this text at the center's workshop in November 2022 and supported its finalization. I would also like to thank Blagoja Mladenovski, Goran Sadikarijo, Jovan Tegovski,

Tomislav Osmanli, and Besnik Emini for sharing their insights, as well as Roumen Avramov, Dina Iordanova, Katarina Kolozova, Viktor Jovanovski, Mišo Dokmanović, and Filip Laypov for reading and commenting on the draft versions of this chapter. The state name of North Macedonia as well as the ethnic and national adjectives related to Macedonia are brought in accordance with the 2018 Greco-Macedonian agreement. I did all the translations throughout the text: the Macedonian-English and Bulgarian-English translations, as well as the translations from Serbian, Croatian, and Serbo-Croatian to English. All the shortcomings that might remain in the text are my responsibility.

1 The annual day of mourning for the Macedonian Jews is a late 1990s informal initiative that was endorsed by state institutions in the early 2000s. About the developments in 2018, see "Holokaustot vo Makedonija nikogaš nema da bide zaboraven," *NovaTV*, March 11, 2018.

2 "Sednica po povod 75 godini od deportacijata na Evreite od Republika Makedonija vo logorot na smrtta Treblinka," *Sobranie na Republika Makedonija*, March 12, 2018.

3 In 2018, there were three separate "Marches of the Living" in the Macedonian cities of Skopje, Bitola, and Štip. The events mimic the "International March of the Living" in its commemorative scope and rituals. For more on the 2018 Macedonian "March of the Living," see "So poveḱe nastani na 11 i 12 mart vo Skopje, Bitola i Štip ḱe bide odbeležana 75-godišninata od holokaustot na makedonskite Evrei," *Vlada na Republika Severna Makedonija*, March 10, 2018. For the reception of the 2018 events commemorating the Holocaust, see Katerina Blaževska, "Bojko Borisov kako Vili Brant: Počit za žrtvite od Holokaustot," *Deutsche Welle—Macedonian*, March 12, 2018. See Veselina Yordanova, "Borisov v Skopie: Da ne zabravyame greshkite, da rabotim zaedno," *Dnes*, March 12, 2018, and Marina Cekova, "Borisov pochete v Skopie pametta na zaginalite makedonski evrei," *Nova*, March 12, 2018, for an overview of the Bulgarian public reception of the 2018 commemorative ceremony in Skopje.

4 The full name of the declarations reads—"Declaration on the occasion of the 75th anniversary of the deportation of the Jews of the Republic of Macedonia in the death camp Treblinka." The declaration was tabled by a group of ten MPs from different party coalitions on March 1, 2018, and published in the forty-first edition of the *Official Gazette of the Republic of Macedonia*, issued on March 6, 2018. More in "Predlog-Deklaracija po povod 75 godni od deportacijata na Evreite od Makedonija vo logorot na

smrtta Treblinka," *Sobranie na Republika Makedonija*, March 1, 2018, and "Sednica po povod 75 godini."

5 "Bulgaria sends a memorandum on 'state-sponsored anti-Bulgarian ideology' in North Macedonia," *European Western Balkans*, September 22, 2020.

6 Svetoslav Todorov, "Bulgarian Ruling Coalition Cracks over North Macedonia Dispute," *Balkan Insight*, June 8, 2022.

7 Lepa Džundeva, "Povtorno debata: Dali Bugarija bila fašistička zemja vo Vtorata svetska vojna," *TV24*, February 6, 2022.

8 Elizabeta Damjanoska-Spesenovska, "Reakcija na Evrejskata zaednica," *Sloboden pečat*, December 10, 2022.

9 Saško Panajotov, "Reakcija na Evrejskata verska zaednica i Fondot na holokaustot na Evreite od Makedonija," *MIA*, September 24, 2021.

10 Soon after the opening of the Bitola club, which was attended by the highest-ranking Bulgarian officials, a German journalist revealed that the house of the club belonged to a Bitola Jewish family whose members had been killed in Treblinka. More in Žaneta Zdravkovska, "Se istražuva dali bila na deportirani Evrei kukjata vo koja e bugarskiot klub," *Sakam da kažam*, August 9, 2022. For the Jewish community reaction to the Ohrid club, see "Evrejskata zaednica zgrozena od registracijata na Združenieto Car Boris III vo Ohrid," *Radio Slobodna Evropa*, August 10, 2022.

11 See Sławomir Kapralski, "The Role Played by the Auschwitz-Birkenau State Museum in Public Discourse and the Evolving Consciousness of the Holocaust in Polish Society," in *Jewish Presence in Absence: The Aftermath of the Holocaust in Poland, 1944–2010*, ed. F. Tych and M. Adamczyk-Grabowska (Jerusalem: Yad Vashem/International Institute for Holocaust Research/Diana Zborowski Center for the Study of the Aftermath of the Shoah, 2014).

12 See Jay Winter and Emmanuel Sivan, "Setting the Framework," in *War and Remembrance in the Twentieth Century*, ed. Jay Winter and Emmanuel Sivan (Cambridge: Cambridge University Press, 2000); Harold Marcuse, *Legacies of Dachau: The Uses and Abuses of a Concentration Camp, 1933–2001* (Cambridge: Cambridge University Press, 2011); and Zofia Wóycicka, *Arrested Mourning: Memory of the Nazi Camps in Poland, 1944–1950* (Frankfurt am Main: Peter Lang, 2013), 9–16.

13 Galena Kuculovska, "Interegnumot vo Skopje—April 1941," *Muzejski Glasnik* 4 (1979): 149–54. For more on the interwar and war history of Macedonia, see Michael Lee Miller's *Bulgaria during the Second World War* (Stanford, CA: Stanford University Press, 1975).

14 For more on the wartime history of the Macedonian Jews, see Aleksandar Matkovski, *Istorijata na Evreite vo Makedonija* (Skopje: Makedonska revija, 1983); Jamila Kolonomos and Vera Vesković-Vangeli, *Evreite vo Makedonija vo Vtorata svetska vojna 1941–1945* (Skopje: Macedonian Academy of Sciences and Arts, 1986); and Vera Vesković-Vangeli, "Treblinka, zbornik na dokumenti," in *Evreite od Makedonija i Holokaustot: Istorija, teorija, kultura*, ed. S. Grandakovska (Skopje: Evro Balkan Press, 2011), 9–402.

15 See Ivo Goldstein, "The Jews in Yugoslavia 1918–1941: Anti-Semitism and the Struggle for Equality," *Jewish Studies at the Central European University* 2, no. 1 (2002): 51–64. In 1940 the "Act for registering people with Jewish origins" was passed by the Yugoslav prewar minister of education, Antun Korosec, which allowed the registration of ten Jewish students in Bitola, four in Skopje, and three in Štip. From July to November 1941, the Bulgarian laws for single taxation of Jewish properties, the prohibition against Jews engaging in trade and industry, and the infamous "Law for the protection of the nation" were implemented in the territory of wartime Macedonia. In 1942 and 1943, the Bulgarian authorities passed a law allowing for the confiscation of Jewish properties, an order for taking Jewish properties, a rule mandating that Jews wear yellow armbands, a restriction on Jews visiting public restaurants, parks, and stores, as well as an order for the liquidation of Jewish craft stores. See Kolonomos and Vesković-Vangeli, *Evreite vo Makedonija*, and Vesković-Vangeli, "Treblinka, zbornik na dokumenti."

16 See Nadège Ragaru, "Contrasting Destinies: The Plight of Bulgarian Jews and the Jews in Bulgarian-occupied Greek and Yugoslav Territories during World War Two," *Online Encyclopedia of Mass Violence* (2017).

17 Brannik Youth was formed after the Bulgarian parliament passed a law on December 29, 1940. The state youth organization was "clearly oriented towards the German Hitler Youth and the Italian Balilla." See Björn Opfer-Klinger, "Bulgaria's Collaboration with the Axis Powers in World War II," in *Complicated Complicity: European Collaboration with Nazi Germany during World War II*, ed. M. Bitunjac and J. H. Schoeps (Berlin: De Gruyter, 2021), 161–92.

18 See Irena Steinfeldt, "Rescue in Bulgaria and Macedonia through the Perspective of the Files of the Righteous Among the Nations," *Yad Vashem* (2014).

19 More in Michael Berenbaum, *The Jews in Macedonia during World War II* (Skopje: Holocaust Fund of the Jews of Macedonia, 2016), 60–61.

Berenbaum further argues that the "Macedonian Jews who avoided death were: those who hid, those who fought with the partisans and survived, and those who were released because they were physicians and pharmacists or foreign nationals of Axis or neutral countries."

20 For an overview of the recent scholarship on the Holocaust and the Macedonian Jews, see Jovan Ḱulibrk, "Holokaustot na makedonskite Evrei vo istoriografijata," in *Evreite od Makedonija i Holokaustot: Istorija, teorija, kultura*, ed. S. Grandakovska (Skopje: Evro Balkan Press, 2011); Stefan Troebst, "Macedonian Historiography on the Holocaust in Macedonia under Bulgarian Occupation," *Südosteuropäische Hefte* 1 (2013): 107–14; Holly Case, "The Combined Legacies of the 'Jewish Question' and the 'Macedonian Question,'" in *Bringing the Dark Past to Light: The Reception of the Holocaust in Postcommunist Europe*, ed. J-P. Himka and J. B. Michlic (Lincoln: University of Nebraska Press, 2013), 352–76; Bartłomiej Rusin, "Deportacja Żydów z Macedonii Wardarskiej, Bełomoria i Pirotu w historiografii bułgarskiej," *Zagłada Żydów. Studia i Materiały* 11 (2015): 255–68; Nadège Ragaru, "Bordering the Past: The Elusive Presences of the Holocaust in Socialist Macedonia and Socialist Bulgaria," *Südost-Forschungen* 76 (2017): 241–72; and "Nationalizing through Internationalization: Writing, Remembering and Commemorating the Holocaust in Macedonia and Bulgaria after 1989," *Südosteuropa* 65, no. 2 (2017): 284–315.

21 Based on the Instructions of the Land Commission for the Investigation of War Crimes of the Occupiers and Their Collaborators (August 25, 1944), pursuant to the decision of the Antifascist Council of National Liberation of Yugoslavia from November 20, 1943, on the establishment of a State Commission for Investigation of War Crimes of the Occupiers and Their Collaborators and Article 9 of the Operating Rules of the State Commission adopted by the National Committee of the Liberation of Yugoslavia on May 6, 1944, the principal tasks of the investigative body of the commission were "gathering evidence on criminal acts perpetrated by the occupiers and their collaborators," to "conduct all necessary hearings and, if necessary, on-site inspections." The research agenda issued by the commission stated that "it is the duty of each citizen to report to the commission," while the materials were also gathered "from house to house," with the "aid of literate youths or members of the Antifascist Women's Front." More in Martina Grahek Ravančić, "The Work of the Land Commission for the Investigation of War Crimes of the Occupiers and Their Collaborators: Analysis Based on Set Tasks and Cases," *Review*

of Croatian History 8, no. 1 (2012): 123–49, and Stijn Vervaet, *Holocaust, War and Transnational Memory: Testimony from Yugoslav and Post-Yugoslav Literature* (New York: Routledge, 2018).

22 Zdenko Löwenthal, ed., *The Crimes of the Fascist Occupants and Their Collaborators against Jews in Yugoslavia* (Belgrade: Federation of Jewish Communities of Federative People's Republic of Yugoslavia, 1957), 190–95.

23 Case, "The Combined Legacies," 363.

24 Aleksandar Matkovski, "Tragedijata na Evreite od Makedonija," *Glasnik na Institutot za nacionalna istorija* 2 (1958).

25 David-Dale Levi, "Bitoljski Jevreji u Narodnooslobodilačkoj borbi," in *Jevrejski Almanah 1957–1958* (Beograd: Savez Jevrejskih Opština Jugoslavije, 1959), 109–15. See, as well, Aleksandar Matkovski, "The Destruction of Macedonian Jewry in 1943," *Yad Vashem Studies* 3 (1959).

26 Troebst, "Macedonian Historiography on the Holocaust," 108.

27 Kolonomos and Veskoviḱ-Vangeli, *Evreite vo Makedonija.*

28 Ragaru, "Nationalizing through Internationalization."

29 Troebst, "Macedonian Historiography on the Holocaust," 108–109.

30 Ḱulibrk, "Holokaustot na makedonskite Evrei," 599–606.

31 For more on the Jewish communal identity and Holocaust history-writing in Yugoslavia, see Jaša Romano, *Jevreji Jugoslavije 1941–1945: Žrtve genocida i učesnici narodnooslobodilačkog rata* (Beograd: Savez jevrejskih opština Jugoslavije, 1980); Ivo Goldstein, "Restoring Jewish Life in Communist Yugoslavia, 1945–1967," *East European Jewish Affairs* 34, no. 1 (2006): 58–71; Renata Jambrešić-Kirin, "Politika sjećanja na Drugi svjetski rat u doba medijske reprodukcije socijalističke culture," in *Devijacije i promašaji: Etnografija domaćeg socijalizma*, ed. L. Feldman and I. Prica (Zagreb: Institut za etnologiju i folkloristiku, 2006); and Milan Koljanin, "Istraživanje holokausta u Jugoslaviji," in *Izraelsko-srpska akademska razmena u istraživanju Holokausta*, ed. J. Mirković (Beograd: Muzej žrtava genocida, 2008).

32 For more on the developments in the Macedonian postwar historiography, see Stefan Troebst, "Yugoslav Macedonia 1943–1953: Building the Party, the State, and the Nation," in *State-Society Relations in Yugoslavia, 1945–1992*, ed. M. K. Bokovoy, J. A. Irvine, and C. S. Lilly (New York: St. Martin's Press, 1997), and "Historical Politics and Historical 'Masterpieces' in Macedonia before and after 1991," *New Balkan Politics* 6 (2003); Ulf Brunnbauer, "Historiography, Myths and the Nation in the Republic of Macedonia," in *(Re)Writing History: Historiography in*

Southeast Europe after Socialism, ed. U. Brunnbauer (Münster: LIT Studies on South East Europe, 2004), "Ancient Nationhood and the Struggle for Statehood: Historiographic Myths in the Republic of Macedonia," in *Myths and Boundaries in South-Eastern Europe*, ed. P. Kolstø (London: Hurst & Company, 2005), and "Pro-Serbians vs. Pro-Bulgarians: Revisionism in Post-Socialist Macedonian Historiography," *History Compass* 3, no. 1 (2005): 1–17; Irena Stefoska, "Why the Institute of National History? The Beginnings of the Institutionalized Form of Historiography in the Process of Building the Macedonian Nation," in *The Echo of the Nation*, ed. Z. Trajanovski et al. (Skopje: Templum, 2009).

33 See Isak Sion, "Učestvoto na Evreite od Štip vo Narodnoosloboditelnoto dviženje," in *Evreite od Makedonija i Holokaustot: Istorija, teorija, kultura*, ed. S. Grandakovska (Skopje: Evro Balkan Press, 2011), 425–35.

34 The whole text of the proclamations can be read in Kolonomos and Veskovik-Vangeli, *Evreite vo Makedonija*, 962–63.

35 Matkovski mentions the names of Aleksandar Todorov and the Hadži Mitkov family, already recognized by Yad Vashem, as well as Dr. Smiljan Franjo Čekada, Vlado Petrov (who was recognized as an honorary member of the postwar Macedonian Jewish religious organization in 1945, but not as a Righteous), and the case of ten-year-old Rudi (Rud) Konfino, who was "almost certainly hiding in a non-Jewish family according to the Bulgarian police." On March15, in the midst of the roundups of Macedonian Jewry in Skopje, the district police chief officer, G. Guškarov, issued a note to the local authorities to confine Rud Marko Konfino, who "escaped the detainment in the Jewish camp" and was suspected to be hiding in the house of Marijana Baruh. More in J. Kolonomos and V. Veskovik-Vangeli, *Evreite vo Makedonija*, 818. See, as well, "Todorov Family," *Righteous Among the Nations Database* M.31.2/1766 (1980), and "Hadži-Mitkov Family," *Righteous Among the Nations Database* M.31.2/1036 (1976). Matkovski's account on the individual rescue histories can be found in *Istorijata na Evreite vo Makedonija*, 129.

36 Kolonomos and Veskovik-Vangeli introduce the stories of the rescuers Boro Altiparmak and Stojan-Bogoja Siljanovski, both recognized by Yad Vashem as Righteous Among the Nations in 1989.

37 Matkovski, *Istorijata na Evreite vo Makedonija*, and Kolonomos and Veskovik-Vangeli, *Evreite vo Makedonija*. For a general overview of the Yugoslav physicians and pharmacists of Jewish origins during World War II, see Jaša Romano, "Jevreji zdravstveni radnici Jugoslavije

1941–1945. Žrtve fašističkog terora i učesnici u NOR-u," in *Zbornik 2* (Beograd: Jevrejski Istorijski Muzej, 1973), 73–257.

38 More on the conferences in the three-volume *Skopje vo NOV*, published by the Skopje-based Gradski odbor na SZB NOV from 1973 to 1980.

39 More in Mustafa Karahasan, "Turskata i albanskata narodnost vo vooruženiot otpor na gradot protiv okupatorot vo 1941 godina," in *Skopje vo NOV 1941* (Skopje: Gradski odbor na SZB NOV, 1973), 247.

40 Jacqueline Nießer, "Which Commemorative Models Help? A Case Study from Post-Yugoslavia," in *Replicating Atonement: Foreign Models in the Commemorations of Atrocities*, ed. M. Gabowitsch (Cham: Palgrave Macmillan, 2017).

41 Emil Kerenji, "'Your Salvation Is the Struggle Against Fascism': Yugoslav Communists and the Rescue of Jews, 1941–1945," *Contemporary European History* 25, no. 1 (2016): 57–74.

42 Jelena Subotić, *Yellow Star, Red Star: Holocaust Remembrance after Communism* (Ithaca, NY: Cornell University Press, 2019): 30.

43 Romano, *Jevreji Jugoslavije*, 52–53, 88.

44 More in Dalia Ofer, "Tormented Memories: The Individual and the Collective," *Israel Studies* 9, no. 3 (2004): 137–56. More on Lebl's writings and activism in Aleksandar Lebl et al., eds., *Ženi* (Beograd: Čigoja, 2013), and Katarzyna Taczyńska, "A Scattered Mosaic of Records and Reminiscences: Ženi Lebl's War Odyssey in Her Personal Writings," in *An Introspective Approach to Women's Intercultural Fieldwork: Female Researchers' Narrations Based on Their Intercultural Experiences from the Field*, ed. U. Markowska-Manista and J. Pilarska (Warsaw: Akademia Pedagogiki Specjalnej, 2017).

45 More in Ženi Lebl, *Plima i Slom* (Skopje: Fond na Holokaustot na Evreite od Makedonija, 2013), 371.

46 Kolonomos, *Dviženjeto na otporot.*

47 Aside from her autobiography, Kolonomos shared her memories in several biographical interviews in the post-Yugoslav period. See, for instance, her interview for the US Holocaust Memorial Museum, conducted by Jaša Almuli, and "Nejzinion život—Film za Jamila Kolonomos," an educational project produced by the Institute of History–Skopje and the elementary school Kočo Racin–Skopje.

48 Žamila-Anđela Kolonomos, "In Battle from Day One," in *We Survived . . . : Yugoslav Jews on the Holocaust*, vol. 3, ed. A. Gaon (Belgrade: Jewish Historical Museum/Federation of Jewish Communities of Serbia, 2009), 17.

49 Kolonomos's collaboration with the US Holocaust Memorial Museum, as well as her involvement in transnational debates and international expert networks, largely contributed to the initial Jewish memory activism in North Macedonia, a factor that was crucial in the envisioning of the Holocaust Memorial Centre in Skopje in the 1990s and early 2000s. She was also one of the initiators of the Holocaust Fund and the Skopje-based Macedonian-Israeli Friendship Society, which, alongside the HMC, became the major memory agents in post-Yugoslav North Macedonia as far as the memory of the Holocaust and the rescue of Macedonian Jews are concerned.

50 Todor Čepreganov, "Was the PO in Macedonia Able to Save the Jews?" in *Diplomacy and Deportation*, ed. V. Gaber (Skopje: Diplomatski klub—Memorijalen centar na holokaustot na Evreite od Makedonija—Institut za nacionalna istorija pri Univerzitetot "Sv. Kiril i Metodij," 2017), 55–61.

51 Ljubica Spaskovska, "Report on Macedonia," *CITSEE Europeanisation of Citizenship in the Successor States of the Former Yugoslavia* (2012), 1.

52 More in Galena Kuculovska, "Izložbata Tragedijata na makedonskite Evrei," *Muzejski Glasnik* no. 5 (1982): 127.

53 Ljubica Sazdova Kondijanova, *Muzej na grad Skopje 1949–2011* (Skopje: Muzej na grad Skopje, 2011), 123–46.

54 A similar ethnographic exhibition, "The Ethnic Colorfulness of Skopje from the Late 19th Century to the Beginning of WWII" (Maced., Etničkoto šarenilo na Skopje od krajot na 19. do početokot na Vtorata svetska vojna), was opened to the public in 2005. The exhibition featured the history of the peaceful coexistence of the multicultural and multiconfessional population of Skopje as a major theme. More in Sazdova Kondijanova, *Muzej na grad Skopje.*

55 Marica Jovanovska, *Ehoto na makedonskite Sefardi* (Skopje: Muzej na Makedonija, 2003).

56 Bojan Ivanov, "Voved," in *Ehoto na makedonskite Sefardi*, ed. M. Jovanovska (Skopje: Muzej na Makedonija, 2003).

57 Jasminka Namičeva et al., *Po tragite na Feniksot* (Skopje: Muzej na grad Skopje, 2003).

58 Barbara Kirshenblatt-Gimblett, "Why Jewish Museums? An International Perspective," *Studia Judaica* 16, no. 2/32 (2013): 77–100.

59 Attendees of the initial meeting that took place in Kolonomos's house were Viktor and Sara Komras, Ljubomir Gajdov, Avram and Samuel Sadikario, as well as Jamila Kolonomos. More in Kolonomos, *Dviženjeto na*

otporot, 108. A similar account can be found in the interview with Avram Sadikario in Avram Sadikario and Rachel Chanin Asiel, "Avram Sadikario," *Centropa*, March 2005. See Viktor Gaber, *Feniksot na nepokorot: 75 godini od obnovuvanjeto na Evrejskata zaednica vo Makedonija* (Skopje: Fond na holokaustot na Evreite od Makedonija, 2019).

60 Lea David, "Lost in Transaction in Serbia and Croatia: Memory Content as a Trade Currency," in *Replicating Atonement: Foreign Models in the Commemorations of Atrocities*, ed. M. Gabowitsch (Cham: Palgrave Macmillan, 2017).

61 Melpomeni Korneti et al., *Holocaust Memorial Center of the Jews from Macedonia* (Skopje: Holocaust Fund of the Jews from Macedonia, 2014).

62 James E. Young, *The Textures of Memory: Holocaust Memorials and Meaning* (New Haven, CT: Yale University Press, 1993), 2.

63 More in Magdalena Bogusławska, "Powrót do Čivutany. Otwarcie Centrum Pamięci o Zagładzie Żydów z Macedonii," *Zagłada Żydów. Studia i Materiały* 7 (2011): 540–45; Dragica Popovska, "Muzejot na holokaustot vo Skopje: Mesto na seḱavanje," *Journal of History* 49, no. 1 (2014): 281–91, and "Symbolic Representations of Identity and the History of the Jews in Macedonia's Public Space," *Studia Środkowoeuropejskie i Bałkanistyczne* 26 (2017): 83–88. Popovska, for instance, applies Nora's *lieu de mémoire* as an entry point to the discussion of the "situatedness" and the "ambiental totality" the Holocaust Memorial Center is reflecting. More in Popovska, "Muzejot na holokaustot," 281–83.

64 Berenbaum, *The Jews in Macedonia*, 8. See, as well, the interview with Berenbaum about the HMC in Paweł Sawicki, "We Remember the Past to Transform the Future," *Memoria: Memory—History—Education* 18, no. 3 (2019): 6–15.

65 Michael Berenbaum, "The Rescuers: When the Ordinary Is Extraordinary," in *The Routledge History of the Holocaust*, ed. J. C. Friedman (London: Routledge, 2011), 315–25.

66 "The Lost Sephardic World of the Western Balkans: A Project by Centropa and the Holocaust Memorial Center for the Jews of Macedonia—Jewish Stories from Split, Dubrovnik, Belgrade, Bitola, and Sarajevo" (2017), available at: https://lostsephardicworld.org/.

67 Irena Stefoska and Darko Stojanov, "A Tale in Stone and Bronze: Old/New Strategies for Political Mobilization in the Republic of Macedonia," *Nationalities Papers* 45, no. 3 (2017): 357.

68 More on the project in Goran Janev, "Narrating the Nation, Narrating the City," *Cultural Analysis* 10, no. 3 (2011): 3–21; James McEvoy, "Managing

Culture in Post-Conflict Societies," *Contemporary Social Science* 6, no. 1 (2011): 55–71; Maja Muhiḱ and Aleksandar Takovski, "Redefining National Identity in Macedonia: Analyzing Competing Origin Myths and Interpretations through Hegemonic Representations," *Etnološka Tribina* 37, no. 44 (2014): 138–52; and Piotr Majewski, "Project 'Skopje 2014'—À la recherche du temps perdu," *Ethnologia Balkanica* 19 (2016): 167–83.

69 An overview of the Bulgarian debate over the Jewish deportations can be found in Roumen Avramov et al., *Balgariya i antisemitizmat* (Berlin: Ekstaz, 2018). See also Roumen Avramov, *"Spasenie" i padenie. Mikroikonomika na darzhavniya antisemitizam v Balgariya, 1940–44* (Sofia: UI Sv. Kliment Ohridski, 2012); Nadya Danova and Roumen Avramov, *Deportiraneto na evreite ot Vardarska Makedoniya, Belomorska Trakiya i Pirot* (Sofia: Obedineni izdateli, 2013); Steven F. Sage, "The Holocaust in Bulgaria: Rescuing History from 'Rescue,'" *Dapim: Studies on the Holocaust* 31, no. 2 (2017): 139–45; Daniela Koleva, "On the (In)convertibility of National Memory into European Legitimacy: The Bulgarian Case," in *Of Red Dragons and Evil Spirits: Post-Communist Historiography between Democratization and New Politics of History*, ed. O. Luthar (Budapest: Central European University Press, 2017), 11–33; and Nadège Ragaru, "The Prosecution of Anti-Jewish Crimes in Bulgaria: Fashioning a Master Narrative of the Second World War (1944–1945)," *East European Politics and Societies* 20, no. 10 (2019): 941–75.

70 Iva Ivanova, "Skopie ni 'zahapa' i za evreite," *News.bg*, March 10, 2011.

71 More in Ivanova, "Skopie ni 'zahapa' i za evreite."

72 Spas Tashev, *The Deportation of the Jews from Vardar Macedonia and Aegean Region: Facts and Myths* (Sofia: Macedonian Scientific Institute, 2012).

73 Ḱulibrk, "Holokaustot na makedonskite Evrei," 603. See, as well, the concept of "the Holocaust template" promoted by Liljana Radonić in "The Holocaust Template—Memorial Museums in Hungary, Croatia and Bosnia-Herzegovina," *Anali* 15, no. 1 (2018): 131–54. See Teodor Borisov, "Makedonskite klubove v sistema na balgarkiya futbol v perioda na Vtorata svetovna voyna. Sluchayat na Makedoniya (Skopie)," *Makedonski Pregled* 4 (2018): 91–108, for an overview of the Bulgarian debate on the movie. The film was also discussed in Nevena Daković and Aleksandra Milovanović, "Narativi sećanja: Holokaust na ekranima bivše Jugoslavije," *Umjetnost riječi* 60, nos. 1–2 (2016): 1–26, and Ragaru, "Nationalization through Internationalization," 301–2. See Elena Ǵeroska, "Četvro poluvreme: Propagandata i neiskrenosta na Darko Mitrevski osakatija eden

odličen film," *Okno*, September 26, 2012, and Nikola Gelevski, "Treto poluvreme: Kradcite na zagubeniot kovčeg," *Okno*, October 2, 2012, for the Macedonian criticism on the film.

74 More on the "nationalistic turn" in Robert Alağozovski, "The Nationalistic Turn and the Visual Response in Macedonian Art and Cinema," in *Retracing Images: Visual Culture after Yugoslavia*, ed. D. Šuber and S. Karamanić (Leiden: Brill, 2012), and Naum Trajanovski, "Contra Omnia Discrimina: Treto Poluvreme vo kontekst na makedonskiot istoriski revizionizam," *Filozofska Tribina* 21, no. 40 (2017): 125–42.

75 The home stadium of FC "Makedonija" was described as the first "liberated territory in occupied Skopje" by Macedonian historians, while the club matches were depicted as platforms for promoting antiregime, pro-liberation agendas. More in Galena Kuculovska, "Aktivnosta na partiskata organizacija vo Skopje preku legalnite kulturno-prosvetni organizacii, sportski i drugi društva vo 1941–1942 godina," and Mile Todorovski, "Formi na otpor vo Skopje i Skopsko vo 1942 godina," both in *Skopje vo NOV 1942* (Skopje: Gradski odbor na SZB NOB, 1973); Vančo Cvetkovski, "Fudbalot vo Skopje za vreme na NOV," in *Fudbalski Klub Vardar* (Skopje: FK Vardar, 1988); and Ivko Pangovski, *Skopski fudbalski nezaboravi* (Skopje: Studentski zbor, 1994).

76 On April 1, 1943, FC "Makedonija" issued a letter to the delegate of Skopje's Commissariat for Jewish Affairs, asking to be awarded with the confiscated Jewish properties in the name of the "large number of members and competitors" and "having in mind the great sport activity of the club and the role it performs in the formation of a strong and powerful sporting youth of the unified fatherland." More in Kolonomos and Vesković-Vangeli, *Evreite vo Makedonija*, 856–57.

77 See the interview with the director for an overview of the events in Deana Kjuka, "Director of Controversial Holocaust Film Rejects 'Revisionist' Criticism," *Radio Free Europe—Macedonian Program*, December 21, 2012, and for a more recent account, Sinisa Jakov Marusic, "Macedonian Medieval Epic Annoys Bulgaria," *Balkan Insight*, February 17, 2014.

78 See, for instance, Daut Dauti, "Debatata 'Čij e Goce Delčev?'—ne vodi nikade," *Deutsche Welle—Macedonian*, June 24, 2019, and Martin Dimitrov and Sinisa Jakov Marusic, "Long-Dead Hero's Memory Tests Bulgarian-North Macedonian Reconciliation," *Balkan Insight*, June 25, 2019.

79 Namely, in 2011, "Shalom" issued a political statement stressing that "the German authorities, along with the Bulgarian pro-Nazi government, as

well as the lack of resistance by the local population," are "culpable for the deportation of the Jews" from the territories of East Thrace, Vardar Macedonia, and the town of Pirot. The author thanks Goran Sadikarijo, the director of the Holocaust Memorial Center, for shedding light on this matter. "Shalom" has not, thus far, officially published a revised statement. However, in 2021, "Shalom" amended its statement with a harsher wording—this happened in the context of the escalation in the Bulgaro-Macedonian dispute over history in 2020 described earlier.

80 See, for instance, Marjan Nikolovski, "75 godini od holokaustot na Evreite—Borisov žali, no ne se izvinuva," *Sitel*, March 12, 2018, and Jasen Bojadžiev, "Deportacijata na makedonskite Evrei- ḱe pobara li Bugarija proška," *Deutsche Welle—Macedonian*, March 12, 2018.

81 Sage, "The Holocaust in Bulgaria," 141.

82 "Kaloyan Pargov, BSP—Sofiya: V Denya na spasyavaneto na balgarskite evrei tryabva da si spomnim vremenata, kogato po ulitsite shestvashe omrazata, i da ne gi dopuskame," *Fokus*, March 10, 2019.

83 John-Paul Himka and Joanna Beata Michlic, "Introduction," in *Bringing the Dark Past to Light: The Reception of the Holocaust in Postcommunist Europe*, ed. J-P. Himka and J. B. Michlic, 17.

84 I thank Prof. Roumen Avramov for sharing more details with me about this initiative.

85 "Bugarija ima interes od makedonskiot napredok," *Globus*, July 24, 2012.

86 Steinfeldt, "Rescue in Bulgaria and Macedonia."

87 "Memorijalen centar na holokaustot na Evreite od Makedonija," *Holocaust Fund*, 2019.

Bibliography

Alaǵozovski, Robert. "The Nationalistic Turn and the Visual Response in Macedonian Art and Cinema." In *Retracing Images: Visual Culture after Yugoslavia*, ed. Daniel Šuber and Slobodan Karamanić, 171–94. Leiden: Brill, 2012.

Avramov, Roumen. *"Spasenie" i padenie. Mikroikonomika na darzhavniya antisemitizam v Balgariya, 1940–44*. ("Salvation" and abjection. Microeconomics of state antisemitism in Bulgaria, 1940–44.) Sofia: UI Sv. Kliment Ohridski, 2012.

Avramov, Roumen, et al. *Balgariya i antisemitizmat*. Berlin: Ekstaz, 2018.

Berenbaum, Michael. *The Jews in Macedonia during World War II*. Skopje: Holocaust Fund of the Jews of Macedonia, 2016.

———. "The Rescuers: When the Ordinary Is Extraordinary." In *The Routledge History of the Holocaust*, ed. Jonathan C. Friedman, 315–25. London: Routledge, 2011.

Blaževska, Katerina. "Bojko Borisov kako Vili Brant: Počit za žrtvite od Holokaustot." (Bojko Borisov as Willy Brandt: Respect for the victims of the Holocaust.) *Deutsche Welle—Macedonian*, March 12, 2018, https://tinyurl.com/5n7kp69v, accessed July 2023.

Bogusławska, Magdalena. "Powrót do Čivutany. Otwarcie Centrum Pamięci o Zagładzie Żydów z Macedonii." (Return to Čivutana. Opening of the Holocaust Memorial Center for the Jews of Macedonia.) *Zagłada Żydów. Studia i Materiały* 7 (2011): 540–45.

Bojadžiev, Jasen. "Deportacijata na makedonskite Evrei—ḱe pobara li Bugarija proška." (The deportation of the Macedonian Jews—Will Bulgaria ask for forgiveness.) *Deutsche Welle—Macedonian*, March 12, 2018, https://tinyurl.com/ms65c7hu, accessed July 2023.

Borisov, Teodor. "Makedonskite klubove v sistema na balgarkiya futbol v perioda na Vtorata svetovna voyna. Sluchayat na Makedoniya (Skopie)." (Macedonian clubs in the Bulgarian football system during World War II. The case of Macedonia [Skopje].) *Makedonski Pregled* 4 (2018): 91–108.

Brunnbauer, Ulf. "Ancient Nationhood and the Struggle for Statehood: Historiographic Myths in the Republic of Macedonia." In *Myths and Boundaries in South-Eastern Europe*, ed. Pål Kolstø, 262–96. London: Hurst & Company, 2005.

———. "Historiography, Myths and the Nation in the Republic of Macedonia." In *(Re)Writing History: Historiography in Southeast Europe after Socialism*, ed. Ulf Brunnbauer, 165–200. Münster: LIT Studies on South East Europe, 2004.

———. "Pro-Serbians vs. Pro-Bulgarians: Revisionism in Post-Socialist Macedonian Historiography." *History Compass* 3, no. 1 (2005): 1–17.

"Bugarija ima interes od makedonskiot napredok." (Bulgaria has an interest in the Macedonian progress.) *Globus*, July 24, 2012.

"Bulgaria Sends a Memorandum on 'State-sponsored Anti-Bulgarian Ideology' in North Macedonia." *European Western Balkans*, September 22, 2020, https://europeanwesternbalkans.com/2020/09/22/bulgaria-sends-a-memorandum-on-north-macedonian-eu-accession-on-their-state-sponsored-anti-bulgarian-ideology/, accessed April 2023.

Case, Holly. "The Combined Legacies of the 'Jewish Question' and the 'Macedonian Question.'" In *Bringing the Dark Past to Light: The Reception of the Holocaust in Postcommunist Europe*, ed. John-Paul Himka and Joanna Beata Michlic, 352–76. Lincoln: University of Nebraska Press, 2013.

Cekova, Marina. "Borisov pochete v Skopie pametta na zaginalite makedonski evrei." (Borisov honored the memory of the dead Macedonian Jews in Skopje.) *Nova*, March 12, 2018, https://tinyurl.com/yrkrrcd6, accessed July 2023.

Čepreganov, Todor. "Was the Partisan Organization in Macedonia Able to Save the Jews?" In *Diplomacy and Deportation*, ed. Viktor Gaber. Skopje: Diplomatski klub—Memorijalen centar na holokaustot na Evreite od Makedonija—Institut za nacionalna istorija pri Univerzitetot "Sv. Kiril i Metodij," 2017.

Cvetkovski, Vančo. "Fudbalot vo Skopje za vreme na NOV." (Football in Skopje during the People's Liberation War.) In *Fudbalski Klub Vardar*. Skopje: FK Vardar, 1988.

Daković, Nevena, and Aleksandra Milovanović. "Narativi sećanja: Holokaust na ekranima bivše Jugoslavije." (Narratives of remembering: The Holocaust on the screens in former Yugoslavia.) *Umjetnost riječi* 60, nos. 1–2 (2016): 1–26.

Damjanoska-Spesenovska, Elizabeta. "Reakcija na Evrejskata zaednica." (Reaction of the Jewish community.) *Sloboden pečat*, December 10, 2022, https://www.slobodenpecat.mk/stav-na-evrejskata-zaednicza-za-ulogata-na-czarstvoto-bugarija-vo-deportaczijata-na-makedonskite-evrei-vo-treblinka/, accessed April 2023.

Danova, Nadya, and Roumen Avramov, eds. *Deportiraneto na evreite ot Vardarska Makedoniya, Belomorska Trakiya i Pirot.* (The deportation of the Jews from Vardar's Macedonia, Western Thrace, and Pirot.) Sofia: Obedineni izdateli, 2013.

Dauti, Daut. "Debatata 'Čij e Goce Delčev?'—ne vodi nikade." (The debate "Whose is Goce Delčev?"—leads nowhere.) *Deutsche Welle—Macedonian*, June 24, 2019, https://tinyurl.com/mrxudxyc, accessed July 2023.

David, Lea. "Lost in Transaction in Serbia and Croatia: Memory Content as a Trade Currency." In *Replicating Atonement: Foreign Models in the Commemorations of Atrocities*, ed. Mischa Gabowitsch, 73–98. Cham: Palgrave Macmillan, 2017.

Dimitrov, Martin, and Sinisa Jakov Marusic. "Long-Dead Hero's Memory Tests Bulgarian-North Macedonian Reconciliation." *Balkan Insight*, June 25, 2019, https://balkaninsight.com/2019/06/25/long-dead-heros-memory-tests-bulgarian-north-macedonian-reconciliation/, accessed July 2023.

Džundeva, Lepa. "Povtorno debata: Dali Bugarija bila fašistička zemja vo Vtorata svetska vojna." (A debate anew: Was Bulgaria a fascist state in World War II.) *TV24*, February 6, 2022, https://24.mk/details/povtorno-debata-dali-bugarija-bila-fashistichka-zemja-vo-vtorata-svetska-vojna, accessed April 2023.

"Evrejskata zaednica zgrozena od registracijata na Združenieto Car Boris III vo Ohrid." (The Jewish community disgusted by the registration of the Association

Tsar Boris III in Ohrid.) *Radio Slobodna Evropa*, August 10, 2022, https://www.slobodnaevropa.mk/a/31981707.html, accessed April 2023.

Gaber, Viktor. *Feniksot na nepokorot: 75 godini od obnovuvanjeto na Evrejskata zaednica vo Makedonija*. (The phoenix of defiance: 75 years from the renewal of the Jewish community in Macedonia.) Skopje: Fond na holokaustot na Evreite od Makedonija, 2019.

Gaon, Aleksandar, ed. *We Survived . . . : Yugoslav Jews on the Holocaust*. Belgrade: Jewish Historical Museum, 2005.

Gelevski, Nikola. "Treto poluvreme: Kradcite na zagubeniot kovčeg." (Third half: The thieves of the lost ark.) *Okno*, October 2, 2012, https://okno.mk/node/22430, accessed July 2023.

Ǵeroska, Elena. "Četvrtoto poluvreme, propagandata i neiskrenosta na Darko Mitrevski osakatija eden odličen film!" (The fourth half, Darko Mitrevski's propaganda and dishonesty ruined a great movie!) *Okno*, September 26, 2012, https://okno.mk/node/22317, accessed July 2023.

Goldstein, Ivo. "The Jews in Yugoslavia 1918–1941: Anti-Semitism and the Struggle for Equality." *Jewish Studies at the Central European University* 2, no. 1 (2002): 51–64.

———. "Restoring Jewish Life in Communist Yugoslavia, 1945–1967." *East European Jewish Affairs* 34, no. 1 (2006): 58–71.

Grahek Ravančić, Martina. "The Work of the Land Commission for the Investigation of War Crimes of the Occupiers and Their Collaborators: Analysis Based on Set Tasks and Cases." *Review of Croatian History* 8, no. 1 (2012): 123–49.

"Hadži-Mitkov Family." The Righteous Among the Nations Database, M.31.2/1036 (1976), https://righteous.yadvashem.org/?search=mitkov&searchType=righteous_only&language=en&itemId=4043739&ind=0, accessed July 2023.

"Holokaustot vo Makedonija nikogaš nema da bide zaboraven." (The holocaust in Macedonia will never be forgotten.) *NovaTV*, March 11, 2018, https://novatv.mk/holokaustot-vo-makedonija-nikogash-nema-da-bide-zaboraven/, accessed April 2023.

Ivanov, Bojan. "Voved." In *Ehoto na makedonskite Sefardi* (The echo of the Macedonian Sephardim), ed. Marica Jovanovska. Skopje: Muzej na Makedonija, 2003.

Ivanova, Iva. "Skopie ni 'zahapa' i za evreite." (Skopje "bit" us for the Jews too.) *News.bg*, March 10, 2011.

Jambrešić-Kirin, Renata. "Politika sjećanja na Drugi svjetski rat u doba medijske reprodukcije socijalističke culture." (The politics of memory of World War II in the era of media reproduction of socialist culture.) In *Devijacije i promašaji:*

Etnografija domaćeg socijalizma, ed. Lada Feldman and Ines Prica, 149–78. Zagreb: Institut za etnologiju i folkloristiku, 2006.
Janev, Goran. "Narrating the Nation, Narrating the City." *Cultural Analysis* 10, no. 3 (2011): 3–21.
Jovanovska, Marica. *Ehoto na makedonskite Sefardi*. (The Echo of the Macedonian Sephardim.) Skopje: Muzej na Makedonija, 2003.
"Kaloyan Pargov, BSP—Sofiya: V Denya na spasyavaneto na balgarskite evrei tryabva da si spomnim vremenata, kogato po ulitsite shestvashe omrazata, i da ne gi dopuskame." (Kaloyan Pargov, BSP—Sofia: On the day of the salvation of the Bulgarian Jews we should evoke the times when violence was marching in the streets.) *GlasNews*, March 10, 2019, https://glasnews.bg/ot-poslednite-minuti/kaloian-pargov-bspsofiia-denia-spasiavaneto-balgarskite-333161/, accessed July 2023.
Kapralski, Sławomir. "The Role Played by the Auschwitz-Birkenau State Museum in Public Discourse and the Evolving Consciousness of the Holocaust in Polish Society." In *Jewish Presence in Absence: The Aftermath of the Holocaust in Poland, 1944–2010*, ed. Feliks Tych and Monika Adamczyk-Grabowska, 605–34. Jerusalem: Yad Vashem/International Institute for Holocaust Research/Diana Zborowski Center for the Study of the Aftermath of the Shoah, 2014.
Karahasan, Mustafa. "Turskata i albanskata narodnost vo vooruženiot otpor na gradot protiv okupatorot vo 1941 godina." (The Turkish and the Albanian nationalities in the armed struggle of the city against the occupier in 1941.) In *Skopje vo NOV 1941*. Skopje: Gradski odbor na SZB NOV, 1973.
Kerenji, Emil. "'Your Salvation Is the Struggle Against Fascism': Yugoslav Communists and the Rescue of Jews, 1941–1945." *Contemporary European History* 25, no. 1 (2016): 57–74.
Kirshenblatt-Gimblett, Barbara. "Why Jewish Museums? An International Perspective." *Studia Judaica* 16, no. 2/32 (2013): 77–100.
Kjuka, Deana. "Director of Controversial Holocaust Film Rejects 'Revisionist' Criticism." *Radio Free Europe—Macedonian Program*, December 21, 2012.
Koleva, Daniela. "On the (In)convertibility of National Memory into European Legitimacy: The Bulgarian Case." In *Of Red Dragons and Evil Spirits: Post-Communist Historiography between Democratization and New Politics of History*, ed. Oto Luthar, 11–33. Budapest: Central European University Press, 2017.
Koljanin, Milan. "Istraživanje holokausta u Jugoslaviji." (The research of the Holocaust in Yugoslavia.) In *Izraelsko-srpska akademska razmena u istraživanju Holokausta*, ed. Jovan Mirković, 284–315. Beograd: Muzej žrtava genocida, 2008.

Kolonomos, Jamila. *Dviženjeto na otporot i Evreite od Makedonija. Skopje: Fond na holokaustot na Evreite od Makedonija.* (The resistance movement and the Jews from Macedonia.) Skopje: Holocaust Fund for the Jews of Macedonia, 2013.

Kolonomos, Jamila, and Vera Veskoviḱ-Vangeli. *Evreite vo Makedonija vo Vtorata svetska vojna 1941–1945.* (Jews in Macedonia during World War II, 1941–1945.) Skopje: Macedonian Academy of Sciences and Arts, 1986.

Korneti, Melpomeni, et al. *Holocaust Memorial Center of the Jews from Macedonia.* Skopje: Holocaust Fund of the Jews from Macedonia, 2014.

Kucia, Marek. *Auschwitz jako fakt społeczny.* (Auschwitz as a social fact.) Krakow: Universitas, 2005.

Kuculovska, Galena. "Aktivnosta na partiskata organizacija vo Skopje preku legalnite kulturno-prosvetni organizacii, sportski i drugi društva vo 1941–1942 godina." (The activity of the partisan organization in Skopje via the cultural-educational organizations, sports and other associations during 1941–1942.) In *Skopje vo NOV 1942.* Skopje: Gradski odbor na SZB NOB, 1973.

———. "Interegnumot vo Skopje—April 1941." (The interregnum in Skopje—April 1941.) *Muzejski Glasnik* 4 (1979): 149–54.

———. "Izložbata Tragedijata na makedonskite Evrei." (The exhibition "The tragedy of Macedonian Jewry.") *Muzejski Glasnik* no. 5 (1982): 149–54.

Ḱulibrk, Jovan. "Holokaustot na makedonskite Evrei vo istoriografijata." (The Holocaust of the Macedonian Jews in historiography.) In *Evreite od Makedonija i Holokaustot: Istorija, teorija, kultura*, ed. Sofija Grandakovska, 592–610. Skopje: Evro Balkan Press, 2011.

Lebl, Aleksandar, et al., eds. *Ženi.* Beograd: Čigoja, 2013.

Lebl, Ženi. *Plima i Slom.* (Tide and Wreck.) Skopje: Fond na Holokaustot na Evreite od Makedonija, 2013.

Levi, David-Dale. "Bitoljski Jevreji u Narodnooslobodilačkoj borbi." (Bitola Jews in the peoples' liberation war.) In *Jevrejski Almanah 1957–1958*, 109–15. Beograd: Savez Jevrejskih Opština Jugoslavije, 1959.

Löwenthal, Zdenko, ed. *The Crimes of the Fascist Occupants and Their Collaborators against Jews in Yugoslavia.* Belgrade: Federation of Jewish Communities of Federative People's Republic of Yugoslavia, 1957.

Majewski, Piotr. "Project 'Skopje 2014'—À la recherche du temps perdu." *Ethnologia Balkanica* 19 (2016): 167–83.

Marcuse, Harold. *Legacies of Dachau: The Uses and Abuses of a Concentration Camp, 1933–2001.* Cambridge: Cambridge University Press, 2011.

Marusic, Sinisa Jakov. "Macedonian Medieval Epic Annoys Bulgaria." *Balkan Insight*, February 17, 2014, https://balkaninsight.com/2014/02/17/macedonian-medieval-epic-angers-bulgaria/, accessed July 2023.

Matkovski, Aleksandar. "The Destruction of Macedonian Jewry in 1943." *Yad Vashem Studies* 3 (1959).

———. *Istorijata na Evreite vo Makedonija*. Skopje: Makedonska revija, 1983.

———. "Tragedijata na Evreite od Makedonija." (The tragedy of the Jews from Macedonia.) *Glasnik na Institutot za nacionalna istorija* 2 (1958).

McEvoy, James. "Managing Culture in Post-conflict Societies." *Contemporary Social Science* 6, no. 1 (2011): 55–71.

"Memorijalen centar na holokaustot na Evreite od Makedonija." *Holocaust Fund*, 2019, https://www.holocaustfund.org.mk/posts/details/1, accessed July 2023.

Miller, Michael Lee. *Bulgaria during the Second World War*. Stanford, CA: Stanford University Press, 1975.

Muhiḱ, Maja, and Aleksandar Takovski. "Redefining National Identity in Macedonia: Analyzing Competing Origin Myths and Interpretations through Hegemonic Representations." *Etnološka Tribina* 37, no. 44 (2014): 138–52.

Namičeva, Jasminka, et al. *Po tragite na Feniksot*. (The phoenix trail.) Skopje: Muzej na grad Skopje, 2003.

Nikolovski, Marjan. "75 godini od holokaustot na Evreite—Borisov žali, no ne se izvinuva." (75 years from the Holocaust of the Jews—Borisov regretful, but fails to apologize.) *Sitel*, March 12, 2018, https://sitel.com.mk/75-godini-od-holokaustot-na-evreite-borisov-zhali-no-ne-se-izvinuva, accessed July 2023.

Ofer, Dalia. "Tormented Memories: The Individual and the Collective." *Israel Studies* 9, no. 3 (2004): 137–56.

Opfer-Klinger, Björn. "Bulgaria's Collaboration with the Axis Powers in World War II." In *Complicated Complicity: European Collaboration with Nazi Germany during World War II*, ed. M. Bitunjac and J. H. Schoeps, 161–92. Berlin: De Gruyter, 2021.

Panajotov, Saško. "Reakcija na Evrejskata verska zaednica i Fondot na holokaustot na Evreite od Makedonija." (Reaction of the Jewish religious community and the Holocaust Fund of the Jews of Macedonia.) *MIA*, September 24, 2021, https://tinyurl.com/25sb2rvt, accessed July 2023.

Pangovski, Ivko. *Skopski fudbalski nezaboravi*. (Skopje football memories.) Skopje: Studentski zbor, 1994.

Popovska, Dragica. "Muzejot na holokaustot vo Skopje: Mesto na seḱavanje." (The Museum of the Holocaust in Skopje: Memory site.) *Journal of History* 49, no. 1 (2014): 281–91.

———. "Symbolic Representations of Identity and the History of the Jews in Macedonia's Public Space." *Studia Środkowoeuropejskie i Bałkanistyczne* 26 (2017): 83–88.

"Predlog-Deklaracija po povod 75 godni od deportacijata na Evreite od Makedonija vo logorot na smrtta Treblinka." (Draft declaration on the 75th anniversary of the deportation of the Macedonian Jews in the deathcamp Treblinka.) *Sobranie na Republika Makedonija*, March 1, 2018.

Radonić, Liljana. "The Holocaust Template—Memorial Museums in Hungary, Croatia and Bosnia-Herzegovina." *Anali* 15, no. 1 (2018): 131–54.

Ragaru, Nadège. "Bordering the Past: The Elusive Presences of the Holocaust in Socialist Macedonia and Socialist Bulgaria." *Südost-Forschungen* 76 (2017): 241–72.

———. "Contrasting Destinies: The Plight of Bulgarian Jews and the Jews in Bulgarian-occupied Greek and Yugoslav Territories during World War Two." *Online Encyclopedia of Mass Violence* (2017), https://www.sciencespo.fr/mass-violence-war-massacre-resistance/en/document/contrasting-destinies-plight-bulgarian-jews-and-jews-bulgarian-occupied-greek-and-yugoslav-.html, accessed July 2023.

———. "Nationalizing through Internationalization: Writing, Remembering and Commemorating the Holocaust in Macedonia and Bulgaria after 1989." *Südosteuropa* 65, no. 2 (2017): 284–315.

———. "The Prosecution of Anti-Jewish Crimes in Bulgaria: Fashioning a Master Narrative of the Second World War (1944–1945)." *East European Politics and Societies* 20, no. 10 (2019): 941–75.

Romano, Jaša. *Jevreji Jugoslavije 1941–1945: Žrtve genocida i učesnici narodnooslobodilačkog rata*. (The Jews of Yugoslavia 1941–1945: Victims of genocide and participants in the people's liberation war.) Beograd: Savez jevrejskih opština Jugoslavije, 1980.

Rosoux, Valerie. "Reconciliation Narrative: Scope and Limits of the Pax Europeana." *Journal of Contemporary European Studies* 25, no. 3 (2017): 325–39.

Rusin, Bartłomiej. "Deportacja Żydów z Macedonii Wardarskiej, Bełomoria i Pirotu w historiografii bułgarskiej." (The deportation of the Jews from Vardar Macedonia, Belomoria and Pirot in the Bulgarian historiography.) *Zagłada Żydów. Studia i Materiały* 11 (2015): 255–68.

Sadikario, Avram, and Rachel Chanin Asiel. "Avram Sadikario." *Centropa*, March 2005, https://www.centropa.org/en/biography/avram-sadikario, accessed July 2023.

Sage, Steven F. "The Holocaust in Bulgaria: Rescuing History from 'Rescue.'" *Dapim: Studies on the Holocaust* 31, no. 2 (2017): 139–45.

Sawicki, Paweł. "We Remember the Past to Transform the Future." *Memoria: Memory—History—Education* 18, no. 3 (2019): 6–15.

Sazdova Kondijanova, Ljubica. *Muzej na grad Skopje 1949–2011*. (The museum of the city of Skopje 1949–2011.) Skopje: Muzej na grad Skopje, 2011.

"Sednica po povod 75 godini od deportacijata na Evreite od Republika Makedonija vo logorot na smrtta Treblinka." (Meeting on the 75th anniversary of the deportation of the Jews from the Republic of Macedonia in the deathcamp Treblinka.) *Sobranie na Republika Makedonija*, March 12, 2018, https://www.sobranie.mk/2016-2020-srm-ns_article-sednica-po-povod-75-godini-od-deportacijata-na-evreite-od-republika-makedonija-vo-logorot-na-smrtta.nspx, accessed July 2023.

Sion, Isak. "Učestvoto na Evreite od Štip vo Narodnoosloboditelnoto dviženje." (The participation of the Jews from Štip in the Peoples' Liberation movement.) In *Evreite od Makedonija i Holokaustot: Istorija, teorija, kultura*, ed. Sofija Grandakovska, 425–35. Skopje: Evro Balkan Press, 2011.

"So poveḱe nastani na 11 i 12 mart vo Skopje, Bitola i Štip ḱe bide odbeležana 75-godišninata od holokaustot na makedonskite Evrei." (Multiple events on 11 and 12 March in Skopje, Bitola and Štip will mark the 75th anniversary of the Holocaust of Macedonian Jews.) *Vlada na Republika Severna Makedonija*, March 10, 2018.

Spaskovska, Ljubica. "Report on Macedonia." *CITSEE Europeanisation of Citizenship in the Successor States of the Former Yugoslavia*, 2012, https://cadmus.eui.eu/bitstream/handle/1814/19624/RSCAS_EUDO_CIT_2012_6.pdf?sequence=3&isAllowed=y, accessed July 2023.

Stefoska, Irena. "Why the Institute of National History? The Beginnings of the Institutionalized Form of Historiography in the Process of Building the Macedonian Nation." In *The Echo of the Nation*, ed. Žarko Trajanovski, 76–92. Skopje: Templum, 2009.

Stefoska, Irena, and Darko Stojanov. "A Tale in Stone and Bronze: Old/New Strategies for Political Mobilization in the Republic of Macedonia." *Nationalities Papers* 45, no. 3 (2017): 356–69.

Steinfeldt, Irena. "Rescue in Bulgaria and Macedonia through the Perspective of the Files of the Righteous Among the Nations." *Yad Vashem* (2014), https://www.yadvashem.org/righteous/resources/rescue-in-bulgaria-and-macedonia.html, accessed July 2023.

Subotić, Jelena. *Yellow Star, Red Star: Holocaust Remembrance after Communism*. Ithaca, NY: Cornell University Press, 2019.

Taczyńska, Katarzyna. "A Scattered Mosaic of Records and Reminiscences: Ženi Lebl's War Odyssey in Her Personal Writings." In *An Introspective Approach to Women's Intercultural Fieldwork: Female Researchers' Narrations Based on Their Intercultural Experiences from the Field*, ed. Urzula Markowska-Manista and Justyna Pilarska, 68–102. Warsaw: Akademia Pedagogiki Specjalnej, 2017.

Tashev, Spas. *The Deportation of the Jews from Vardar Macedonia and Aegean Region: Facts and Myths*. Sofia: Macedonian Scientific Institute, 2012.

"Todorov family." The Righteous Among the Nations Database, M.31.2/1766 (1980), https://righteous.yadvashem.org/?search=todorov&searchType=righteous_only&language=en&itemId=4024079&ind=0, accessed July 2023.

Todorov, Svetoslav. "Bulgarian Ruling Coalition Cracks over North Macedonia Dispute." *Balkan Insight*, June 8, 2022, https://balkaninsight.com/2022/06/08/bulgarian-ruling-coalition-cracks-over-north-macedonia-dispute/, accessed April 2023.

Todorovski, Mile. "Formi na otpor vo Skopje i Skopsko vo 1942 godina." (Resistance forms in Skopje and the Skopje region in 1942.) In *Skopje vo NOV 1942*. Skopje: Gradski odbor na SZB NOB, 1973.

Trajanovski, Naum. "Contra Omnia Discrimina: Treto Poluvreme vo kontekst na makedonskiot istoriski revizionizam." (Contra Omnia Discrimina: Third Half in the context of the Macedonian historical revisionism.) *Filozofska Tribina* 21, no. 40 (2017): 125–42.

Troebst, Stefan. "Historical Politics and Historical 'Masterpieces' in Macedonia before and after 1991." *New Balkan Politics* 6 (2003), http://www.newbalkanpolitics.org.mk/item/Historical-Politics-and-Historical-%E2%80%9CMasterpieces%E2%80%9D-in-Macedonia-before-and-after-1991#.ZCG8ZnZBy3A, accessed July 2023.

———. "Macedonian Historiography on the Holocaust in Macedonia under Bulgarian Occupation." *Südosteuropäische Hefte* 1 (2013): 107–14.

———. "Yugoslav Macedonia, 1943–1953: Building the Party, the State, and the Nation." In *State-Society Relations in Yugoslavia, 1945–1992*, ed. Melissa K. Bokovoy, Jill A. Irvine, and Carol S. Lilly, 243–66. New York: St. Martin's Press, 1997.

Vervaet, Stijn. *Holocaust, War and Transnational Memory: Testimony from Yugoslav and Post-Yugoslav Literature*. New York: Routledge, 2018.

Vesković-Vangeli, Vera. "Treblinka, zbornik na dokumenti." (Treblinka, a collection of documents.) In *Evreite od Makedonija i Holokaustot: Istorija, teorija, kultura*, ed. Sofija Grandakovska, 9–402. Skopje: Evro Balkan Press, 2011.

Winter, Jay, and Emmanuel Sivan. "Setting the Framework." In *War and Remembrance in the Twentieth Century*, ed. Jay Winter and Emmanuel Sivan, 6–39. Cambridge: Cambridge University Press, 2000.

Wóycicka, Zofia. *Arrested Mourning: Memory of the Nazi Camps in Poland, 1944–1950*. Frankfurt am Main: Peter Lang, 2013.

Yordanova, Veselinka. "Borisov v Skopie: Da ne zabravyame greshkite, da rabotim zaedno." (Borisov in Skopje: We shall not forget the mistakes, we should work together.) *Dnes*, March 12, 2018, https://www.dnes.bg/politika/2018/03/12/borisov-v-skopie-da-ne-zabraviame-greshkite-da-rabotim-zaedno.370396, accessed July 2023.

Young, James E. *The Textures of Memory: Holocaust Memorials and Meaning*. New Haven, CT: Yale University Press, 1993.

Zdravkovska, Žaneta. "Se istražuva dali bila na deportirani Evrei kukjata vo koja e bugarskiot klub." (It is being investigated whether the house of the Bulgarian club was from deported Jews.) *Sakam da kažam*, August 9, 2022, https://sdk.mk/index.php/dopisna-mrezha/se-istrazhuva-dali-bila-evrejska-kukata-vo-koja-e-bugarskiot-klub-vo-bitolskoto-evrejsko-maalo/, accessed April 2023.

PART II

National Memory—Local Memory

4

Bringing the State Back into Memory Studies

Commemorating the Righteous in France, 2007–20

SARAH GENSBURGER

The official commemoration of the Righteous Among the Nations, the gentiles who helped Jews during the Holocaust, commenced on May 1, 1962, in Jerusalem with the inauguration of the Avenue of the Righteous on the site of Yad Vashem. Almost sixty years later, on September 12, 2019, a new Avenue of the Righteous was unveiled, this time in the French spa city of Vichy. Between 1940 and 1944, the city was the seat of the French government of the Vichy regime, which collaborated with the German occupiers in implementing the Final Solution. While the 1962 Jerusalem Avenue of the Righteous celebrated rescuers as a courageous minority, the 2019 Vichy Avenue of the Righteous was said to memorialize the behavior of a majority of the French people during the Holocaust. The symbolic gap between these two sites commemorating the Righteous calls for an in-depth study of the ways in which memory categories travel from one place to another and the substantial changes they undergo in that process.

Both the appropriation and the change in the meaning of the category of "Righteous" in the commemoration of the Holocaust in France can be traced back to a government intervention. This chapter, therefore, examines the influence of the state and the way transnational, local, and national dynamics of memory interact. In doing so, it takes a stand in the debate on the best scale for analyzing the transnationalization of memory in the contemporary world.[1] Indeed, despite the development of the third phase of memory studies focusing on the transnational dimension, until now few scholars have addressed the "tension between the production of remembrance through transnational processes and its grounding in concrete locations."[2] Locating transnational memory still constitutes a challenge for the field.[3] To overcome it, this chapter will suggest putting the state back into memory studies as a way of understanding this articulation between transnational dynamics and local appropriations: "The increasing importance of transnational and local in memory studies seems to have made the nation a less relevant starting point from which to conceptualize memory. Yet, states progressively attempt to administer memory."[4] Since the beginning of the 1990s, governments across the world have, indeed, been implementing a large and increasing number of public memory policies.[5] What follows calls for a reintroduction of the state into the study of memory dynamics, yet not through a national lens, as implied in the expression of "national memory," which was key in the first phase of memory studies, but as an organizational framework that plays an active role in the articulation of local and transnational levels of memorialization. To do so, this chapter will examine the development of commemorative sites and landmarks commemorating the Righteous which have emerged all over France since 2007.

This essay was not meant to be written. In July 2006, I defended a dissertation on the process of remembrance through the concept of Righteous Among the Nations, focusing on the French case. I analyzed how and to what extent the Israeli commemorative practice had been appropriated in the French context, at the intersection of state public policies, collective mobilization, and individual testimonies. I described how the French state, its government, and its administration had progressively transformed the Israeli category of "Righteous Among the Nations" into a French one, while transforming its symbolic meaning. As a perfect illustration of this dynamic that I had highlighted in my dissertation, a "National Homage to the Righteous of France" was organized within the walls of the Pantheon, the most prestigious mausoleum for figures of importance to the French nation, just a few months after I defended my thesis. On January 18, 2007, an honorific inscription appeared in the crypt of this temple of the Republic. French television broadcast the ceremony live, and access to the monument was free for seven days following the event. During that time, 42,131 people came to see the new commemorative plaque.[6] The ceremony and its apparent success seemed to be the final point in the process I had been studying for many years. The commemoration of the Righteous Among the Nations had become French, complemented by its own national site of memory.[7]

However, it has since become clear that this "National Homage to the Righteous of France" was only one more step in an ongoing process of diffusing the commemoration of the Righteous in the country. Indeed, from 2007 to 2020, more than four hundred places were named after a Righteous gentile or given the category of the "Righteous" per se.[8] This chapter examines this local diffusion of the transnational category in France as a way of investigating how transnational memory locates itself. Based on interviews, analysis of public documentation and archives, as well as participant observation fieldwork, it calls for the state to be brought back into the study of both processes—the transnationalization and localization of memory—and argues for their interconnectedness.[9]

The Creation of the First Avenues of the Righteous in France

The first Avenue of the Righteous on French soil was not the one in Vichy. In fact, an Avenue of the Righteous was inaugurated as early as October 8, 2000, in the 4th district of Paris, when this name was attached to the pedestrian street running alongside the building of the Shoah Memorial.[10] Seven years before the Pantheon ceremony, this was the first territorial appropriation of the Israeli category of Righteous by the French state.[11]

Indeed, the French state had begun to appropriate the concept of the Righteous earlier. On July 16, 1995, on the anniversary of the Vel d'Hiv roundup,[12] the newly elected French president Jacques Chirac finally acknowledged the role of the French state in the mass deportation of Jews during the Holocaust. He then used the expression "Righteous Among the Nations" for the first time in his new role as head of state. In doing so Chirac forged a new dichotomy between the Vichy government, on the one hand, and the Righteous as true Frenchmen, on the other, between the good and the bad, the light and the dark. He praised the image of France, which in his words was "present, one and indivisible, in the hearts of these French citizens, these 'Righteous Among the Nations,' who at the darkest moment of agony, as Serge Klarsfeld writes, at the risk of their lives, saved three-quarters of the Jewish community resident in France, and gave life to its better qualities: humanist values, values of freedom, justice and tolerance, on which French identity is founded, to which we remain bound in the future."[13]

Beginning in July 1995, Jacques Chirac, as head of state, continuously repeated this new narrative on any occasion he could. In December 1997, the president evoked the Righteous again, this time when submitting the "Jewish File"[14] to the Shoah Memorial:

> Of course, there was a France that resisted and fought for our honor. There were the fishermen of the Ile de Sein who answered the call of General de Gaulle. There were all the units engaged alongside the

> Allies on the Freedom front. There was the daily discreet heroism of all the "Righteous" [. . .] these anonymous people from all walks of life, all religions, who saved, often at risk to their lives, three quarters of the French Jewish population. Yes, happily there was the best, a France that was generous, courageous and proud, a France of hope. And it was this France, this France of light, General de Gaulle, the Free French, the Resistance and the Righteous which finally won the day.[15]

From one presidential speech to another, the "Righteous" became central characters in the new state narrative of World War II and the Holocaust in France. They were meant to embody the majority of the French population. Encouraged by this new official involvement of the French state in the commemoration of the Righteous (which until then was exclusively the responsibility of Israel), Daniel Marcovitch, a Jewish member of the French parliament, suggested in July 2000 that the category of Righteous should be introduced into French law. Following his lead, parliament established the novel concept of the "Righteous of France." It referred to the Israeli term while at the same time setting itself apart. Tellingly, July 16—marking the anniversary of the Vel d'Hiv roundup in 1942—became a national day of commemoration "in honor of the victims of the racist and antisemitic crimes of the French state and in honor of the 'Righteous' of France."[16] The state implemented a new public policy making the Righteous the protagonists of the official narrative.

Although the first French Avenue of the Righteous in Paris was inaugurated a few months after the creation of this new day of national commemoration, these events were linked beyond any chronological conjunction. First, Daniel Marcovitch—a French Jew with close family ties to Israel—who was both a socialist MP and a representative of the city of Paris, played an important role in the articulation of the different levels of public action and commemoration. The involvement of the state in the commemoration of the Righteous paved the way for that of the city of Paris. This direct causal relation is reflected in the original choice of the name in 2000 as the "Avenue of the Righteous of France" rather than the "Avenue of the Righteous" as in Yad Vashem.[17] The decision was made by the Paris City Council. Second, the commitment of the new French government under President Chirac to the commemoration of the Righteous not only led to a new configuration but also legitimized an increasing number of social actors, who became committed to and began to invest in this commemoration.

In 2000, fostering the creation of new "Avenues of the Righteous" on French soil became a way for local political actors and NGO representatives to claim legitimacy in the eyes of the French state. Since the mid-1980s the task of submitting claims for the recognition of Righteous by the Israeli state and the organization of local ceremonies in France belonged exclusively to the French Committee for Yad Vashem, a French NGO gathering French Jews, mainly former Jewish resistance fighters, with close links to Israel. Through their commitment, these social actors sought to promote a positive image of Israel in France and vice versa.[18] However, they had never advocated for the creation of a permanent site of memory for the Righteous in France.

Shortly after Chirac's speech of 1995,[19] the Central Consistory of France—the main representative organization of French Jewry as a religious community and the partner of the state in this matter—created the "French Association of Righteous Among the Nations," an association to pay public homage to the French Righteous. Its statute was officially registered in October 1996.[20] The association sought to encourage nominating more French citizens as Righteous by publicizing the existence of this title among French Jews and assisting them in filling in the Yad Vashem applications. In this, it was similar to the objectives of the French Committee for Yad Vashem. However, the leaders of the French Association of Righteous Among the Nations considered themselves complementary to the latter, with which they did not have direct relations. While most members of the French Committee for Yad Vashem were liberal in their religious practice, the French Association of Righteous Among the Nations and the Central Consistory were Jews practicing religion in a traditional way. The latter two groups sought to establish a parallel form of national recognition for those who had helped Jews during the war but were unable to obtain the Israeli title because of the complex and demanding procedure required by Yad Vashem. In other words, they wanted the commemoration of the Righteous to "become French." Its leaders referred to President Chirac's July 1995 speech as the trigger for their initiative. In their view, the state appropriation of the Israeli category of the Righteous opened up a new era enabling the development of a new and specifically French commemoration.

For the French Association of Righteous Among the Nations, the territorial diffusion of the commemoration of the Righteous within the French borders became one of the main concerns. They saw it as a way to anchor the title of Righteous in French society. When I interviewed one of the leaders of the French Association of Righteous Among the Nations, he had a rather strong response to my observation that such monuments already existed in Israel: "They have a memorial at Yad Vashem, the Avenue of the Righteous. But for us, it was important to create that in France."[21] In response to the question about the purpose of a French site in comparison with the Avenue of the Righteous in

Jerusalem, he again answered rather emotionally: "Listen, not everyone goes to Israel. I think there are lots of French people who support the creation of this monument in France."[22]

On November 2, 1997, the Central Consistory of France and its French Association of the Righteous Among the Nations unveiled a "Memorial to Honor the French Righteous" in Thonon-les-Bains—the region known for its resistance to the Germans during the war. The event enjoyed official support and was attended by several representatives of the French government. The minister of culture and the *prefet* (the local representative of the state) both made speeches during the ceremony. This first local memorial did not have a large impact in the country as a whole, however, as it was situated in the countryside, far away from the actual city of Thonon. As a result, it did not attract much interest either from the local population or visitors. However, the story was quite different in Nancy. After the inauguration of the Avenue of the Righteous of France in Paris, the Central Consistory of France and the French Association of the Righteous joined together with the city of Nancy to create an "Avenue of the Righteous" there. Due to the location of the space that was made available, it ultimately became a "Square of the Righteous" (Place des Justes), with the project officially inaugurated in September 2002, by the mayor of Nancy together with Gérard Blum, then president of both the Consistorial French Association of the Righteous Among the Nations and the Nancy Jewish community.

Through its commitment to the territorial dissemination of commemorative sites for the Righteous in France, the consistory changed the traditionally assumed work division between Jewish community institutions with regard to their actions toward, and interactions with, the state. Indeed, since the end of World War II, the Representative Council of Jewish Institutions in France (CRIF) had traditionally been in charge of the relations with the state concerning Jewish culture and rights, including memory and compensation issues in relation to the Holocaust, while the consistory was involved only in matters of religion and religious practice. Through their involvement in promoting the creation of commemorative sites for the Righteous in France, the consistory broke with this traditional division. So, in reaction to the inauguration in Nancy and in an effort to reclaim its role vis-à-vis the state, the CRIF in turn created a local "Avenue of the Righteous" in Toulouse in 2003. Its local branch contacted the city administration, with which it had been working closely for some time, to suggest the creation of a memorial street.

Thus between 2000 and 2003, three "Avenues of the Righteous" were inaugurated in France: in Paris, Nancy, and Toulouse. The spread of this kind of commemorative site from Israel to France illustrates the double process of transnationalization and localization of memory. The transnational expansion in France of the Israeli spatial tool of commemorating the Righteous was the result of local initiatives taking place at the level of three French cities. At the same time, this process of simultaneous transnationalization and localization corresponds first and foremost with the state policy and the social configuration built by the state. When looked at more closely, it becomes clear that this spread was triggered by the transformation of state public policy, which not only changed the official narrative in relation to the Holocaust in France but also brought about a change in the social configuration of actors involved in the field of the commemoration of the Righteous.

Competing for State Legitimization

From 2008 onward, the French state again took the initiative in appropriating the transnational memory of the Righteous. Its policies indirectly contributed to the second phase of the territorial diffusion of the commemoration of the new heroes in local contexts.

In 1990 Yad Vashem substituted the ceremony of planting a tree by a Righteous in Jerusalem with inscribing the laureates' names on a wall situated in a commemorative garden dedicated to the Righteous. Similarly, the ceremony that took place in Paris in the "Avenue of the Righteous of France" on June 14, 2006, involved engraving the names of the "Righteous of France" on the outside wall of the Shoah Memorial. This new wall was inaugurated jointly by French prime minister Dominique de Villepin and his Israeli counterpart, Ehud Olmert. The ceremony in the Pantheon just a few months later marked an additional step in the further appropriation of the Israeli commemorative ritual by the French state. The addition of the category of the "National Homage to the Righteous of France" in the crypt of the Pantheon completed the process of rooting the term "Righteous" on French soil. Although government officials and civil servants working in the central agencies of the French state had had no intention of promoting the local dissemination of this new model for memory sites, the "National Homage" generated a localization of the memory of the Righteous.

Indeed, new social actors saw the "National Homage to the Righteous of France" as official encouragement for mobilization around initiatives first and foremost embedded in the French context and therefore different from the one originally framed by the Yad Vashem Institute. In the immediate aftermath of the Pantheon ceremony and as a direct reaction to it, two new French associations, Anonymous, Righteous, and Persecuted of the Nazi Era in the French Cities (Anonymes, Justes et persécutés durant la période nazie, or AJPN) and

Tribute to the Villages of France (Hommage aux villages de France), were created with the purpose of promoting the recognition of the Righteous beyond the strict definition formulated by Yad Vashem. They also planned to develop commemorative initiatives beyond the Israeli and French capital cities. Each of them began their work by referring to the French state's memory policy and the recent inauguration of the plaque inside the Pantheon. Significantly, the headquarters of these new NGOs were both located far away from Paris, decentralizing, for the first time, the dynamics of commemoration of the Righteous in France.

The AJPN was formed on the initiative of a group of former hidden Jewish children, as well as children and grandchildren of the French Righteous,[23] from various regions of France. Its president, Hellen Kaufmann, lives in Bordeaux and its vice president, François Dru, in Annecy. This association has aimed at providing "an open platform for contributions, exchanges and encounters between all people wanting to contribute their testimonies in order to enrich, complete and publicize a story or an incident of rescue during World War II."[24] It focuses on narratives, and aims at making them available online to a broad public.

On the other hand, Tribute to the Villages of France—the second NGO to emerge from the 2007 Pantheon ceremony—has focused on the development of local commemorations and sites of memory as a way to give collective meaning to the strictly individual recognition of the Righteous by Yad Vashem.[25] Its aim is to "locate villages in France that took in and saved Jews hunted by the Nazis; honor the villagers and their villages; extend the memory work to other generations; create pedagogical instruments based on history; erect a plaque honoring the rescuers."[26] This association was also created by former hidden children based far from Paris; in this instance, its president, Maurice Barefeld, lives in Cannes. This NGO has been looking for villages where Jews were rescued, seeking to shift the recognition and rescue narrative from an individual level to a collective one. Even more, both organizations have stressed two main characteristics of the French state's redefinition of the category of Righteous, by introducing the category of "anonymous people" and thus stressing a collective dimension in the commemorative initiatives, going beyond honoring individuals formally recognized by Yad Vashem. While the scale of activities and narratives suggested by these two new French associations differed, each of them mentioned the involvement of the French state in the commemoration of the Righteous as the point of departure for their own work. Both decided to get involved because they felt legitimized to do so by the recent state initiatives concerning public memory policies. At the same time, each of these new social actors developed their own narrative and did not reproduce the "official" one promoted by the state. One focuses on making historical information about individual rescuers available online. The other wants to honor villages and cities, promoting the idea that the rescue of Jews was a collective act rather than an individual one. However, they are nonetheless both influenced by the French state, because of its roles in promoting the category of Righteous as a French one and in developing a public arena for public actors who want to commemorate rescuers in a French context, without explicit links with Yad Vashem and Israel.

The emergence of the two groups profoundly changed the configuration of social actors involved in the commemoration of the Righteous in France. Moreover, it created new challenges for the French Committee for Yad Vashem. Since 2000 the committee had been the only interlocutor of the French government in charge of policy concerning Holocaust memory, although it diverged from the state narrative, criticizing, for example, the transformation of the initial Israeli concept of the Righteous Among the Nations into the "Righteous of France" or the application of the title to groups, such as the inhabitants of an entire village. They were a state auxiliary for the participation of the Righteous and their families in the Pantheon ceremony of 2007 and for the organization of the annual commemoration of the Vel d'Hiv roundup on July 16. However, more than sixty years after the end of the war, the number of individuals who could provide testimony necessary for the application for recognition as a Righteous has steadily decreased. Therefore, the original justification for the committee's existence was at risk. Moreover, and maybe more important, the emergence of new memory activists with a strong and explicit connection to French sites weakened the French committee's legitimacy and diminished its administrative and political significance for the state.

In 2010, the new association Homage to the Villages of France organized two local ceremonies, obtaining extensive media coverage. In June they honored the village of Mauroux, in the southern department Lot, unveiling a commemorative plaque on the wall of the village hall.[27] In October the following year, they repeated the operation in the Corsican village of Canari. Jean Wohl, a Jewish man who had been rescued in Corsica and represented the NGO during the ceremony, described the association's agenda:

> Things are very clear in our mind. Through Canari, we honour all Corsican villages, and indeed all of Corsica. This land was exemplary, in a time of fear and sometimes famine, by saving Jews and also showing the way forward to free France from the yoke of the occupying forces. The term Righteous is not excessive for them. The celebration of courage, engraved in stone, also has a pedagogical aspect for all young generations who must preserve the precious memory of their

> grandparents' sacrifices and their human values of generosity and altruism. The dead are never completely dead when we remember them.[28]

In 2008 the French Committee for Yad Vashem had begun reorganizing its work and sending more representatives to the different regions of France. In 2010, likely in reaction to the initiatives of Homage to the Villages of France but without referring to it, it went one step further. In its annual report the French Committee for Yad Vashem declared its goal for 2011 to be: "to inscribe the tributes [individual recognitions of the Righteous] both locally and publicly: with plaques or by renaming a street, a square, with the names of these Righteous of France, honoured by Yad Vashem. From this came the idea of inscribing these values of courage, tolerance, fraternity more durably, by bringing these villages and towns together in a network within our Committee."[29]

Thus their Network of Sites of Memory of the Righteous, Towns and Villages of France (Le Réseau des lieux de mémoire des justes, villes et villages de France) aimed at "bringing together the towns and villages that named a place of memory—a road, a square, an alley, a garden, a plaque—in order to perpetuate the memory of these 'Righteous Among the Nations.'"[30]

When asked to retrace the emergence of this project, the general secretary of the French Committee for Yad Vashem explained that the idea came up during the inauguration of a "Plaza of the Righteous Among the Nations" and a commemorative stele on May 5, 2010, at Saint-Amand-Montrond. On this occasion, the head of the French committee became aware of the "infinite opportunities" offered by this form of commemoration tied to permanent localization: "Since then, the development of the network has become a top priority for the Committee and the best way to ensure its future."[31] Indeed, when researching this initial idea, the team composed of members of the committee determined that only 101 French towns and villages had a site of memory like this, even though more than two thousand of them in the past had hosted a recognition ceremony for one of their inhabitants (see Map 4.1). The French committee then decided to systematically invite these towns and villages to join the network.

The official launch ceremony of the network on September 12, 2012, at the City Hall in Paris illustrates the way the localization of the action of the French committee has been intertwined with an effort to reaffirm its state legitimacy. In this instance, it was strengthened by the presence of several state representatives and mayors from more than forty towns and villages who attended the ceremony.

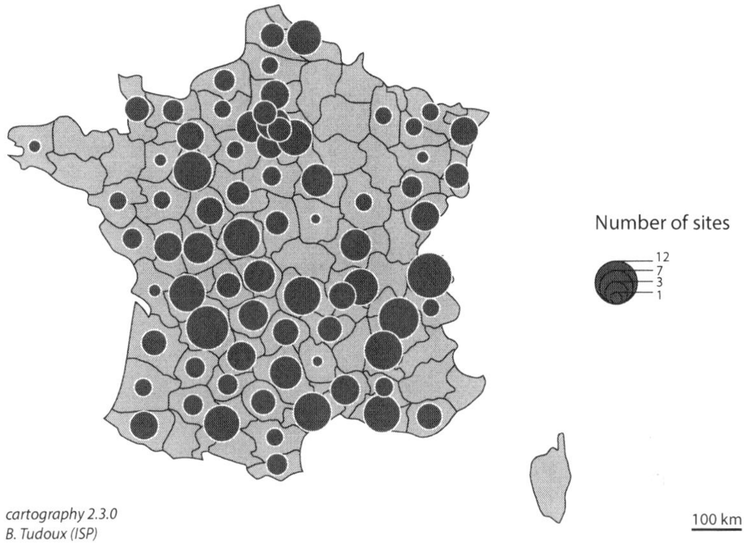

Map 4.1. Number of sites of memory for each district (French *département*). Cartography: B. Tudoux (ISP). Additional design: Clara Gensburger.

As a doctoral student, I volunteered with the committee, doing some participatory observation fieldwork. In 2011 the French committee asked me to design the digital content to be displayed during this ceremony. I explained that I wanted to continue reflecting on the issues I had examined in my dissertation. As a result I was able to take notes during conversations and to conduct informal interviews with several volunteers who participated in the committee's activities. Indeed, the committee linked the membership in the network Towns and Villages of Righteous of France for each town or village with their inauguration of a site of memory and the creation of a digital exhibition. In doing so, the committee positioned the network at the exact intersection of the digital activity developed by AJPN and of the creation of local sites of memory promoted by the Homage to the Villages of France. Already by spring 2013, the network Towns and Villages of Righteous of France had brought together forty-seven cities. Six years later, in October 2019, it had grown to 122 members, representing 386 existing sites of memory and forty-eight more under construction (see Map 4.2).[32]

While the state played a central role in the process of localization of the transnational memory of the Righteous Among the Nations, it did not intervene directly through such institutions as major museums or school programs.

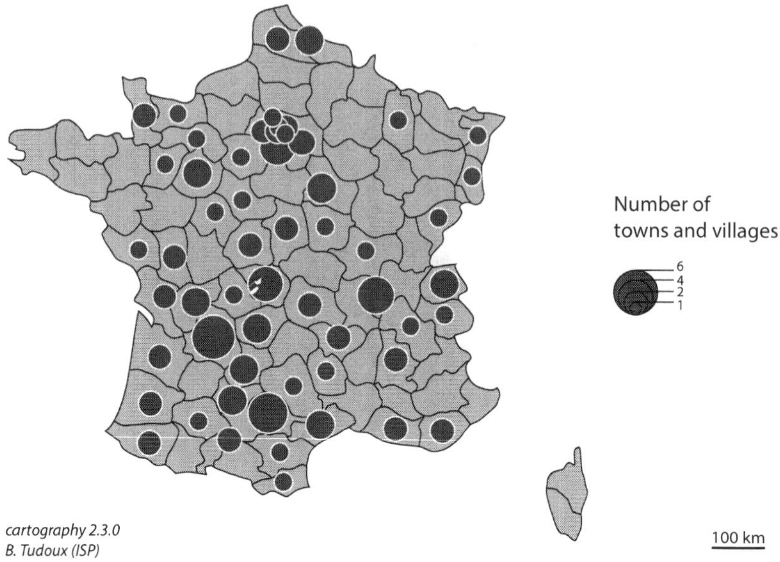

Map 4.2. Number of French towns and villages belonging to the network. Cartography: B. Tudoux (ISP). Additional design: Clara Gensburger.

Rather, the state narrative created a counterbalance to the Vichy involvement in the deportation of Jews by stressing the very existence of Righteous who are said to have contributed to the survival of three-quarters of the Jews from France. If this narrative has gained such a broad popularity, it is because it corresponded with the views of numerous and diverse social actors who had been sharing this view for years before the French government and its representatives verbalized it. Thus the main impact of the state memory policy occurred by way of its commitment to the commemoration of the Righteous of France. In turn, this commitment transformed the configuration of social actors interested in this public commemoration.

Significantly, the French Committee for Yad Vashem systematically referred to the state memory policy whenever it presented the network Towns and Villages of Righteous of France (as the AJPN and Homage to the Villages of France NGOs did in their official statutes in 2008). A close reading of the annual reports of the French Committee for Yad Vashem from the years 2011–19 reveals that, from the very beginning, the presentation and realization of the network project went hand in hand with other steps taken by the French state in developing public policies of memory about the Righteous. For example, the 2011 annual report of the French Committee for Yad Vashem stated:

> We must remember that on January 18, 2007, in the Crypt of the Pantheon, then President Jacques Chirac, following the proposition of Simone Veil, awarded France's "Righteous Among Nations," whether anonymous or publicly recognized, a legitimate place among the illustrious figures of France. He had their collective action inscribed on a plaque in the Pantheon, with these words: "[. . .] heedless of the risks they faced, they incarnated the honor of France, the values of justice, tolerance and humanity." [. . .] Among the 9 ceremonies recorded in the calendar of national commemorations, which are the subject of legislative or regulatory texts recorded in the *Journal Officiel* is the "National Day for the memory of victims of racist and anti-Semitic crimes committed by the French state, and homage to the Righteous of France."

A third state-related justification for the French committee's decision to create the network of Towns and Villages of the Righteous of France appeared for the first time in the 2012 annual report: "On July 10, 2012, five years after the inauguration of the plaque commemorating the Righteous of France in the Pantheon, the medal of 'Righteous Among Nations' was officially included in the Museum of the Legion of Honour in Paris."[33] Here, the inclusion of the Yad Vashem medal in a museum dedicated to the main civil honorific distinction given by the state in France is once again put forward to illustrate how the local actions of the French Committee is implemented side by side with the French state memory policy regarding the Righteous.

On the other hand, in the informal conversations I had with the volunteers working for the French committee, I was told that they did not share all the aspects of the official state interpretation of the Righteous Among the Nations. For example, they insisted on the individual nature of the title and criticized the rhetoric encouraged by Jacques Chirac's speeches and the suggestion that the Righteous embodied the majority of the French people. In all public speeches given by representatives of the committee, when they appeared in their official framework, they referred to both the individual nature and the Israeli origin of the title of Righteous and cited the sentence: "The title of Righteous Among the Nations was created by Yad Vashem and the State of Israel in order to honor individuals who saved Jews during the Holocaust."

These tensions suggest that state memory policy should be investigated as a way to better understand the link between transnationalization and localization of memory. Here the dynamic differs from the classic concepts of "national," or even "official," memory which are most often considered equivalent to any state intervention in the field of memory and focuses mainly on the official narrative and the way it is transmitted (or not). In the present case, the influence of the national public policy is more relational than content-related. The localization of the memory of the Righteous is a direct consequence of this central state action to the extent that the French state's appropriation of the Israeli commemoration of the Righteous Among the Nations profoundly transformed the configuration of the French social actors committed to the public celebration of these heroes and therefore created a new social field legitimizing and facilitating the diffusion of the memory of the Righteous at the local level, whatever narrative may be offered in this passing. While this dynamic of transnational memory in the local context implies neither a shared adhesion to a common narrative of the past or a unified way of commemorating the Righteous, it was nevertheless first made possible by the implication of the nation-state actors into the process.

Polysemic Commemoration of the Righteous in France

It was precisely these multiple readings of the commemoration of the Righteous in France that facilitated its diffusion throughout the country. Following the French committee's invitation, Thierry Vinçon, mayor of Saint-Amand-Montrond, a midsized city of the Centre-Val de Loire region, became the first president of the Towns and Villages of Righteous of France network. Saint-Amand-Montrond was the place where, in 2010, the very idea of the network was born, through a conversation between the president of the French Committee for Yad Vashem and the city mayor. Since then, on various occasions, Vinçon has made public speeches explaining his motivation for inaugurating a site of memory for the Righteous Among the Nations and participating in the creation of the network Towns and Villages of Righteous of France. Each time, he has repeated: "I have decided to honour the Righteous Among the Nations from the Cher [Department] and from Saint-Amand-Montrond to give our town a sense of pride in its history!" On the day of the ceremony in 2010, it rained heavily. The mayor used the rain as a metaphor, stating that the occasion provided the city with the opportunity to "wash away" or cleanse its past.[34]

Indeed during the war, while some inhabitants rescued Jews, welcoming them into their homes, others denounced Jews and were accomplices of the Milice (a paramilitary organization composed of French volunteers who actively collaborated with the German occupiers, assisting them in their antisemitic crimes and the fight against the Resistance). After the war, from 1971 to 1983, the city repeatedly elected as mayor Maurice Papon, who had participated in organizing deportations of Jews during the war. During the war, he acted as *prefet*, the main representative of the central state, in Bordeaux and its district. During the Algerian War, Papon served as *prefet* of Paris, and as such he was responsible for the murderous repression of the Algerians on the streets of Paris at the time, and more specifically on October 17, 1961, when hundreds of demonstrators were thrown in the River Seine and drowned. As late as 1997–98, he stood trial for his role in the deportation of Jews during the Holocaust and was convicted for his "collaboration in committing a crime against humanity."[35]

In this context, the symbolic and collective meaning given to the Righteous Among the Nations by Thierry Vinçon is the exact opposite of the one envisioned by the Yad Vashem Institute, which considers the actions of the Righteous as an exception, in contrast to those of a generally hostile society. The tension between these two opposing narratives sheds light on the variety of historical and symbolic narratives on which both the transnationalization and the localization of the memory of the Righteous in France rest.

A similar appropriation occurred in 2000 when another institution, the Memorial du Martyr Juif in Paris, soon to become the Shoah Memorial, began to act as a major actor in the commemoration of the Righteous in France. In this case, it operated on a European rather than a local level, building close relationships with heritage sites not only in France but also elsewhere in Europe. The Shoah Memorial became the French representative in the Europeanization of the memory of the Righteous, while increasing its local presence on French territory. In February 2020, the village council of Chambon-sur-Lignon, a little village in southeastern France, voted to delegate the managing of its local museum, called Lieu de mémoire au Chambon-sur-Lignon, to the Shoah Memorial.[36] The museum, which opened in 2013, is dedicated to people from the village and its vicinity who sheltered Jews fleeing from Nazi persecutions during World War II. Established with the financial support of several governmental and nongovernmental organizations, it was until then an institution of the local community. An important argument for the shift was the international status of the Shoah Memorial in Paris and the hope for more visibility on a European level. The involvement of the Shoah Memorial resulted in a more prominent sharing of the narrative expressed by the French state, giving the Righteous a more collective rather than individual interpretation. On the list of names of the French Righteous engraved on the external wall of the Shoah Memorial in Paris, Chambon-sur-Lignon has always been referred to as an actual recipient of the title of Righteous Among the Nations, even though Yad Vashem grants this title only to individuals. The French Committee for Yad Vashem has been complaining about this ever since 2006, claiming, correctly, that Chambon-sur-Lignon as such has never been awarded a medal by Yad Vashem. Although, on October 14, 1990, during a grand official ceremony, Yad Vashem bestowed a collective certificate of honor on Chambon, the village never received the official title Righteous Among the Nations.[37]

The joint dynamic of localization and transnationalization works both ways. The French Committee for Yad Vashem popularized the memory of the Righteous throughout France as a way to maintain its central position in relation to the French state. At the same time, the local developments in the memory of the Righteous proved to be symbolic resources reinforcing the committee's legitimacy vis-à-vis Yad Vashem. In April 2013, during the annual Yom HaShoah commemoration,[38] the committee organized a trip to Israel for twenty mayors and representatives of French towns and villages belonging to the network. This timing was very symbolic, because the year marked the anniversary of the founding of Yad Vashem and of the creation of the Department of the Righteous, which took place sixty and fifty years earlier, respectively. The Israeli media as well as the French regional press (but significantly not the national one) covered the visit of the French representatives extensively.[39] Similar excursions were organized in the years 2015–19, each time involving ten to fifteen representatives of French localities. During these encounters, the national, international, and local institutions and memory agents reinforced one another and strengthened one another's legitimacy.

Bringing the State Back into Memory Studies

Almost ten years ago, Astrid Erll indicated the existence of three different phases in the study of memory.[40] In the first phase, the founding fathers from Bartlett to Halbwachs gave rise to collective memory as a topic of research. The second period was epitomized by Pierre Nora's work on "realms of memory."[41] It focused on the national level and saw the development of numerous studies on national memory. The third, and current, period has been dedicated to the study of "traveling memories," as Erll puts it, and what is also called "transcultural,"[42] "planetary,"[43] "multidirectional,"[44] "globital,"[45] or simply "transnational"[46] memory. As it happens, the second and third phases share the approach to studying memory mainly through the analysis of cultural content and artifacts. The most recent works, however, paid attention to the social actors whose activities have resulted in the "traveling" of memory. Jessica Rapson and Lucy Bond, for example, speak of "forums of remembrance" to describe these configurations of social actors instrumental in the transnationalization of memory.[47] However, this new consideration for the actual actors of this travel of memory has neglected the state, associating it with the second phase on "national memory."

The French case study highlights how the state memory policy plays a crucial role in the dual process of transnationalization and localization of memory of the Righteous Among the Nations in the country. It encourages studying memory not only through the lens of cultural history but also through those of political science.[48] The typology established by Michael Mann, one of the major theoreticians of political power, which distinguishes the two powers of the state—the despotic one and the infrastructural one—is particularly enlightening here.[49] The French state's memory policy has exercised its influence on the localization of the commemoration of the Righteous in France, not through a "despotic power" and content-related memory policy, but rather through its infrastructural power, guiding and organizing society. Of course, given that French society is state-centered,[50] it may not be possible to replicate this very pattern in every other context. It nevertheless suggests the need for bringing the state back into memory studies, and not merely reducing it to the production of a "national" or "official" memory.

Notes

The maps included in this text have been designed by Benoit Tudoux. Katharine Throssell and Nicolas Hodge edited the English language of this text.

1 The main relevant publications that delimited this subfield of research are, in chronological order, Daniel Levy and Natan Sznaider, "Memory Unbound: The Holocaust and the Formation of Cosmopolitan Memory," *European Journal of Social Theory* 5, no. 1 (February 2002): 87–106, and *The Holocaust and Memory in the Global Age* (Philadelphia: Temple University Press, 2006); Chiara De Cesari and Ann Rigney, eds., *Transnational Memory: Circulation, Articulation, Scales* (Berlin: De Gruyter, 2014); Astrid Erll and Ann Rigney, "Cultural Memory Studies after the Transnational Turn," *Memory Studies* 11, no. 3 (2018): 272–73; and, more specifically regarding the topic of this book, Sarah Gensburger, "La diffusion internationale de la catégorie de 'Juste parmi les Nations.' Repenser l'articulation entre diffusion des droits de l'homme et globalisation de la mémoire," *Revue internationale de politique comparée* 22, no. 4 (2015): 537–55.

2 Jenny Wüstenberg, "Locating Transnational Memory," *International Journal of Politics, Culture and Society* (July 2019): 1–12. Here page 1 and regarding the topic of this book, Zofia Wóycicka, "Global Patterns, Local Interpretations: New Polish Museums Dedicated to the Rescue of Jews during the Holocaust," *Holocaust Studies: A Journal of Culture and History* 25, no. 3 (2019): 248–72.
3 Laura Hasunuma and Mary McCarthy, "Creating a Collective Memory of the Comfort Women in the USA," *International Journal of Politics, Culture and Society* 32, no. 2 (2019): 145–62.
4 Sara Dybris McQuaid and Sarah Gensburger, "Administrations of Memory: Transcending the Nation and Bringing Back the State in Memory Studies," *International Journal of Politics, Culture and Society* 32, no. 2 (2019): 125–43, and Laurie Boussaguet and Florence Faucher, "The Politics of Symbols: Reflections on the French Government's Framing of the 2015 Terrorist Attacks," *Parliamentary Affairs* 71, no. 1 (2017): 169–95.
5 Sarah Gensburger and Sandrine Lefranc, *Beyond Memory: Can We Really Learn from the Past?* (London: Palgrave, 2020).
6 This was the official number given by the Pantheon administrator at the end of January 2007.
7 Sarah Gensburger, *National Policy, Global Memory: The Commemoration of the "Righteous" from Jerusalem to Paris, 1942–2007* (New York: Berghahn Books, 2016).
8 This number was obtained using the database of street names made available by the French government on https://www.data.gouv.fr/fr/, accessed March 2022.
9 Peter B. Evans, Dietrich Rueschemeyer, and Theda Skocpol, eds., *Bringing the State Back In* (Cambridge: Cambridge University Press, 1985).
10 Which by then was still known as "the Memorial of the Unknown Jewish Martyr—Centre for Contemporary Jewish Documentation."
11 Gensburger, *National Policy, Global Memory.*
12 This term refers to the roundups of July 16, 1942, that led to the arrest of 12,884 Jews in Paris. The name "Vel d'Hiv" comes from the fact that 8,160 of them were initially held in the Velodrome d'Hiver cycling stadium in Paris. The reader will find more details on this event, along with others that are mentioned here, in Serge Klarsfeld, *Le Calendrier de la persécution des Juifs de France* (Paris: Fayard, 2003).
13 Speech by Jacques Chirac, president of the French Republic, delivered during the ceremony commemorating the roundup of Jews on July 16 and 17, 1942.

14 René Rémond, *Un fichier juif: Rapport de la commission présidée par René Rémond au Premier ministre* (Paris: Plon, 1996).

15 Speech by Jacques Chirac, president of the French Republic, on the occasion of the official transfer of the police census files concerning Jews in Occupied France to the national archives into the Memorial to the Unknown Jewish Martyr, which has since become the Shoah Memorial, Paris, December 5, 1997.

16 Law of July 10, 2000, Journée nationale à la mémoire des victimes des crimes racistes et antisémites de l'Etat français et d'hommage aux "Justes" de France.

17 See the city council decision no. 101 of 2000: https://a06-v7.apps.paris.fr/a06/jsp/site/Portal.jsp?page=ods-solr.display_document&id_document=51073&items_per_page=20&sort_name=&sort_order=&terms=all%C3%A9e%20des%20justes&query=all%C3%A9e%20des%20justes. The name was changed in 2019, returning to the formal Israeli expression Allée des Justes parmi les Nations (Avenue of the Righteous Among the Nations). See the city council decision no. 116 of 2019: https://a06-v7.apps.paris.fr/a06/jsp/site/plugins/solr/modules/ods/DoDownload.jsp?id_document=148842&items_per_page=20&sort_name=&sort_order=&terms=all%C3%A9e%20des%20justes&query=all%C3%A9e%20des%20justes. Both links were accessed April 4, 2023.

18 For more details on these groups, see Sarah Gensburger, "The Righteous Among the Nations as Elements of Collective Memory," *International Social Science Journal* 62, nos. 203–4 (2012): 135–46.

19 The first correspondence found in the archives of the association preserved at the consistory, and the archives of the French Committee for Yad Vashem, are dated March 1996, but they present an initial project formulated in autumn 1995. Moreover, in 1998 the leaders of the association said they had been working on this project for two and a half years; interview with Gérard Blum and Jules Bloch, February 25, 1998, Paris.

20 Statutes of the French Association of Righteous Among the Nations, no. 127392P, registered October 16, 1996, Prefecture of Police Paris, Office of Associations.

21 Interview with Gérard Blum and Jules Bloch, February 25, 1998, Paris.

22 Interview with Jules Bloch, May 25, 1998, Paris.

23 Official declaration made under the NGO identification number 332005861, made on August 18, 2008, in Bordeaux (Gironde).

24 http://www.ajpn.org, accessed December 2020.

25 For more details on the procedure and a presentation of the actual status of the special diploma given to the Chambon-sur-Lignon village, see Gensburger, *National Policy, Global Memory*.

26 Official declaration made under the NGO identification number 2007 0048 on October 25, 2007, in Cannes (Alpes-Maritimes).

27 https://www.mauroux46.fr/histoire and https://www.ladepeche.fr/article/2010/06/28/863470-mauroux-hommage-a-un-village-de-justes.html, accessed February 2020.

28 https://www.corsematin.com/article/bastia/canari-village-symbole-de-laction-des-corses-pendant-loccupation, accessed February 2020 (now unavailable).

29 *Annual Report of the French Committee for Yad Vashem* (Paris: French Committee for Yad Vashem, 2010).

30 *Annual Report of the French Committee for Yad Vashem* (Paris: French Committee for Yad Vashem, 2010).

31 *Annual Report of the French Committee for Yad Vashem* (Paris: French Committee for Yad Vashem, 2011).

32 *Annual Report of the French Committee for Yad Vashem* (Paris: French Committee for Yad Vashem, 2019).

33 *Annual Report of the French Committee for Yad Vashem* (Paris: French Committee for Yad Vashem, 2012).

34 https://artsandculture.google.com/exhibit/les-justes-parmi-les-nations-de-saint-amand-montrond%C2%A0/gQaoyNxG, accessed March 2022.

35 The accusation did not include his actions against the Resistance any more than his role in the assassination of Algerian demonstrators in Paris on October 17, 1961, because these crimes took place too long ago. In 1998, only the "crime against humanity" could have given rise to a trial, because it is not subject to statutory limitations.

36 https://www.memorialdelashoah.org/la-gestion-du-musee-du-chambon-sur-lignon-confiee-au-memorial-de-la-shoah.html, accessed March 2023.

37 See, for example, the report in the article published by Ilana Cicurel in *L'Arche* (November 1990). For more information, see Gensburger, *National Policy, Global Memory*.

38 Created in April 1951, and set on Nissan 27, this day was formerly called "Day of the Commemoration of the Genocide and the Ghetto Uprising." In April 1959 it took its new name, "Yom HaShoah," or Holocaust Remembrance Day.

39 https://actu.fr/occitanie/cahors_46042/pradines-le-maire-et-son-adjointe-rentrent-dun-sejour-en-israel_4052020.html, accessed March 2023.

40 Astrid Erll, "Travelling Memory," *Parallax* 17, no. 4 (2011): 4–18.
41 Pierre Nora, *The Realms of Memory: Rethinking the French Past* (New York: Columbia University Press, 1997).
42 Lucy Bond and Jessica Rapson, *The Transcultural Turn: Interrogating Memory between and beyond Borders* (Berlin: De Gruyter, 2014).
43 Lucy Bond, Ben De Bruyn, and Jessica Rapson, "Planetary Memory in Contemporary American Fiction," *Textual Practice* 31, no. 5 (2017): 853–66.
44 Michael Rothberg, *Multidirectional Memory: Remembering the Holocaust in the Age of Decolonization* (Stanford, CA: Stanford University Press, 2009).
45 Ann Reading, *Gender and Memory in the Globital Age* (Basingstoke: Palgrave Macmillan, 2016).
46 Wulf Kansteiner, "Transnational Holocaust Memory, Digital Culture and the End of Reception Studies," in *The Twentieth Century in European Memory: Transcultural Mediation and Reception*, ed. Tea Sindbaek Andersen and Barbara Törnquist-Plewa (Leiden: Brill, 2017), 305–43.
47 Lucy Bond and Jessica Rapson, *The Transcultural Turn*, 19.
48 On this marginalization of political science in this research field, see Sarah Gensburger, "Halbwachs's Studies in Collective Memory: A Founding Work for Contemporary 'Memory Studies'?" *Journal of Classical Sociology* 16, no. 4 (2016): 396–413.
49 Michael Mann, *The Sources of Social Power*, vol. 4, *Globalizations, 1945–2011* (Los Angeles: University of California Press, 2012).
50 Pierre Birnbaum, *La logique de l'État* (Paris: Les Éditions Fayard, 1982).

Bibliography

Birnbaum, Pierre. *La logique de l'État*. (How the state thinks.) Paris: Les Éditions Fayard, 1982.

Bond, Lucy, Ben De Bruyn, and Jessica Rapson. "Planetary Memory in Contemporary American Fiction." *Textual Practice* 31, no. 5 (2017): 853–66.

Bond, Lucy, and Jessica Rapson. *The Transcultural Turn: Interrogating Memory between and beyond Borders*. Berlin: De Gruyter, 2014.

Boussaguet, Laurie, and Florence Faucher. "The Politics of Symbols: Reflections on the French Government's Framing of the 2015 Terrorist Attacks." *Parliamentary Affairs* 71, no. 1 (2017): 169–95.

De Cesari, Chiara, and Ann Rigney, eds. *Transnational Memory: Circulation, Articulation, Scales*. Berlin: De Gryuter, 2014.

Erll, Astrid. "Travelling Memory." *Parallax* 17, no. 4 (2011): 4–18.

Erll, Astrid, and Ann Rigney. "Cultural Memory Studies after the Transnational Turn." *Memory Studies* 11, no. 3 (2018): 272–73.

Evans, Peter B., Dietrich Rueschemeyer, and Theda Skocpol, eds. *Bringing the State Back In*. Cambridge: Cambridge University Press, 1985.

Gensburger, Sarah. "La diffusion internationale de la catégorie de 'Juste parmi les Nations.' Repenser l'articulation entre diffusion des droits de l'homme et globalisation de la mémoire." (The international circulation of the "Righteous among the Nations" category. Rethinking the articulation between the Human Rights diffusion and the globalization of memory.) *Revue internationale de politique comparée* 22, no. 4 (2015): 537–55.

———. "Halbwachs's Studies in Collective Memory: A Founding Work for Contemporary 'Memory Studies'?" *Journal of Classical Sociology* 16, no. 4 (2016): 396–413.

———. *National Policy, Global Memory: The Commemoration of the "Righteous" from Jerusalem to Paris, 1942–2007*. New York: Berghahn Books, 2016.

———. "The Righteous Among the Nations as Elements of Collective Memory." *International Social Science Journal* 62, no. 203–4 (2012): 135–46.

Gensburger, Sarah, and Sandrine Lefranc. *Beyond Memory: Can We Really Learn from the Past?* London: Palgrave, 2020.

Hasunuma, Laura, and Mary McCarthy. "Creating a Collective Memory of the Comfort Women in the USA." *International Journal of Politics, Culture and Society* 32, no. 2 (2019): 145–62.

Kansteiner, Wulf. "Transnational Holocaust Memory, Digital Culture and the End of Reception Studies." In *The Twentieth Century in European Memory: Transcultural Mediation and Reception*, ed. Tea Sindbaek Andersen and Barbara Törnquist-Plewa, 305–43. Leiden: Brill, 2017.

Klarsfeld, Serge. *Le Calendrier de la persécution des Juifs de France*. (The Calendar of the persecution of the Jews in France.) Paris: Fayard, 2003.

Levy, Daniel, and Natan Sznaider. *The Holocaust and Memory in the Global Age*. Philadelphia: Temple University Press, 2006.

———. "Memory Unbound: The Holocaust and the Formation of Cosmopolitan Memory." *European Journal of Social Theory* 5, no. 1 (February 2002): 87–106.

Mann, Michael. *The Sources of Social Power*, vol. 4, *Globalizations, 1945–2011*. Los Angeles: University of California Press, 2012.

McQuaid, Sara Dybris, and Sarah Gensburger. "Administrations of Memory: Transcending the Nation and Bringing Back the State in Memory Studies." *International Journal of Politics, Culture and Society* 32, no. 2 (2019): 125–43.

Nora, Pierre. *The Realms of Memory: Rethinking the French Past*. New York: Columbia University Press, 1997.

Reading, Ann. *Gender and Memory in the Globital Age*. Basingstoke: Palgrave Macmillan, 2016.

Rémond, René. *"Un fichier juif": Rapport de la commission présidée par René Rémond au Premier ministre*. ("Jewish records." The report of the committee presided by René Rémond to the Prime Minister.) Paris: Plon, 1996.

Rothberg, Michael. *Multidirectional Memory: Remembering the Holocaust in the Age of Decolonization*. Stanford, CA: Stanford University Press, 2009.

Wóycicka, Zofia. "Global Patterns, Local Interpretations: New Polish Museums Dedicated to the Rescue of Jews during the Holocaust." *Holocaust Studies: A Journal of Culture and History* 25, no. 3 (2019): 248–72.

Wüstenberg, Jenny. "Locating Transnational Memory." *International Journal of Politics, Culture and Society* (July 2019): 1–12.

5

The "Righteous Resisters"

Memory of Holocaust Rescue in Slovakia

HANA KUBÁTOVÁ

Speaking at a gathering marking the seventy-fifth anniversary of the Slovak National Uprising (Slovak, *Slovenské národné povstanie*), the then state secretary, Branislav Ondruš, had only words of gratitude for those who took part in the 1944 rebellion.[1] Philosophizing about how big events always rest "on the shoulders of the little people," Ondruš praised the courage of the partisans while drawing attention to the heroism of those who provided the rebels with water, food, and shelter. Many Slovaks exhibited their bravery by hiding people in danger, Ondruš continued, without being specific about whom this concerned or whom they feared. Saying what was expected from a politician on that national holiday, Ondruš included a rhetorical twist in his speech when he added that Slovakia has more Righteous Among the Nations per capita than any other country.[2] The connections made between rescue and resistance have some grounds in reality: Most Slovak recipients of the Righteous title, awarded by Yad Vashem, the Holocaust Martyrs' and Heroes' Authority in Jerusalem, to gentiles who "assumed the entire responsibility for the Jews' survival,"[3] received the honor for actions during 1944–45.

By linking the Slovak National Uprising to Holocaust rescue, Ondruš inadvertently exposed the broader agenda of the recent attempts to secure "feel-good" narratives relating to World War II by presenting the Slovaks as righteous resisters.[4] As shown here, while records of resistance have long served to denounce fascism, the Righteous trope invites nationalism back in. This is why the "righteous turn" is examined in my chapter as part of a broader nativist populist appeal that sees all others, both persons and ideas, as "fundamentally threatening to the homogeneous nation state."[5] Whereas nationalism builds on prejudice against those who do not match the indigenous or founding ethnic group, nativism targets enemies both within and outside: people, institutions, doctrines, or beliefs.[6] In Western Europe, nativism, populism, and authoritarianism form the ideological core of the radical right.[7] In Eastern Europe, nativism has become increasingly mainstream, feeding off the 2007–8 economic crisis and, above all, the 2015 migration crisis, often crossing ideological boundaries.[8] Whether coming from the right or the left, in Slovakia as elsewhere, nativist politicians mobilize identity-based grievances. They appeal and mobilize deep-seated human emotions, especially anxiety and fear. Claiming to represent the overlooked "silent majority" against the corrupt political elite, nativist politicians pledge to protect "the people" from their adversaries. These adversaries may take the form of immigrants who allegedly challenge the homogeneity of the nation, but increasingly also supranational bodies, such as the European Union, seen as advancing multiculturalism, liberalism, and minority rights at the expense of the titular group.

Slovakia serves as a particularly poignant example of how the reshaping of self-pleasing narratives of World War II coincides with the shifting role these tropes have in (and on) identity politics in much of Eastern Europe today. "Historically determined dividing lines" have always played a role in the country, with societal cleavages often being politicized.[9] While it is certainly not atypical for historical narratives to be picked up by politicians in Slovakia,[10] there is more to why issues of collaboration, complicity, and rescue have been made into a public concern, and why now. By examining how the narrative of heroic helpers has expanded resistance mythology, my chapter claims that the return of an ethnic reading of the past is also a rejection of the more nuanced interpretations of World War II and the Holocaust, and of emotions of shame that are embedded in supranational historical narratives of the European project.[11]

Understanding the Holocaust as a communal, intimate genocide, to reference historians Omer Bartov and Natalia Aleksiun, and as an in-group transgression that in hindsight is more often avoided than acknowledged, to point to the works of social psychologists Nyla Branscombe and Michael J. A. Wohl, my chapter examines the penetration of Holocaust rescue into the official narratives of World War II in Slovakia.[12] Several avoidance strategies have been applied across Europe in the aftermath of the Holocaust, seeking to place the troubled past in parenthesis or to shift the blame onto others, be they "fascists," "traitors of the nation," or the victims themselves.[13] In postwar Europe, most countries have also exaggerated the scope of their antifascist resistance. As historian Tony Judt aptly noted, for a country to be considered "innocent" during the war, "a nation had to have resisted and to have done so in its overwhelming majority."[14]

This chapter builds on the understanding that what complicates coming to terms with one's past, in Eastern Europe in general and in Slovakia in particular, is the communal or intimate character of the Holocaust. In Eastern Europe, gentiles' choices directly impacted the lives of their Jewish neighbors. Not only has there been more of what there is to remember and forget in post-1945 Eastern Europe, but there has also been more of what is at stake here when it comes to how the Holocaust is made sense of years later, and this is precisely because of how implicated the majority societies were in the Nazis' Final Solution. As the continuous mnemonic battles over World War II history suggest, interpreting the Holocaust matters across Eastern Europe, provoking "a sense that wider social identities are at stake" seven decades after the events.[15]

I begin with a brief historical introduction to the troubled past of Slovakia. The focus here is on the period between August 1944 and spring 1945, placing the Slovak National Uprising at its center. Discussion of the antifascist resistance, embodied by the 1944 uprising, has been the dominant strategy for avoiding questions about local collaboration in the Holocaust. Representing a significant resistance action in Nazi-dominated Europe, lasting from August 29 until late October 1944, and involving more than sixty thousand army officers and eighteen thousand partisans on the side of the rebellion, the uprising came to serve as evidence that the majority of society rejected the collaborationist state from the beginning. After evaluating the links between rescue and resistance, including how these links are being politically activated, I lay out the theoretical framework of my argument, consisting of the mechanisms of moral disengagement when facing responsibility for harm caused to others.[16] Pointing to broader trends in avoidance strategies, I follow the shifts in how the 1944 uprising and Holocaust rescue have been appropriated in Slovakia since 1993. I then turn to those recognized as Righteous, made into symbols of the nation's alleged innocence during the Holocaust. Contextualizing the recipients' files, I argue that these complicate rather than purify the Slovak past. I conclude by addressing the theoretical and methodological implications of my work for the study of how the national "good name" is being activated today in Slovakia and elsewhere.

1944 and the Troubled Past of Slovakia

Placing the merits of the uprising aside, wartime Slovakia was a model Nazi ally. The country's collaboration with Nazi Germany was structural, going beyond practical considerations. Slovakia accepted a defensive treaty (German, *Schutzvertrag*) with Nazi Germany within days of its "independence" declaration in

March 1939, aligning its foreign, military, and economic policy with that of Berlin. Slovakia became the only country to join Nazi Germany in its attack on Poland in September 1939, which marked the beginning of World War II. As a member of the Axis powers, Slovakia joined the Nazi attack on the Soviet Union in June 1941, and on Great Britain and the United States in December 1941.[17] The country's contribution to Nazi Germany's war effort may have been limited, but Berlin understood the "practical value" of Slovakia, whether this was in 1938–39, in relation to the destruction of Czechoslovakia, or in 1944–45, given that its territory was a wedge between advancing Soviets and retreating Germans.[18]

Wartime Slovakia was also an ideological ally of Nazi Germany. Until the outbreak of the uprising and the German occupation, the country was governed by a national administration, perceived as legitimate by the majority of the population.[19] The regime attempted to bridge Catholic and fascist principles in its rule,[20] and the different wings within the state party, the Hlinka Slovak People's Party (Slovak, *Hlinkova slovenská ľudová strana*), competed with each other for Hitler's attention and approval. Headed by Jozef Tiso, who enjoyed both secular power as the president and religious authority as a priest in a country where most identified with the Roman Catholic Church, Slovakia introduced harsh anti-Jewish laws, at times surpassing the severity of contemporary Nazi legislation. By presenting the so-called Jewish Question as an opportunity for the majority of society to enhance their social standing, large sections of the population participated in "limiting Jewish influence in the social and economic life of Slovakia," a euphemism for a wide range of discriminatory measures, including the restriction of Jewish employment, confiscation of Jewish farmland and forests, liquidation and seizure of Jewish businesses, and the sale of Jews' personal property, including clothes, shoes, and household items at auctions that often overlapped with Jews being deported in cattle cars, most of them to imminent death. Indeed, the widespread complicity in robbing the Jews, long awaited by many and carried out in broad daylight, has been linked to anti-Jewish violence, institutional and communal, during the war and its aftermath.[21] The Slovak government played an active role in the 1942 deportations, in which local gendarmes (Slovak, *žandári*), assisted by military personnel, including the paramilitary Hlinka Guard (Slovak, *Hlinkova garda*), transported approximately 58,000 Jews (out of 89,000 Jews living in Slovakia in 1940) to Auschwitz and the Lublin area. The 1944 deportations, in which an additional 13,000 Jews were deported from Slovakia, most of them to Auschwitz and Theresienstadt, were orchestrated by the German occupying forces, especially the Einsatzgruppe H of the Security Police and SD. In locating the Jews in hiding, they often, however, relied on local paramilitary formations, particularly the Emergency Divisions of the Hlinka Guard (Slovak, *Pohotovostné oddiely Hlinkovej gardy*). Members of the Hlinka Guard participated in the most vicious German-orchestrated atrocities in Slovakia, targeting real or alleged partisans, many of them Jews, in Kremnička (November 1944–March 1945) and Nemecká (January 1945).[22]

In spite of the uprising being memorialized as "Slovak" and "national," it was very much an international and collaborative endeavor, with some thirty different nationalities fighting on the side of the partisans and selected Slovak army units.[23] Estimates of how many Jews were in Slovakia at the outbreak of the uprising vary from 18,000 to 25,000 (including about 3,000 Jews who had escaped there from Hungary),[24] and so do estimates of how many of them joined the rebellion (between 800 and 1,200).[25] The Jews were present in virtually every rebel group, despite their particularly vulnerable position. Persecuted by their own state, often also betrayed by their gentile neighbors, Jewish partisans were typically former detainees of labor camps, released at the outbreak of the uprising. Ill equipped and malnourished, the Jews were hunted down as both political and "racial" enemies, fearing the Germans as much as their Slovak henchmen.

In the two parts of the country—one controlled by the partisans and the other controlled by the Germans—the situation of the Jews differed. In the territory under the control of the partisans, the Slovak National Council (Slovak, *Slovenská národná rada*), as the official authority, repealed the nondemocratic legislation of the Tiso regime, invalidating thereby all anti-Jewish laws.[26] Conversely, German forces rushed not only to reestablish control over Slovakia but also to "solve the Jewish Question" there. Assisted by the Emergency Divisions of the Hlinka Guard but often also by locals, the Germans hunted down the remainder of Slovak Jewry. By October 1944, the uprising had been brutally crushed, with some ninety villages and towns burned down, and deportations renewed.[27] From the approximately 5,000 individuals murdered in reprisals for the uprising, many of them hanged, strangled, burned or buried alive, about 2,000 were Jews.[28] In short, when it comes to who fought and died in the glorified Slovak National Uprising, this was very much a Jewish rebellion, too.

The uprising not only accelerated the erosion of the regime, manifested in a governmental reshuffle, but also contributed to the decline of its popular support, observable in what the official reports called a "defeatist," "doubtful" mood in society.[29] Situation reports indicate that by late 1943 and early 1944 only a few believed that Nazi Germany would be victorious, and later developments, in Slovakia but also on the Eastern Front, sealed the fate of the regime. Whether as a result of a genuine awakening or a pragmatic choice, many now reconsidered their allegiance to the collaborationist state. Scholars of Jewish-gentile relations, including myself, have also noted a shift in popular responses to state-sponsored and religiously sanctioned antisemitism in the last months of the war.[30] Some went even further in their assessments of how the attitudes of the Slovaks changed around late 1944 and early 1945. Examining eyewitness testimonies, for instance, the ethnographer Peter Salner claimed that there was an "increase in the number of those who were willing to risk [their lives] and help."[31] Coming to a similar conclusion, but relying on institutional written materials, historians Jean-Marc Dreyfus and Eduard Nižňanský argued that "Slovaks risked their lives at the end of the war to rescue Jews whose fate they had not previously cared about."[32] The idea that the rescue of Jews accelerated following the German occupation has also been advocated by public figures such as Pavol Mešťan, then director of the Museum of Jewish Culture.[33] When asked why so few cases of assistance could be traced to 1942, Mešťan responded that this is because at that time there was "no knowledge of Jews being exterminated outside of the Slovak State."[34]

What, if any, is the link between rescue and resistance? When assessing this question, we need to consider that, to avoid the 1944 deportations, Jews needed outside help. Whether by obtaining false papers and passing as gentiles, hiding in attics or improvised shelters, in hay sheds or mountain bunkers, in rectories, hidden behind the walls of convents and church orphanages whose sanctuary was at least partially respected by the occupying troops, in isolated villages or cities, Jews needed assistance to survive.[35] In both oral and written testimonies, Jewish survivors from Slovakia mention that rescue manifested itself in various ways, ranging from direct acts on their behalf (when their former neighbors, friends, but also complete strangers provided them with shelter, food, clothing, and other material resources) to "refraining from action" (typically knowing of the Jews in hiding but not reporting them).[36] The thesis that the willingness to help Jews or unwillingness to harm them increased toward the end of the war seems to be also supported by statistics. Yad Vashem has recognized twice as many Slovaks for their actions on behalf of the Jews taken in the midst of or following the 1944 uprising than in the period between the establishment of the Slovak State in March 1939 and the first deportation wave of March–October 1942.[37] However, although the most reported cases of rescue have indeed been linked to the Slovak National Uprising or the German occupation, this was not the only increase for that time. A rise in cases has also been documented with respect to denunciations, including the betrayal of the Jews in hiding from around the same period.[38] Police stations were flooded with people reporting on Jews and their local helpers, whether actual or assumed.[39] "Aryanizations" of the little property that was left briefly resumed in 1944, and the looting now also targeted assets of Jews previously protected by exemptions, now disregarded by the Germans. Jewish partisans recall not only comradeship in the rebel groups but also prejudice.[40] This explains why some Jewish partisans decided to conceal their identities while fighting the fascists.[41]

Examining the Slovak National Uprising without taking into account its broader historical context allows for the interpretation of the Holocaust as something that happened to, rather than in, Slovakia. It enables the Holocaust in Slovakia to be framed as a crime for which the Germans were solely responsibly, and for which they themselves should bear guilt and shame. Making claims about Slovak-Jewish relations on the basis of what transpired in the last months of the war is also ahistorical, as it overlooks what preceded and what followed. This included not only years of discrimination during the war but also the refusal to correct the wrongs in the postwar reality, especially regarding the return of looted property, something that occurred both on the institutional and the individual level.[42] It is not only that the postwar leadership of Slovakia obstructed the introduction of restitution laws; the return of a handful of Jewish survivors also triggered anti-Jewish violence in the aftermath of the conflict, such as the infamous September 1945 pogrom in Topoľčany.[43] Institutional sources and witness accounts leave little doubt about the presence of antisemitism in postwar Slovakia. I will come back to these arguments when addressing the selected stories of the Righteous in the last section of my chapter.

Protecting the Moral Image of the Nation

Slovakia's mnemonic battles are not unique in their attempts to distance the country from its troubled past, just as there is nothing surprising about the lingering resistance mythology either. On the contrary, social psychologists working on experiences of collective guilt tell us that dissociation from the wrongdoer, even if clearly representative of the group in question, is a typical strategy for avoiding feelings of responsibility.[44] Historians of France, most notably Henry Rousso, have called the failure to come to terms with the collaborationist regime of Philippe Pétain "the Vichy syndrome,"[45] a term that came to symbolize the difficulty of European states to acknowledge what transpired during the war. To protect the moral image of the nation, a number of countries placed their peripheral resistance "movements at the center of historical memory[;] such accounts redeemed nations after years of Nazi occupation; they absolved them of any complicity in the crimes of the Nazis' New Order."[46] Scholars of Western Europe, especially postwar France and Italy, noticed that these countries avoided questions of complicity in the Holocaust by fostering an image of the goodhearted people who stood in opposition, if not resistance, to the fascists who supposedly represented the fringes of their national communities. As the historian Rebecca Clifford argued, for example, the "notions of the *bons Français/italiani, brava gente* played important roles in postwar national identity, and the power and persistence of these myths held in check public discussions of the extent of French and Italian cooperation with and participation in the persecution of Jews."[47] The process of divorcing the allegedly antifascist nation from the politicians in power, many of whom were tried for collaboration in the postwar years, was utilized in Eastern Europe as well. Historian Nadège Ragaru, for instance, observed the emergence of the "another Bulgaria" trope in the 1944–45 trials of perpetrators of the Holocaust, leading to the construction of public accounts in which the innocent Bulgarian people stood apart from the "fascists" on trial.[48] A similar tale of the two Slovak nations, in which the majority of goodhearted people supposedly clashed with the handful of traitors in power, can also be traced to the proclamations of the Czechoslovak government-in-exile in London, seeking to promote the democratic image of the once joint state abroad.[49] While condemning the Nazi and Slovak anti-Jewish policies, exiled politicians were careful enough to assign responsibility, in the Czech case, solely to the Germans, and, in the Slovak case, to the higher-ups whose actions supposedly did not reflect the sentiments of the ordinary people.[50] The tale of the two Slovakias was readily received in postwar Czechoslovakia, and together with the resistance mythology has served to deflect questions of responsibility for the Holocaust until the present day.

Slovakia is also not the only country in which Holocaust rescue has been gaining political momentum, as this volume testifies to. By introducing memory laws that criminalize allegations of local participation in the Holocaust, weaponizing education for ideological purposes, using government funding to install institutions "protecting" historical legacies of the country while cutting funding from those that do not bow to fabrications mandated from above, resorting to smear tactics against academics who supposedly slander the "good name" of the nation when they point to instances of collaboration and complicity, Poland represents the most extreme case of distorting the record of the Holocaust for a nativist future. For nativist politicians across Eastern Europe, Poland is setting the tone, including on how to enforce historical policies that highlight the good in the national sphere. The replacing of Jewish victims by noble gentiles in official narratives of World War II illustrates my point here, and the expansion of exhibitions dedicated to Holocaust rescue across Europe is one example of how this is being done. In the last two decades, museums dedicated to the memory of those who saved Jews during World War II—conveying different messages and serving different purposes, of course—mushroomed across Europe, to be found now in Poland, Latvia, Lithuania, Bulgaria, Germany, and France.[51] In Italy, a new museum and memorial commemorating the rescue of seventy-three Jewish children in Nonantola, in the north of the country, has been under construction since late 2019.[52] A number of countries, Slovakia included, have also opened expositions devoted to rescue in existing or new Holocaust and Jewish museums, often occupying a prominent place in the public space.

Not only did memorials to the Righteous become more widespread, but the very concept has also been stretched. As Wóycicka shows, there is now a "wider tendency to universalize the concept of the Righteous by giving it a broader meaning not restricted to gentiles rescuing Jews during the Holocaust as defined by Yad Vashem."[53] Again, with its series called "Encyclopedia of the Righteous," broadcast on the public Radio Slovakia, and including stories of both those recognized as rescuers by Yad Vashem and the "brave Slovaks" who did not receive the award but who "nevertheless helped save human lives during World War II," Slovakia is a good example of how the understanding of the Righteous has come to include an ever wider group.[54] As the moderator and producer of the Radio Slovakia series, Dagmar Mozolová tells listeners at the end of each recording that "taking the population size into consideration, we belong to the countries that have received the highest number of awards in the world."[55] The bigger the number of the recipients, the clearer the conscience of the nation, seems to be the argument here.

Examining the mnemonic battles in Slovakia allows us to pinpoint how the meaning assigned to resistance and rescue shifted over time: The official doctrine of the modern Slovak republic, established January 1, 1993, draws on an antifascist tradition, epitomized by the Slovak National Uprising.[56] The country considers itself a successor to the Czechoslovak federation (1989–92), claiming no legal ties to the wartime state (1939–45).[57] The reality is more complicated. Although the uprising has always held an important place in the Slovak national calendar, whether this was acknowledged by the existence of a national holiday or not,[58] its legacy has often been contested on the political level. Similar political ambivalence may also be observed with respect to the history of the wartime state.

Scholars, including the prominent historian of the rebellion Jozef Jablonický, demonstrated how the history of the uprising has been twisted to serve ideological purposes, especially in the four decades of communist rule in Czechoslovakia (1948–89).[59] Others, including ethnographers Juraj Zajonc and Monika Vrzgulová, have explored how various political actors approached the

Slovak National Uprising since the 1990s.[60] Political scholar Samuel Abrahám, while examining the first general elections (1994) in modern Slovakia, argued that how parties treated controversial periods, especially the wartime past, superseded ideology when it came to party alliances at the time.[61]

On the cultural front, the revisionist agenda has been carried forward by organizations such as Matica slovenská, established in the nineteenth century to foster Slovak scholarship, or the Roman Catholic Church, whose numerous local leaders have expressed positive views on the then president-priest Tiso, presenting him as a savior of both the Slovaks and the Jews, also with the assistance of exiled historians. On the party level, a positive outlook on the wartime history was promoted by the Slovak National Party (Slovak, *Slovenská národná strana*), in government during 1993–94, 1994–98, 2006–9, and 2016–20. Throughout the 1990s, when the party was also in charge of the ministry of education (1994–98) and pushed revisionist textbooks into the curriculum, its representatives referred to Tiso as a martyr, claimed the wartime state was an outcome of the will of the people, rather than a byproduct of Nazi plans in the region, and treated the regime as instrumental for building Slovak statehood, which in turn supposedly outweighed any "mishandlings," such as the Holocaust. Not surprisingly, then, the Slovak National Party was critical of the uprising, blaming it for allegedly terminating the country's independence and for paving the way for a communist takeover in 1948.[62]

The Slovak National Party and the ethnonationalists it represented also shared a very specific view of Holocaust rescue. As historian Nina Paulovičová stated, "The wave of public righteous awards since the 1990s has led to different responses within society. For ethno-nationalists the presence of the 'Righteous' rescuers in political discourse was rather problematic," as they presented the Slovaks as victims and only victims.[63] Assisted by former émigrés, especially František Vnuk and Milan Stanislav Ďurica, the ethnonationalists cleared the Slovaks of all guilt and shame, and shifted the blame for the Holocaust onto the Jews themselves and their alleged hostility toward the Slovak nation.[64] Their revisionism centered not so much on "the Slovaks" but the higher-ups, especially Tiso. As historian James M. Ward wrote in the preface to his extensive biography of the president-priest:

> In the 1990s, Tiso was the object of an aggressive attempt to rehabilitate him and a symbol of everything seemingly wrong about post-Communist Slovakia: nationalism, authoritarianism, xenophobia, bigotry, neofascism. These were the years of the greatest social debate about Tiso, discussions that were typified by their confusion and

> stridency. What you thought about him said a lot about the direction in which you wanted the country to go and how you imagined yourself as a person. What you knew about him depended on which side you read of an extraordinarily polarized literature.[65]

In their defense of Tiso, the ethnonationalists went as far as to present him as the "savior of the Jews," citing his alleged generosity in granting exemptions from the 1941 Jewish Code (Slovak, *Židovský kódex*). The code, a series of harsh anti-Jewish laws, allowed the president to relieve individual Jews from its discriminatory provisions but also from the very definition of "a Jew" it introduced. An exemption could decide between life and death, as it implied being spared—often together with the immediate family—from the 1942 deportations. Despite meticulous historical research showing that the presidential exemptions were not only scarce but granted first and foremost to the "economically important," and hence intended to benefit the state rather than to protect the Jews,[66] assertions that Tiso was a rescuer of the Jews continue to be spread until today. One of the most bizarre yet persistent lies is the claim that a statue of Tiso was erected in Jerusalem, supposedly ordered by the Israeli government as "a token of gratitude for saving lives."[67]

With the governmental change in 1998 that brought down the authoritarian rule of Vladimír Mečiar and his People's Party–Movement for a Democratic Slovakia (Slovak, *Ľudová strana–Hnutie za demokratické Slovensko*, or HZDS), and as part of the country's efforts to join the European Union, the new, moderate center-right government of Mikuláš Dzurinda turned to the uprising to underline the democratic traditions of the country. In contrast to the rhetoric of the Slovak National Party, typical speeches on the rebellion now highlighted the courage of the partisans to take up arms against the Nazis and their local henchmen, placing the uprising in a broader European context. Resistance mythology helped to support the claim that the majority of Slovaks rejected fascism and ethnic nationalism, not only in the distant but also the recent past. As part of the accession strategy, the government made policy decisions and gestures to further prove the country was serious about recognizing the importance of the Holocaust. Those included official apologies of the Slovak parliament for the role the country played in the persecution of Jews (1990), the opening of the Museum of Jewish Culture in Bratislava and the launch of its scholarly journal, *Acta Judaica Slovaca* (1994), the opening of the Institute of Judaism as part of the Comenius University in Bratislava (1996), and the erection of Holocaust plaques and memorials, including the Central Memorial to the Holocaust of Jews in Slovakia, in Bratislava (1997).

In 2001, September 9 was turned into the Memorial Day to the Victims of the Holocaust and Racial Violence to commemorate the adoption of the Jewish Code in 1941. In 2002, the Nation's Memory Institute (Slovak, *Ústav pamäti národa*) was established and mandated to explore the period of the two "totalitarian" regimes that held power between 1939 and 1989. The institute initially launched important historical inquiries into "Aryanization" of Jewish property and collaboration, including databases of looted Jewish businesses and of former members of the Hlinka Guard. The new political elite also adopted a different view on Holocaust rescue. As Paulovičová writes, the moral capital of the Righteous was used as "a building block of identity politics and democracy and as a means of furthering the process of Europeanization. In the hands of the liberals, the category of rescuers has served as a transfer ticket to European Union structures."[68]

The country's politics became increasingly populist and nativist in time, and this shift became especially visible around the 2015 migration crisis.[69] Approaching societal cleavages around cultural issues as an opportunity to take over the nationalist agenda, the nominally leftwing SMER–Social Democracy presented itself as the defender of a Christian, national, and socially conscious state.[70] In government with the Slovak National Party, SMER pushed forward a number of historical falsehoods, including claims that Slovakia's history extends to the ninth century, calling those who dared to challenge these claims "national nihilists," "pseudo-historians" who allegedly despised everything Slovak.[71] While turning to history as a means of strengthening national identity, narratives of the past communicated on the supranational level have also come into question.[72] In the recent evocations of Holocaust rescue in Slovakia, it is not the Jews but the goodhearted Slovak people who are at the center of the World War II narratives. This turn is manifested in governmental efforts to erect statues to those who saved Jews during World War II,[73] televised galas dedicated to the Righteous, attended by the political elite, and the opening of an exhibition dedicated to the Righteous as part of the new Holocaust Museum in Sereď, the only museum of its kind in the country.[74]

Indeed, the righteous resister trope no longer avoids the Holocaust but misuses its legacy, turning complicity into rescue and perpetrators into victims. Whether in their public speeches, as we saw with Ondruš, or Mozolová's public radio broadcasts, politicians and public figures have treated the Righteous Among the Nations awards as an international competition. The words of Mešťan, former director of the Museum of Jewish Culture, illustrate my point here: "When it comes to the size of the population, Slovakia is among those with most recipients of the Righteous Among the Nations title. Of course, there would have been even more recipients if such a possibility had existed before [the revolution of] 1989."[75] Looking beyond the bare numbers, what story do the files of the Righteous really tell?

Contextualizing the Righteous

The six hundred files pertaining to Slovakia's Righteous Among the Nations are a testament to the heroism and bravery on the part of the individuals who risked their lives to help their Jewish neighbors, friends, but also complete strangers, amid World War II. Nevertheless, a close reading of the individual stories complicates how the personal and family sacrifices are being nationalized, and how choices made by individuals and their networks are being presented as proof of a particular Slovak national character. Situating stories of rescue in an institutional and historical framework does not diminish the merit of these acts. Quite the reverse, it is the context that illuminates why these instances of rescue deserve recognition, albeit one that acknowledges the courage the recipients showed as they stood up not so much against an imported fascism but a very intimate one, engrained in the complicity and collaboration of the state they lived in and of the majority of their fellow citizens.

The story of František Gucman, recognized as a Righteous in early 1995, exemplifies the danger of treating the Slovak National Uprising and the German occupation in isolation. During the course of the war, Gucman worked as an income tax clerk in the town of Hlohovec, in western Slovakia. As part of his agenda, Gucman oversaw arranging the local storage of goods left behind by deported Jews. These goods, including furniture and clothing but also household items, such as duvets and pillows, were then sold at public auctions. For those without political and family ties to the regime that would enable them to take over the more lucrative Jewish businesses, such auctions were an opportunity for the "ordinary people" to get hold of things in short supply and for a cheap price. The goods that did not sell, principally religious books, were gathered in a warehouse in the Hlohovec income tax offices, for which Gucman was also responsible. In a regime clogged by nepotism and corruption, this position gave access not only to goods but also to local elites, including members of the Hlinka Slovak People's Party and the Hlinka Guard. A man of humble origins, Gucman remembered his former Jewish neighbors and their kindness, and this prompted him to help those in need. Around 1942, Gucman employed a number of Jews to assist him in classifying and cataloging the religious scripts, and intentionally prolonged their employment so they would not be deported. Then, in 1944, as the Germans disregarded any exemptions and the deportations were renewed, Gucman hid five Jews in the attic of the storage space he was supervising.[76]

While Gucman's decision to offer a helping hand to local Jews endangered him and his family, the threat emanated not only from the Slovak State and from the Germans, who brought another layer of terror as they were occupying the country, but also from the locals, many of whom continued to loot Jewish property and betrayed Jews in hiding.[77] When read closely, the Righteous collection exemplifies not only heroism but also complicity and collaboration, almost as two sides of the same coin. Indeed, many recipients mention not only the "fascists" or Hlinka Guard members as those who represented fascism for them, but the "locals" too.[78]

Alexander Potok survived the war hiding together with his parents in a stable owned by the family of Zuzana Mosná and Rudolf Mosný. When he approached Yad Vashem to have the deeds of his rescuers recognized, he recalled the "painful wandering" from one place to another, as "the villagers were afraid to let them into their houses" and he himself was afraid of being betrayed.[79] A few months after his petition on behalf of the Mosný family, Yad Vashem contacted Alexander Potok and requested that he support his letter with "at least one eyewitness account from an independent source." Approaching his rescuer first, Potok wrote back to Yad Vashem explaining, in broken English, why this was not possible: "He told me, our concealment was kept in strict secrecy (even from the neighbors), one could not trust anyone. We did not leave our hiding place till the end of the war, therefore there may not even be an independent witness."[80]

That being said, the actual Yad Vashem criteria behind the award also lead scholars and the general public to conclusions that muddy rather than illuminate the heroism that rescuers personify. Yad Vashem lists four conditions for granting the title, these being, first, the "active involvement of the rescuer in saving one or several Jews from the threat of death or deportation to death camps," second, "risk to the rescuer's life, liberty or position," third, "the initial motivation being the intention to help persecuted Jews: i.e., not for payment or any other reward such as religious conversion of the saved person, adoption of a child, etc.," and finally fourth, "the existence of testimony of those who were helped or at least unequivocal documentation establishing the nature of the rescue and its circumstances."[81]

Scholars, including historian Bob Moore, have since demonstrated how "the very criteria used by the Commission for the Designation of the Righteous have served to create anomalies in the distribution of awards," pointing to the fact that while there are far more Righteous recipients in the Netherlands than in Belgium, Jews had a much higher chance of surviving the Holocaust in the latter.[82] Whereas Moore explains this inconsistency by the different approach the two postwar administrations took with respect to gathering documentation concerning the plight of the Jews, including survival testimony, he points to yet another interpretative problem connected to the formal criteria behind the award, and that is how to access the very motivation behind rescue. From what we know of rescuers from the West and the motivation they disclosed, religious incentives override all others.[83] Most rescuers from Slovakia also mention humanitarianism and Christian faith as the key reasons for extending help to Jews.[84] This should, however, raise questions. If faith and altruism made the difference, why have religious groups, parishes, and communities that identified as Christian not been more prominent in rescue? And if religion is the answer, how do we then explain the popularity Tiso enjoyed, and the implication of many religious figures in excusing the dehumanization of and discrimination against the Jews in Slovakia? Similarly to Moore, yet pointing to tipping as a "moral normality" in 1944–45 Budapest, historian Istvan Pal Adam suggests that the Yad Vashem criteria may contradict wartime reality. He refers specifically to Budapest building managers, some of whom helped Jews and were given tips for their work. The historian argues that it "does not seem fair to undervalue the courage of the helping building managers when tipping was part of normal life and honouring good service by tipping was the *comme il faut*."[85] The Slovak documentation supports this criticism and suggests that the criteria applied by Yad Vashem have often been in conflict with the situation on the ground, and that these principles have also been bent in the application process.

This is the case of Ján Turčok and his wife, Elizabeta Turčeková, who lived together with their daughter, Mária, in Hliník, then a small village in central Slovakia. Turčok supported his family working as a seasonal worker. He spent much of the year away from his family, on a large estate in Podunajské Biskupice, near the capital, Bratislava. It was here that Turčok befriended Ferdinand Szusz, a Jew who was managing the estate. Szusz survived the 1942 deportations as an "economically important Jew," and this exemption also protected his wife, Vilma Szusz, and their two daughters, Mira and Lili. Following the 1944 occupation of Slovakia and the renewed threat of deportations, the two families made an arrangement: The Turčoks would take the two Susz daughters to live with them as their distant relatives. A monetary transaction was made, which more than forty years later Lili Szusz (now Pasternak) disclosed to Yad Vashem. In her written plea, Pasternak reiterated that she "grew up being told Mr. and Mrs. Turcok saved us not because they were paid, but because they knew it was the right thing to do." The admission of a payment complicated the decision process. Pasternak responded to further inquiries explaining:

> Mr. Turcok was paid for his promise to hide us (we don't know how much), but the money was not the reason for his brave action. Please understand that he was very poor, and to feed and shelter two extra children for an unknown length of time would have been a hardship for him, and since my parents had the money, it was only natural for them to offer the Turcoks some payment. The fact that Mr. and Mrs. Turcok were endangering their lives, and the lives of their own children if they were caught harbouring Jews was something that they were willing to do EVEN WITHOUT A MONETARY REWARD.[86]

In these and other instances, peasants who helped Jews were poor, and whether they were offered money, valuables, or a promise to of reward when the war ended, they clearly acted out of more than economic motives. Indeed, while survivors' accounts, oral or written, provide evidence that establishing what guided their rescuers' actions is practically impossible, they seem to be in agreement that money was never the only motivation behind the choices taken by their gentile rescuers.[87] Despite procedural doubts, and bending their own rules, the commission at Yad Vashem in February 2002 agreed to honor the deeds of the Turčok couple, and their certificate as Righteous Among the Nations was issued in late June of that year.

In this and many other cases, Yad Vashem's insistence on clear proof of altruism behind the acts of the rescuers often tested the patience of the survivors. In 1990, the Holocaust Martyrs' and Heroes' Authority in Jerusalem received a letter from Anton Roček, who approached Yad Vashem after hearing on the radio in Slovakia that they were looking for gentiles who had saved Jews during the war. Writing down what transpired during World War II, Roček appended his testimony with two affidavits supporting his case. It was in mid-1944 when a gentile friend approached Roček, asking whether he and his wife, Žofia Ročeková, would agree to hide Erika Rosenberg, a teenage daughter of a Jewish couple from Bardejov, a spa town in eastern Slovakia. There seemed to be no connection between the two families prior to when the Ročeks made a decision that could endanger their lives. The Roček family took Erika under their roof, registering her at the district office under the name of Magda Šoltésová. We do not know how long it took the Ročeks to decide on whether to offer shelter to Rosenberg, or whether they discussed it with anyone in their family circle apart from that friend. Neither do we know much about the deliberation process at Yad Vashem. It was certainly lengthy and demeaning. As a result, ten years after the original petition was filed, Emanuel Rohan (formerly Rosenberg), the brother of Erika Rosenberg, addressed Yad Vashem with strong words:

> I have made various attempts to ask you to consider Mr. Anton Roček to be included among the Righteous among the Nations. The answer I receive, did he do it for money? My sister did not have any money to pay, she worked as a maid, went to church with the family she was with, etc. Mr. Roček is over 80 years of age. Time is of the essence. Thank G-d my sister is here to give testimony. Please act immediately.[88]

It took an additional nine years for Yad Vashem to decide on the matter and award the Ročeks the title of Righteous. The extensive process, the questions posed in the course of the investigation, in which relatives of the rescuer needed to explain at length that "the term 'to work' on the farm is equal to the term 'to be hidden,'"[89] made both survivors and rescuers not only have misgivings about the process but also take care in how they addressed the awarding authority. This explains why much of the correspondence in the collection—letters sent by both Jewish survivors and their gentile helpers—followed the same pattern, insisting that the help put the gentiles in mortal danger, and that the rescuers "were not tempted by any material rewards, they were motivated strictly only by human kindness and love for their fellow men."[90]

Conclusion

Holidays, traditions, and rituals allow for the performance and reproduction of national attachments; these are "occasions to remember, celebrate, and, to a certain extent, construct a glorious (and glorified) national past."[91] This also applies to the national holiday marking the outbreak of the Slovak National Uprising of August 29, 1944, including the festivities in 2019 that opened my chapter. The annual rallies, the wreath-laying ceremonies, and the predictable speeches of politicians, the symbols of the uprising etched in plaques, statues, monuments, and public places, offer an opportunity to "fuse the imagined community of the nation into the actual community of the nation."[92] What is more, national holidays are very often also a projection of the future. When lecturing the public on historical events and their legacies, politicians turn to the past to enforce a particular vision of tomorrow.

As shown, while the meaning assigned to the uprising has evolved with the political context, its symbolic role has hardly been diminished. Already during World War II and increasingly thereafter, the Slovak National Uprising served as a means of avoiding uncomfortable questions about local collaboration and complicity, a tool used in attempts to restore the image of a "moral nation" by painting the Slovaks as a nation of resistance fighters. At the same time, a number of politicians have, beneath the façade of antifascism, always looked up to the wartime "Christian and national" state as the only available historical model of Slovak independence. In doing so, the ethnonationalists not only challenged the legacy of the uprising but also twisted the history of the Holocaust, because both cast a shadow on a regime they hope to legitimize. The ethnonationalists were so thorough in their whitewashing of the past that they turned the collaborator Tiso into a Jewish rescuer.

Eager to join the structures of the European Union, Slovakia's new moderate representatives adjusted both the rhetoric and the historical policies to what was expected of them. Apologies were issued, memorials unveiled, institutions founded, all to demonstrate that Slovakia was serious in recognizing the Holocaust and its role in the persecution of the Jews. The last decade has brought a significant shift in the appropriation of the Holocaust, though. It has also revealed that many have never believed in the cosmopolitan narratives of World War II and the Holocaust. At the same time, the idealized story of the uprising helped and continues to help align the nation around an example of courage and resilience to fight fascism, in the past and today.

Amid a global landscape of economic instability, mass migration, and heated discourse surrounding race and culture, a mounting number of political leaders spanning the ideological spectrum have resorted to invoking nostalgia-laden rhetoric in an effort to assuage public anxieties. This discourse not only emphasizes positive sentiment but also posits the replacement of shame with pride. Rhetoric about the "good old days" has now also incorporated the history of World War II, with "the good people" at its center. Inviting nationalism back in, nativist politicians revived revisionist claims, making use of a trope of an enemy system that seeks to destroy everything familiar, and in particular "our" national and cultural heritage. Narratives about the past and in particular about the troubled past of World War II came to play a key political role. Social historians of the Holocaust, not satisfied with catchall categories of perpetrators, bystanders, and victims when examining the situation on the ground, have become among the representatives of the liberal-progressive order now being targeted.

Analyzing the shifting narratives of World War II together with the stories of the Righteous allows us to follow the ways in which rescue and resistance became intertwined. It also reveals which notions of the past are being mobilized, by whom, and to what political end. It is not only that the trope of the Righteous needs to be contextualized; we also need to finally "break free from the idea that the occupation period itself has to be treated in isolation and unrelated to events before or after the war."[93] While the tying of the Righteous to the ritualized antifascist resistance "feels good," it is rescue in the midst of wartime complicity and collaboration that represents the actual "good" in this story.

Notes

My chapter was supported by the European Regional Development Fund project "Beyond Security: Role of Conflict in Resilience-Building" (reg. no.: CZ.02.01.01/00/22_008/0004595).

1 Member of the party SMER–Social Democracy (Slovak, SMER–*Sociálna demokracia*), in government between 2006 and 2010 and 2012 and 2020, Branislav Ondruš held the office of the state secretary at the Ministry of Labor, Social Affairs and Family between 2012 and 2020.

2 Zlatica Gregorová, "Štátny tajomník Branislav Ondruš: Odkaz SNP si treba vždy pripomínať," *Sala.dnes24.sk*, August 29, 2019, https://sala.dnes24.sk/statny-tajomnik-branislav-ondrus-odkaz-snp-si-treba-vzdy-pripominat-339672.

3 Yad Vashem, "About the Righteous," http://www.yadvashem.org/righteous/about-the-righteous, accessed August 20, 2020,

4 On "feel-good" narratives, see e.g., Jan Grabowski and Dariusz Libionka, "Distorting and Rewriting the History of the Holocaust in Poland: The Case of the Ulma Family Museum of Poles Saving Jews during World War II in Markowa," *Yad Vashem Studies* 45, no. 1 (2017): 29–32.

5 Cas Mudde, *Populist Radical Right Parties in Europe* (Cambridge: Cambridge University Press, 2007), 19.

6 See Mudde, *Populist Radical Right Parties in Europe*; Cas Mudde, "Introduction to the Populist Radical Right," in *The Populist Radical Right: A Reader*, ed. Cas Mudde (London: Routledge, 2017), 1–10. On nativism or "majority ethnic nationalism," see also, e.g., Eric Kaufmann, *Whiteshift: Populism, Immigration, and the Future of White Majorities* (New York: Abrams, 2019).

7 The Austrian Freedom Party and the Geert Wilders' Party of Freedom in the Netherlands can serve as examples of this mixture.

8 See the agenda-setting of, e.g., the Fidesz–Hungarian Civic Alliance (Hungarian, Fidesz–Magyar Polgári Szövetség) in Hungary; the Law and Justice Party (Polish, Prawo i Sprawiedliwość) in Poland; and the Kotlebists–People's Party Our Slovakia (Slovak, *Kotlebovci–Ľudová strana Naše Slovensko*) in Slovakia, blurring the boundaries among mainstream, radical right, and extreme right parties and movements in Eastern Europe.

9 See, e.g., Samuel Abrahám, "Early Elections in Slovakia: A State of Deadlock," *Government and Opposition* 30, no. 1 (1995): 86–100.

10 See, e.g., Bartek Pytlas, "Radical-Right Narratives in Slovakia and Hungary: Historical Legacies, Mythic Overlaying and Contemporary Politics," *Patterns of Prejudice* 47, no. 2 (2013): 162–83.

11 George Soroka and Félix Krawatzek, "Nationalism, Democracy, and Memory Laws," *Journal of Democracy* 30, no. 2 (2019): 157–71.

12 Omer Bartov, "Communal Genocide: Personal Accounts of the Destruction of Buczacz, Eastern Galicia, 1941–44," in *Shatterzone of Empires: Coexistence and Violence in the German, Habsburg, Russian, and Ottoman Borderlands*, ed. Omer Bartov and Eric D. Weitz (Bloomington: Indiana University Press, 2013), 399–420; Omer Bartov, *Anatomy of a Genocide: The Life and Death of a Town Called Buczacz* (New York: Simon & Schuster, 2018); Natalia Aleksiun, "Intimate Violence: Jewish Testimonies on Victims and Perpetrators in Eastern Galicia," *Holocaust Studies: A Journal of Culture and History* 23, nos. 1–2 (2017): 17–33; Nyla B. Branscombe, Ben Slugoski, and Diane M. Kappen, "The Measurement of Collective Guilt: What It Is and What It Is Not," in *Collective Guilt: International Perspectives*, ed. Nyla B. Branscombe and Bertjan Doosje (Cambridge: Cambridge University Press, 2004), 16–34; Michael J. A. Wohl and Nyla R. Branscombe, "Forgiveness and Collective Guilt Assignment to Historical Perpetrator Groups Depend on Level of Social Category Inclusiveness," *Journal of Personality and Social Psychology* 88, no. 2 (2005): 288–303; Michael Wohl, Nyla Branscombe, and Yechiel Klar, "Collective Guilt: Emotional Reactions When One's Group Has Done Wrong or Been Wronged," *European Review of Social Psychology* 17, no. 1 (2006): 1–37.

13 For a brief overview of memory politics in postwar Europe, see, e.g., Richard Ned Lebow, "The Memory of Politics in Postwar Europe," in *The Politics of Memory in Postwar Europe*, ed. Richard Ned Lebow, Wulf Kansteiner, and Claudio Fogu (Durham, NC: Duke University Press, 2006), 1–39.

14 Tony Judt, "The Past Is Another Country: Myth and Memory in Postwar Europe," *Daedalus* 121, no. 4 (1992): 90–91.

15 Soroka and Krawatzek, "Nationalism, Democracy, and Memory Laws," 158.

16 Nyla B. Branscombe and Bertjan Doosje, "International Perspectives on the Experience of Collective Guilt," in *Collective Guilt: International Perspectives*, ed. Nyla B. Branscombe and Bertjan Doosje (Cambridge: Cambridge University Press, 2004), 3.

17 Ivan Kamenec, "The Slovak State, 1939–1945," in *Slovakia in History*, ed. Mikuláš Teich, Dušan Kováč, and Martin D. Brown (New York: Cambridge University Press, 2011), 175–92.

18 Valerián Bystrický, "Slovakia from the Munich Conference to the Declaration of Independence," in *Slovakia in History*, ed. Mikuláš Teich, Dušan Kováč, and Martin D. Brown (New York: Cambridge University Press, 2011), 158.

19 See, e.g., Hana Kubátová, *Nepokradeš! Nálady a postoje slovenské společnosti k židovské otázce, 1938–1945* (Praha: Academia, 2013); Hana Kubátová, "Popular Responses to the Plunder of Jewish Property in Wartime Slovakia," *Jewish Studies at the Central European University* 7 (2013): 109–26.

20 Hana Kubátová and Michal Kubát, "The Priest and the State: Clerical Fascism in Slovakia and Theory," *Nations and Nationalism* 27, no. 734–749 (2021).

21 Complicity in the widely defined Aryanization process and fear of the return of Jewish survivors, seen as uncomfortable witnesses, were also among the triggers of the infamous September 1945 anti-Jewish pogrom in Topoľčany. See, e.g., Hana Kubátová and Michal Kubát, "Were There 'Bystanders' in Topoľčany? On Concept Formation and the 'Ladder of Abstraction,'" *Contemporary European History* 27, no. 4 (2018): 528–81; Hana Kubátová, "Teraz alebo nikdy: Povojnové protižidovské násilie a väčšinová spoločnosť na Slovensku," *Soudobé dějiny* 3 (2016): 321–46; Anna Cichopek-Gajraj, *Beyond Violence: Jewish Survivors in Poland and Slovakia, 1944–48* (Cambridge: Cambridge University Press, 2014).

22 Lenka Šindelářová, *Einsatzgruppe H: působení operační skupiny H na Slovensku 1944/1945 a poválečné trestní stíhání jejích příslušníků* (Praha/Banská Bystrica: Academia/Múzeum Slovenského národného povstania, 2015), 160–69.

23 Dušan Halaj, "SNP a európska rezistencia," in *SNP v pamäti národa. Materiály z vedeckej konferencie k 50. výročiu SNP, Donovaly 26.–28. apríla 1994* (Bratislava: NKV International, 1994), 249–71.

24 Yeshayahu Jelinek, "The Role of the Jews in Slovakian Resistance," *Jahrbücher für Geschichte Osteuropas* 15, no. 3 (1967): 419; Ladislav Lipscher, *Židia v slovenskom štátě: 1939–1945* (Bratislava: Print-Servis, 1992), 161–62; Katarína Hradská, "Deportácie slovenských Židov v rokoch 1944–1945 so zreteľom na transporty do Terezína," *Historický časopis* 45, no. 3 (1997): 456.

25 Jelinek, "The Role of the Jews in Slovakian Resistance," 415–22.

26 Katarína Zavacká, “K tradícii nariaďovacej právomoci na Slovensku (II. časť),” *Právny obzor* 86, no. 1 (2003): 38–64.
27 Stanislav Mičev et al., *Fašistické represálie na Slovensku* (Bratislava: Vydavateľstvo Obzor, 1990), 96.
28 James Mace Ward, *Priest, Politician, Collaborator: Jozef Tiso and the Making of Fascist Slovakia* (Ithaca, NY: Cornell University Press, 2013), 253.
29 See, e.g., Kubátová, *Nepokradeš!*
30 Kubátová, *Nepokradeš!* 159–77
31 Peter Salner, *Prežili holokaust* (Bratislava: Veda, Ústav etnológie Slovenskej akadémie vied, 1997), 69.
32 Jean-Marc Dreyfus and Eduard Nižňanský, “Jews and Non-Jews in the Aryanization Process: Comparison of France and the Slovak State, 1939–45,” in *Facing the Catastrophe: Jews and Non-Jews in Europe during World War II*, ed. Beate Kosmala and Georgi Verbeeck (Oxford; New York: Berg, 2011), 30.
33 Pavol Mešťan stepped down from his position on September 30, 2020. The museum is currently run by an interim director, Michal Vaněk. The Museum of Jewish Culture is part of the Slovak National Museum, founded by the Ministry of Culture.
34 Miroslav Čaplovič, “Židia si chcú pamätať z vojny aj nezištnú pomoc,” *Pravda.sk*, December 6, 2017, sec. Žurnál, https://zurnal.pravda.sk/rozhovory/clanok/450173-zidia-si-chcu-pamatat-z-vojny-aj-nezistnu-pomoc/, accessed January 3, 2023.
35 Ivan Kamenec, “Changes in the Attitude of the Slovak Population to the So-Called Jewish Question during the Period 1938–1945,” in *Nazi Europe and the Final Solution*, ed. David Bankier and Israel Gutman (Jerusalem: Yad Vashem, 2003), 336; see also a similar argument in Ivan Kamenec, *Po stopách tragédie* (Bratislava: Archa, 1991), 275; Salner, *Prežili holokaust*, 69–98. For a fascinating instance of rescue behind the walls of a convent, see Yad Vashem Archives, RG M.31.1.—Files of the Department for the Righteous Among the Nations, file number 8700 (Čermaňová Vilma, Šinská Imberta).
36 Salner, *Prežili holokaust*, 69–118.
37 Nina Paulovičová, “Rescue of Jews in the Slovak State (1939–1945)” (PhD diss., University of Alberta, Department of History and Classics, 2012), 49, http://hdl.handle.net/10402/era.25987, accessed June 3, 2022. This calculation rests on the 2007 *Encyclopedia of the Righteous*; see Yisrael Gutman, ed., *The Encyclopedia of the Righteous Among the Nations: Rescuers of Jews during the Holocaust* (Jerusalem: Yad Vashem, 2007).

38 See, e.g., Kamenec, *Po stopách tragédie*, 265–79.

39 See, e.g., District Archive Topoľčany, RG Okresný úrad Bánovce, file D1-424/44, box 84, anonymous letters reporting on the Jews, June 18, 1944, and July 13, 1944.

40 Yad Vashem Archives, RG Documentation Centre of the Central Union of Jewish Communities in Bratislava (M.5), testimony of Ladislav Rybár on the situation of Jews in Brezno nad Hronom, April 30, 1946.

41 See, e.g., Jelinek, "The Role of the Jews in Slovakian Resistance," 420.

42 Cichopek-Gajraj, *Beyond Violence*, 90–113.

43 Kubátová, "Teraz alebo nikdy: Povojnové protižidovské násilie a väčšinová spoločnosť na Slovensku."

44 See, e.g., Branscombe and Doosje, "International Perspectives on the Experience of Collective Guilt"; Branscombe, Slugoski, and Kappen, "The Measurement of Collective Guilt: What It Is and What It Is Not"; Wohl and Branscombe, "Forgiveness and Collective Guilt Assignment to Historical Perpetrator Groups Depend on Level of Social Category Inclusiveness"; Wohl, Branscombe, and Klar, "Collective Guilt."

45 Henry Rousso, *Le Syndrome de Vichy: 1944–198 . . .* (Paris: Éditions de Seuil, 1987).

46 Martin R. Gutmann, *Building a Nazi Europe: The SS's Germanic Volunteers* (Cambridge: Cambridge University Press, 2018), 54.

47 Rebecca Clifford, *Commemorating the Holocaust: The Dilemmas of Remembrance in France and Italy* (Oxford: Oxford University Press, 2013), 6.

48 Nadège Ragaru, "Juger les crimes antisémites avant Nuremberg: L'expérience du Tribunal populaire en Bulgarie (novembre 1944–avril 1945)," *Histoire@Politique* 26, no. 2 (2015), http://www.histoire-politique.fr/index.php?numero=26&rub=dossier&item=250, accessed April 3, 2022.

49 Hana Kubátová, "On the Image of the Jew in Postwar Slovakia," *Annual of Language & Politics and Politics of Identity* 9 (2015): 71–85; Hana Kubátová and Jan Láníček, *The Jew in Czech and Slovak Imagination, 1938–89: Antisemitism, the Holocaust, and Zionism* (Boston: Brill, 2018), 123–68.

50 See, e.g., Kubátová and Láníček, *The Jew in Czech and Slovak Imagination, 1938–89: Antisemitism, the Holocaust, and Zionism*, 136–37.

51 Zofia Wóycicka, "Global Patterns, Local Interpretations: New Polish Museums Dedicated to the Rescue of Jews during the Holocaust," *Holocaust Studies: A Journal of Culture and History* 25, no. 3 (2019): 254.

52 "Winning Design for Nonantola's Jewish Children Museum Announced," *Inexhibit* (blog), November 21, 2019, https://www.inexhibit.com/marker/

winning-design-nonantolas-jewish-chidren-museum-announced/, accessed April 1, 2022.

53 Wóycicka, "Global Patterns, Local Interpretations," 243.

54 Recordings of the *Encyclopedia of the Righteous* are available at "Rádio Slovensko: Encyklopédia spravodlivých," slovensko.rtvs.sk, https://slovensko.rtvs.sk/rubriky/encyklopedia-spravodlivych, accessed January 31, 2021

55 See the closing words at the end of each segment. "Rádio Slovensko: Encyklopédia spravodlivých."

56 Oľga Gyarfašová and Grigorij Mesežnikov, "Actors, Agenda, and Appeal of the Radical Nationalist Right in Slovakia," in *Transforming the Transformation? The East European Radical Right in the Political Process*, ed. Michael Minkenberg (London: Routledge, 2015), 231. See also Grigorij Mesežnikov, "National Populism in Slovakia—Defining the Character of the State and Interpreting Select Historic Events," in *National Populism and Slovak-Hungarian Relations in Slovakia 2006–2009*, ed. Kálmán Petöcz (Šamorín: Forum Minority Research Institute, 2009), 39–66.

57 See also Oľga Gyarfašová, "Radicalization of Radical Right: Nativist Movements and Parties in the Slovak Political Process," in *Radical Right Movement Parties in Europe*, ed. Ondřej Císař and Manuela Caiani (Abingdon: Routledge, 2018), 199–215.

58 August 29 was first made into a national holiday in July 1945 by the postwar legislative Slovak National Council (Slovak, *Slovenská národná rada*) but was soon dropped in the reborn Czechoslovakia. As of 1952, August 29 was recognized as a day of significance in Czechoslovakia, and in September 1992, a law was adopted that turned August 29 into a national holiday in Slovakia.

59 For how the history of the uprising was politically utilized during 1948–89, see esp. Jozef Jablonický, *Glosy o historiografii SNP: zneužívanie a falšovanie dejín SNP* (Bratislava: NVK International, 1994).

60 "Sviatky a zákon NR SR č. 241/1993 o štátnych sviatkoch, dňoch pracovného pokoja a pamätných dňoch v monitoringu médií 1999-2011. Výskumná správa projektu VEGA 2/0069/11.," Archív textov Ústavu etnológie SAV, 2013; Monika Vrzgulová, "Komu patrí Slovenské národné povstanie," in *Čo je to sviatok v 21. storočí na Slovensku?*, ed. Katarína Popelková (Bratislava: Ústav etnológie SAV, 2014), 66–108.

61 Abrahám, "Early Elections in Slovakia," 97.

62 Grigorij Mesežnikov and Oľga Gyárfášová, *National Populism in Slovakia* (Bratislava: Institute for Public Affairs, 2008), 17–18.

63 Paulovičová, "Rescue of Jews in the Slovak State (1939–1945)," 26.
64 Yeshayahu A. Jelinek, "Slovaks and the Holocaust: Attempts at Reconciliation," *Soviet Jewish Affairs* 19, no. 1 (1989): 57–68. See also, e.g., Abrahám Samuel, "Ďurica, postmodernizmus a Európská Únia," *Kritika & Kontext* 2, nos. 2–3 (1997): 26–32.
65 Ward, *Priest, Politician, Collaborator*, xi.
66 James Mace Ward, "'People Who Deserve It': Jozef Tiso and the Presidential Exemption," *Nationalities Papers: The Journal of Nationalism and Ethnicity* 30, no. 4 (2002): 571–601.
67 Igor Cagáň, "K údajnému pamätníku Jozefovi Tisovi v Jeruzaleme apel k stanovisku izraelského veľvyslanca na Slovensku," November 30, 2014, http://jozeftiso.sk/jt/ludovy-kultus/267-k-udajnemu-pamatniku-jozefovi-tisovi-v-jeruzaleme, accessed January 31, 2021.
68 Paulovičová, "Rescue of Jews in the Slovak State (1939–1945)," 37.
69 These arguments draw from Hana Kubátová and Jan Láníček, "Memory Wars and Emotional Politics: 'Feel Good' Holocaust Appropriation in Central Europe," *Nationalities Papers* (forthcoming).
70 Petra Burzova, "Towards a New Past: Some Reflections on Nationalism in Post-Socialist Slovakia," *Nationalities Papers* 40, no. 6 (2012): 879–94.
71 Burzova, "Towards a New Past: Some Reflections on Nationalism in Post-Socialist Slovakia," 883.
72 Jelena Subotic, "Political Memory, Ontological Security, and Holocaust Remembrance in Post-Communist Europe," *European Security* 27, no. 3 (2018): 302. See also Subotic, *Yellow Star, Red Star*.
73 This idea was voiced by Robert Fico, head of SMER–Social Democracy and prime minister between 2006 and 2010 and 2012 and 2016, meeting with Rabbi Andrew Baker in 2009, the American Jewish Committee's director of international Jewish affairs and personal representative of the OBSE chairmanship on combating antisemitism. See "Pri školách by sme mali stavať pamätníky holokaustu, vyhlásil Fico," Pravda.sk, September 7, 2009.
74 "Múzeum Holokaustu v Seredi, Slovenské Národné Múzeum," snm.sk, https://www.snm.sk/?muzeum-holokaustu-uvodna-stranka, accessed March 7, 2021.
75 Čaplovič, "Židia si chcú pamätať z vojny aj nezištnú pomoc."
76 Yad Vashem Archives, RG M.31.1, file number 11439 (Klimová Eva); Yad Vashem Archives, RG M.31.2, file number 6445 (Gucman František).
77 Nina Paulovičová and Jozef Urminský, "Židovská komunita v dejinách mesta Hlohovec (1938–1945). Príbeh, ktorý prešiel tmou" (Hlohovec: Občianske združenie Ex Libris Ad Personam Hlohovec, 2009), 182–83.

78 Yad Vashem Archives, RG M.31.2, file number 11439 (Mosná Zuzana).
79 Yad Vashem Archives, RG M.31.2, file number 11439 (Mosná Zuzana).
80 Yad Vashem Archives, RG M.31.2, file number 11439 (Mosná Zuzana).
81 Yad Vashem, "FAQs: The Righteous Among the Nations Program," https://www.yadvashem.org/righteous/faq.html, accessed February 1, 2021. See also, e.g., Mordecai Paldiel, *Sheltering the Jews: Stories of Holocaust Rescuers* (Minneapolis, MN: Fortress Press, 1996); Mordecai Paldiel, "Righteous Gentiles and Courageous Jews: Acknowledging and Honoring Rescuers of Jews," *French Politics, Culture & Society* 30, no. 2 (2012): 134–49.
82 Bob Moore, "The Rescue of Jews in Nazi-Occupied Belgium, France and the Netherlands," *Australian Journal of Politics & History* 50, no. 3 (2004): 385.
83 Moore, "The Rescue of Jews in Nazi-Occupied Belgium, France and the Netherlands," 389.
84 See, e.g., Margita, 1998, Interview by USC Shoah Foundation Institute for Visual History and Education, University of Southern California, Rimavská Sobota, Slovakia, February 13; Peter Z., 1998, Interview by USC Shoah Foundation Institute for Visual History and Education, University of Southern California, Bratislava, Slovakia, January 19.
85 Istvan Pal Adam, *Budapest Building Managers and the Holocaust in Hungary* (Basingstoke: Palgrave Macmillan, 2016), 116, 114.
86 Yad Vashem Archives, RG M.31.1.—Files of the Department for the Righteous Among the Nations, file number 9635 (Turčok Ján).
87 See Ivan Kamenec, 1996, Interview by USC Shoah Foundation Institute for Visual History and Education, University of Southern California, Bratislava, Slovakia, July 12, cassette 3, 03:00–05:00.
88 Yad Vashem Archives, RG M.31.1.—Files of the Department for the Righteous Among the Nations, file number 11887 (Roček Anton).
89 Yad Vashem Archives, RG M.31.1.—Files of the Department for the Righteous Among the Nations, file number 5602 (Hučko Ján).
90 Yad Vashem Archives, RG M.31.1.—Files of the Department for the Righteous Among the Nations, file number 3162 (Hajtáš Geza). See also Yad Vashem Archives, RG M.31.2, file number 11439 (Klimová Eva); YVA, RG M.31.2, file number 7939 (Čiefová Emília).
91 Jon E. Fox, "National Holiday Commemorations: The View from Below," in *The Cultural Politics of Nationalism and Nation-Building: Ritual and Performance in the Forging of Nations*, ed. Rachel Tsang and Eric Taylor Woods (Abingdon: Routledge, 2013), 39. For what are now classic works on the role of holidays and other rites in nationalist agenda, see

esp. Anthony D. Smith, *The Ethnic Origins of Nations* (Oxford: Blackwell, 1986); Eric Hobsbawm and Terence O. Ranger, eds., *The Invention of Tradition* (Cambridge: Cambridge University Press, 1983); Eric J. Hobsbawm, *Nations and Nationalism since 1780: Programme, Myth, Reality* (Cambridge: Cambridge University Press, 1991).

92 Fox, "National Holiday Commemorations: The View from Below," 39. On commemorations of the Slovak National Uprising, see also Vrzgulová, "Komu patrí Slovenské národné povstanie."

93 Moore, "The Rescue of Jews in Nazi-Occupied Belgium, France and the Netherlands," 388.

Bibliography

Abrahám, Samuel. "Early Elections in Slovakia: A State of Deadlock." *Government and Opposition* 30, no. 1 (1995): 86–100.

Adam, Istvan Pal. *Budapest Building Managers and the Holocaust in Hungary*. Basingstoke: Palgrave Macmillan, 2016.

Aleksiun, Natalia. "Intimate Violence: Jewish Testimonies on Victims and Perpetrators in Eastern Galicia." *Holocaust Studies: A Journal of Culture and History* 23, nos. 1–2 (2017): 17–33.

Bartov, Omer. *Anatomy of a Genocide: The Life and Death of a Town Called Buczacz*. New York: Simon & Schuster, 2018.

———. "Communal Genocide: Personal Accounts of the Destruction of Buczacz, Eastern Galicia, 1941–44." In *Shatterzone of Empires: Coexistence and Violence in the German, Habsburg, Russian, and Ottoman Borderlands*, ed. Omer Bartov and Eric D. Weitz, 399–420. Bloomington: Indiana University Press, 2013.

Branscombe, Nyla B., and Bertjan Doosje. "International Perspectives on the Experience of Collective Guilt." In *Collective Guilt: International Perspectives*, ed. Nyla B. Branscombe and Bertjan Doosje, 3–15. Cambridge: Cambridge University Press, 2004.

Branscombe, Nyla B., Ben Slugoski, and Diane M. Kappen. "The Measurement of Collective Guilt: What It Is and What It Is Not." In *Collective Guilt: International Perspectives*, ed. Nyla B. Branscombe and Bertjan Doosje, 16–34. Cambridge: Cambridge University Press, 2004.

Burzova, Petra. "Towards a New Past: Some Reflections on Nationalism in Post-Socialist Slovakia." *Nationalities Papers* 40, no. 6 (2012): 879–94.

Bystrický, Valerián. "Slovakia from the Munich Conference to the Declaration of Independence." In *Slovakia in History*, ed. Mikuláš Teich, Dušan Kováč, and Martin D. Brown, 157–74. New York: Cambridge University Press, 2011.

Cagáň, Igor. "K údajnému pamätníku Jozefovi Tisovi v Jeruzaleme apel k stanovisku izraelského veľvyslanca na Slovensku." (To the alleged memorial of Jozef Tiso in Jerusalem, an appeal to the position of the Israeli ambassador to Slovakia.) November 30, 2014. http://jozeftiso.sk/jt/ludovy-kultus/267-k-udajnemu-pamatniku-jozefovi-tisovi-v-jeruzaleme, accessed January 31, 2021.

Čaplovič, Miroslav. "Židia si chcú pamätať z vojny aj nezištnú pomoc." (Jews want to remember selfless aid during the war.) *Pravda.sk*, December 6, 2017, sec. Žurnál, https://zurnal.pravda.sk/rozhovory/clanok/450173-zidia-si-chcu-pamatat-z-vojny-aj-nezistnu-pomoc/, accessed January 3, 2023.

Cichopek-Gajraj, Anna. *Beyond Violence: Jewish Survivors in Poland and Slovakia, 1944–48*. Cambridge: Cambridge University Press, 2014.

Clifford, Rebecca. *Commemorating the Holocaust: The Dilemmas of Remembrance in France and Italy*. Oxford: Oxford University Press, 2013.

Dreyfus, Jean-Marc, and Eduard Nižňanský. "Jews and Non-Jews in the Aryanization Process: Comparison of France and the Slovak State, 1939–45." In *Facing the Catastrophe: Jews and Non-Jews in Europe during World War II*, ed. Beate Kosmala and Georgi Verbeeck, 13–40. Oxford: Berg, 2011.

Fox, Jon E. "National Holiday Commemorations: The View from Below." In *The Cultural Politics of Nationalism and Nation-Building: Ritual and Performance in the Forging of Nations*, ed. Rachel Tsang and Eric Taylor Woods, 38–52. Abingdon: Routledge, 2013.

Grabowski, Jan, and Dariusz Libionka. "Distorting and Rewriting the History of the Holocaust in Poland: The Case of the Ulma Family Museum of Poles Saving Jews during World War II in Markowa." *Yad Vashem Studies* 45, no. 1 (2017): 29–32.

Gregorová, Zlatica. "Štátny tajomník Branislav Ondruš: Odkaz SNP si treba vždy pripomínať." (State Secretary Branislav Ondruš: The message of the Slovak National Uprising should always be remembered.) *Sala.dnes24.sk*, August 29, 2019, https://sala.dnes24.sk/statny-tajomnik-branislav-ondrus-odkaz-snp-si-treba-vzdy-pripominat-339672, accessed January 31, 2021.

Gutman, Yisrael, ed. *The Encyclopedia of the Righteous Among the Nations: Rescuers of Jews during the Holocaust*. Jerusalem: Yad Vashem, 2007.

Gutmann, Martin R. *Building a Nazi Europe: The SS's Germanic Volunteers*. Cambridge: Cambridge University Press, 2018.

Gyarfašová, Oľga. "Radicalization of Radical Right: Nativist Movements and Parties in the Slovak Political Process." In *Radical Right Movement Parties in Europe*, ed. Ondřej Císař and Manuela Caiani, 199–215. Abingdon: Routledge, 2018.

Gyarfašová, Oľga, and Grigorij Mesežnikov. "Actors, Agenda, and Appeal of the Radical Nationalist Right in Slovakia." In *Transforming the Transformation? The East European Radical Right in the Political Process*, ed. Michael Minkenberg, 224–48. London: Routledge, 2015.

Halaj, Dušan. "SNP a európska rezistencia." (SNP [Slovak National Uprising] and European resistance.) In *SNP v pamäti národa. Materiály z vedeckej konferencie k 50. výročiu SNP, Donovaly 26.–28. apríla 1994*, 249–71. Bratislava: NKV International, 1994.

Hobsbawm, Eric J. *Nations and Nationalism since 1780: Programme, Myth, Reality*. Cambridge: Cambridge University Press, 1991.

Hobsbawm, Eric, and Terence O. Ranger, eds. *The Invention of Tradition*. Cambridge: Cambridge University Press, 1983.

Hradská, Katarína. "Deportácie slovenských Židov v rokoch 1944–1945 so zreteľom na transporty do Terezína." (Deportation of Slovak Jews in the years 1944–1945 with regard to transports to Terezín.) *Historický časopis* 45, no. 3 (1997): 455–71.

Inexhibit. "Winning Design for Nonantola's Jewish Children Museum Announced," November 21, 2019, https://www.inexhibit.com/marker/winning-design-nonantolas-jewish-chidren-museum-announced/, accessed April 1, 2022.

Jablonický, Jozef. *Glosy o historiografii SNP: zneužívanie a falšovanie dejín SNP*. (Essays on the historiography of the Slovak National Uprising: The abuse and falsification of the history of the SNP.) Bratislava: NVK International, 1994.

Jelinek, Yeshayahu. "The Role of the Jews in Slovakian Resistance." *Jahrbücher für Geschichte Osteuropas* 15, no. 3 (1967): 415–22.

———. "Slovaks and the Holocaust: Attempts at Reconciliation." *Soviet Jewish Affairs* 19, no. 1 (1989): 57–68.

Judt, Tony. "The Past Is Another Country: Myth and Memory in Postwar Europe." *Daedalus* 121, no. 4 (1992): 83–118.

Kamenec, Ivan. "Changes in the Attitude of the Slovak Population to the So-Called Jewish Question during the Period 1938–1945." In *Nazi Europe and the Final Solution*, ed. David Bankier and Israel Gutman, 327–38. Jerusalem: Yad Vashem, 2003.

———. *Po stopách tragédie*. Bratislava: Archa, 1991.

———. "The Slovak State, 1939–1945." In *Slovakia in History*, ed. Mikuláš Teich, Dušan Kováč, and Martin D. Brown, 175–92. New York: Cambridge University Press, 2011.

Kaufmann, Eric. *Whiteshift: Populism, Immigration, and the Future of White Majorities*. New York: Abrams, 2019.

Kubátová, Hana. *Nepokradeš! Nálady a postoje slovenské společnosti k židovské otázce, 1938–1945.* (You shall not steal! Moods and attitudes of Slovak society toward the Jewish question, 1938–1945.) Praha: Academia, 2013.

———. "On the Image of the Jew in Postwar Slovakia." *Annual of Language & Politics and Politics of Identity* 9 (2015): 71–85.

———. "Popular Responses to the Plunder of Jewish Property in Wartime Slovakia." *Jewish Studies at the Central European University* 7 (2013): 109–26.

———. "Teraz alebo nikdy: Povojnové protižidovské násilie a väčšinová spoločnosť na Slovensku." (Now or never: Postwar anti-Jewish violence and the majority society in Slovakia.) *Soudobé dějiny* 3 (2016): 321–46.

Kubátová, Hana, and Michal Kubát. "The Priest and the State: Clerical Fascism in Slovakia and Theory." *Nations and Nationalism* 27, no. 3 (2021): 734–49.

———. "Were There 'Bystanders' in Topoľčany? On Concept Formation and the 'Ladder of Abstraction.'" *Contemporary European History* 27, no. 4 (2018): 528–81.

Kubátová, Hana, and Jan Láníček. "Memory Wars and Emotional Politics: 'Feel Good' Holocaust Appropriation in Central Europe." *Nationalities Papers* (forthcoming).

———. *The Jew in Czech and Slovak Imagination, 1938–89: Antisemitism, the Holocaust, and Zionism.* Boston: Brill, 2018.

Lebow, Richard Ned. "The Memory of Politics in Postwar Europe." In *The Politics of Memory in Postwar Europe*, ed. Richard Ned Lebow, Wulf Kansteiner, and Claudio Fogu, 1–39. Durham, NC: Duke University Press, 2006.

Lipscher, Ladislav. *Židia v slovenskom štátě: 1939–1945.* (Jews in the Slovak State: 1939–1945.) Bratislava: Print-Servis, 1992.

Mesežnikov, Grigorij. "National Populism in Slovakia—Defining the Character of the State and Interpreting Select Historic Events." In *National Populism and Slovak-Hungarian Relations in Slovakia 2006–2009*, ed. Kálmán Petöcz, 39–66. Šamorín: Forum Minority Research Institute, 2009.

Mesežnikov, Grigorij, and Oľga Gyárfášová. *National Populism in Slovakia.* Bratislava: Institute for Public Affairs, 2008.

Mičev, Stanislav, Ján Stanislav, Jozef Rodák, and Dušan Halaj. *Fašistické represálie na Slovensku.* (Fascist repressions in Slovakia.) Bratislava: Vydavateľstvo Obzor, 1990.

Moore, Bob. "The Rescue of Jews in Nazi-Occupied Belgium, France and the Netherlands." *Australian Journal of Politics & History* 50, no. 3 (2004): 385–95.

Mudde, Cas. "Introduction to the Populist Radical Right." In *The Populist Radical Right: A Reader*, ed. Cas Mudde, 1–10. London: Routledge, 2017.

———. *Populist Radical Right Parties in Europe.* Cambridge: Cambridge University Press, 2007.

Paldiel, Mordecai. "Righteous Gentiles and Courageous Jews: Acknowledging and Honoring Rescuers of Jews." *French Politics, Culture & Society* 30, no. 2 (2012): 134–49.

———. *Sheltering the Jews: Stories of Holocaust Rescuers*. Minneapolis, MN: Fortress Press, 1996.

Paulovičová, Nina. "Rescue of Jews in the Slovak State (1939–1945)." PhD diss., University of Alberta, Department of History and Classics, 2012. http://hdl.handle.net/10402/era.25987, accessed June 3, 2022.

Paulovičová, Nina, and Jozef Urminský. "Židovská komunita v dejinách mesta Hlohovec (1938–1945). Príbeh, ktorý prešiel tmou." (The Jewish community in the history of the city of Hlohovec [1938–1945]: A story that passed through the darkness.) Hlohovec: Občianske združenie Ex Libris Ad Personam Hlohovec, 2009.

Pravda. "Pri školách by sme mali stavať pamätníky holokaustu, vyhlásil Fico." (Fico stated that we should build Holocaust memorials near schools.) September 7, 2009. https://spravy.pravda.sk/domace/clanok/163278-pri-skolach-by-sme-mali-stavat-pamaetniky-holokaustu-vyhlasil-fico/, accessed August 20, 2021.

Pytlas, Bartek. "Radical-Right Narratives in Slovakia and Hungary: Historical Legacies, Mythic Overlaying and Contemporary Politics." *Patterns of Prejudice* 47, no. 2 (2013): 162–83.

Rádio Slovensko. "Rádio Slovensko: Encyklopédia spravodlivých." (Radio Slovakia: Encyclopedia of the Righteous.) 2021. https://slovensko.rtvs.sk/rubriky/encyklopedia-spravodlivych, accessed January 31, 2021.

Ragaru, Nadège. "Juger les crimes antisémites avant Nuremberg: l'expérience du Tribunal populaire en Bulgarie (novembre 1944–avril 1945)." (Judging antisemitic crimes before Nuremberg: The experience of the People's Tribunal in Bulgaria [November 1944–April 1945].) *Histoire@Politique* 26, no. 2 (2015), http://www.histoire-politique.fr/index.php?numero=26&rub=dossier&item=250, accessed April 3, 2022.

Rousso, Henry. *Le Syndrome de Vichy: 1944–198 . . .* (The Vichy Syndrome: 1944–198 . . .) Paris: Éditions de Seuil, 1987.

Salner, Peter. *Prežili holokaust*. (They survived the Holocaust.) Bratislava: Veda, Ústav etnológie Slovenskej akadémie vied, 1997.

Samuel, Abrahám. "Ďurica, postmodernizmus a Európská Únia." (Durica, postmodernism, and the European Union.) *Kritika & Kontext* 2, nos. 2–3 (1997): 26–32.

Šindelářová, Lenka. *Einsatzgruppe H: působení operační skupiny H na Slovensku 1944/1945 a poválečné trestní stíhání jejích příslušníků*. (Einsatzgruppe H: The activities of Operational Group H in Slovakia 1944/1945 and the postwar criminal prosecution of its members.) Praha/Banská Bystrica: Academia/Múzeum Slovenského národného povstania, 2015.

Slovak National Museum Website. "Múzeum Holokaustu v Seredi, Slovenské Národné Múzeum," https://www.snm.sk/?muzeum-holokaustu-uvodna-stranka, accessed March 7, 2021.

Smith, Anthony D. *The Ethnic Origins of Nations*. Oxford: Blackwell, 1986.

Soroka, George, and Félix Krawatzek. "Nationalism, Democracy, and Memory Laws." *Journal of Democracy* 30, no. 2 (2019): 157–71.

Subotic, Jelena. "Political Memory, Ontological Security, and Holocaust Remembrance in Post-Communist Europe." *European Security* 27, no. 3 (2018): 296–313.

———. *Yellow Star, Red Star: Holocaust Remembrance after Communism*. Ithaca, NY: Cornell University Press, 2019.

"Sviatky a zákon NR SR č. 241/1993 o štátnych sviatkoch, dňoch pracovného pokoja a pamätných dňoch v monitoringu médií 1999–2011. Výskumná správa projektu VEGA 2/0069/11." (Holidays and the Law of the National Council of the Slovak Republic No. 241/1993 on state holidays, days of rest from work, and memorial days in media monitoring from 1999–2011.) Research report of the VEGA 2/0069/11 project Archív textov Ústavu etnológie SAV, 2013.

Vrzgulová, Monika. "Komu patrí Slovenské národné povstanie." (To whom does the Slovak national uprising belong?) In *Čo je to sviatok v 21. storočí na Slovensku?*, ed. Katarína Popelková, 66–108. Bratislava: Ústav etnológie SAV, 2014.

Ward, James Mace. "'People Who Deserve It': Jozef Tiso and the Presidential Exemption." *Nationalities Papers: The Journal of Nationalism and Ethnicity* 30, no. 4 (2002): 571–601.

———. *Priest, Politician, Collaborator: Jozef Tiso and the Making of Fascist Slovakia*. Ithaca, NY: Cornell University Press, 2013.

Wohl, Michael, Nyla Branscombe, and Yechiel Klar. "Collective Guilt: Emotional Reactions When One's Group Has Done Wrong or Been Wronged." *European Review of Social Psychology* 17, no. 1 (2006): 1–37.

Wohl, Michael J. A., and Nyla R. Branscombe. "Forgiveness and Collective Guilt Assignment to Historical Perpetrator Groups Depend on Level of Social Category Inclusiveness." *Journal of Personality and Social Psychology* 88, no. 2 (2005): 288–303.

Wóycicka, Zofia. "Global Patterns, Local Interpretations: New Polish Museums Dedicated to the Rescue of Jews during the Holocaust." *Holocaust Studies: A Journal of Culture and History* 25, no. 3 (2019): 248–72.

Yad Vashem. "About the Righteous." http://www.yadvashem.org/righteous/about-the-righteous, accessed August 20, 2020.

———. "FAQs: The Righteous Among the Nations Program." https://www.yadvashem.org/righteous/faq.html, accessed February 1, 2021.

Zavacká, Katarína. "K tradícii nariaďovacej právomoci na Slovensku (II. časť)." (The tradition of administrative authority in Slovakia.) *Právny obzor* 86, no. 1 (2003): 38–64.

6

Constructing a Legacy

The Memory of Andrei Sheptytsky in Contemporary Ukraine

LILIANA HENTOSH

TRANSLATED BY ASIA FRUMAN

Metropolitan Andrei Sheptytsky was a prominent church leader, public figure, and major Ukrainian philanthropist of the first half of the twentieth century. During World War II, he helped rescue a number of Jewish men, women, and children in Lviv (Ger., Lemberg; Pol., Lwów; Russ., Lvov). Despite applications submitted to Yad Vashem, Sheptytsky has not been recognized as Righteous Among the Nations, while several people who worked with him in the rescue efforts, often acting under his guidance, have been awarded the title. In Soviet times his name was mostly mentioned in a negative context, and the traces of his manifold activities were almost completely erased from history. In recent years, however, Sheptytsky has been increasingly gaining attention in Ukraine. Scholars, cultural activists, and laypeople have participated in passionate discussions about his legacy and ways of honoring him. In 2015 the 150th anniversary of his birth was celebrated in Ukraine at the highest level, with the program of commemorative events approved by a resolution of the parliament.[1] Outside Ukraine—particularly in Poland—Sheptytsky's political views and actions, especially during World War II, have been strongly criticized. So why are the life and accomplishments of this person perceived and interpreted so differently in different parts of Ukraine and beyond?

In this essay I will first discuss Andrei Sheptytsky's life and his most significant endeavors. In particular I will focus on his political beliefs and attitudes and provide an in-depth analysis of his activities during World War II, which continue to be viewed as controversial both in Ukraine and abroad. The second part of the chapter will shed light on how the image of Metropolitan Sheptytsky as a historical figure was created, and how the memory of him was shaped first by the Soviet authorities and then in independent Ukraine. For this purpose I will analyze studies, academic and educational publications on Sheptytsky that appeared in Ukraine after 1991, as well as public commemorations dedicated to him.

Multidimensional regional differences present an important context for researching any aspect of life in contemporary Ukraine, including the role played by the memory of Sheptytsky and the shaping of his image in Ukrainian public consciousness.[2] Over the last few years, memorial initiatives devoted to Sheptytsky have become particularly popular in western Ukraine, contributing to the process of constructing his legacy.[3] During the three decades of independence, there have been periods when the ruling elites tried particularly hard to influence the formation of a nationally homogenous state. They believed that measures aimed at "ukrainizing" historical memory would help consolidate Ukrainian society. Nevertheless, different attitudes toward Metropolitan Sheptytsky continue to persist in different regions of Ukraine and abroad.[4]

Andrei Sheptytsky: A Biographical Outline

Count Roman Aleksander Maria Sheptytsky (Szeptycki) was born in 1865 in the kingdom of Galicia and Lodomeria—a crownland of the Austro-Hungarian Empire.[5] His mother, Sofia, was the daughter of the renowned Polish author Aleksander Fredro, and his father, Jan Sheptytsky, was of Ruthenian/Ukrainian descent. Roman Sheptytsky was brought up with the values typical of his milieu—Roman Catholicism and Polish patriotism. However, already in his youth, Sheptytsky decided to convert and become a priest of the Greek Catholic Church. In 1899, at the age of thirty-four, on the initiative of and with active support from the Apostolic Capital, Sheptytsky was nominated bishop of Stanyslaviv (Pol., Stanisławów; Ger. Stanislau; currently Ivano-Frankivsk), and in 1900–1901 he became archbishop of Lviv and metropolitan of Galicia. Sheptytsky never placed himself within a framework of one identity only, be it Polish or Ukrainian. Rather, he considered himself an heir to the historical tradition of the Polish–Lithuanian commonwealth, to a nationhood composed of Poles, Lithuanians, and Ruthenians. He hoped for a future in which Poles and Ukrainians would be able to coexist in harmony. Such views were not uncommon in the era of empires. The Great War, the fall of the Habsburg Empire, and the Polish-Ukrainian war that followed put his political vision to the test. Owing to the Polish-Ukrainian conflict, which escalated in the early twentieth century, he felt compelled to take a stand. Faced with a clear-cut choice, he decided to follow the Ukrainian path, driven by his role as a spiritual leader and his understanding of a bishop's duty to share the life of his congregation.

The metropolitan had a complex attitude toward Ukrainian nationalism. The ukrainization of the Greek Catholic Church took place in a period when radical nationalism was quickly gaining popularity, especially among the younger generation. Sheptytsky supported the activities of youth organizations, as well as cultural and political movements. He believed that moderate nationalism could have a positive influence on the formation of Ukrainian national identity. However, he was critical of extreme nationalism, considering it unchristian and totalitarian, and opposed attempts to instrumentalize the Greek Catholic Church for its cause. In 1934 he openly condemned the Organization of Ukrainian Nationalists (OUN) in the Ukrainian press, denouncing its ideology and terrorist methods.[6]

As a young man, Andrei Sheptytsky became interested in Jewish history, languages, and culture. Later, as metropolitan, he maintained good relations with Jewish scholars and rabbis from Galicia, continuing to do so after the dissolution of the Austro-Hungarian Empire in 1918 and the absorption of this territory into the reborn Polish state. His intellectual interest in Jewish spiritual and cultural heritage, as well as his willingness to bring about a rapprochement with representatives of the Jewish community, reflected his sympathy for the Jewish people in general—an attitude that was more an exception than a rule among the Roman and Greek Catholic clergy in Poland. Moreover, Sheptytsky was acquainted and maintained contact with those representatives of the Western European Catholic clergy who formed the Association of Friends of Israel. The association requested that the Roman Catholic Church remove antisemitic statements from the liturgy.[7]

The beginning of World War II brought yet another change of political regimes in the region that had once formed the eastern portion of Habsburg Galicia: Pursuant to the secret supplementary protocol of the German-Soviet Nonaggression Pact of August 23, 1939, part of this territory was annexed by the Soviet Union. This posed a serious challenge for Sheptytsky, who regarded communism as the principal danger to the existence of his church and his congregation. Between September 1939 and June 1941, following the occupation of the eastern territories of the Second Polish Republic, the Soviet government persecuted—among other denominations—the Greek Catholic Church, closing down all monasteries, nationalizing church property, and banning religion from the public space and educational institutions. Members of the clergy were arrested and deported. The experience of Soviet persecutions influenced the metropolitan's attitude toward the German troops that entered Lviv in June 1941.[8] The surrounding region, duly dubbed *Distrikt Galizien* (the District of Galicia), became part of the German occupation zone General Government, which had been established after the invasion of Poland.

Like most of the Ukrainian population of Lviv, Sheptytsky also regarded the arrival of German troops first and foremost as a liberation from the Bolsheviks. The German army was expected to establish some form of law and order, and therefore was given a solemn welcome.[9] In early July 1941, Sheptytsky published two pastoral letters in which he welcomed the Wehrmacht as liberators and called on the Ukrainian people to be obedient.[10] His signature also appears on a letter that the leaders of the Ukrainian National Council in Lviv sent to Adolf Hitler in January 1942.[11] In this letter, the UNC recognized the German occupying forces of the newly expanded General Government, as well as their occupation of neighboring parts of western Ukraine, and offered to support Nazi Germany in its fight against the Soviet Union. At the same time, the authors of the letter criticized German policy toward Ukrainians and declared their adherence to the idea of Ukrainian statehood. These documents were the basis for later accusations that Sheptytsky had collaborated with the Third Reich.

During the first months after the German invasion of the Soviet Union, Sheptytsky continued to see the Germans as guarantors of the two things most important to him: liberation from Soviet atheism and the revival of Ukrainian nationhood.[12] However, his illusions concerning the German regime were dispelled quite swiftly. His church was not given complete freedom to preach, and its ecclesiastical territory was limited to Galicia. Sheptytsky's activity was restricted and controlled. His public appeals and pastoral letters were censored, as were the periodicals of the Ukrainian Greek Catholic Church (UGCC), including its official mouthpiece, *Lvivski Arkhiyeparkhialni Vidomosti* (Lviv archdiocesan news).[13] Moreover, the metropolitan quickly realized that the German authorities had no intention of supporting Ukrainian statehood. The German occupying regime put quite an abrupt end to attempts to declare the formation of a Ukrainian state by OUN (B), one of the two factions of OUN. Many members of both factions of OUN were arrested.

Sheptytsky became critical of the new occupying authorities. He was deeply shocked by the violence, atrocities, and murders committed in his archdiocese. In September 1941, as Ludwig Losacker, chief of staff of the Galicia district administration later recollected, Sheptytsky met him and Karl Lasch, governor of the Galicia district, to declare that he considered the murder of Jews unacceptable.[14] He was also one of the first to inform the Vatican about the German plans to carry out the total annihilation of the Jewish population. On March 28, 1942, he wrote a letter to Pope Pius XII to warn him about the mass murder of Jews in Ukraine.[15] A draft of this letter is preserved in the Central State Historical Archive of Lviv. However, as the Vatican archives spanning World War II were still closed when this essay was written, we do not know whether they reached Rome.

Between August 29 and 31, 1942, through the mediation of confidants, Sheptytsky managed to send two further letters to Pope Pius XII and Cardinal Eugène Tisserant, secretary of the Congregation for the Oriental Churches.[16] In these letters he described the suffering of Jews and pointed out that they were "the first victims" of the Nazi terror.[17] He openly criticized and condemned the criminal nature of the German occupying regime: "This is a system of lies, deception, injustice, plundering, a caricature of every idea of civilization and order. This is a system of extreme egotism . . . totally insane national chauvinism, hatred for everything that is honest and good."[18]

Some of Sheptytsky's pastoral letters, namely the one "On Mercy," from June 1942, and the letter "Thou Shalt not Kill," published in November 1942, can also be interpreted as direct responses to the events of the Holocaust.[19] In the first letter, he challenged Nazi racial theory by emphasizing the unity of the human race: "Each neighbor—is your brother, a member of one human family, descended from the family of the first man."[20] In both documents he stressed the sacredness of human life and the equal right to life, which could not be taken away by any other human being. In his opinion, those who committed murder were putting themselves beyond the pale of the community.[21] Sheptytsky taught that compassion must be offered to anyone in need, "to neighbors in general, also to strangers, to non-Christians, to atheists and to enemies."[22] In his opinion, the highest manifestation of love was to sacrifice yourself for one's own neighbor. None of the letters mentioned Jews explicitly; seemingly the metropolitan did not refer to any specific events at all, since the Germans censored his writings.[23] However, when he wrote about loving one's neighbor whose ethnicity and religion are different from one's own, it is clear that he meant, first and foremost, the Jews.

Furthermore, Sheptytsky tried to organize aid for Jews. The first people he helped directly were probably the children of Rabbi Kalman Chameides, Herbert and Leon. Other families followed. Some were sheltered in Sheptytsky's residence on St. George's Hill in Lviv. Additional people were hidden in the Studion, belonging to the Studite monastic order, the church's printing house, and in the basement of the "Solid" Shoe Factory, which partly belonged to the church.[24] Johannes Peters, a German Studite, ran the factory at Sheptytsky's request. After Peters's arrest in the autumn of 1942, the factory building (where 16 Jews were hiding) was sealed off. Sheptytsky bribed German officials and bought out the factory within twenty-four hours.[25] Thanks to this, both the people in hiding and those involved in aiding them were saved. His most successful efforts were those aimed at saving Jewish children. The metropolitan's closest associate, his brother Archimandrite Klymentiy Sheptytsky, governed Studite monasteries and orphanages, which became shelters for Jews, mostly children. The exact number of Jewish children and adults saved through the metropolitan's mediation is unknown but estimated at around 150.[26] It is also known that Sheptytsky encouraged members of the Greek Catholic clergy to engage in rescue efforts. People from his immediate circle—including his personal secretaries Fr. Volodymyr Hrytsay and Fr. Ivan Kotiv—were involved in hiding Jews. He knew which priests from his diocese issued false birth certificates and allowed the practice to continue.[27] Metropolitan Sheptytsky died in Lviv on November 1, 1944, several months after Soviet troops liberated the city.

The Soviet Defamation Campaign and the Creation of the Negative Image of Sheptytsky

After the Red Army entered Lviv on July 27, 1944, Andrei Sheptytsky and his immediate circle found themselves under close scrutiny by the Soviet security services. Following his death, a campaign to dismantle the Ukrainian Greek Catholic Church began. Sheptytsky's successor, Metropolitan Josyf Slipyj, and all the other Greek Catholic bishops were arrested. In March 1946 Soviet secret services and local authorities, in cooperation with the leaders of the Russian Orthodox Church, held the Lviv Synod, which decreed that the UGCC should cease to exist. All the priests, monks, and nuns who did not convert to Orthodoxy were arrested and sentenced to long-term imprisonment in Soviet camps.[28]

To justify these policies, the Soviets launched a defamation campaign against the UGCC. Since Sheptytsky had been its leader for decades and enjoyed great authority among the Ukrainian population of the region, he became the principal target of these attacks. Soviet propagandists accused the metropolitan of collaboration with Nazi Germany. In the immediate postwar years, as noted by Iryna Sklokina, Soviet propaganda established "a clear association between collaboration and nationalism."[29] Such an associative approach allowed for the interpretation of Sheptytsky's activities related to the development of the Ukrainian community as support for radical nationalist movements and therefore as an activity that promoted or simply was collaboration with Nazi

Germany. Indeed, Soviet propagandists developed a narrative portraying Sheptytsky as a Ukrainian "bourgeois nationalist," fascist, and Nazi collaborator.

The foundations of the metropolitan's negative image—a formula Soviet authorities would rely on during the entire Soviet period—were laid by Yaroslav Halan.[30] Halan became well known for his pamphlets and articles that, in the language typical of Soviet propaganda, "unmasked Ukrainian bourgeois nationalism" and accused "radical Ukrainian nationalists" of committing crimes against the "Soviet people." A committed atheist, Halan wrote critically of the UGCC and religion in general. On April 8, 1945—a few months after Sheptytsky's death and three days before the arrest of the UGCC leaders—*Vilna Ukraina*, a regional newspaper, published an article by Halan titled "With a Cross or with a Knife?"[31] In this piece the Greek Catholic clergy was characterized as "enemies of the Ukrainian people, clad in the cassocks of Uniate priests," "servants of the gods of swastika and tryzub," and "organizers of Ukrainian-German nationalist gangs." The text was reprinted in other Ukrainian periodicals and then published as a separate brochure with a circulation of more than 150,000 copies.[32] Between 1945 and 1949, Halan wrote a few more pamphlets that "unmasked the anti-people essence" of the Greek Catholic Church and its leader, Andrei Sheptytsky.[33] Translated into Russian, his work was published and distributed in hundreds of thousands of copies all over the USSR and widely read at schools and universities. The image of Sheptytsky created by Halan continued to be propagated during the entire Soviet period.

Another author actively involved in discrediting Sheptytsky in the 1970s and 1980s was Yevstafiy Halsky, a Ukrainian historian and KGB colonel who published his nonfiction pieces, circulated in many thousands of copies, under the pen name Klym Dmytruk.[34] Halsky used both original documents authored by Sheptytsky as well as falsifications and memoirs of dubious origin. He claimed that Sheptytsky had been responsible for the crimes committed against civilians by Greek Catholic police officers in the wartime district of Galicia. The truth is that Sheptytsky was quite vocal in his disapproval of the Ukrainian police. As early as the autumn of 1941, he verbally instructed his priests to warn their parishioners against joining these units. He likewise asked the clergy to tell those who had already enrolled not to carry out orders that contradicted the Ten Commandments.[35]

Yet another cocreator of Sheptytsky's black legend was Serhii Karin, likewise a Ukrainian KGB colonel, who published under the pen name Serhii Danylenko. The accusations that Sheptytsky was a collaborator were worded in general terms and employed clichés typical of Soviet propaganda, including statements that he allegedly "inspired people to collaborate," was "the spiritual father of the Ukrainian nationalists," "cordially welcomed the [German] occupiers," and "blessed Ukrainian policemen."[36] While the topic of the Holocaust as such did not appear in these publications, their authors mentioned that Soviet citizens of Jewish descent had been among the victims of the Ukrainian nationalists.

Sheptytsky's image as a collaborator was also spread in popular culture. One such example was a 1959 feature film, *Ivanna*, directed by Viktor Ivchenko, whose artistic legacy reflected a clear ideological bias. Shown for many years, with special screenings held at schools and universities, the movie propagated the trope of the metropolitan as a prime enemy of the Soviet government and the Soviet lifestyle and as the mastermind of collaboration with the Nazi regime. Ivanna, the protagonist of the film, is a young Ukrainian woman who enters a convent; later, during the war, she witnesses the collaboration of Ukrainian nationalists, Greek Catholic priests (including the metropolitan himself), and the German authorities. Ivanna joins a Soviet partisan unit and dies a heroic death, betrayed by her Greek Catholic acquaintances.[37] The film became the cornerstone of Sheptytsky's tarnished reputation, and it largely accounts for why many associated his name, first and foremost, with nationalism and collaboration.[38] Today a significant part of the population of Ukraine, especially the older generation, still sees Sheptytsky as a someone who had ties to Ukrainian nationalists and cooperated with the Germans.

In Independent Ukraine

In independent Ukraine, beginning in the early 1990s in its western part, another image of the metropolitan emerged, in stark contrast to the established Soviet portrayal. This image was not entirely new. During the entire Soviet period, clandestine Greek Catholic priests, bishops, and monks had continued to operate in western Ukraine and Transcarpathia with the support of the local population, despite the Soviet authorities' persecution of the UGCC. Some renowned figures of the dissident movement in western Ukraine were in close contact with the clandestine clergy. The Greek Catholic underground cherished the memory of Sheptytsky as that of a religious and national leader.[39] The UGCC's reemergence from the underground in the late 1980s coincided with the process of democratization in the USSR.[40] Western Ukrainian NGOs demanded radical sociopolitical reforms to improve the quality of life in the Soviet Union; in particular, they sought the rehabilitation of the UGCC and the return of its property.[41] Serving as a powerful mobilizing factor, these demands were also voiced at almost every rally in western Ukraine during the late 1980s.[42] Church leaders who returned from exile and the clergy that emerged from the underground became visible and prominent public activists and important agents in reshaping historical memory in western Ukraine.

In the 1990s the public discourse in western Ukraine increasingly stressed the centrality of Ukrainian ethnic identity and argued for Ukrainian as the sole state language.[43] Those promulgating this ethnically oriented historical memory, including the local elites who helped establish this narrative, harshly criticized the Soviet past and its memory politics. Their approach manifested in the rapid de-sovietization of the public space and in numerous press publications that condemned the Soviet system and uncritically praised the activity of nationalist organizations of the 1930s and 1940s. This nationalistic narrative did not gain popularity in other parts of Ukraine. What prevailed outside western Ukraine was what could be called an "eastern Slavic narrative," which stressed the cultural affinity between Russians and Ukrainians.[44] Adherents of these two historical narratives had opposite standpoints on many historical issues, especially on such questions as the activity of the OUN and the Ukrainian Insurgent Army (UPA) and the legacy of Andrei Sheptytsky.

In the Ukrainian ethnocentric historical narrative, the Holocaust played a minor role, perceived as an event not directly related to Ukrainian history.[45] At the same time, attitudes toward antisemitism remained ambiguous. Indeed, organizations and historical figures who as early as the 1990s were put on a pedestal as national heroes in western Ukraine were often those who adhered to the ideology of radical Ukrainian nationalism and antisemitism. In particular, members of the OUN and the UPA, which waged guerrilla warfare against the Soviet authorities in that region until the early 1950s, were often the same people who had served in the Ukrainian police units as the Germans' auxiliaries during the Holocaust.

The UGCC has shared the Ukrainian ethnocentric narrative to which the majority of its congregation has adhered. Since the beginning of the 1990s, its leaders have made significant efforts to challenge the claims of Soviet propaganda about the UGCC and particularly about Andrei Sheptytsky and Josyf Slipyj. The first popular conference on Sheptytsky's legacy was held in Lviv as early as the spring of 1990. The main speakers were social and political activists with close ties to the dissident movement and the newly formed People's Movement of Ukraine.[46] In 1994 the first academic conference on Sheptytsky took place in Ukrainian. It was hosted by the Institute of Church History (Lviv), the Kyiv-Mohyla Academy (Kyiv), and the Metropolitan Andrey Sheptytsky Institute of Eastern Christian Studies (Ottawa, Canada).[47] Academic papers on the history of the Greek Catholic Church and on Sheptytsky himself, as well as reprints of books written by Ukrainian exiles, such as Lonhyn Tsehelskyi and

Vasyl Lentsyk, began to appear.[48] They presented the metropolitan in a different light from that portrayed in publications available in Soviet times. Further, the publication of a manual for schoolteachers popularized a more positive image of Sheptytsky among the younger generation.[49] As a result, within only fifteen years Sheptytsky's name became renowned not only in western Ukraine but also, though to a lesser extent, in other parts of the country.

Most of the educational publications concerning Sheptytsky sought to establish his image as a "national leader," "ardent Ukrainian patriot," and "head of the Ukrainian Church." Depending on the intended purpose of each publication, some essential characteristics of Sheptytsky's biography and work were omitted. For example, the texts intended for a Greek Catholic audience in western Ukraine generally bypass his Polish aristocratic lineage and ties to Polish culture, as well as his criticism of the OUN. The proceedings of the previously mentioned Lviv conference, organized in the spring of 1990 and intended for the general audience, painted an idealized picture of Sheptytsky as a Ukrainian patriot and national and religious leader.[50] They failed to mention the metropolitan's critical view of radical Ukrainian nationalism. Meanwhile, Vasyl Lentsyk only briefly mentioned that the metropolitan had helped and saved Jews during the war.[51] This voluminous book, produced by an ecclesiastical publishing house and actively disseminated, influenced many other writers.[52] Moreover, publications intended for a general Ukrainian audience usually did not highlight the fact that Sheptytsky had advocated for papal primacy, nor did they accentuate his support for Austria-Hungary and Germany during World War I.

In recent years Sheptytsky's life and work have fostered a distinct field of academic research, beginning with Sheptytsky's 150th anniversary in 2015. Several scholarly monographs, collected papers, editions of source materials, and albums were issued on this occasion.[53] Academic conferences were held in Lviv, Kyiv, and Poltava to celebrate this anniversary. The educational literature that best represents the topic includes an illustrated volume, *The Moses of the Ukrainian Spirit*, and *Via Romana* by Serhii Herman, an interesting fictionalized biography of the metropolitan.[54]

Important indicators of how the image of Sheptytsky has changed in independent Ukraine are the results of opinion polls ranking prominent Ukrainians. In "Great Ukrainians," an ambitious media project conducted by the national TV channel Inter in the years 2007–8, Sheptytsky was ranked nineteenth.[55] In one survey conducted in 2012 by the sociological group Rating, Metropolitan Sheptytsky was ranked fifty-second in a list of the hundred most prominent Ukrainians.[56] Despite the considerable degree of subjectivity involved, such rankings show that, in the course of the last two decades, the metropolitan's name has successfully returned to Ukrainian history: From a negative character on the margins, he has transformed into a hero.

However, in most academic and popular publications in Ukraine, Sheptytsky's role during World War II, and in particular his aid to Jews, attracted very little attention. Indeed, these aspects were sometimes ignored entirely. Instead, authors strongly emphasized those facets of Sheptytsky's work that contributed to the Ukrainian national movement and state-building before World War II.[57] This approach can be explained, first, by the fact that Ukrainian historical studies and the policy of publishing academic or popular works on history were and partly still are dominated by the ethnocentric paradigm. Typically, the events of World War II are described in passing, sketchily, and without due examination of the history of the Holocaust. Second, paying closer attention to the metropolitan's efforts to help and rescue Jews would require an unwelcome examination of the Holocaust in present-day western Ukraine, including the study of the attitudes of the Ukrainian population and Ukrainian political and civil organizations toward the Holocaust and, in particular, the participation of the Ukrainian police in the extermination of local Jewish communities.[58]

Nevertheless, several books have been published in Ukraine that do delve into Sheptytsky's role in the rescue of Jews during the Holocaust. Two are of particular importance: an educational guidebook by Kyrylo Kindrat, which refers to the metropolitan as a "Righteous of Ukraine," and a monograph authored by Zhanna Kovba. The latter is the first Ukrainian academic publication about the actions of the non-Jewish population in the context of the Holocaust across the area that once constituted eastern Galicia.[59] Furthermore, two memoirs appeared in Ukrainian translation, one by Rabbi David Kahane, the other by Kurt Lewin, both of whom owed their lives to Sheptytsky.[60] The most recent publication is a book by Yurii Skira entitled *Those with a Calling: Monks of the Studite Order and the Holocaust*.[61] Skira's book is the first academic monograph on the Studite monks' efforts to rescue Jews and the role played in this endeavor by Andrei Sheptytsky and his brother Klymentiy. Despite these publications, Sheptytsky's activities during World War II and his efforts to provide aid to Jews still remain both under-researched and underexposed.

Sheptytsky in the Public Space: Street Names, Monuments, and Museums

Sheptytsky has become visible in western Ukraine not only in historiography but also in public spaces. As early as the 1990s, streets and squares in numerous towns of western Ukraine were named after him, his brother Klymentiy, and the

Sheptytsky family. The naming of streets after Sheptytsky reflected the first stage of the decommunization of public spaces in Ukraine.[62] Following that, schools, libraries, hospitals, and other public institutions were named after Sheptytsky in Lviv, Ternopil, Ivano-Frankivsk, and other towns in the region. One of the most recent examples is the inauguration of the Andrei Sheptytsky memorial library of the Ukrainian Catholic University (UCU) in 2017.

In other parts of Ukraine, streets and squares named after Sheptytsky appeared only much later, inspired by the Euromaidan Revolution (referred to in Ukraine as the Revolution of Dignity) of 2013–14, which stimulated further decommunization of the public space. This decommunization was enshrined in the 2015 Law on Condemning the Communist and National Socialist (Nazi) Totalitarian Regimes in Ukraine and Prohibiting Their Symbols. This Ukrainian law vested municipal authorities with the duty to rename streets whose names still bore a relation to communist ideology, the Soviet past, or sometimes even Russian history and culture. City councils and municipal executive bodies, in their search for appropriate names, chose the name of a Greek Catholic metropolitan out of a small pool of exclusively Ukrainian historical figures with no connection to Soviet or Russian culture and history. For example, when in 2016 the mayor of Kyiv, Volodymyr Klychko, proposed renaming Anatoly Lunacharsky Street (Lunacharsky was a Russian/Soviet writer) Andrei Sheptytsky Street, 278 of 341 deputies present at the Kyiv city council session voted in favor.[63] In the same year, in Dubno, Rivne Oblast, even Pushkin Street was renamed Sheptytsky Street.

However, although Sheptytsky's name has gradually appeared on the maps of Ukrainian cities, the cities' residents have not always approved of these changes. Quite typical was the situation in Mykolaiv, an oblast capital in southern Ukraine. In February 2016, 129 streets were "decommunized" there. Among them Karl Marx Street was renamed Andrei Sheptytsky Street, at the suggestion of the Renaming Committee and the mayor, who emphasized the metropolitan's broad philanthropic activities, assistance to the victims of Holodomor, and efforts to save Jews during World War II.[64] Nevertheless, this proposal caused serious discontent among those living on the street, who gathered signatures and filed protests. During the entire process, political debates continued at the Mykolaiv city council, whose members representing the party "Opposition Bloc" strongly supported the grassroots protests.[65] At the same time, representatives of the Ukrainian Orthodox and Greek Catholic churches requested that the city council support the new name of the street.[66] Eventually the municipal authorities renamed the disputed street again in March 2017, this time designating it Tradytsiyna ("Traditional"), although it is hard to tell what traditions this name was supposed to perpetuate.[67] In order not to insult Greek Catholic citizens, the municipal authorities gave Sheptytsky's name to a different street.[68]

What happened in Mykolaiv indicates that the figure of Sheptytsky is still not accepted by a significant number of Ukrainian citizens, especially those from the south and east of the country and those belonging to the Ukrainian Orthodox Church of the Moscow Patriarchate. A prominent exception in this respect was the creation of a space dedicated to the metropolitan at the Jewish Memory and the Holocaust in Ukraine museum in Dnipro (2012).[69] The museum includes a room commemorating the Righteous Among the Nations, where the curators recreated a part of the metropolitan's study in his Lviv residence. This was where Sheptytsky hid Rabbi David Kahane and the sons of Rabbi Ezekiel Lewin.

The Conflict between Russia and Ukraine and the Sheptytsky Anniversary

In 2015 Ukraine celebrated the 150th anniversary of Andrei Sheptytsky's birth. The celebrations occurred in the context of the conflict between Ukraine and Russia: In January–March 2014, the Russian Federation annexed Crimea, and in April that year, the war in Donbass began. The celebrations took place in accordance with a decree of the Ukrainian parliament that had been issued on July 17, 2014. It seems that during the ongoing political and military crisis of 2014, the Ukrainian authorities tried to call on the legacy of those who were most distant from the Russian or Soviet past.

The Ukrainian elites that came to power in 2014 following the Euromaidan Revolution wanted to break with the Soviet and post-Soviet past, as well as with the "Russian world." Moreover, Russia's annexation of Crimea and its military aggression in eastern Ukraine necessitated a search for new moral reference points, and new national heroes. Many of the public and academic initiatives organized to celebrate the 150th anniversary of Sheptytsky's birth bore the hallmarks of politically motivated events. The memorial initiatives included the issuing of a commemorative coin by the National Bank of Ukraine and the opening of exhibitions dedicated to Sheptytsky at museums in Lviv, Kyiv, and Odessa. Commemorative events were also organized in smaller cities, such as Zhytomyr, Chernihiv, Vinnytsia, and Boyarka.

In some of these commemorative enterprises, the subject of Sheptytsky's assistance to the Jews became more prominent. On Sheptytsky's anniversary, the Ukrainian Institute of National Remembrance published a biographical note on its website providing a brief overview of his philanthropic and educational activities, emphasizing the fact that "he had to combine his service to God with his service to Ukrainian national interests."[70] The article also highlighted the metropolitan's efforts to save Jews during World War II. Almost half of the text seek to determine why Yad Vashem did not award Sheptytsky the title of Righteous Among the Nations and why the Roman Curia did not beatify him.[71]

There were several successful attempts to "build a bridge" between the past and the present, thus making Sheptytsky's legacy relevant to the younger generation. A children's illustrated book about the metropolitan's activities came out, making a connection between his life and those of contemporary young Ukrainians in comprehensible terms.[72] It also mentioned that the metropolitan had helped save Jewish children during the war. Students of the journalism school at the Ukrainian Catholic University in Lviv created the film *Our Metropolitan*, which included remarks made by students about their views on Sheptytsky and his teachings.[73] They praised his courage and commented on his morality in the context of the assistance he rendered to Jews during World War II.

In March 2015 a statue of the metropolitan was unveiled in Lviv in the presence of Ukraine's president, Petro Poroshenko. In his speech Poroshenko stressed Sheptytsky's activities in terms of Ukrainian state-building.[74] Neither his nor other inaugural speeches mentioned the aid the metropolitan gave to Jews during the Holocaust. The preparations for this event had begun several years earlier. As early as 2010 a committee comprised of representatives of the UGCC, municipal authorities, and local artists selected a design based on the 1932 statue of Sheptytsky by Andrii Koverko. Contemporary Ukrainian artists Mykhaylo Fedyk and Ihor Kuzmak suggested placing a reproduction of Koverko's sculpture across from the entrance to St. George's Cathedral. This would have required a significant reconfiguration of the urban space, which likewise would have to be financed from the city's budget.[75] The proposal sparked controversy among activists, who protested that the project would entail the destruction of the historic park where the statue was to be installed. Others criticized the project as being artistically uninspired and aesthetically outdated.[76] Voices were also raised that such an expensive project should not be implemented while the war was being fought in eastern Ukraine. Eventually it was decided to alter the project so that the construction affected only a part of the park. However, this compromise did not satisfy any of the parties. It seems that the ongoing war considerably heightened the tension in the debate. Supporters of the project, many of whom were active members of the UGCC congregation, perceived any criticism as unpatriotic and accused their adversaries of acting on orders of the Kremlin.[77] Those in opposition accused them of conservatism, jingoism, and obscurantism.[78] A generational conflict played a role as well, as there were many young people among the critics. However, it is worth noting that, despite the strong disagreements, nobody questioned the idea of erecting a monument to Sheptytsky as such.

Indeed, the statue in Lviv was not the only monument to Sheptytsky inaugurated in Ukraine in 2015. In the same year, a statue of Sheptytsky was erected in Ivano-Frankivsk, and a memorial plaque was unveiled in Kyiv at the Teachers' House, the building where the first national parliament of Ukraine formerly held its meetings; Sheptytsky spoke there in 1917.

Opposition to revising Sheptytsky's memory in the public sphere came also from religious and political circles. State support for the celebration of Sheptytsky's anniversary aroused opposition from the clergy and congregation of the Russian Orthodox Church (the Moscow Patriarchate). Critical publications on Sheptytsky appeared on related web pages.[79] They presented Sheptytsky as a figure hostile to both Russia and the Russian Orthodox Church.[80] For instance, the Union of Orthodox Journalists published an article on its homepage by Nazar Holovko, titled "Andrei Sheptytsky: A Schizophrenic or a Coward?"[81] In his article, Holovko returned to the familiar tropes accusing Sheptytsky of collaboration with Nazi Germany. Dmitry Vedeneyev repeated these accusations in his article, "Soviet [Military] Intelligence and the Church Schisms in Occupied Ukraine," published in the online magazine *Pravoslavnaya Zhizn* (Christian Orthodox life).[82] Interestingly, these texts do not discuss Sheptytsky's attitude toward Jews and his help for the Jewish community during the Holocaust. Despite these controversies, the anniversary celebrations, which took place in the context of the Ukrainian-Russian military conflict, helped solidify Sheptytsky's public image as a prominent Ukrainian figure and an important contributor to Ukraine's state-building. However, this vision was more nuanced than the national patriotic image of the metropolitan formed in western Ukraine in the 1990s.

International Resonance

While the history of the Holocaust still plays a minor although increasingly visible role in the discussions in Ukraine, the international resonance of Sheptytsky has been closely connected with his activities during World War II. The Yad Vashem commission that considered Sheptytsky's case in the 1970s and 1980s ultimately declined to award him the designation of Righteous Among the Nations in 1991. The main reasons for the refusal were his alleged support for Nazi ideology and a broadly defined "collaboration with the Nazi regime," including the blessing he gave to the 14th Waffen Grenadier Division of the SS (1st Galician).[83] The commission also pointed out that he never explicitly mentioned the massacre of Jews in his public statements. Moreover, as a Ukrainian political and spiritual leader, Sheptytsky was held responsible for the immoral behavior of segments of Ukrainian society.[84] The Yad Vashem commission did not take into account that, as of 1932–34, Sheptytsky was in confrontation with OUN, and that his opposition continued during the war. Furthermore, Sheptytsky's actions should be considered from the perspective of his religious office: He was responsible for the Greek Catholic Church. Contacts with representatives of the Soviet and Nazi regimes were, from his standpoint, necessary to secure its survival. An open condemnation of German crimes could have had grave consequences for the members of his congregation. Nevertheless, his pastoral letters were courageous and comprehensible to his congregation as his response to the persecution of the Jews.

Sheptytsky's case remains unresolved. In the last decades, a number of people who were rescued by Sheptytsky, including Kurt Lewin, David Kahane, Oded Amarant, Adam Daniel Rotfeld, and Lili Stern-Pohlmann, have lobbied on his behalf at Yad Vashem. For some of them, the nonrecognition of Sheptytsky as Righteous is painful. Poland's former foreign minister, Adam Daniel Rotfeld, who survived the war as a young child in the Univ Greek Catholic monastery headed by Andrei Sheptytsky's brother Klymentiy, believes that Yad Vashem's decision regarding the metropolitan is unfair and harmful to the reputation of this institution.[85] There has also been an increasing interest in this issue in Ukraine and abroad, first and foremost among the Jewish and Greek Catholic communities. The Ukrainian-Jewish Encounter (UJE)[86], a project launched in Canada, has been striving to publicize Sheptytsky's rescue efforts for several years.[87] In 2012 the UJE produced the documentary *Saved by Sheptytsky*, based on interviews with Lili Stern-Pohlmann, Oded Amarant, and Leon Chameides.[88] In 2013 the UJC and the Jewish Confederation of Ukraine cofounded a special award, the Metropolitan Andrei Sheptytsky Medal, which was bestowed by the head of the Ukrainian Greek Catholic Church. The medal is granted to politicians and public figures who have contributed to the development of Jewish-Ukrainian relations.[89]

In November 2019, UGCC priests and representatives of Ukrainian civil society signed a collective letter to Yad Vashem asking the commission to reconsider Sheptytsky's case.[90] In January 2020, Moshe Reuven Azman, chief rabbi of Ukraine, sent a letter to Avner Shalev, chairman of the Yad Vashem directorate, asking him to award the metropolitan the title of Righteous Among the Nations.[91] Azman called Sheptytsky a "giant of true humanism" and argued that the rescued human lives were more important than Sheptytsky's telegrams and letters conveying greetings to Hitler. During his visit to Poland on the seventy-fifth anniversary of the liberation of Auschwitz, on January 27, 2020, Ukraine's president, Volodymyr Zelensky, publicly expressed his support for this appeal "for the sake of historical justice."[92]

In response, Katya Gusarova, from the Yad Vashem Department of the Righteous Among the Nations, stated that the institute did not have fundamental objections to reconsidering the metropolitan's case. However, this would require that previously unseen historical documents and materials be submitted to the commission that would disprove the collaboration charges against Sheptytsky.[93] As a matter of fact, during previous hearings, many historical documents were not included in Sheptytsky's Yad Vashem case file. During the Soviet era it was impossible to view documents from Soviet archives. In contrast, before February 2022, all Ukrainian archives were accessible, including those of the security service of the USSR, which contain a collection of documents on Sheptytsky. The Vatican archives covering World War II opened in March 2020. They contain letters Sheptytsky sent to the Roman Curia, which should help shed light on his attitude toward the German occupiers.

Moreover, some of the documents the commission did consider before must be analyzed for authenticity. During World War II, texts were circulated in Sheptytsky's name that were not authored by him. For instance, the newspapers *Krakivski Visti* and *Ukrainski Shchodenni Visti* published two forged appeals in his name. One of them, "To Grain Growers," urged peasants to donate their agricultural products to the German army. The metropolitan's ordinariate lodged a protest over the forgery with *Ukrainski Shchodenni Visti*, but the publication never published a disclaimer.[94]

Yad Vashem's attitude toward Sheptytsky's case might have been partly influenced by biases born out of Soviet propaganda. Moshe Reuven Azman pointed to this phenomenon in his letter to Shalev. He wrote that Jews from Israel and the diaspora must dismiss "Soviet propaganda myths and stereotypes concerning Sheptytsky."[95] There are also myths and stereotypes that Ukrainians have to dismiss, in particular the myth of Sheptytsky as a Ukrainian nationalist, which misrepresents his attitude toward radical nationalism, as represented by OUN and the UPA.

Still, Sheptytsky did receive a degree of international recognition. In 2012 the House of Commons of Canada adopted a motion to recognize "Sheptytsky's courageous actions, compassion for his oppressed Jewish Ukrainian countrymen, and enduring example of commitment to fundamental human rights as humankind's highest obligation."[96] Members of the All-Ukrainian Council of Churches and Religious Organizations visited the Canadian parliament to attend the event. The delegation was composed of representatives from all

Ukrainian churches, except for the Ukrainian Orthodox Church of the Moscow Patriarchate. A year later, in 2013, the Anti-Defamation League posthumously bestowed on Sheptytsky the Jan Karski Courage to Care Award.

Conclusions

Views about Andrei Sheptytsky's life and his influence have changed over time. In Ukraine, he has been gradually presented as a complex figure who played an important role in the lives of Ukrainians not only as the head of the local UGCC but also as the most significant local philanthropist; he thus enjoyed considerable social and political influence. During World War II, the metropolitan called on his congregation to respect every person's right to life. Moreover, he personally rescued a number of Jews and gave directions to his associates to help them. This marked a departure from the Soviet propaganda. In the USSR, Sheptytsky's efforts aimed toward Ukrainian nation-building were seen as support for radical nationalist movements—for what was called "bourgeois nationalism" in Soviet parlance—and therefore as actions that promoted collaboration with fascists or, indeed, amounted to such collaboration. The image of Sheptytsky as a collaborator was circulated and replicated for decades, influencing the opinions of people who studied at Soviet schools and universities.

After the UGCC's emergence from the underground in 1989–90 and Ukraine's declaration of independence in 1991, the situation changed radically. Especially in western Ukraine, Metropolitan Sheptytsky regained his place in Ukrainian history as one of the most prominent church figures and, to a certain extent, the founder of the modern Ukrainian nation and state. Recent initiatives have sought to popularize the metropolitan's ethos as well as knowledge about his legacy across the country. Ukrainian government officials, leaders of the Greek Catholic Church, NGOs, and cultural organizations have supported these efforts. Gradually, they established Sheptytsky's legacy as an important factor in Ukrainian nation-building. Thus the negative perception of his role as a "Ukrainian nationalist," promulgated in the Soviet period, morphed into a radically different legacy depicting Sheptytsky as a national hero who struggled for the creation of the independent Ukrainian state.

This image of Sheptytsky, however, continues to be contested by some segments of Ukrainian society, for whom he remains a controversial figure. Both regional and denominational differences are at play here. Sheptytsky was a Greek Catholic archbishop, while a significant part of the Ukrainian population identifies as Orthodox (or as culturally and religiously close to the traditions of the Christian Orthodox Church). The inhabitants of Ukraine's eastern and southern regions in particular do not recognize Sheptytsky as a hero, due to the legacy of Soviet propaganda in these regions. Another obstacle is the Ukraino-centric nature of Sheptytsky's image as it was formed in the 1990s.

Both the critical and the national-heroic readings had a common drawback: They saw Sheptytsky mainly through the lens of his role in Ukrainian nation- and state-building. This marginalized some essential aspects of his work and elements of his spiritual legacy. In the 1990s the Holocaust was still perceived by both Ukrainian academics and the general public as peripheral to Ukrainian history[97] This tendency influenced the research on, and popularization of, Sheptytsky's life and work: His assistance to Jews during the Nazi occupation was downplayed or only mentioned *en passant*, since it "did not fit" the upbeat national narrative.

While certain actions that Sheptytsky committed during World War II remain controversial and might be seen as unacceptable, they should not prevent anyone from recognizing the evidence of his courage and humanism beyond racist or religious differences. Clearly, however, the status of Sheptytsky as a Ukrainian national hero has negatively influenced his international image. Complicating the legacy of Andrei Sheptytsky by recovering the memory of his help for Jews will help to form a fuller—not just Ukrainocentric—account of his activities, a vision that can then begin functioning in the Ukrainian collective memory. Indeed, in the last few years, Sheptytsky's actions in the context of the Holocaust have increasingly attracted interest among Ukrainians, including Ukrainian Jews, especially those of the younger generation. An important role in this regard is being played by such public figures as the chief rabbi of Ukraine, Moshe Reuven Azman, and the Ukrainian president, Volodymyr Zelensky. Their appeals to Yad Vashem to award Sheptytsky with the title Righteous Among the Nations were given wide coverage in the media and turned the public's attention to these issues. With these developments, Sheptytsky's image as an aid giver and rescuer of Jews is becoming an important part of his legacy.

The 2022 Russian invasion of Ukraine has had and continues to have a profound impact on Ukrainian collective memory, including the memory of World War II and the Holocaust. Since the very first days of the war, public figures and media personalities used events and images of World War II as points of reference or comparison. The memory of the Holocaust has also undergone a transformation. It has become relatable for Ukrainian citizens, who see themselves as victims of a genocidal project and genocidal practices employed by the Russian government and army. It is symbolic that, in the first days of this war, Russian missiles partially destroyed Babyn Yar—the murder and burial site of tens of thousands of Holocaust victims in Kyiv and the most famous Holocaust memorial in Ukraine.

As part of this transformation, the Russian-Ukrainian war will likely influence the perception of the person and the legacy of Metropolitan Sheptytsky in the country. Institutions founded by or named after him, such as the Ukrainian Catholic University and the National Museum in Lviv, have started a number of initiatives referring to Sheptytsky's ethos. Through their work providing material help and defending cultural values, they strive to ensure Ukrainian victory. Staff and students of the Ukrainian Catholic University, where young people from all regions of Ukraine study, regardless of religious affiliation, raised four million dollars in the first six months of the war to help Ukrainian wounded (civilians and soldiers) and refugees, and to support the military and volunteers. In July 2022 the National Museum opened an exhibition of the works of the artist Maria Prymachenko (1909–97), whose house-museum had been destroyed during the Russian offensive on Kyiv in March 2022. On August 18, 2022, the president of Ukraine, Volodymyr Zelensky, visited the museum during his one-day visit to Lviv as he met with UN Secretary-General António Guterres and the president of Turkey, Recep Tayyip Erdogan. These facts symbolically emphasize that the institutions founded personally by Sheptytsky have become important for Ukrainian resistance and will play an important role in a future reconstruction of Ukraine. Likewise, the postwar rethinking of the constituent components of Ukrainian identity by citizens of Ukraine from different regions and of different ethnic backgrounds will likely strengthen the centrality of Sheptytsky as a historical figure. Thanks to his mixed ethnic origins, multiculturalism, and the fact that his Ukrainian identity was a matter of his personal choice, and to a large extent thanks to his humanism and humanitarian activism, Sheptytsky is well poised to continue gaining popularity among the citizens of Ukraine.

Notes

1 Visnyk Verkhovnoi Rady (Herald of the Ukrainian parliament), 2014, no. 29, 953.

2 The most common kind of Ukrainian regional analysis is a simplistic consideration of the country's extreme east/west dichotomy, i.e., the Lviv/Donetsk dichotomy. Publicly released data from surveys conducted in these cities in 1994, 1999, and 2004 will be used in the present study. For the results of these surveys ("Lviv-Donetsk: Sociological Analysis of Group Identities and Hierarchies of Social Loyalties," conducted by the Historical Research Institute of Lviv University), see "L'viv-Donec'k:

social'ni identychnosti v suchasnij Ukrayini," *Ukraina Moderna*, no. 12/(2) (2007).

3 Volodymyr Kulyk, "Nacionalistychne proty radyans'kogo: istorychna pamyat' v nezalezhnij Ukrayini" (National versus Soviet: Historical Memory in Independent Ukraine), http://www.historians.in.ua/index.php/en/istoriya-i-pamyat-vazhki-pitannya/379-volodymyr-kulyk-natsionalistychne-proty-radianskoho-istorychna-pamiat-u-nezalezhnii-ukraini, accessed January 21, 2020; Yaroslav Hrytsak, "National Identities in Post-Soviet Ukraine: The Case of L'viv and Donetsk," in *Cultures and Nations of Central and Eastern Europe: Essays in Honor of Roman Szporluk* (Cambridge, MA: Harvard University Press, 1998), 263–81.

4 This chapter relies on my publications: Liliana Hentosh, *Vatykan i vyklyky modernosti. Shidnoevropeiska polityka papy Benedykta XV ta ukrainsko-polskyi konflikt v Halychyni, 1914–1923* (The Vatican and challenges of modernity: East European politics of Pope Benedict XV and Ukrainian-Polish conflict in Galicia) (Lviv: Klasyka, 2006); Liliana Hentosh, *Metropolyt Andrei Sheptyts'kyj, 1923–1939: Vyprobuvannya idealiv* (Metropolitan Andrei Sheptyts'kyj, 1923–1939: A Trial of Ideals) (Lviv: Klasyka, 2015). Further important publications on Sheptytsky include Andrii Krawchuk, *Christian Social Ethics in Ukraine: The Legacy of Andrei Sheptytsky* (Edmonton: Canadian Institute of Ukrainian Studies Press, 1997); Paul Magocsi, ed., *Morality and Reality: The Life and Times of Andrei Sheptyts'kyi* (Edmonton: Canadian Institute of Ukrainian Studies Press, 1989).

5 For more on Sheptytsky, see Magocsi, ed., *Morality and Reality*; Hentosh, *Metropolyt Andrei Sheptyts'kyj, 1923–1939*; Magdalena Nowak, *Dwa Światy. Zagadnienie identyfikacji narodowej Andrzeja Szeptyckiego w latach 1865–1914* (Two Worlds: The problem of the national identity of Andrei Sheptyts'kyi, 1865–1914) (Gdańsk: Wydawnictwo Universytetu Gdańskiego, 2018).

6 Hentosh, *Metropolyt Andrei Sheptyts'kyj, 1923–1939*, 159, 419–20. In an interview he gave to *Tygodnik Ilustrowany* (Warsaw, May 5, 1935), Sheptytsky said that nationalism "is close to paganism" and that it is "harmful from the Church's point of view." In his open letter titled "A Word to Ukrainian Youth" ("Слово до української молоді," 1932), Sheptytsky characterizes totalitarian political movements of that epoch without using the word *totalitarianism*. However, when talking about Ukrainian nationalism, he remarks, "This is a global movement that has created—on the one hand—fascism and a tendency toward

dictatorship, which is so articulate in many states, and—on the other hand—Bolshevism." ("Mytropolyt Andrei Sheptytskyi: Zhyttia i Dialnist'" [Metropolitan Andrei Sheptytsky: Life and work], in *Tserkva i Suspilne Pytannia. Dokumenty i Materialy 1899–1944* [The church and the social issues: Documents and materials 1899–1944] [Lviv: Misioner, 1998], vol. 2, pt. 1, 358–59).

7 Hubert Wolf, *Pope and Devil: The Vatican's Archives and the Third Reich* (Cambridge, MA: Harvard University Press, 2010), 91–93; Hentosh, *Metropolyt Andrei Sheptyts'kyj, 1923–1939*, 424–26.

8 J. Bussgang's article is important for understanding the metropolitan's actions during World War II. See Julian J. Bussgang, "Metropolitan Sheptytsky: A Reassessment," *Polin*, no. 21 (2008): 401–35.

9 "Mytropolyt Andrei Sheptytskyi: Zhyttia i Dialnist,'" 517–18.

10 The metropolitan's view of the political situation was influenced by his health and his isolation—he acquired information from only a limited range of sources, and his informants sometimes tried to manipulate his views and actions. After a grave illness—presumably a stroke—that he suffered in the autumn of 1931, Sheptytsky lost his mobility and had to use a wheelchair; he was unable to leave his chambers. Some have doubts about the original texts and signatures on the two pastoral letters. The original copy of Sheptytsky's pastoral letter from July 1, 1941, preserved in the Lviv Central State Historical Archive (CDIAL), has his handwritten signature. The copy of the pastoral letter from July 5, 1941, stored in the same archive and published by *Krakivski Visti*—a Ukrainian language newspaper controlled by Nazi authorities in Krakow—was not signed by Sheptytsky. Because of his stroke, Sheptytsky could hardly write, and his signatures in those years were very indistinct. See also Andrii Bolianovskyi, "Mizh khrystyianskoiu moralliu i neliudskym zlom (Reaktsiia mytropolyta Andreia Sheptytskoho na okupatsiinu polityku natsional-sotsialistychnoi Nimechchyny v Halychyni 1941–1944 rr.: vid formalnoi loialnosti do krytyky i protestiv.)" (Between the Christian ethics and inhuman evil [Response of metropolitan A. Sheptytsky to the occupation policy of Nazi Germany in Galicia 1941–1944: From formal loyalty to criticism and protests]), in *The Second World War and the Fate of the Civil Population in Eastern Europe: Papers of the International Conference in the Memory of Metropolitan Andrei Sheptytsky*, ed. Leonid Finberg (Kyiv: Dukh i Litera, 2016), 11–12, 59–60.

11 Ukrainian National Council in Lviv (Ukrainska Natsionalna Rada, or UNC): a body formed in Lviv out of the Council of Seniors on July 30,

1941, to represent the interests of the Ukrainian population of Galicia, part of Volhynia, and the Holm region before the German authorities. The president of the UNC was Kost Levytskyi, and Metropolitan Sheptytsky was its honorary president. The council was banned by the Germans on March 3, 1942. I will discuss the authenticity of this letter later in this chapter.

12 Canadian church historian Andrii Krawchuk believes that in his attitude toward the German occupying regime, Metropolitan Sheptytsky went through several stages, starting out "with an initially positive perception of the German takeover" and eventually taking a stance of "a fundamental opposition to the Nazi regime." Krawchuk, *Christian Social Ethics in Ukraine*, 208.

13 See Andrii Bolianovskyi, "Mizh khrystyianskoiu moralliu i neliudskym zlom," 20–21.

14 See Hansjakob Stehle, "Sheptyts'kyi and the German Regime," in *Morality and Reality*, ed. Magocsi, 131. See also: Andrii Bolianovskyi, "Mizh khrystyianskoiu moralliu i neliudskym zlom," 41–42.

15 CDIAL. F. 201, op. 2r, f. 90, pp. 25–26.

16 *Actes et Documents du Saint Siège relatifs à la Seconde Guerre Mondiale*, ed. Pierre Blet (Vatican City: Libreria Editrice Vaticana, 1967), vol. 3, part 1, 168–73, and part 2, 625–29.

17 *Actes et Documents du Saint Siège relatifs à la Seconde Guerre Mondiale*, 982–83. On the significance of the letters, see also Robert Ventresca, *Soldier of Christ* (Cambridge, MA: Harvard University Press, 2015), 171–72.

18 "Mytropolyt Andrei Sheptytskyi: Zhyttia i Dialnist'," 985.

19 "Mytropolyt Andrei Sheptytskyi: Zhyttia i Dialnist'," 243–59, 259–68. On this see also John-Paul Himka, "Metropolitan Andrey Sheptysky and the Holocaust," *Polin*, 26 (2014): 345–46.

20 "Mytropolyt Andrei Sheptytskyi: Zhyttia i Diialnist'," 257.

21 "Mytropolyt Andrei Sheptytskyi: Zhyttia i Diialnist'," 261–64, 267–68.

22 "Mytropolyt Andrei Sheptytskyi: Zhyttia i Diialnist'," 255.

23 Scholars have at their disposal different printed versions of the metropolitan's letters that contain traces of censorship.

24 Eliyahu Yones, *Smoke in the Sand: The Jews of Lvov in the War Years, 1939–1944* (Jerusalem, 2004 Gefen Publishing House), 252. We know the names of some people who were hiding in the "Solid" Shoe Factory: Solomon Hilfer, Jacob and Dania Heller, Abraham, Feyga, and Anna Fink.

25 See Yurii Skira, *Poklykani. Monahy Studiiskoho Ustavu ta Holokost* (Those with the calling: Monks of the Studite order and the Holocaust) (Kyiv: Dukh i Litera, 2019), 128–29.

26 Shimon Redlich, "Metropolita Andrzej Szeptycki i wspólnota żydowska," in *Kościół, naród, państwo. Działanośćé i dziedzictwo Metropolity Andrzeja Szeptyckiego (1865–1944)*, ed. Andrzej Roman Szeptycki (Warszawa: Wydawnictwo KEW, 2011): 110; Bussgang, "Metropolitan Sheptytsky: A Reassessment," 427.

27 Sheptytsky once received a note from an unknown person who recounted the information received from Dr. Sanocki about Germans planning to arrest several Greek Catholic priests for giving Jews false birth certificates. "Mytropolyt Andrei Sheptytskyi: Zhyttia i Dialnist," vol. 2, pt. 2, 976.

28 See Bohdan Bociurkiw, *The Ukrainian Greek Catholic Church and the Soviet State (1939–1950)* (Edmonton: Canadian Institute of Ukrainian Studies Press, 1996), 62–101. Until the collapse of the USSR in 1991, the UGCC was considered an illegal and hostile religious organization; its priests and adherents, who held clandestine church services, were constantly faced with the threats of arrest and imprisonment.

29 Iryna Sklokina, "Radianska polityka pam'iati pro kolaboratsiiu periodu natsystskoi okupatsii yak instrument natsionalnoi polityky: rehionalnyi aspekt" (Soviet memory politics concerning collaborationism as an instrument of national policy: Regional aspect), *Natsionalna ta istorychna pam'iat: zbirnyk naukovykh prats* (National and historical memory: Collections of articles), no. 3 (2013): 118–41.

30 Yaroslav Halan (1902–49) was born in Galicia and studied at the University of Vienna and the Jagiellonian University of Kraków. He was a talented author known for his great affection for the USSR. In 1924 he joined the Communist Party of western Ukraine. From 1941 to 1944, he worked for the *Radyanska Ukraina* (Soviet Ukraine) radio station in Moscow; from 1945 to 1946, he was a special correspondent for the newspaper *Radyanska Ukraina* at the Nuremberg trials. Halan was murdered in October 1949 in his Lviv apartment. The Soviet security services arrested and tried two young men, allegedly members of the Ukrainian Nationalist Underground, for the crime. Halan's murder was followed by a wave of arrests of the Ukrainian intelligentsia. During the Soviet period, streets and squares were named after Halan; in Lviv, a huge monument to Halan remained standing until the early 1990s.

31 Yaroslav Halan, *Tvory v 4 tomakh* (Collection of works in four volumes) (Kyiv: Naukova Dumka, 197), v. 2, 440–41. Halan wrote this article under the pen name V. Rosovych.

32 Larysa Kapitan, "Pidhotovka hromadskoi dumky naperedodni likvidatsii Hreko-katolytskoi tserkvy u Zakarpatti" (Influencing public opinion before the elimination of the Greek Catholic Church in the Transcarpathian region), *Naukovyi visnyk Uzhhorodskoho nauionalnoho univer-sytetu* (2017): 7–9.

33 Halan, *Tvory v 4 tomakh*, vol. 2, 536–52.

34 Klym Dmytruk, *Svastika na sutanakh* (Swastikas on cassocks) (Moscow: Politizdat, 1976); Klym Dmytruk, *S krestom i trezubtsem* (With a cross and a trident) (Moscow: Politizdat, 1979); Klym Dmytruk, *Pid chornymy sutanamy. Pravda pro zviazky iierarkhii uniatskoi tserkvy z fashystskymy zaharbnykamy* (The black cassocks: The truth about the connections between the hierarchy of the Uniate Church and the Nazi aggressors) (Kyiv: Politizdat Ukrainy, 1975); Klym Dmytruk, *In Holy Robes: The Truth about the Contacts between the Hierarchy of the Uniate Church and the Nazi Aggressors* (Kiev: Ukraina Society, 1978).

35 The metropolitan's instructions are documented in the transcripts of the Synods of the Lviv archdiocese of the Greek Catholic Church for the period 1941–44.

36 These phrases occur repeatedly in the works of such authors as Klym Dmytruk, Volodymyr Dobrychev, Serhiy Danylenko, and others.

37 The film received an award at the All-Union Film Festival.

38 Noa Sigal, an employee of Yad Vashem, mentioned the strong influence of this film on the formation of the stereotype about Sheptytsky as a collaborator/criminal, https://varianty.lviv.ua/21622-noa-sihal-shchepko-i-tonko-ne-vidchuvaly-sebe-ni-poliakamy-ni-yevreiamy-ni-ukraintsiamy-vony-buly-lvivianamy, accessed January 20, 2020.

39 These were, first and foremost, Ivan Hel and Myroslav Marynovych, founders of the Ukrainian Helsinki Group.

40 In the late 1980s, the underground UGCC in the Soviet Union was comprised of ten bishops, more than a thousand priests, and more than two thousand monks and nuns. See Stepan Kobuta, "Politychni aspekty lehalizatsii Ukrainskoi Hreko-Katolytskoi Tserkvy (1987–1991)" (Political aspects of the legalization of the Ukrainian Greek Catholic Church in 1987–1991) *Ludyna i Polityka* 3 (1993): 23–24.

41 The formal act of legalization took place on October 20, 1989, when the clandestine Greek Catholic clergy held a synod in Lviv, proclaiming the revival of their aboveground activity.

42 See Padraic Kenney, "Lviv's Central European Renaissance, 1987–1990," *Harvard Ukrainian Studies* 24 (2000): 304–9.

43 Volodymyr Kulyk, "Nacionalistychne proty radyans'kogo: istorychna pamyat' v nezalezhnij Ukrayini" (The nationalist versus the Soviet: Historical memory in independent Ukraine), http://www.historians.in.ua/index.php/en/istoriya-i-pamyat-vazhki-pitannya/379-volodymyr-kulyk-natsionalistychne-proty-radianskoho-istorychna-pamiat-u-nezalezhnii-ukraini, accessed January 20, 2020.

44 The concepts characteristic of this narrative are the shared cultural and historical identity of Russians and Ukrainians, bilingualism, and "Russian" Orthodox Christianity as the traditional religion of Ukraine.

45 John-Paul Himka, "The Reception of the Holocaust in Postcommunist Ukraine," in *Bringing the Dark Past to Light: The Reception of the Holocaust in Postcommunist Europe*, ed. John-Paul Himka and Joanna Michlic (Omaha: University of Nebraska Press, 2013), 626–61.

46 *Materialy konferentsii, prysviachenoi zhyttiu ta diialnosti mytropolyta Andreia Sheptytskoho* (Proceedings of the conference on the life and work of Metropolitan Andrei Sheptytsky) (Lviv: Atlas, 1990). This small (65-page) book enjoyed a circulation of 10,000 copies.

47 Conference, "Metropolitan Andrei Sheptytsky (1865–1944)," Kyiv, 1994.

48 In 1993, the first collection of academic papers was published on Sheptytsky and the history of the Greek Catholic Church; these were Ukrainian translations of works by foreign scholars (Yaroslav Hrytsak and Borys Gudziak, eds., *Kovcheg. Zbirnyk statey z tserkovnoi istorii* [Ark: A collection of articles on church history] [Lviv: Institute for Historical Research at the Ivan Franko National University of Lviv, 1993]; Lonhyn Tsehelskyi, *Mytropolyt Andrei Sheptytskyi. Korotkyi zhyttiepys i ohliad yoho tserkovno-narodnoi diyalnosti* [Metropolitan Andrei Sheptyts'kyi: A short biography and overview of his clerical and social activity] [Lviv: Misioner, 1995]; Wasyl Lentsyk, *Vyznachni postati Ukrainskoi Tserkvy Mytropolyt Andrei Sheptytskyi i Patriarkh Yosyf Slipyi* [Outstanding personalities of the Ukrainian Church—Metropolitan Andrei Sheptyts'kyi and Patriarch Josyf Slipyi] [Lviv: Svichado, 2001]).

49 *Slidamy Mytropolyta. Metodychnyi posibnyk dlia provedennia zakhodiv, prysviachenykh roku Mytropolyta Andreia* (Following in the steps of the Metropolitan: A manual for organizing events dedicated to Metropolitan Andrei) (Lviv: Vydannia Komisii v Spravakh Katehisatsii UHKTs, 2001). This manual was prepared by teachers in Lviv who worked on programs for teaching Christian ethics in schools, and was published by the commission for catechesis of the Ukrainian Greek Catholic Church. The manual was distributed among teachers of western Ukraine.

50 See *Materialy konferentsii, prysviachenoi zhyttiu ta diialnosti mytropolyta Andreia Sheptytskoho*, 7–8; Lentsyk, *Vyznachni postati Ukrainskoi Tserkvy Mytropolyt Andrei Sheptytskyi i Patriarkh Yosyf Slipyi*, 284; see also 12, 19–20, 25, 128.

51 Lentsyk, *Vyznachni postati Ukrainskoi Tserkvy Mytropolyt Andrei Sheptytskyi i Patriarkh Yosyf Slipyi*, 217–18.

52 *Slidamy Mytropolyta*.

53 Hentosh, *Metropolyt Andrei Sheptyts'kyj, 1923–1939: Vyprobuvannya idealiv*; *"Blazhen toi muzh . . .": Fotoalbom do 150-littia z dnia narodzhennia mytropolyta A. Sheptytskoho* (Blessed is that man . . . : Photo-album dedicated to the Metropolitan's 150th anniversary) (Lviv: Manuskript, 2015).

54 Olha Myhailuk, ed., *Moisei ukrainskoho Dukha. Naukovo-mystetske vydannia v dvoi tomakh* (Ukrainian Moses: Academic/artistic edition in two volumes) (Lviv: Artklas, 2015); Serhii Herman, *Via Romana. Zhyttia Mytropolyta Andreia Sheptytskoho* (Via romana: The life of Metropolitan Andrei Sheptytsky) (Kyiv: Yaroslaviv Val, 2017).

55 The show followed the format of the BBC's series "100 Greatest Britons." It was aired on Inter during 2007–8, in prime time on Sundays, in the form of a talk show lasting 1.5 to 3 hours. The Kyiv International Institute of Sociology selected the audience according to random sampling, so that it was representative of the entire population of Ukraine. The audience was able to vote during the talk show.

56 The Religious Information Service of Ukraine: https://risu.org.ua/ua/index/all_news/community/social_questioning/48239/, accessed January 20, 2020.

57 Zoya Suhanova and Nina Sulyma-Matlashenko, *Andrei Sheptytskyi: Realii khresnoho shliakhu—Storinky istorii Ukrainy. Posibnyk dlia vchyteliv* (Andrei Sheptyts'kyi: His via crucis—Pages of the history of Ukraine. A manual for teachers) (Kyiv: Osvita, 1992); Orest Krasivskyi, *Za ukrainsku derzhavu i tserkvu. Hromadska i supilno- politychna diialnist mytropolyta A. Sheptytskoho v 1918–1923 rr.* (For the Ukrainian state and church: Social and political activity of Metropolitan A. Sheptyts'kyi in 1918–1923) (Lviv: Lohos, 2006); Ivan Hel, "Mytropolyt Andrei Sheptytskyi i ukrainska natsionalna ideia" (Metropolitan Andrei Sheptyts'kyi and the Ukrainian national idea), *Literaturna Ukraina* (February 8, 1996); Yaroslav Bilas, "Mytropolyt Andrei Sheptytskyi i problema natsionalno-vyzvolnoho rukhu ukraintsiv" (Metropolitan Andrei Sheptyts'kyi and the problem of the Ukrainian national liberation

movement, Abstract of the dissertation for the degree in Religious studies defended in Lviv National University), (Kyiv, 2003).

58 Dieter Pohl, "Ukrainische Hilfskrafte beim Mord an den Juden," in *Die Täter der Shoah: Fanatische Nationalsozialisten oder ganz normale Deutsche?* ed. Gerhard Paul (Gottingen: Wallstein Verlag, 2002, 211–19).

59 *Mytropolyt Andrei Sheptytskyi—pravednyk Ukrainy. Knyha pam'iati*, ed. Kyrylo Kindrat (Metropolitan Andrei Sheptytskyi—A Righteous of Ukraine: Book of Memory) (Rivne-Lviv: PF "Lista," 2001); Zhanna Kovba, *Liudianist' u bezodni pekla. Povedinka mistsevoho naselennia Skhidnoi Halychyny v roky "ostatochnoho rozv'iazannia yevreiskoho pytannia"* (Humanity in the depth of hell: Behavior of the population of Eastern Galicia in the years of the "final solution of the Jewish problem") (Kyiv: Dukh i Litera, 2000).

60 *Shchodennyk Lvivskoho getto: Spohady rabyna Davyda Kakhane* (Lviv ghetto diary: Memories of Rabbi David Kahane) (Kyiv: Dukh i Litera, 2009); Kurt Lewin, *Mandrivka kriz iliuzii* (trans. from English) (A journey through illusions) (Lviv: Svichado, 2008).

61 Skira, *Poklykani. Monahy Studiiskoho Ustavu ta Holokost.*

62 Liliana Hentosh and Bohdan Tscherkes, "Lviv in Search of Its Identity: Transformations of the City's Public Space," in *Cities after the Fall of Communism: Reshaping Cultural Landscapes and European Identity*, ed. J. Czaplicka, N. Gelazis, and B. Ruble (Washington, DC: Woodrow Wilson Center Press, 2009), 255–80.

63 Kyiv Municipal Administration, https://forum.kyivcity.gov.ua, accessed January 20, 2020.

64 News portal *Depo.ua*, https://mk.depo.ua/ukr/nikolaev/stali-vidomi-vsi-dekomunizovani-nazvi-vulits-u-mikolaevi-26022016105500, accessed January 20, 2020.

65 Opposition Bloc has united (both at the parliamentary and local levels) different political groups dissatisfied with the Ukrainian government's policy.

66 Religious Information Service of Ukraine, https://risu.org.ua/ua/index/all_news/state/church_state_relations/66429/, accessed January 20, 2020.

67 Ukrainski Novyny (Ukrainian news), https://ukranews.com/ua/news/485703-u-mykolayevi-pereymenuvaly-svizhodekomunizovanu-vulycyu-sheptyckogo-na-tradyciynu, accessed January 20, 2020.

68 Ukrainski Novyny (Ukrainian news), https://ukranews.com/ua/news/485703-u-mykolayevi-pereymenuvaly-svizhodekomunizovanu-vulycyu-sheptyckogo-na-tradyciynu, accessed January 20, 2020.

69 Anna Medvedovska, "Obraz mytropolyta A. Sheptytskoho v suchasnii suspilnii dumtsi Ukrainy" (The image of Metropolitan A. Sheptytsky in contemporary Ukrainian public opinion), *Naddniprianska Ukraina: istorychni procesy, podii, postati* 11 (2013): 221–28.

70 Ukrainian Institute of National Remembrance, http://www.memory.gov.ua/news/mitropolit-andrei-yuvilyar-blazhennii-pravednik, accessed January 20, 2020.

71 Ukrainian Institute of National Remembrance, http://www.memory.gov.ua/news/mitropolit-andrei-yuvilyar-blazhennii-pravednik, accessed January 20, 2020.

72 Oksana Dumanska and Halyna Tereshchuk, *Sheptytskyi vid A do Ya* (Sheptytsky from A to Z) (Lviv: Vydavnytstvo Staroho Leva, 2015).

73 Catholic social and religious news portal *Credo*, https://credo.pro/2015/11/146789, accessed January 20, 2020.

74 *Daily Lviv News*, https://dailylviv.com/news/kultura/u-lvovi-urochysto-vidkryly-pamyatnyk-mytropolytu-andreyu-sheptytskomu-21382, accessed January 20, 2020.

75 Lviv news portal *Zaxid.net*, https://zaxid.net/pamyatnik_sheptitskomu_konsensus_znaydeno_n1351184. Accessed January 20, 2020. City council members discussed the heavy costs involved in the project—30 million UAH, while that year's city budget allocated to the preservation of Lviv's historical sites amounted to only 14.5 million UAH. Kateryna Slipchenko, "Prystrasti za Sheptytskym" (The passion of Sheptytsky), zaxid.net/pristrasti_za_sheptitskim_n1343798, accessed January 20, 2020.

76 See Mykhaylo Ivanyk, "Pamyatnyk Sheptytskomu: velyke ne totozhne velychnomu" (Monument to Sheptytskyi: Big is not equal to majestic), https://zbruc.eu/node/30590; https://zaxid.net/pamyatnik_sheptitskomu_konsensus_znaydeno_n1351184, accessed January 20, 2020. See also Yaroslav Nazar, "Borotba za skver u Lvovi: doroha, dereva ta Sheptytsky" (Struggling for a park in Lviv: The road, the trees and Sheptytsky), https://www.bbc.com/ukrainian/society/2015/09/150831_lviv_park_conflict_ms, accessed January 20, 2020.

77 Oles Horodetsky, "Pamyatnyk Sheptytskomu u Lvovi: hibrydna viyna na terenakh Halychyny" (The monument to Sheptytsky in Lviv: A hybrid war in the Galician lands), https://www.radiosvoboda.org/a/26922012.html, accessed January 20, 2020.

78 Horodetsky, "Pamyatnyk Sheptytskomu u Lvovi: hibrydna viyna na terenakh Halychyny," https://www.radiosvoboda.org/a/26922012.html, accessed January 20, 2020.

79 See also Vladimir Petrushko, "Mitropolit Andrei Sheptytskyi: evoliutsyia mirovozzrenyia" (Metropolitan Andrei Sheptytsky: Evolution of his views), https://www.religion.in.ua/main/history/152-mitropolit-andrej-sheptickij-yevolyuciya.html, accessed January 20, 2020.

80 Vladimir Petrushko, "Aspid: O beatifikatsii Mitropolitf Andreia Sheptytskoho" (Viper: On beatification of Metropolitan Andrei Sheptytsky), http://donetsk.church.ua/aspid/, accessed January 20, 2020.

81 Nazar Holovko, "Mitropolit Andrei Sheptytskyi—shizofrenik ili trus?" (Metropolitan Andrei Sheptytsky: A schizophrenic or a coward?), https://spzh.news/ru/istorija-i-kulytrua/34283-mitropolit-andrey-sheptitskiy-shtrikhi-k-portretu, accessed January 20, 2020.

82 https://pravlife.org/ru/content/sovetskaya-razvedka-i-cerkovnye-raskoly-v-okkupirovannoy-ukraine-chast-1, accessed January 20, 2020.

83 https://ukrainianjewishencounter.org/en/hromadske-radio-no-holocaust-one-nation-holocaust-applies/, accessed January 20, 2020.

84 Interview of Prof. Shimon Redlich with Rev. Adam Boniecki, *Tygodnik Powszechny* (November 11, 2008), https://www.tygodnikpowszechny.pl/nie-boj-sie-dziecko-133592, accessed January 20, 2020.

85 https://sprawiedliwi.org.pl/en/news/debate-righteous-and-unrecognized-rescuers-brothers-andrzej-and-klemens-szeptycki, accessed January 20, 2020. See also Roald Hoffmann's interview with the participants of the public initiative "Ukrainian Jewish Encounter," published in the Ukrainian weekly *Fokus*, September 14, 2015, https://focus.ua/politics/337025/, accessed January 20, 2020.

86 The UJE is a privately organized initiative aimed at facilitating mutual understanding between Ukrainians and Jews. https://ukrainianjewishencounter.org/en/, accessed January 20, 2020.

87 Furthermore, in October 2018 UJE and the Ukrainian Catholic University co-organized a commemorative event, "Metropolitan Sheptytsky and the Holocaust," featuring Prof. Wold Moskovich and Lili Stern-Pohlmann, which took place in the Ukrainian Catholic Cathedral of the Holy Family in Exile in London: http://ukrainianinstitute.org.uk/news_710/, accessed January 20, 2020 (now unavailable).

88 https://ukrainianjewishencounter.org/uk/врятовані-шептицьким/, accessed January 20, 2020.

89 https://ukrainianjewishencounter.org/en/the-sheptytsky-award; https://jcu.org.ua/projects/medal-imeni-mitropolita-sheptickogo, accessed January 20, 2020.

90 https://synod.ugcc.ua/data/naukovtsi-i-duhovenstvo-zvernulysya-do-yad-vashem-z-prohannyam-vyznaty-mytropolyta-andreya-sheptytskogo-pravednykom-narodiv-svitu-1909/, accessed January 20, 2020.

91 https://zaxid.net/miy_obovyazok_u_tomu_shhob_stati_na_zahist_andreya_sheptitskogo_n1496350, accessed January 20, 2020 (the full text of the letter in Ukrainian).

92 https://www.ukrinform.ua/rubric-society/2863854-zelenskij-pidtrimav-zvernenna-sodo-viznanna-septickogo-pravednikom-narodiv-svitu.html, accessed January 21, 2020.

93 The author of the present chapter received an electronic version of Ms. Gusarova's letter from Rev. Yustyn Boyko, who also wrote a petition to Yad Vashem and gathered signatures from representatives of the intelligentsia.

94 *Mytropolyt Andrei Sheptytsky: Dokumenty i Materialy*, ed. Zhanna Kovba (Kyiv: Dukh i Litera), 16, 19.

95 https://zaxid.net/miy_obovyazok_u_tomu_shhob_stati_na_zahist_andreya_sheptitskogo_n1496350 (the full text of the letter in Ukrainian), accessed January 21, 2020.

96 https://openparliament.ca/debates/2012/4/24/jason-kenney-2, accessed January 21, 2020.

97 Adam Daniel Rotfeld, "Wzór ludzkiej przyzwoitości i cywilnej odwagi: O roli Klemensa Szeptyckiego w czasie II woiny światowej," in *Arystokrata ducha. Życie i dziedzictwo błogosławionego ojca Klemensa Szeptyckiego (1869–1951)*, ed. Andrzej Szeptycki (Warsaw: KEW, 2017), 18–19.

Bibliography

Archival Sources

Central State Historical Archive of Lviv (CDIAL). Collection 201 (F. 201), op. 2r, f. 90.

Published Archival Sources

Actes et Documents du Saint Siège relatifs à la Seconde Guerre Mondiale. Vol. 3, parts 1 and 2. Ed. Pierre Blet. Vatican City: Libreria Editrice Vaticana, 1967.

Mytropolyt Andrei Sheptytsky: Dokumenty i Materialy. Ed. Zhanna Kovba. Kyiv: Dukh i Litera, 2003.

Mytropolyt Andrei Sheptytskyi: Zhyttia i Dialnist. Tserkva i Suspilne Pytannia. Dokumenty i Materialy 1899–1944. (Metropolitan Andrei Sheptytsky: Life and work, the church and the social issues: Documents and materials 1899–1944.) Vol. 2, parts 1 and 2. Lviv: Misioner, 1998.

Books

"Blazhen toi muzh . . .": Fotoalbom do 150-littia z dnia narodzhennia mytropolyta A. Sheptytskoho. ("Blessed is that man . . .": Photo-album dedicated to the metropolitan's 150th anniversary.) Lviv: Manuskript, 2015.

Bociurkiw, Bohdan. *The Ukrainian Greek Catholic Church and the Soviet State (1939–1950).* Edmonton: Canadian Institute of Ukrainian Studies Press, 1996.

Dmytruk, Klym. *In Holy Robes: The Truth about the Contacts between the Hierarchy of the Uniate Church and the Nazi Aggressors.* Kiev: Ukraina Society, 1978.

———. *Pid chornymy sutanamy. Pravda pro zviazky iierarkhii uniatskoi tserkvy z fashystskymy zaharbnykamy.* (The black cassocks: The truth about the connections between the hierarchy of the Uniate Church and the Nazi aggressors.) Kyiv: Politizdat Ukrainy, 1975.

———. *S krestom i trezubtsem.* (With a cross and a trident.) Moscow: Politizdat, 1979.

———. *Svastika na sutanakh.* (Swastikas on cassocks). Moscow: Politizdat, 1976.

Dumanska, Oksana, and Halyna Tereshchuk. *Sheptytskyi vid A do Ya.* (Sheptytsky from A to Z.) Lviv: Vydavnytstvo Staroho Leva, 2015.

Halan, Yaroslavю. *Tvory v 4 tomakh.* (Collection of works in four volumes.) Vol. 2. Kyiv: Naukova Dumka, 1977.

Hentosh, Liliana. *Metropolyt Andrei Sheptyts'kyj, 1923–1939: Vyprobuvannya idealiv.* (Metropolitan Andrei Sheptyts'kyj, 1923–1939: A trial of ideals.) Lviv: Klasyka, 2015.

———. *Vatykan i vyklyky modernosti. Shidnoevropeiska polityka papy Benedykta XV ta ukrainsko-polskyi konflikt v Halychyni, 1914–1923.* (The Vatican and challenges of modernity: East European politics of Pope Benedict XV and Ukrainian-Polish conflict in Galicia.) Lviv: Klasyka, 2006.

Herman, Serhii. *Via Romana. Zhyttia Mytropolyta Andreia Sheptytskoho.* (Via Romana: The life of metropolitan Andrei Sheptytsky.) Kyiv: Yaroslaviv Val, 2017.

Krasivskyi, Orest. *Za ukrainsku derzhavu i tserkvu. Hromadska i supilno-politychna diialnist mytropolyta A. Sheptytskoho v 1918–1923 rr.* (For the

Ukrainian state and church: Social and political activity of Metropolitan A. Sheptyts'kyi in 1918–1923.) Lviv: Lohos, 2006.

Krawchuk, Andrii. *Christian Social Ethics in Ukraine: The Legacy of Andrei Sheptytsky*. Edmonton: Canadian Institute of Ukrainian Studies Press, 1997.

Kovba, Zhanna. *Liudianist' u bezodni pekla. Povedinka mistsevoho naselennia Skhidnoi Halychyny v roky "ostatochnoho rozv'iazannia yevreiskoho pytannia."* (Humanity in the depth of hell: Behavior of the population of eastern Galicia in the years of the "final solution of the Jewish problem.") Kyiv: Dukh i Litera, 2000.

Kovcheg. Zbirnyk statey z tserkovnoi istorii. (Ark: A collection of articles on church history.) Ed. Yaroslav Hrytsak and Borys Gudziak. Lviv: Lviv University Press, 1993.

Lentsyk, Wasyl. *Vyznachni postati Ukrainskoi Tserkvy Mytropolyt Andrei Sheptytskyi i Patriarkh Yosyf Slipyi.* (Outstanding personalities of the Ukrainian church—Metropolitan Andrei Sheptyts'kyi and patriarch Josyf Slipyi.) Lviv: Svichado, 2001.

Lewin, Kurt. *Mandrivka kriz iliuzii.* (A journey through illusions.) Lviv: Svichado, 2008.

Materialy konferentsii, prysviachenoi zhyttiu ta diialnosti mytropolyta Andreia Sheptytskoho. (Proceedings of the conference on the life and work of Metropolitan Andrei Sheptytsky.) Ed. Yurii Turkevych. Lviv: Atlas, 1990.

Moisei ukrainskoho Dukha. Naukovo-mystetske vydannia v dvoi tomakh. (Ukrainian Moses: Academic/artistic edition in two volumes.) Ed. Olha Myhailuk. Lviv: Artklas, 2015.

Morality and Reality: The Life and Times of Andrei Sheptyts'kyi. Ed. Paul Magocsi. Edmonton: Canadian Institute of Ukrainian Studies Press, 1989.

Mytropolyt Andrei Sheptytskyi—pravednyk Ukrainy. Knyha pam'iati. (Metropolitan Andrei Sheptytskyi—A righteous of Ukraine: Book of memory.) Ed. Kyrylo Kindrat. Rivne-Lviv: PF "Lista," 2001.

Nowak, Magdalena. *Dwa Światy. Zagadnienie identyfikacji narodowej Andrzeja Szeptyckiego w latach 1865–1914.* (Two worlds: The problem of the national identity of Andrei Sheptyts'kyi, 1865–1914.) Gdańsk: Wydawnictwo Universytetu Gdańskiego, 2018.

Shchodennyk Lvivskoho getto: Spohady rabyna Davyda Kakhane. (Lviv ghetto diary. Memories of Rabbi David Kahane.) Ed. Zhanna Kovba. Kyiv: Dukh i Litera, 2009.

Skira, Yurii. *Poklykani. Monahy Studiiskoho Ustavu ta Holokost.* (Those with the calling: Monks of the Studite order and the Holocaust.) Kyiv: Dukh i Litera, 2019.

Slidamy Mytropolyta. *Metodychnyi posibnyk dlia provedennia zakhodiv, prysviachenykh roku Mytropolyta Andreia.* (Following in the steps of the metropolitan: A manual for organizing events dedicated to Metropolitan Andrei.) Lviv: Vydannia Komisii v Spravakh Katehisatsii UHKTs, 2001.

Suhanova, Zoya, and Nina Sulyma-Matlashenko. *Andrei Sheptytskyi: Realii khresnoho shliakhu—Storinky istorii Ukrainy. Posibnyk dlia vchyteliv.* (Andrei Sheptyts'kyi: His via crucis—Pages of the history of Ukraine. A manual for teachers.) Kyiv: Osvita, 1992.

Tsehelskyi, Lonhyn. *Mytropolyt Andrei Sheptytskyi. Korotkyi zhyttiepys i ohliad yoho tserkovno-narodnoi diyalnosti.* (Metropolitan Andrei Sheptyts'kyi: A short biography and overview of his clerical and social activity.) Lviv: Misioner, 1995.

Ventresca, Robert. *Soldier of Christ.* Cambridge, MA: Harvard University Press, 2015.

Wolf, Hubert. *Pope and Devil: The Vatican's Archives and the Third Reich.* Cambridge, MA: Harvard University Press, 2010.

Yones, Eliyahu. *Smoke in the Sand: The Jews of Lvov in the War Years, 1939–1944.* Jerusalem: Gefen Publishing, 2004.

Chapters in Edited Volumes

Bolianovskyi, Andrii. "Mizh khrystyianskoiu moralliu i neliudskym zlom. (Reaktsiia mytropolyta Andreia Sheptytskoho na okupatsiinu polityku natsional-sotsialistychnoi Nimechchyny v Halychyni 1941–1944 rr.: vid formalnoi loialnosti do krytyky i protestiv.") (Between the Christian ethics and inhuman evil. [Response of Metropolitan A. Sheptytsky to the occupation policy of Nazi Germany in Galicia 1941–1944: From formal loyalty to criticism and protests].) In *The Second World War and the Fate of the Civil Population in Eastern Europe: Papers of the International Conference in the Memory of Metropolitan Andrei Sheptytsky*, ed. Leonid Finberg, 12–72. Kyiv: Dukh i Litera, 2016.

Hentosh, Liliana, and Bohdan Tscherkes. "Lviv in Search of Its Identity: Transformations of the City's Public Space." In *Cities after the Fall of Communism: Reshaping Cultural Landscapes and European Identity*, ed. J. Czaplicka, N. Gelazis, and B. Ruble, 255–80. Washington, DC: Woodrow Wilson Center Press, 2009.

Himka, John-Paul. "The Reception of the Holocaust in Postcommunist Ukraine." In *Bringing the Dark Past to Light: The Reception of the Holocaust in Postcommunist Europe*, ed. John-Paul Himka and Joanna Michlic, 626–61. Omaha: University of Nebraska Press, 2013.

Hrytsak, Yaroslav. "National Identities in Post-Soviet Ukraine: The Case of L'viv and Donetsk." In *Cultures and Nations of Central and Eastern Europe: Essays in Honor of Roman Szporluk*, ed. Zvi Gitelman, Lubomyr A. Hajda, John-Paul Himka, and Roman Solchanyk, 263–81. Cambridge, MA: Harvard University Press, 1998.

Pohl, Dieter. "Ukrainische Hilfskrafte beim Mord an den Juden." In *Die Täter der Shoah: Fanatische Nationalsozialisten oder ganz normale Deutsche?* ed. Gerhard Paul, 211–19. Gottingen: Wallstein Verlag, 2002.

Redlich, Shimon. "Metropolita Andrzej Szeptycki i wspólnota żydowska." In *Kościół, naród, państwo. Działanośċ i dziedzictwo Metropolity Andrzeja Szeptyckiego (1865–1944)*, ed. Andrzej Roman Szeptycki, 107–114. Warszawa: Wydawnictwo KEW, 2011.

Rotfeld, Adam Daniel. "Wzór ludzkiej przyzwoitości i cywilnej odwagi: O roli Klemensa Szeptyckiego w czasie II woiny światowej." In *Arystokrata ducha. Życie i dziedzictwo błogosławionego ojca Klemensa Szeptyckiego (1869–1951)*, ed. Andrzej Szeptycki, 13–24. Warsaw: Wydawnictwo KEW, 2017.

Sklokina, Iryna. "Radianska polityka pam'iati pro kolaboratsiiu periodu natsystskoi okupatsii yak instrument natsionalnoi polityky: rehionalnyi aspekt." (Soviet memory politics concerning collaborationism as an instrument of national policy: Regional aspect.) In *Natsionalna ta istorychna pam'iat: zbirnyk naukovykh prats* (National and historical memory: Collections of articles), ed. Volodymyr Soldatenko, 118–41. Kyiv: NVC "Priorytety," 2013.

Stehle, Hansjakob. "Sheptyts'kyi and the German Regime." In *Morality and Reality: The Life and Times of Andrei Sheptyts'kyi*, ed. Paul Magocsi, 181–99. Edmonton: Canadian Institute of Ukrainian Press, 1989.

Journal Articles

Boniecki, Adam. "Nie bój się dziecko." (Rev. Adam Boniecki interviews Prof. Shimon Redlich.) *Tygodnik Powszechny*, November 18, 2008, https://www.tygodnikpowszechny.pl/nie-boj-sie-dziecko-133592, accessed January 21, 2020.

Bussgang, Julian J. "Metropolitan Sheptytsky: A Reassessment." *Polin* 21 (2008): 401–35.

Hel, Ivan. "Mytropolyt Andrei Sheptytskyi i ukrainska natsionalna ideia." (Metropolitan Andrei Sheptyts'kyi and the Ukrainian national idea.) *Literaturna Ukraina* 6 (February 1996): 3–4.

Kapitan, Larysa. "Pidhotovka hromadskoi dumky naperedodni likvidatsii Hreko-katolytskoi tserkvy u Zakarpatti." (Influencing public opinion before the elimination of the Greek Catholic Church in the Transcarpathian region.) *Naukovyi visnyk Uzhhorodskoho nauionalnoho universytetu. History* 2 (2017): 6–15.

Kenney, Padraic. "Lviv's Central European Renaissance, 1987–1990." *Harvard Ukrainian Studies* 24 (2000): 303–12.

Kobuta, Stepan. "Politychni aspekty lehalizatsii Ukrainskoi Hreko-Katolytskoi Tserkvy (1987–1991)." (Political aspects of the legalization of the Ukrainian Greek Catholic Church in 1987–1991.) *Ludyna i Polityka* 3 (1993): 20–28.

Medvedovska, Anna. "Obraz mytropolyta A. Sheptytskoho v suchasnii suspilnii dumtsi Ukrainy." (The image of metropolitan A. Sheptytsky in contemporary Ukrainian public opinion.) *Naddniprianska Ukraina: istorychni procesy, podii, postati* 11 (2013): 221–28.

"Sheptytskyi Has to Be Granted Righteous." *Fokus*, September 14, 2015, https://focus.ua/politics/337025/, accessed January 21, 2020.

Visnyk Verkhovnoi Rady. (Herald of the Ukrainian parliament), no. 29 (2014): 953.

Website Articles

Azman, Moshe Reuven. "Mii oboviazok staty na zahyst Andreia Sheptytskoho." (It is my duty to stand for Andrei Sheptytskyi.) *Zaxid.net*, January 21, 2020, https://zaxid.net/miy_obovyazok_u_tomu_shhob_stati_na_zahist_andreya_sheptitskogo_n1496350, accessed April 19, 2023.

"Forum, Kyiv Municipal Administration." *Kyivcity.gov*, https://forum.kyivcity.gov.ua, accessed October 20, 2019.

Holovko, Nazar. "Mitropolit Andrei Sheptytskyi—shizofrenik ili trus?" (Metropolitan Andrei Sheptytsky: A Schizophrenic or a coward?) *SPZH.News*, September 11, 2016, https://spzh.news/ru/istorija-i-kulytrua/34283-mitropolit-andrey-sheptitskiy-shtrikhi-k-portretu, accessed January 21, 2020.

Horodetsky, Oles. "Pamyatnyk Sheptytskomu u Lvovi: hibrydna viyna na terenakh Halychyny." (The monument to Sheptytsky in Lviv: A hybrid war in the Galician lands.) *Radiosvoboda*, March 26, 2015, https://www.radiosvoboda.org/a/26922012.html, accessed January 21, 2020.

Ivanyk, Myroslava. "Pamyatnyk Sheptytskomu: Velyke ne totozhne velychnomu." (Monument to Sheptytskyi: Big is not equal to majestic.) *Zbruc*, December 16, 2014, https://zbruc.eu/node/30590, accessed January 21, 2020.

Kenney, Jason. "Metropolitan Andrey Sheptytsky." *Openparliament*, April 27, 2012 https://openparliament.ca/debates/2012/4/24/jason-kenney-2/.

Kulyk, Volodymyr. "Nacionalistychne proty radyans'kogo: istorychna pamyat' v nezalezhnij Ukrayini." (National versus Soviet: Historical memory in independent Ukraine.) September 20, 2012, http://www.historians.in.ua/index.php/en/istoriya-i-pamyat-vazhki-pitannya/379-volodymyr-kulyk-natsionalistychne-proty-radianskoho-istorychna-pamiat-u-nezalezhnii-ukraini, accessed April 19, 2023.

Magoci, Robert Paul. "Vriatovani Sheptytskym" (Saved by Sheptytskyi.) https://ukrainianjewishencounter.org/uk/врятовані-шептицьким/, accessed April 19, 2023.

"Mytropolit Andrei—blazhennii pravednyk." (Metropolitan Andrei—blessed and righteous.) Ukrainian Institute of National Remembrance, July 24, 2015, http://www.memory.gov.ua/news/mytropolit-andrei-yuvilyar-blazhennii-pravednik, accessed January 21, 2020.

"Nash mytropolit. Film about A. Sheptytskyi." *Credo* [Catholic social and religious news portal], November 23, 2015, https://credo.pro/2015/11/146789, accessed April 19, 2023.

"Naukovtsi ta duhovenstvo zvernulisa do Yad Vashem z prohanniam vyznaty mytropolyta Andreya Sheptytskoho pravednykom narodiv svitu." (Scholars and clergy asked Yad Vashem to honor metropolitan Andrei Sheptytsky by title of the righteous among the nations.) *Synod.ugcc*, November 17, 2019, https://synod.ugcc.ua/data/naukovtsi-i-duhovenstvo-zvernulysya-do-yad-vashem-z-prohannyam-vyznaty-mytropolyta-andreya-sheptytskogo-pravednykom-narodiv-svitu-1909/, accessed 19, 2023.

Nazar, Yaroslav. "Borotba za skver u Lvovi: doroha, dereva ta Sheptytsky." (Struggle for a park in Lviv: The road, the trees and Sheptytsky.) *BBC News/Ukraine*, September 3, 2015, https://www.bbc.com/ukrainian/society/2015/09/150831_lviv_park_conflict_ms, accessed April 19, 2023.

"Pamiatnyk Sheptytskomu: konsensus znaideno." (Monument to Sheptytskyi: Consensus was found.) *Zaxid.net.*, May 13, 2015, https://zaxid.net/pamyatnik_sheptitskomu_konsensus_znaydeno_n1351184, accessed January 21, 2020.

Petrushko, Vladimir. "Aspid: O beatifikatsii Mitropolitf Andreia Sheptytskoho." (Viper: On beatification of metropolitan Andrei Sheptytsky.) *Donbas Pravoslavnyi*, July 25, 2010, http://donetsk.church.ua/aspid/, accessed April 19, 2023.

———. "Mitropolit Andrei Sheptytskyi: evoliutsyia mirovozzrenyia." (Metropolitan Andrei Sheptytsky: Evolution of his views.) *Religion*, April 13, 2009, https://www.religion.in.ua/main/history/152-mitropolit-andrej-sheptickij-yevolyuciya.html, accessed January 21, 2021.

"The Sheptytsky Award." *Ukrainian Jewish Encounter*, June 1, 2016, https://ukrainianjewishencounter.org/en/the-sheptytsky-award, accessed January 21, 2020.

Sigal, Noa. "Shchepko i Ton'ko ne vidchuvaly sebe ni poliakamy, ni evreiamy, ni ukraintsiamy, vony buly lvivianamy." (Shchepko and Ton'ko did not identify themselves with Jews, Poles or Ukrainians, they were inhabitants of Lviv.) September 2, 2014, https://varianty.lviv.ua/21622-noa-sihal-shchepko-i-tonko-ne-vidchuvaly-sebe-ni-poliakamy-ni-yevreiamy-ni-ukraintsiamy-vony-buly-lvivianamy, accessed January 21, 2020.

Slipchenko, Kateryna. "Prystrasti za Sheptytskym." (The passion of Sheptytsky.) *Zaxid.net*, March 11, 2015, http://zaxid.net/prystrasti_za_sheptitskim_n1343798, accessed January 21, 2020.

"There Is no Holocaust of One Nation—the Holocaust Applies to All." *Ukrainian Jewish Encounter*, October 11, 2015, https://ukrainianjewishencounter.org/en/hromadske-radio-no-holocaust-one-nation-holocaust-applies/Ukrinform, accessed January 21, 2020.

"U Lvovi urochysto vidkryly pamiatnyk mytropolytu Andreyu Sheptytskomu." (Monument to Andrei Sheptytskyi was solemnly unveiled in Lviv.) *Daily Lviv News*, July 29, 2015, https://dailylviv.com/news/kultura/u-lvovi-urochysto-vidkryly-pamyatnyk-mytropolytu-andreyu-sheptytskomu-21382, accessed April 19, 2023.

"U Mykolayevi pereymenuvaly vulycyu Sheptyckogo na tradyciynu." (Street named after Sheptytskyi was renamed into Traditional in Mykolaiv.) *Ukrainski Novyny*, November 3, 2019, https://ukranews.com/ua/news/485703, accessed January 21, 2020.

"Vidomi vsi novi nazvy vulyts u Mykolaevi." (New names of streets in Mykolaiv were announced.) *MkDepo*, February 26, 2016, https://mk.depo.ua/ukr/nikolaev/stali-vidomi-vsi-dekomunizovani-nazvi-vulits-u-mikolaevi-26022016105500, accessed April 19, 2023.

"Vulytsia Sheptytskoho vestyme do pershoho khramu UGCC in Mykolaivi." (Sheptytskyi's street will lead to the first Greek-Catholic church in Mykolaiv.) *Religious Information Service of Ukraine*, March 21, 2017, https://risu.org.ua/ua/index/all_news/state/church_state_relations/66429/, accessed January 21, 2020.

"Zelenskyi pidtrymav zvernennia shchodo vznannia Sheptytskoho 'righteous among the nations.'" (Zelenskyi supported appeal to honor Sheptytskyi as righteous among the nations.) January 27, 2020, https://www.ukrinform.ua/rubric-society/2863854-zelenskij-pidtrimav-zvernenna-sodo-viznanna-septickogo-pravednikom-narodiv-svitu.html, accessed January 21, 2020.

Dissertation

Bilas, Yaroslav. "Mytropolyt Andrei Sheptytskyi i problema natsionalno-vyzvolnoho rukhuukraintsiv" (Metropolitan Andrei Sheptyts'kyi and the problem of the Ukrainian national liberation movement: Abstract of the dissertation defended at Lviv National University, 2003) Kyiv, 2003.

7

Belated and Incomplete

Recognizing the Righteous Among the Nations in Belarus

ANIKA WALKE

The Righteous Among the Nations exemplify the possibility to disavow and withstand Nazi ideology. Too few acted on this possibility, yet those who did ought to be remembered. The further the Holocaust recedes into the past, and the more complex the history of the genocide and its aftermath are, the more difficult it is to recognize the women and men who did assist Jews in evading the Nazi regime. Belarus, a territory where up to 90 percent of the prewar Jewish population fell victim to systematic killings and violence during the occupation, is a case in point. In this area, rescuers themselves were often the targets of wartime violence and did not survive. Other rescuers rejected efforts to identify and honor them because they feared that persistent antisemitic resentment among their neighbors would make them the targets of greed or hatred. The Cold War schism that effectively cut off communication between Soviet citizens and Israeli institutions further prevented the documentation of Belarusian Righteous Among the Nations. As a result, few received the honor in Belarus before 1991, and the story of those who helped Jews to survive remains incomplete.[1]

Inna Gerasimova, the founder of the Museum of the History and Culture of Jews in Belarus in Minsk, suggests that the trappings of Nazi ideology, antisemitism, and the plan to destroy European Jewry continued to shape relations between Jews and non-Jews in the immediate postwar period and fueled, for instance, the Soviet antisemitic campaigns of the late 1940s and early 1950s.[2] She lists these effects of the Nazi genocide as inhibiting the identification and honoring of those who aided Jews in their struggle for survival. This state of affairs was compounded by official policies favoring a focus on the heroic and victorious aspects of the war, and neither Jews who survived the Holocaust nor those who helped them felt comfortable or compelled to speak about their experiences in postwar Belarus. The period of *glasnost* and, later, the breakup of the Soviet Union marked openings for such revelations. Yet even though rescuers have been identified in fits and starts since the early 1990s, many of them have preferred to receive their medals at events in Minsk, the country's capital, rather than in their hometown or village, where they might be stigmatized as "Jew-helpers."[3]

While some bemoan that the neglect of the history of Jewish rescue marks a missed opportunity to utilize their "educational and moral potential,"[4] one should acknowledge that the fears of newly recognized Righteous indicate a continuing animosity, if not outright hatred, toward Jews residing in Belarus—experiences that are well documented for the imperial and Soviet periods as well as for recent Belarusian history. The reluctance to accept honors in public is paralleled by a noticeable absence—until recently—of state authorities in identifying and honoring Belarusian Righteous among the Nations. This is in stark contrast to many other Eastern European countries for whom the active search for and celebration of people who supported their Jewish compatriots seems to have been instrumental in achieving recognition as a valuable member of the European community and, eventually, the European Union—an endeavor long-term president Alexander Lukashenko actively disavows. At the same time, the fundamental ambivalence inherent in both remembering and not remembering the Righteous reveals a desire to conveniently brush aside uncomfortable phenomena, a desire seemingly shared by the country's leadership and large parts of the population. If the Righteous can be forgotten, so can greed, or the thirst for power that drove locals to report on their Jewish neighbors during the German occupation, to help hunt them down and transport them to execution sites, or to appropriate their homes and belongings, all of which left little room for Jews to escape mass murder and required unique strategies of survival, including the assistance of gentiles.

Evaluating the history of recognizing the Righteous Among the Nations in Belarus thus demands a broad perspective that considers the wartime experience of the Holocaust as much as postwar dynamics, including state-sponsored antisemitism and Soviet and Belarusian politics of memory, which have continuously skirted confronting the collaboration and complacency of Belarusians with German policies during the occupation. Conversely, this avoidance results in indifference toward those who actively supported Jews seeking survival options, with state authorities' engagement limited to the participation of representatives in award ceremonies organized by entities such as the Israeli embassy or Yad Vashem.[5]

Following the suspension of diplomatic relations between Israel and the USSR in the aftermath of the Six-Day War in 1967, a situation that lasted until the breakup of the Soviet Union, the identification of rescuers in Belarus was nearly impossible. Only Jews who had been Polish citizens before 1939 and who had immigrated to Israel via Poland could safely submit evidence to Yad Vashem. However, even if Yad Vashem approved these applications, rescuers who still resided in the Belorussian Soviet Socialist Republic (BSSR) were unable to accept the award in person. Although that obstacle was removed with the breakup of the Soviet Union in 1991, the identification of people who assisted Jews' efforts to survive remains a fraught and difficult process. Belarusian authorities offer little support, and it depends on volunteers and survivors themselves to track down the Righteous. The delay in identifying helpers also defers a more comprehensive account of just how many Righteous Among the Nations there were in Belarus, and thus of our understanding of Jewish survival.

This chapter examines three stories of people who helped Jews during the German occupation, and traces their fates after the war. These case studies emphasize this region's specificity regarding Jewish survival. They do not embrace the full range of help offered to Jews in Belarus, but they shed light on strategies that rescuers developed and employed to assist Jews. Such strategies include providing shelter during killing actions in urban ghettos and organizing escape routes to partisan units in the surrounding forests, providing transitional shelter for ghetto fugitives in rural areas and while en route to partisan units, and direct cooperation with the partisan movement to secure shelter, food, and protection. Moreover, these stories show the different conditions governing Jewish survival in either urban or rural settings. They emphasize that the Soviet partisan movement played a crucial role in facilitating the rescue of Jewish lives, which sets Belarus apart from other regions under German occupation. Last but not least, the three case studies pose questions concerning the recognition of those who aided Jewish survivors in the years since the breakup of the Soviet Union.

I reconstruct the process of identifying the Righteous by drawing on media reports, secondary scholarship, and expert interviews with individuals who have been involved in documenting the help given by Belarusians to Jews. The work of these individuals laid the foundations for what we know to date. I therefore briefly introduce major activists and offer a chronology before turning to the case studies and, finally, analyze the history and celebration of aid for

Jews against the backdrop of more general dynamics of Holocaust memory in present-day Belarus.

Politics of Memory and the Recognition of Righteous Among the Nations in Belarus

The great personal risks involved in saving Jewish lives in Belarus remained unacknowledged as a result of the Soviet politics of memory. The authorities' portrayal of the Great Patriotic War denied that Jews were specifically targeted by the occupying regime and also bore the brunt of violence committed by Soviet citizens who collaborated with the Germans.[6] As a result, even the efforts of Soviet partisans to rescue Soviet and other Jews were covered up and not commonly popularized among the general public.[7] These omissions contributed to a widespread perception that everyone did indeed suffer equally and made the identification of people who helped persecuted Jews appear irrelevant, if not misplaced. When in the early 1990s survivors and members of the waning Jewish community in Belarus began to collect evidence and track down people who hid Jews or otherwise helped them to survive the Holocaust, they were confronted with a widespread, yet distorted, understanding of the war and the occupation that had been propagated during the Soviet era. The silence over the systematic assault on Jews in Belarus continues to prevent a wider acknowledgment that some Belarusians, in fact, participated in persecuting their Jewish neighbors.

Perestroika and the breakup of the Soviet Union triggered great efforts by survivors to identify and honor the Righteous, especially in the mid-1990s. By 1997 Yad Vashem had awarded the title Righteous Among the Nations to 124 Belarusians.[8] By January 2022, 680 Belarusian Righteous had been included in Yad Vashem's database.[9] The sharp increase in numbers stems from hard work by survivors, volunteers, and the Israeli embassy in Belarus. The first Israeli ambassador, Eliahu Valk, assigned to Minsk in 1992, together with his wife, Aviva, was instrumental in locating and identifying the helpers and their descendants.[10] They actively sought to rectify the decades-long delay and contacted survivors living in Belarus to find out about their rescuers. As mentioned previously, only Jews who held Polish citizenship in 1939—because they were living in what became the western part of Belarus, which the USSR annexed after the outbreak of World War II—and who emigrated from Belarus in the early postwar years, could file their cases with Yad Vashem, either from Poland, Israel, or elsewhere. However, even if their rescuers were identified, they could not leave the country to attend the award ceremony.[11] For instance, Andrei Stanko and his wife, Natalia Zakharovna, had rescued Eli Kozinets, his wife, and their two sons after they had fled the Dolginovo ghetto. Stanko and Zakharovna hid them in their home in Rechki (Vileiskii district). The Kozinets family, after immigrating to Israel in 1965, applied for the title for the Stankos, and it was granted in 1966. However, it was not until 1994 that the Stankos's daughter was able to accept the honor in person, by which time her parents had long passed away.[12]

During the same period, and parallel to the ambassador's efforts, survivors like Maia Krapina and Frida Raisman—and volunteers including Inna Gerasimova, Elizaveta (Liza) Kiril'chenko, and Arkadii Shul'man—began to search systematically for those who had assisted Jews in their quest for survival. Inna Gerasimova, a historian, was deeply involved in reviving Jewish communal life in Belarus, and in documenting Belarusian Jewish history. Among other projects, she founded the Museum of the History and Culture of Jews in Belarus in 2002, which was sponsored by the Union of Belarusian Jewish Public Associations and Communities and the American Joint Distribution Committee.[13] The museum, which is located on premises shared with local Jewish community services such as "Hesed Rachamim," would eventually provide a home for the project to identify the Righteous of Belarus. It offered space for conducting research, filling out applications, and storing documentation. In 2010 the museum housed an exhibition that for the first time popularized information on the Righteous Among the Nations in Belarus. "Pamiatniki Pamiati" (Memorials to memory), devoted primarily to documenting memorials and monuments commemorating victims of the Holocaust, noted memorials to those who aided Jews on a separate exhibition panel that displayed a map of the republic.[14] Moreover, in 2004, Gerasimova and her team published a book documenting everyone whose role in aiding Jews during the German occupation had been verified. A new, updated edition was released in 2015.[15]

Alongside these volunteer efforts, a few scholars have published materials on the history of assisting Jews during the Holocaust.[16] However, these researchers either live and work abroad or work as freelancers or for independent organizations such as the Minsk-based Istoricheskaia Masterskaia "Leonid Levin," an educational and research center ("History Workshop") named after Leonid Levin (1936–2014), an award-winning architect of several memorials and former chair of the Union of Belarusian Jewish Public Associations and Communities. The History Workshop is an educational center housed in the last remaining building that was part of the ghetto, and it is funded by the International Center for Education and Exchange (IBB), a German organization hosting transnational educational programs and support networks.[17] In 2009 the History Workshop organized a conference in Minsk that represents the sole attempt to date to systematically discuss the issue of Jewish rescue.[18]

Research that has laid the foundations for uncovering and honoring hundreds of people who sought to save Jewish lives from Nazi genocide has brought to the fore a more complex narrative of World War II than the hegemonic Soviet portrayal of the war had let on. The portrayal and documentation of rescue activities reveal the often limited sympathy toward Jews, as well as the dangers posed to them by other Soviet citizens who thwarted efforts to support Jews who had escaped from ghettos or eluded mass executions. As such, this research contradicts the emphasis on the unified struggle of the Soviet population against the German occupiers. The belated interest in and recognition of the helpers might signal a changing public discourse toward greater awareness of the history of the Holocaust and its local implications.

Yet attention paid to the lives and memories of the Righteous in Belarus is largely limited to Jewish community organizations. There is neither governmental effort to support the search for the rescuers nor a recognition that this history might serve to teach students and schoolchildren about the Belarusian wartime experience or the flawed postwar memory, in order to reckon with the complex history of wartime terror, genocide, collaboration, resistance, and rescue.

Contextualizing the Righteous Among the Nations in Belarus

German troops crossed the demarcation line between the German and Soviet occupation zones of Poland on June 22, 1941, and quickly advanced through the Belorussian Soviet Socialist Republic (BSSR), defeating millions of Soviet troops. Local residents experienced the invasion as a surprise attack that destroyed their homes in a matter of days, displacing thousands and shattering a society that was embroiled in deep political, social, and cultural transformation as a result of the revolution in 1917 and, in the case of the western parts of the BSSR, the annexation of formerly eastern Polish territory in September 1939.

Air raids and the swift advance of German troops cost hundreds of thousands of lives, and few people were able to evacuate or flee before being caught under the rule of the German occupying authorities. Locals had to report to work for the new regime, which included continuing to fulfill their roles as farmers and workers. Much of the agricultural yield was confiscated, and locals received limited food rations instead of payment. In the Reich Commissariat Ostland and, to a lesser extent, in the Reich Commissariat Ukraine, the civilian administration established by the occupiers regulated the use of the local labor force and natural and other resources, primarily with the goal of supporting the ongoing war effort. The eastern parts of Belarus remained under military administration for the duration of the war. Ongoing military operations, battles between German and Soviet troops, and a growing and increasingly effective partisan movement sabotaged the German efforts to bring the area under control. In the attempt to crush the movement and subjugate the local population, the Germans identified not only the actual partisans—that is, combatants—as their enemy, but anyone who might *potentially* support the partisans. In practice, civilians in certain areas were collectively subsumed under these groups; Jews were considered enemies by definition and thus were primary targets for what was labeled antipartisan warfare—but was, in fact, a series of military operations that targeted civilians as much as combatants. As a result of this brutal war, Belarus lost between one quarter and one third of its population during World War II. In addition to the population loss, by the end of the war, 1,200,000 residential houses in the countryside had been destroyed; 90 percent of urban houses and public buildings had become uninhabitable.[19] In 1945 three million people found themselves homeless or living in makeshift dwellings dug into the soil, 85 percent of the industrial plants were damaged, the economy's capacity had decreased by 95 percent, crop space had been nearly halved, and 80 percent of the cattle had been destroyed.[20]

The Germans embedded the genocide of the Jews in this war of extermination. On the eve of the German invasion, about 700,000 Jews were residing within the borders of present-day Belarus, including about 320,000 who had become Soviet citizens when the eastern parts of Poland were annexed by the USSR in 1939. In addition, more than 65,000 Jews had escaped from western Poland (which was under German occupation) and sought shelter in the BSSR. Many of them stayed without official registration, while others were deported to the Soviet interior alongside other Polish citizens who refused to accept Soviet citizenship or were deemed a threat to Soviet power. Thus we can only estimate how many Jews were caught by the German occupation of Belarus, but most scholars settle on the number of approximately 800,000.[21] Over the course of the three-year long occupation, 90 percent of this population were killed.

The deadly violence against Jews commenced as soon as the invasion began. Beginning in late summer 1941, German special units, the so-called *Einsatzgruppen*, launched the systematic destruction of whole Jewish communities. Often within days of the arrival of German troops, Jewish residents were ghettoized, which cut them off from food supplies, medical care, and access to other necessities and networks of mutual support. Depending on the size of the Jewish population and the local conditions, the makeshift ghettos consisted of several street blocks, some residential houses, and schools or synagogues, either cordoned off by barbed wire or guarded by Belarusian auxiliary police.[22] Overcrowding in residential buildings increased the suffering, especially in the urban ghettos in Minsk, Mogilev, Vitebsk, Bobruisk, and Białystok, where thousands died of hunger and disease.

During roundups, local communities were assembled and collectively marched to antitank trenches, natural ravines, or pits prepared in advance just outside of their hometowns, where Jewish men and women of all ages, as well as children, were shot indiscriminately and buried in mass graves. As a result most Jewish inhabitants of the region had been killed by spring 1942; the remaining individuals and small communities were destroyed before the fall of 1943. The ghetto in Minsk, the capital, survived longer than any other ghetto in Belarus but was also liquidated in October 1943. In many instances locals helped identify Jews, dragged them out of hiding places, or participated in the roundups and even the shootings. In other words, the Holocaust was deeply embedded in an all-encompassing regime of violence, and it was perpetrated by occupiers together with local collaborators. Moreover, it was very visible, as it took place where people lived.[23]

The dynamics of World War II and the murder campaigns against Jews residing in Belarus posed unique challenges to any effort to secure survival. The speed and brutality of the invasion and occupation and the quick succession of invasion and mass murder left the victims very little time to prepare or make arrangements to flee or obtain help. It required lifesaving efforts on the spot, under the extremely difficult conditions of widespread hunger and near-constant military and partisan activity. Seeking shelter with non-Jewish Belarusians, finding refuge in the woods, or joining the ranks of a partisan unit offered the only opportunities to survive. The experience of shared suffering and danger intensified bonds between Jews and their helpers, which in many cases had developed before the war and turned out to be crucial for survival under the occupation. For some Jews, friends, coworkers, business partners, patients, domestic aides, or neighbors proved reliable supporters in their time of need. These relationships not only persisted in the face of Nazi ideology and terror, but also often continued after the war. In the aftermath of the war, they ran counter to a climate in which Jewish experiences were silenced, marginalized, or even declared to be untrue. State-sponsored antisemitic campaigns destroyed the infrastructure of Jewish life in Belarus, yet some friendships between Jews and their rescuers seem to have persevered, despite renewed ideological mobilization.[24]

Olga Glazebnaia and Varvara Simon: Urban Rescue in the Minsk Ghetto

German troops occupied Minsk, the capital of the BSSR, as early as June 28, 1941. Many residents tried to flee the city, as it was targeted by heavy air raids, but they were stopped by German troops that had advanced quickly, and thus had to turn around and return. Among them were up to eighty thousand Jews, who within days found themselves ordered to move into a ghetto, cramming into often half-destroyed houses with few possessions. Forced labor was instituted for those older than fifteen, and only those who worked received regular food rations. Others—children, the elderly, or the sick—relied on the goodwill of those workers. The presence of staff members of the General Commissariat Weißruthenien (a subdivision of the Reich Commissariat Ostland) and several military units that were stationed in the city created a volatile situation for Jews, inside and outside the ghetto. In addition to the deprivation and overcrowding, German patrols regularly entered the Jewish district, assaulting individuals or breaking into homes to abuse and rob. Beginning in late July, SS and auxiliary troops, formed by locals, conducted systematic raids on designated sections of the ghetto. In late August, during two of those roundups, hundreds of Jewish men were arrested and shot, and in November residents of several streets were detained and killed. These and the following killing actions in the spring and summer of 1942 quickly decimated the ghetto population; by the summer of 1942, only twenty thousand residents deemed "capable of work" of the initial eighty thousand or so ghetto inhabitants were still alive, even though in the fall of 1942 several thousand Jews were deported from Germany, Austria, and several occupied countries to the ghetto. Starvation, disease, and terror created an untenable situation in the ghetto that few could survive.[25]

For the few who did survive, the help of non-Jews outside the ghetto proved essential. The experiences of two Jewish sisters, Roza Zelenko (née Tsukerman) and Liubov' Sokolova (née Tsukerman, usually called Lusia), give insight into the harsh conditions and show that only the help of their friend Olga Glazebnaia (née Simon) and her sister Varvara Simon made their survival possible. These young women's prescribed national identities—Olga and her sister being Ukrainian and Roza and her family being Jewish—turned out to be decisive for their fate under the German occupying regime, since Olga and her sister's non-Jewish identity allowed them to help their friends and maintain important connections with the world beyond the ghetto.

Olga, born in 1922, had moved to Minsk from Kiev together with her older sister Varvara in 1935. Varvara Simon, then twenty-three years old, was raising two children at the time; her husband worked out of town, and she needed help. Roza and Olga had met in school and became close friends, even though Roza was four years younger. They were part of a larger circle of friends that included Roza's sister Lusia (born 1923) and others. The teenagers met regularly to listen to music and dance.[26] During the air raids in the first few days of the war, Roza, Lusia, their father, and several other family members fled Minsk. At the time, their mother was out of town with a younger sister and ended up on an evacuation train that took them to Kyrgyzstan, effectively separating the family until after the war. Those family members who fled Minsk on foot did not make it very far and had to return to the city after a few days, only to find their house completely destroyed. They settled in a house that was half-intact, but had to move again in late July, when the German occupying regime ordered the creation of a "Jewish residential district"—a ghetto. Olga, her sister Varvara Simon, and the two young children also left Minsk to seek shelter from air raids and the German terror. But they, too, had to return to the city in the late fall of 1941. Olga was surprised to find her friends behind barbed wire, separated from her and other non-Jews: "I did not understand this at first, why they were in a ghetto. We went to school together. It had never occurred to me that they were Jews and that that was at all important."[27]

Olga and Varvara realized that the situation of Minsk Jews was becoming increasingly desperate when they observed a group of them working at a construction site adjacent to their own home on Sovietskaia Street. Varvara began smuggling food to them, at times by crawling through holes in the ghetto fence.[28] Later, Varvara joined the efforts of the emerging underground movement to evacuate adolescents from the ghetto and place them with partisan units outside the city.[29]

In the ghetto, Roza, Lusia, and other friends suffered from crowded conditions and insufficient food. As of the late summer of 1941, they were exposed to the direct threat of terror, mass arrest, and killing operations orchestrated by the SS. During these *Aktionen*, SS and auxiliary troops rounded up and killed groups of Jews (sometimes hundreds, sometimes thousands) at shooting sites on the outskirts of the city or with the help of gas vans in which Jews were suffocated while being transported to, for instance, Blagovshchina or Shashkova, where they were buried in mass graves.

Olga and Varvara tried to support their friends in various ways. For example, they supplied them with food that Varvara procured. Having worked in retail before the war, she knew several farmers outside of Minsk who lived in small villages or so-called *khutors* (Russ., homesteads or hamlets detached from villages). Together with a group of other women, Varvara regularly took valuables, clothes, or other useful items, which Roza and Lusia had given them, to these farmers and exchanged them for food.[30] Olga took bags full of potatoes or flour, crawled through a hole in the barbed wire that separated the ghetto from the rest of the city, and delivered them to her friends and others. Sometimes, Zelenko remembers, Olga also "joined our column when we were marched to our workplace in the morning, and she gave us a loaf of bread or a bottle of milk. She took a lot of risks."[31] Indeed, Olga once had to hide in one of the so-called *malinas*, hiding places Jewish families created in their homes, because a German patrol had noticed her in the ghetto.[32] Roza, Lusia, and other Jews had used such *malinas* several times during roundups, when Germans and collaborators roamed the ghetto to snatch Jews from the streets or drag them out of their homes. Soon the sisters realized that it would be safer to hide outside the ghetto, and during one of the German roundups in the winter of 1941, they made their way to Olga and Varvara's home and asked for shelter for the duration of the raid. The two sisters opened their door, this and many other times, and as Olga recalls, this was a natural decision, not the result of deliberate planning: "They came, all in tears, shivering, what were we to do? We didn't think about it. . . . We didn't plan to rescue anyone, but the girls came, sometimes together, sometimes one of them. And they usually came when bad things were happening in the ghetto, there were often pogroms. And when they came, of course we hid them."[33] In September 1943, Roza and a friend spent several days at their friends' place:[34] They huddled in a hiding place underneath an unused bathroom, a hollow space that the women had fitted out with some fabric and old clothes and covered with loose wooden floorboards.[35] They thus hoped to escape brutal raids that targeted the ghetto and the whole city because Wilhelm Kube, the General Commissar of Weißruthenien, had been assassinated by members of the city's underground movement. German forces used this as a pretext for a wave of violence, killing a number of people as hostages while ostensibly searching for members of the underground.[36]

In the fall of 1941, an underground movement began to develop in Minsk, consisting of members on both sides of the ghetto fence. Alongside the evacuation of children from the ghetto, the underground sought to establish connections with partisan detachments that were emerging in the forests and wetlands of Belarus, so as to organize escape routes for ghetto fugitives. The groups also supported partisans by collecting necessary items such as shoes, clothing, medical supplies, tools, and ammunition, and by helping Soviet prisoners of war to flee from Minsk-based prisons and camps. Varvara was among those who maintained such connections. During her trips to the countryside to procure food, she frequently met with partisans, either bringing supplies for them or receiving information or goods to be sent to Minsk. Roza, Lusia, and their friend Lilia

Glezer collected clothes in the ghetto, which they would then pass on to Olga or Varvara, who transported these items to their final destinations.[37] Partisans also stayed over at Varvara and Olga's house when they visited Minsk.[38] This connection with the organized underground and the partisan movement turned out to be instrumental for securing Rosa and Lusia's survival.

Roza and Lusia lost their entire family during the German roundups and mass killings that began in 1941, and like many others realized that only an escape from the ghetto would offer a chance to make it through the war. Varvara arranged for Lusia's escape from the ghetto in the spring of 1943, together with Lilia Glezer. Both young women joined the "Bolshevik" detachment of the "Belarus" brigade, a combat unit active in the Minsk region, where they worked as cooks and nurses for about a year, until the liberation.[39] Roza, who was several years younger, had to stay behind—a combat unit did not admit her, as supposedly she would not have been useful for their efforts. In her account, Roza also pointed out that she "looked more Jewish than her sister":[40] Lusia had fair hair and skin and could pass as a gentile.[41] Olga and Varvara continued to support her until the final days of the ghetto's existence. Together with her uncle and her cousin, Roza survived the liquidation of the ghetto in October 1943 in a *malina*. Varvara was then able to organize their safe passage out of town and into the woods, where the three ghetto escapees joined the "Ponomarenko" unit of the "Ponomarenko" Brigade.[42] This unit appears to have been more inclined to admit ghetto fugitives than others, possibly because a Jewish man, Zakhar Boiko, occupied an important leadership position within the unit.[43]

Throughout the two years of aiding their Jewish friends, Olga and Varvara took many risks by entering the ghetto, hiding Roza and others in their house, interacting and working with partisans, and organizing the escape from the ghetto of several young Jewish women and men. They also struggled to make ends meet, feeding Varvara's two young children and another Jewish woman who had moved in with them once she had lost her whole family. This woman, Revekka (Riva) Vishnevetskaia, at some point ran into a former classmate who had taken up work for the police and recognized her. Varvara managed to organize her timely escape, but as Roza Zelenko points out, this moment of alarm demonstrates that not only Germans posed a threat but locals as well. German patrols regularly tried to arrest Olga and send her away to carry out forced labor. An older neighbor, also named Olga, even pretended to be her while the "real" Olga hid in the basement, and was so able to deflect the danger. Olga Glazebnaia believes that many neighbors knew what she and her sister were doing, but nobody reported them, "they were like gold."[44] In fact, her sister Varvara explains that some of her neighbors and other acquaintances were also involved in efforts to evacuate Jewish adolescents from the ghetto and took them to partisan units.[45] These seemingly contradictory reports about non-Jews' responses to the persecution of Jews demonstrate the varying attitudes of the Belarusian population toward Germans, Jews, and partisans, and just how much Jewish survival depended on those around them—they could be trusted allies, or they could come forward to denounce and report Jews and thereby condemn them to death.

Roza and Lusia were among the few Jews of Minsk who survived the occupation and returned to the city after the war with their partisan units. They immediately sought out Olga and Varvara and moved in with them for a short period. Minsk was in ruins, and up to eight people shared one bedroom. What mattered, however, was that they were alive: "I still remember those onions," Roza explained. "Yes, we sat on the bed with a plate in front of us with a little bit of oil in it, we dipped the onions into that oil and took a bite of bread—it was wonderful!" Olga added, "And we laughed, and everything was great. We didn't own anything beyond the clothes on our backs, we had no money, but we had survived."[46] The friendship continued for several decades; Olga and Roza remained close. Roza Zelenko and Lusia Sokolova ensured that her friends Olga Glazebnaia and Varvara Simon were recognized as Righteous Among the Nations. Both women received the honor in September 1997.[47]

By offering hiding places, providing food, organizing escape from the ghetto, and even leading Jews to safety, a number of non-Jews who lived next to the Minsk Ghetto supported Jewish friends, former neighbors, and coworkers, but also strangers, and thus provided invaluable aid that was instrumental for a good number of the estimated ten thousand Jews who survived the Minsk Ghetto. Many of these relationships were rooted in prewar connections and continued throughout the postwar period.[48] Often, the rescue of Jewish adolescents or children was initiated by their peers, Russian or Belarusian children or teenagers who had gone to school with them and developed friendships and who rejected the notion of racial hatred that singled out Jews for extermination.[49] Urban modernization and the creation of Soviet institutions, including schools that actively promoted overcoming national segregation in the 1920s, certainly played a role in the emergence and persistence of these networks. Many especially young Jews who lived in prewar Minsk were deeply integrated, and their ties with non-Jews proved essential for survival.[50] At the same time, rescue and aid efforts were complicated by this urban context. Close interaction with and residence next to others who might not be as supportive or even hostile bore the danger of discovery, which could lead to severe punishment, including death. Food shortages were felt harshly and required dangerous and prolonged efforts to secure provisions in the countryside. Lastly, while urban-rural mobility such as Varvara's was an asset to the partisan movement and to the Jews she was able to evacuate to the partisans, it also heightened the possibility of being discovered and reported to the Germans.

This case of aiding Jews in German-occupied Belarus reveals if not a blurred line between rescue and resistance, then how closely they were connected. Aiding survival and rescue work was a deliberate way to counter German-led policies and the practice of extermination, but it took place alongside—and in several ways thanks to—work with organized resistance groups such as partisans. This interconnectedness helped save Jews by offering them a destination after fleeing the ghetto, and activities such as gathering food or other supplies provided cover for transmitting messages. The following two examples from the rural areas of eastern Belarus further illustrate this phenomenon.

Foma and Elena Kuiko and Elena Kezha: Rural Rescue as Transition

Leonid Gol'braikh grew up in Beshankovichy, a former shtetl in Vitebskaia *oblast* (Russ., province) in eastern Belarus. German troops reached the area in early July 1941 and, as elsewhere, introduced a regime of violence that included the ghettoization of all individuals categorized as Jews, their forced labor, and the looting and destruction of Jewish property. In the early hours of February 11, 1942, all the Jews in Beshankovichy were rounded up and led toward a killing site in a nearby forest. More than one thousand people, including children and the elderly, were marched through the town, past the homes of neighbors, former classmates, and others.[51] Eleven-year-old Leonid Gol'braikh managed to slip out of the column of people and hide in the forest. Later that day, he crawled out and ran away, leaving behind his hometown and his mother and two sisters, who were shot together with other Jews. "I went to this family about ten kilometers away, and I only made it there at night, because I tried to avoid villages and settlements. I arrived there in the middle of the night, I was in such a state, I was shaking violently. The woman held me in her arms for the whole night."[52] Leonid had made his way to Foma and Elena Kuiko, who lived in the village of Svecha. Leonid's father had been friends with Foma Kuiko before the war, and the family had supported the Gol'braikhs throughout the first few months of the German occupation. Their daughter Elena brought food to the fence around the ghetto of Beshankovichy, and picked up items to exchange for food.

When young Leonid knocked at their door that night, they took him in without hesitation and provided shelter, food, and a change of clothes. Eventually the boy had to move on, because his hosts feared denunciation by other residents who had also known Leonid before the war. Nina Dashkevich, Kuiko's younger daughter, remembers that the local mayor warned the family that others might report them to the Germans. But when the mayor himself attempted to arrest Leonid, the father refused to hand over the child. "He said, 'No, I won't give him to you.'"[53] For several months, Leonid worked as a farmhand for families in the area, surviving on the payments in kind he received for tending cattle and helping with the harvest. By the fall of 1942, the Kuikos and the boy had decided that it would be safer for him to join a partisan unit to avoid continuous scrutiny. They successfully made contact with partisans and arranged for his admission into a detachment, where he participated in a number of missions, caring for the unit's horses, and saw the liberation in the summer of 1944.[54] Before Leonid joined the unit, its commander, Mikhail Sol'nikov, recommended that he change his name. Knowing that some locals and partisans harbored antisemitic sentiments, Leonid L'vovich Gol'braikh became Leonid Vasilevich Andrichenko, a fact that of course obscured the main reason for Golbraikh's presence in the detachment—that is, his escape from Nazi persecution based on his Jewish identity.[55]

As in the case of Roza Zelenko and Liubov' Sokolova, Gol'braikh's survival reveals the crucial importance of local non-Jewish residents—many of them former family friends and coworkers, but also chance acquaintances who provided refuge and support. In small towns and villages, their homes served as transitional hiding places; others offered food, clothes, medical aid, or even forged documents that would allow the ghetto escapee to pass as a non-Jew. Others were in touch with partisans and arranged for their charges to join them and thus leave villages or towns that were frequently controlled by German forces or Belarusian auxiliaries. The only places where Jews could live for a longer period were the so-called *khutors* or *zastenki* (Russ., farmstead, literally "behind the wall")—small settlements beyond proper village boundaries that due to their location escaped regular surveillance.[56]

This transitionary help, independent of its duration, was vital, since "sometimes a few hours played a decisive role in saving a person's life."[57] Longer-lasting aid, over months or even years, carried an even deadlier risk for the helpers and their families. Whereas those who reported on Jews in hiding and their helpers often received rewards from the Germans in the form of food, vodka, tobacco, and money, the helpers and their families faced harsh punishment, usually death.[58] In some instances, all residents of a given village were killed and their settlement razed in retaliation. For example, all 280 villagers of Skirmontovo (Koidanovskii district) were killed during a German punitive campaign in the summer of 1943, presumably for their aid to Jews en route to a nearby partisan unit.[59] The Kuiko family's fear that Leonid might be discovered was thus well justified, and his departure a logical solution.

After liberation in July 1944, Gol'braikh returned to Beshankovichy, but he did not find any surviving members of his family. After a short year of schooling, he embarked on a journey through several towns and cities all over the USSR, settling eventually in Leningrad. Nevertheless, he regularly visited Beshankovichy and maintained a powerful emotional bond with his rescuers. He sent them photographs and letters, and he visited them every summer, together with his wife and son. The feeling was mutual: Nina Dashkevich described her relationship to Gol'braikh as that of a sibling.[60] Marina Dashkevich, Kuiko's granddaughter, even moved to Leningrad when Gol'braikh encouraged her to do so, and for a while lived with his family there.[61]

In 2016 I shared Gol'braikh's story with Stanislav Leonenko, then director of the local history museum in Beshankovichy. He suggested that Foma and Elena should be recognized as Righteous Among the Nations. Based on the interview I conducted with Kuiko's daughter, supplemented by interviews I had done more than a decade earlier with Gol'braikh, Leonenko compiled a case file that he passed on to Liza Kiril'chenko at the Minsk Museum of Jewish History, who expertly shepherded the case through to its successful conclusion.[62] Because Gol'braikh passed away in 2012, his son Lev submitted the official request to recognize the Kuikos as Righteous Among the Nations to Yad Vashem. The close relationship between Dashkevich's daughter and Lev Gol'braikh was instrumental in arranging this step, as by that time Lev was living in Germany—without the close relationship between the two families, the necessary paperwork would have been difficult to secure.[63] In July 2018, Foma and Elena Kuiko and their daughter Elena received the honor posthumously.[64] Nikolai Kezha, Foma and Elena's grandson, and his family came to Minsk to accept the medal from Alon Shoham, Israel's ambassador to Belarus, during the annual Holocaust remembrance ceremony on May 2, 2019. As they told a journalist from Beshankovichy, they were touched that somebody remembered their relatives.[65]

Poreche: Communal Rescue Efforts in the Wetlands

By the time Yad Vashem recognized the Kuiko family as Righteous Among the Nations, they had all passed away—like many of the Belarusians and others who had helped save Jewish lives during the German occupation. This delay, as mentioned earlier, is primarily a result of the Cold War. It is therefore all the more commendable that until today, survivors and allies in the countries of the former

Soviet Union, including Belarus, work toward making the names of rescuers known publicly and documenting their stories for posterity. Among the first to do so in Belarus was Maria Levina-Krapina (born 1935), a resident of Minsk widely known as Maia Krapina. As a child, Maia Krapina benefited from an extraordinary collective effort to save dozens of children from the Minsk Ghetto.

In the early 1990s, Maia Krapina began to work in the newly founded Jewish community center "Hesed Rachamim" in Minsk. Retired by that time, she and others of her generation began to revive Jewish communal life in Belarus and to support elderly Jews who were struggling with health or other problems. They also began to collect the stories of loss and survival that Soviet Jews had passed on only privately. Among these were hundreds of accounts of assistance and rescue efforts by non-Jews. Spurred on by the opening of the Israeli embassy in Minsk, Krapina and others took on the difficult task of collecting the necessary documents, especially the survivors' own accounts about the help extended to them. For Krapina, this was a personal issue and a chance to show her gratitude to Anastasia Khurs, the woman who had saved her life when she escaped from the Minsk Ghetto.[66]

In the fall of 1943, Maia Krapina's older brother Iosif, who had already joined a partisan unit, arranged for a group of children aged eight to thirteen, many of them orphans, to leave the Minsk Ghetto and seek shelter in the Belarusian countryside. Iosif had fled the ghetto to join a partisan unit, but had then taken up the difficult task of guiding others from Minsk safely to the partisans, namely to the M. I. Kutuzov unit of the Second Minsk Brigade, which had its base in the Pukhovichi district. The unit had been founded by other escapees from the ghetto, including Israil Lapidus, who was now leading the brigade. When Iosif realized that the liquidation of the Minsk Ghetto was drawing near in October 1943, he gathered his sister and forty other children and led them to safety. His hope was that Lapidus would support them, and the leadership of the brigade indeed did.[67] When the children arrived in Porech'e after a sixty-mile trek on foot, the partisans were awaiting them, together with several village residents. The combatants then asked each resident to shelter as many children as possible, and almost all of them did. Some invited one, others two, others even three of the ghetto escapees into their homes. Those who were unable to do so because of spatial constraints or other matters helped out in other ways.[68]

Many of the adolescents had been suffering from malnutrition for a long time or needed medical care; others were deeply traumatized by what had transpired in the ghetto. Mikhail Pekker, for instance, had been among the several thousand children and women who were shot at the so-called Iama, a pit in Minsk, in March 1942. He miraculously survived but had ceased to speak as a result of the trauma. He regained his speech only after several months of being affectionately cared for by the villagers.[69] Several families took in two or more children, sharing what little food they had with these Jewish escapees. Sometimes, partisans brought supplies to the village. Those who had sufficiently recovered from malnutrition and trauma began helping with farmwork. However, they were not safe. Due to its proximity to partisan activity, the village was regularly visited by German patrols, moments in which the locals would leave their homes to hide in the nearby marshes and forests, sometimes only to find their homes burned down or their cattle stolen when they returned.[70] As Krapina points out, "Poreche could have shared the fate of Khatyn," the village that was razed in March 1943 with more than a hundred residents burned to death in a barn, as a form of retaliation for the villagers' aid to partisans.[71] And yet the village as a whole and its residents survived. Krapina marvels at the solidarity of the villagers: "But even in the neighboring villages, where everyone knew who was hidden in Poreche, nobody reported on us. Nobody!"[72] Toward the end of the war, many older Jewish boys joined the Soviet army, and some of them fell on the front. Those who returned home, however, maintained close relationships with their rescuers. These long-lasting relationships facilitated the recognition of the villagers as Righteous, if belatedly. To date, Yad Vashem has recognized twelve men and women who took in Jewish children from Minsk. The last people to receive the title were Agrippina and Aleksei Shashok, who were honored posthumously in 2016.[73]

Poreche is the place in Belarus where the first memorial to the Righteous Among the Nations was erected. In 2000 Maia Krapina and Frida Raizman, another child survivor who had been sheltered in the village, established and funded a memorial to the rescuers of Poreche.[74] The dedication of the memorial brought together prominent local politicians, representatives of the Jewish community in Belarus, and delegates from several NGOs, including the chairman of the local council of delegates, the deputy chairperson of the local executive committee, the heads of the Union of Belarusian Jewish Public Associations and Communities, the Jewish Agency in Belarus, the chairman of the Belarusian Foundation "Mutual Understanding and Reconciliation," and the president of the Foundation "Holocaust."[75] The inscription on the memorial reads: "During the Great Patriotic War (1941–1944), residents of Poreche heroically rescued Jewish children who had fled the Minsk Ghetto. From the rescued."[76] For years afterward, Raisman, Krapina, and other survivors assisted the local school by providing equipment and supplies, and they regularly visited the village to tell their story.

Krapina reiterates the opinion of some survivors that the whole village should be honored collectively as a Village of the Righteous, given the communal effort it took to care for a whole group of children.[77] Of course, according to Yad Vashem's bylaws, the title and medal of the Righteous Among the Nations is only awarded to individuals. Additionally, Inna Gerasimova suggests that because of the involvement of a nearby partisan unit, even the basic requirement that aides helped of their own volition may prove a challenge here, since the decision to support the Jewish children may not have been made by the residents.[78]

The support for ghetto escapees in Porech'e illustrates a distinct pattern of help for Jews in search of shelter in German-occupied Belarus: The partisan movement played a crucial role, either as the final destination for those seeking shelter outside the ghettos (e.g., Roza Zelenko and Leonid Gol'braikh), or, as in the case of the forty children from the Minsk Ghetto, as a safety guard and provider of food and other supplies. This is not to say that all partisans and leaders of partisan units or brigades were willing to do so; indeed there is ample evidence to the contrary. In fact, partisans killed many ghetto fugitives.[79] But it was nearly unthinkable to secure shelter and safety *without* them, just as the help of non-Jews was essential in general.

The stories of Pavel Proniagin and Nikolai Kiselev exemplify the complex role of the Soviet partisan movement in assisting Jews and the difficulties Yad Vashem has had with classifying such cases. As partisans, both men were instrumental in organizing survival options for Jews, but one of them was not recognized as a Righteous, and the other received the title only after a long and contested process of documentation. Pavel Proniagin commanded a partisan unit that rescued a number of Jews from the Kossovo Ghetto. He was not recognized because Yad Vashem determined that, as a commander of a military organization, he did not risk particular danger by extending help to the Jews.[80] However, Leonid Smilovitsky argues that the assumption that the helper faced a significant personal risk when assisting Jews (a stipulation of the Yad Vashem bylaws) should apply here. There were many instances in which partisan commanders were reprimanded by their superiors for helping civilians, especially Jews, and of course rescuing Jews from the ghettos was risky under any circumstance.

Nikolai Kiselev's experience shows this very clearly. Kiselev led more than two hundred Jews from Dolginovo to safety across occupied territory, and he did so in the face of substantial resistance from his superiors.[81] Like Proniagin, he did not receive any kind of recognition for these rescue efforts from the Soviet authorities after the war, and he even omitted any mention of his rescue efforts in his memoirs and personnel file, for fear of retribution for violating military orders. When Proniagin published a memoir in 1979, Soviet censors redacted his portrayal of the rescue of ghetto residents.[82] Yad Vashem recognized Kiselev as Righteous Among the Nations in 2005, after Inna Gerasimova, who had researched the rescue operation, and a group of survivors who had participated in the march began to press the case in the early 2000s.[83]

These case studies of long-term support in an urban context, shelter from persecution in a rural area, and a group rescue effort in cooperation with a partisan unit exemplify the kinds of aid offered to Jews in Belarus. Directors of orphanages who took in Jewish children who lived under different identities, priests and other religious personnel who created hiding places in churches and chapels, clerks who forged documents, nannies or domestic workers who continued to support their former employers and charges—there is a long list of other men and women who could have been named here. A survey of these various efforts has been provided in a handful of publications devoted to the Righteous Among the Nations in Belarus. They suggest that more often than not the efforts a group of people were necessary to help save one or more Jewish lives.[84] A large number of the Righteous were women, many of them childless and rather poor.[85] Most men of draft age had been mobilized into the Red Army; others had joined the partisans. Left behind, the women thus had space to offer, and at times they were actually in need of help with house- or farmwork, so the presence of young Jews could be practical or even beneficial.

Overall, and this is not unique to the Belarusian context, the rescue of Jews usually consisted of providing shelter, food, and care in secrecy. Such mundane, seemingly unspectacular acts appear to pale next to the visible, dramatic, public acts of partisans and the military, which formed the core of the Soviet memory and commemoration of the Great Patriotic War.[86] As a result, these efforts have remained largely unacknowledged outside the personal relationships between the rescued and their helpers. These relationships, on the other hand, often lasted for decades and were, in the end, the foundation for a belated public recognition of these risky acts to undermine the Nazi genocide.

Post-Soviet Recognition: The Belarusian Righteous Among the Nations

Although Pavel Proniagin has not been officially recognized as a Righteous Among the Nations, in 1996 Israeli ambassador Valk presented him with a commemorative medal, and Yad Vashem expressed deep gratitude for his heroism.[87] Survivors and local activists deemed this insufficient and planned to subvert the exclusion of Proniagin from the register of the Righteous Among the Nations by including a tree in his honor in the Alley of the Righteous Among the Nations in Minsk, a row of trees near the memorial at the "Iama" that is reminiscent of the Yad Vashem Memorial complex. The alley in Minsk was initiated by Ambassador Valk and his wife, Aviva, in 2000.[88] Given Yad Vashem's final decision, a tree for Proniagin was not included.[89] Nevertheless, the survivors' disagreement with Yad Vashem's classification of Proniagin's deeds suggests that their assessment of what counts as valuable assistance sits uncomfortably outside the Yad Vashem bylaws.

The Belarusian efforts to document the Righteous Among the Nations may be partly driven by the desire to inscribe the country in a globalized discourse on the rescue of Jews while highlighting some national specificities. However, while in some other European countries the commemoration of the Righteous is financed and supported by the state, in Belarus these initiatives are the result of a Holocaust memory discourse that is propelled by grassroots initiatives and runs parallel to state authorities' lackluster approach to documenting and commemorating the Nazi genocide against Jews.

Survivors and activists are driven by a profound sense of gratitude, of personal and communal debt and moral obligation to identify and track down the women and men who helped several hundred Jews residing in Belarus to survive the Holocaust.[90] Their efforts have been successful. Hundreds of individuals have been identified, bringing the deeds of the helpers into the public sphere: The ten trees that were planted in 2000 at the Alley of the Righteous Among the Nations in Minsk have reached maturity and cannot go unnoticed. At the moment, there are efforts underway to redesign the memorial and ensure that the large number of Righteous is made more widely known.[91] Signs of recognition for those who aided Jewish survival are visible outside of Minsk as well: Since 1992, several memorial plaques have been installed at homes and churches where Jews were hidden during the German occupation in Borisov, Staroe Selo, and Kobrin, among others.[92] In 2005 the Jewish community of Bobruisk unveiled a memorial to the sixteen officially registered Righteous Among the Nations of the town and district, and there is also an Alley of the Righteous.[93] The earlier-mentioned memorial in Porech'e is thus one of several in the rural areas of the republic, where perhaps the majority of Belarusian Jews survived.

At the same time, the history of these rural memorials reveals the limitations of Yad Vashem regulations in honoring those who helped Jews survive. For instance, in 2002 Iosif Gel'fand erected a monument in memory of all those who helped save his family in the village of Medvezhino (Starodorozhski district).[94] When Inna Gerasimova and Liza Kiril'chenko began to research the story, they realized that more people were involved in hiding and caring for the Gel'fand family than had been recognized by Yad Vashem thus far.[95] Since no survivors were alive, there were no witnesses who could support further inclusions into the registry of the Righteous Among the Nations, one of the conditions for granting the title.[96] The rupture of diplomatic relations between the Soviet Union and Israel, and the resulting delay in recognizing those who assisted Jewish survival, contributed to the fact that many of these helpers will forever remain unknown and unhonored.

Beyond the difficulty of collecting evidence and the resulting gaps in our knowledge about aid to Jews, there is also a dispute over numbers. Over the years, the number of Belarusian citizens recognized as Righteous by Yad Vashem has increased steadily; the late 1990s were the years with the highest recognition quota: 58 in 1996, 77 in 1997, 64 in 1998, 42 in 1999, and 60 in 2000. Over the past decade, yearly numbers have been in the single digits.[97] Overall, 680 women and men have been entered into the database (as of January 2022). However, a 2015 book edited by Inna Gerasimova and others gives the number of 794 "Pravedniki" (Righteous), and recent media reports indicate that the number of Righteous Among the Nations of Belarus has crossed the threshold of 800.[98] The discrepancy results from different perspectives on how to classify a given rescue as Belarusian. Gerasimova and her collaborators decided to base their count on the place of rescue, applying the borders of 1991. Therefore, their count includes inhabitants of the former Polish eastern territories annexed by the Soviet Union in 1939. Many of them resettled in Poland after World War II. This method of counting is historically justified. According to Gerasimova, the *location* of where help was given is relevant, since it determined the circumstances and risks of saving Jewish lives. To her, Belarus stands out because of the speed of ghettoization and mass murder in the German-occupied Soviet territories, and because "there were partisans everywhere, there was war all around, and that made it all the more difficult and dangerous."[99] Given that aid to Jews was rarely an individual act and usually required the involvement of more than one person, the role of the social environment was decisive. For example, it made a big difference whether the rescue action took place in former Polish territories, where nationalism and antisemitism were already widespread in the prewar decades, or in territories that had been part of the Soviet Union since the early 1920s and where people were less likely to denounce Jews, where there was a strong Soviet partisan movement, and where residents were themselves the targets of mass terror. All these factors posed unique challenges or, conversely, decisive opportunities for aiding Jewish survival.

The dispute over numbers also reflects the complex history of statehood in the area that is characterized by many border-redrawings and the multiethnic composition of the population, and it points toward the political dimension of commemorating the Righteous. While Belarusian researchers and activists increase the number of Belarusian Righteous by adding ethnic Poles living in Polish territories annexed by the USSR in 1939, the efforts of Polish state authorities go in the opposite direction. They are seeking to commemorate all ethnic Poles recognized by Yad Vashem, no matter where they lived and what their citizenship at the time of war was. Doing so, the Polish government, led by the Law and Justice party, has tried to reshape national and international Holocaust memory by aggrandizing Poles' support for Jews and, simultaneously, downplaying and disputing Polish involvement in the Holocaust.[100] Moreover, as the Belarusian government shows little interest in claiming the history of aid for Jews for commemorative or political purposes, the hard work of identifying rescuers in Belarus is performed by volunteers, activists, and an ever smaller number of survivors. The situation is quite different in Poland, where state resources are mobilized for the same efforts, which are therefore more effective. This creates a competitive environment that deflects from the actual purpose of honoring those who helped Jews to survive.

Many of the recent titles of Righteous Among the Nations have been awarded posthumously, and therefore the rescuers themselves will not experience public recognition. Moreover, many of those who were rescued have passed away. Nevertheless, as Maia Krapina and Frida Raizman suggested, telling the story of rescuing Jewish children in Poreche and elsewhere offers an opportunity to talk about the ethical dilemmas that present themselves in the context of extreme violence against individuals and communities. Unfortunately, in Belarus such conversations remain limited to a small community of survivors and former helpers and their descendants, and to the still slim number of scholars and activists engaged in elevating Belarus's Jewish history and the history and memory of the Holocaust.

Even though Belarus regained its sovereignty in 1991, public awareness of both the extermination of Jews and rescue efforts has remained at the margins of official policies regarding commemoration and education about the past. While in the 1990s many award ceremonies were held in the Jewish Community Center, more recent events have taken place in more prominent public venues, such as the new Museum for the Great Patriotic War or the Belarusian State Philharmonic.[101] They are typically organized by the embassy of Israel, at times supported by other embassies, such as the Polish one.[102] Apart from the 2010 exhibition in the Museum of the History and Culture of Jews in Belarus, exhibitions on the topic are organized only by foreign organizations such as the United Nations or the Czech embassy.[103] On the other hand, individual activists, local schoolteachers and students, even residents who have access to a telephone and can help transmit information from or to elderly rescuers living in rural areas, drive the search for the Righteous and thereby help shape a narrative of wartime experiences that reflects the impact of occupation and genocide on large parts of the civilian population.[104] To date, apart from the Museum of the History and Culture of Jews in Belarus, the History Workshop is the only institution in Belarus that makes information about Belarusians who rescued Jews available to a larger public.[105]

The state authorities show little interest in the matter. So far, President Alexander Lukashenko has mentioned the issue of the Righteous only once, in a speech held on the sixty-fifth anniversary of the destruction of the Minsk Ghetto, on October 20, 2008. The official narrative of the war continues to focus on the victorious Soviet military and partisan movement, which is on open display during the yearly victory parades on May 9, the anniversary of the end of World War II, and in the Museum of the Great Patriotic War that opened in 2014 to replace the original Museum of the Great Patriotic War of 1966.[106] The new, modern-looking museum does include a few rather general displays on the extermination of Jews and the suffering of civilians. Yet it does little to illuminate the history of the Minsk Ghetto (whose territory is within walking distance of the museum grounds) or other ghettos around the country, or local responses including rescue or collaboration. The efforts of the members of the ghetto underground movement that cooperated with the partisan movement have been made visible, whereas the efforts of civilians who helped persecuted Jews remain invisible in the museum exhibit. Most important, the larger implications of war and occupation that brought destruction and death to millions of people are not discussed.

Beginning in the early 1990s, Belarus has seen increasing efforts to commemorate Jewish victims. Hundreds of memorials at mass shooting sites have been erected, filling an important gap in the historical memory. A number of memorials had been established in the years since the end of World War II.[107] However, like the memorials to the Righteous in Minsk, Bobruisk, or Porech'e, these memorials are typically sponsored by private initiatives, often from abroad. Austrian and German organizations and governments initiated the building of a memorial complex at Maly Trostenets, a former death camp that consisted of several sites. Donation campaigns in Austria and Germany in the 2010s provided major funding, without which the project would not have been realized, and it opened in 2015 (first stage) and 2018 (second stage). The Belarusian government agreed to the establishment of the memorial, yet it did so reluctantly and with mixed results: The Jewishness of the local victims has been downplayed on official signage. Overall, governmental approval and involvement were motivated more by the desire to improve Belarus's international reputation than by a commitment to unearth and acknowledge Belarusian history in all its complexity.[108]

On the surface, the lack of official attention to the history of rescue may seem like a denial of the specificity of the persecution of the Jewish population under the German occupation. In addition, and on a deeper level, this ignorance results from the widespread celebration of only the visible and spectacular acts of heroism and combat that are associated with the military and partisan movement's victory. The difficult conditions under which civilians, Jewish and non-Jewish, tried to survive, and what it took to survive, remain marginalized. The mundane acts of labor for survival, of everyday efforts to procure food and clothing, and the demonstration of empathy were essential to withstand Nazi terror and the Holocaust, but perhaps they are not spectacular enough to be noticed and recognized. In addition, the Jewish experience of the war continues to be separated from that of the general population. Facing up to the history of aid and rescue would require an honest confrontation with a history of local residents' complicity in the persecution and extermination of Belarusian and other Jews, and the tremendous difficulty and risks faced by those who tried to counter the mass murder. The instrumentalization of Holocaust memory when it is opportune, such as in the case of the Maly Trostenets memorial complex just described, and the use of antisemitic imagery in denouncing protests against the fraudulent elections that held Alexander Lukashenko in power feed concerns that such an honest and transparent approach to the extermination of Jews in Belarus is a distant prospect.[109] The recent intensification of state repression in the wake of the election protests in 2020 and the Russian war of aggression against Ukraine, in which Belarus has played an important role as a staging ground for Russian military advances, suggest that progress with regard to a widely accepted and shared memory of the Holocaust is rather unlikely.

In the spring of 2022, the Belarusian president signed a new law criminalizing the denial of the genocide of the Belarusian people by German occupiers and their accomplices during World War II. Simultaneously, Belarusian protesters against government repression and election fraud are portrayed as the successors of wartime collaborators, *ipso facto*, as potential genocidaires.[110] Prior deliberations and the text of the law have mentioned the Holocaust only marginally. While the new law arises from a political agenda to discredit opposition movements, the omission is inscribed into a long history of neglecting the extermination of Belarus's Jewish population. Despite the government's pretending otherwise, the new memory laws addressing Belarus's history and the memory of World War II will likely perpetuate this disregard for years to come, further obliterating the history and memory of Jewish victims of Nazi persecution and those who tried to support them, and undoing much of the progress that had been made in this realm over the preceding twenty years.

Notes

1 I am deeply grateful to Inna Gerasimova and Elizaveta (Liza) Kiril'chenko, who generously shared their perspective on the topic during phone interviews and by email. Several years ago, Iryna Kashtalian kindly shared several interviews that she had conducted with Righteous Among the Nations; several of these interviews are now available at "Arkhiv svidetelei Minskoi istoricheskoi masterskoi—Pravedniki narodov mira," http://zeitzeugenarchiv.gwminsk.com/ru/archiv/gerechte, accessed October 25, 2023.

2 Inna Gerasimova, "Pravedniki—gordost' Belarusi," in *Pravedniki Narodov Mira Belarusi*, ed. I. N. Gerasimova, E. M. Kiril'chenko, M. A. Movzon, and A. L. Shul'man (Minsk: Medizont, 2015), 6.

3 Gerasimova, "Pravedniki—gordost' Belarusi," 6.

4 Il'ia Al'tman, *Zhertvy Nenavisty: Kholokost v SSSR, 1941–1945gg* (Moscow: Kovcheg, 2002), 453.

5 "Ob uchastii Posla Belarusi v Izraile E. Vorob'eva v tseremonii vruchenia medali i gramoty Pravednikov narodov mira," Ministerstvo inostrannykh del Respubliki Belarus, May 25, 2022, https://mfa.gov.by/press/news_mfa/c09e1d0eb56ceb10.html, accessed October 3, 2022.

6 Bernhard Chiari, *Alltag hinter der Front: Besatzung, Kollaboration und Widerstand in Weißrussland 1941–1944* (Düsseldorf: Droste, 1998), e.g., 248–49.

7 See Anika Walke, *Pioneers and Partisans: An Oral History of Nazi Genocide in Belorussia* (New York: Oxford University Press, 2015), chaps. 4 and 5; Inna Gerasimova, *Marsh zhizni. Kak spasali dolginovskikh evreev* (Moscow: AST, 2016).

8 Leonid Smilovitsky, "Righteous Gentiles, the Partisans, and Jewish Survival in Belorussia, 1941–1944," *Holocaust and Genocide Studies* 11, no. 3 (1997): 321.

9 The Righteous Among the Nations—Names of Righteous by Country, https://www.yadvashem.org/righteous/statistics.html, accessed October 24, 2023.

10 Smilovitsky, "Righteous," 323; Gerasimova, "Pravedniki—gordost' Belarusi," 7.

11 Gerasimova, "Pravedniki—gordost' Belarusi," 7.

12 Gerasimova, "Pravedniki—gordost' Belarusi," 7. See also the Righteous Among the Nations Database, Stanko, Andrey, and Stanko, Natalya, https://righteous.yadvashem.org/?search=stanko&searchType=righteous_only&language=en&itemId=4021576&ind=3, accessed October 5, 2020.

13 Inna Gerasimova, phone interview with the author, September 23, 2020. For more information on the museum, see https://www.jewishmuseum.by, accessed March 30, 2023.

14 Inna Gerasimova, email to the author, March 11, 2021.

15 I. P. Gerasimova and A. L. Shul'man, eds., *Pravedniki Narodov Mira Belarusi* (Minsk: OGOD Tonpik, 2004); I. P. Gerasimova, E. M. Kiril'chenko, M. A. Movzon, and A. L. Shul'man, eds., *Pravedniki Narodov Mira Belarusi* (Minsk: Medizont, 2015).

16 Smilovitsky, "Righteous Gentiles"; . . . *Na perekrestkakh sudeb: Iz vospominanii byvshikh uznikov getto i pravednikov mira*, ed. O. M. Arkad'eva, L. L. Geller-Martynova, T. S. Kurdadze, and D. I. Rusakovskaia (Minsk: Chetyrie Chetverty, 2001); K. I. Kozak, M. I. Krapina, I. S. Prostak, R. K. Semashko and Minskii mezhdunarodnyi obrazovatel'nyi tsentr imeni Iokhannesa Rau/Dortmundskii mezhdunarodnyi obrazovatel'nyi tsentr, eds., *Pravedniki Narodov Mira: Zhivye svidetel'stva Belarusi. Sbornik dokumentov, materialov i statei* (Minsk: Logvinov, 2009); Katrin Reichelt, *Der Wald war ein letzter Ausweg: Hilfe für verfolgte Juden im deutsch besetzten Weißrussland 1941–1944* (Berlin: Lukas Verlag, 2017).

17 For more information on the History Workshop "Leonid Levin" and the IBB, see http://gwminsk.com, accessed May 10, 2021.

18 See the conference documentation in Kozak et al., eds., *Pravedniki Narodov Mira: Zhivye svidetel'stva Belarusi.*

19 Leonid Smilovitskii, "Bor'ba evreev Belorussii za vosvrat svoego imushchestvo i zhilishch' v pervoe poslevoennoe desiatiletie, 1944–1954gg.," in *Belarus V XX Stagoddzi*, ed. V. I. Andreev (Minsk: Vodolei, 2002), 167f.

20 Christian Gerlach, *Kalkulierte Morde: Die deutsche Wirtschafts- und Vernichtungspolitik in Weißrussland, 1941–1944* (Hamburg: Hamburger Edition, 1999), 11.

21 Sara Bender and Pearl Weiss, eds., *The Encyclopedia of the Righteous Among the Nations: Rescuers of Jews during the Holocaust: Europe*, part 2 (Jerusalem: Yad Vashem, 2011), xlix.

22 For a concise portrayal of ghettoization in the German-occupied Soviet territories, see Christopher Browning, "Introduction," in *Encyclopedia of*

Camps and Ghettos, 1933–1945, vol. 2: *Ghettos in German-Occupied Eastern Europe*, ed. Martin Dean (Bloomington: Indiana University Press, 2012), esp. xxxi–xxxv.

23 For portrayals of the German occupation of Belarus, the Holocaust, and collaboration, see e.g., Gerlach, *Kalkulierte Morde*; Chiari, *Alltag hinter der Front*; Barbara Epstein, *The Minsk Ghetto 1941–1943: Jewish Resistance and Soviet Internationalism* (Berkeley: University of California Press, 2008); Leonid Rein, *The Kings and the Pawns: Collaboration in Byelorussia during World War II* (New York: Berghahn, 2011); Walke, *Pioneers and Partisans.*

24 Leonid Smilovitsky, *Jewish Life in Belarus: The Final Decade of the Stalin Regime, 1944–1953* (New York: Central European University Press, 2014).

25 For a concise account of the conditions and history of the Minsk Ghetto, see Anne Speckhard, "Minsk," *Encyclopedia of Camps and Ghettos, 1933–1945*, vol. 2: *Ghettos in German-Occupied Eastern Europe*, ed. Martin Dean (Bloomington: Indiana University Press, 2012), 1233–37.

26 Roza Zelenko and Olga Glazebnaia, interview with the author, Minsk, October 11, 2002.

27 Zelenko and Glazebnaia, interview.

28 Yad Vashem Archives (YVA), M. 31-7727-9089, p. 2.

29 YVA, M. 31-7727-9089, pp. 2 and 30. A detailed study of these efforts can be found in: Epstein, *The Minsk Ghetto*, ch. 5, 171–80.

30 Zelenko and Glazebnaia, interview. See also Olga Glazebnaia and Svetlana Nikolaichik, interview with Iryna Kashtalian, Minsk, October 13, 2014.

31 Zelenko and Glazebnaia, interview.

32 Glazebnaia and Nikolaichik, interview.

33 Glazebnaia and Nikolaichik, interview. The word "pogrom," while typically used to describe mob violence targeting particular groups, especially Jews, is widely used by survivors and witnesses in the former Soviet Union to describe the killing actions conducted by German troops and their auxiliaries.

34 YVA, M. 31-7727-9089, p. 17.

35 Zelenko and Glazebnaia, interview; YVA, M. 31-7727-9089, p. 24.

36 YVA, M. 31-7727-9089, p. 7.

37 Epstein, *The Minsk Ghetto*, 181.

38 Glazebnaia and Nikolaichik, interview.

39 Liubov' Efimovna Tsukerman, interview with Iryna Kashtalian, Minsk, November 2011. For the sake of transparency, I must mention an unsolvable contradiction: In all interviews that were conducted with Liubov' Efimovna or her sister, the date of her escape from the ghetto is given as spring or early summer 1943. In her letter to Yad Vashem, however, Ms. Tsukerman suggests that she fled after hiding, with Roza, in the room under Varvara and Olga's bathroom to hide from the raids in the aftermath of Wilhelm Kube's assassination, which took place in September 1943. I do not believe that the inconsistent timeline mars the overall account of the Simon sisters' aid efforts; it does, however, hinder a complete reconstruction of these efforts.

40 Zelenko and Glazebnaia, interview.

41 Epstein, *The Minsk Ghetto*, 183

42 Zelenko and Glazebnaia, interview.

43 See Emanuil G. Ioffe, "Belorusskie Evrei v Bor'be s Natsizmom v 1941–1945gg.," *Zhurnal rossiiskikh i vostochnoevropeiskikh istoricheskikh issledovanii* 11, no. 4 (2017): 81. Ioffe lists Boiko as chief of staff of the "Ponomarenko" brigade, but a more recent publication by the National Archive of the Republic Belarus and the publisher "Belarus Today" identifies Boiko as the commissar of the Ponomarenko unit of the brigade with the same name; see "Partizany Belarusi: Boiko Zakhar Antonovich," https://partizany.by/partisans/30256/, accessed March 2021.

44 Glazebnaia and Nikolaichik, interview.

45 YVA, M. 31-7727-9089, pp. 2 and 30.

46 Zelenko and Glazebnaia, interview.

47 The Righteous Among the Nations Database, Glazebnaya Olga; Sister: Simon Varvara, https://righteous.yadvashem.org/?search=glazebnaya&searchType=righteous_only&language=en&itemId=4015024&ind=0, accessed October 24, 2023.

48 See, for instance, Tamara Iakovlevna Osipova, interview with Iryna Kashtalian, November 3, 2014; Tatiana Polikarpovich, interview with Iryna Kashtalian, n.d.; Ivan Ivanovich Bovt, interview with Iryna Kashtalian, December 11, 2014.

49 Leonid Smilovitskii, "Kholokost i spasenie evreev v Belarusi," in *Evrei Belarusi: iz nashei obshchei istorii, 1905–1953gg.* (Minsk: Arti-Feks, 1999), 157. See Bovt, interview with Iryna Kashtalian, December 11, 2014; Raisa Kirillovna Semashko, interview with Iryna Kashtalian, Minsk, November 26, 2014.

50 See Epstein, *The Minsk Ghetto*; Walke, *Pioneers and Partisans*, chaps. 2 and 3.
51 For a concise summary of the events related to the persecution and extermination of Jews in Beshankovichy, see Daniel Romanovsky, "Beshankovichy," in *Encyclopedia of Camps and Ghettos, 1933–1945*, vol. 2: *Ghettos in German-Occupied Eastern Europe*, ed. Martin Dean (Bloomington: Indiana University Press, 2012), 1647–49; Anika Walke, "Split Memory: The Geography of Holocaust Memory and Amnesia in Belarus," *Slavic Review* 77, no.1 (2018): 174–97.
52 Leonid Gol'braikh, interview with the author, St. Petersburg, May 5, 2001.
53 Nina Dashkevich, interview with the author, Beshankovichy, June 6, 2016.
54 Gol'braikh, interview, May 5, 2001. For more on Leonid's experience in the partisan unit, please see Walke, *Pioneers and Partisans*, chap. 5.
55 See Walke, *Pioneers and Partisans*, 132.
56 Elizaveta Kiril'chenko, phone interview with the author, September 24, 2020.
57 Gerasimova, "Pravedniki—gordost' Belarusi," 6.
58 Al'tman, *Zhertvy Nenavisty*, 439, 440; Smilovitskii, "Kholokost i spasenie," 148; Kuzma Kozak, "Spasenie evreev kak odna iz form antigermanskogo nevooruzhennogo soprotivlenia v gody Vtoroi mirovoi voiny," in *Pravedniki Narodov Mira: Zhivye svidetel'stva Belarusi*, 47.
59 "A Meeting in Minsk: Accounts of Tamara Gershakovich, Captain Lifshitz, and Sofia Disner. Recorded by L. Katzovich," in *The Unknown Black Book: The Holocaust in the German-occupied Soviet Territories*, ed. Joshua Rubenstein and Ilya Altman (Bloomington: Indiana University Press, 2008), 260.
60 Dashkevich, interview.
61 Dashkevich, interview; Gol'braikh interview, May 11, 2005.
62 Kiril'chenko explained later that she regularly encounters cases in which scholars have conducted interviews about the Holocaust with survivors but failed to ensure that those who were central for Jewish survival were recognized by Yad Vashem (Kiril'chenko, interview). It behooves us as scholars to reflect carefully on this failure.
63 Kiril'chenko, interview.
64 The Righteous Among the Nations Database, Foma Kuyko and Yelena, Daughter, https://righteous.yadvashem.org/?search=kuyko&searchType=righteous_only&language=en&itemId=13295588&ind=0, accessed February 14, 2021.

65 Anzhela Liudino, "Chislo belorusskikh pravednikov mira popolnili zhiteli Beshenkovichiny," *Zaria*, May 20, 2019, http://www.gztzara.by/2019/05/chislo-belorusskih-pravednikov-narodov-mira-popolnili-zhiteli-beshenkovichchiny/, accessed October 5, 2020.

66 The Righteous Among the Nations Database, Anastasia Khurs, https://righteous.yadvashem.org/?search=khurs&searchType=righteous_only&language=en&itemId=4014346&ind=0, accessed October 5, 2020.

67 Maia Isakovna Levina-Krapina, *Trizhdy Rozhdennaia: Vospominania byvshei uznitsy minskogo getto* (Minsk: Isdatel' Emizer Kolas, 2008), 27–29. See also Reichelt, *Der Wald*, 111–59, which is largely based on Levina-Krapina's account.

68 Levina-Krapina, *Trizhdy Rozhdennaia*, 30–35.

69 Levina-Krapina, *Trizhdy Rozhdennaia*, 31.

70 Levina-Krapina, *Trizhdy Rozhdennaia*, 35.

71 On Khatyn, see Per Anders Rudling, "The Khatyn Massacre in Belorussia: A Historical Controversy Revisited," *Holocaust and Genocide Studies* 26, no. 1 (2012): 29–58.

72 Levina-Krapina, *Trizhdy Rozhdennaia*, 76.

73 The Righteous Among the Nations Database, Aleksey and Agrippina Shashok, https://righteous.yadvashem.org/?search=Porechye&searchType=righteous_only&language=en&itemId=12486161&ind=3, accessed October 5, 2020.

74 Levina-Krapina, *Trizhdy Rozhdennaia*, 77.

75 Levina-Krapina, *Trizhdy Rozhdennaia*, 77.

76 Levina-Krapina, *Trizhdy Rozhdennaia*, 78.

77 Levina-Krapina, *Trizhdy Rozhdennaia*, 78.

78 Gerasimova, interview.

79 Leonid Smilovitsky, "Antisemitism in the Soviet Partisan Movement, 1941–1944: The Case of Belorussia," *Holocaust and Genocide Studies* 20, no. 2 (2006): 207–34.

80 Smilovitskii, "Kholokost i spasenie," 174.

81 For details on Kiselev's rescue activity and its postwar reception, see Inna Gerasimova, *Marsh zhizni. Kak spasali dolginovskikh evreev.*

82 Smilovitsky, "Righteous Gentiles," 322.

83 The Righteous Among the Nations Database, Nikolai Kiselev, https://righteous.yadvashem.org/?search=kiselev&searchType=righteous_only&language=en&itemId=5262517&ind=1, accessed October 5, 2020.

84 Sara Bender and Pearl Weiss, eds., *The Encyclopedia of the Righteous: Europe*, part 2, li. For case studies that show the variety of rescue efforts,

see for instance, O. M. Arkad'eva et al., . . . *Na perekrestkakh sudeb*; Smilovitskii, "Kholokost i spasenie"; Kozak, "Spasenie evreev," 28–48.

85 Smilovitskii, "Kholokost i spasenie," 144; Kozak, "Spasenie evreev," 28; Evgenii Rozenblat, "Spasenie evreev Belarusi v gody Kholokosta: nekotorye teoreticheskie aspekty temy," in *Pravedniki Narodov Mira: Zhivye svidetel'stva Belarusi*, 67.

86 Kozak, "Spasenie evreev," 17, 27; see also "Belorusskie Pravedniki narodov mira: nezametnyi podvig 'malen'kogo cheloveka,'" DW.com, May 9, 2011, https://www.dw.com/ru/белорусские-праведники-народов-мира-незаметный-подвиг-маленького-человека/a-15063075, accessed February 14, 2021.

87 Smilovitsky, "Righteous Gentiles," 322.

88 Tatiana Gaiduk, "Memorializatsia Kholokosta v Belarusi," http://gwminsk.com/contributions/articles/memorializaciya-holokosta-v-belarusi, accessed March 18, 2021. See also Inna Gerasimova, email to the author, March 11, 2021.

89 Smilovitsky, "Righteous Gentiles," 323. More on Proniagin's deeds and postwar life can be found in Ella Maksimova, "Zhil li pravednik po pravde," *Izvestia*, no. 39, March 1, 1995, available at *Biblioteka Istoki*, https://sources.ruzhany.info/083.html, accessed October 12, 2020.

90 "Ot sostavitelei," in *Pravedniki Narodov Mira Belarusi*, ed. I. N. Gerasimova et al., 5; Levina-Krapina, *Trizhdy Rozhdennaia*, 69.

91 Gerasimova, interview.

92 Inna Gerasimova, email to the author, March 11, 2021.

93 Gaiduk, "Memorializatsia;" Inna Gerasimova, email to the author, March 11, 2021. For an image of the Bobruisk memorial, see https://wiki.bobr.by/Аллея_Праведников, accessed March 30, 2023.

94 Inna Gerasimova, email to the author, March 11, 2021.

95 Inna Gerasimova, "O pamiatnikakh," unpublished manuscript, 2010.

96 See Yad Vashem's explanation of the process establishing the eligibility of helpers for receiving the title of the Righteous Among the Nations at https://www.yadvashem.org/righteous/faq.html, which seemed to have determined the outcome of Gerasimova and Kiril'chenko's efforts.

97 This statistical snapshot is based on the author's analysis of Yad Vashem's statistics available at https://www.yadvashem.org/righteous/statistics.html, accessed October 24, 2023. See also data available in I. G. Gerasimova et al., eds., *Pravedniki Narodov Mira Belarusi*. This cursory account is of necessity incomplete and likely inaccurate since both sources draw on differing transliteration tables and it is next to

impossible to compare accurately. Despite inaccuracies in the details, I am confident that the larger picture is reliable.

98 "Zvanie 'Pravednikov narodov mira' prisvoeno uzhe 808 urozhentsam Belarusi," Naviny.BY, 4.5.2016, https://naviny.by/rubrics/society/2016/05/04/ic_news_116_474536, accessed October 5, 2020.

99 Gerasimova, interview.

100 See Elisabeth Wassermann, "The Polish Discourse about the Righteous Among the Nations: Between Commemoration, Education and Justification?" *Politeja* 52, no. 1 (2018): 125–44.

101 "Medali 'Pravednik narodov mira' vrucheny belorusskim grazhdanan, spasavshim evreev v gody Vtoroi Mirovoi Voiny," BelaPAN, April 16, 2015, https://belapan.by/archive/2015/04/16/media_pravedniki/, accessed October 12, 2020.

102 Tatiana Kuznechenkova, "V Grodno vruchili sertifikat i imennuiu medal 'Pravednik narodov mira' i vspomnili sobytia Kholokosta," *Zara nad Nёmanam*, November 22, 2016, http://www.mosty-zara.by/ru/news/v-grodno-vruchili-sertifikat-i-imennuyu-medal-pravednik-narodov-mira-i-vspomnili-sobytiya-holokosta.html, accessed October 12, 2020.

103 "V Muzee istorii goroda Minska otkrylas' unikal'naia fotovystavka," OON Belarus, January 28, 2013, https://un.by/novosti-oon/v-belarusi/371-ru-2f6e039d8e034, accessed October 12, 2020; "V Minske prezentovali vtoroe izdanie knigi 'Pravedniki narodov mira Belarusi,'" Belarus.by, May 19, 2015, https://www.belarus.by/ru/press-center/70th-anniversary-of-the-great-victory/v-minske-prezentovali-vtoroe-izdanie-knigi-pravedniki-narodov-mira-belarusi_i_23296.html, accessed October 12, 2020.

104 Kiril'chenko, interview. See also Ksenia Domashevich, "Tsilia i Masha. Kak zhivut devochki, 'rasstreliannye' 76 let nazad," Imena, April 30, 2017, https://imenamag.by/posts/uchitelnica-i-holocost, accessed February 14, 2021.

105 Arkhiv svidetelei Minskoi istoricheskoi masterskoi—Pravedniki narodov mira, http://zeitzeugenarchiv.gwminsk.com/archiv/gerechte, accessed October 12, 2020.

106 An initial version of the museum was opened in 1944, consisting primarily of artifacts and documentation of the local partisan movement.

107 Arkadi Zeltser, *Unwelcome Memory: Holocaust Monuments in the Soviet Union* (Jerusalem: Yad Vashem, 2018).

108 See Magdalena Waligórska, "Remembering the Holocaust on the Fault Lines of East and West-European Memorial Cultures: The New Memorial

Complex in Trastsianets, Belarus," *Holocaust Studies: A Journal of Culture and History* 24, no. 3 (2018): 3.

109 "'Propaganda perestupaet granitsy prilichia.' Kak rezhim ispol'zuet temu Kholokosta v bor'be s protestuiushchimi. Interviu s Aleksandrom Fridmanom," BELSAT.TV, March 5, 2021, https://belsat.eu/ru/news/05-03-2021-propaganda-perestupaet-granitsy-prilichiya-kak-rezhim-ispolzuet-temu-holokosta-v-borbe-s-protestuyushhimi/, accessed June 20, 2022.

110 "Lukashenko podpisal zakon o genotside belorusskogo naroda v gody Vekikoi Otechestvennoi voiny," BELTA, January 5, 2022, https://www.belta.by/president/view/lukashenko-podpisal-zakon-o-genotside-belorusskogo-naroda-v-gody-velikoj-otechestvennoj-vojny-478199-2022/, accessed October 3, 2022. See also Felix Ackermann, "'Der Genozid am Belarusischen Volk' als politischer Diskurs und Strafverfolgungspraxis," *Belarus-Analysen* no. 56 (2022), https://www.laender-analysen.de/belarus-analysen/56/der-genozid-am-belarusischen-volk-als-politischer-diskurs-und-strafverfolgungspraxis/, accessed October 3, 2022.

Bibliography

Ackermann, Felix. "'Der Genozid am Belarusischen Volk' als politischer Diskurs und Strafverfolgungspraxis." (The "Genocide of the Belarusian people" as political discourse and practice of criminal prosecution.) *Belarus-Analysen* 56 (2022), https://www.laender-analysen.de/belarus-analysen/56/der-genozid-am-belarusischen-volk-als-politischer-diskurs-und-strafverfolgungspraxis/, accessed October 3, 2022.

Al'tman, Il'ia. *Zhertvy Nenavisty: Kholokost v SSSR, 1941–1945gg.* (Victims of hate: The Holocaust in the USSR, 1941–1945.) Moscow: Kovcheg, 2002.

Arkad'eva, Ol'ga M., L. L. Geller-Martynova, T. S. Kurdadze, and D. I. Rusakovskaia, eds. . . . *Na perekrestkakh sudeb: Iz vospominanii byvshikh uznikov getto i pravednikov mira.* (. . . At the crossroads of fate: Memories of former ghetto prisoners and Righteous Among the Nations.) Minsk: Chetyrie Chetverty, 2001.

Bender, Sara, and Pearl Weiss, eds. *The Encyclopedia of the Righteous Among the Nations: Rescuers of Jews during the Holocaust: Europe*, part 2. Jerusalem: Yad Vashem, 2011.

Browning, Christopher. "Introduction." In *Encyclopedia of Camps and Ghettos, 1933–1945*, vol. 2: *Ghettos in German-Occupied Eastern Europe*, ed. Martin Dean, xxvii–xxxix. Bloomington: Indiana University Press, 2012.

Chiari, Bernhard. *Alltag hinter der Front: Besatzung, Kollaboration und Widerstand in Weißrussland 1941–1944.* (Everyday life in the rear: Occupation, collaboration, and resistance in Belarus, 1941–1944.) Düsseldorf: Droste, 1998.

Dean, Martin, ed. *Encyclopedia of Camps and Ghettos, 1933–1945*, vol. 2: *Ghettos in German-Occupied Eastern Europe.* Bloomington: Indiana University Press, 2012.

Domashevich, Ksenia. "Tsilia i Masha. Kak zhivut devochki, 'rasstreliannye' 76 let nazad." (Tsilia and Masha: The current life of girls who "were shot" 76 years ago.) *Imena*, April 30, 2017. https://imenamag.by/posts/uchitelnica-i-holocost, accessed February 14, 2021.

Epstein, Barbara. *The Minsk Ghetto 1941–1943: Jewish Resistance and Soviet Internationalism.* Berkeley: University of California Press, 2008.

Gaiduk, Tatiana. "Memorializatsia Kholokosta v Belarusi." (The memorialization of the Holocaust in Belarus.) *Istoricheskaia Masterskaia im. "Leonid Levina."* N.d. http://gwminsk.com/contributions/articles/memorializaciya-holokosta-v-belarusi, accessed March 18, 2021.

Gerasimova, Inna. *Marsh zhizni. Kak spasali dolginovskikh evreev.* (March of life: How the Jews of Dolginov were rescued.) Moscow: AST, 2016.

———. "O pamiatnikakh." (On memorials.) Unpublished manuscript, 2010.

———. "Pravedniki—gordost' Belarusi." (The Righteous Among the Nations: The pride of Belarus.) In *Pravedniki Narodov Mira Belarusi*, ed. Inna Gerasimova, E. M. Kiril'chenko, M. A. Movzon, and A. L. Shul'man, 6–7. Minsk: Medizont, 2015.

Gerasimova, Inna P., E. M. Kiril'chenko, M. A. Movzon, and A. L. Shul'man, eds. *Pravedniki Narodov Mira Belarusi.* (The Righteous Among the Nations of Belarus.) Minsk: Medizont, 2015.

Gerasimova, Inna P., and A. L. Shul'man, eds. *Pravedniki Narodov Mira Belarusi.* (The Righteous Among the Nations of Belarus.) Minsk: OGOD Tonpik, 2004.

Gerlach, Christian. *Kalkulierte Morde: Die deutsche Wirtschafts- und Vernichtungspolitik in Weißrussland, 1941–1944.* (Calculated murders: German economic politics and the politics of extermination in Belarus, 1941–1944.) Hamburg: Hamburger Edition, 1999.

Ioffe, Emanuil G. "Belorusskie Evrei v Bor'be s Natsizmom v 1941–1945gg." (Belarusian Jews struggling against the Nazi regime, 1941–1945.) *Zhurnal rossiiskikh i vostochnoevropeiskikh istoricheskikh issledovanii* 11, no. 4 (2017): 69–104.

Kozak, Kuzma. "Spasenie evreev kak odna iz form antigermanskogo nevooruzhennogo soprotivlenia v gody Vtoroi mirovoi voiny." (The rescue of Jews as a form of unarmed resistance against the Germans during World

War II.) In *Pravedniki Narodov Mira: Zhivye svidetel'stva Belarusi*, ed. Kuzma Kozak et al., 13–54. Minsk: Logvinov, 2009.

Kozak, Kuzma I., M. I. Krapina, I. S. Prostak, R. K. Semashko, and Minskii mezhdunarodnyi obrazovatel'nyi tsentr imeni Iokhannesa Rau/Dortmundskii mezhdunarodnyi obrazovatel'nyi tsentr, eds. *Pravedniki Narodov Mira: Zhivye svidetel'stva Belarusi. Sbornik dokumentov, materialov i statei.* (The Righteous Among the Nations: Belarusian living witnesses. A collection.) Minsk: Logvinov, 2009.

Kuznechenkova, Tatiana. "V Grodno vruchili sertifikat i imennuiu medal 'Pravednik narodov mira' i vspomnili sobytia Kholokosta." (Awarding the certificate and medal "Righteous Among the Nations" and remembering the Holocaust in Grodno.) *Zara nad Nëmanam*, November 22, 2016. http://www.mosty-zara.by/ru/news/v-grodno-vruchili-sertifikat-i-imennuyu-medal-pravednik-narodov-mira-i-vspomnili-sobytiya-holokosta.html, accessed October 12, 2020.

Levina-Krapina, Maia Isakovna. *Trizhdy Rozhdennaia: Vospominania byvshei uznitsy minskogo getto*. (Born three times: The memories of a former female prisoner of the Minsk Ghetto.) Minsk: Isdatel' Emizer Kolas, 2008.

Liudino, Anzhela. "Chislo belorusskikh pravednikov mira popolnili zhiteli Beshenkovichiny." (Residents of Beshankovichy join the ranks of the Righteous Among the Nations.) *Zaria*, May 20, 2019. http://www.gztzara.by/2019/05/chislo-belorusskih-pravednikov-narodov-mira-popolnili-zhiteli-beshenkovichchiny/, accessed October 5, 2020.

"Lukashenko podpisal zakon o genotside belorusskogo naroda v gody Vekikoi Otechestvennoi voiny." (Lukashenko signs law on the genocide of the Belarusian people during World War II.) BELTA, January 5, 2022, https://www.belta.by/president/view/lukashenko-podpisal-zakon-o-genotside-belorusskogo-naroda-v-gody-velikoj-otechestvennoj-vojny-478199-2022/, accessed October 3, 2022.

Maksimova, Ella. "Zhil li pravednik po pravde." (Did the Righteous Among the Nations live truthfully?) *Izvestia*, March 1, 1995, no. 39, *Biblioteka Istoki*, https://sources.ruzhany.info/083.html, accessed October 12, 2020.

"Medali 'Pravednik narodov mira' vrucheny belorusskim grazhdanan, spasavshim evreev v gody Vtoroi Mirovoi Voiny." (Medal "Righteous Among the Nations" awarded to Belarusians who saved Jews during World War II) BelaPAN, April 16, 2015, https://belapan.by/archive/2015/04/16/media_pravedniki/, accessed October 12, 2020.

"Ob uchastii Posla Belarusi v Izraile E. Vorob'eva v tseremonii vruchenia medali i gramoty Pravednikov narodov mira." (Belarusian ambassador to Israel, E. Vorobev, participates in award ceremony for Righteous Among the Nations.)

Ministerstvo inostrannykh del Respubliki Belarus. May 25, 2022. https://mfa.gov.by/press/news_mfa/c09e1d0eb56ceb10.html, accessed October 3, 2022.

"'Propaganda perestupaet granitsy prilichia.' Kak rezhim ispol'zuet temu Kholokosta v bor'be s protestuiushchimi. Interviu s Aleksandrom Fridmanom." ("The propaganda crosses the lines of decency:" How the regime instrumentalizes the Holocaust in the fight against protesters. An interview with Alexander Friedman.) BELSAT.TV March 52021, https://belsat.eu/ru/news/05-03-2021-propaganda-perestupaet-granitsy-prilichiya-kak-rezhim-ispolzuet-temu-holokosta-v-borbe-s-protestuyushhimi/, accessed June 20, 2022.

Ptitsina, Polina. "Belorusskie Pravedniki narodov mira: nezametnyi podvig 'malen'kogo cheloveka.'" (Belarusian Righteous Among the Nations: The invisible deeds of ordinary people.) DW.com, May 9, 2011, https://www.dw.com/ru/белорусские-праведники-народов-мира-незаметный-подвиг-маленького-человека/a-15063075, accessed February 14, 2021.

Reichelt, Katrin. *Der Wald war ein letzter Ausweg: Hilfe für verfolgte Juden im deutsch besetzten Weißrussland 1941–1944.* (The forest was the last way out: Help for persecuted Jews in German-occupied Belarus, 1941–1944.) Berlin: Lukas Verlag, 2017.

Rein, Leonid. *The Kings and the Pawns: Collaboration in Byelorussia during World War II.* New York: Berghahn, 2011.

Romanovsky, Daniel. "Beshankovichy." In *Encyclopedia of Camps and Ghettos, 1933–1945*, vol. 2: *Ghettos in German-Occupied Eastern Europe*, ed. Martin Dean, 1647–1649. Bloomington: Indiana University Press, 2012.

Rozenblat, Evgenii. "Spasenie evreev Belarusi v gody Kholokosta: nekotorye teoreticheskie aspekty temy." (The rescue of Belarusian Jews during the Holocaust: Some theoretical considerations.) In *Pravedniki Narodov Mira: Zhivye svidetel'stva Belarusi*, ed. Kuzma Kozak et al., 55–67. Minsk: Logvinov, 2009.

Rubenstein, Joshua, and Ilya Altman, eds. *The Unknown Black Book: The Holocaust in the German-occupied Soviet Territories*. Bloomington: Indiana University Press, 2008.

Rudling, Per Anders. "The Khatyn Massacre in Belorussia: A Historical Controversy Revisited." *Holocaust and Genocide Studies* 26, no. 1 (2012): 29–58.

Smilovitskii, Leonid. "Antisemitism in the Soviet Partisan Movement, 1941–1944: The Case of Belorussia." *Holocaust and Genocide Studies* 20, no. 2 (2006): 207–34.

———. "Bor'ba evreev Belorussii za vosvrat svoego imushchestvo i zhilishch' v pervoe poslevoennoe desiatiletie, 1944–1954gg." (Belarusian Jews' fight for the return of their property and homes during the first postwar decade,

1944–1954.) In *Belarus V XX Stagoddzi*, ed. V. I. Andreev, 168–78. Minsk: Vodolei, 2002.

———. "Kholokost i spasenie evreev v Belarusi." (The Holocaust and the rescue of Jews in Belarus.) In *Evrei Belarusi: iz nashei obshchei istorii, 1905–1953gg.* (The Jews of Belarus: Our common history, 1905–1953), 128–77. Minsk: Arti-Feks, 1999.

Smilovitsky, Leonid. *Jewish Life in Belarus: The Final Decade of the Stalin Regime, 1944–1953*. New York: Central European University Press, 2014.

———. "Righteous Gentiles, the Partisans, and Jewish Survival in Belorussia, 1941–1944." *Holocaust and Genocide Studies* 11, no. 3 (1997): 301–29.

Speckhard, Anne. "Minsk." In *Encyclopedia of Camps and Ghettos, 1933–1945*, vol. 2: *Ghettos in German-Occupied Eastern Europe*, ed. Martin Dean, 1233–37. Bloomington: Indiana University Press, 2012.

"V Minske prezentovali vtoroe izdanie knigi 'Pravedniki narodov mira Belarusi.'" (Second edition of the book "Righteous Among the Nations of Belarus" launched in Minsk.) Belarus.by, May 19, 2015, https://www.belarus.by/ru/press-center/70th-anniversary-of-the-great-victory/v-minske-prezentovali-vtoroe-izdanie-knigi-pravedniki-narodov-mira-belarusi_i_23296.html, accessed October 12, 2020.

"V Muzee istorii goroda Minska otkrylas' unikal'naia fotovystavka." (Unique photo exhibition opens in the Museum of the History of the City of Minsk.) OON Belarus, January 28, 2013, https://un.by/novosti-oon/v-belarusi/371-ru-2f6e039d8e034, accessed October 12, 2020.

Waligórska, Magdalena. "Remembering the Holocaust on the Fault Lines of East and West-European Memorial Cultures: The New Memorial Complex in Trastsianets, Belarus." *Holocaust Studies: A Journal of Culture and History* 24, no. 3 (2018): 329–53.

Walke, Anika. *Pioneers and Partisans: An Oral History of Nazi Genocide in Belorussia*. New York: Oxford University Press, 2015.

———. "Split Memory: The Geography of Holocaust Memory and Amnesia in Belarus." *Slavic Review* 77, no.1 (2018): 174–97.

Wassermann, Elisabeth. "The Polish Discourse about the Righteous Among the Nations: Between Commemoration, Education and Justification?" *Politeja* 52, no. 1 (2018): 125–44.

Zeltser, Arkadi. *Unwelcome Memory: Holocaust Monuments in the Soviet Union*. Jerusalem: Yad Vashem, 2018.

"Zvanie 'Pravednikov narodov mira' prisvoeno uzhe 808 urozhentsam Belarusi." (808 natives of Belarus have been named Righteous Among the Nations already.) Naviny.by, May 4, 2016, https://naviny.by/rubrics/society/2016/05/04/ic_news_116_474536, accessed October 5, 2020.

Interviews

Bovt, Ivan Ivanovich. Interview with Iryna Kashtalian. Minsk, December 11, 2014.

Dashkevich, Nina. Interview with the author. Beshankovichy, June 6, 2016.

Gerasimova, Inna. Phone interview with the author. Wiesbaden/St. Louis, September 23, 2020.

Glazebnaia, Olga, and Svetlana Nikolaichik. Interview with Iryna Kashtalian. Minsk, October 13, 2014.

Gol'braikh, Leonid. Interview with the author. St. Petersburg, May 5, 2001.

Gol'braikh, Leonid. Interview with the author, St. Petersburg, May 11, 2005.

Kiril'chenko, Elizaveta. Phone interview with author. Minsk/St. Louis, September 24, 2020.

Osipova, Tamara Iakovlevna. Interview with Iryna Kashtalian. Minsk, November 3, 2014.

Polikarpovich, Tatiana. Interview with Iryna Kashtalian. Minsk, n.d.

Semashko, Raisa Kirillovna. Interview with Iryna Kashtalian. Minsk, November 26, 2014.

Tsukerman, Liubov' Efimovna. Interview with Iryna Kashtalian. Minsk, November 2011.

Zelenko, Roza, and Olga Glazebnaia. Interview with the author. Minsk, October 11, 2002.

Archival Sources

Yad Vashem Archives, RG M. 31—Files of the Department for the Righteous Among the Nations.

Web Sources

Alleia Pravednikov. https://wiki.bobr.by/Аллея_Праведников.

Archive of Witnesses of the History Workshop Minsk. (Arkhiv svidetelei Minskoi istoricheskoi masterskoi—Pravedniki narodov mira.) http://zeitzeugenarchiv.gwminsk.com/ru/archiv/gerechte.

The History Workshop "Leonid Levin." (Istoricheskaia Masterskaia im. "Leonida Levina.") http://gwminsk.com.

Museum of the History and Culture of the Jews of Belarus. (Muzei Istorii i Kultury Evreev Belarusi.) https://www.jewishmuseum.by.
Partisans of Belarus. (Partizany Belarusi.) https://partizany.by.
The Righteous Among the Nations: Names of Righteous by Country. https://www.yadvashem.org/righteous/statistics.html.
The Righteous Among the Nations Database. https://righteous.yadvashem.org.

PART III

Individual Memory—Public Remembrance

8

Commemorating and Remembering Jewish Rescue in Greece

ANNA MARIA DROUMPOUKI

One may say that the individual remembers by placing himself in the perspective of the group, but one may also affirm that the memory of the group realizes and manifests itself in individual memories.

—Maurice Halbwachs, *On Collective Memory*

The Jewish presence in Greece has been longstanding and, until the Holocaust, diverse, reflecting the different cultural backgrounds of Jews settling in the area. Small communities of Romaniote Jews, who mainly settled in central Greece and the Ionian islands, were among the first Jews to put down roots in Europe, arriving prior to the Byzantine period. Sephardic Jews came later, having been expelled from Spain in 1492, and they settled in great numbers in the city of Thessaloniki, forming a distinctive group that became predominant both numerically and culturally among the Jewish inhabitants of the Ottoman Empire.[1] The example of the city of Thessaloniki is representative: Thessaloniki was the capital of Sephardic Judaism for more than four centuries.[2] However, the creation of a modern Greek nation-state in the nineteenth century created a different kind of challenge.[3]

Greek Jews lived, and continue to live, in an ethnically, religiously, and linguistically homogenous society. Religion in particular has played a crucial role in the formation of modern Greek national identity. To be considered Greek, one had to be born in Greece or be of Greek ancestry, speak Greek, and be an Orthodox Christian.[4] This ethnic focus highlights the difficulties inherent in being Jewish in a nation-state. In addition, during the nineteenth century, the concept of the "Jewish Other" was developed within the Greek Orthodox clergy to stand for the notion of the "national enemy."[5] In modern Greece, had Jews been recognized within the Greek national consciousness, they might have been given the freedom and opportunity to affirm their Greek identity.[6] This traditionally problematic situation of the Jewish communities in Greece had consequences during World War II, when the German occupying authorities set the Holocaust in motion.

The Holocaust in Greece claimed a heavy toll on the Jewish population—about 84 percent of Greek Jews were killed, one of the highest annihilation rates in Nazi Europe—and witnessed both the destruction of entire communities and remarkable survival statistics on a local scale. By far the largest Jewish community was in Thessaloniki, with about seventy thousand Jewish inhabitants before World War II. Twenty-four Jewish communities remained after the war, yet in eleven communities, 90 percent or more of the population was lost, while six communities still had more than 50 percent of their former Jewish population.[7] Such discrepancies are discussed extensively in recent historiography, forming an ever-expanding field that is fueled by competing memory discourses, political debates, and interdisciplinary methodology, and only in recent years has the dissemination of evidence and particularly survivors' testimonies, accompanied by a proliferation of educational initiatives and commemorative practices, provided new perspectives on the history of the catastrophe of Greek Jews.[8]

This essay will not examine the phenomenon of rescue by the resistance, the church, or individuals, as most cases have been extensively recorded. In the Yad Vashem Righteous Among the Nations digital database, which is organized by country, the stories of some 328 Righteous in Greece have been recorded to date.[9] Instead, I seek to understand the different ways Jews experienced rescue, and to identify those influences that shaped the rescue narratives, by examining the parallel and contradictory points in the official Greek and collective Jewish memories. Following what has been characterized as the "coming out" of Jewish history in Greece,[10] a number of new academic monographs, edited volumes, and scholarly articles have been devoted to studying the Greek Jewish experience during the Holocaust and its aftermath. These publications have explored sensitive, previously underexplored subjects, such as local collaboration, appropriation of Jewish property, and the destruction of Jewish cultural and religious heritage by local actors. Together, these and other topics have generated innovative approaches, opening new avenues for future research. Nevertheless, current research exploring the memory and postmemory of the rescue of Jews has remained framed largely by Greek national narratives. Indeed, the Greek Jewish experience of rescue has not yet been a focus of academic research. This chapter seeks to fill this gap.

The aim of this essay is therefore twofold. On the one hand, I argue that this sudden rise in interest in the Greek Righteous Among the Nations constitutes an official policy with the explicit purpose of promoting an official narrative of tolerance and the peaceful coexistence of Jews and non-Jews in the overall context of contemporary discourse on the theme of Jewish rescue. As such, it can be perceived as a diplomatic tool used by governmental institutions, especially the Greek ministry of foreign affairs. These national "agents of memory" emphasize collective action and solidarity, often blurring the specifics of particular rescue actions. By emphasizing specific aspects of the past over others, or enhancing them to stress the narrative of Greek solidarity, they foster an inherently unbalanced "selective remembrance." On the other hand, I map out the main features of the ways the Righteous are remembered by survivors and their descendants. By examining sixteen oral history testimonies of Holocaust survivors held at the Visual History Archive (VHA) of the USC Shoah Foundation Collection and the Oral History Project "Memories of the Occupation in Greece" of the Free University of Berlin, I explore how these individual accounts are connected to collective representations and vice versa.[11] I argue that the perception of rescue has become enhanced through the personal beliefs and experiences of those survivors who construct our understanding of the events. I also identify rescue as a formative component of Greek Jewishness in the postwar period. The purpose of this text is to depict rescue not as a common story but as a common field of symbolic activity, borrowing Andrew Buckser's expression,[12] and a common field of individual constructions of the past and of one's Jewish identity.

For Greek Jews the issue of rescue assumes a major significance as their social and cultural assimilation has always been contested on the legal basis, as exemplified by passage of the 1949 law that permitted immigration to Israel only under the condition of renouncing one's Greek citizenship. The perception that Greek Jews are different and separate from the rest of the population is not confined to the average citizen even today, especially among the local population in outlying provinces. This is a normative part of a Greek Orthodox society that identifies Jews as strangers who do not belong to the national family or to the religious patterns of the majority group. Therefore, rescue stories serve the need for self-assurance and reflect the uneasy feeling among the Jews living in a country that bears all the marks of a state religion.

Among those Jews interviewed by British anthropologist Bea Lewkowicz during her 1990s study of the Jewish experience in Thessaloniki, none sought to blame the Greek people for the advent, or extent, of the Holocaust in Greece. This was the result, perhaps, of the need to highlight the relationships between Greeks and Jews living together in Greece like "brothers and sisters."[13] Indeed, I would argue similarly that feelings of insecurity among Greek Jews stem from a perceived exclusion from the Greek "ethnos" (nation) I outlined earlier. Their narratives reflect a defining myth produced mostly by the national agents of memory. Therefore, the official commemorative agenda, constructed by the Greek state and followed by the Jewish communities and their official representatives, is inherently unbalanced and—in emphasizing specific aspects of the past over others, or enhancing them to stress the narrative of Greek solidarity—results in a "selective remembrance."[14] The state initiatives played a major role in the creation of a commemorative mechanism that exists until today. The timing of this morality narrative can be traced back to 2016, with the first official ceremonies organized by the state and the Central Board of Jewish Communities in Greece serving as the catalysts, and it continues until today.

Thus this chapter also seeks to rethink the way memory and history are intertwined by focusing on the very processes and the numerous complex historical, political, and aesthetic axes on which memory of Jewish rescue is constructed. Post-1945 Greece was built on policies of oblivion and unification. As everywhere in postwar Europe, the nation emphasized victories, heroes and heroic events, resistance, endurance, and national values to sustain its continuity in the highly antagonistic Cold War environment. The questions I seek to answer are related to the multidimensional entanglement of history and memory and the ways of signification, resignification, and rhetorical transformations of rescue, focusing on the policies of managing the memory of the Holocaust in Greece.

The "Morality Narrative" in Greece

The topic of Jewish rescue was largely ignored in Greece prior to 2016. The topic gathered momentum as of 2016, when forms of official memorialization and commemoration began. In spite of the official commemorations and the existence of many individual stories and histories, there is no larger overview or study of the topic in Greece. There remains only a single published academic work on the subject, released in 2012,[15] a far cry from the relatively large corpus of material available in other European countries.[16] The story of Jewish rescue is, fundamentally, one concerned with the issue of Jewish hiding places during the German occupation of Greece, a topic that has not yet been granted a separate treatment in Greek historiography and literature and which remains somehow outside the scope of the interest of researchers, despite the fact that it is an important and common experience of the Shoah. We know little about Jewish hiding places from the time of the occupation—the places that became a space for the salvation of hundreds of people. The topics of rescue and hiding were, and remain, absent, as the escapees were stigmatized as undignified and treacherous relative to those who remained in the ghettos and camps.[17] Hidden Jews experienced a degree of "displaced" guilt because of the processes of adaptation and compliance they underwent to subsist.[18]

The year 2016 proved decisive in the creation of an "official" memory of Jewish rescue in Greece. In January 2016 the prefecture of Athens and the Jewish community of Athens organized a series of events to commemorate International Holocaust Remembrance Day. The main theme of the 2016 events was the Righteous Among the Nations, a topic that had not been broached before. On Wednesday, January 27, 2016, a memorial to the 328 Greek Orthodox Righteous, financed by the Jewish community of Athens, was unveiled in the courtyard of Athens's Beth Shalom Synagogue. The monument was inaugurated by the president of the Hellenic Republic, Prokopis Pavlopoulos, in the presence of a handful of Greek Righteous and Holocaust survivors, and a far larger number of their descendants. The design of the monument is well within the established symbolic canon of such monuments: It shows a book, the cover of which is decorated with the image of a tree—a Jewish symbol of life; its metal pages are engraved with the names of the 328 Greek Righteous Among the Nations, and its base bears the inscription: "He who saves one life, saves the whole world." In the course of the ceremony, both the president of the Jewish community of Athens, Minos Moissis, and the president of the Central Board of the Jewish Communities in Greece, Moissis Konstantinis, paid tribute to "these heroes." Minos Moissis highlighted the significance of the monument's location on Melidoni Street: "the very heart of the Jewish neighborhood of Athens [where], in March 1944, the Jews who were not lucky enough to be protected by such people as the Righteous, were arrested, loaded onto trucks bound for the Chaidari Camp and, from there, onto trains headed for the concentration camps."[19] In his speech Moissis juxtaposed fear and persecution with the contrasting qualities of solidarity and heroism that had been displayed by those "who selflessly saved many Jews by risking their life and the lives of their families." Moreover, Moissis stressed the "true Greekness" of Greek Jews by emphasizing their long presence in Greece.[20] Konstantinis's speech propounded the same narrative: "Those who managed to escape deportation during the persecution experienced the full scope of human nature: indifference, treachery, enmity, self-interest and profiteering, but also their opposites, self-sacrifice, heroism, solidarity, support. . . . The first were the rule, the second the exception. . . . Our saviors were our only hope, the light amidst the darkness."

The commemoration of the Righteous by the Greek Jewish community shows us that the Jews and the institutions representing them comply, at least to some extent, with the aspects of the official commemoration and the proposed narrative of the ministry of foreign affairs. This particular commemorative theme celebrates singular acts of bravery and heroism, and the emphasis is on the exemplary significance of people's actions. It is important to point out that this is a monument to those who rescued Jews—it does not commemorate Jewish survivors. In fact, there is only one such monument in Greece: a wall at the Jewish Museum of Thessaloniki which bears the names of the city's survivors (and contains a number of mistakes).[21] January 2016 was also significant because it was then that the Greek parliament honored International Holocaust Remembrance Day for the first time by devoting a special parliamentary session to the issue, with emphasis on the Greek Righteous. The speaker and minister of education addressed the plenary of the parliament on the Holocaust and the need to remember. On the same day, following a decree of the ministry of education, a two-hour session on the Holocaust was made mandatory in every Greek school, also something that had never taken place before in Greece.[22]

As laid out earlier, since 2016 Greece has witnessed a proliferation of initiatives organized by the state and the Israeli embassy in Athens. The number of such initiatives is difficult to assess, but it is definitely on the rise. Greece's "discovery" of rescuers is also a part of its building new diplomatic relations with Israel, as over the last years Greece has become a close ally. The two countries have established a fully fledged alliance in which they conduct joint military exercises and coordinate on security operations in the eastern Mediterranean.[23] Thus the Israeli embassy plays a pivotal role in most of the ceremonies honoring the rescuers. Some examples include the May 2017 ceremony at the residence of the Israeli ambassador to Greece, where Katina and Ioannis Perakis were posthumously recognized as Righteous Among the Nations for their efforts in sheltering the ten-year-old Moise Battino at their home in Piraeus between August 1943 and October 1944.[24] On November 14, 2018, Nikolaos Athanasoulis and Athanasios Dimopoulos were awarded the title of "Greek Righteous" for rescuing Abraham Camhis's family during the Holocaust. The award ceremony took place at the Kryoneri Multinational Center in Corinth, in the presence of the president of the Kryoneri Community of Corinth and the Israeli ambassador to Greece. Celebrations of Jewish rescue serve both as a form of family reunion and as a homecoming that entails the recognition of and identification with one's roots, in this case the families of Jewish survivors and the families of the rescuers. Relatives of Camhis's family traveled from Israel to Kryoneri to attend the event, and the ceremony was attended by many members of the Athanasouli and Dimopoulos families. An Israeli air force plane flew over Kryoneri to honor the occasion.[25]

Pupils from primary and secondary schools are also involved in these projects. One such example is the initiative of Elefsina Secondary School, which with the participation of the ministry of education, and, once again, the Israeli embassy, hosted an event on May 2018 in honor of George, Chariklia, and Vasilis Dararas, who saved Victor Levy and his son, Sam.[26] Again in 2018, on January 18, a ceremony took place in the theater of the Lauder Jewish Community School of Athens. The students worked diligently with their teachers to prepare the story of the Assimakopoulos family, who saved Delia Ferro during the German occupation. Dignitaries among the guests were the attaché of the German embassy in Athens, representatives from the Israeli embassy in Athens, the commander of the Psichiko police force, representatives from the central Jewish board, as well as the chief rabbi of Athens.[27] The most recent school ceremony was held in the Athens College Theater on Monday, February 11, 2019, honoring the father of one the most distinguished politicians of recent times, Tasos Giannitsis. The occasion recognized Constantine Giannitsis's pivotal role in saving the lives of members of the Asher Raphael Moissis family during the Holocaust. The event was co-organized by Athens College, the ministry of education, research, and religious affairs, and the Israeli embassy. The honor was accepted on behalf of the late Constantine Giannitsis by his children: his son, former minister Tasos Giannitsis, and his daughter, Eleni Kappetou. Welcome speeches were given by the then minister of education, research, and religious affairs, Kostas Gavroglou; the Israeli ambassador to Greece, Irit Ben-Abba; and the president of the Central Board of Jewish Communities in Greece, David Saltiel. The ceremony was attended by former prime ministers, MPs, mayors, the governor of the Bank of Greece, the US ambassador to Greece, as well as members of the church, the armed forces, and the business community.[28]

Though at present we cannot evaluate the extent to which these projects have influenced the historical consciousness of the young pupils, the very fact that schools participate in these events represents a positive development in a country where Holocaust education in schools hasn't yet found its place in the curricula. In the speeches delivered during all these ceremonies, the "Righteous" have been framed as offering lessons to both young and old that the fight against discrimination and prejudice is a conscientious choice, an individual and societal imperative.[29]

This broad, public support for such commemorations since 2016 lies in the reaffirmation of the rescuers' deeds as honorable and heroic aspects of Greek wartime history, creating a morality narrative that emphasizes the "heroic acts of Greeks" during the German occupation. Borrowing Joanna Beata Michlic's argument about the Polish case, we see that the subject of rescuers is usually brought up not for its intrinsic intellectual and moral merits but predominantly to defend the good name of Greeks.[30] This boom in interest finds expression in the old pattern of thinking about and manipulating rescuers for particular political, social, and moral aims. The topic has attracted the attention of the general public, appealing to those interested in popular depictions in both print and digital media that promote an uncomplicated, linear narrative of bravery. Such treatments provide relatively unproblematic access points to the Holocaust of Greek Jews. Television documentaries such as *Life Will Smile* by Steven Priovolos (2019), a history of three hundred Jews who evaded the Nazis on the Greek island of Zakynthos, perpetuate the narrative of Greeks' purported "total solidarity," where they appear as Good Samaritans helping their Jewish neighbors.

The discourse in Greek historiography takes two divergent paths: One argues that Greek society was indifferent to the suffering of Jews and provided little help. Some historians have disputed the significance of acts of rescue themselves, arguing that the help provided by the Greek Peoples' Liberation Army (ELAS), the military wing of the leftist resistance organization EAM (National Liberation Front), was done for financial compensation.[31] These arguments have complicated the historically oversimplified understanding of rescuing Jews. The second tendency is to depict the people of Greece as providers of consistent, decisive, and moral help to their Jewish neighbors.[32] This narrative reinforces the self-aggrandizing Greek image of peaceful coexistence with minorities by emphasizing "diachronic" tolerance as a predominant element of Greekness, and as a moral principle continually recognized in national narratives. According to this interpretation, the general population's attitudes toward Jews were invariably positive; there was a lack of anti-Jewish violence, and Jews were fully integrated into society.

The public debate over Jewish rescue culminated in 2017, when the Greek ministry of foreign affairs, in collaboration with Yad Vashem, published a volume titled *The Greek Righteous Among the Nations*, with the explicitly stated aim of "restoring the historical truth" about the Greek Jewish experience.[33] The volume posited that there was a silence concerning the topic of Jewish rescue. Edited by the former director of the archives of the ministry of foreign affairs, Foteini Tomai, the book explores the positive roles played by the Greek state, the church, the national resistance, representatives of the local administration, the police, and other authorities in saving Greek Jews during the German occupation. The book is a good example of the official historical narrative of peaceful coexistence between gentiles and Jews which, according to the Greek-Jewish historian Rika Benveniste, relies on a kind of Greek exceptionalism.[34] This official narrative finds support in the tenuous nature of Jewish communities, which find themselves in a double bind: condemning antisemitic speech and actions and at the same time negating the existence of antisemitism.[35] As an agent of the state narrative, Foteini Tomai directed the foreign ministry's archives from 1996 to 2018 and was appointed the country's special envoy for Holocaust issues in 2013. She has supported the narrative of a pre- and postwar harmonious coexistence between Greek Jews and non-Jews, a simplistic interpretation most historians find inaccurate.[36] Since the publication of Tomai's book in 2017, the Greek ministry of foreign affairs has seen the task of commemorating the Righteous Among the Nations as a process involving symbolic and rhetorical strategies. These public representations acquire considerable political authority.

Tomai and other scholars argue that modern Greece's establishment on the "principle of full emancipation and freedom of religion for all citizens" forms the foundational myth of full Jewish integration, which was to serve as the basis for their rescue.[37] According to this argument, the Jews enjoyed the full support of the church during the German occupation, as well as the sympathies of the overwhelming majority of their non-Jewish compatriots. Likewise, supposedly age-old tolerance in smaller cities, where the local population was helpful and hid the persecuted Jews, proved instrumental in the Jews' rescue. Tomai claims, moreover, that the Greek state was "the only one in Europe to return abandoned Jewish properties to their owners," highlighting, in positive terms, the "international uniqueness of Greek legislation regarding the post-war legal settlement of property restitution."[38] Her earlier work, *Documents on the History of the Greek Jews: Records from the Historical Archives of the Ministry of Foreign Affairs* (1998), is an important example of the tendency to emphasize the aid provided by Greek people.[39] This is a narrative characteristic of all official publications of the Greek ministry of foreign affairs. As Andrew Buckser shows in the example of the rescue of Danish Jews, studies of the rescue have tended to depict it in epic terms, as a battle of tolerance and democratic values against prejudice and inhumanity. This accords with a general tendency in the social sciences to cast Holocaust rescue in universal terms, and to depict its heroes as exemplars of universal values.[40] This argument enables a richer understanding of the official narrative produced by the Greek ministry of foreign affairs.

Another image the Greek ministry of foreign affairs publicly promotes is one where Orthodox priests demonstrated impeccably pro-Jewish attitudes during the war. The Jewish Museum of Greece in Athens (JMG) recently hosted a temporary exhibition, *The Good Shepherds: Metropolitans and Chief Rabbis in the Face of the Holocaust* (January 23–October 4, 2019), which aimed to "research the conditions under which senior members of the Greek Orthodox clergy and eminent rabbis decided and acted in various ways to assist persecuted Jews during the years of the Nazi Occupation."[41] The exhibition showcased the positive actions of members of the Orthodox church who either carried out public anti-German protests, such as Archbishop Damaskinos in Athens, or offered gestures of sympathy or support, promoting their public status as moral role models at the time. The Jewish Museum "reveals these examples in order to honor those involved and inspire us today."[42] The exhibition also aimed to highlight the importance of individual choice within an oppressive, often contradictory, and extremely complex context. In several cases, assistance rendered to Jews was recognized by the exhibition as only one element of an individual's positive character, rather than as a defining characteristic. Clergymen are portrayed in the exhibition as patriotic, altruistic, and highly motivated, even though the church ultimately failed to take meaningful steps to oppose deportations.[43] Attitudes of the members of the Orthodox church toward the persecuted Jews were ambiguous: Many bishops were pro-German, others remained neutral, and a handful refused to cooperate. Positions also varied greatly among the lowest ranks of the clergy.[44] The exhibit's representation of the Orthodox church is key to Holocaust memory in Greece, as today more than 90 percent of Greeks define their national identity based on their shared Orthodox faith. The Greek Orthodox Church is thus implicitly linked to the state. As in the case within the European Union, where attitudes toward Jews often serve as public barometers of morality, the commemorative practices of the state and the Jewish Museum of Greece frame the church as a fundamental opponent of Jewish persecution and reaffirm the implicit morality of the church in general, thereby exonerating the church's actions during the German occupation.

Founded in 1977, the Jewish Museum has received substantial financial support from the Greek ministry of culture, the Greek ministry of foreign affairs, and the associations of its donors and supporters. The museum has had an especially consistent cooperative relationship with the ministry of foreign affairs, which with it has been working since 2000. But this relationship also reveals that Greek Jews are still perceived as not belonging to the national community, thus all topics related to Greek Jewry fall within the remit of the Greek ministry of foreign affairs. The Greek ministry of foreign affairs has also taken over the development and financing of the permanent Greek exhibition about the Greek Jews who were deported to Auschwitz, at the Memorial and Museum Auschwitz-Birkenau.[45]

How Individuals Remember: Common Features in Rescue Narratives

This section presents several accounts that deal with rescue, underscoring the similarity between individual and collective narratives concerning the topic of Jewish rescue within the Jewish experience. My goals here are to point out the ways rescue is narrated and how the similarities between different types of rescue are contextualized. Most of the sixteen interviewees described in this section live in Greece, with the exception of two living in the United States and Canada. Four of these narrators were interviewed twice after a break of many years, thereby providing an opportunity to investigate how they renarrate and reshape their experiences. (At the end of this essay, I have included an analytical appendix with basic data about all the testimonies cited.) My aim is to show how accounts of the experience of rescue relate to one another in terms of the content of testimonial strategies.

The accounts of individual experiences of hiding and rescue share common traits with the official memory expressed by Jewish institutions and representatives. Generally, the ways Greek Jews elaborate and reshape their narratives of the past within oral testimony have seldom been explored. Andrew Buckser has sought to explore the topic of Jewish rescue by analyzing the ways members of the Jewish community of Denmark narrate their stories of rescue. Such stories, he suggests, help to define the individual by enabling them to locate themselves in the social world and in a temporal order: "To tell the history of one's group is to ground one's identity."[46] This is extremely helpful for understanding how Greek Jews remember acts of assistance, and particularly the exclusionary or inclusionary relationship between the Jewish communities of Greece and the outside world. Testimonies of survivors are collected from two different periods: in the years 1994–98 (interviews from Visual History Archive) and 2016–18 ("Memories of the Occupation in Greece"), shedding light on the perception of Greek Jewish men and women who survived the Holocaust in Greece.

A number of commonalities emerge from a close reading of the sixteen individual Greek Jewish testimonies examined for this study. First and foremost, antisemitism features only tangentially in recollections of the German occupation or of the time spent in hiding. Survivors also recall the hospitality shown during their postwar life in Greece. Second, all interviewees emphasize the cordial relationship between Jews and gentiles prior to the outbreak of war. A third common element is the emphasis given to the postwar maintenance of relations between saviors and the saved. This latter element, in particular, underlines the sense of belonging and reciprocity between national groups as important components in the perception of sameness as shared humanity. Solidarity narratives reinforce bonds with fellow members of the same national group by portraying the allegedly high degree of Jewish assimilation in Greece, by underlining the bonds between Christians and Jews, and by illustrating the lack of religious or demographic divisions. This is the reality that, according to the narrators, made the rescue possible. Lastly, interviewees express gratitude to the church or the resistance, which proved so crucial to their survival. To be acknowledged as Greek themselves, narrators accommodate the collective image of Greek national suffering alongside that of Greek resistance and heroism.[47]

By comparing or cross-mapping a sample of narratives to see what they share, we can recognize thematic similarities. The following examples of testimonies illustrate the self-affirming nature of the established narrative of morality. The key aspect is the emphasis on both the rescued and the rescuer having stayed in touch after the war, which lends credibility to stories of altruism and human kindness. The Jewish narrators argue that they identify strongly with the larger Greek culture and that the larger society always regarded them as "Greeks." Thus the reason rescue occurred in Greece derived in large part from the integration and acceptance of Jews into the larger Greek society, an argument that does not have a great deal of truth in it, as Greek Jews were never strongly assimilated into the Greek national context. Even today, beyond general stereotypes and the antisemitic rhetoric that rightist anti-immigrant parties adopt, most Greeks have very little contact with or knowledge of Jews or Judaism. Jews are not present in popular culture, and most Greeks know next to nothing about them. What's more, to say that Greek Jews were simply Greek like any other Greek, and to attribute rescue to the depth of assimilation, fails to account for the diversity of Greek Jewry. The explanation of cultural similarity may be an appealing one, particularly in the context of the moral debate surrounding the Holocaust of Greek Jews, but it also involves a serious oversimplification of the rather complicated Greek Jewish history. Nevertheless, it is difficult not to attribute moral stature to the rescuers, as antisemitism was far from unknown in prewar Greece, even though the following testimonies argue to the contrary.

Even when gently pressed on her experience of pre- and postwar discrimination, Miranda Alkalay, a Jewish woman born in Trikala in 1929, emphasized the hospitality of the Greek state and its people. Her rescue story is one of the hospitality of and acceptance by gentiles.[48] Alkalay's interview, which took place in Athens in 2016, provides an important perspective on those Jewish families who had sought refuge in the Greek mountains, revealing their lived experience and their survival practices during the occupation. In 1943, at the beginning of the German occupation, the Alkalay family fled to the village of Kapourna in Thessaly, where they stayed for thirteen months in a rented house shared with Miranda's uncle and aunt. Recent studies have highlighted the actions of "sudden rescuers-protectors" in instances where the lives of Jewish children were under immediate threat. These individuals, strangers or acquaintances, protected the children from mistreatment and malnutrition.[49] In Miranda's case, the "sudden rescuers-protectors" were her neighbors, who helped where they could, warned her of any German presence, and provided her and her family with food: "They loved us and they selflessly protected us. They were our heroes; they risked their lives to save us who were complete strangers. I will never forget them. I visit them with my children almost every year."[50] The narrative of flawless relations falters slightly when she reveals that the food was not obtained unconditionally, but through barter.

Heinz Kounio, a Jew born in Carlsbad (Karlovy Vary), western Bohemia, in 1927, was deported to Auschwitz from Thessaloniki at the age of fifteen. He and his family, along with twenty-eight hundred others, were on the first Greek transport from Thessaloniki on March 15, 1943. Heinz survived the war together with his mother, Chella, his father, Salvator, and his sister, Erika, because they could speak German and were employed at Auschwitz as translators. He has lived in Thessaloniki, Greece, since 1945. His testimony was given, in Greek, in 2017 on a visit to Berlin to promote his autobiography, which had been translated into German.[51] He recalls the postwar assistance provided to the family by the Greek chief of police, who helped them regain their photographic studio in Thessaloniki. With the help of his daughter, who gave him cues during the interview, Kounio recalled that his Christian neighbors had returned cameras taken from his family shop.[52] He thus considers both those who returned his stock and the chief of police as personal rescuers. He did not recall antisemitic acts or the confiscation of Jewish property by gentiles in Thessaloniki, even though historical research has shown confiscated property to have formed the basis of Greek-German commerce—which benefited Christian "conscientious heads of families," businessmen, shop-owners, collaborators, and sympathizers, while still maintaining a semblance of legitimacy.[53] Jewish-owned spaces in Thessaloniki were violently occupied, and a new economy was built on the leftovers of the departing Jewish community and its material remains.[54] Heinz Kounio gave an interview to the Shoah Foundation in 1998 in which he references his experience of prewar and postwar antisemitic discrimination in Thessaloniki, though he avoids repeating the same assertions during the interview conducted in 2017.[55] The other three interviews that were examined for this study—taken in two different periods—don't vary much, and the testimonial context remains the same, with the exception of one case that will be analyzed shortly.

Recent Holocaust scholarship has explored whether and how survivor testimonies can change over time, as well as the context in which the testimony originated and the ways context could have affected the structure and content of the testimonial text.[56] Anja Tippner addresses the possibilities and benefits of testimonial comparisons in her essay "Worlds Apart? Cross-mapping Camp Literature from the Gulag and Nazi Concentration Camps" by referring to the changing emphases of testimonies from the same individual. Such changes can illustrate the testimonial context's dependence on the emotional, cultural, and political needs of different societies.[57] The discrepancies between the different testimonies of the same person have to do with memories recorded at different points of distance from the events they describe. These discrepancies have nothing to do with accuracy and reflect rather the different perceptions of the same event in different contemporaneities. Heinz Kounio gave an interview in 1998, and he may have felt more comfortable speaking since he was addressing a foreign audience, in this case an American one. In 1998, Greek antisemitism was not established as a topic for public discussion, so Kounio may have wished to help the society come to terms with a difficult past by addressing it. As a witness, he brings the topic to light as the facts have not taken hold within a public culture of remembrance. A collective discourse on the topic of Greek antisemitism started only after 2000, opening up a subject that had been taboo for a long time. Kounio's testimony records a shift from individual experience to public memory, a transformation that first took place within the field of historiography.[58] However, when I interviewed him in 2017, I asked him if he had encountered antisemitism in Thessaloniki, and he answered with a flat negative: "We have never been attacked, discriminated against or insulted by Greeks—my Jewishness was never the basis of an insult."[59]

Zafeiria Kone, born in Larisa in 1936, first hid with her family in Karalaka, near Mount Olympus, and then at Karya and Ampelonas. She received false baptismal records and changed her name to Roula in 1943.[60] Passing as non-Jews, the family survived in peasant huts, which were small and often overcrowded. Many Jewish families from Larisa stayed at Ampelonas, and the resistance played a decisive role in their rescue, as many Jews joined the partisans or worked alongside villagers as liaisons, in the ancillary services of the resistance army, or assumed secretarial duties in the National Solidarity Organization, which gathered and distributed food. She recounts: "If there hadn't been the resistance, we wouldn't be alive now. [. . .] Generally, everybody helped us and opened their houses to us."[61] Even if her life story gives an account of painful experiences of prolonged starvation and exhaustion, of a harshness that goes beyond the average experience during the German occupation, the traumatic experiences remain somehow hidden in her narrative, and her focus is on the people who helped her. She sees herself more as a passive victim, given her reliance on the resistance and the people who hid her and her family for survival: "They were all very compassionate. They knew we were Jews and they helped us, we wouldn't be alive without them."[62] But hiding required immense determination, knowledge, physical strength, and skill to survive in inhospitable conditions with none of the conveniences of civilization and a limited access to outside help—it was a fragile state of loneliness. Organizing a long period of time in a hiding place required an enormous effort and a combination of coordination, ingenuity, and luck, as everything could be put in jeopardy by careless or reckless behavior.[63]

This account differs from the previous testimony given by Zafeiria Kone in 1998 for the Shoah Foundation Institute. There she concentrated her narrative on the people of the village, stating that *nobody* wanted to provide them with shelter, a memory very different from the one recorded in 2016.[64] As in the case of Heinz Kounio, we have to fill in the narrative gaps with our own interpretation. This particular case study of two interviews given by the same person, stretching over a period of almost twenty years, is a typical example of the increasing similarity between individual and collective narratives concerning the topic of Jewish rescue. The narrative patterns she used in 2016 coincide with the official memory of Jewish rescue that was formulated that same year. For some survivors, the first testimony they give is seen as a direct continuation of efforts to document the events. Narratives are obviously more complex than one can assume. In the course of time, according to Henry Greenspan, survivors search for a world that was sufficiently responsive, and recollections of war experiences are being shaped by postwar affirmations. They assert and celebrate solidarity. On another level, survivors invest hope in the collective impact of their testimony, especially when they are very old and think this may be their last chance to share their individual experience.[65] It is this form of narrative legacy they hope to express. In her 2016 interview, Zafeiria Kone mentioned that she experienced antisemitism in school during the postwar years, though it seems to have had little effect on her: "The teacher at school told me all the time that I should go to the Jewish school, not there. But it was OK for me."[66] After the war, the family stayed with a colleague of her father while looking for a house of their own, though the homeowner resented their presence and even at one point physically attacked them, scalding them with boiling water. Asked whether this was an antisemitic act, Zafeiria chose to downplay the attack by mentioning that there were relatively few houses in postwar Larissa. The family continues to return to the village, and they maintain a friendship with those who sheltered them.

Yehouda Chaki, born in Athens in 1938, hid in the suburb of Aigaleo-Attika with his mother and father at the house of the Papadopoulos family. In the interview recorded in 1996, he repeatedly addresses the meaning of Greekness. An intellectual and a successful painter in Canada, Chaki sought to restore, as quickly as possible, the vision of an ideal world in which the humanistic belief in solidarity among the oppressed prevails. For him, memory was not a process of recollection of past events, conditions, and sensations but a practice of selecting and repeating some events that manifest his Greek identity, even though, unconsciously, he maintains in his narrative a distinction between the categories of "Greek" and "Jew": "We were accepted, they gave us a lot of food, and after the war there was some food left, and my father went back to this area and distributed the food to the locals. They were good to us, they were communists in this area. We were treated well by the Greeks. . . . We were also Greeks, we spoke the language the same way they spoke the language, we were not different. The Jews were assimilated, they looked like Greeks and they were merchants like the Greeks."[67] Chaki maintained a relationship with the family that had sheltered him. Indeed, Andreas Papadopoulos had wanted to adopt him and is referred to by Yehouda as "nonos," a word that, in Christian Orthodoxy, means "godfather." The local priest baptized him in 1943, knowing that the boy was Jewish: "Everything went very smoothly."[68] They too stayed in contact after the war. Yehouda, who immigrated to Canada after the war and resumed his Jewish identity, visited the United States Holocaust Memorial Museum on its inauguration in 1993 and saw the name of the family that had saved him in the permanent collection—an experience he found particularly moving: "[The reason that] some of the Jews survived is because of the Greeks. They were very good."[69] His testimonial record seems to be a story addressed, first and foremost, to the Papadopoulos family and only second to a broader audience: "It is my duty and an obligation to testify on behalf of this family, I have a personal motivation to tell the story. It's all about them."[70]

Lena Yosafat, born in Katerini in 1912, hid under a false identity in the small village of Skouterna in Pieria, and maintained a similar gratitude to those "Good Samaritans" who helped her: "They all treated us very well. They gave us pork, eggs, cheese, everything."[71] Remembering the time spent in hiding, she spoke about the solidarity of people and the strength of the bonds created in the village. She felt like a member of the community, and the people gave her medicine, shoes, and clothes. Moreover, she formulated universal characteristics of Jewish rescue by referring to the rescuers as models of religious tolerance: "We were Jews and they were Christians; we were different but we all believed in the same god. They saved us because they were Christians."[72] After the war, she returned to the village and visited the people who had helped her; she stayed in contact with them, and, like Yehuda, she unequivocally says that "Greeks were good to us."[73] In her interview, she referred quite frequently to religion, suggesting that she and other survivors felt uncertain whether they could blend physically, culturally, and socially into the Christian world. In 1951, Lena left Greece together with her husband, David, and immigrated to the United States, where she started working at a tailor shop in Cincinnati, Ohio.

Born in Larissa in 1935, Ioudas-Leon Magrizos was the youngest member of a poor Jewish family. His father, Symeon, kept a thrift store, and his mother, Sarah, was a housewife. He had three siblings: Isaac, Eleonora, and Eriketi. In 1941 his family moved to Kileler to escape the bombardment, which had killed his uncle, David. In 1943, faced with Jewish deportations in Thessaloniki and the Bulgarian occupation zone, the Magrizos family sought safety in Gounitsa. They sheltered with another Jewish family named Kalderon who had escaped the deportations from Thessaloniki and were en route to Athens. The Magrizos family subsequently relocated to the convent of Tsouma, then home to approximately eighty Larissan Jews. A few months before the liberation, following the advice of local partisans, all these families left the difficult conditions of Tsouma and moved to the isolated village of Megalo Eleftherochori.

Ioudas-Leon and his family returned to Larissa after the war. In 1990 he was recognized as an active member of the Jewish community of Larissa, having administered it for thirty years and served as a member of the city's Zionist association, even though he did not immigrate to Israel like many of those who shared his faith. His sister belonged to EAM.[74] In his testimony, the leitmotif of continuity of relations looms large again: The Magrizos family maintained contact with the Arzoumanidou family, which had rendered assistance at Kileler, the daughter of the latter even learning dressmaking from Ioudas's wife. Acknowledging the gratitude that Greek Jews have to the Orthodox church, Magrizos's narrative depicted rescue as a collective moral achievement on behalf of the resistance and the church: "I must be clear about this: the resistance helped us a lot, the church as well. They acted morally in such difficult times, something that today would not happen so easily. [. . .] I want to emphasize that hiding somebody wasn't a simple thing. They were such good people that they don't even think that they did something terrific, they don't advertise themselves. They were heroes."[75] The compelling moral force behind the rescue of Jews, the universal insistence that what mattered was the victim's position of dependence and subjection to unjust persecution, are combined in Ioudas's testimony to make the meaning of these actions universal. In a sense it was this moral force and duty that motivated the rescuers, according to Ioudas, independent of personal likes or dislikes: "Whoever came to us helped us. It was like it was their duty to help us. It was not because we were Jews. It was because we were people, like them."[76]

Born in the coastal town of Volos in 1938, Rachil Papadrianou was the daughter of a local banker named Isidoros Varouch. At the beginning of the war, her father had been falsely identified to the Germans as an intelligence service agent by some of his own employees, and he was imprisoned. On his release, the family fled to the mountains. They survived with the assistance of the Chatzidakis family who, Rachil recounts, "stood against tyranny and risked their own safety."[77] Their belongings were kept safe for the duration of the war by their Christian friends, Alekos and Marika Kataropoulou. Rachil later converted to Christianity and, in 1977, married a Christian, Evaggelos Papadrianou, in an Orthodox ceremony. Despite her conversion at the request of her future husband and against her parents' wishes, Rachil always considered herself first and foremost a Jew, and she regularly attends synagogue services. She claims her only experience of antisemitism was a recent one, when, during Easter in Nafplio, an Orthodox priest publicly admonished the Jews for the death of Jesus. This, she recalled, made clear to her the existence of a fundamental religious antisemitism, and it angered her greatly.[78] In contrast to the form of "censorship" that prevails in the previously discussed testimonies, Rachil breaks the usual silence about antisemitism and challenges the hagiographic narrative of impeccable Greek-Jewish relations.

By centering his narrative on the key aspect of staying in touch after the war with the people who rescued them, Michail Nachman lends credibility to humanitarianism and kindness. At the end of his interview, Nachman, born in Piraeus in 1936, presented a photo, dated 1948, of a family excursion with the Kontopanou family, with whom he hid at Karpenisi.[79] His brother, Telis-Israel Nachman (born 1928), emphasized that the Kontopanou family were still friends.[80] The wife of Michail Nachman, Ioulia Solomon-Nachman, born in Trikala in 1938, was hidden with her family in various locations around Athens by the Andreopoulou and Moumoutzi families; her grandmother pretended to be deaf because she could not speak Greek. They, like the others, remained close friends after the war: The Christian families consider her children as their own; her children call them "uncle and aunt," and Ioulia considers Mrs. Andreopoulou as her second mother. Motivated by gratitude, the Nachman family successfully nominated both the Andreopoulou and Moumoutzi families for recognition as Righteous Among the Nations.[81]

Having left the Thessaloniki ghetto alone, Andreas Sephiha (born in 1929) spent the occupation in Argos, located in the Peloponnese region, and Athens, living under the assumed name "Andreas Sfikas," a false identity provided to him by the former chief of police at Thessaloniki, Mouschoundis. He grew up in a world of change; it was his thirty-year association with the Jewish community of Thessaloniki that provided the catalyst for his memoir of the Jewish communities in Thessaloniki and across the wider diaspora.[82] He remained grateful to those who had sheltered him: "Seeking nothing for themselves and with no ulterior motive or hope of personal gain, they risked life and limb and opened the doors of their home to us, total strangers though we were."[83] Sephiha's children, like those of other families, maintain contact with the families who saved him: "We remained in touch with Maria Tsiapouris and still have close ties with her family. Though she herself has died, we are still in touch with her lawyer son, the incumbent deputy prefect of Argolis, Sotiris Kotsovos. Sotiris still talks about the time he first met our family."[84] The Sephardim, Sephiha maintains, never let the flame of their love for their homeland die. Through the testimonial act, Sephiha strengthens a reconstructed identity and reinforces it by drawing from his narrative a legacy: He feels as if he were part of the first generation to be born on Greek soil after the expulsion of Sephardi Jews from Spain in 1492, and since neither of his parents had been to a Greek school, he needed a proper Greek education: "Not only was it a good Greek school, but it instilled in me the ability to feel Greek, which I have maintained throughout my life. When I was president of the Jewish community and watched parades as its representative, I was moved to tears when the flag of the Greek commandos was paraded past; that was the unit I served in when I was in the Greek army."[85]

Many accounts of being rescued essentially end with emphasis on the friendships that arose between the Greek rescuers and the rescued Jews, mostly because the rescuers were self-effacing men and women who performed these incredible, heroic deeds. Solomon Antzel, born in Thessaloniki in 1930, lived under an assumed identity in Athens, in the apartment of the Kefala family; after the occupation, he became best friends with the Kefalas's children.[86] Moris Leon, born in Thessaloniki in 1928, was able to obtain false documents before the introduction of anti-Jewish measures. He fled with his family to the island of Skopelos, where he survived with the help of the island's inhabitants. Like many survivors cited here, Leon also emphasizes solidarity with the people of Skopelos. At the end of the interview, he presented photos of the Mitzeliotis family from 1945 and 1996, as well as photographs showing him in front of a monument bearing the names of his rescuers.[87] These photographs have acquired a documentary power, and the visual medium intensifies the power of Moris

Leon's message. The image of the monument serves as a device of memory, with both a personal and a historical significance.

The varied experiences of hiding and rescue help to reconstruct the microcosm of Jewish persecution, with oral interviews revealing different patterns and trajectories. Still, themes such as betrayal, exploitation, and Greek antisemitism do not fit easily into the established narrative and do not follow the general pattern. Lela Kosti-Koymeri, born in Chalkida in 1922, offers a complex, and ultimately tragic, picture of rescue. Two of her brothers, Chaim and Iakovos, left for Palestine with the partisans. With her mother, Eftihia, her father, Jeshua, her sister, Hanna, and her brother Isaak, she stayed for a year at Steni Evoias, in a small room belonging to a Christian client of her father. Having had his offer of marriage to Lela rebuffed, a local peasant named Michelis (later mayor of Psachna Evoias) began a campaign of blackmail against Lela's family and later burned down the home of the family who had taken them in, forcing them to flee to the mountains. After the war, her father sued Michelis, but owing to the death threats that Jeshua received from the collaborationist Greek Security Battalions, he provided a false testimony.[88]

Not surprisingly, few explicit instances of Greeks blackmailing Jews have come to light.[89] Revenge would have been an unlikely action to take at the time of liberation and during the civil war that followed. Competing political priorities left little space for acts of revenge on behalf of Jews. Lela's experience illustrates the complex nature of interactions between Jews and gentiles, though she expresses only gratitude, despite her bitter memories of the blackmail and threats; fondly remembering those who helped her, she overlooked those who did not: "The people who helped us were selfless and noble people. Even though we were afraid for our life because Michelis threatened to kill us and we had to pay some people to give us back our property after the war, because they stole from us, mercilessly. In periods of war people become relentless. But anyway, I have forgotten them, I only remember the good people that helped us."[90]

Within the study sample, there are exceptions to the general pattern of brushing aside antisemitic incidents. While the rescue story of Rosa Asser Pardo, born in 1933 in Thessaloniki, seems typical in many ways, she openly discusses both her Greekness and her experience of Greek antisemitism. In April 1943, the Pardo family (Rosa, her sister, and her parents) took refuge in the third-floor apartment of George Karakotsos, his wife, Phaedra, and their child, Philon, at 113 Tsimiski Street in Thessaloniki. They stayed hidden there for 548 days. Rosa, sharing a single room with her family, kept a diary and changed her name to Roula Karakotsos.[91] She recalls Greek antisemitism and denunciations by gentiles in Thessaloniki: "It is a strange country, Greece. Whether they like us or not."[92] She does not consider herself a "passionate Greek," rather, she is Greek "because everyone calls her a Greek."[93] After the war, Rosa studied law in Paris before taking up a post practicing law in the Athens law office of Asher Moissis (1899–1975). Moissis was a Greek Zionist leader and honorary consul of the State of Israel in Greece. Rosa talked with him about Zionism and Judaism and became personally active in Zionist matters. Rosa considers Zionism the ideology by which the Jews of the Diaspora maintain their links with the Jewish people. Still, she chose to stay in Greece and live in Athens, because she did not want to leave her family. Reflecting on her own rescue, Rosa expressed gratitude to the Karakotsos family. Her testimony does not fit neatly into any of the themes identified earlier.

The case of Alexandros Simha, born in Thessaloniki in 1937, is equally interesting. In 1941, Alexandros, along with his father, mother, and two brothers, fled to Athens; they stayed first in a basement at Mouseion in Athens before moving to Pagkrati. The family took false identity papers, provided to them by Athenian police chief Angelos Evert. In 1942, his father joined the forces of the Greek government-in-exile in the Middle East. His mother and his brothers, Saul (Pavlos) and Tzakos (Gerasimos), sought refuge in the area of Akropoli and left Alexandros with a Christian family named Aiginiti in the city center, at Ippokratous and Tsimiski, and he remained with them until the end of the occupation. The family reunited after the war. Between 1953 and 1961 Alexandros studied in Switzerland, first at a boarding school and then at a commercial school. In 1961 he graduated with a degree in finance and returned to Athens to start his own business as a tobacco trader. He did not maintain contact with the Aiginitis family, and his memories of them are overwhelmingly negative, characterized by domestic disputes and frequent beatings.

Alexandros's testimony is one of only two in the collection of the Free University which recalls Greek antisemitism (the other being Rosa Asser Pardo's account). Antisemitism led him to conceal his identity and to harbor feelings of personal shame. His father retained his false name, Simihas; the preservation of his Christian name was something almost instinctive in postwar Greece. In the army Alexandros experienced fervent antisemitism. His commanding officer used to say that "Hitler, fortunately, got rid of the Jews." In 1998 he was married to a non-Jewish wife. At the end of his interview, he stated that the Greek people ought to have shown some understanding of the State of Israel, because although Israel is very small—"the size of the Peloponnese"—everyone wants to destroy it. Even though he declared his love of Greece, in his eyes "Israel serves as a safety net in the event of any future threat."[94] The Zionist sympathies of the two narrators are complex and rooted in their traumatic experiences. Their pro-Zionist feelings influence their perceptions of the people who rescued them, who remain somehow hidden, while antisemitism occupies a central place in their narratives. The identities they adopted after the war, forged in the context of their travels, foreign education, and interactions with non-Jewish groups, are also formative for their Jewishness and a reason for their lack of interest in manifesting their Greek national identity.

Conclusion: "Narrative Legacies" in Greece

The story of Jewish rescue in Greece is fundamentally one concerned with gentile-Jewish relations. The accounts examined here were shaped by the long-held beliefs of the Jewish survivors, and they either exaggerated solidarity or praised those institutions or individuals who provided help, in line with the official memory produced by the institutions of the Greek state. Since the 1990s, there has been a growing body of literature about the rescue of Jews in Nazi-occupied Europe.[95] But there has been no such study to date of Jewish rescue in Greece and specifically about the psychosocial characteristics of Greek rescuers: their motivations, their class or social affiliations, or their personal relationships to the victims. In many testimonies, for example, we learn that the rescuers were friends of the families or business partners of the parents. Equally remarkable is the absence of memoirs of the rescuers themselves, with the exception of one testimony in the Visual History Archive.[96] There is a level of complexity to the retelling of events, as the reflections of one person often "speak" to the reflections of another. While the narrators stand at the center of the rescue story, most of the narrative revolves around the rescuers—their motivations, their moral courage, and their selflessness. The Jews appear as relatively passive, a general tendency that is maybe understandable, given the rhetorical uses to which the rescue has generally been put, especially in the national narrative.[97]

The narratives of Greek Jewish survivors presented here consist of a body of symbols, a set of references that individuals use to construct their understandings of the self and the world.[98] The sense of rootedness features prominently in the narratives concerning rescue, reflecting the hagiographic image of flawless Greek-Jewish relations, while there are only a few narratives that break this mold. This pattern becomes essential, as survivors' narratives are affected by listeners and their expectations, and sometimes survivors shape their accounts to meet these expectations.[99] The voices in testimonies increasingly complement each other as their individuality unfolds. In exploring survivors' voices, we become aware of the connections among stories of survival, as survivors act as custodians of memory by shedding light on the past. The predominant feature of their narratives is solidarity, and in this way they discern a coherent structure and consistency regarding the experiences they communicate. Henry Greenspan's concept of "narrative legacies" can be helpful here, as it suggests all stories are narratives of survival and that they have always been linked with the concept of legacy.[100] By recounting their stories, the narrators express their conviction of faith in the shared survival of Christians and Jews, by emphasizing the positive sides of this coexistence. This is conceived by the narrators as their legacy, a contribution to intergenerational continuities, a reaffirmation of endurance and duration. In this way narrative legacies are made actual, in every age and in every society; the narrators know their stories will be preserved and will contribute to the creation of general sentiments and reflections. Their stories and experiences reflect the social worlds within which they live, and by emphasizing generosity instead of animosity or racial discrimination, they shape a form of narrative legacy that will contribute to a mutual understanding in a world that is rapidly changing. Thus the struggle between meaning and memory continues.

The particular accounts that have been chosen for this essay are not intended to be representative; rather, they give a sense of the intimate connection between personal experience and official constructions of the past. They convey a standard set of moral and historical lessons, similar to the official state narrative. According to Andrew Buckser, the past often plays an important role in self-definition for Jewish communities, offering a symbolic language through which to express ideas of common origin. In this way narratives of rescue become allegories for the relationship between gentiles and Jews within a country.[101] The conventional narrative of the past produced by the state should not be considered a simple counterpart to the individual memories concerning rescue. The state is not the only memory agent, but it undoubtedly holds an exclusive position in this field because it can support its interpretations of the past by speaking in the international arena, and because it has the power, tools, and funds to propagate its narrative. In consequence, the symbolic activity of the official actors gains special significance, becoming a common point of reference. When the official interpretations of the past seem inconsistent, the repertoire of the past becomes an instrument for achieving political aims. Thus historical events are interpreted in terms of heroism, national glory, and achievements.

Appendix

Name	Date and place of birth	Interview date and location	Interviewer and digital repository
Miranda Alkalay Interviews in Greek	1929, Trikala, Greece	1. 1998, Athens, Greece 2. 2016, Athens, Greece	1. Sara Levy, Visual History Archive (VHA) 2. Anna Maria Droumpouki, Memories of the Occupation in Greece (MOG)
Ioudas-Leon Magrizos Interview in Greek	1935, Larissa, Greece	2016, Larissa, Greece	Ersi Malagiorgi, MOG
Heinz Kounio Interviews in Greek	1927, Karlsbad (Karlovy Vary), western Bohemia	1. 1998, Thessaloniki, Greece 2. 2016, Thessaloniki, Greece	1. Rena Molho, VHA 2. Anna Maria Droumpouki, MOG
Zafeiria (Roula) Kone Interviews in Greek	1936, Larissa, Greece	1. 1998, Volos, Thessaly, Greece 2. 2016, Volos, Thessaly Greece	1. Pavlina Matathia, VHA 2. Antonis Antoniou, MOG
Yehouda Chaki Interview in English	1938, Athens, Greece	1996, Canada	
Lena Yosafat, maiden name Taboh Interview in English	1912, Katerini, Greece	1995, Cincinnati, Ohio	Joanne Centa, VHA
Rachil Papadrianou Interview in Greek	1938, Volos, Greece	1998, Glyfada, Athens, Greece	Daisy Allalouf, VHA

Name	Date and place of birth	Interview date and location	Interviewer and digital repository
Michail Nachman Interview in Greek	1936, Piraeus, Greece	1998, Athens, Greece	Nelly Nadjary Leon, VHA
Telis-Israel Nachman Interview in Greek	1928, Athens, Greece	1998, Athens, Greece	Mathilde Nachmias, VHA
Ioulia Solomon-Nachman Interview in Greek	1938, Trikala, Greece	1998, Athens, Greece	Nelly Nadjary Leon, VHA
Andreas Sephiha Interview in Greek	1929, Thessaloniki, Greece	1998, Thessaloniki, Greece	Elias Matalon, VHA
Solomon Antzel Interview in Greek	1930, Thessaloniki, Greece	1998, Athens, Greece	Regina Kounio, VHA
Moris Leon Interview in Greek	1928, Thessaloniki, Greece	1998, Athens, Greece	Marilyn Pizante, VHA
Lela Kosti-Koymeri Interview in Greek	1922, Chalkida, Greece	1998, Athens, Greece	Yvette Leon, VHA
Rosa Asser Pardo Interviews in Greek	1933, Thessaloniki, Greece	1. 1998, Thessaloniki, Greece 2. 2016, Athens, Greece	1. Nelly Nadjary Leon, VHA 2. Anna Maria Droumpouki, MOG
Alexandros Simha Interview in Greek	1937, Thessaloniki, Greece	2016, Athens, Greece	Anna Maria Droumpouki, MOG

Notes

1 See Efi Avdela, "Towards a Greek History of the Jews of Salonica?" *Jewish History* 28 (November 2014): 405–10. Efi Avdela argues that Greek historiography has demonstrated a relentless ethnocentrism in conceptualizing difference in Greek society at large, as a result of which Greek Jews were rendered invisible in the Greek historical narrative and were, occasionally, treated as a homogenous, isolated entity. Greek historiography has largely overlooked questions of Jewish identity, the relationship of Jews to non-Jews, the nature of Jewishness, and the construction of a

common past with non-Jews in the Greek context. As noted by Avdela, the popularity of the topic can hardly be doubted; hundreds of books and articles have been published on the Jewry of Thessaloniki. Yet historiographical analysis has revealed several problematic characteristics of the corpus: The majority of relevant studies concern the Ottoman period; two-thirds are written by non-Greek historians; most were published after the 1990s; and, finally, few consider internal heterogeneity and the character of conflicts or relationships with the city's other ethnic groups.

2 Rena Molho, "The Jewish Community of Thessaloniki and Its Incorporation into the Greek State, 1912–1919," *Middle Eastern Studies* 24 (1988): 122. According to Efi Avdela, the bibliography about Jewry in Thessaloniki amounts to hundreds of books and articles.

3 Among the basic studies on the history of the Greek Jews: Bernard Pierron, *Juifs et Chrétiens de la Grèce Moderne. Histoire des relations intercommunautaires de 1821 à 1945* (Paris: Harmattan, 2000); Katherine E. Fleming, *Greece: A Jewish History* (Princeton, NJ: Princeton University Press, 2008); Rena Molho, *The Jews of Thessaloniki 1856–1919: A Unique Community* (Athens: Themelio, 2001); Joseph Néhama, *Histoire des Israélites de Salonique*, 7 vols. (Paris: Durlacher/Molho, 1935–78); Esther Benbassa and Aron Rodrigue, *Die Geschichte der sephardischen Juden: Von Toledo bis Saloniki* (Bochum: Dr. Dieter Winkler, 2005).

4 Harris Mylonas, *The Politics of Nation-Building: Making Co-Nationals, Refugees, and Minorities* (Cambridge: Cambridge University Press, 2012), 121.

5 Philip Carabott, "State, Society and the Religious 'Other' in Nineteenth-Century Greece," *Κάμπος: Cambridge Papers in Modern Greek* 18 (2011): 1, 27.

6 Katerina Kralova, "'Being Traitors': Post-War Greece in the Experience of Jewish Partisans," *Southeast European and Black Sea Studies* 17, no. 2 (2017): 263–80.

7 Joshua Eli Plaut, *Greek Jewry in the Twentieth Century, 1913–1983: Patterns of Jewish Survival in the Greek Provinces before and after the Holocaust* (London: Associated University Presses), 70.

8 Articles and books of particular note include Andrew Apostolou, "The Exception of Salonica: Bystanders and Collaborators in Northern Greece," *Holocaust and Genocide Studies* 14, no. 2 (2000): 165–96; Minna Rozen, "Jews and Greeks Remember Their Past: The Political Career of Tzevi Koretz (1933–1943)," *Jewish Social Studies* 12, no. 1 (2005): 111–66; Bea Lewkowicz, *The Jewish Community of Salonika: History, Memory,*

Identity (London: Valentine Mitchell, 2006); Katherine Fleming, *Greece: A Jewish History* (Princeton, NJ: Princeton University Press, 2008), Karina Lampsa and Jacov Schibi, *Η ζωή απ' την αρχή. Η μετανάστευση των Ελλήνων Εβραίων στην Παλαιστίνη (1945–1948)* (Life from the beginning. The migration of Greek Jews in Palestine, 1945–48) (Athens: Alexandria, 2010); George Antoniou, Stratos Dordanas, Nikos Zaikos, and Nikos Marantzidis, eds., *Το Ολοκαύτωμα στα Βαλκάνια* (The Holocaust in the Balkans) (Salonica: Epikentro, 2011); Avdela, "Towards a Greek History of the Jews of Salonica?" 405–10; Leon Saltiel, "Dehumanizing the Dead: The Destruction of Thessaloniki's Jewish Cemetery in the Light of New Sources," *Yad Vashem Studies* 42, no. 1 (2014): 1–35; Maria Kavala, *Η Καταστροφή των Εβραίων της Ελλάδας (1941–1944)* (The destruction of the Jews of Greece, 1941–1944) (Athens: Kallipos: Open Academic Editions, 2015); Rena Molho, *Der Holocaust der griechischen Juden. Studien zur Geschichte und Erinnerung* (Hamburg: Dietz, 2016); Katerina Kralova, "In the Shadow of the Nazi Past: Post-War Reconstruction and the Claims of the Jewish Community in Salonica," *European History Quarterly* 46, no. 2 (2016): 262–90; Leon Saltiel, "Professional Solidarity and the Holocaust: The Case of Thessaloniki," in *Jahrbuch für Antisemitismusforschung*, ed. Werner Bergmann et al. (Berlin: Metropol, 2015), 229–48; Pothiti Hantzaroula, "Children after the Holocaust and the Reconstruction of Jewish Communities in Post-War Greece," *Holocaust Studii şi Cercetări* 7, no. 1 (2015): 217–39; Rika Benveniste, *Λούνα. Δοκίμιο ιστορικής βιογραφίας* (Luna: A historical biography) (Athens: Polis, 2017); Rika Benveniste, *Die Überlebenden. Widerstand, Deportation, Rückkehr. Juden aus Thessaloniki in den 1940er Jahren* (Berlin: Edition Romiosini, 2017; first published in Greek in 2014); Evanghelos Chekimoglou and Anna Maria Droumpouki, eds., *Την επαύριον του Ολοκαυτώματος* (The day after the Holocaust) (Salonica: Jewish Museum of Thessaloniki, 2017); Katerina Kralova, "'Being Traitors': Post-war Greece in the Experience of Jewish Partisans," *Southeast European and Black Sea Studies* 17, no. 2 (2017): 263–80; George Antoniou and Dirk Mosses, eds., *The Holocaust in Greece* (Cambridge: Cambridge University Press, 2018); Leon Saltiel, ed., *«Μη με ξεχάσετε»: Τρεις Εβραίες μητέρες γράφουν στους γιους τους από το γκέτο της Θεσσαλονίκης* ("Don't forget me": Three Jewish mothers write to their sons from the Salonica ghetto) (Athens: Alexandria, 2018); Leon Nar, *Ξανά στη Σαλονίκη: Η μετέωρη επιστροφή των Ελλήνων Εβραίων στον γενέθλιο τόπο (1945–1946)* (Again in Salonica: The return of Greek Jews to their birthplace, 1945–1946)

(Athens: Polis, 2018); Paris Papamichos Chronakis, "A National Home in the Diaspora? Salonican Zionism and the Making of a Greco-Jewish City," *Journal of Levantine Studies* 8, no. 2 (Winter 2018): 59–84.

9 The Visual History Archive has expanded to include testimonies from rescuers. For Greece, one can access the testimony of Sotiris Papastratis from Evia, a member of the leftist resistance organization EAM, who helped many Jews to escape from Evia to the Middle East. See Sotiris Papastratis, ID Number 47258, VHA, USC Shoah Foundation, interview date Dec. 9, 1998.

10 Rika Benveniste, "The Coming Out of Jewish History in Greece" (2008), http://anciensiteusagespublicsdupasse.ehess.fr/index.php?id=130, accessed March 2, 2020 (now unavailable).

11 http://www.occupation-memories.org/en/index.html, accessed March 24, 2023. The collection of video interviews contains life-story interviews with ninety-three contemporary witnesses of the German occupation of Greece (1941–44). The interviews were conducted in Greece, Germany, and Israel from 2016 to 2018. Contemporary witnesses from a variety of backgrounds have been interviewed for the project, allowing a variety of experiences to be documented from different angles. Reports come, for example, from Jews who were in hiding, Shoah survivors, people who were arrested during raids in Athens or other places and deported to Germany, members of the resistance, survivors of massacres, etc.

12 Andrew Buckser, "Modern Identities and the Creation of History: Stories of Rescue among the Jews of Denmark," *Anthropological Quarterly* 72, no. 1 (January 1999): 3.

13 Lewkowicz, *The Jewish Community of Salonika: History, Memory, Identity*, 192.

14 Kobi (Yaakov) Kabalek, "The Rescue of Jews and the Memory of Nazism in Germany, from the Third Reich to the Present" (PhD diss., University of Virginia 2013), 7.

15 Yakov Shimby and Karina Lampsa, *I diasosi: I siopi tou skomou, I antistasi sta ghetto kai sta stratopeda, oi Ellines Evraioi sta hronia tis Katohis* (The rescue: The silence of the people, resistance at ghettos and camps, Greek Jews during the German occupation) (Athens: Kapon, 2012), in Greek.

16 Yakov Shimby and Karina Lampsa, *I diasosi*. In international historiography: Wolfgang Benz and Juliane Wetzel, *Solidarität und Hilfe für Juden während der NS-Zeit Rettungsversuche—Regionalstudien Slowakei, Bulgarien, Serbien, Kroatien mit Bosnien und Herzegowina, Belgien, Italien* (Berlin: Metropol Verlag, 2004); John J. Michalczyk, ed., *Resisters,*

Rescuers and Refugees: Historical and Ethical Issues (Kansas City, MO: Sheed & Ward, 1997).

17 Marta Cobel-Tokarska, *Desert Island, Burrow, Grave: Wartime Hiding Places of Jews in Occupied Poland* (Berlin: Peter Lang, 2018), 22.

18 David M. Seymour and Mercedes Camino, eds., *The Holocaust in the Twenty-First Century: Contesting/Contested Memories* (New York: Routledge, 2017), 5.

19 https://en.gariwo.net/photo-galleries/events/unveiling-of-greek-righteous-among-the-nations-monument-14535.html, accessed March 24, 2023.

20 https://en.gariwo.net/photo-galleries/events/unveiling-of-greek-righteous-among-the-nations-monument-14535.html, accessed August 9, 2019.

21 Philip Carabott, "The New Center of Jewry in Greece, Athens 1941–1947," Netherlands Institute of Athens, lecture, March 22, 2018.

22 http://athjcom.gr/english/news/holocaust-remembrance-day-january-27th-2016/, accessed December 9, 2019.

23 Eric Cortellessa, "How Greece Became One of America's—and Israel's—Closest Allies," *Washington Monthly*, June 18, 2019, https://washingtonmonthly.com/2019/06/18/how-greece-became-one-of-americas-and-israels-closest-allies/, accessed March 24, 2023.

24 https://www.efsyn.gr/politiki/110647_brabeia-toy-giant-basem-se-ellines-iroes-poy-diesosan-ebraioys, accessed December 9, 2019.

25 https://tinyurl.com/2p8dftbm, accessed December 9, 2019.

26 https://www.liberal.gr/apopsi/oi-isondikaioi-ton-ethnonsin-sto-2o-gumnasio-eleusinas/205750, accessed December 9, 2019.

27 https://lauderfoundation.com/righteous-among-the-nations-award-athens-greece/, accessed December 9, 2019.

28 http://athenscollege.org/2019/02/13/righteous_among_nations/, accessed December 9, 2019 (now unavailable).

29 https://www.constitutionalism.gr/2020-01-27-giannitsis-dikaioi-ethnon/, accessed March 24, 2023.

30 Joanna Beata Michlic, "Memories of Jews and the Holocaust in Post-Communist Eastern Europe," in *The Holocaust in the Twenty-First Century: Contesting/Contested Memories*, ed. David M. Seymour and Mercedes Camino (New York: Routledge, 2017), 140.

31 Shimby and Lampsa, *I diasosi*, 289–96.

32 Paul Isaac Hagouel, "Framework and Historical Context of Jewish Greeks and Jews in Occupied Greece: Indicative Localities Thessaloniki, Athens,

Corfu, Xanthi & Zakynthos" (paper presented at "Nations of Occupied Europe and the Holocaust" conference, Warsaw, December 6–8, 2017).

33 https://www.mfa.gr/epikairotita/eidiseis-anakoinoseis/anakoinose-gia-te-nea-ekdose-tou-upourgeiou-exoterikon-oi-ellenes-dikaioi-ton-ethnon.html, accessed March 24, 2023.

34 Benveniste, "The Coming Out of Jewish History in Greece."

35 Benveniste, "The Coming Out of Jewish History in Greece."

36 See, for example, the article by historian Hagen Fleischer about the activities of Foteini Tomai, "The Humiliation of the Official Memory of the Holocaust," https://chronos.fairead.net/chronos-archives-01, accessed March 24, 2023.

37 Hagouel, "Framework and Historical Context of Jewish Greeks and Jews in Occupied Greece."

38 Fotini Tomai-Constantopoulou, "Property of Jewish Greeks in Context of the Holocaust: Legal Status, German Occupation and Post-War Restitution and Memory" (lecture delivered at the "Nationalization, Confiscation and Restitution: Historical, Legal, Economic and Political Issues" conference organized by the New Balkans Institute, Belgrade, Serbia, February 25–26, 2014).

39 Foteini Tomai and Thanos Veremis, *Documents on the History of the Greek Jews: Records from the Historical Archives of the Ministry of Foreign Affairs* (Athens: Kastaniotis, 1998).

40 Andrew Buckser, "Rescue and Cultural Context during the Holocaust: Grundtvigian Nationalism and the Rescue of the Danish Jews," *Shofar: An Interdisciplinary Journal of Jewish Studies*19, no. 2 (Winter 2001): 2.

41 https://www.jewishmuseum.gr/en/the-good-shepherds-metropolitans-and-chief-rabbis-in-the-face-of-the-holocaust/, accessed June 10, 2019.

42 https://www.jewishmuseum.gr/en/the-good-shepherds-metropolitans-and-chief-rabbis-in-the-face-of-the-holocaust/.

43 Philip Carabott, "Stance and Reactions of the Greek Orthodox Society Towards the Persecution of Its Greek-Jewish Co-Citizens During the Nazi Occupation," in *To Olokautoma sta Balkania* (The Holocaust in the Balkans), ed. Giorgos Antoniou, Stratos N. Dordanas, Nikos Zaikos, and Nikos Marantzidis (Thessaloniki: Epikentro, 2011), 253–95.

44 Carabott, "Stance and Reactions of the Greek Orthodox Society Towards the Persecution of its Greek-Jewish Co-Citizens During the Nazi Occupation."

45 About the close cooperation between JMG and its director with the ministry of foreign affairs and Foteini Tomai, see the video published on the

fortieth anniversary of the foundation of the JMG, especially after 16:09: https://www.jewishmuseum.gr/evraiko-moyseio-tis-ellados-i-istoria-40-chronon/, accessed August 11, 2019.

46 Buckser, "Modern Identities and the Creation of History: Stories of Rescue among the Jews of Denmark," 3.

47 Katerina Kralova, "Being a Holocaust Survivor in Greece: Narratives of the Postwar Period, 1944–1953," in *The Holocaust in Greece*, ed. Giorgos Antoniou and A. Dirk Moses (Cambridge: Cambridge University Press, 2018), 323.

48 Miranta Alkalai, Interview mog040, September 9, 2016, interviewer: Anna Maria Droumpouki, interview archive "Memories of the Occupation in Greece," https://archive.occupation-memories.org/de, DOI: 10.17169/mog.mog040, accessed March 15, 2018.

49 Joanna B. Michlic, *Jewish Children in Nazi-Occupied Poland: Survival and Polish-Jewish Relations during the Holocaust as Reflected in Early Postwar Recollections* (Jerusalem: Yad Vashem, 2008).

50 Miranta Alkalai, Interview mog040, September 9, 2016.

51 https://www.juedische-allgemeine.de/juedische-welt/unbedingter-wille-zu-berichten/, accessed December 10.

52 Heinz Kounio, Interview mog051, December 1, 2016, interviewer: Anna Maria Droumpouki, interview archive "Memories of the Occupation in Greece," https://archive.occupation-memories.org/de, DOI: 10.17169/mog.mog051, accessed March 15, 2018.

53 Stratos N. Dordanas, "Exontosi kai leilasia: I ipiresia diaxeiriseos israilitikon periousion (YDIP)" (Annihilation and plundering: The service for the disposal of Jewish property), in *To Olokautoma sta Balkania* (The Holocaust in the Balkans), ed. Giorgos Antoniou, Stratos N. Dordanas, Nikos Zaikos, and Nikos Marantzidis (Thessaloniki: Epikentro, 2011), 331–52; Iasonas Chandrinos, "Gia na min ploutisoun adika se varos ton Evraion . . . I diaxeirisi ton evraikon periousion tis Thessalonikis kai oi germano-ellinikes emporikes sinallages 1943–1944" (So that they won't get rich unfairly on account of the Jews . . . : The Jewish properties and the German-Greek commercial transactions, 1943–1944), in *Tin epavrion tou Olokaftomatos* (The day after the Holocaust), ed. Evaggelos Hekimoglou and Anna Maria Droumpouki (Thessaloniki: Jewish Museum of Thessaloniki, 2017), 166–74.

54 Kostis Kornetis, "Expropriating the Space of the Other: Spoliations of Thessalonican Jews in the 1940s," in *The Holocaust in Greece*, ed. Giorgos

Antoniou and A. Dirk Moses (Cambridge: Cambridge University Press, 2018), 228–51.

55 Heinz Kounio, ID No. 41892, VHA, USC Shoah Foundation, date of interview May 29, 1998.

56 For analyses of interviews and changes in their recounting over time, see Henry Greenspan, *On Listening to Holocaust Survivors: Recounting and Life History* (Westport, CT: Praeger, 1998); Laurence L. Langer, *Holocaust Testimonies: The Ruins of Memory* (New Haven, CT: Yale University Press, 1991); Jürgen Matthäus, ed., *Approaching an Auschwitz Survivor: Holocaust Testimony and Its Transformations* (Oxford: Oxford University Press, 2009); Henry Greenspan, *The Awakening of Memory: Survivor Testimony in the First Years after the Holocaust and Today* (Washington, DC: USHMM, 2001).

57 Anja Tippner, "Worlds Apart? Cross-mapping Camp Literature from the Gulag and Nazi Concentration Camps," in *Narratives of Annihilation, Confinement, and Survival*, ed. Anja Tippner and Anna Artwinska (Berlin: De Gruyter, 2019), 43.

58 See Aristotle A. Kallis, "The Jewish Community of Salonica under Siege: The Antisemitic Violence of the Summer of 1931," *Holocaust and Genocide Studies* 20, no. 1 (Spring 2006): 34–56.

59 Heinz Kounio, Interview mog051, December 1, 2016.

60 Zafiria Kone, Interview mog049, January 5, 2017, interviewer: Antonis Antoniou, interview archive "Memories of the Occupation in Greece," https://archive.occupation-memories.org/de, DOI: 10.17169/mog.mog049, accessed March 15, 2018.

61 https://www.jewishmuseum.gr/en/the-greek-resistance-and-the-jews-1941-1944/, accessed August 11, 2019.

62 Zafiria Kone, Interview mog049, January 5, 2017.

63 Marta Cobel-Tokarska, *Desert Island, Burrow, Grave: Wartime Hiding Places of Jews in Occupied Poland* (Berlin: Peter Lang, 2018), 10.

64 Zafiria Kone, ID No. 45261, VHA, USC Shoah Foundation, date of interview June 23, 1998.

65 Greenspan, *The Awakening of Memory: Survivor Testimony in the First Years after the Holocaust and Today*, https://collections.ushmm.org/search/catalog/bib49303, accessed March 24, 2023.

66 Zafiria Kone, Interview mog049, January 5, 2017.

67 Yehouda Chaki, ID No. 53873, VHA, USC Shoah Foundation, date of interview November 18, 1996.

68 Yehouda Chaki, ID No. 53873, date of interview November 18, 1996.
69 Yehouda Chaki, ID No. 53873, date of interview November 18, 1996.
70 Yehouda Chaki, ID No. 53873, date of interview November 18, 1996.
71 Lena Zosafat, ID No. 10300, VHA, USC Shoah Foundation, date of interview December 17, 1995.
72 Lena Zosafat, ID No. 10300, date of interview December 17, 1995.
73 Lena Zosafat, ID No. 10300, date of interview December 17, 1995.
74 Ioudas Magrizos, Interview mog065, April 20, 2017, interviewer: Kerasia (Ersi) Malagiorgi, interview archive "Memories of the Occupation in Greece," https://archive.occupation-memories.org/de, DOI: 10.17169/mog.mog065, accessed March 21, 2018. I would like to thank the interviewer, Ersi Malagiorgi, for providing me with the detailed protocols of the interview.
75 Ioudas Magrizos, Interview mog065, April 20, 2017.
76 Ioudas Magrizos, Interview mog065, April 20, 2017.
77 Rachil Papadrianoy, ID No. 46032, VHA, USC Shoah Foundation, date of interview May 22, 1998.
78 Rachil Papadrianoy, ID No. 46032, date of interview May 22, 1998.
79 Michail Nachman, ID No. 43234, VHA, USC Shoah Foundation, date of interview April 15, 1998.
80 Telis-Israel Nachman, ID No. 38559, VHA, USC Shoah Foundation, date of interview February 26, 1998.
81 Ioylia Nachman, ID No. 40863, VHA, USC Shoah Foundation, date of interview April 15, 1998.
82 Andreas Sephiha, ID No. 48935, VHA, USC Shoah Foundation, date of interview December 13, 1998.
83 Andreas Sephiha, ID No. 48935, date of interview December 13, 1998.
84 Andreas Sephiha, *Remembering a Life and a World* (Thessaloniki: Ianos, 2015).
85 Sephiha, *Remembering a Life and a World*, 34.
86 Solomon Anzel, ID No. 37993, VHA, USC Shoah Foundation, date of interview February 8, 1998.
87 Moris Leon, ID No. 43190, VHA, USC Shoah Foundation, date of interview April 14, 1998.
88 Lela Koymeri, ID No. 47767, VHA, USC Shoah Foundation, date of interview October 21, 1998.
89 Philip Carabott, "The Traitors Should Be Vanished from the Face of the Earth: Jewish Collaborators and the Shadow of Treason," in *The Day after*

the Holocaust, ed. Anna Maria Droumpouki and Evaggelos Hekimoglou (Thessaloniki: Jewish Museum of Thessaloniki, 2016), 102–22.

90 Lela Koymeri, ID No. 47767, VHA, USC Shoah Foundation, date of interview October 21, 1998.

91 Rosa Asser Pardo, *548 Days with Another Name: Salonika 1943. A Child's Diary, an Adult's Memories of War* (New York: American Friends of the Jewish Museum of Greece and Bloch Publishing, 2005).

92 Rosa Asser Pardo, Interview mog046, December 20, 2016, interviewer: Anna Maria Droumpouki, interview archive "Memories of the Occupation of Greece," https://archive.occupation-memories.org/de, DOI: 10.17169/mog.mog046 accessed March 15, 2018.

93 Rosa Asser Pardo, Interview mog046, December 20, 2016.

94 Alexandros Simha, Interview mog045, December 12, 2016, interviewer: Anna Maria Droumpouki, interview archive "Memories of the Occupation in Greece," https://archive.occupation-memories.org/de, DOI: 10.17169/mog.mog045, accessed March 19, 2018.

95 See Michalczyk, ed., *Resisters, Rescuers and Refugees: Historical and Ethical Issues.*

96 Sotiris Papastratis, ID Number 47258, VHA, USC Shoah Foundation, date of interview December 9, 1998.

97 Similar complexities of Jewish experience that very seldomly appear in the rescue literature are present in the case of Danish Jewry. See Andrew Buckser, *After the Rescue: Jewish Identity and Community in Contemporary Denmark* (New York: Palgrave Macmillan, 2003), 199.

98 Buckser, *After the Rescue*, 4.

99 Greenspan, *On Listening to Holocaust Survivors*, 43.

100 Greenspan, *On Listening to Holocaust Survivors*, 182.

101 Buckser, *After the Rescue*, 210.

Bibliography

Antoniou, George, Stratos Dordanas, Nikos Zaikos, and Nikos Marantzidis, eds. *Το Ολοκαύτωμα στα Βαλκάνια*. (The Holocaust in the Balkans.) Salonica: Epikentro, 2011.

Antoniou, George, and Dirk Mosses, eds. *The Holocaust in Greece*. Cambridge: Cambridge University Press, 2018.

Apostolou, Andrew. "The Exception of Salonica: Bystanders and Collaborators in Northern Greece." *Holocaust and Genocide Studies* 14, no. 2 (2000): 165–96.

Avdela, Efi. "Towards a Greek History of the Jews of Salonica?" *Jewish History* 28 (November 2014): 405–10.

Benbassa, Esther, and Aron Rodrigue. *Die Geschichte der sephardischen Juden: Von Toledo bis Saloniki*. (History of the Sephardic Jews. From Toledo to Thessaloniki.) Bochum: Dr. Dieter Winkler, 2005.

Benveniste, Rika. *Λούνα. Δοκίμιο ιστορικής βιογραφίας*. (Luna: A historical biography.) Athens: Polis, 2017.

———. *Die Überlebenden. Widerstand, Deportation, Rückkehr. Juden aus Thessaloniki in den 1940er Jahren*. Berlin: Edition Romiosini, 2017; first published in Greek in 2014.

Benz, Wolfgang, and Juliane Wetzel. *Solidarität und Hilfe für Juden während der NS-Zeit Rettungsversuche—Regionalstudien Slowakei, Bulgarien, Serbien, Kroatien mit Bosnien und Herzegowina, Belgien, Italien*. (Solidarity and help for Jews during the Nazi era—regional studies Slovakia, Bulgaria, Serbia, Croatia with Bosnia and Hercegovina, Belgium, Italy.) Berlin: Metropol, 2004.

Buckser, Andrew. *After the Rescue: Jewish Identity and Community in Contemporary Denmark*. New York: Palgrave Macmillan, 2003.

———. "Modern Identities and the Creation of History: Stories of Rescue among the Jews of Denmark." *Anthropological Quarterly* 72, no. 1 (January 1999): 1–17.

———. "Rescue and Cultural Context during the Holocaust: Grundtvigian Nationalism and the Rescue of the Danish Jews." *Shofar: An Interdisciplinary Journal of Jewish Studies* 19, no. 2 (Winter 2001): 1–25.

Carabott, Philip. "The New Center of Jewry in Greece, Athens 1941–1947." Netherlands Institute of Athens, lecture, March 22, 2018.

———. "Stance and Reactions of the Greek Orthodox Society Towards the Persecution of Its Greek-Jewish Co-Citizens during the Nazi Occupation." In *To Olokautoma sta Balkania* (The Holocaust in the Balkans), ed. Giorgos Antoniou, Stratos N. Dordanas, Nikos Zaikos, and Nikos Marantzidis, 253–95. Thessaloniki: Epikentro, 2011.

———. "State, Society and the Religious 'Other' in Nineteenth-Century Greece." *Κάμπος: Cambridge Papers in Modern Greek* 18 (2011): 1–27.

———. "The Traitors Should Be Vanished from the Face of the Earth: Jewish Collaborators and the Shadow of Treason." In *The Day after the Holocaust*, ed. Anna Maria Droumpouki and Evaggelos Hekimoglou, 102–22. Thessaloniki: Jewish Museum of Thessaloniki, 2016.

Chandrinos, Iassonas. "Gia na min ploutisoun adika se varos ton Evraion . . . I diaxeirisi ton evraikon periousion tis Thessalonikis kai oi germano-ellinikes emporikes sinallages 1943–1944." (So that they won't get rich unfairly on account of the Jews . . . : The Jewish properties and the German-Greek commercial transactions, 1943–1944.) In *Tin epavrion tou Olokaftomatos* (The day after the Holocaust), ed. Evaggelos Hekimoglou and Anna Maria Droumpouki, 166–74. Thessaloniki: Jewish Museum of Thessaloniki, 2017.

———. "Oi dikaioi tou antifasismou. To EAM kai oi prospatheies diasosis ton Ellinon Evraion." (The righteous of antifascism. EAM and the efforts of saving the Jews.) In *Oi Evraikes koinotites anamesa se Anatoli kai Disi. 15os–20os aionas* (Jewish communities between east and west, 15th–20th century), ed. Anna Mahaira and Leda Papastefanaki, 282–94. Ioannina: Isnafi, 2016.

———. *Synagonistis: Ellines Evraioi stin Ethniki Antistasi.* (Greek Jews in national resistance.) Athens: Jewish Museum of Greece, 2013.

Chekimoglou, Evanghelos, and Anna Maria Droumpouki, eds. *Την επαύριον του Ολοκαυτώματος.* (The day after the Holocaust.) Salonica: Jewish Museum of Thessaloniki, 2017.

Chronakis, Paris Papamichos. "A National Home in the Diaspora? Salonican Zionism and the Making of a Greco-Jewish City." *Journal of Levantine Studies* 8, no. 2 (Winter 2018): 59–84.

Cobel-Tokarska, Marta. *Desert Island, Burrow, Grave: Wartime Hiding Places of Jews in Occupied Poland.* Berlin: Peter Lang, 2018.

Dordanas, Stratos N. "Exontosi kai leilasia: I ipiresia diaxeiriseos israilitikon periousion (YDIP)." (Annihilation and plundering: The service for the disposal of Jewish property.) In *To Olokautoma sta Balkania* (The Holocaust in the Balkans), ed. Giorgos Antoniou, Stratos N. Dordanas, Nikos Zaikos, and Nikos Marantzidis, 331–52. Thessaloniki: Epikentro, 2011.

Fleming, Katherine E. *Greece: A Jewish History.* Princeton, NJ: Princeton University Press, 2008.

Greenspan, Henry. *The Awakening of Memory: Survivor Testimony in the First Years after the Holocaust and Today.* Washington, DC: USHMM, 2001.

———. *On Listening to Holocaust Survivors: Recounting and Life History.* Westport, CT: Praeger, 1998.

Hantzaroula, Pothiti. "Children after the Holocaust and the Reconstruction of Jewish Communities in Post-War Greece." *Holocaust Studii și Cercetări* 7, no. 1 (2015): 217–39.

Kabalek, Kobi (Yaakov). "The Rescue of Jews and the Memory of Nazism in Germany, from the Third Reich to the Present." PhD diss., University of Virginia, 2013.

Kallis, Aristotle A. "The Jewish Community of Salonica under Siege: The Antisemitic Violence of the Summer of 1931." *Holocaust and Genocide Studies* 20, no. 1 (Spring 2006): 34–56.

Kavala, Maria. *Η Καταστροφή των Εβραίων της Ελλάδας (1941–1944)*. (The destruction of the Jews of Greece, 1941–1944.) Athens: Kallipos: Open Academic Editions, 2015.

Kralova, Katerina. "Being a Holocaust Survivor in Greece: Narratives of the Postwar Period, 1944–1953." In *The Holocaust in Greece*, ed. Giorgos Antoniou and A. Dirk Moses, 304–27. Cambridge: Cambridge University Press, 2018.

———. "'Being Traitors': Post-War Greece in the Experience of Jewish Partisans." *Southeast European and Black Sea Studies* 17, no. 2 (2017): 263–80.

———. "Expropriating the Space of the Other: Spoliations of Thessalonican Jews in the 1940s." In *The Holocaust in Greece*, ed. Giorgos Antoniou and Dirk Moses, 228–51. Cambridge: Cambridge University Press, 2018.

———. "In the Shadow of the Nazi Past: Post-War Reconstruction and the Claims of the Jewish Community in Salonica." *European History Quarterly* 46, no. 2 (2016): 262–90.

Lampsa, Karina, and Jacov Schibi, *Η ζωή απ' την αρχή. Η μετανάστευση των Ελλήνων Εβραίων στην Παλαιστίνη (1945–1948)*. (Life from the beginning. The migration of Greek Jews in Palestine, 1945–48.) Athens: Alexandria, 2010.

Langer, Laurence L. *Holocaust Testimonies: The Ruins of Memory*. New Haven, CT: Yale University Press, 1991.

Lewkowicz, Bea. *The Jewish Community of Salonika: History, Memory, Identity*. Elstree: Vallentine Mitchell, 2006.

Matthäus Jürgen. *Approaching an Auschwitz Survivor: Holocaust Testimony and Its Transformations*. Oxford: Oxford University Press, 2009.

Michalczyk, John J., ed. *Resisters, Rescuers and Refugees: Historical and Ethical Issues*. Kansas City, MO: Sheed & Ward, 1997.

Michlic, Joanna Beata. *Jewish Children in Nazi-Occupied Poland: Survival and Polish-Jewish Relations during the Holocaust as Reflected in Early Postwar Recollections*. Jerusalem: Yad Vashem, 2008.

———. "Memories of Jews and the Holocaust in Post-Communist Eastern Europe." In *The Holocaust in the Twenty-First Century: Contesting/Contested Memories*, ed. David M. Seymour and Mercedes Camino, 135–59. New York: Routledge, 2017.

Molho, Rena. *Der Holocaust der griechischen Juden. Studien zur Geschichte und Erinnerung*. Hamburg: Dietz, 2016.

———. "The Jewish Community of Thessaloniki and Its Incorporation into the Greek State, 1912–1919." *Middle Eastern Studies* 24 (1988): 39–403.

———. *The Jews of Thessaloniki 1856–1919: A Unique Community*. Athens: Themelio, 2001.

Mylonas, Harris. *The Politics of Nation-Building: Making Co-Nationals, Refugees, and Minorities*. Cambridge: Cambridge University Press, 2012.

Nar, Leon. *Ξανά στη Σαλονίκη: Η μετέωρη επιστροφή των Ελλήνων Εβραίων στον γενέθλιο τόπο (1945–1946)*. (Again in Salonica: The return of Greek Jews to their birthplace, 1945–1946.) Athens: Polis, 2018.

Néhama, Joseph. *Histoire des Israélites de Salonique*. (History of Jews in Thessaloniki.) Paris: Durlacher/Molho, 1935–78.

Pardo, Rosa Asser. *548 Days with Another Name: Salonika 1943. A Child's Diary, an Adult's Memories of War*. New York: American Friends of the Jewish Museum of Greece and Bloch Publishing, 2005.

Pierron, Bernard. *Juifs et Chrétiens de la Grèce Moderne. Histoire des relations intercommunautaires de 1821 à 1945*. (Jews and Christians in modern Greece. History of intercommunity relations, 1821–1945.) Paris: Harmattan, 2000.

Plaut, Joshua Eli. *Greek Jewry in the Twentieth Century, 1913–1983: Patterns of Jewish Survival in the Greek Provinces before and after the Holocaust*. London: Associated University Presses, 1996.

Rozen, Minna. "Jews and Greeks Remember Their Past: The Political Career of Tzevi Koretz (1933–1943)." *Jewish Social Studies* 12, no. 1 (2005): 111–66.

Saltiel, Leon. "Dehumanizing the Dead: The Destruction of Thessaloniki's Jewish Cemetery in the Light of New Sources." *Yad Vashem Studies* 42, no. 1 (2014): 1–35.

———. "Professional Solidarity and the Holocaust: The Case of Thessaloniki." In *Jahrbuch für Antisemitismusforschung*, ed. Werner Bergmann et al., 229–48. Berlin: Metropol, 2015.

Saltiel, Leon, ed. *«Μη με ξεχάσετε»: Τρεις Εβραίες μητέρες γράφουν στους γιους τους από το γκέτο της Θεσσαλονίκης*. ("Don't forget me": Three Jewish mothers write to their sons from the Salonica ghetto.) Athens: Alexandria, 2018.

Sephiha, Andreas. *Remembering a Life and a World*. Thessaloniki: Ianos, 2015.

Seymour, David M., and Mercedes Camino, eds. *The Holocaust in the Twenty-First Century: Contesting/Contested Memories*. New York: Routledge, 2017.

Shimby, Yakov, and Karina Lampsa. *I diasosi: I siopi tou skomou, I antistasi sta ghetto kai sta stratopeda, oi Ellines Evraioi sta hronia tis Katohis*. (The rescue: The silence of the people, resistance at ghettos and camps, Greek Jews during the German occupation.) Athens: Kapon, 2012.

Tippner, Anja. "Worlds Apart? Cross-mapping Camp Literature from the Gulag and Nazi Concentration Camps." In *Narratives of Annihilation, Confinement, and Survival*, ed. Anja Tippner and Anna Artwinska, 30–47. Berlin: De Gruyter, 2019.

Tomai, Foteini, and Thanos Veremis. *Documents on the History of the Greek Jews: Records from the Historical Archives of the Ministry of Foreign Affairs*. Athens: Kastaniotis, 1998.

9

Irena Sendler from Żegota

The Heroine and Her Myth

ANNA BIKONT

TRANSLATED BY JASPER TILBURY

History

"She is the mother of two-and-a-half thousand children saved from the Warsaw Ghetto. I do not use the term 'foster mother,' just 'mother,' because she gave them a second life," wrote Anna Mieszkowska in her authorized biography of Irena Sendler.[1] Her protagonist, who received the Righteous Among the Nations medal in 1965, was "discovered" by a wider audience at the beginning of the twenty-first century. Since then, the story of how Irena Sendler saved twenty-five hundred children from the Warsaw Ghetto has been recounted in fiction, biographies, children's books, comics, and in documentary and feature films (including *The Courageous Heart of Irena Sendler*, produced in the United States and starring Oscar-winning actress Anna Paquin).[2] Numerous schools, streets, and squares in Poland are named after her. The Polish parliament designated 2018 as the Year of Irena Sendler. In my book, *Sendler: In Hiding*, published in 2017, I tried to separate the facts from the myths that have arisen around her.[3]

Before and during World War II, Irena Sendler was employed as a social worker at the Warsaw City Council's Department of Social Welfare and Public Health. From the beginning of the war, she and her female colleagues at the welfare department helped their friends from work who had been thrown out of their jobs on account of being Jews. They continued to look after Jewish children who had been excluded from the municipal care system and needed assistance.[4] This is how Sendler described the activities initiated by her friend

Jadwiga Piotrowska: "Community interviews were the basis for providing assistance in the social care system. The idea was to fake these interviews. So we would enter a fictitious Polish surname and use it to get money and clothes. These items were collected by trusted people and taken to Jewish families."[5] Piotrowska also proposed that the welfare department should continue to help a group of Jewish children who had been under its care before the war by falsifying their papers by giving them non-Jewish surnames. First the child had to be classified as an orphan and placed in one of the fourteen welfare centers in Warsaw. In Sendler's words, "It was necessary to secure the assistance of a desk officer and a guardian and to conduct a fictitious interview and a fictitious medical examination; in short, it was necessary to circumvent, consciously and deliberately, all of the social welfare regulations."[6] For a short period of time (the first months of the war), this was all that needed to be done.

Toward the end of 1939, the Nazi occupiers began to tighten their grip. Now all adult Jews for whom Sendler and her departmental colleagues were securing illegal aid from the city had to have their papers forged in three places. First there were the registration books kept by building administrators—it was necessary to find someone willing to register tenants they had never seen. Then there was the city records department, where residents were registered—it was necessary to have an accomplice who worked there. And finally, there was the welfare department, where a file was kept for every person under its care. Sendler and her female colleagues would alter the files by assigning dangerous infectious diseases to their Jewish friends who were hiding under assumed names, so that no one would think of inspecting the places where they were registered.[7]

In 1993, at an international conference in honor of the Righteous in Warsaw, Sendler said: "Many times I heard people who had been driven to extreme poverty and exhaustion ask in despair, sobbing: 'Why have all of our acquaintances, even friends, our comrades with whom we fought in a common cause for decades, our neighbours, some of whom benefited from our help for years—why have they abandoned us? Why can they not even bring themselves to send a brief note, a small acknowledgment that they remember us? Why, why?'"[8] This estrangement, which happened very quickly, before the ghettos were even created, was described in numerous diaries and memoirs. Irena Sendler and her colleagues were among the few who did not succumb to the general trend.

That was the situation until November 16, 1940, the day the Warsaw Ghetto was sealed off. The Nazis crammed three hundred thousand of Warsaw's residents, one-third of the population, into a space that covered less than 2.5 percent of the city's area and was bordered by a three-meter-high wall. Sendler could enter the ghetto legally. The director of the Municipal Sanitary Works,

Juliusz Majkowski, had a large batch of permits for use by the sanitary services. The Nazis were terrified of typhus, which was spreading in the crowded ghetto, and it was Majkowski who was responsible for keeping the disease under control. Together with Irena Schultz, who also worked at the welfare department, Sendler would bring medicines and cleaning products into the ghetto under the guise of being a sanitary service employee—with the documentation to prove it. The women smuggled in clothes by wearing them. Sendler was petite. She could put on a few sweaters or blouses without attracting any attention and still have room to hide some food. Ration cards were issued in the ghetto—the daily ration was around three hundred calories. Food that could be purchased legally lasted for, at most, the first few days in a month. "It initially began with us providing a very small amount of help to our friends," Sendler said. "It offends me when people see this as an example of great heroism. You know, such praise is completely exaggerated. My friend Ewa Rechtman was there, as was the lawyer Zysman, who ended up in the ghetto with his whole family. Going to the ghetto opened my eyes to what was happening. As a result, those support networks began to expand."[9]

"I remember her visit to the ghetto," recalled Michał Głowiński, a nephew of the lawyer Józef Zysman with whom Sendler had worked before the war.[10] "She was young, petite, and pretty—definitely pretty. My grandmother said to her: 'Irena, when you come to this apartment, it is as if a smile has entered the house.' I found this idea of smile entering the house somewhat puzzling. I took it literally, and for a long time I wondered what it meant. That is why I remembered both the phrase and Sendler herself."[11]

Initially, help for the ghetto meant bringing in food, medicines, and cleaning products. Sendler did not just visit the ghetto in a hurry to deliver something and leave. She would accompany her friends in their desperate attempts to lead a normal life—organizing activities for children, attending lectures and concerts, celebrating religious holidays, publishing underground newspapers. She observed—to use Rachela Auerbach's phrase—"death walking in broad daylight through the streets of a closed city,"[12] and this was part of her everyday life. Few non-Jewish Poles experienced the ghetto as intensely and personally as Sendler did.

As the situation in the ghetto worsened dramatically, some individuals tried to escape. Sendler describes the actions she took on their behalf, without specifying the dates.

> Thanks to my permit, I was able to bring food into the ghetto during those difficult times, especially dairy products and fat, but I was also

> able to set up a rescue organization. We had three safe houses on the Polish side: a) Wronia Street (between Krochmalna Street and Chłodna Street), b) Dworska Street (rag warehouses), and c) Grójecka Street (a factory, corner of Kopińska Street). We led people out along established routes. Together with Irena Schultz, I would arrange all the details inside the ghetto (number of people, meeting point, route, group). Wanda Wyrobkowa and I would direct people to the three safe houses mentioned above. There were three types of people we helped escape. First there were those who mainly needed to be led out and possibly taken to a predetermined location. Sometimes they needed a little financial help too. The second type wanted to reach a safe house outside Warsaw. In this case the aim would be to get through the ghetto cordon and provide them with shelter for a few days. The third type, the most common, were people who had no one outside the ghetto and were almost or completely penniless. For these people, life had to be organized from scratch. Adults were assigned to appropriate jobs, usually in the provinces.[13]

Working at the welfare department before the war, Sendler—unlike most of her female colleagues—had looked after adults. (She had been responsible for homeless shelters and had also trained social workers.) From her testimony preserved in the archive of the Ghetto Fighters' House (Kibbutz Lohamei HaGeta'ot) in Israel, it appears that this was also the case at the beginning of the war and during the *Grossaktion Warschau*, which the Nazis carried out between July 22 and September 21, 1942: Sendler mainly cared for adults and "older children"—that is, children who could pass for adults when dressed in several layers of clothing. At the same time, she was in constant contact with her friends from the welfare department, who had looked after children before the war and who were now trying to help their female colleagues and their young charges on the other side of the ghetto wall.

It should be noted that going over to the "Aryan" side, which Sendler describes, did not mean that she (or Schultz or Wyrobkowa) would leave through the ghetto gate together with the designated person. Her role, and that of her female colleagues, was to coordinate contacts between those going to work on the Aryan side, among whom the escapees were to be smuggled out, and people on the Aryan side, who were to provide refuge for the escapees in Warsaw or in the provinces. Jews knew far better how to get out of the ghetto than the Poles did. On the other side of the wall, however, the help of Poles was invaluable.

Jonas Turkow, a Jewish actor, director, and theater producer, who in 1965 nominated Irena Sendler for the Righteous Among the Nations medal in Yad Vashem, described how he came across her while looking for ways to save his daughter. Turkow wound up in the Warsaw Ghetto together with his wife, Diana Blumenfeld, and daughter Margarita. Someone told him that "a Christian partner with whom he did business knew a certain woman by the name of Wanda who had previously asked about Jewish children who could be placed in convents and orphanages." This is how he met Wanda Wyrobkowa, who was also from the City Council's Department of Social Welfare and Public Health, and it was through her that he met Sendler.[14] "A whole series of conversations took place. In the final phase they were attended by, among others, Irena Sendler, a wonderful, luminous figure," wrote Turkow. "Ms. Sendler had already made contact with our own Ala Gołąb-Grynbergowa and had visited the ghetto several times."[15] "Sendler," Turkow continued, "wanted to present to the ghetto leadership her plan for saving the children. She and her female colleagues were willing to take on a few children, but it would be possible to take on many more if only the money could be found. She discussed the plan with Ala Gołąb-Grynbergowa and Dawid Guzik, who became very interested in it, but her contact with them was interrupted by the *Grossaktion*." During the *Grossaktion* (the liquidation of the Warsaw Ghetto carried out by the Nazis in the summer and autumn of 1942), 265,000 Jews were transported from the Umschlagplatz to the Treblinka extermination camp, and another 10,000 were killed on the spot. As Turkow recalled, Dawid Guzik, a social activist in the ghetto and deputy director of the American Joint Distribution Committee in Warsaw, the most important Jewish self-help organization, went half-mad after his wife, daughter, and son-in-law were taken to the Umschlagplatz. Perhaps that is why Sendler tried a different approach and found her way to Turkow via Wanda Wyrobkowa. Turkow promised to look for funds, but contact with him also quickly broke off during the *Grossaktion*.

When, following the liquidation of the ghetto, the Council to Aid Jews (Żegota) was established in late 1942, its chairman, Julian Grobelny, contacted Sendler as the representative of a group of women from the welfare department involved in helping Jews. Żegota was a Polish-Jewish organization established by the Polish government-in-exile. It included representatives of political parties connected with the London-based government and representatives of Jewish political parties, and it was through them that Żegota distributed money: Each party, whether Polish or Jewish, received funds in proportion to the number of people in its care.[16] Grobelny represented the Polish Socialist Party (PPS), with which Sendler had also been associated before the war, but he heard about her not through the PPS but from an acquaintance who looked after Jewish children.[17] Existing structures that were aiding Jews but which were not affiliated with political parties were also able to benefit from Żegota's help. This is what happened with Irena Sendler's network of colleagues from the welfare department. They had already been helping the Jewish inhabitants of Warsaw of their own accord, but it was Żegota that enabled them to combine their efforts and expand their activities.

The first Żegota document mentioning Sendler dates from August 16, 1943: "Trojan proposes the formation of a committee consisting of Iza, Jolanta, D., Mikołaj, and Borowski to manage the affairs of the Children's Section. The motion passed."[18] "Trojan" is Julian Grobelny, who headed Żegota; "Iza" is Izabella Kuczkowska from the welfare department; "Jolanta" is Irena Sendler's underground alias; "D" is Aleksandra Dargielowa, head of one of the Warsaw offices of the Central Welfare Council, a charitable organization that operated officially under the German occupation; and "Mikołaj" and "Borowski" are Leon Feiner of the Bund and Adolf Berman of the Jewish National Committee, both of whom were members of the presidium of Żegota.

From the moment the Żegota money appeared, one could legitimately speak of "Sendler's liaison officers," although that is not how her colleagues would have described themselves at the time. Sendler could now say to each of them: "If you have Jewish children or adults in your care, I know someone who will enable me to provide you with money each month. I can help you with documents, doctors, or a sudden change of accommodation." Years later, the employees of the welfare department described, in a collective volume, the Department's work: "The most active person and main organizing force behind our efforts [to rescue Jewish children] was Irena Sendler (indeed, she was employed in another section of the Department)."[19] "None of my liaison officers knew that I worked for Żegota," explained Sendler to her biographer.[20] When asking for help, Sendler and the women liaison officers usually did not reveal to the people they contacted that they were trying to assist Jewish children. "I have to say that we only received help when we used the pretext that our campaign was Polish and patriotic," wrote Sendler in the aforementioned account, which is preserved in the archive of the Ghetto Fighters' House. "We knew from experience not to disclose the fact that the children were Jewish. We merely said that they were Polish children, the offspring of independence fighters. We were afraid not of blackmail or betrayal, but of the social welfare staff refusing to cooperate."[21]

In the spring of 1943, during the Warsaw Ghetto Uprising, Sendler's group set up a network of emergency shelters—apartments where children and adults could be housed for a few days or weeks. During that time, Żegota would obtain documents for them and help them find more permanent accommodation. Most of Sendler's female colleagues lived modestly, in a single room with a kitchen; if they lived in two rooms, it would be with their entire family, but this did not stop them from giving temporary refuge to escapees. Sendler lived with her sick mother, who would be visited by a caregiver, and thus had no ability to hide anyone. "Many children passed through my house. I cannot name them because most of the time I did not know who they were," wrote Sendler's colleague, Izabella Kuczkowska, in a statement for Yad Vashem.[22] The villa on Lekarska Street where Jadwiga Piotrowska and her family lived served as an emergency shelter. A record number of fifty children were accommodated there at various times.[23] Of the people in Sendler's circle, Zofia Wędrychowska and Stanisław Papuziński also had a bigger apartment. It was located on Mątwicka Street, and although there were already a dozen or so people living there, including Jewish children, it was likewise used as an emergency shelter.[24]

It is worth mentioning at this juncture that the aforementioned people, as well as Sendler's other colleagues, all came from the same milieu—the College of Social and Educational Work, which operated as part of the Free Polish University (Wolna Wszechnica Polska). The latter, founded in Warsaw in 1918, was an eminent institution of interwar Poland that was independent of the educational and religious authorities. It was a modern and exceptional university for its time, free from antisemitic excesses; it never imposed the "ghetto benches" system.[25] Workers, communists, a few people with criminal convictions, and a great many Jews studied at the College of Social and Educational Work, which had the reputation of being a leftwing institution; its founder was Professor Helena Radlińska. Sendler, meanwhile, prior to working for the City Council, had been employed in the legal department of the Mother and Child Welfare Section, which was established under the auspices of the college.[26]

At a meeting in September 1943, Aleksandra Dargielowa, the first head of the Children's Section of Żegota, tendered her resignation and proposed that Irena Sendler take her place.[27] According to a report by Żegota's auditing committee from February 1944, the Children's Section received 238,000 zlotys in the last quarter of 1943, that is, when Sendler was its director. As noted in the report, 6 percent of its funds were donated to the section, which looked after ninety-nine children.[28] Żegota spent more on rescuing children, but many of its activities were carried out by other departments, and this remained the case even after the establishment of the Children's Section. There was no point in increasing risks unnecessarily. Sendler was in constant contact with Julian Grobelny (until his arrest in March 1944) and with Leon Feiner and Adolf

Berman. She was able to pay out 500 zlotys per month for each child, or 1,000 zlotys in exceptional situations. These were the financial guidelines, but—as she recounted—"the position I managed to establish for myself in Żegota was such that I didn't really follow those guidelines, because I believed that there were some families who didn't need to be given anything, and others who needed more than 1,000 zlotys."[29]

From the outset, the section also provided emergency assistance to children who received no regular support, including those hiding in convents and in institutions run by the Central Welfare Council (RGO), when a child had to be taken away and placed in new accommodation. Sendler was in charge of aid logistics. She transferred money to a network of liaison officers (she mentions 8–10 liaison officers), organized housing and urgent medical assistance, and transported children from place to place when the situation became dangerous for them.

On October 18, 1943, a few days after Sendler became head of the Children's Section, she was paid a visit by the Gestapo. Her detention was probably the result of a denunciation that was not connected with her work in saving Jews.[30] Three weeks later, on November 13, 1943, Sendler was released.[31] The bribe paid by Żegota worked. In mid-December, after a month of clandestine quarantine following her release from Pawiak prison, Sendler returned to her duties as head of Żegota's Children's Section, but from that moment on remained in hiding.[32] She continued to move around the city, but always used false documents. She did not spend nights at home and never showed up at work, although there was a paycheck waiting for her there for the time she had spent in detention.[33]

In the archive of the Ghetto Fighters' House, I found a report on Irena Sendler's work at the Żegota Children's Section after her release from Pawiak prison—one small piece of paper. The signature of "Jolanta" does not appear under the table entitled "The nursery from 1 January to 31 May [1944]," but it may be assumed, with a high degree of certainty, that she was the author of that document. Listed in the table are children "in establishments on the account of the Żegota Children's Section." There were twenty-eight such children in January, and thirty in May. Sendler notes that fifty of them each received 1,000 zlotys per month. There were sixty-seven children "at home on the account of the Section" in January, rising to almost twice as many (131) by May. A further five to six children received "emergency clothing allowances." The Children's Section had 105,000 zlotys at its disposal in January, this sum increasing to 170,000 zlotys by May. Sendler calculated that the section needed 281,000 zlotys for the month of June.[34] Comparing these figures with the data from October

1943, it is apparent that the Children's Section was gradually expanding its activities. The accounts show (if the section's income is divided by the sums it paid out—usually 500 zlotys per child per month) that initially financial support was provided to around one hundred children, in January to more than two hundred, and in May to more than three hundred.

In her postwar articles, Sendler described two occasions on which the chairman of Żegota, Julian Grobelny, asked for her help. "Once he called me away from some very important work and interrupted a meeting of the Żegota Council's presidium simply because he had received information that somewhere in the Wawer district (he didn't have the exact address) there was a girl whose mother had been murdered in such a brutal way that for several days it had been impossible to bring the child to its senses. We were *en route* to Wawer by train when the Germans suddenly started rounding people up at the Eastern Railway Station. We were lucky to escape arrest." They managed to find the girl.[35] On another occasion "he told me to go immediately with a trusted doctor and some medicines to the woods between Otwock and Celestynów, because there, in a rubbish pit, a mother was hiding with her baby. Food was being brought to her by a teacher from the neighboring village, but the baby was very sick and needed medical attention."[36]

Finding people who were ready to give shelter to a Jewish child, even when Żegota was paying something for it, was extremely difficult. New problems arose, which had to be dealt with immediately to save the child's life. This is well illustrated by a letter from the guardian of Margarita Turkow, mentioned earlier. Without Żegota's knowledge, this guardian, Mrs. Borcińska, established contact with Margarita's father and attempted to blackmail him into paying her money. (Margarita's name in hiding was Marysia.)

> Do you want to ask Marysia if she's healthy, if she's not coughing? Well, I can tell you that she is healthy and she is not coughing. Indeed, she is as fit as a fiddle, and may God grant her such good health until the end of the war. Do you also want to ask how she spent her birthday?—no doubt rather uneventfully. I can tell you that no one beats her here, no one abuses her. She has a roof over her head, something to eat, and a warm bed to sleep in, but she is here with strangers. And now what you should be asking is whether someone is paying for her. She has been with me since 20 August, and yet only 2,100 zlotys has arrived for her. I estimate that her upkeep is 60 zlotys per day, thus I am owed a great deal of money. Who in fact is her guardian? Ms. Sendler [spelled: Sejdler], but she has only been here once. Then she sent

> money through other people. They have given me 2,100 zlotys so far. Why should I be looking after Marysia for free? I could take her out into the street and leave her there to God's mercy.
>
> Please consider her fate, because my conditions are as follows: 60 zlotys per day, paid a year-and-a-half in advance, including for the time I have already looked after her. If you decline, then please take her away. Otherwise I shall do as I said, for I do not wish to put myself at risk and gain nothing from it.
>
> *Marysia's guardian*[37]

Many of those in Sendler's care fell victim to blackmailers—this was the rule more than the exception—and once again accommodation had to be found for the children. And so it was that Sendler found lodgings for some of Józef Zysman's family, mentioned earlier—his two sisters and his nephew Michał Głowiński. In an unheated garret on Srebrna Street, little Michał diligently learned to recite his Catholic prayers. One morning there was a vigorous knocking at the door. In walked a young, blond-haired man, a picture of wartime elegance: mustache, herringbone jacket, Tyrolean hat. The family didn't have enough money to buy themselves out. One of Zysman's sisters, Teodora, went to look for cash, while Michał and his mother stayed as hostages. Michał was moving pieces on the chessboard when the blackmailer offered him a game. They played for several hours, waiting to see if Aunt Teodora would return. "There is a motif in art, that of playing cards with Death. From that day on, I lost my interest in chess," recounted Głowiński.[38] The money was arranged, and Sendler continued to take care of the Zysman family. "Sendler, a secular saint, placed me in an orphanage run by the Felician Sisters," explained Głowiński.[39] She also found accommodation for his mother—as a maid in the service of the Otwock police commander's widow.

Another story concerns Chaja Estera Sztajn. "Tereska"—her name during and after the war—suddenly had to be taken away from the place where she was hiding. Sendler arranged for her to be put in a summer camp organized by the Central Welfare Council in Świder, where of course she had to pretend that she was a Polish orphan. Before leaving Tereska there, Sendler handed her a small, empty suitcase. The whole operation was carried out in a great hurry. Tereska didn't get along with the other girls. They didn't like her and used every pretext to accuse her of stealing. Looking for evidence, they opened her suitcase, but found nothing. However, the empty suitcase immediately made the children suspect that Tereska was Jewish. And so, once again, Sendler had to quickly remove her from the summer camp.[40]

Żegota was established late on, when most Polish Jews had already been murdered; the Children's Section operated under Sendler's leadership from July 1944. With the outbreak of the Warsaw Uprising on August 1, 1944, the aid network fell apart. Sendler worked as a nurse during the uprising. Immediately after the war she became head of the City Council's Department of Social Welfare and Public Health. She subsequently worked in the field of education, first as a high-ranking ministry official and later as the principal of various schools in Warsaw.[41] She died in 2008, aged ninety-eight.

Memory

For years, Irena Sendler was not widely known, except among a very narrow circle of Holocaust scholars who were aware of her distinguished role.[42] This situation did not change until four girls from Uniontown, a small town in Kansas largely inhabited by white Protestants, wrote a very moving ten-minute play about Sendler for a school assignment; it was entitled *Holocaust: Life in a Jar*, and news of it filtered through to Poland.[43] In February 2000, Sabrina, Megan, Elisabeth, and Gabrielle wrote to Irena Sendler to inform her that "we have written a play about you and will be performing it in a school competition."[44] Sendler replied immediately, adding that she didn't need the money for the return postage, as she could afford to buy stamps from her pension.[45] That was the beginning of a correspondence in which Sendler patiently answered the girls' questions about saving Jewish children and corrected the more naive aspects of the play. "You write that Irena will tell the guards that the children have typhus and that she will put them in a hospital. She wouldn't have been able to say that because the Nazis killed anyone who was sick with typhus," Sendler explained to them.[46] She also sent a receipt for the three dollars the girls had forwarded for the return postage, which she instead donated to charity.

Back in 2001, a national debate on Polish-Jewish relations, provoked by Jan Tomasz Gross's book *Neighbors*, was underway in Poland. The book tells the story of an event that took place on July 10, 1941, when, shortly after the Germans had entered an area previously occupied by the Soviet Union in September 1939, the Polish residents of Jedwabne, a small town in northeastern Poland, burned their Jewish neighbors alive in a barn. Gross stated that sixteen hundred Jews had been murdered in Jedwabne alone.[47] In the American play, Sendler leads twenty-five hundred children out of the ghetto, writes down their names—both their real names and the ones they used in hiding—and buries the list in a jar. This figure of twenty-five hundred rescued Jewish children masked the terrible figure of sixteen hundred men, women, and children murdered in Jedwabne (in fact, the number of Jews killed in Jedwabne on that day was somewhat lower[48]) and became a collective antidote to the story described by Gross. And so, this largely forgotten ninety-year-old lady, still living in Warsaw, suddenly became very famous.

In Poland, therefore, the story of Irena Sendler has served as an counter-narrative to the revelations delivered by Gross's book. This is not the only such case. The political instrumentalization of the Righteous has a long tradition.[49] One of the earliest instances occurred after the Kielce pogrom of July 1946. Even *Tygodnik Powszechny*, a progressive Catholic weekly known for its decency and opposition toward the communists, responded to the pogrom by publishing a front-page editorial about Poles helping Jews.[50]

The propaganda reached its peak in the years 1967–68. To appease the public and distract attention from current political and social problems, the communist authorities launched an antisemitic campaign that forced several thousand Polish Jews into emigration. The proposition that during World War II Poles helped Jews on a massive scale was an integral part of the official narrative of that time. The Righteous were to serve as proof of the alleged lack of gratitude and perfidy of the Jews, who were supposedly slandering Poles instead of showing appreciation. The Polish press published lists compiled by the Security Service of Poles who were said to have aided Jews.[51] "Despite the high blood toll, the Polish nation has not failed. The stream of martyred Polish blood mingled with the martyred Jewish blood,"[52] wrote a well-known propagandist. At the time, Irena Sendler refused to give a radio interview on her aid activities. However, many former members of Żegota allowed their stories to be exploited by the state authorities to confirm the narrative about the self-sacrificial help delivered by Poles to Jews.[53] The press quoted figures of 100,000 Poles murdered by the Germans for helping Jews.[54] According to recent estimates, the actual number was much lower—we currently know of 341 to 346 Poles killed for their involvement in aid activities.[55] After the publication of *Neighbors*, the "Righteous" once again moved into the limelight and became a part of Polish historical memory of World War II awareness for good.[56] This also had positive effects. The Righteous—unfortunately only few of them were still alive—were finally honored and appreciated. They were invited by President Lech Kaczyński to the presidential palace and given awards. However, at the same time, their individual stories were transposed into a collective experience, becoming a synecdoche for the stance of the entire national community.

Today, the story of the Righteous—promoted by state authorities and disseminated in school textbooks—has become the standard narrative of Polish-Jewish relations during World War II. It is almost the only thing you can learn about through Polish media during International Holocaust Remembrance Day. As formulated by the Holocaust historian Jan Grabowski, "The Holocaust becomes a theatre that provides a stage upon which righteous gentiles can perform noble deeds on the largely undefined and obscure crowd of anonymous Jews in need."[57] On the territory of the former Warsaw Ghetto, on the grounds surrounding POLIN Museum of the History of Polish Jews, one can sit down on a Jan Karski bench and walk along the Irena Sendler Avenue. All these commemorations overwrite the experience of the solitude of those who perished in the Holocaust, as expressed by the Monument to the Ghetto Heroes unveiled nearby already as early as in 1948.

It is estimated that, of the nearly one million Jewish children who lived in Poland in 1939, only five thousand survived in the Polish territories occupied by Nazi Germany (and some scholars claim that even this number is inflated).[58] The five thousand include children found in the camps of Majdanek and Auschwitz whom the Nazis did not have time to kill as well as children who survived in other camps, forests, private homes, and convents. It is highly unlikely that twenty-five hundred of them were saved by Sendler alone, but this number had a soothing effect, and everyone in Poland—politicians, journalists, historians—wanted to believe it. Sendler believed it, too. "After Jedwabne we needed a hero"—this is how Sendler described being thrust into the limelight to a group of her friends. "I am a national alibi," she said, as ever-greater accolades were bestowed on her.[59] But publicly she didn't object.

Where did the figure of twenty-five hundred children saved by Irena Sendler and the story of the buried bottles or jars containing their names come from? In my book, *Sendlerowa. W ukryciu*, I traced the origins of the myth.[60] Sendler mentioned this number for the first time in 1979 in a statement submitted to Teresa Prekerowa, author of the pioneering book about Żegota, *Konspiracyjna Rada Pomocy Żydom w Warszawie 1942–1945* (The clandestine Council to Aid Jews in Warsaw 1942–1945). In the statement Sendler wrote that five hundred children were saved in convents, another five hundred in institutions run by the Central Welfare Council, and two hundred in the so-called Boduen House;[61] a further thirteen hundred children were placed in Polish families, and one hundred young Jews were sent to fight alongside the partisans.[62]

These figures were certainly provided by Sendler in good faith, but the statement gives no indication as to how she arrived at them. At one point she adds that the numbers include both children and adults. Nor is there anything in the statement to suggest that Sendler was the driving force behind saving these people. On the contrary, she lists twenty-four members of staff who were responsible for specific aid departments.

Thus the figure of twenty-five hundred children appeared only thirty-four years after the war. In 1965, in a letter to the Department for the Righteous Among the Nations, the secretary of Żegota, Adolf Berman, wrote that Sendler had "with great courage saved numerous Jewish children from the Nazis' clutches."[63] Neither Berman nor Turkow made any mention in their statements of the figure of twenty-five hundred children. Szymon Datner, a Holocaust survivor, historian, and director of the Jewish Historical Institute in Warsaw, dedicated part of a text published in 1970 in the institute's bulletin to "Jolanta" (Irena Sendler), but he, too, omitted mention of the twenty-five hundred children.[64] And in a long interview from 1967, Sendler herself made no reference to the twenty-five hundred saved children or to the idea that she herself had led them out of the ghetto ("Irena Schultz was the expert in that," she recalled).[65]

Despite the enormous dedication of Żegota activists, the scale of the assistance they provided was much smaller than what one might imagine from hearing that a single Żegota activist saved twenty-five hundred children. Indeed, the actual level of assistance provided is known from the reports of the council's meetings that were transmitted to the Polish government-in-exile in London. Initially, Żegota operated mainly in Warsaw, where in the winter of 1943 it gave financial support to two hundred to three hundred people (according to data for January–February 1943), and after the Ghetto Uprising in June 1943, this number rose to a total of one thousand people.[66] From the moment Żegota began helping people outside Warsaw too, the only available data relate to the total number of people who received financial support. There were one thousand to fifteen hundred such people in October 1943, rising to between three thousand to four thousand in the first half of 1944.[67] In the 1980s–90s, before she became famous, Sendler herself would tell friends about the twenty-five hundred children she had saved and about the list of children she had given to Berman after the war so that their families or Jewish institutions could find them.[68] "It was impossible for anyone to remember two-and-a-half thousand names—they had to be written down. I kept the list on rolls of thin tissue paper," she said in an interview for *Nowiny Kurier*, an Israeli Polish-language newspaper.[69] On many occasions Sendler said she had stored the list in two bottles that she had buried in the garden of Jadwiga Piotrowska's house at 9 Lekarska Street. One of the bottles survived. (The girls from Kansas mistakenly thought that they were jars, hence the title of their play: *Life in a Jar*.) "I took the contents of the second bottle," she said, "to the chairman of the Central Committee of Jews in Poland, Adolf Berman. I couldn't find out to whom Berman forwarded the list."[70] In his statement written in connection with the award of the Righteous Among the

Nations medal to Sendler, Berman mentioned nothing about the list of names purportedly given to him.

While searching for Sendler's list, I came across dozens of other lists of Jews who had been saved or whom relatives were trying to find. Some of these lists were written during the war, on cards or tissue paper, sometimes in code; others, created just after the war, were handwritten on huge sheets of paper; still others, of a slightly later provenance, were typewritten, such as the "Alphabetical List of Polish Jews."[71] When one considers that Poland's Jewish community before the war was three-and-a-half-million strong, the mere fact that an alphabetical list of its surviving members could be written down on just a few pages of typing paper is tragic in the extreme. Sendler's official biographer maintained that her list of twenty-five hundred children was in Israel, in the archive of the Ghetto Fighters' House.[72] This sounded likely, for that is where the Adolf Berman archive is located, and Berman was the person to whom Sendler, in her own words, had handed the list.

However, I found no trace of the list there. I talked to the Israeli researchers Nahum Bogner, author of *At the Mercy of Strangers*, a book about children in hiding in wartime Poland, and Noam Rachmilevitch, who was cataloging the Berman archive. They both assured me that the list was not there. I also searched the Central Zionist Archives in Jerusalem as well as the archives of Yad Vashem, the Holocaust Museum in Washington, and the Jewish Historical Institute in Warsaw.

Żegota used meticulous (and dangerous) methods when making payments. The liaison officers would write down the real names and addresses of the people they gave money to and the amounts paid. All the receipts from a particular cell would be checked by the audit committee. When Irena Sendler became head of the Children's Section, she was accountable to Julian Grobelny, who would forward a summary of the expenditures to the committee. As established by Prekerowa, the financial records of the Children's Section were most likely lost, along with the records of the Polish Socialist Party cell headed by Grobelny. They were buried in the basement of a house in Warsaw's Boernerowo district, which was destroyed during the Warsaw Uprising.[73] Besides, most of the children received money not through the Children's Section but through the organs of the parties that contributed to Żegota's budget; entrusting the lists of those children to Sendler would have created an unnecessary additional risk.

However, Sendler's colleague, Jadwiga Piotrowska, mentioned on several occasions the list that she had buried in her garden: "At one time—Oh, the folly of youth!—I kept my own coded statistics. I put my notes in a squat bottle that I buried in the garden. After liberation I looked for it, but couldn't find anything."[74] "Around fifty or so children passed through my house. I had a list, which I buried in my back garden during the war. Someone must have been looking for something there, because after the war I couldn't find it. The list was in a bottle and the bottle broke. The paper must have been destroyed by the rain."[75] "The list containing the children's real and assumed names was lost during the Warsaw Uprising."[76]

Hanna Rechowicz, Jadwiga Piotrowska's daughter, told me the following: "I heard about a broken bottle in which my mother had kept the names of children. Perhaps those names were preserved in my mother's memory and also in Irena's, I don't know, my mother didn't mention it. When Irena became famous, that story about a list of two-and-a-half thousand children's names hidden under an apple tree began to circulate. It's probably an urban myth."[77]

The list buried in the garden on Lekarska Street must have been a list of the children who passed through Piotrowska's house. It might also have included a few other children who were under the care of Piotrowska's colleagues at the department and to whom Sendler gave money.

The canon of stories about Sendler includes not just the twenty-five hundred children but also tales about how she got children out of the ghetto. They describe a terrifying ordeal, a transition from darkness into light: "She put some of them to sleep with drugs to make them appear dead, thanks to which they were taken out in sacks as victims of typhus. Others were told to curl up into a ball and pack themselves into a suitcase. Sometimes she would put children in crates and cover them with bricks."[78]

In the 1990s, Sendler first told the story of how she had transported children hidden in crates in an ambulance accompanied by a barking dog. When she became famous, she repeated it many times, including to her biographer, Anna Mieszkowska, and to the director Andrzej Wolf, who made a documentary film about her.[79] This is probably the most common motif in stories about Irena Sendler, which has made its way into numerous films, articles, and internet entries. It more or less goes like this: Sendler enters the ghetto in a sanitary service ambulance, in which sits a big Alsatian dog. On leaving, the driver squeezes the Alsatian's paw as the ambulance approaches the ghetto gate. The dog whines and thus drowns out the crying of the babies hidden in the ambulance inside wooden crates.[80] I have not, however, come across any facts confirming that Sendler herself was involved in taking children out of the ghetto. As I mentioned earlier, she first looked after adults, and when she became head of Żegota's Children's Section, she was in charge of aid logistics.

Myth

The need to sentimentalize the Holocaust gives rise to moving stories that do not necessarily have to be true. Irena Sendler's actions were in keeping with the narrative of the rescuers and the rescued that prevails in Poland. In 1993 *Tygodnik Powszechny* published a report on an international conference about the Righteous that had taken place in Warsaw. "The Jews present were deeply moved by the words of the wheelchair-bound Sendler, the Righteous Gentile," wrote the author, quoting a story that Sendler had apparently recounted off the cuff (it does not appear in her conference notes)[81]: "During the war a woman went to see a priest and asked him the following question: 'Is it a terrible sin to help the Jews? My neighbors say that I shall go to hell because of it.' The priest replied: 'On the contrary, you will go straight to heaven.' A few days later, the woman returned to the priest: 'I am grateful that you replied in the way that you did. I repeated your words to my neighbors. Now a whole group of Jewish children is being looked after by the parish, because everyone wants a good place in heaven.'"[82]

I knew the origin of this story, and it has nothing to do with Poland's wartime reality. It is based on the recollections of Halina Grubowska, a Holocaust survivor, who, at that time, in the early 1990s, would meet with Sendler on a regular basis. Her real name was Chana Grynberg. She was nine years old when she left the Białystok ghetto and was placed in the care of the Leszczyński family in Suraż by Polish friends of her father's. She immediately became the favorite of Mrs. Leszczyńska, who considered her an orphaned Polish child. The Leszczyńskis' son, who was older than Chana, suspected that the girl was Jewish and tried to catch her out. The truth was revealed when he told her to describe her mother's funeral. (Jews, unlike Christians, were buried not in a coffin but placed on a bier and wrapped in white linen.) When he triumphantly announced his discovery to his parents, Mrs. Leszczyńska stopped speaking to Chana altogether. The family no longer ate with her at the same table, and they demanded that the person who had brought Chana to them take her away as soon as possible. A week passed, but no one showed up, so Mrs. Leszczyńska went to see the local priest for advice. The priest said: "The girl must be baptized, and you, woman, shall go to heaven for having saved the girl's soul for Christ." Little Chana stayed with the Leszczyńskis until the end of the war, but they did not let on to their neighbors, and there was no group of Jewish children being looked after by the parish. The story had a rather different conclusion. After the war Chana's father came to fetch her. And it was then that the priest told Mrs. Leszczyńska that he would not grant her absolution for having sheltered the Jewish child, since the child was no longer Christian.[83] Sendler knew the denouement. Why, then, did she so often feel compelled to descend into sentimental guff in the middle of a story? She wanted recognition for what she had achieved. Was it therefore the case that, to be elevated to the status of a heroine, she knew she had to stick to a narrative that her compatriots would find appealing?

A national heroine must have a biography that suits the nation at a given moment in its history. This is also true of Sendler's biography, and not just her wartime stories. She is presented as a Catholic and as a victim of persecution by the communist authorities. Her life, however, from beginning to end, does not befit the type of heroine to whom people want to raise monuments in Poland today.

Throughout her life, Sendler was a woman of the left. Among friends she would say that she was not a religious person. Born into a middle-class home, she embarked on her professional career before the war as a young rebel, providing legal aid to distressed mothers and children. She helped unemployed women, servants who had been raped by their masters, and prostitutes who didn't know who the fathers of their children were. She boldly went to the places where they lived: cellars, basements, conditions reminiscent of the nineteenth century. She told them about contraception and urged them to fight for maintenance payments and the acknowledgment of paternity.[84]

Sendler's official biography, as well newspaper articles, stress that she suffered terrible persecution at the hands of the communists. She herself said that she had been brutally interrogated by the security services (Urząd Bezpieczeństwa, UB) during the Stalinist period, as a result of which her baby had died shortly after birth, and that in the postwar years she had been sentenced to death for sheltering Home Army (Armia Krajowa, AK) soldiers.[85] But Sendler was not persecuted during the Stalinist period. She was a member of the postwar Polish United Workers' Party (Polska Zjednoczona Partia Robotnicza, PZPR) from its inception in 1948 until its dissolution in 1990, and even briefly served on various committees connected with the upper echelons of the party.[86]

Even in her early youth, Sendler was drawn to the left because socialists and communists treated Jews as fellow citizens with equal rights. A person's attitude toward Jews was always a fundamental moral criterion for her. Sendler remained leftwing throughout her life and thoroughly detested the right, whom she associated with antisemitism. (The left's role in saving Jews is a topic that still awaits an author.)

In Poland, the enduring image of Irena Sendler is that of an elderly lady with dove-white hair, gentle, lively eyes, and a warm smile. Her true image has been lost in the sentimental myth of a noble woman who took children by the hand and led them out of the ghetto. She is portrayed as a modest person with a huge heart, which is the standard way women are generally portrayed. Sendler was not particularly modest, though. Indeed, she was always adding something to her biography, embellishing it, changing it. She liked to be in the limelight. Besides a good heart, she had outstanding managerial skills. That is why she managed to save so many children and to create an efficient support network for them.

The representation of women in the Polish canon also includes the trope of a man who is killed or arrested, after which his wife or beloved becomes involved in clandestine activities. It was therefore emphasized that Sendler's husband, Mieczysław Sendler, was held in a German prisoner of war camp (*Oflag*) for the duration of the war. Having been mobilized in August 1939, he was indeed taken prisoner during the September campaign and spent the next five-and-a-half years incarcerated in the Woldenberg POW camp.[87] Irena Sendler, meanwhile, had a passionate wartime affair and hid her Jewish lover, Adam Celnikier, on the Aryan side. After the war she divorced her first husband (whom she would later remarry) and married Celnikier, who continued to use his false identity papers, going by the name Stefan Zgrzembski. They had three children, one of whom died shortly after birth. Sendler never told anyone that her husband was Jewish, nor did she tell her children, although at the beginning of the 1960s—Celnikier had passed away by then—she considered immigrating to Israel, as she was unable to put up with Polish antisemitism any longer.[88]

To make Sendler fit the obligatory model of a Polish heroine, many facts about her life had to be pruned, supplemented, and given new emphasis. The purpose was not only to elevate Sendler to the pantheon of national saints, but also to transform the experience of the Righteous—their overwhelming sense of loneliness, the feeling that they were fighting not just the Nazi occupiers but Polish society, too—into the experience of the Polish nation as a whole. It was thus a way of extolling the virtues of the Poles *en bloc*. As *Niedziela*, a popular Catholic weekly, so aptly put it, "Today the story of her life is presented in the media and in history lessons as a beautiful example of Polish people's attitude towards the Holocaust."[89]

When the right won the elections in Poland in 2015, its leaders proclaimed an end to the "pedagogy of shame." In the words of one leading rightwing columnist, the "pedagogy of shame" was "an attempt to drastically undermine Poles' self-esteem by depriving us of our pride in our past, especially the pride associated with our struggle and martyrdom during World War II; a time when our fathers and grandfathers said NO to two godless, pagan totalitarianisms:

German and Soviet; a time of heroism and sacrifice."[90] The government proposed replacing the "pedagogy of shame" with a new pedagogy of national pride.

The time has come to speak of all the good that Poles have done for Jews—this is now the task of state institutions, the ministry of foreign affairs, and the government-controlled media. Polish-Jewish relations during the Holocaust are the sensitive issue, the raw nerve, that has damaged the Polish ego, and what is now crucial in the context of the Holocaust is to prove to the world that Poles behaved in an exemplary fashion all along.

The fact of the matter is that Sendler saved Jews not only from the Nazis but also from Polish blackmailers and ordinary neighbors. She operated in a sea of indifference, resentment, and hatred. Her decision to help Jews flew in the face of the popular view that one should only help "one's own"—that is, native Poles. Together with her colleagues, she formed a secret clan. They led a double conspiracy, not only against the Germans but also against the Poles. When finding homes for the children in her care, as long as the child had a "good appearance" (in other words, did not look Jewish), she would say that she was looking to house the child of a Polish officer who had perished in the war.

"Lost in the cacophony of the 'optimistic' narrative is the plain truth that Poles who saved Jews during the Holocaust were a terrified minority who were exposed not only to the terror of the occupier, but also to the hostility of broad swathes of Polish society, in which there was simply no consent for such activities," writes the Holocaust historian Jan Grabowski. "It is characteristic that—decades after the war—many Polish Righteous preferred to receive their awards in secret, so that their neighbors would not find out."[91]

Sendler did not correct any of the myths that grew around her; rather, she bolstered them, assuming the role of a heroine who symbolized the courageous attitude of Poles toward saving Jews during World War II. Only occasionally would she tell her friends: "During the war it was easier to ask someone to store a tank under their living room carpet than to give shelter to one small Jewish child."[92]

Notes

1 Anna Mieszkowska, ed., *Matka dzieci Holocaustu. Historia Ireny Sendlerowej* (Warsaw: Wydawnictwo Literackie, 2004), 19.
2 *The Courageous Heart of Irena Sendler*, directed by John Kent Harrison (K&K Selekt Film and Baltmedia, 2009).
3 Anna Bikont, *Sendlerowa. W ukryciu* (Wołowiec: Czarne 2017).

4 On November 1, 1939, the Nazis ordered all aid to Jewish citizens of Warsaw to cease. Jews were to be taken care of solely by the Jewish community. Anna Chmielewska et al., "Miejska służba opieki społecznej Warszawy w latach wojny i okupacji 1939–1945," in *Warszawa lat wojny i okupacji 1939–1944*, ed. Krzysztof Dunin-Wąsowicz and Halina Winnicka (Warsaw: Państwowe Wydawnictwo Naukowe, 1971).
5 Irena Sendler, "'Jaga.' Wspomnienie o Jadwidze Piotrowskiej," *Słowo Żydowskie*, July 15–29, 1994.
6 Irena Zgrzembska (Sendler's postwar married surname), Zeznanie [no date], Adolf Berman collection, Holdings Registry 19355. Archive of the Ghetto Fighters' House (hereafter AGFH), Israel (hereafter cited as Zgrzembska, Zeznanie).
7 Zgrzembska, Zeznanie.
8 Notes for Irena Sendler's speech during the conference "'Can Indifference Kill?' First International Conference in Honor of Those Who Saved Jews During the Holocaust," Warsaw, July 5–7, 1993, S/353/12, Sendler collection, Materiały zebrane w latach 1995–2003, Archive of the Jewish Historical Institute (hereafter AŻIH), Warsaw, Poland.
9 Interview conducted with Irena Sendler as part of a research project on children who survived the Holocaust, led by Judith Kestenberg of Child Development Research at New York University, April 1985, S/353/10, Sendler collection, Materiały, AŻIH. See also Irena Sendler, Relacja, February 26, 1969, 301/6466, AŻIH; Józef Goldkorn, ". . . kto ratuje jedno życie ludzkie . . . ," *Prawo i Życie*, April 23, 1967.
10 Józef Zysman, chairman of the Association of Court and Bar Trainees, who in addition to his private practice defended unemployed workers against eviction and fought for the rights of illegitimate children. He worked together with Sendler in the legal aid clinic of the Mother and Child Welfare Section of the Citizens' Committee for Helping the Unemployed, Sendler's first employer.
11 Teresa Torańska, *Śmierć spóźnia się o minutę. Trzy rozmowy Teresy Torańskiej* (Warsaw: Agora, 2010).
12 Rachela Auerbach, *Pisma z getta warszawskiego*, Karolina Szymaniak, ed., and trans. Karolina Szymaniak and Anna Ciałowicz (Warsaw: Żydowski Instytut Historyczny, 2016), 93. At Emanuel Ringelblum's request, Rachela Auerbach wrote what she described as ghetto reportage for his archive. Some of her notebooks were discovered after the war inside metal containers, in which the archive was buried.
13 Zgrzembska, Zeznanie.

14 Turkov does not give the date of his meeting with Sendler, but it seems to have taken place just before the *Grossaktion*, that is, in the spring of 1942.
15 Jonas Turkov, *C'etait ainsi: 1939–1943, la vie dans le ghetto de Varsovie*, trans. Maurice Pfeffer (Paris: Austral, 1995). Ala Gołąb-Grynbergowa was the nurse matron in the Warsaw Ghetto. Before the war she had been an employee of the Welfare Department. In Turkow's book, Wanda Wyrobkowa is referred to as Wanda Wyrubowa, and Irena Sendler as Irena Sandler.
16 Teresa Prekerowa, *Konspiracyjna Rada Pomocy Żydom w Warszawie 1942–1945* (Warsaw: Państwowy Instytut Wydawniczy, 1982); Władysław Bartoszewski, *O Żegocie relacja poufna sprzed pół wieku* (Warsaw: Wydawnictwo Naukowe PAN, 2013).
17 Irena Sendler, "Ci, którzy pomagali Żydom. (Wspomnienia z czasów okupacji hitlerowskiej)," *Biuletyn ŻIH*, nos. 45–46, 1963.
18 Minutes of the session of the Żegota Council Presidium held on August 16, 1943, 202/XV-2, Government Delegation for Poland, Central Archives of Modern Records (hereafter AAN), Warsaw, Poland.
19 Statement by Jadwiga Piotrowska, "Pogwarki socjalne. Spotkania z przeszłością," in *Opieka Społeczna w Warszawie 1923–1947. Opracowania i materiały*, ed. Małgorzata Gładkowska et al. (Warsaw: Interart, 1995), 147.
20 Mieszkowska, *Matka dzieci Holocaustu*, 68.
21 Zgrzembska, Zeznanie.
22 Izabella Kuczkowska, Statement of February 22, 1967, 349/24/177, AŻIH.
23 Jadwiga Piotrowska, Statement of March 23, 1987, 349/24/1903, AŻIH; interview with Hanna Rechowicz, 2016, author's private archive.
24 Irena Sendler, "Zofia i Stanisław Papuzińscy. Wspomnienie," *Gazeta Wyborcza*, November 26, 1999; interview with Joanna Papuzińską-Beksiak, 2016, author's private archive.
25 This refers to the segregated seating of Jewish students at Polish universities, introduced in 1935.
26 Ignacy Myślicki, *Wolna Wszechnica Polska. Cel i zadania. Ustrój. Uprawnienia* (Warsaw: Towarzystwo Przyjaciół Wolnej Wszechnicy Polskiej, 1930); interview with Janina Pogonowską-Goldhar 2005, author's private archive.
27 Prekerowa, *Konspiracyjna Rada Pomocy Żydom*.
28 Cash report of the Council to Aid Jews for the fourth quarter of 1943, submitted to the Jewish Department of the Government Delegation of February 7, 1944, 202/XV-2, Government Delegation for Poland, AAN.

29 Interview with Irena Sendler from April 1985, S/353/10, Sendler collection, Materiały zebrane w latach 1995–2003, AŻIH (hereafter cited as Sendler, Interview).
30 Interview with Władysław Bartoszewski, 2014, author's private archive.
31 Association of Former Political Prisoners of Pawiak Prison, 233/65, Archive of the Museum of Pawiak Prison (hereafter AMWP), Warsaw, Poland.
32 Sendler, Interview.
33 Mayor's staff, File no. 56, p. 169, Archives of the City of Warsaw (hereafter APMSW), Warsaw, Poland. The letter was found by Jan Grabowski; see Jan Grabowski, "Przyczynek do biografii Ireny Sendlerowej (z dokumentów warszawskiego Ratusza)," *Zagłada Żydów. Studia i Materiały* 10 (2014): 623.
34 Children's section, settlement for January–May 1944, 5882., Adolf Berman collection, AGFH.
35 Sendler, "Ci, którzy pomagali Żydom."
36 Sendler, "Julian Grobelny i jego żona Helena. Wspomnienie," *Gazeta Wyborcza*, April 18, 2003.
37 S. Borcińska, letter to Diana Blumenfeld and Jonas Turkow, no date [1942], Adolf Berman collection, Collection's Section 77, AGFH.
38 Michał Głowiński, recording from August 23, 1996, Interview Code: 19205, Visual History Archive (hereafter VHA) (hereafter Głowiński, Recording)
39 Głowiński, Recording.
40 Teresa Körner, Testimony of October 28, 1965, 03/2824, Yad Vashem Archives (hereafter YVA), Jerusalem, Israel.
41 Bikont, *Sendlerowa*.
42 In Lewinówna and Bartoszewski's book, the most important book about the Righteous to be published in Poland, consisting of several hundred accounts, Sendler appears second, just after Adolf Berman. Władysław Bartoszewski and Zofia Lewinówna, eds., *Ten jest z ojczyzny mojej. Polacy z pomocą Żydom 1939–1945* (Kraków: Znak, 1967).
43 Marcin Fabjański, "'Życie w słoiku' trwa 10 minut," *Gazeta Wyborcza*, May 19, 2001.
44 Irena Sendler, S/353/19, Materiały zebrane w latach 1995–2003, AŻIH.
45 Extensive correspondence between the high school girls and Sendler can be found in S/353/19-20, Sendler collection, AŻIH. See also Jack Mayer, *Życie w słoiku. Ocaleni Ireny Sendlerowej*, trans. Robert Stiller (Warsaw: AMF, 2011).

46 Bikont, *Sendlerowa.*
47 Jan T. Gross, *Sąsiedzi. Historia zagłady żydowskiego miasteczka* (Sejny: Pogranicze, 2000).
48 It has not been possible to establish the exact number of people murdered, but it is likely to have been somewhere between six hundred and nine hundred victims. Anna Bikont, *My z Jedwabnego* (Warsaw: Prószyński i S-ka, 2004).
49 On this see Tomasz Żukowski, *Wielki retusz. Jak zapomnieliśmy, że Polacy zabijali Żydów* (Warsaw: Wielka Litera, 2018).
50 "Zbrodnia kielecka," *Tygodnik Powszechny,* July 21, 1946, 1. Cited in Żukowski, *Wielki retusz,* 190.
51 Wykaz Polaków ukrywających Żydów w czasie okupacji hitlerowskiej i korespondencja 1939–1945 (List of Poles hiding Jews during World War II and correspondence, 1939–1945), IPN, BU 1804/52.
52 Tadeusz Kur, "Ten jest z ojczyzny mojej," *Prawo i Życie,* April 23, 1967.
53 See Krzysztof Głogowski, "W służbie humanizmu i patriotyzmu. Rozmowa z Jadwigą Piotrowską," *Słowo Powszechne,* April 20, 1968.
54 In Poland, the Germans introduced the death penalty for those helping Jews. The ordinance announced by Warsaw district governor Ludwig Fischer on November 10, 1941, declared the death penalty for Jews leaving the ghettos unauthorized. The same penalty applied "to those who knowingly provide such Jews with shelter or help them in any other manner (e.g., providing overnight accommodation, support, or transporting them in any type of vehicle, etc.)." Quoted in Władysław Bartoszewski and Zofia Lewinówna, eds., *Ten jest z ojczyzny mojej. Polacy z pomocą Żydom 1939–1945* (Kraków: Wydawnictwo Znak, 2007), 646.
55 Martyna Grądzka-Rejak and Aleksandra Namysło, eds., *Represje za pomoc Żydom na okupowanych ziemiach Polski w czasie II wojny światowej,* vol. 1 (Warsaw: Instytut Pamięci Narodowej, 2019).
56 See Alicja Podbielska, "Toruńskie Yad Vashem," *Zagłada Żydów. Studia i Materiały* 16 (2020): 874–83.
57 Jan Grabowski, "The Holocaust as a Polish Problem," in *Poland and Polin: New Interpretations in Polish-Jewish Studies,* ed. Irena Grudzińska-Gross and Konrad Matyjaszek (Frankfurt am Main: Peter Lang, 2016), 23.
58 According to the historian Lucjan Dobroszycki, this figure, established in 1945 by the Central Committee of Jews in Poland, is an overestimate. There was no comprehensive census—the survivors were registered in district committees and the numbers were then added up. At the time, however, many people, including children, were moving around

in search of family members, leaving messages here and there. A child might therefore be registered in several places. Lucjan Dobroszycki, *Survivors of the Holocaust in Poland: A Portrait Based on Jewish Community Records 1944–1947* (Armonk: M.E. Sharpe, 1994).

59 Interviews with Michał Głowiński (2015), Anna Mieszkowska (2015), and J. Sobolewska-Pyz (2015), author's private archive.

60 Bikont, *Sendlerowa*.

61 The Father Baudouin Educational Institution, known as the Boduen House, was a large Warsaw orphanage with a heroic wartime record of rescuing Jewish children. It is not known, however, how many Jewish children were placed there; after the war, a few of the children who had taken refuge at the Boduen House were found after the war by Jewish organizations.

62 Prekerowa, *Konspiracyjna Rada Pomocy Żydom*.

63 Adolf Berman, Statement of May 28, 1965, catalog no. 153, Irena Sendler, Files of the Department for the Righteous Among the Nations, YVA.

64 Szymon Datner, "Materiały z dziedziny ratownictwa Żydów w Polsce w okresie okupacji hitlerowskiej," *Biuletyn ŻIH*, nos 75–76 (1970).

65 Goldkorn, ". . . kto ratuje jedno życie ludzkie . . ."

66 Prekerowa, *Konspiracyjna Rada Pomocy Żydom*.

67 Prekerowa, *Konspiracyjna Rada Pomocy Żydom*.

68 She told Irena Kowalska about the list and Michał Głowiński about the twenty-five hundred rescued children. Bikont, *Sendlerowa*.

69 "Z Ireną Sendlerową z Żegoty rozmawia Anna Ćwiakowska," *Nowiny Kurier*, June 17, 1983.

70 Irena Kowalska, unpublished oral history interview with Irena Sendler conducted in the 1990s, manuscript, author's private archive. Berman died in 1978. Prekerowa corresponded with him for the purposes of her book. Nowhere does she write about Berman receiving a list of rescued children from Sendler after the war.

71 Jewish Survivors Residing in Warsaw at the End of June 1945, Documents of the Jewish Emigrant Aid Society of Canada, BU 1268/7134U, Records of the former Chief Commission for the Prosecution of Crimes against the Polish Nation concerning Adolf Berman, Institute of National Remembrance (IPN), Warsaw, Poland. The list was prepared by the Records and Statistics Department of the Central Committee of Jews in Poland. It was translated into English because the committee sent copies to Jewish organizations in Palestine, the United States, the United Kingdom, and Sweden.

72 Anna Mieszkowska, oral conversation with author, 2015.
73 Prekerowa, *Konspiracyjna Rada Pomocy Żydom.*
74 Romuald Teyszerski, "50 razy kara śmierci. Rozmowa z Jadwigą Piotrowską," *Kierunki*, May 11, 1986.
75 Plater Robinson, "Jadwiga: Just from our Hearts," in *Teaching the Holocaust* (New Orleans: Southern Institute for Education and Research, Tulane University, 1989), 27.
76 Jadwiga Piotrowska, Statement of March 23, 1987, 349/24/1903, AŻIH.
77 Hanna Rechowicz, oral conversation with the author, 2006.
78 A "fact" added on April 19, 2013, under the entry "Irena Sendlerowa" in the Polish version of Wikipedia, accessed March 1, 2015.
79 Mieszkowska, *Matka dzieci Holocaustu*; Andrzej Wolf, dir., *Historia Ireny Sendlerowej* (Wolfilm, 2015).
80 Sendler recounts the story to Andrzej Wolf in a recording from August 1, 2007 (footage from 2005–8 for the film about Irena Sendler; the footage is kept at the Polish Center for Holocaust Research). In the film there is a dramatization with an Alsatian.
81 Jan Grosfeld, "Czy obojętność może zabijać," *Tygodnik Powszechny*, July 18, 1993.
82 Grosfeld, "Czy obojętność może zabijać."
83 Halina Grubowska, *Haneczko, musisz przeżyć* (Montreal Polish-Jewish Heritage Foundation of Canada, 2007). Interview with Halina Grubowska, 2005; interview with Józef Leszczyński, 2005, author's archive.
84 Sendler described her work at the legal aid clinic of the Mother and Child Welfare Section of the Citizens' Committee for Helping the Unemployed in Irena Sendler, "O dziecko nieślubne," in *Dla przyszłości: praca zespołowa* (Warsaw: Obywatelski Komitet Pomocy Społecznej, 1934).
85 Mieszkowska, *Matka dzieci Holocaustu.*
86 Sendler joined the Polish Workers' Party (PPR) in 1946. In 1947 she was, among other roles, a member of the Social Welfare Section in the Social and Occupational Department of the Central Committee of the Polish Workers' Party. Irena Sendler-Zgrzembska, Questionnaire sent to party cadres dated December 16, 1949, catalog no. 46158, Warsaw Committee of the Polish United Workers' Party (hereafter PZPR), Personal file of Irena Sendler-Zgrzembska, State Archives in Warsaw (hereafter APW), Warsaw, Poland. In 1949 she was a member of the Social Welfare Section in the Social and Occupational Department of the Central Committee of the Polish United Workers' Party, the successor of the

PPR. Transcript of a meeting of the Social Welfare Section in the Social and Occupational Department of the Central Committee of the PZPR held on April 26, 1949, catalog no. 237, Central Committee of the PZPR in Warsaw, AAN.

87 Mieczysław Sendler, 477, List of prisoners of the Woldenberg POW camp, catalog no. 5637, Archive of the Central Prisoner of War Museum in Łambinowice-Opole (hereafter WASt).

88 "[Irena Sendler] asked me to find out in Israel whether she could arrange to live there, because her children are Jewish and she is having problems with her neighbors." Körner, Testimony.

89 Sławomir Błaut, "Egzamin z człowieczeństwa," *Niedziela*, no. 21 (2008): 35.

90 Michał Karnowski, editor-in-chief of the rightwing weekly *W sieci*, quoted in Jakub Majmurek, "Pedagogika wstydu, którego nie było," *Oko. press*, August 6, 2016, https://oko.press/pedagogika-wstydu-ktorej-nigdy-bylo/, accessed March 23, 2023.

91 Jan Grabowski, "Ustawa o IPN. Historia Holocaustu należy do świata," *Gazeta Wyborcza*, February 4, 2018.

92 Note to Wanda Rotenberg from March 1994, catalog no. 29481, Bela Elster collection, AGFH.

Bibliography

Auerbach, Rachela. *Pisma z getta warszawskiego.* (Writings from the Warsaw Ghetto.) Ed. Karolina Szymaniak. Trans. Karolina Szymaniak and Anna Ciałowicz. Warsaw: Żydowski Instytut Historyczny, 2016.

Bartoszewski, Władysław. *O Żegocie relacja poufna sprzed pół wieku.* (On Żegota—A confidential testimony from half a century ago.) Warsaw: Wydawnictwo Naukowe PAN, 2013.

Bartoszewski, Władysław, and Zofia Lewinówna, eds. *Ten jest z ojczyzny mojej. Polacy z pomocą Żydom 1939–1945.* (This one is from my homeland. Poles helping Jews 1939–1945.) Kraków: Znak, 1967.

———. *Ten jest z ojczyzny mojej. Polacy z pomocą Żydom 1939–1945.* (This one is from my homeland. Poles helping Jews 1939–1945.) Kraków: Wydawnictwo Znak, 2007.

Bikont, Anna. *My z Jedwabnego.* (We from Jedwabne.) Warsaw: Prószyński i S-ka, 2004. (Eng. ed. *The Crime and the Silence: The Quest for the Truth of a Wartime Massacre.* London: William Heinemann, 2015.)

———. *Sendlerowa. W ukryciu.* (Sendler: In hiding.) Wołowiec: Czarne 2017.

Błaut, Sławomir. "Egzamin z człowieczeństwa." (An exam in humanity.) *Niedziela*, no. 21 (2008), https://m.niedziela.pl/artykul/85564/nd/Egzamin-z-czlowieczenstwa, accessed March 23, 2023.

Chmielewska, Anna, et al. "Miejska służba opieki społecznej Warszawy w latach wojny i okupacji 1939–1945." (Municipal welfare service in Warsaw during World War II, 1939–1945.) In *Warszawa lat wojny i okupacji 1939–1944* (Warsaw during the war and occupation 1939–1944), ed. Krzysztof Dunin-Wąsowicz and Halina Winnicka, 149–91. Warsaw: Państwowe Wydawnictwo Naukowe, 1971.

Datner, Szymon. "Materiały z dziedziny ratownictwa Żydów w Polsce w okresie okupacji hitlerowskiej." (Materials on the rescue of Jews in Poland under Hitlerite occupation.) *Biuletyn ŻIH*, no. 1/73 (1970): 135–40.

Dobroszycki, Lucjan. *Survivors of the Holocaust in Poland: A Portrait Based on Jewish Community Records 1944–1947*. Armonk: M.E. Sharpe, 1994.

Fabjański, Marcin. "'Życie w słoiku' trwa 10 minut." ("Life in the jar" lasts 10 minutes.) *Gazeta Wyborcza*, May 19, 2001.

Głogowski, Krzysztof. "W służbie humanizmu i patriotyzmu. Rozmowa z Jadwigą Piotrowską." (In the service of humanism and patriotism. A conversation with Jadwiga Piotrowska.) *Słowo Powszechne*, April 20, 1968.

Goldkorn, Józef. ". . . kto ratuje jedno życie ludzkie . . ." (. . . *whoever* saves one life . . .) *Prawo i Życie*, April 23, 1967.

Grabowski, Jan. "The Holocaust as a Polish Problem." In *Poland and Polin: New Interpretations in Polish-Jewish Studies*, ed. Irena Grudzińska-Gross and Konrad Matyjaszek, 17–27. Frankfurt am Main: Peter Lang, 2016.

———. "Przyczynek do biografii Ireny Sendlerowej (z dokumentów warszawskiego Ratusza)." (A contribution to the biography of Irena Sendler. Documents from the files of the mayor of Warsaw.) *Zagłada Żydów. Studia i Materiały* 10 (2014): 622–25.

———. "Ustawa o IPN. Historia Holocaustu należy do świata." (The IPN Law. The history of the Holocaust belongs to the world.) *Gazeta Wyborcza*, February 4, 2018.

Grądzka-Rejak, Martyna, and Aleksandra Namysło, eds. *Represje za pomoc Żydom na okupowanych ziemiach Polski w czasie II wojny światowej*. (Reprisals for aiding Jews in Poland during World Wat II.) Vol. 1. Warsaw: Instytut Pamięci Narodowej, 2019.

Grosfeld, Jan. "Czy obojętność może zabijać." (Can indifference kill.) *Tygodnik Powszechny*, July 18, 1993.

Gross, Jan T. *Sąsiedzi. Historia zagłady żydowskiego miasteczka*. (Neighbors: The history of the destruction of a Jewish community.) Sejny: Pogranicze, 2000.

(Eng. ed. *Neighbors: The Destruction of the Jewish Community in Jedwabne, Poland*. Princeton, NJ: Princeton University Press 2001.)

Grubowska, Halina. *Haneczko, musisz przeżyć*. (Haneczka, you have to live.) Montreal: Polish-Jewish Heritage Foundation of Canada, 2007.

Harrison, John Kent, director. *The Courageous Heart of Irena Sendler*. K&K Selekt Film and Baltmedia, 2009, 96 min.

Kowalska, Irena. Unpublished oral history interview with Irena Sendler, conducted in the 1990s, manuscript, author's private archive.

Kur, Tadeusz. "Ten jest z ojczyzny mojej." (This one is from my homeland.) *Prawo i Życie*, April 23, 1967.

Majmurek, Jakub. "Pedagogika wstydu, którego nie było." (Pedagogy of shame that never existed.) *Oko.press*, August 6, 2016, https://oko.press/pedagogika-wstydu-ktorej-nigdy-bylo/, accessed March 23, 2023.

Mayer, Jack. *Życie w słoiku. Ocaleni Ireny Sendlerowej*. (Life in a jar. People saved by Irena Sendler.) Trans. Robert Stiller. Warsaw: AMF, 2011. (Eng. ed.: *Life in a Jar: The Irena Sendler Project: A Novel*. Middlebury, VT: Long Trail Press 2010.)

Mieszkowska, Anna, ed. *Matka dzieci Holocaustu. Historia Ireny Sendlerowej*. (Mother of the children of the Holocaust. The story of Irena Sendler.) Warsaw: Wydawnictwo Literackie, 2004.

Myślicki, Ignacy. *Wolna Wszechnica Polska. Cel i zadania. Ustrój. Uprawnienia*. (Free Polish University: Aim and objectives, constitution, rights.) Warsaw: Towarzystwo Przyjaciół Wolnej Wszechnicy Polskiej, 1930.

Piotrowska, Jadwiga. "Pogwarki socjalne. Spotkania z przeszłością." (Social chats. Encounters with the past.) In *Opieka Społeczna w Warszawie 1923–1947. Opracowania i materiały*. (Social welfare in Warsaw 1923–1947. Studies and materials.), ed. Małgorzata Gładkowska et al., 79–174. Warsaw: Interart, 1995.

Podbielska, Alicja, "Toruńskie Yad Vashem." (Yad Vashem in Toruń.) *Zagłada Żydów. Studia i Materiały* 16 (2020): 874–83.

Prekerowa, Teresa. *Konspiracyjna Rada Pomocy Żydom w Warszawie 1942–1945*. (The clandestine Council to Aid Jews in Warsaw 1942–1945.) Warsaw: Państwowy Instytut Wydawniczy, 1982.

Robinson, Plater. "Jadwiga: Just from Our Hearts." In *Teaching the Holocaust*. Brochure, author's private archive. New Orleans: Southern Institute for Education and Research, Tulane University, 1989.

Sendler, Irena. "Ci, którzy pomagali Żydom. (Wspomnienia z czasów okupacji hitlerowskiej)." (Those who aided Jews. Memoires from the Hitlerite occupation.) *Biuletyn ŻIH* 45–46 (1963): 234–47.

———. "'Jaga.' Wspomnienie o Jadwidze Piotrowskiej." ("Jaga": Recollections of Jadwiga Piotrowska.) *Słowo Żydowskie*, July 15–29, 1994.

———. "Julian Grobelny i jego żona Helena. Wspomnienie." (Julian Grobelny and his wife. Recollections.) *Gazeta Wyborcza*, April 18, 2003.

———. "O dziecko nieślubne." (For the illegitimate child.) In *Dla przyszłości: praca zespołowa*. (For the future: Team work.) Brochure, Aniela Uziembło's private archive. Warsaw: Obywatelski Komitet Pomocy Społecznej, 1934.

———. "Z Ireną Sendlerową z Żegoty rozmawia Anna Ćwiakowska." (Irena Sendler from Żegota.) Interview by Anna Ćwiakowska. *Nowiny Kurier*, June 17, 1983.

———. "Zofia i Stanisław Papuzińscy. Wspomnienie." (Zofia and Stanisław Papuziński. Recollections.) *Gazeta Wyborcza*, November 26, 1999.

Teyszerski, Ramuald. "50 razy kara śmierci. Rozmowa z Jadwigą Piotrowską." (50 times the death penalty. An interview with Jadwiga Piotrowska.) *Kierunki*, May 11, 1986.

Torańska, Teresa. *Śmierć spóźnia się o minutę. Trzy rozmowy Teresy Torańskiej*. (The death comes a minute late. Three interviews by Teresa Torańska.) Warsaw: Agora, 2010.

Turkov, Jonas. *C'etait ainsi: 1939–1943, la vie dans le ghetto de Varsovie*. (It was like this: 1939–1943, life in the Warsaw Ghetto.) Trans. Maurice Pfeffer. Paris: Austral, 1995.

Wolf, Andrzej, director. *Historia Ireny Sendlerowej*. (The story of Irena Sendler.) Wolfilm, 2015, 27 min.

Żukowski, Tomasz. *Wielki retusz. Jak zapomnieliśmy, że Polacy zabijali Żydów*. (The great retouch. How we forgot that Poles killed Jews.) Warsaw: Wielka Litera, 2018.

Archival Materials

Association of Former Political Prisoners of Pawiak Prison, 233/65. Archive of the Museum of Pawiak Prison (Archiwum Muzeum Więzienia Pawiak, hereafter AMWP), Warsaw, Poland.

Berman, Adolf. Statement of May 28, 1965, Files of the Department for the Righteous Among the Nations, Irena Sendler, 153. Yad Vashem Archive (hereafter YVA), Jerusalem, Israel.

Borcińska, S. Letter to Diana Blumenfeld and Jonas Turkow, no date [1942], Adolf Berman collection, Collections Section 77. Archive of the Ghetto Fighters' House (hereafter AGFH), Israel.

Cash report of the Council to Aid Jews for the fourth quarter of 1943, submitted to the Jewish Department of the Government Delegation of February 7, 1944,

Government Delegation for Poland, 202/XV-2, Central Archive of Modern Records (Archiwum Akt Nowych, hereafter AAN), Warsaw, Poland.
Children's section, settlement for January–May 1944, Adolf Berman collection, 5882, AGFH.
Correspondence between the high school girls and Irena Sendler, Sendler collection, S/353/19-20, Archive of the Jewish Historical Institute (Archiwum Żydowskiego Instytutu Historycznego, hereafter AŻIH), Warsaw, Poland.
Documents of the Jewish Emigrant Aid Society of Canada, Records of the former Chief Commission for the Prosecution of Crimes against the Polish Nation concerning Adolf Berman, BU 1268/7134U. Institute of National Remembrance (Instytut Pamięci Narodowej, hereafter IPN), Warsaw, Poland.
Głowiński, Michał. Interview recording from August 23, 1996, Interview Code: 19205. Visual History Archive (hereafter VHA).
Körner, Teresa. Testimony of October 28, 1965, 03/2824, YVA.
Kuczkowska, Izabella. Statement of February 22, 1967, 349/24/177, AŻIH.
Minutes of the session of the Żegota Council Presidium held on August 16, 1943, Government Delegation for Poland, 202/XV-2, AAN.
Note to Wanda Rotenberg from March 1994, catalogue no. 29481, Bela Elster collection, AGFH.
Piotrowska, Jadwiga. Statement of March 23, 1987, 349/24/1903, AŻIH.
Sendler, Irena. Interview conducted with Irena Sendler as part of a research project on children who survived the Holocaust, led by Judith Kestenberg of Child Development Research at New York University, April 1985, Sendler collection S/353/10, AŻIH.
———. Interview from April 1985, Sendler collection, Materiały zebrane w latach 1995–2003 (Materials collected in the years 1995–2003), S/353/10, AŻIH.
———. Notes for her speech during the conference "'Can Indifference Kill?' First International Conference in Honor of Those Who Saved Jews During the Holocaust." Warsaw, July 5–7, 1993, Sendler collection, Materiały zebrane w latach 1995–2003 (Materials collected in the years 1995–2003), S/353/12, AŻIH.
———. Relacja (Witness account), February 26, 1969, 301/6466, AŻIH.
Sendler, Mieczysław. List of prisoners of the Woldenberg POW camp, catalog no. 5637. Archive of the Central Prisoner of War Museum in Łambinowice-Opole.
Sendler-Zgrzembska, Irena. Questionnaire sent to party cadres dated December 16, 1949, Warsaw Committee of the Polish United Workers' Party (hereafter PZPR), personal file of Irena Sendler-Zgrzembska, 46158. State Archives

in Warsaw (Archiwum Państwowe w Warszawie, hereafter APW), Warsaw, Poland.

Transcript of a meeting of the Social Welfare Section in the Social and Occupational Department of the Central Committee of the PZPR held on April 26, 1949, Central Committee of the PZPR in Warsaw, 237, AAN.

Wykaz Polaków ukrywających Żydów w czasie okupacji hitlerowskiej i korespondencja 1939–1945. (List of Poles hiding Jews during World War II and correspondence 1939–1945), BU 1804/52, IPN.

Zgrzembska, Irena. Zeznanie (Testimony) [no date], Adolf Berman collection, Holdings Registry 19355, AGFH.

10

Rescue from Memory

Wartime Experience in Postwar Perspective

MARK ROSEMAN

A Speech in the Aftermath of War

> *We celebrate today the victory of the world over National Socialism. Only those who have lived under this terrible physical and psychological pressure, always fending off attacks from the system, always in danger, can understand what that means.*
>
> —Artur Jacobs, "Ansprache zur Maifeier 1945"

On May 1, 1945, Artur Jacobs gave a speech. His audience was the twenty or so members of the "Bund Gemeinschaft für sozialistisches Leben" (The League–Community for Socialist Life), who saw out the end of war in a guest house owned by the group's members, on the shore of Lake Constance. Normally based in the Ruhr, and some two hundred members strong on the eve of Nazi rule, the "Bund," as its members referred to it, had managed to sustain an active existence through the vicissitudes of Nazi persecution and war.[1] The group dated back to 1924 and had originally emerged as an outgrowth of Artur's classes at Essen's adult education institute. Over the following years it had attracted workers, teachers, middle-class women with a social conscience, and others, among them quite a few Jews. Through meetings, joint study, physical exercise, and excursions, they sought to develop a holistic and uplifting communal life. They also reached out to others through adult education, experiments in alternative schooling, gymnastics training, and political meetings. In the heady years of the 1920s, the Bund's members were hoping to be the crucible for a future, better Germany. They were certainly not preparing for life under a future fascist dictatorship.

The advent of the Third Reich hit the group hard, and it took Artur and his followers a while to establish a new modus vivendi. Most of the Jewish members managed to emigrate by 1938, but from Kristallnacht onward the Bund reached out to other Jews in the Ruhr region, offering psychological support, assistance in emigration, then in preparing for deportation, then sending more than a thousand parcels to deported Jews in Poland and Theresienstadt, and saving the lives of probably eight who stayed behind, some surviving illegally for two to three years. Artur's Jewish wife, Dore, was among those protected. Now, just two days after a hair-raising day when the battle front had passed by the house on Lake Constance, Artur shared his thoughts with his fellow Bundists.

In this, his first public address on International Labor Day in thirteen years, Artur reminded the comrades of all they had withstood in the darkest period of their lives. As difficult as the direct threats from the regime had been the pressure to conform and the challenge of standing alone. They had gained, he argued, the profound insights into humankind reserved for those who confronted a dictatorship in full consciousness of what they were doing, and had emerged intact. With their "knowledge gained through suffering" (*erlittene Erkenntnis*),[2] as Jacobs dubbed it, they would be armed for the new world that was to come. A fine orator and charismatic, youthful personality, despite his sixty-five years of age, Artur no doubt moved and inspired his listeners. But whether he accurately conveyed what they had gone through is another question. The narrative departed in some significant respects from the reality of their lives under Nazi rule, and it did so in ways that characterize also subsequent accounts penned by the group. The speech thus constitutes an unusual opportunity to observe the moment when the experience of a group of rescuers was transformed into memory. Using Artur's address and other wartime and postwar documents, this essay is about the pressures and incentives to rewrite the experience of helping others. It pursues an issue that has been largely neglected until now—namely, how the rescuers' own view of what they had done changed over time—and it asks how recognizing this might affect our broader understanding of rescue and resistance.

Rescue and Memory. A Microstudy

As the editors of this volume have argued, over the last few years historians have begun to "rescue" rescue, that is, to recover a history partially eclipsed by memory. As will be explored in the pages that follow, the Bund's story also belongs to the history and memory of resistance, but it is rescue that is currently receiving greater historiographical attention, and it is in relation to rescue that historians are becoming aware of just how powerfully postwar representation and commemoration refracted or colored our understanding. Other chapters in this volume demonstrate how heroic myths of rescue emerged in some places, dead silences in others, as different national and international political constellations laid claim to the memory of war and Holocaust. In nations liberated from Nazi rule, anti-Nazi resistance was often overblown in ways that belied a far murkier history of collaboration. Rescue might be celebrated and exaggerated as part of the heroic anti-Nazi narrative, but it might also be ignored so that Jewish fates should not overshadow national or communist suffering. In postwar Germany the dynamics of memory were clearly different from those of the occupied countries. For much of the first decade of the Federal Republic of Germany's existence, memory of resistance to Hitler was publicly taboo. Rescue was, true enough, not tainted with the same whiff of unpatriotic disloyalty. However, when denazification ground to a halt at the end of the 1940s and individual stories of helping Jews thus lost their exculpatory function, it became more convenient for West Germans to claim that no one had known anything about the Jewish fate and that assistance had been impossible. In East Germany, Jewish suffering was drowned out by the threnody to communist martyrs. With respect to resistance, the idea that Germans had opposed their *Führer* slowly became respectable in West Germany, and from the late 1950s onward the forms of resistance that could be celebrated steadily broadened. However, for those on the left now seeking to recover working-class opposition to the regime, help for Jews did not figure as "real" resistance. For others, talking about rescue would have involved painful acknowledgment of past knowledge and choices.[3] With the solitary exception of a program of recognition in West Berlin, rescue of Jews was very slow to gain much recognition.

From the 1980s, Yad Vashem's model of the Righteous came to exercise a powerful resonance in West Germany just as elsewhere in Europe, as Sarah Gensburger has demonstrated.[4] But while Yad Vashem's growing, carefully curated list of cases worthy of recognition drew international attention to rescuers' heroism, historians are now coming to see how far it also unbalanced our understanding of rescue. Ethicists and psychologists interested in altruism took Yad Vashem's morally upstanding individual rescuer as their model and indeed drew their interview subjects from Yad Vashem's list of honorees.[5] In doing so they excluded a great deal of nonaltruistic activity that helped save lives and neglected the central role of social structures, networks, and environments in prompting or impeding help.[6] "Rescue" was understood as a self-contained, morally uplifting act, an understanding that belied the haphazard and unpredictable trajectories of those who, with help here and there, eventually survived. In many cases (though less so in Germany than in parts of occupied Europe), "rescue" was prompted or abetted by behind-the-scenes self-help from underground Jewish organizations.[7] Even when it was not, survival usually depended not only on multiple gestures from multiple sources but also on a great deal of self-help and initiative from the survivors themselves. This complex history is only now being recovered.

What has received relatively little attention in this reappraisal, however, is how those involved themselves came to remember or represent their actions after the war. We know from Buchenwald, for example, that political groupings might consciously whitewash the story of their solidarity.[8] We know, too, that resistance heroes, particularly those with postwar political pretensions, often aided and abetted the manufacture of national myths.[9] But away from such pivotal mythmakers at the fulcrum of national memory, what happened to the individual or, as in the Bund's case, group experience of rescue and opposition? As far as the scholarship on rescue is concerned, the psychologists and ethicists who long dominated the field relied almost exclusively on interviews recorded decades after the event and did not spend much time worrying about how experience metamorphized into memory.

Certainly, they had good reasons for trusting what they heard. The sociologist Nechama Tec, whose work on rescue remains influential, justified her reliance on interviews by arguing that memories of such dramatic events were too powerful to be clouded over time.[10] One might counter that, precisely *when* they are traumatic, events can be subject to significant reworking in memory, yet Holocaust scholarship in general is rediscovering testimony's reliability.[11] As Christopher Browning found in his work on the Starachowice labor camp, where survivors recorded testimonies at multiple points in time, those accounts remained remarkably consistent.[12] But the questions posed by this essay are not about the accurate retention of facts. The kinds of paradigm shift that Bund sources reveal are interesting precisely because they did *not* involve major changes to the raw story of what the group had done (unless by "changes" we mean foregrounding some elements and occluding others). Instead, they alert us to moral, political, and perspectival forces that worked on individual and group memory in the transformed conditions of the postwar world. Given that the rescuers' psychological and ethical frameworks have been central concerns for scholars, it is surprising that we have not asked how, when, and why rescuers' views and interpretations might be subject to change.[13]

This essay analyzes texts from leading figures in the Bund as they sought to make sense of their lives under Nazi rule. The first example looks at the Bund's attitudes toward Jews and help for Jews, exploring the contrast between Artur's correspondence from the late 1930s, in the wake of Kristallnacht, when the Bund was in the thick of its first serious involvement in helping Jews, on the one hand, and postwar accounts of its help for Jews, on the other. The second example, using the speech with which this chapter opened, shows the remarkable disappearance of the *war* (as against Nazi persecution) from Artur's account of the Bund's activities, a disappearance that meant a vital context of the Bund's help for Jews was no longer visible. The last of the three examples revolves around the group's uncertainty about whether and how to describe the history of its actions under Nazism, including its rescue of Jews, as "resistance." Some of the changes captured in these examples were no doubt idiosyncratic, peculiar to this particular group, but others seem more generalizable and responded to broader shifts in perception and memory. A concluding section considers the larger implications for our understanding of the memory of rescue and resistance under Nazi rule, both within the (West) German context in which most Bund members spent their postwar lives, but also beyond.

Personal Connections and Principles

In the early postwar period, the Bund produced a number of different accounts of its actions and experiences under the Nazis. Initially these, like Artur's May 1 speech, were for internal use, to celebrate the group's achievement and inspire its members to provide moral leadership in a shattered postwar Germany. Later the group produced a series of pamphlets aimed initially at the Allies, in the hope that (West) Germany's new rulers would recognize the Bund's leadership potential, and later at a German audience. In his May address, Artur did not say anything specifically about help for Jews, but he did lay out what he believed had been the key prerequisite for the group's willingness and ability to sustain itself in opposition during the Nazi era: "The only people who could remain committed were those who could look beyond their own selves, their immediate circle, and any personal advantages and disadvantages for themselves, and instead hold in view the true needs of the German people and humanity as a whole."[14]

A pamphlet produced in 1946 or 1947 about the Bund's "Jewish Aid Work" offered a more detailed account not only of the Bund's actions on behalf of Jews, but also of the group's reasons for acting. We are not sure for whom the report was intended, possibly German political elites at local and regional levels to whom the western Allies were beginning to give more responsibility. The pamphlet rejected the idea that the group had acted "out of cheap sentimentality" ("aus billigen Mitleidsgefühlen") and emphasized the principles that had enjoined it to oppose injustice wherever it occurred.[15] Just as the Bund had campaigned for women, Black people, colonial peoples, minorities, and other oppressed in the pre-Nazi era, the report said, under the Nazis it had had to intervene on behalf of Jews, and for the Jews above all, as the group hardest hit by persecution. Far from acting out of mere sympathy, it claimed, the group had in fact felt obliged to help those whose way of life it found "distant and alien and, yes, even antipathetic." Decades later, the Zenkers, a leading Mülheim couple in the Bund, said the same thing, namely, that they had had actively to surmount their reluctance to help people with very different political views and from a radically different social milieu.[16]

During the Nazi era itself, the Bund had for obvious reasons been very circumspect in describing what it was doing. Nevertheless, there are clear insights to be gleaned from contemporary sources, not least from the private correspondence between the Bund's leading couple, Artur and Dore Jacobs, and their only son, Friedl (Gottfried.) Under the Nuremberg laws, Friedl counted as "mixed race of the first degree," since two of his grandparents were Jews. He was not subject to the full punitive treatment reserved for "full Jews," which under the convoluted regulations would have been the case had his parents raised him as a Jew. Even so, by 1938, increasing restrictions on the "Mischlinge" (and brutal assaults by fellow students) had stymied Friedl's efforts to study in Germany. In the summer of 1938, with the help of Dore's Dutch relatives, the then twenty-year-old moved to the Netherlands. His parents hoped their son's chances would be better served abroad, even if higher education no longer seemed within reach. The family kept in touch by mail, and seemingly all of Artur's and Dore's letters have been preserved.[17] The couple were mindful of censorship, and the Bund is never mentioned explicitly, but for those in the know it is obvious when it is being referred to, and the letters are a remarkable source of experiences and feelings captured in the moment.

At the end of 1938, Artur felt battered not only by the tragic fates he and other Bund members encountered among Kristallnacht's victims but also by the waves of antisemitic ordinances that affected Dore, his Jewish wife. The only consolation, he wrote, was to act: "We can offer a lot of help, give advice, offer material support, suggest ways forward. That gives one's life a special accent, a certain satisfaction. How impoverished, how hopelessly impoverished all these people are who had nothing but their family and their bourgeois lives. That's gone now. And now every hour they are confronted with an abyss of emptiness."[18]

By January 1939, though uncertainty lay ahead "like a great Sphinx," things had settled down a little.[19] Artur could take a breath and talk about the situation in which they found themselves, and in doing so convey a sense of the context and rewards for the Bund's work. For someone familiar with the group's post-war accounts, two things stand out. The first is that, not least through Dore, the Jacobses were connected to many Jews in the region struggling to escape. There were, Artur wrote on January 21, 1939, the Herzfelds, the in-laws of Dore's brother Robert:

> More and more people are disappearing from view. The Herzfelds have now just upped and gone, the house not sold, taking only the absolute minimum with them. The mother of Mrs Herzfeld was 84. She is now swimming along on the Mediterranean, unbowed like a youngster. The Sunday before we dropped by for a short visit. Words cannot express all the feelings that run through your mind. That is the fate of a family for whom family was everything, and whose lives seemed completely secure. The one son in Brazil, the second in Paris, the girl in Palestine, and the youngest just crossed the water to a new Heimat. And now the older generation, who had seemed to be irrevocably rooted here, held by a thousand ties, are gone, almost overnight.

Or, he went on, there were the Levis, the uncle and aunt of Bund member Berthold Levi. (Berthold himself had already managed to immigrate to Sweden.)

> The same thing happened with Dr L., Berthold's uncle, the doctor. Both he and his wife are about 70. Even just a few months ago they did not even dream of leaving, despite everything. Now they are readying themselves for departure to Argentina. And they should be happy if they succeed. The disruption, destruction, suffering, the attempts to hold on before being shaken loose that is required to make old people tear themselves away from the soil they know so well, cannot be expressed.
>
> You can well imagine that under such circumstances we have our hands full, helping, giving advice, offering consolation, keeping despair at bay and a small spark of hope alive. All our energies and those of our friends are focused on this sphere of life.

The Bund's help was often directed at those with whom the Jacobses' personal acquaintance and family links had brought them into contact.

Of course, many Bund members were not Jewish and did not have the same set of acquaintances. So it was crucial here that a "mixed marriage" couple headed the Bund, and that they were able to share their personal experiences, knowledge, and connections, which made palpable to the rest of the group what Jews were going through. In January 1940, after learning of the Jacobses' worries about their son, and after observing what the Jacobses themselves were going through, a non-Jewish Bund member, Karlos Morgenstern, wrote: "What you and Gottfried [Friedl] are going through—and we experience through you—is truly a battlefront. On one side is the individual with his spiritual mission, and on the other all the entanglements which society and nature impose on him."[20] Mindful of the censor, Morgenstern was careful, but his meaning was clear. It was through the Jacobses, the individuals with the "spiritual mission" (in the Kantian understanding of *Geist* as humanity's intellectual and moral essence), who were at the same time discriminated against as a mixed-race family, that the whole group came to understand what Jews were enduring.

All this might seem somewhat obvious, but this world of Jewish connections is entirely absent from the scene the group painted after the war. Viewed through the lens of Artur's wartime correspondence, the Bund's actions were embedded in a dense network of personal ties. Viewed through the group's postwar self-accounts, by contrast, we learn that self-sacrifice and earnest principle had been the driving forces for their actions, at times overcoming barriers to help those who felt so alien.

The two accounts are not wholly incompatible. As a socialist avant-garde, the Bund had in the 1920s been deeply at odds with conservative opinion and bourgeois attitudes. The Ruhr's Jews, like the majority of those in Germany, were solidly middle-class and engaged in trade. Patriotic, respectable, and for the most part socially conservative, their lifestyle bore no resemblance to the Bundists'. In that sense, a perceived social chasm did have to be bridged.[21] The Jacobses' and other Jewish members' prewar personal connections, so visible in the letters, were thus all the more important in rendering persecution visible and palpable for the group.

That social chasm is in some sense visible in Artur's letters, but in a quite different way from the postwar accounts. After the sentence about trying to keep the spark of hope alive cited earlier, Artur goes on:

> One can often do only the small things, the big ones are beyond our reach. But at the right time, done in the right way, they can sometimes work miracles. If anything in these dark times can set our spirits in motion once more and remind us of that spark of spiritual strength

> within, it is these small moments when we see our words landing upon fertile soil. People learn to see their lives from a completely different perspective. Hammered by fate, the old quest for a pleasurable life, a good position, security and affluence, suddenly falls apart. In its place, real life emerges, with other goals and possibilities.[22]

Several times in these years, even as late as 1942, we find in Bund letters and diaries this trope of philistine circles overcoming their materialism and recovering the essential core of humanity. It is hard to say how much it was influenced by antisemitic notions of commercially money-grubbing Jews and how much it responded to the group's general antimaterialism, be it in the form of its anticapitalism, be it in its Kantian emphasis on *Geist*. "I saw rich Jewish women sitting in the rubble of their homes," Tove Gerson told her listeners in Bartlesville, Oklahoma, in a talk about Kristallnacht given in March 1942. Gerson, a Bund member, had immigrated to the United States in 1939 to join her "mixed-race" Jewish husband. She went on:

> What I was most conscious of was that these women, who like all of us had once clung to their possessions and their homes, seemed no longer to even see their destroyed home, and seemed to be completely uninterested in "stuff," seemed to have completely moved beyond "stuff," and had space within them for only one thing and that was the question: how is this possible? How is it possible that human beings can do this to people who have never done anything to them, whom they don't even know. How is this possible?[23]

As the Bund came to fully apprehend the murderousness of the Nazi project, the notion that hardship might be beneficial in any way became unpalatable. Gerson's comments in 1942 probably reflect a moment of transition. She begins with the theme of leaving materialism behind, but probably aware that was becoming unseemly, she moves on, not to the "spiritual liberation" of former materialists but to search for the reasons for the violence. The "alienness" of the Jewish community emerges in postwar accounts as an obstacle to empathy that the group overcame with its principled solidarity; but the idea that the group could participate in helping the victims shed their materialism for something more authentic has completely gone.

What's clear is just how significantly the Holocaust affected the group's relationship to Jews and Judaism. A leftwing Jewish milieu had been an important part of the Bund's pre-Nazi social world. Yet that milieu, so important for recruitment and social relationships, had coexisted with critical attitudes within the group toward the social character of German Jews in general, and toward all organized religions. By 1945, both milieu and attitudes had been profoundly affected. On the one hand, the Nazis had expelled or murdered the region's Jews. The milieu was gone forever. On the other, revelations about the Holocaust, which reached a crescendo at the end of the war, made the group's earlier critical attitudes obsolete and untoward. Even without the Holocaust, the group's narrative would probably have inclined it to be selective in presenting its experience, because the Bund felt it so important to emphasize the ethical roots (as against the contingent circumstances) behind its activities. Taken together, the result was that the Bund's prewar and wartime Jewish connections, connections that were so important in creating bonds with the persecuted, remain invisible.

The War That Went into Hiding

Let us return now to the May 1 speech. Artur reminded his listeners of all the risks they had faced—losing their jobs, house searches, Gestapo surveillance, imprisonment, inhumanly hard incarceration, and horrific, punitive, concentration camps. Harder still, he argued, had been avoiding being somehow suborned by the system. When every sphere of life had been claimed by the regime, maintaining one's distance had meant living like an outcast. The temptation to find a niche had been great. But they had understood that, even if one was engaged in seemingly harmless activity, the fruits of one's labors would be claimed by the regime. Just as hard as resisting the regime's embrace had been wishing for the defeat of one's own country, welcoming the bombing attacks that set one's house on fire, or cheering for the ground-attack aircraft that turned every rail journey into Russian roulette.

All this, Artur declared, would have been too difficult for any individual on their own: "That we remained strong, that not a single one of us fell by the wayside, even among those who lived far from us, that is a glorious page in the Bund's history. And that we remained alive, that we lived through this time awake, that we matured and grew—we owe all that to the Bund." Even then, all their intense work would not have been enough to prevent them from feeling utterly marginalized if they had not learned as a group to discern the laws of world history in action, ultimately dooming the Nazi regime by its own hand. It was this understanding that equipped them to witness not just victory over the regime but the beginnings of a new world. "This," he concluded, "is our first of May."[24]

Artur's powerful address marked his first opportunity to view the experience of the Third Reich in the rear-view mirror. Not that the yesterdays of the dictatorship had already receded into the distance. They were etched into consciousness—into body and soul. But the end of the war and the fall of the Third Reich marked such a dramatic rupture that afterward nothing looked quite the same. To speak about Nazi Germany was no longer to speak about the present—and for Artur, on May 1, 1945, it was to speak with an eye to an open, but very uncertain, future. Artur's speech established many of the accents of the group's postwar accounts of its recent past, accents that differed from the sources that we have from the Nazi years themselves.

For now let us address just one significant issue: The focus in Artur's speech is so relentlessly on the Nazi regime that it takes a while for a rather striking fact to register—the war has virtually disappeared. For the vast majority of the Bund's members, it had been the war that had tested them to the utmost. The Ruhr had seen more than three years of ever more intense air raids. In March 1943, Bund member Friedel Kette wrote an unforgettable account of a massive air raid over Essen, and of her walk through the destroyed city. Horror gave way to disorientation and to grief as Kette and her Bund friend Sonja Schreiber lost their way in a city they had known since birth, surrounded by collapsed buildings, twisted metal, still-burning interiors, and ghostly human presences dragging their few remaining goods to nowhere in particular. A few months later, Artur vividly described the breathless rush from the group's Wuppertal apartment, as he and his fellow residents scrambled down into the cellar moments before an incendiary bomb set the house on fire, then broke through into a neighboring cellar, and then, as fire followed them, into the cellar beyond that, finally fleeing to an unbuilt hillside across from the house. Well away from any major metropolitan center, nestled on the shore of Lake Constance, Meersburg offered respite from the air raids, but not from the war. Just two days before Artur gave his speech, he and his fellow residents had experienced the most traumatic day, as French forces and the Waffen SS fought it out literally on their doorstop. Shells were landing just in front of the house. In barely legible pencil-scrawled handwriting, Dore captured the "Sunday we will not forget." The group faced life or death choices—whether to hang out a white flag or not. If they did not, the house might be destroyed by French artillery. If they did, perhaps the French would spare them, but the Waffen SS on the other side of the hill would have them in its sights. In the end, they put up the flag and got away with it.

Back in 1943, in the face of the titanic forces unleashed by war, Bund members had become increasingly conscious of their powerlessness. In July, a bit more than a month after narrowly escaping with his life in Wuppertal,

Artur began drafting an address for the next group retreat in the Sauerland, the wooded and hilly landscape to the east of the Ruhr.[25] They had just emerged, he wrote, from days utterly dominated by worries about the most basic things in life, cares that had absorbed most of their energies and pursued them through the day like hunted animals. Besieged by terror, they had learned what it was like to be on the front line of total war. Now, here they were in the quiet world they knew so well. Clouds drifted across the sky, the trees whispered in the wind, the birds sang. Everything was familiar. But they could no longer be the same. The images of burning cities, of a world of horror and suffering, were indelibly inscribed on their souls. Their task was to understand these images for what they were: the battleground of a global transformation. Since they themselves were caught up in the maelstrom, the only choice they had was between being uncomprehending, complaining victims, on the one hand, and engaging with the cataclysmic global forces that were leading toward a new and better world, on the other.

Reeling under the impact of total war, the group came to reinterpret its own historical role. In the Weimar era, it had seen itself as a model and catalyst of change. To be sure, its radius of action was small, but nonetheless it had aspired to be an agent of social transformation. The massive scale of the war, however, brought home the enormity of the forces reshaping the globe, forces that dwarfed the national class struggle, which the Bund had once imagined would serve as the motor for change. Implicitly, the group's own role had been downgraded. The ordinary person, as Bund member Else Bramesfeld put it, was no longer the agent of change but rather its servant. The group's sense of its own power was vastly diminished.[26] What remained to them was an almost spiritual task: to genuflect with awe before the historical power reshaping the world.[27] "It's a strange feeling," Artur confided to his diary in February 1944. "On the one hand I become ever smaller and less important, but the thing that draws my life into its orbit, and that I am drawn to serve, becomes more and more significant, powerful, distant, unreachable, yes infinite."[28] For all their courage and their activism, the lesson Bund members were learning—on one level surprising, on another logical—was a new appreciation of their powerlessness. In the face of a conflict of such shocking, terrifying, awe-inspiring magnitude, their former hopes of changing the world looked like youthful folly.

The war's impact on the Bundists' lives was total, and it formed the critical backdrop to all their actions, be it helping Jews or trying to maintain group life. Bund members threw themselves into help for others as a way of mastering their fears. Lisa Jacob, a Jewish Bund member whom the group protected in hiding throughout the war, remembered coping with the sense of threat by working on the collections of foodstuffs she was readying for the next parcel to be sent to deported Jews.[29] "Again and again, only one thing remains to give one courage, drive, and a sense of energy, despite one's powerlessness," wrote Artur. "'Work, create, do something that is meaningful!'"[30] The disruptions of war made assisting others all the more difficult—hindering travel and communication, impacting rations, and destroying living space. But toward the end, the chaos of war also created certain opportunities, above all for Jews to pass as refugees or bombed-out evacuees, something of which Dore took advantage, using a forged ID. Yet, returning to Artur's speech again, two days after the war was over, virtually all the transformative shocks of war—separations, combat, bombing raids, and the general disruption of ordinary life—disappear from the story, and indeed from all testimonies the group would produce after 1945.

One way of understanding this narrative choice is to say that Artur and the group wanted to foreground their distinctive collective achievement, the moral test to which they had been subjected, and the political lessons they had learned. The war (ignoring the Holocaust) had for the most part not presented a distinctive moral test for the group.[31] Enduring the war was not something that differentiated the group from its neighbors. Presenting a history to highlight the Bund's distinctive stance therefore necessarily excluded all such massive threats and tests. This was logical—but a central and transformative part of the Bund's experience thereby went missing.

In Bund texts produced a year or two into the postwar period, texts aimed at a larger audience and not just the Bund faithful, the refusal to highlight the war experience probably also took on a moral and pedagogic function. The "First Letter Abroad" observed that "everything is judged only from today's perspective, as though there had been no past, no provocation of war, no Lidices, no extermination camps, no Night and Fog decrees, no millions murdered."[32] The group thus had strong motives for underplaying German suffering in wartime. In his influential book, *War Stories*, Robert Moeller notes the ubiquity of war narratives in the 1940s and 1950s, as older pre-Nazi tropes about Germany's unfair treatment at the hands of the world were transmuted into less revanchist but no less trenchant accounts of its unrivaled suffering.[33] Seen in this light, Artur's emphasis can be seen as a deliberate corrective to a nation concealing its complicity underneath the ruins of its own catastrophic defeat.

And yet the almost uncanny absence of the war in Bund accounts feels like something more than a positive moral or narrative choice. In an insightful if controversial lecture given at the University of Zurich in 1997 and later published, the writer W. G. Sebald argued that the postwar period was characterized by a striking inability to engage with the real terror of the bombing war.[34] Certainly, city after city produced local publications that detailed the extent of destruction.[35] Yet the formalistic language accompanying such texts seemed only to bury the real experience deeper under the rubble. Perhaps because they felt it would contradict the image they wished to present of a group full of vigor and promise, perhaps because of a rather old-fashioned understanding of the psyche that predated modern understandings of trauma, Bund members almost never wrote after the war about their fears and their vulnerability—except where doing so strengthened an argument about how the group had been stronger together than each individual alone.

This interpretation is, of course, speculative. What is not speculative is that speeches and texts produced in good faith, even in the first days of liberation, offered a version of history that was already highly selective. The war had in so many different ways been the essential frame for the Bund's help for Jews. Sometimes the disruptions of war had impeded actions, sometimes they had created niches and opportunities to help. War in a way had galvanized the group to act—with a philosophy of mastering fear through helping others, the Bund found in its limited agency the antidote to war's terrors. None of this is accessible in the postwar narrative.

Resisting Definitions

Incautious as the Bund's diarists and letter-writers sometimes were under Nazi rule, they were not so foolhardy as to declare their opposition on paper (even if, as we have seen, they found oblique ways to convey what they were doing). Thus we find the word "resistance" (*Widerstand*) used for the first time only after liberation, in the May 1, 1945, speech, when Artur declared that to "live in resistance for twelve years, resolute, acting on one's own free-will and rejecting all temptations—that would have been too difficult for any individual on their own."[36]

But what exactly did "living in resistance" mean? A later passage of the speech offers clarity:

> Not lifting a finger on behalf of the system and yet at the same time living fully in the world, with all one's mental faculties, experiencing everything, being a part of everything, as though one were oneself directly involved. Registering everything that was happening, analyzing it, tirelessly forging weapons for the coming battle, not forgetting for an instant that National Socialism represents the collapse of all

> highest values [*Götterdämmerung aller höchsten Werte*], and that were it to be victorious, life would not be worth living.

Artur did not understand resistance in terms of actively fighting the regime. Instead, he was connoting what in German might be termed *Widerständigkeit*, resilience, fortitude, an ability to withstand pressure and at the same time be fully immersed in life. The "weapons" were intellectual ones—above all gaining a complete understanding of Nazism so as to eradicate it in the future. Lisa Jacob too used resistance in the sense of resilience when she wrote in an early postwar account that "what always filled me with new resilience [*Widerstandskraft*] was life in the Bund."[37] In the same vein, one of the most reflective of the Bund's postwar publications, in which the group sought to lay out how it had stood against the Nazis, talked about its members' "inner resilience" (*innere Widerstandskraft*)[38] and their ability "to resist twelve terrible years unbroken."[39] In elaborating what this meant, the report offered a similar exposition to Artur's May 1945 speech: "Not a life alongside the system, not a life withdrawn, and certainly not the 'happiness of the niche,' as it were, a respite from the horrors of real life, but instead a life amid these horrors, permanently contending with the system, in the struggle and through struggle, through the shocks, suffering and uncertainties which it brings."[40] Given this emphasis on resilience, on learning, and on dissecting the system, it is not surprising that the group often spoke of its "illegal life" and "illegal work" rather than claiming resistance per se. Certainly, its members were aware of what they had done in helping Jews, but they saw it as the extension of their effort to live by their values, unswayed by Nazism.

At the same time, however, the group felt under pressure in the early postwar period to assert its relevance and its record. The more it sought to establish its credentials vis-à-vis the claims and expectations of other leftwing groups, the more the language of resistance and of active struggle took center stage. In June 1946, for example, Artur submitted a questionnaire to establish his status as a victim of persecution. This was necessary to receive supplementary rations and the reinstatement of his pre-Nazi pension.[41] Artur presented himself as the head of an illegal "antifascist-fighting league" (*antifaschistischen Kampfbund*) that had "actively fought against National Socialism."[42] When the leftwingers on the committee responsible for allocating supplementary rations proved skeptical, Artur doubled down, describing his "danger-filled battled against National Socialism."[43] Later exchanges with the restitution authorities resonated with similar language.

We see the same pressures at work in the group's efforts to reach a wider public, beginning with three "Letters Abroad." The first of these pamphlets, written in 1946 and never published, was directed primarily at the Allies, whom the Bund hoped to access through members living in exile in the United States. The later ones, aiming at a more domestic audience, were produced in 1947–48 and mass-printed in 1948. It was in these pamphlets that the group laid out its readiness to provide leadership in postwar Germany, as established by its record under Nazism. The "Second Letter Abroad" was particularly outspoken:

> During the whole twelve years of darkness the Bund continued illegally to fight on and deployed its full force against the criminal Nazi system. Permanently in fear of their lives, its members pursued in the most varied of places and in forms continually adapted to changing conditions, a tireless enlightenment and demasking work. Not for an instant did this illegal activity stop, on the contrary, in the course of 12 years it simply grew stronger, more fundamental, more lively and more comprehensive.[44]

Another pamphlet detailed the group's "Aid Work for Jews."[45] In 1947, learning that the resistance figure Günther Weisenborn was planning to write a book about opposition to Hitler, the group sent him some of its writing.[46] Citing the Bund's own materials, Weisenborn would report that the Bund

> remained 12 years long in illegal opposition, during which it systematically demasked the regime and enlightened others through carefully thought-out help actions for the victims of fascism, particularly for Jews and foreign workers. Key figures in the Bund immigrated, many others were in prison, others traveled around illegally for years. The Bund carried out a well-planned correspondence and package service for deported Jews. Thousands of parcels assisted the persecuted in their suffering. Identity Papers were organized, those on the run given a place to stay, and foreign workers protected from forced measures.[47]

Here, the Bund text on which Weisenborn drew evidently used the terminology of "illegal opposition." While much of what followed hewed closely to the reality, the language also offered more than a touch of exaggeration regarding the group's activities, particularly the scope of its efforts to enlighten others about the real character of the regime, the degree to which the reality of (brave and generous) help for a number of individuals evolved into systematic machinery, and finally how far and how long the Bund's own leadership had been in danger.

After the flurry of early postwar pamphleteering, the group moved on. Having failed to secure itself a place of influence and a new following, it ceased projecting itself collectively onto the larger world or publicly reflecting on its history. When Weisenborn's paean to the grassroots opposition to Nazism appeared in 1953, amid the Cold War climate of the early Federal Republic, the book was already out of sync with the times, indeed represented almost the sole exception to a near decade of West German silence about leftwing resistance. In the later 1950s, as it became more acceptable to recognize German opposition to Hitler, discussions rarely went beyond the holy trinity of the army, the Kreisau Circle, and the Confessing Church.[48] During the 1960s, however, student unrest and the revival of interest in Marxist thought at West German universities created a new willingness to recover the heroism of Nazism's leftwing opponents. In 1969 two major well-researched books heralded what would become a flood of publications detailing resistance and opposition at the grassroots level. The most important was the history of resistance in Essen, the Bund's heartland, produced by the social-democratic historian Hans-Josef Steinberg, who would later become the Federal Republic's first professor of labor history, at the University of Bremen. Steinberg's account remains the most substantial and thoroughly researched narrative of political resistance to the Nazis in that city and, indeed, one of the best local studies on resistance anywhere in Germany.[49]

Steinberg was surprisingly hard on the Bund. Probably Weisenborn's rather unfortunate characterization of them as a nonsocialist (*bürgerliche*) group (though the Bundists had almost all been members of the KPD or SPD and described themselves as a "socialist order") had inclined Steinberg to be skeptical from the start, conscious as he was of a great deal of overblown writing about spiritual resistance and inner emigration in the early postwar period. Moreover, because the Bund had done much that was unusual, without careful additional research their record could easily seem implausible. The Bund's most significant and risky activity had been helping Jews, which in the understanding of leftwing historiography in the 1960s was not seen as resistance, since it did not aim at toppling the regime. And on top of all that, Steinberg detected the whiff of exaggeration that pervaded the Bund's attempts to establish their oppositional bona fides. The result was that Steinberg cited the group only once in the whole book, in an early footnote, and only as an example (and as the *only* example) of the dangers of retrospective exaggeration.

Thus, just as in the early postwar period (and partly because of its rhetorical exaggerations in the early postwar period), the Bund had fallen short of others' expectations of what resistance should look like. Artur did not live to see Steinberg's publication, having died in 1968. Some years later, however,

Dore, her own health failing, sought to record the group's history, its early days, its experiences under Nazism, and its postwar years. The 232-page typewritten manuscript, titled "Gelebte Utopie" (Lived utopia), which Dore compiled with the help of other Bund members not long before her death in 1978, consists of articles, speeches, letters, diary entries, poems, and other documents produced by the group—assembled into chapters with introductions written by Dore.[50] It is a wonderful collection for anyone seeking to write the Bund's history. Given the preponderance of contemporaneous source material, if anything would appear to be a neutral record of the past, this would seem to be it. And yet Dore's selection and narrative differ significantly in emphasis from earlier group accounts—particularly from the ones the Bund produced in the immediate aftermath of war.

As in the earlier postwar texts, the Nazi years continue to be the heart of the story, but Steinberg's book, though never acknowledged (unlike Weisenborn's), had had a major impact on Dore's account. The word "resistance" does not appear once, and despite its seemingly comprehensive collection of Bund texts, none of the "Letters Abroad," nor the text on the "Aid Work for Jews," the group's most decisive postwar statements about its experience, are included. Dore's introduction to the section on the Nazi years, titled "Illegal Life," in some respects returned to the ground of Artur's speech on May 1, 1945 (included in the collection), focusing on the group's efforts to make sense of National Socialism, though not ignoring its efforts to help others. The one significant gesture toward chronicling rescue was the text "Freundestreue," in which Lisa Jacob offered a detailed account of her years on the run and her debt to the group. But many of the selected texts emphasized the more spiritual side of the group. Dore and her colleagues thus played it safe in making claims about the group's anti-Nazi activities. From the vantage point of this text, the Nazi period appeared above all as a period of internal transformation and maturation, in which, under the greatest stresses, the Bund survived, grew, and gained a new kind of faith in the workings of history.

Dore was disappointed that the group could not find a publisher. Only in 1990, after she had died, did a group of surviving Bundists manage to see a version of *Gelebte Utopie* in print. This was a different work again. The impetus for publication came from outside, thanks to the interest of younger friends of the Bund, above all Karin Gerhard, the director of the school for gymnastics that Dore had founded (by then called the Dore Jacobs School—now the Dore Jacobs Berufskolleg). The outsiders ensured that the revised version of the book was attuned to the interests of a new, younger German readership.[51] The spiritual undercurrent in Dore's account was largely gone. Since the 1980s, West

Germany had seen a wave of studies and school projects recovering everyday resistance in Nazi Germany. Although there was some effort to distinguish among outright resistance, nonconformity, and immunity to Nazi ideas, *Widerstand* as a term became far more encompassing. Following the publication of Inge Deutschkron's *I Wore the Yellow Star*, there had also been an explosion of interest in hiding and rescue, and an increasing tendency to see in rescue a form of resistance, even if the term *Rettungswiderstand* (rescue-resistance) would be coined only later.[52] It is not surprising, therefore, that *Widerstand* made a modest comeback in the published version of *Gelebte Utopie*, featuring in the text on the book's back cover. One of the "Letters Abroad" was also now included in the volume. As in all the earlier versions from Artur's speech onward, the Bund's close links to a leftwing Jewish scene were largely absent, as were the trials of war.

Rescue in Experience and Memory

Postwar reinvention is a familiar topic, particularly in the German context, but we have tended understandably to focus on those with something to hide. Large parts of German society were under pressure to rewrite their personal history. This might take the form of cynical whitewashing to circumvent denazification, subtler self-deceptions to master the cognitive dissonance between one's former beliefs and postwar expectations, or sometimes more profound and honest reappraisals of the ethical roots of one's earlier behavior. All this, we know, took place both at the individual level and at the highest levels of politics and public discourse, as the postwar Germanies struggled to find a place in the international alliance systems of their former enemies.[53] Yet the Bund reminds us that the end of the war was a key moment of reinvention even for those who now found themselves on the "right side" of history.

Why should that be? For one thing, it was in many cases, and certainly for the Bund, only now, as the war ended, that rescue and resistance groups began to turn their experiences into narrative. It was only at that point (as far as the sources tell us) that the group felt both the pressure and the opportunity to make sense of what they had done so that they could communicate it to others. But this was not easy to do. Above all, how to reconcile the sense of having surmounted a supreme challenge with the modest results they had to show for it? They did not even know at this stage if most of those whom they had helped had survived. In May 1945, drafting a letter to friends overseas, Dore acknowledged how difficult it was to render intelligible what they had been through to those who had not shared the experience. The mixture of security and threat, of everydayness and extraordinariness, had been a daily puzzle and now in retrospect was even more so. How could they ever convey the difficulty and danger of small gestures and the measure of small achievements?

Moreover, as Artur ventured his first, seminal effort at constructing the group's narrative in the May 1945 speech, the world around him already looked very different compared with the one the group had faced just a short while earlier. First, and most obviously, the outcome of their story was now clear—the Nazis were on the verge of total defeat, and the group had survived. Second, Artur could look forward to action in a postwar German society that would need new guides and leaders. The isolation and impotence of life under dictatorship now gained new meaning and a new political function in Artur's speech, namely, as preparation and character formation for postwar leadership. Aspects of wartime life thus had to be trimmed and refracted to emphasize principle and character. And so, as the group crafted a narrative for the future, key elements of the world it had recently inhabited drifted out of view. Nothing that Artur and others said after the war, to remind ourselves of one example, recognized the crucial fact that its leading couple was in a "mixed" marriage and had a "mixed-race" son, and thus had very personal reasons for acting that were not the result of abstract principles. This is not at all to deny the principled character of the Bund, but rather to argue that it, like other groups, foregrounded moral principle over personal ties in its postwar story. Again, this was not unique to the Bund.

An additional characteristic of the immediate postwar moment—particularly for German rescuers who had been often less well-informed about the horrors the Nazis were inflicting in the east than had been their counterparts living under German occupation elsewhere—was that the emerging revelations about the Holocaust's scale and character went beyond even their worst fears and significantly affected their understanding of Jewish fates. After the war, when radio broadcasts revealed to the Bund members the nature of Auschwitz, the encouraging words they had once given Jewish neighbors whom they had bravely accompanied to deportation centers, or the parcels they had courageously taken to the post office to send to deportees in the east, took on a different meaning. Unlike their actions then, everything they wrote after the war was in the full knowledge of the monstrous policy of extermination. Some of the hopes and beliefs that had once motivated the group's assistance for Jews—that the recipients would seize the opportunity of adversity to find their true, spiritual selves, for example—were no longer thinkable or sayable.

Earlier, this essay presented Artur's speech as offering us the opportunity to see how, almost overnight, the group's "experience" was being transmuted into "memory." Yet to talk of memory blurs *recall* with *narrative choice*. If the portrait of the group's achievements Artur painted in May 1945 was selective, then it was not because anything had been forgotten. The basic human tendency to impose agency and continuity on often very contingent life-stories, familiar to biographers and oral historians, was reinforced in this case by the group's sense of mission and principle. Above all, the future beckoned. New postwar perspectives, the *Erwartungshorizont* (horizon of expectations), to use Reinhart Koselleck's terminology, cast the group's experience in a different light.[54] Even in the mid-1970s, when the political stakes for the group were no longer significant, one might still argue that Dore and her fellow compilers were actively curating the group's image for posterity as much as they were "remembering" per se. (Though how self-conscious this process was, is another matter.) It is thus true to say that the past was "remembered" differently, but often more with an eye to the future than because of forgetting.

The reference to Dore's account reminds us that, important as the end of the war was for laying down the group's postwar narrative, the story did not remain static. The Bund was used to standing on the sidelines and being the odd one out, and so to a certain extent remained unmoved by the changing currents of postwar German attitudes. Yet they could not be impervious. In particular, as we have seen, shifting public understandings of what constituted resistance had important consequences for the way the group told its story.

In some respects the Bund's postwar trajectory resembles that of other political groups involved in resistance more than that of rescuers. Like other resistance groups, the Bund sought to mobilize its wartime record with an eye to influencing the postwar world. Rescue networks were often more informal and impromptu than the Bund, less obviously political, and with less interest in developing an agenda for the postwar period. Moreover, the Bund was writing in an era in which "rescue" as such was not yet a powerful public theme, so it was the tropes and heroic models associated with resistance that influenced (and disrupted) its narrative. As the group competed to establish its anti-Nazi credentials, the language of active resistance, of concerted outreach and battle (*Kampf*), entered its discourse, reaching a high point in 1947. Yet the group had difficulty being taken seriously as a resistance group, and in later years pulled back from claiming to have waged resistance at all.

However, we should not overdo the distinction between resistance and rescue when it comes to the purposeful crafting of narrative. As the ethicist and political scientist Michael Gross has shown, those involved in rescue networks, even informal ones with no programmatic aspirations after the war, have often been tempted to emphasize the principled moral reasoning behind their actions, and to downplay or lose sight of the many situational and other factors that galvanized them into motion or enabled them to act.[55] Analyzing the responses of those involved in the extraordinary rescue operation at Le Chambon-sur-Lignon in the Auvergne, for example, we can see that group dynamics, internal group incentives and pressures, and the particular stance of a few of the foremost individual leaders all had a part to play—much of which disappears in the later interviews conducted by Pierre Sauvage and others. In part this is a sign that Kantian ethics were by no means restricted to the Bund, but more probably reflects the basic human need to impose a narrative of agency and principle onto chaotic and complex events, particularly in the light of the new expectations of the postwar period.

In fact, I would argue that it is to our understanding of rescue that this analysis of the group's narrative has most to contribute. This is, above all, because the scholarship on rescue has, as intimated at the beginning of this essay, paid so little attention to questions of narrative and memory. In another recent publication, I argued that our notion of rescue is in some respects too retroactive: Working backward from the fact that a potential victim of the Holocaust survived, we impose a teleological concept, which we dub "rescue," on what were often multiple and far more piecemeal acts of help and self-help undertaken in particular moments with a limited horizon of intent.[56] But the examples from the Bund add a second dimension of retroactive distortion. They suggest that in taking later "memories" or narratives for granted, we fail to ask how they might occlude our understanding of earlier experience.

What we learn from the Bund, in fact, is the group's challenge in conveying both what it had meant to live in opposition under a dictatorship and how difficult it had been to extend even small gestures toward those in need. By looking carefully at its early postwar speeches and pamphlets, we see that the effort of corralling wartime experience into a narrative fit for purpose in the postwar era very rapidly reshaped the terms in which its anti-Nazi action came to be understood and communicated to others. Shifting public discourse about the Nazi past in postwar Germany, and emerging revelations about the Holocaust, also influenced the Bund's narrative. It sought to reeducate a public that it felt was dwelling on Germany's own woes and ignoring its wrongs. And it also wanted to make its own record fit the mold of leftwing narratives of resistance. The result, I suspect invisibly for the protagonists, was to produce continued subtle modulations of its story.

No doubt the colors that entered the Bund's accounts were often idiosyncratic, the result of views about man, society, and history that were not at all characteristic of other resistance and rescue groups. Moreover, recollections of individual rescuers will follow different patterns from that of such self-conscious group histories as the Bund's. Yet examining the Bund at the very least make us wonder whether the motives and vistas that once guided helpers' actions might, like the Bund's own accounts, be refracted by the changing expectations of the postwar world. It is hard to believe, for example, that the self-understanding of those now celebrated as "rescuers" and their interpretation of who they were and what they did can be unaffected by the powerful norms and heroic archetypes that have been disseminated by Yad Vashem and others in the public realm.

Notes

1 On the Bund, see Mark Roseman, *Lives Reclaimed: A Story of Rescue and Resistance in Nazi Germany* (New York: Metropolitan Books, 2019).

2 Artur Jacobs (henceforth AJ), "Dunkel und dennoch Licht. Lichtfest-Ansprache 1941," reproduced in Dore Jacobs, "Gelebte Utopie" (unpublished manuscript, no date [1975]), 134–36 (henceforth DJGU). Copies are preserved in the Bund's private collection of files (henceforth BAE), which are now housed in a building belonging to the Dore Jacobs Berufskolleg, Essen.

3 Kobi Kabalek, "The Rescue of Jews and the Memory of Nazism in Germany, from the Third Reich to the Present," PhD diss., University of Virginia, 2013; Dennis Riffel, *Unbesungene Helden: Die Ehrungsinitiative des Berliner Senats 1958 bis 1966. Reihe Dokumente, Texte, Materialien* (Berlin: Metropol, 2007); Michael Geyer, "Resistance as Ongoing Project: Visions of Order, Obligations to Strangers, Struggles for Civil Society," *Journal of Modern History* 64 (1992): 217–41; Peter Steinbach and Johannes Tuchel, *Widerstand gegen die nationalsozialistische Diktatur 1933–1945*, 1. Aufl. ed. (Berlin: Lukas, 2004); Johannes Tuchel, *Der vergessene Widerstand: Zu Realgeschichte und Wahrnehmung des Kampfes gegen die NS-Diktatur*, Dachauer Symposien zur Zeitgeschichte (Göttingen: Wallstein, 2005), in particular Tuchel's essay, "Vergessen, verdrängt, ignoriert: Überlegungen zur Rezeptionsgeschichte des Widerstandes gegen den Nationalsozialismus im Nachkriegsdeutschland," in *Der vergessene Widerstand*, 7–38.

4 On Yad Vashem's history, see Sarah Gensburger, "L'émergence de la catégorie de Juste parmi les nations comme paradigme mémoriel: Réflexions contemporaines sur le rôle socialement dévolu à la mémoire," in *Culture et Mémoire*, ed. Carola Hähnel-Mesnard, Marie Liénard-Yeterian, and Cristina Marinas (Paris: Éditions de l'École Polytechnique,

2008), 25–32; Sarah Gensburger, *Les Justes de France. Politiques publiques de la mémoire* (Paris: Presses de Sciences Po, 2010); and Kobi Kabalek, "The Commemoration Before the Commemoration: Yad Vashem and the Righteous Among the Nations, 1945–1963," *Yad Vashem Studies* 39, no. 1 (2011): 169–211.

5 This is true of Samuel P. Oliner and Pearl Oliner, *The Altruistic Personality: Rescuers of Jews in Nazi Europe* (New York: Free Press, 1988); Eva Fogelman, *Conscience and Courage: The Rescuers of the Jews during the Holocaust* (New York: Anchor Books, 1994); Kristen R. Monroe, *The Heart of Altruism: Perceptions of a Common Humanity* (Princeton, NJ: Princeton University Press, 1998); Kristen R. Monroe, *The Hand of Compassion: Portraits of Moral Choice during the Holocaust* (Princeton, NJ: Princeton University Press, 2004).

6 See, among many recent studies, Suzanne Beer, "Aid Offered Jews in Nazi Germany: Research Approaches, Methods, and Problems," Violence de masse et Résistance—Réseau de recherche, https://www.sciencespo.fr/mass-violence-war-massacre-resistance/en/document/aid-offered-jews-nazi-germany-research-approaches-methods-and-problems; Christian Gudehus, "Helping the Persecuted: Heuristics and Perspectives Exemplified by the Holocaust," *Online Encyclopedia of Mass Violence* (2016); Marten Düring, *Verdeckte soziale Netzwerke im Nationalsozialismus: Die Entstehung und Arbeitsweise von Berliner Hilfsnetzwerken für verfolgte Juden* (Berlin: De Gruyter Oldenbourg, 2015).

7 Konrad Kwiet and Helmut Eschwege, *Selbstbehauptung und Widerstand: Deutsche Juden im Kampf um Existenz und Menschenwürde, 1933–1945*, Hamburger Beiträge zur Sozial und Zeitgeschichte (Hamburg: Christians, 1984). Bob Moore, *Survivors: Jewish Self-Help and Rescue in Nazi-Occupied Western Europe* (Oxford: Oxford University Press, 2010).

8 Lutz Niethammer, Karin Hartewig, Harry Stein, and Leonie Wannenmacher, *Der "gesäuberte" Antifaschismus: Die SED und die roten Kapos von Buchenwald: Dokumente* (Berlin: Akademie Verlag, 1994).

9 Robert Gildea, *Fighters in the Shadows: A New History of the French Resistance* (Cambridge, MA: Belknap Press of Harvard University Press, 2015); Eve Rosenhaft, "The Uses of Remembrance: The Legacy of the Communist Resistance in the German Democratic Republic," in *Germans against Nazism: Nonconformity, Opposition and Resistance in the Third Reich—Essays in Honour of Peter Hoffmann*, ed. Francis R. Nicosia and Lawrence D. Stokes (New York: Berghahn Books, 2015).

10 Nechama Tec, *When Light Pierced the Darkness: Christian Rescue of Jews in Nazi-Occupied Poland* (New York: Oxford University Press, 1986), 204.
11 Mark Roseman, "Surviving Memory: Truth and Inaccuracy in Holocaust Testimony," *Journal of Holocaust Education* 8, no. 1 (1999): 1–20.
12 Christopher R. Browning, *Remembering Survival: Inside a Nazi Slave-Labor Camp*, 1st ed. (New York: W. W. Norton & Co., 2010).
13 See the excellent discussion in Beer, "Aid Offered Jews in Nazi Germany," and Gudehus, "Helping the Persecuted."
14 AJ, "Ansprache zur Maifeier 1945," reprinted in DJGU, 176.
15 Institut für Zeitgeschichte, ED 106/97, "Bericht über das Judenhilfswerk des 'Bundes' Gemeinschaft für sozialistisches Leben," typewritten manuscript, no date.
16 Inge Olesch, "Widerstand in Mülheim an der Ruhr," master's thesis (diplomarbeit), specifically 332, note 319.
17 Artur and Dore's letters to Friedl (Gottfried) are preserved in Alte Synagoge, Essen, Bestand 45–2AS, Nachlaß Gottfried Jacobs (henceforth NGJ). Quotation here "schauert einen bis ins Gebein."
18 NGJ, AJ to FJ, December 2, 1938.
19 The following is taken from Artur's letter sent January 21, 1939.
20 NGJ, Karlos Morgenstern to AJ, January 10, 1940.
21 Though because the group's high-minded philosophizing appealed to those with a higher education, ironically in the end the Jews the group remained in close contact with were largely educated and middle class.
22 NGJ, AJ to FJ, January 21, 1939.
23 Schlesinger Library, Cambridge, Mass, MC447 Box 2, Folder 31, manuscript titled "Rede vor der American Association of University Women. Bartlesville," March 9, 1942.
24 AJ, "Ansprache zur Maifeier 1945."
25 Entry in Artur Jacobs's diary (henceforth AJD), after the entry July 6, 1943. The diary is preserved for the most part in the Stadtarchiv Essen, Nachlass Jacobs, Bestand 626. Some parts are in the BAE.
26 BAE, typewritten manuscript, "Verpflichtungstag 1944. Ansprache von Else." See also AJD, Abschnitt "Blutopfer der Soldaten," one of several meditations that follow a diary entry from August 15, 1943, nachfolgen. See also an undated letter from Karlos Morgenstern; and a letter from Karlos to Karin, Hildesheim, January 1943, both in the possession of Karlos's daughter, Barbara Martin, in Marl.
27 AJD, 4. December 1943, August 8, 1943, and an appendix, "Aufriss zu einer neuen Schrift: Objektive Mächte als Helfer zum wahren Leben."

28 AJD, 10. February 1944.

29 Herself on the run, Lisa Jacob spoke of dealing with fear by putting things in a suitcase ready for the next package to be sent out to deported Jews. BAE, Kotik, "Sie wussten was sie tun," 4.

30 Artur Jacobs, letter, reproduced as "Brief in der Nazizeit (1942)," in DJGU, 146.

31 Given the threat to life involved, the group does not seem to have considered the extreme choice of refusing to serve.

32 BAE, undated, typewritten text, "Der Bund. Gemeinschaft für sozialistisches Leben. Erster Auslandsbrief," 3–4. In terms of dating this document, from Artur's letter to Kurt Desch, it is clear that by May 1947 at least one, and probably two, subsequent reports had already been completed—the "Aid Work for Jews" (*Judenhilfswerk*) (henceforth JHW) and the "Second Letter Abroad."

33 Robert G. Moeller, *War Stories: The Search for a Usable Past in the Federal Republic of Germany* (Berkeley: University of California Press, 2001).

34 Published in English as Winfried Georg Sebald, *On the Natural History of Destruction* (New York: Random House, 2003).

35 David F. Crew, *Bodies and Ruins: Imagining the Bombing of Germany, 1945 to the Present* (Ann Arbor: University of Michigan Press, 2017).

36 AJ, "Ansprache zur Maifeier 1945," reprinted in DJGU, 176.

37 Lisa Jacob, "'Der Bund,' Gemeinschaft für sozialistisches Leben und meine Errettung vor der Deportation," *Das Münster am Hellweg*, 37 (1984): 1:105–34, at 113.

38 BAE, undated printed text, Der Bund, "Leben in der Illegalität. Dritter Auslandsbrief" (1947), 21.

39 BAE, Der Bund, "Leben in der Illegalität. Dritter Auslandsbrief," 2.

40 BAE, Der Bund, "Leben in der Illegalität. Dritter Auslandsbrief," 3.

41 For the British Zone, in December 1945, Zonal Policy Instruction no. 20 established a common framework for short-term help for victims. Victims were now entitled to extra rations, priority in the allocation of jobs and housing, and rent support for a transitional period. Initially restricted to concentration camp survivors, within a few weeks the policy was de facto extended to others who could claim to have suffered equivalent hardship. The policy was intended not just to provide help but also to explicitly demonstrate to the German public that opponents of the Nazi regime were being given appropriate recognition. It was now that Artur submitted his request for support. Susanna Schrafstetter,

"Von der Soforthilfe zur Wiedergutmachung: Die Umsetzung der Zonal Policy Instruction Nr 20 in der britischen Besatzungszone," in *"Arisierung" und "Wiedergutmachung" in deutschen Städten*, ed. Christiane Fritsche and Johannes Paulmann (Köln: Böhlau Verlag, 2014), 309–34, specifically 311–15. Julia Volmer-Naumann, "'Betrifft: Wiedergutmachung': Entschädigung als Verwaltungsakt am Beispiel Nordrhein-Westfalen," in *"Arisierung" und "Wiedergutmachung" in deutschen Städten*, 335–62, specifically 338.

42 Stadtarchiv Essen (StAE), File WG 158, J103 (Artur Jacobs), Fragebogen. June 6, 1946.

43 StAE, WG 158, J103, AJ to Militärregierung Fürsorgeamt für politische Opfer, July 22, 1946.

44 BAE, Der Bund, "Gemeinschaft für sozialistisches Leben. Aus der illegalen Arbeit des Bundes. Zweiter Auslandsbrief" (printed copy, no date.), 6.

45 JHW, see note 32.

46 Artur Jacobs to Kurt Desch, Zinnen-Verlag, May 30, 1947. The correspondence can be found in the Weisenborn Nachlass, Akademie der Künste, Berlin. I am grateful to Kobi Kabalek for alerting me to this.

47 Günther Weisenborn, ed., *Der lautlose Aufstand. Bericht über die Widerstandsbewegung des deutschen Volkes 1933–1945* (Hamburg, 1953), S.102f.

48 On the historiography and reception of resistance, see the references in note 3.

49 Hans-Josef Steinberg, *Widerstand und Verfolgung in Essen, 1933–1945* (Bonn: Verlag Neue Gesellschaft, 1969). The other was Kurt Klotzbach, *Gegen Den Nationalsozialismus: Widerstand Und Verfolgung in Dortmund 1930–1945; Eine Historisch-Politische Studie. Schriftenreihe Des Forschungsinstituts Der Friedrich-Ebert-Stiftung B: Historisch-Politische Schriften* (Hannover: Verlag für Literatur und Zeitgeschehen, 1969).

50 DJGU, see note 2.

51 BAE, "Mitteilungen an die Bundesfreunde, No.9. Herbsttagung, November 9, 1988," 10.

52 Inge Deutschkron, *Ich trug den gelben Stern* (Köln: Verlag Wissenschaft und Politik, 1978). The subsequent play was called "Ab heute heißt Du Sara."

53 A couple of important examples from an expansive literature include Norbert Frei, *Adenauer's Germany and the Nazi Past: The Politics of Amnesty and Integration* (New York: Columbia University Press, 2002);

Norbert Frei, *1945 Und Wir: Das Dritte Reich Im Bewusstsein Der Deutschen* (Munich: C.H. Beck, 2005).

54 Reinhart Koselleck, "'Erfahrungsraum' und 'Erwartungshorizont'—zwei historische Kategorien," in *Vergangene Zukunft: Zur Semantik Geschichtlicher Zeiten* (Frankfurt am Main: Suhrkamp Verlag, 1979), 352–75.

55 Michael L. Gross, *Ethics and Activism: The Theory and Practice of Political Morality* (Cambridge: Cambridge University Press, 1997).

56 Mark Roseman, "Die Rettung der Geschichte. Der 'Bund: Gemeinschaft sozialistisches Leben' und sein 'Judenhilfswerk,'" in *ÜberLeben im Dritten Reich. Handlungsspielräume und Perspektiven von Juden und ihren Helfern* (Göttingen: Wallstein, 2020), 85–126, especially 116–17.

Bibliography

Beer, Suzanne. "Aid Offered Jews in Nazi Germany: Research Approaches, Methods, and Problems," *Violence de masse et Résistance—Réseau de recherche*, https://www.sciencespo.fr/mass-violence-war-massacre-resistance/en/document/aid-offered-jews-nazi-germany-research-approaches-methods-and-problems, accessed April 9, 2023.

Borgstedt, Angela. "Hilfe Für Verfolgte: Judenretter Und Judenhelfer." (Help for the persecuted: Rescuers and helpers of Jews.) In *Widerstand gegen die nationalsozialistische Diktatur 1933–1945*, ed. Peter Steinbach and Johannes Tuchel, 307–21. Berlin: Lukas, 2004.

Browning, Christopher R. *Remembering Survival: Inside a Nazi Slave-Labor Camp*. 1st ed. New York: W. W. Norton & Co., 2010.

Crew, David F. *Bodies and Ruins: Imagining the Bombing of Germany, 1945 to the Present*. Ann Arbor: University of Michigan Press, 2017.

Deutschkron, Inge. *Ich trug den gelben Stern*. (I wore the yellow star.) Cologne: Verlag Wissenschaft und Politik, 1978. English edition: *Outcast: A Jewish Girl in Wartime Berlin*. New York: Fromm International Pub. Corp., 1989.

Düring, Marten. *Verdeckte soziale Netzwerke im Nationalsozialismus: Die Entstehung und Arbeitsweise von Berliner Hilfsnetzwerken für verfolgte Juden*. (Hidden social networks in National Socialism: The emergence and operation of networks of aid for persecuted Jews in Berlin.) Berlin: De Gruyter Oldenbourg, 2015.

Florath, Bernd. "Die Europäische Union." (The European Union.) In *Der vergessene Widerstand: Zu Realgeschichte und Wahrnehmung des Kampfes gegen die NS-Diktatur*, ed. Johannes Tuchel, 114–39. Dachauer Symposien zur Zeitgeschichte, Bd 5. Göttingen: Wallstein, 2005.

Fogelman, Eva. *Conscience and Courage: The Rescuers of the Jews during the Holocaust*. New York: Anchor Books, 1994.

Frei, Norbert. *1945 Und Wir: Das Dritte Reich Im Bewusstsein Der Deutschen*. (1945 and us: The Third Reich in the German consciousness.) Munich: C.H. Beck, 2005.

———. *Adenauer's Germany and the Nazi Past: The Politics of Amnesty and Integration*. New York: Columbia University Press, 2002.

Gensburger, Sarah. "L'émergence de la catégorie de Juste parmi les nations comme paradigme mémoriel: Réflexions contemporaines sur le rôle socialement dévolu à la mémoire." (The emergence of the category of the righteous as a paradigm of memory: Contemporary reflections on the societal role ascribed to memory.) In *Culture et Mémoire*, ed. Carola Hähnel-Mesnard, Marie Liénard-Yeterian, and Cristina Marinas, 25–32. Paris: Éditions de l'École Polytechnique, 2008.

———. *Les Justes de France. Politiques publiques de la mémoire*. (The righteous of France: The politics of memory.) Paris: Presses de Sciences Po, 2010. English edition: *National Policy, Global Memory: The Commemoration of the "Righteous" from Jerusalem to Paris, 1942–2007*. New York: Berghahn, 2016.

Geyer, Michaekl. "Resistance as Ongoing Project: Visions of Order, Obligations to Strangers, Struggles for Civil Society." *Journal of Modern History* 64 (1992): 217–41.

Gildea, Robert. *Fighters in the Shadows: A New History of the French Resistance*. Cambridge, MA: Belknap Press of Harvard University Press, 2015.

Gross, Michael L., *Ethics and Activism: The Theory and Practice of Political Morality*. Cambridge: Cambridge University Press, 1997.

Gudehus, Christian. "Helping the Persecuted: Heuristics and Perspectives Exemplified by the Holocaust." *Online Encyclopedia of Mass Violence* (2016), https://www.sciencespo.fr/mass-violence-war-massacre-resistance/en/document/helping-persecuted-heuristics-and-perspectives-exemplified-holocaust.html, accessed April 9, 2023.

Jacob, Lisa. "'Der Bund,' Gemeinschaft für sozialistisches Leben und meine Errettung vor der Deportation." (The Bund: Community for Socialist life and how I was saved from deportation.) *Das Münster am Hellweg* 37, no. 1 (1984): 105–34.

Kabalek, Kobi. "The Commemoration Before the Commemoration: Yad Vashem and the Righteous Among the Nations, 1945–1963." *Yad Vashem Studies* 39, no. 1 (2011): 169–211.

———. "The Rescue of Jews and the Memory of Nazism in Germany, from the Third Reich to the Present." PhD diss., University of Virginia, 2013.

Klotzbach, Kurt. *Gegen Den Nationalsozialismus: Widerstand Und Verfolgung in Dortmund 1930–1945; Eine Historisch-Politische Studie. Schriftenreihe Des Forschungsinstituts Der Friedrich-Ebert-Stiftung B: Historisch-Politische Schriften.* (Against National Socialism: Resistance and persecution in Dortmund, 1930–1945.) Hannover: Verlag für Literatur und Zeitgeschehen, 1969.

Koselleck, Reinhart. "'Erfahrungsraum' und 'Erwartungshorizont'—zwei historische Kategorien." (Experience and the horizon of expectations—Two historical categories.) In *Vergangene Zukunft: Zur Semantik Geschichtlicher Zeiten*, 352–75. Frankfurt am Main: Suhrkamp Verlag, 1979.

Kosmala, Beate, and Claudia Schoppmann, eds. *Solidarität Und Hilfe Für Jüden Während Der NS-Zeit. Band 5. Überleben Im Untergrund. Hilfe Für Juden in Deutschland.* (Solidarity and help for Jews during the Nazi period. Vol. 5. Survival underground. Help for Jews in Germany.) Reihe Solidarität Und Hilfe 5. Berlin: Metropol, 2002.

Kwiet, Konrad, and Helmut Eschwege. *Selbstbehauptung und Widerstand: Deutsche Juden im Kampf um Existenz und Menschenwürde, 1933–1945.* (Agency and resistance: German Jews in the struggle for survival and dignity.) Hamburger Beiträge zur Sozial und Zeitgeschichte. Hamburg: Christians, 1984.

Lutjens, Richard N. *Submerged on the Surface: The Not-so-Hidden Jews of Nazi Berlin, 1941–1945.* 1st ed. New York: Berghahn, 2019.

Moeller, Robert G. *War Stories: The Search for a Usable Past in the Federal Republic of Germany.* Berkeley: University of California Press, 2001.

Monroe, Kristen R. *The Hand of Compassion: Portraits of Moral Choice during the Holocaust.* Princeton, NJ: Princeton University Press, 2004.

———. *The Heart of Altruism: Perceptions of a Common Humanity.* Princeton, NJ: Princeton University Press, 1998.

Moore, Bob. "The Rescue of Jews from Nazi Persecution: A Western European Perspective." *Journal of Genocide Research* 4, no. 3 (2003): 293–308.

———. *Survivors: Jewish Self-Help and Rescue in Nazi-Occupied Western Europe.* Oxford: Oxford University Press, 2010.

Niethammer, Lutz, Karin Hartewig, Harry Stein, and Leonie Wannenmacher. *Der "gesäuberte" Antifaschismus: Die SED und die roten Kapos von Buchenwald: Dokumente.* (Whitewashed antifascism: The SED and the red kapos of Buchenwald. Documents.) Berlin: Akademie Verlag, 1994.

Oliner Samuel P., and Pearl Oliner. *The Altruistic Personality: Rescuers of Jews in Nazi Europe.* New York: Free Press, 1988.

Paldiel, Mordecai. *German Rescuers of Jews.* London: Vallentine Mitchell, 2017.

Riffel, Dennis. *Unbesungene Helden: Die Ehrungsinitiative des Berliner Senats 1958 bis 1966. Reihe Dokumente, Texte, Materialien.* (Unsung heroes: The efforts to honor [the rescuers] by the Berlin Senate, 1958–1966.) Berlin: Metropol, 2007.

Roseman, Mark. *Lives Reclaimed: A Story of Rescue and Resistance in Nazi Germany*. New York: Metropolitan Books, 2019.

———. "Surviving Memory: Truth and Inaccuracy in Holocaust Testimony." *Journal of Holocaust Education* 8, no. 1 (1999): 1–20.

———. *ÜberLeben im Dritten Reich. Handlungsspielräume und Perspektiven von Juden und ihren Helfern*. (Survival/About life in the Third Reich. Agency and perceptions of Jews and their helpers.) Göttingen: Wallstein, 2020.

Rosenhaft, Eve. "The Uses of Remembrance: The Legacy of the Communist Resistance in the German Democratic Republic." In *Germans against Nazism: Nonconformity, Opposition and Resistance in the Third Reich—Essays in Honour of Peter Hoffmann*, ed. Francis R. Nicosia and Lawrence D. Stokes. New York: Berghahn Books, 2015.

Schrafstetter, Susanna. *Flucht Und Versteck: Untergetauchte Juden in München. Verfolgungserfahrung Und Nachkriegsalltag*. (Fleeing and hiding: Jews underground in Munich. The experience of persecution and everyday life after the war.) Göttingen: Wallstein Verlag, 2015.

———. "Von der Soforthilfe zur Wiedergutmachung: Die Umsetzung der Zonal Policy Instruction Nr 20 in der britischen Besatzungszone." (From emergency aid to restitution: The implementation of Zonal Policy Instruction Number 20 in the British Zone of Occupation.) In *"Arisierung" und "Wiedergutmachung" in deutschen Städten*, ed. Christiane Fritsche and Johannes Paulmann, 309–34. Köln: Böhlau Verlag, 2014.

Sebald, Winfried Georg. *On the Natural History of Destruction*. New York: Random House, 2003.

Steinbach, Peter, and Johannes Tuchel. *Widerstand gegen die nationalsozialistische Diktatur 1933–1945*. (Resistance to the National Socialist dictatorship.) 1. Aufl. ed. Berlin: Lukas, 2004.

Steinberg, Hans-Josef. *Widerstand und Verfolgung in Essen, 1933–1945*. Bonn: Verlag Neue Gesellschaft, 1969.

Tec, Nechama. *When Light Pierced the Darkness: Christian Rescue of Jews in Nazi-Occupied Poland*. New York: Oxford University Press, 1986.

Tuchel, Johannes. *Der vergessene Widerstand: Zu Realgeschichte und Wahrnehmung des Kampfes gegen die NS-Diktatur*. (The forgotten resistance: History and perception of the fight against the Nazi dictatorship.) Dachauer Symposien zur Zeitgeschichte. Göttingen: Wallstein, 2005.

Volmer-Naumann, Julia. "'Betrifft: Wiedergutmachung': Entschädigung als Verwaltungsakt am Beispiel Nordrhein-Westfalen." ("Concerning restitution":

Compensation as an administrative procedure using the case of North-Rhine Westphalia.) In *"Arisierung" und "Wiedergutmachung" in deutschen Städten*, ed. Christiane Fritsche and Johannes Paulmann, 335–62. Köln: Böhlau Verlag, 2014.

Weisenborn, Günther, ed. *Der lautlose Aufstand. Bericht über die Widerstandsbewegung des deutschen Volkes 1933–1945*. Hamburg, 1953.

Index of Names

Index of Places

Contributors

NATALIA ALEKSIUN is the Harry Rich Professor of Holocaust Studies at the University of Florida, Gainesville. She holds doctoral degrees from the University of Warsaw and NYU. Her research focuses on Jewish history in east-central Europe in the twentieth century and the Holocaust. Aleksiun has written extensively on the history of Polish Jews before, during, and after the Holocaust; Polish-Jewish relations; and Jewish historiography. In addition to her 2021 book, *Conscious History: Polish Jewish Historians before the Holocaust*, she is the author of *Dokąd dalej? Ruch syjonistyczny w Polsce 1944–1950* (Where to? The Zionist movement in Poland, 1944–1950). She edited several volumes, including (with Brian Horowitz and Antony Polonsky) *Polin: Studies in Polish Jewry*, vol. 29, "Writing Jewish History in Eastern Europe"; (with Hana Kubátová) *European Holocaust Studies*, vol. 3, "Places, Spaces, and Voids in the Holocaust"; and (with Eliyana R. Adler) *Entanglements of War: Social Networks during the Holocaust*. She serves as coeditor of *East European Jewish Affairs*.

SOFIE LENE BAK is an associate professor at the Saxo Institute at the University of Copenhagen. She holds a PhD in history from the University of Copenhagen. She is the author of several books and articles on antisemitism, Danish Jewish history, and the Holocaust, including the monograph *Nothing to Speak of: Wartime Experiences of the Danish Jews 1943–1945*, and most recently (with D. Pataricza, S. Muir, B. Følner, V. Kieding Banik, and P. Rudberg,) "Jewish Archives and Sources in the Nordic Countries: The Current State of Affairs and Future Perspectives" in *Nordisk Judaistik*; and "Danish Historical Narratives of the Occupation: The Promises and Lies of April 9th," in *Nordic War Stories: World War II as History, Fiction, Media, and Memory*.

ANNA BIKONT is a Polish journalist and nonfiction writer. In 1989 she cofounded *Gazeta Wyborcza*, the first independent daily in post-communist Europe and the main newspaper in Poland. Her book *The Crime and the Silence: The Quest for the Truth of a Wartime Massacre* was translated into many languages. Published by FSG in 2015, the book won a National Jewish Book Award. In 2017, Bikont received a doctorate honoris causa from the University of Gothenburg. Among her recent publications are *Sendlerowa. W ukryciu* (Sendler: In hiding), and *Cena. W poszukiwaniu żydowskich dzieci po wojnie* (The price: The search for Jewish children after the war).

Anna Maria Droumpouki holds a bachelor's degree in history and archaeology, a master's degree in museology, and a PhD in contemporary Greek and European history (all from the University of Athens). She was a visiting research scholar at the Leibniz Institute for Jewish History and Culture–Simon Dubnow (Leipzig, 2009), and a postdoctoral fellow at the Research Centre for Modern History of Panteion University (Athens, 2014–16). She is the author of *Monuments of Oblivion: Traces of the Second World War in Greece and in Europe*, and *An Endless Negotiation: The Rehabilitation of Jewish Communities in Greece and the German Reparations*. She is also coeditor (with Philip Carabott and Iassonas Chandrinos) of *From Persecution to Rehabilitation: Aspects of the History of Greek Jews*. A founding member of the Workshop on the Study of Modern Greek Jewry, Droumpouki was scientific coordinator of the Greek-German project "Memories of the Occupation in Greece" at the Free University Berlin (2016–18) and a Gerda Henkel fellow, working with Dr. Philip Carabott on the project "The Shoah and the (Re)Making of Greek Jewry: The Case of the Jews in Athens" (2019–21). She is currently a research assistant at the University of Munich, working on the Deutsche Forschungsgemeinschaft–funded project (DFG [German Research Foundation]) "The Worst Times Are Not Yet Over: Jewish Life in Post-War Greece, 1944–1949."

Sarah Gensburger is a social scientist, tenured researcher at the French National Center for Scientific Research (CNRS), and deputy director of the Institute for the Social Sciences of Politics CNRS/Paris Nanterre University/ENS Paris Saclay. She has authored numerous books, including *Witnessing the Robbing of the Jews: A Photographic Album (Paris, 1940–1944)*; *The Commemoration of the "Righteous" from Jerusalem to Paris, 1942–2007*; *Memory on My Doorstep: Chronicles of the Bataclan Neighbourhood (2015–2016)*; and (with Sandrine Lefranc) *Beyond Memory: Can We Really Learn from the Past?*.

Ido de Haan is professor in political history at Utrecht University. Among his publications are a study about the commemoration of the Holocaust in the Netherlands (*Na de ondergang. De herinnering aan de Jodenvervolging in Nederland 1945–1995*) and several essays on Holocaust history and memory, including "Failures and Mistakes: Images of Collaboration in Postwar Dutch Society," in *Collaboration with the Nazis: Public Discourse after the Holocaust*; "An Unresolved Controversy: The Jewish Honor Court in the Netherlands 1946–1950," in *Jewish Honor Courts: Revenge, Retribution, and Reconciliation in Europe and Israel after the Holocaust* (Wayne State University Press); and "Saving the Bystander," in *Probing the Limits of Categorization: The Bystander in Holocaust History*.

Liliana Hentosh is senior research associate at the Institute for Historical Research at Lviv National University. She is the author of *The Vatican and Challenges of Modernity: Eastern Politics of the Vatican and Ukrainian-Polish Conflict in Galicia in 1914–1923* (in Ukrainian) and *Metropolitan Andrei Sheptytsky (1923–1939): A Trial of Ideals* (in Ukrainian). She has also published numerous essays and articles, including (with Bohdan Tscherkes) "Lviv in Search of Its Identity: Transformations of the City's Public Space," in *Cities after the Fall of Communism: Reshaping Cultural Landscapes and European Identity*; and "Rites and Religions: Pages from the History of Interdenominational and Interethnic Relations in Twentieth-Century Lviv," in *Harvard Ukrainian Studies*.

Hana Kubátová is assistant professor and head of the Center for the Transdisciplinary Research of Violence, Trauma and Justice at the Charles University in Prague. Her research interests include majority-minority relations in wartime and postwar Slovakia, identity construction, and microdynamics of (ethnic) violence. She has been the recipient of numerous fellowships, including the Marie Curie Fellowship for Early Research Training, Charles H. Revson Foundation Fellowship, Felix Posen Fellowship, Gisela Fleischmann Scholarship, and, more recently, the Junior Core Fellowship from the Institute of Advanced Study, CEU. Kubátová has published in Slovak, Czech, English, German, and Hungarian. Her contributions have appeared in journals including *Nations and Nationalism*, *Contemporary European History*, *Holocaust Studies: A Journal of Culture and History*, *East European Politics and Societies: and Cultures*, and others. She is coauthor (with Ján Lániček) of *The Jew in Czech and Slovak Imagination, 1938–89: Antisemitism, the Holocaust, and Zionism*, and coeditor (with Ján Lániček) of *Jews and Gentiles in Central and Eastern Europe during the Holocaust: History and Memory*. Most recently she coedited (with Natalia Aleksiun) *Places, Spaces, and Voids in the Holocaust*.

Mark Roseman is Distinguished Professor in history and Pat M. Glazer Chair in Jewish Studies at Indiana University. He is the author of numerous works on the Holocaust and modern European history. His most recent studies include *Lives Reclaimed: A Story of Rescue and Resistance in Nazi Germany* and (with Devin Pendas and Richard Wetzel) *Beyond the Racial State*, as well as the book *ÜberLeben im Holocaust. Handlungsspielräume von Juden und ihren Helfern*. He is the general editor of the Cambridge History of the Holocaust.

Naum Trajanovski is an assistant at the Faculty of Sociology, University of Warsaw. He holds a PhD in sociology from the Institute of Philosophy and Sociology at the Polish Academy of Sciences. He was a research fellow at the Macedonian Academy of Sciences and Arts and the Faculty of Philosophy in Skopje. His academic interests include memory politics in North Macedonia, nationalism studies, and sociological knowledge-transfers in east-central Europe. He is the author of a book, in Macedonian, on the Museum of the Macedonian Struggle and Macedonian memory politics. Some of his most recent publications are "Operation Museum: Memory Politics as 'Populist Mobilization' in North Macedonia (2006–2011)," in *Memory Politics and Populism in Southeastern Europe*, and "'A Patriotic Act for Macedonia': The Mnemohistory of Commemorations of Mara Buneva in Skopje (2001–2018)," in *Contemporary Southeastern Europe*.

Raphael Utz is project group head for the documentation center "German Occupation of Europe in the Second World War" in Berlin. He studied medieval and modern history, Eastern European history, and Slavic studies at Heidelberg University. He holds a MPhil in Russian and Eastern European studies from Oxford University and PhD in history from Heidelberg University. Utz has been a lecturer in Russian and Eastern European history at Cambridge University and Heidelberg University, and a doctoral scholar of the German National Scholarship Foundation. He was a research fellow at Friedrich Schiller University, Jena (2007–10), and managing director of the Imre Kertész Kolleg, Jena (2010–22). He published the monograph *Rußlands unbrauchbare Vergangenheit. Nationalismus und Außenpolitik im Zarenreich*. He has coedited three volumes, including (with Jörg Ganzenmüller) *Orte der Shoah in Polen: Gedenkstätten zwischen Mahnmal und Museum*; (with Jörg Ganzenmüller) *Sowjetische Verbrechen und russische Erinnerung: Orte—Akteure—Deutungen*; and (with Felicitas Fischer von Weikersthal, Frank Gruener, Susanne Hohler, and Franziska Schedewie) *The Russian Revolution of 1905 in Transcultural Perspective: Identities, Peripheries, and the Flow of Ideas*, and coauthored numerous articles.

ANIKA WALKE is Georgie W. Lewis Career Development Professor and associate professor of history at Washington University in St. Louis. Walke's research and teaching interests include World War II and Nazi genocide, migration, nationality policies, and oral history in the (former) Soviet Union and Europe. She has published many articles and book chapters on related themes. Her book, *Pioneers and Partisans: An Oral History of Nazi Genocide in Belorussia*, weaves together oral histories, video testimonies, and memoirs to show how the first generation of Soviet Jews experienced the Nazi genocide and how they remembered it after the dissolution of the USSR in 1991. From 2014 to 2022, Walke served as coprincipal investigator of "The Holocaust Ghettos Project: Reintegrating Victims and Perpetrators through Places and Events," an NEH-funded endeavor of the Holocaust Geographies Collaborative to develop a historical geographical information system of Nazi-era ghettos in Eastern Europe.

ZOFIA WÓYCICKA holds a PhD in history from the University of Warsaw. She is assistant professor at the Centre for Research on Social Memory at the University of Warsaw, where she is currently leading a research project titled "Help Delivered to Jews during World War II and Transnational Memory in the Making." Previously she worked as an educator at POLIN–Museum of the History of Polish Jews, as an exhibition curator at the House of European History/Brussels, and as a researcher at the Centre for Historical Research Berlin of the Polish Academy of Sciences and the German Historical Institute Warsaw. She authored the monograph *Arrested Mourning: Memory of the Nazi Camps in Poland, 1944–1950*. She is also coeditor (with Magdalena Saryusz-Wolska and Joanna Wawrzyniak) of *Memory Studies*, vol. 15, no. 6, "Mnemonic Wars: New Constellations." Her other recent publications include "A Global Label and Its Local Appropriations: Representations of the Righteous Among the Nations in Contemporary European Museums," in *Memory Studies*; and (with Stefan Berger et al.) "Memory Cultures of War in European War Museums," in *Agonistic Memory and Representations of War in Twentieth-Century Europe*.